THE SUNDAY NEWS   FAMILY COOK BOOK

See Recipes on Page 320

The Sunday News

Family Cook Book

By Alice Petersen & Ella Elvin

Food Editors, The New York *News*

Full Color Photography by Harry Warnecke
and his associates in the *News* Color Studios

Rowman and Littlefield, Inc.

NEW YORK

Staff

FOR THE *NEWS*

EDITORIAL
ALICE PETERSEN · ELLA ELVIN
Food Editors
HELEN M. CALITRI · MARIE BURKE · LAMB RYAN · JOSEPHINE HUNT

PHOTOGRAPHIC
HARRY WARNECKE, *Chief*
GUS SCHOENBAECHLER · ROBERT CRANSTON · WILLIAM KLEIN
DANIEL JACINO · LEE ELKINS · ARTHUR SASSE

FOR ROWMAN AND LITTLEFIELD, INC.

GEORGE HORNBY
Editorial and Art Director
NORA McNIALL · YVONNE JOHNSON · GAIL NOVAK · ANN GUILFOYLE

 *For Mary King Patterson*

For text see page 10

Flavor's the Thing

Table of Contents

Foreword

If you were to work day and night for years, testing recipes in a fully-equipped, modern kitchen, you just might come up with 1500 delicious recipes to match those contained in this magnificent book. Of course, to accomplish this, you would need enough food to feed an army . . . original suggestions from thousands of people . . . and a staff of experts to assist you. That's exactly what was needed to complete this ambitious project. In addition, the *News* Color Studio took 337 full-color photographs to illustrate the mouth-watering selections you'll find on the following pages.

So here it is . . . 320 pages of the widest possible variety of recipes, many of them award winners, put together in the most beautiful, useful cook book ever published. All assembled by Alice Petersen and Ella Elvin, brilliant and imaginative Food Editors of the *News*.

SHELF 1

Herb Blend for Salads: Adds a piquant distinctive flavor to your Dressings and Salads.

Herb Blend for Meats: Add enough to taste. For Roasts, Meat Loafs and Stews.

Herb Blend for Fish: For Fish, Peas and all Fish Dishes.

Savory Leaf: Delicious in Soups, Stuffings, Beans, Cabbage, Stewed Meats, Poultry, Game and Lamb.

Saffron: For Fish, Shellfish, Soup, Boiled Rice, Curry and Fish Sauces. Use very sparingly.

Paprika: Adds color and savor to Goulash, Stews, Hashes, Veal Dishes, Salads, Game and Fowl.

Mustard-Ground: Widely used for Meat, Sauces, Fish, Mayonnaise, French Dressing and Cream Salad Dressing.

Bay Leaves: For Beef Stews, Pork, Tomato Aspic and all Tomato Dishes. Also Stuffing for Fish and Fowl.

Chervil: Delicious for Salads, Soups, Fish Sauces and Egg Dishes.

Oregano: Used on many Spanish, Mexican and Italian Dishes—Pork, Fresh Mushrooms, Kidney Stew, Beans and Various Sauces.

SHELF 2

Poppyseed: Use as a topping on Rolls, Cookies and Breads.

Dill: Used in Pickles, Fish and Sauces.

Celery Seed: Adds delicious flavor to Potato Salad, Soups and Stews.

Anise Seed: Sprinkle on Sweet Rolls, Cakes, Cookies and Coffee Cake in baking.

Caraway Seed: Used in the baking of Breads, Cookies, Cakes, Candy, Salads and Cheese.

Whole Cloves: Add a few to Baked Ham, Consomme, Venison, Poultry, Preserves and Baked Apples.

Ginger: Used widely for baking, especially Gingerbread, Cookies, Buns, Puddings and Oriental Dishes.

Nutmeg: Used in Custards, Puddings, Pumpkin and Fruit Pies. Also gives delicate aromatic flavor to Cabbage, Cauliflower and Spinach. Use a sprinkling on "Egg-Nog."

Cinnamon: Indispensable in Apple Pie, Applesauce, Baked Apples, Sweet Rolls, Cinnamon Toast and Game Sauces.

Allspice: Use sparingly to enhance the flavor of Soups, Sauces, Game and Meat.

SHELF 3

Bouquet Garni: For Soups, Gravies, Stews and with Meat.

Basil: Used widely in French and Italian Dressings. Delicious flavoring in Soups, Stews, Fowl, Meat Loaf, and Meat Balls.

Marjoram: For Stuffings, Chopped Meats, Salads and Sauces. Adds zest to Stews and Soups.

Rosemary: Used in Italian Dishes, Soups, Lamb, Eggs, Meat and Fish Sauces.

Tarragon: Indispensable for Turtle Soup, Fish, Eggs and Omelets, Meat Sauces, Salad Greens, Pickled Salads. Flavor for Vinegar and Béarnaise Sauce.

Sage: Use sparingly in Soups and all Bread Stuffings. For Fowl, Fish and Pork.

Thyme: Delicious in Stuffings, Fish Sauces, Eggplant, Beans, Soup, Gumbo, Creole, and Meat Dishes.

Curry Powder: For Lamb, Rice, Fish, Soup, Venison, Kidney Stews, Sauces and Mushrooms.

Creole Seasoning: This is used for Thick Soups, Gumbo and Ragouts.

Pickling Spices: Used in Pickles and Relishes.

SHELF 4

Herb Blend for Soups: Used in Soups sparingly at first, then add to suit your family's taste.

Herb Blend for Vegetables: For Vegetables and Spaghetti—use sparingly at first—add to taste.

Herb Blend for Eggs and Cheese: Use sparingly at first—more to taste. For Eggs and Cheese Dishes.

Pepper (Ground): Most generally used of all spices at table and in cooking.

Pepper-Cayenne: This is very red hot pepper. Delicious to use wth Shrimp and Crab Dishes and Chili Sauce as well as all hot Mexican and Spanish dishes.

White Pepper: Used chiefly in Cheese Sauce and Dishes in which it is preferable not to have the pepper show.

Cracked Pepper: Particularly good in Salads.

Black Peppercorns: Used in Peppermills, Soups, Pickling and in Meat Stews.

Poivre Aromatique: Delightfully pungent taste in Chicken Pot-Pie, and Tomato Juice.

Mixed Peppercorns: Used in Peppermill—also in Soups, Pickling and Meat Stews.

SHELF 5

Hickory Smoked Salt: Sprinkle on both sides of Steaks, Chops, Hamburgers before cooking. It imparts a fine wood-smoked flavor, recalling the taste of outdoor cookery.

Onion Salt: Blend smoothly in Soups, Gravies, Sauces, Salads, Egg Dishes, Roast Meats, Stuffed Peppers, Hashed Brown Potatoes and Meat Pies.

Celery Seasoning Salt: Adds poignant flavor to Salads, Stews, Soups, Meat Loaf, Hash, Cold Meats and Potato Salad.

Seasoning Salt: Used in cooking and on the table. Adds zest to Meats, Soups, Sauces, Salad Dressings and Corn on the Cob.

Poultry Seasoning: Add to your own Bread Stuffing or to a prepared Stuffing for Fowl, Fish and Pork Roast.

White Minced Onion: Use where all dishes call for onion—Salad Dressings, Roast Beef, Steaks, Chops, Hashed Brown Potatoes.

Onion Powder-Roasted: Adds fine flavor to Roast Beef or Lamb, Broiled Chops, Steaks, Home Fries or Hashed Brown Potatoes.

Ginger Garlic Salt: Excellent with Roast Duck, Chinese Dishes, Roast Pork, Beef and Lamb, Barbecues, Steaks and Braised Chicken.

Charcoal Salt: Dust evenly on both sides of Steaks, Chops, and Hamburgers to get that wonderful outdoor barbecue taste and appearance.

Onion Powder: Any recipe calling for onion. Delicious in Sauces, all Potato recipes, Meats and Stews.

SHELF 6

Gumbo File: For Soups, Stews, etc. The glutinous effect of Fresh Okra. Add a minute or two before serving.

Parsley Flakes: Used in Soups, Stews, Meat Loaf, Fish. Also a sprinkle on Hors d'Oeuvres.

Sesame Seed: Exotic flavor sprinkled over Breads and Cakes when baking.

Garlic Powder: Can be used freely in any recipe calling for garlic flavoring. Delicious in Sauces, all Potatoes, Meats and Stews.

Minced Garlic: Used in Meats, Spaghetti Sauces and Salads.

Good Taste: Can be used on the table and in cooking. To season any dish usually calling for salt and pepper.

Chives: Used in Soups, Hors d'Oeuvres and adds savor to Stews and Sauces.

Horseradish Powder: To prepare: Mix 2 tablespoons powder with ¼ cup milk; add 2 teaspoons vinegar and ⅛ teaspoon salt. Blend; let stand 15 minutes. Keep prepared horseradish in the refrigerator.

Garlic Salt: Used for Deviled Eggs, Barbecue, Roasts, Goulash, Broiled or Fried Steaks, Salads, Sauces and Italian Dishes.

Florentine Souffle

One-fourth cup quick cooking tapioca
One teaspoon salt
One-eighth teaspoon pepper
One cup milk, heated
Cooking time: Five to eight minutes in
    a double boiler
One cup drained cooked spinach, minced
One teaspoon grated onion
One-sixteenth teaspoon nutmeg
One-sixteenth teaspoon sage
Three eggs, beaten separately
Oven temperature: 350 degrees
Baking time: Fifty minutes, or until firm
One cup cheese sauce
Servings: Four or five

Cook the tapioca, salt, pepper and milk in a double boiler, stirring constantly, until the tapioca thickens and becomes clear. Add the spinach, onion, nutmeg and sage; take from the hot water. Cool five minutes. Stir in the beaten egg yolks;

fold this mixture into the beaten egg whites. Pile into a greased baking dish (5 cup size); set in a pan of hot water. Bake in a moderate oven until firm in the center and beginning to brown on top. Serve in the baking dish with cheese sauce.

Folded Cheese Omelet

Six eggs, beaten slightly
Six tablespoons milk
Three-fourths teaspoon salt
One-eighth teaspoon pepper
One-sixteenth teaspoon basil
Two dashes tabasco sauce
Two tablespoons margarine
Cooking time: Six to ten minutes
One cup shaved Swiss cheese
Servings: Four

Beat the eggs until whites and yolks are blended. Add the milk and seasonings. Heat the margarine slowly in a heavy skillet. Pour in the egg mixture. It should sizzle. Cook, mixing with a spatula, until it begins to thicken. Then cook until slightly brown on the bottom and almost firm. Sprinkle evenly with the shaved cheese. Fold and slide onto a hot platter. Garnish with parsley and serve at once.

Eggs and Breakfast Dishes

Shirred Eggs au Gratin

One-fourth cup butter
Three tablespoons flour
One-half teaspoon salt
One-sixteenth teaspoon pepper
Two cups milk
One cup grated cheddar cheese
Eight eggs
Oven temperature: 375 degrees
Bake: Fifteen to twenty minutes
Serves: Four

In a saucepan melt the butter. Blend in the flour, salt and pepper. Gradually stir in the milk and cook, stirring constantly until thickened. Add the cheese and stir until melted. Divide sauce between four individual ramekins or oversized custard cups. Break two eggs carefully into each. Cover ramekin with a piece of aluminum foil. Bake in a moderately hot oven for fifteen to twenty minutes or until eggs are set.

A FAVORITE RECIPE
Eggs Andrew

Two tablespoons butter or margarine, melted
One small onion, minced
Cooking time: Five minutes
Four eggs beaten with
One-fourth teaspoon salt
One-fourth cup milk
Two tablespoons dry sherry
Cooking time: Until it starts to get firm
Two ounces American cheese, minced
Cooking time: Two minutes
Servings: Two

Melt the butter in a heavy skillet. Add the onion; cook until glazed. In a bowl beat the eggs with the salt, milk and sherry. Pour over the onions. Cook over a low flame. When the mixture begins to thicken sprinkle the cheese over the top. Continue cooking until the cheese melts. Fold over and serve on a hot platter garnished with sprigs of parsley.

ANDREW CORMAN, *Brooklyn, N.Y.*

A FAVORITE RECIPE
Egg Parmesan

One tablespoon olive oil
Two eggs, mixed with
Three tablespoons grated Parmesan cheese
Three tablespoons catsup
One-sixteenth teaspoon marjoram
One-sixteenth teaspoon salt
Cooking time: Seven minutes, about
Servings: One, or two

Pour the oil into a cold skillet. Mix the eggs, cheese, catsup, marjoram and salt in a bowl. Pour into the cold skillet; place over flame, stir constantly as for scrambled eggs. Serve with hot rolls.

MISS THERESA A. RONGA, *New York, N.Y.*

Poached Eggs Special

One-fourth cup butter or margarine
One-fourth cup flour
One teaspoon salt
One-eighth teaspoon pepper
One teaspoon dry mustard
Two cups milk
Cook: Until thickened
One-fourth cup grated Gruyere or chedder cheese
Four strips bacon
Eight eggs
Four split English muffins, toasted
Servings: Four

In the upper half of a double boiler melt the butter or margarine. Blend in the flour, salt, pepper and dry mustard. Gradually add the milk, stirring constantly, until the sauce is thickened. Add the grated cheese and stir until melted into the sauce. Place over hot water while cooking the bacon, poaching the eggs and toasting the split English muffins. To serve place two toasted English muffin halves on each individual serving plate. Spoon cheese sauce over muffins and top each half with a well drained poached egg. Garnish with crisp strip of bacon and serve at once.

Baked Eggs with Sardines and Spinach

Butter
Two pkgs. (10 oz. each) frozen chopped spinach (defrosted)
One-half cup heavy cream
One teaspoon salt
One-eighth teaspoon pepper
One-eighth teaspoon nutmeg
Four eggs
One can (3¾ oz.) Norway sardines
Oven temperature: 350 degrees
Bake: Fifteen to twenty minutes
Four slices buttered toast
Serves: Four

Butter four individual ramekins. Drain the liquid from the defrosted frozen chopped spinach. In a bowl mix the spinach with the heavy cream, salt, pepper and nutmeg. Spoon mixture into the ramekins, making a depression in the center. Carefully place an egg in each depression. Arrange the drained sardines around the eggs. Cover tightly with a piece of foil. Bake in a moderate oven until eggs are set. Cut buttered toast into triangles and set around the edge of each ramekin. Serve at once.

Mustard Cheese Baked Eggs

One cup grated cheddar cheese
Four eggs
One-half teaspoon dry mustard
One-sixteenth teaspoon cayenne
One-half teaspoon salt
One-third cup milk
One tablespoon butter
Oven temperature: 350 degrees
Bake: Twelve to fifteen minutes
Four pieces crisp hot toast
Serves: Four

Scatter the grated cheese over the surface of a buttered pie plate (9 in.) mounding slightly to create nests for each of the four eggs. Break eggs carefully into hollows. In a cup stir together the dry mustard, cayenne and salt. Blend in the milk and pour over the eggs. Dot with butter and bake in a moderate oven until eggs are set. Serve each egg in cheese on a crisp piece of hot toast.

Pepper and Egg Omelet

Three tablespoons olive or salad oil
Four green peppers, cut in pieces
Sautéing time: Five to ten minutes
Eight eggs
One-fourth cup water
One teaspoon salt
One-eighth teaspoon pepper
Cooking time: Five to ten minutes
Servings: Four

Place the olive or salad oil in a large heavy skillet; add the cut green peppers and sauté until tender. Into a bowl break the eggs, add the water, salt and pepper and beat with a rotary beater. Pour over the tender peppers and cook until set. Stir as necessary until the eggs are as cooked as desired. Serve at once.

Special Scrambled Eggs

One baked pastry shell (8 or 9 in.)
Eight slices bacon
Fry: Crisp
Eight eggs
One teaspoon salt
One-fourth cup sauterne or dry white wine
One-fourth cup heavy cream
One teaspoon instant minced onion
Four tablespoons butter
Cook: Five to ten minutes
One-half cup grated cheddar cheese
Oven temperature: 350 degrees
Heat: Five minutes
Serves: Six

Prepare and bake a pastry shell (8 or 9 in.). If made ahead, reheat shell while scrambling the eggs. Fry the bacon in a heavy skillet until crisp. Drain on absorbent paper. In a bowl beat the eggs slightly and add the salt, wine, cream and minced onion. Heat the butter in a large skillet, add the eggs and cook over low heat, stirring occasionally until the eggs are nearly set. Spoon eggs into the crust and crumble bacon over the top. Sprinkle with the grated cheese and place in a moderate oven just long enough to melt the cheese. Serve at once.

Deviled Tomato Omelet

Six eggs
Two tablespoons water
Salt and pepper to taste
Two tablespoons butter or margarine
Two canned tomatoes, chopped
One can (4½ oz.) deviled ham
Cook: Five to ten minutes
Serves: Four

In a bowl beat the eggs slightly, add the water and salt and pepper to taste. Heat the butter or margarine in a large skillet. Pour in the eggs and cook over moderate heat. Run a spatula around the edge of the cooking egg mixture to permit the liquid portion to run under and come in contact with the heat. Before egg is completely set spoon the mixed chopped tomato and deviled ham over one half. Fold omelet over filling and slide on a heated platter to serve.

Cheese Sauced Puffy Omelet

Six egg whites
Three tablespoons water
One-half teaspoon salt
Six egg yolks
Two tablespoons flour
Dash of black pepper
One and one-half tablespoons butter
Browning time: Six minutes, or more
One-half pound American cheese, grated
One-half teaspoon dry mustard
Three-fourths cup milk
Oven temperature: 300 degrees
Baking time: Ten minutes, or more
Servings: Six

In a bowl beat the egg whites with the water and salt until stiff but not dry. In a smaller bowl beat the yolks with flour and pepper until thick and lemon colored. Carefully fold yolks into whites. In a large skillet heat the butter until melted. Add the egg mixture and cook on top of the stove until omelet is golden brown on the under side, about six minutes. Transfer to a slow oven and bake for ten minutes or until top starts to brown. In the meantime combine the grated cheese with the dry mustard in a saucepan, gradually blend in the milk. Cook over moderate heat until the cheese is thoroughly melted and sauce is smooth. To serve the omelet fold over in half and slide onto a heated platter. Cut into individual portions and serve with the cheese sauce.

Crab Meat Hash Omelet

One and one-half cups diced, raw potato
Boiling, salted water
Cook: Ten minutes, about
Three eggs
One teaspoon salt
One-eighth teaspoon pepper
Three tablespoons finely chopped green
 pepper
Three tablespoons finely chopped onion
One can (7 oz.) crab meat
Two tablespoons butter or margarine
Cook: Five to ten minutes
Serves: Four

Cook the diced, raw potatoes in the boiling, salted water until just tender. Drain. In a bowl beat the eggs with the salt and pepper. Add the chopped green pepper, onion and drained, cooked potatoes. Flake crab meat, removing cartilage, and add to the egg mixture. Melt the butter or margarine in a large heavy skillet. When hot, pour in the egg mixture. Cook, without stirring until the combination is nicely browned on the bottom and egg is set. Cut in four portions to serve. With a very large skillet fold over before portioning if desired.

Fine Herbs Omelet

One tablespoon butter
One tablespoon finely sliced green onion
One tablespoon chopped parsley
One tablespoon chopped chives
Pinch of dried tarragon
Sauté: Three to five minutes
Three eggs
One-half teaspoon salt
Dash of pepper
Cook: Until omelet is set
Serves: Two

In a skillet or omelet pan heat the butter. Add the green onion, parsley, chives and tarragon and sauté briefly over moderate heat. In a bowl fork-beat the eggs with the water, salt and pepper. Heat butter to bubbling point and pour in the egg mixture. Cook over low heat, lifting the cooked portion at edge with a spatula to allow the uncooked portion to run underneath. When creamy, increase the heat slightly to brown the under surface of the omelet lightly. Remove from the heat. Fold over and divide into two portions. Serve at once.

Eggs a la Benedict

Four slices broiled, baked ham or
 Canadian bacon
Four split English muffins, toasted
Four hard-cooked eggs, sliced
One cup Hollandaise sauce
Serves: Four

Place a slice of broiled ham or Canadian bacon on each toasted English muffin half. Arrange sliced hard-cooked eggs on top of each ham slice. Spoon sauce over all.

Hollandaise Sauce

One-fourth pound butter or margarine
 divided into three parts
Two egg yolks
One and one-half tablespoons lemon juice
One-half teaspoon salt
Few grains cayenne
Cook: Five minutes
Yield: One cup

In a heavy saucepan melt a third of the butter. Let stand until cool. Stir in the egg yolks, lemon juice, salt and cayenne. Place over very low heat. Add the second portion of butter; stirring constantly until it is blended into the mixture. Repeat procedure for the third portion of butter. If sauce is to stand, keep it covered in warm bowl in a saucepan with an inch or so of warm, not hot, water in the bottom.

Creamed Chicken Omelet

Four eggs
Two tablespoons cream or milk
One-half teaspoon salt
One can (10½ oz.) condensed cream of
 chicken soup
One tablespoon finely chopped parsley
One-third cup slivered toasted almonds
One tablespoon butter or margarine
Cook: Until eggs are set
Servings: Three

Break the eggs into a bowl, add the cream or milk and salt. Stir with a fork just until mixed. In a bowl combine the condensed cream of chicken soup with the finely chopped parsley and slivered toasted almonds. Heat the tablespoon of butter or margarine in a heavy skillet or omelet pan, pour in the egg mixture. Lower the heat and cook, tipping the pan and lifting the edge of the cooked egg with a spatula to let the uncooked portion run beneath. Place lid on pan for about a minute to set the top surface of egg. Spoon chicken, parsley and almond mixture over the omelet. Fold omelet in half, cut into three portions and serve.

Peppered Shrimp and Eggs

One-half pound cooked, peeled and
 deveined shrimp
Four slices bacon
Fry: Crisp
One-half cup finely chopped onion
Three-fourths cup chopped green pepper
Sauté: Until tender
One-half teaspoon salt
One-fourth teaspoon pepper
Cook: Five minutes
Six eggs
One-fourth cup cream
One teaspoon Worcestershire sauce
Cook: Five to ten minutes
Serves: Four

The small shrimp that are cooked, cleaned and frozen in half pound packages are a good choice for this dish. Thaw them first. At serving time cook the bacon in a large heavy skillet until crisp, remove and crumble. Add the chopped onion and green pepper to the bacon fat in the skillet, sauté until tender. Add the salt, pepper and shrimp. Cook briefly to heat through. In a bowl beat the eggs, add the cream, Worcestershire sauce and crumbled bacon and pour into the shrimp mixture. Cook, stirring occasionally until the eggs are firm. Serve at once.

Accent on Breakfast

Start the day right by having a good breakfast. Vary it by offering a different combination of fruit, cereal, beverage and egg dishes.

Eggs Baked in Toast Cups

Four slices bread
Butter
Catsup
Four eggs
Oven temperature: 375 degrees
Bake: Fifteen minutes
Serves: Four

Trim the crusts from the bread and spread one side with butter. Press each slice, butter side down, into a custard cup. Spread catsup over inner surface of the bread cup and break an egg into each. Bake in a moderately hot oven for fifteen minutes or until the eggs are set. Serve at once.

Scrambled Eggs and Chives

Twelve eggs
Three-fourths cup light cream
One-half teaspoon celery salt
One-eighth teaspoon pepper
Two tablespoons butter
Two tablespoons chopped chives
Scrambling time: Five minutes
One teaspoon paprika
Servings: Six

Beat the eggs slightly with a fork; stir in the cream and seasonings. Heat the butter in a heavy skillet over low heat; when hot pour in the egg mixture and chives. Cook, mixing gently, till the eggs are almost set. Remove to an ovenproof platter; serve over a dish warmer. Garnish with paprika.

Folded Cheese-Chive Omelet

Six eggs, beaten slightly
Six tablespoons water, or milk
Three-fourths teaspoon salt
One-eighth teaspoon pepper
One- sixteenth teaspoon basil
Two dashes tabasco sauce
Two tablespoons butter or margarine
Cooking time: Six to ten minutes
One cup shredded cheddar cheese
One-fourth cup chopped chives
Pimiento strips
Servings: Four

Beat the eggs until yolks and whites are blended. Add the water, or milk, and seasonings. Heat the butter slowly in a heavy skillet or omelet pan. Pour in the egg mixture. It should sizzle. Cook, mixing with a fork, until it begins to thicken. Then cook until slightly brown on the bottom and almost firm. Sprinkle evenly with the shredded cheese and three tablespoons of chives. Fold and slide onto a hot platter. Garnish with chives and pimiento strips. Serve at once.

Plain Omelet

Six eggs, beaten slightly
Six tablespoons milk or water
Three-fourths teaspoon chive salt
One-eighth teaspoon pepper
Three tablespoons margarine
Cooking time: Six to ten minutes
Servings: Four

Beat the eggs until the yolks and whites are blended. Stir in the milk and seasonings. Heat the margarine in a heavy skillet until hot. Pour in the omelet; cook slowly until set. Lift the edges as they cook,

allowing the uncooked portion to run under and around the cooked. When done, fold in half; slip onto a hot platter. Garnish with parsley. Serve immediately.

Ham and Cheese Omelet

Sprinkle three-fourths cup grated American or Parmesan cheese and one-half cup chopped ham over the omelet before folding. Garnish with ham and parsley.

Spanish Omelet

Cook one-half of a chopped onion and green pepper in two tablespoons margarine until soft. Add one can (8 oz.) tomato sauce; reheat. Serve between and around the omelet.

Shrimp Omelet

Heat one cup cooked shrimp and a can (10½ oz.) condensed celery soup. Serve between and around the omelet.

Mushroom Omelet

Bring one can (10½ oz.) condensed mushroom soup, one cup cooked sliced mushrooms and one-half cup cooked peas to a boil. Add one tablespoon sherry. Serve between and around the omelet.

Baked Omelet

Four eggs, separated
One cup thick white sauce
One-half teaspoon salt
One-eighth teaspoon pepper
One-eighth teaspoon marjoram
One tablespoon margarine
Cooking time: Five minutes
Oven temperature: 325 degrees
Baking time: Fifteen minutes (about)
Servings: Four

Beat the egg yolks until thick; add the sauce and seasonings. Beat the egg whites until stiff and fold into yolk mixture. Heat the margarine in a heavy skillet; pour in the omelet. Cook over low heat until a light brown on the bottom. Set in a moderately slow oven; bake until firm in the center and almost dry on the top. Cut part way through the center. Fold; slip onto a hot platter. Serve with a sauce of creamed mushrooms and peas.

A FAVORITE RECIPE
Eggs Mornay

Twelve hard-cooked eggs, shelled
Six tablespoons butter or margarine
Six tablespoons flour
One and three-fourths cups milk
One cup chicken broth
One-fourth cup sherry
Four ounces sharp cheese (cheddar)
One-half cup grated Parmesan cheese
One-half teaspoon salt
One-fourth teaspoon white pepper
One-half teaspoon Worcestershire sauce
Cooking time: Fifteen minutes in a double boiler
One teaspoon minced parsley
One cup croutons
Servings: Six

In a saucepan, cover the eggs with water; cook slowly for 20 to 25 minutes. Peel while hot. Place in a shallow baking dish (10 in.). In a double boiler, blend the butter and flour, add the milk and broth (can be made with bouillon cubes); sherry, cheddar and Parmesan cheese, salt and pepper and Worcestershire sauce; cook stirring until thick and smooth. Pour hot over the hot eggs. Scatter parsley and croutons over top. Serve with a salad and toasted rolls.

MRS. MARIE T. THOMSEN, *Jersey City, N.J.*

Pineapple Upside-Down French Toast

Two tablespoons butter or margarine
One-fourth cup brown sugar
One-fourth cup canned crushed pineapple,
    drained
One tablespoon pineapple syrup
One egg
Three-fourths cup milk
One-eighth teaspoon salt
Four slices bread
Oven temperature: 400 degrees
Bake: Twenty-five minutes
Serves: Four

In a baking pan (9 x 9 x 2 in.) melt the butter or margarine. Blend in the brown sugar and crushed pineapple, spreading evenly over the bottom of the pan. In a bowl beat the egg, add the milk and salt. Dip the bread slices into the egg and milk mixture to coat well, lay over the brown sugar and pineapple. Bake in a quick oven for twenty-five minutes. Remove from oven when lightly browned on top and let stand for about one minute before inverting over a platter. The topping will cling to the toast.

French Toast a l'Orange

One-fourth cup sugar
One-eighth teaspoon salt
Two teaspoons cornstarch
One-half cup orange juice
One-fourth cup dry white wine
Two teaspoons grated orange rind
Cooking time: Five to eight minutes
Two tablespoons butter or margarine
Two eggs
One-half teaspoon salt
One tablespoon sugar
One-sixteenth teaspoon nutmeg
One-fourth cup milk
One-fourth cup dry white wine
Butter or margarine
Six slices bread
Frying time: Five minutes, about
Servings: Three

Prepare the sauce first by combining in a small saucepan the fourth of a cup of sugar, eighth of a teaspoon of salt and cornstarch. Stir in the orange juice, wine and grated rind and cook over moderate heat, stirring constantly until sauce is thickened and clear. Add the butter. In a bowl, beat the eggs with the half teaspoon salt, tablespoon of sugar and nutmeg. Add the milk and remaining dry white wine; blend thoroughly. Melt the butter or margarine for frying in a heavy skillet. When well heated dip the slices of bread quickly into the egg mixture then place in the heated fat. Brown slowly on both sides, adding more butter or margarine to the skillet should it be needed. Serve hot with the hot orange sauce and crisp bacon slices.

Plain Waffles

Two cups sifted flour
Three teaspoons baking powder
One tablespoon sugar
One teaspoon salt
Three egg yolks
One and one-half cups milk
One-third cup salad oil
Three egg whites
Baking time: Three to five minutes
Yield: Six (7 in.) waffles

Sift together into a bowl the flour, baking powder, sugar and salt. In a second bowl beat the egg yolks and combine with the milk and salad oil. Add to the flour mixture, stirring only until blended. Beat egg whites to soft peaks and fold into the batter. Preheat the waffle iron to baking temperature. Pour about four tablespoons of batter into center of the iron, close the grids. Bake until the steam ceases. Serve waffle with butter and syrup.

Pecan Waffles

Two cups sifted flour
Three teaspoons baking powder
One-fourth teaspoon salt
One cup chopped pecans
Two egg yolks
One and one-half cups milk
One-third cup salad oil or melted
    shortening
Two egg whites
Servings: Six

Sift together into a bowl the flour, baking powder and salt. Stir in the chopped pecans. In a second bowl beat the egg yolks, add the milk and salad oil or melted shortening. Stir into the dry ingredients. Beat the egg whites until stiff and fold carefully into the batter. Preheat the waffle iron to baking temperature. Pour the batter into center of heated grids, spread slightly with a spoon. Close grids and bake until steam ceases. Serve waffles immediately with butter and maple syrup.

Pineapple Waffles

Two cups sifted flour
Three teaspoons baking powder
One teaspoon salt
Three egg yolks
Grated rind of one lemon
One and one-half cups canned crushed
    pineapple, drained
One cup milk
One-third cup salad oil
Three egg whites
Baking time: Three to five minutes
Yield: Six (seven-inch) waffles

Sift together into a bowl the flour, baking powder and salt. In a second bowl beat the egg yolks with the grated lemon rind, blend in the canned crushed pineapple, milk and salad oil. Add the flour mixture, stirring just enough to blend.

In a bowl beat the egg whites until they hold soft peaks. Fold into the batter carefully. Preheat the waffle iron to baking temperature. Pour about four tablespoons of batter into center of the iron, close the grids. Bake until the steam ceases. Serve waffles with butter and syrup.

A FAVORITE RECIPE
Corn Cakes

Four tablespoons butter or margarine,
    melted
Fat for frying
Frying time: Ten minutes, about
Two eggs, beaten light
One-half cup milk
One can (10½ oz.) cream-style corn
One small onion, grated
Two cups prepared biscuit mix
Serves: Four

In a bowl beat the eggs. Stir in the milk, corn and onion. Fold in the biscuit mix, stirring just enough to blend. Stir in the melted butter. Heat a griddle and grease lightly. Ladle a generous spoonful of batter for each cake on griddle. Bake until brown; turn, browning the other side. Serve with sausage and syrup.

MRS. HAROLD LANE, *Columbus, Ind.*

Buttermilk Pancakes

One and one-half cups sifted flour
Three-fourths teaspoon baking soda
Three-fourths teaspoon salt
One tablespoon sugar
One and one-half cups sour or buttermilk
Two egg yolks
Two teaspoons vanilla
Three tablespoons butter or margarine,
    melted
Two egg whites
Servings: Four, or five

Sift the flour, baking soda, salt and sugar into a bowl. Stir in the milk, egg yolks, vanilla and melted butter or margarine. Beat the egg whites in a second bowl until they hold soft peaks; fold into the first mixture. Spoon onto a hot greased griddle or skillet and brown pancakes on one side until top is covered with bubbles. Turn and brown second side. Serve hot with syrup.

Miniature Swiss Pancakes

Two egg yolks
One and one-fourth cups grated Swiss
    cheese
One-half cup dairy sour cream
One and one-half tablespoons flour
One-half teaspoon salt
One teaspoon prepared mustard
One tablespoon softened butter, or more
Fry: Until golden
Yield: Sixteen pancakes (2½ in.)

In a bowl beat the egg yolks, stir in the grated cheese, dairy sour cream, flour, salt and mustard. Mix well. In a heavy skillet melt the butter. Drop the batter by heaping teapoonfuls and fry until golden brown on both sides. Serve with fruit sauce or syrup.

Swedish Pancakes

Three eggs
Two tablespoons sugar
One-fourth teaspoon salt
One cup sifted flour
Three cups milk
Standing time: Two hours or more
Butter or margarine for frying
Yield: Forty, or more
Lingonberry preserves
Serves: Six to eight

In a bowl beat the eggs with the sugar and salt with a rotary beater. Gradually beat in the flour and milk, beating smooth. Let stand for two hours in the refrigerator before using. At serving time heat a heavy skillet with enough butter to prevent sticking. Drop spoonfuls of the thin batter in for small three inch pancakes. Brown on both sides. As they are cooked, transfer to a heated platter to keep warm. Serve six for a dessert portion, more for breakfast, spooning the lingonberry preserves over top, or rolling the pancakes over the preserves.

Griddle Cakes

Two and one-half cups sifted flour
Three teaspoons baking powder
One tablespoon sugar
Three-fourths teaspoon salt
Two cups milk
One egg yolk
One teaspoon vanilla
Three tablespoons butter or margarine, melted
One egg white
Servings: Four, or five

Sift the flour, baking powder, sugar and salt into a bowl. Stir in the milk, egg yolk, vanilla and melted butter or margarine. Mix well. Beat the egg white in a second bowl until it holds soft peaks; fold into the first mixture. Spoon onto a hot greased griddle or skillet and brown pancakes on one side until top is covered with bubbles. Turn and brown second side. Serve hot with syrup.

Nut Currant Syrup

Three tablespoons butter or margarine
Three tablespoons chopped pecans
One and one-half cups maple-blended syrup
One-half teaspoon cinnamon
Dash of salt
One-fourth cup currants
Simmer: Ten minutes
Yield: Two cups

In a saucepan melt the butter or margarine. Add the nuts and brown slightly. Add syrup, cinnamon and salt. Add currants, cover and simmer slowly for about ten minutes. Serve hot with hot griddle cakes.

Bran Griddle Cakes

Two cups sifted flour
Three teaspoons baking powder
One teaspoon baking soda
One teaspoon salt
Three tablespoons sugar
One cup ready-to-eat bran cereal
One cup hot water
One egg
One and one-half cups milk
Butter or shortening for frying
Yield: Twelve (6 in.); twenty-four (3 in.)

Sift together the flour, baking powder, soda, salt and sugar. Place the bran cereal in a small bowl and pour on the hot water. In a medium-sized bowl beat the egg, blend in the milk. Stir in the softened bran cereal then the sifted dry ingredients, stirring only until combined. Heat a small amount of butter or shortening in a heavy bottomed skillet or on a griddle. Pour about one-third cup of batter onto the skillet for each of the large pancakes. Turn when surface is studded with air holes. Brown on both sides, turning only once. Serve with syrup, jelly or the following Fig Sherry Sauce. Bake smaller cakes to serve as a dessert.

Fig Sherry Sauce

Three-fourths cup finely chopped dried figs
One-half cup water
Cooking time: Two to three minutes
Two tablespoons cornstarch
One-eighth teaspoon salt
One cup maple-blended syrup
Cooking time: Five minutes, about
Two tablespoons lemon juice
One teaspoon grated lemon rind
Two tablespoons butter
One-fourth cup sherry
Yield: Two cups

In a small saucepan, combine the chopped dried figs and water. Bring to a boil and cook briefly, stirring constantly, until all of the water is absorbed. Stir in the cornstarch, salt and syrup. Continue cooking, stirring constantly, until the mixture thickens, about five minutes. Remove from heat and stir in the lemon juice, rind, butter and sherry. Serve over pancakes, waffles, ice cream or puddings.

Corn Crumb Griddle Cakes

One egg
Two cups milk
Two tablespoons salad oil
One and one-third cups sifted flour
Three teaspoons baking powder
One-half teaspoon salt
Two tablespoons sugar
One-half cup corn flake crumbs
Servings: Four

In a bowl beat the egg. Blend in the milk and salad oil. Sift the flour, baking powder, salt and sugar into a second bowl. Stir in the corn flake crumbs. Add the liquid ingredients, stirring only until combined. Spoon onto a preheated griddle or lightly oiled heavy skillet to bake. Brown on both sides, turning once. Serve with butter and maple syrup or the following combination. This recipe will make about twenty-four three inch griddle cakes, fewer of larger size.

Fresh Corn Griddle Cakes

Two cups fresh corn, cut off the cob (three or four ears)
Three eggs
One teaspoon sugar
One teaspoon salt
One-half teaspoon baking powder
One-third cup corn meal
One-half cup dairy sour cream
Fat for frying
Fry: Five minutes, about
Yield: Ten or twelve

Cut corn from the cob to measure two cups. In a bowl beat the eggs, add the sugar, salt, baking powder and corn meal, mixing well. Fold in the dairy sour cream and the cut corn. Heat small amount of fat on a griddle or in a heavy skillet. Pour fourth cup measures of the mixture for each cake. Brown on both sides. Very good with bacon or ham.

Sour Cream Pancakes

Two eggs
One-half cup sieved cottage cheese
Three-fourths cup dairy sour cream
Three-fourths cup sifted flour
One teaspoon salt
One-half teaspoon baking soda
Standing time: Fifteen minutes
Fat or shortening for frying
Frying time: Five minutes, about
Yield: Twelve four-inch cakes

In a bowl, beat the eggs. Blend in the sieved cottage cheese and dairy sour cream. Sift together the flour, salt and baking soda and blend into the egg and cheese mixture. Let stand for a few minutes. Then spoon onto a lightly greased heated skillet or griddle and cook until browned on both sides, turning once. Serve at once with butter and apple sauce or maple syrup.

Spanish Puffy Omelet

Two tablespoons quick cooking tapioca
Three-fourths cup milk
One-half teaspoon salt
One-eighth teaspoon pepper
Cooking time: Ten minutes
One tablespoon butter
Four eggs, separated
Oven temperature: 350 degrees
Baking time: Fifteen minutes (about)
Two tablespoons minced green pepper
One medium-sized onion, cut into rings
Two tablespoons bacon fat
Cooking time: Five minutes
One can (No. 2) tomatoes
One-fourth cup chopped stuffed olives
One tablespoon sugar
One teaspoon salt
One-eighth teaspoon pepper
Cooking time: Fifteen minutes
Serves: Four, or more

Place a greased iron skillet (9 in.) in a moderate oven to heat. Combine the tapioca, milk, salt and pepper in the top of a double boiler. Cook over boiling water until slightly thick, stirring frequently. Add the butter. Beat the egg yolks until thick and lemon-colored. Fold into the tapioca mixture. Gently fold into the stiffly beaten egg whites. Pour into the hot greased skillet. Bake in a moderate oven until the top is dry and does not retain an impression when lightly pressed with the finger.

In a skillet cook the green pepper and onion rings in the bacon fat until soft. Add the remaining ingredients and cook until slightly thick. When the omelet is done, cut part way through the center. Pour half of the sauce over the omelet. Fold and slip onto a hot platter. Pour the remaining sauce around and on top of the omelet. Cut into wedges and serve. For variety try one of these in place of the Spanish sauce.

CHEESE OMELET: Sprinkle three-fourths cup grated cheddar cheese over cooked omelet just before folding omelet.

CREAMED MEAT OR FISH OMELET: Add one-half cup chopped cooked ham, chicken or tuna to a cup of medium white sauce. Serve omelet arranged on a hot platter with the creamed meat or fish between and over the omelet.

HAM CHIVE OMELET: Add one-fourth cup each of chopped ham and chives to beaten egg yolks.

A FAVORITE RECIPE
Avocado Omelet

One-half cup cubed (¼ in.) ripe avocado
One medium-sized tomato, peeled, seeded, cut into dice
Two teaspoons tomato juice
One-fourth teaspoon garlic salt
One-eighth teaspoon curry powder
Two tablespoons butter, heated
Four eggs, slightly beaten
Cooking time: Until set
Six slices avocado
Servings: Two

Peel a large ripe avocado; cut half into cubes, reserving the remainder for sliced avocado garnish. Place the diced avocado in a bowl; add the tomato, juice, salt, curry powder and eggs. Heat half of the butter in a heavy skillet, add half of the mixture; when omelette is cooked on the bottom, but soft on top, put over as omelette. Slide out of the skillet upon a hot plate. Make the second omelette in the same way. Garnish the omelette with sliced avocado and serve at once.

MRS. GEORGE PIANO, JR., *Tenafly, N.J.*

A FAVORITE RECIPE
Creamed Egg Bake

Four tablespoons butter, melted
One-half teaspoon Ac'cent
Four tablespoons flour
Two cups milk
Cooking time: Ten minutes in a double boiler
One teaspoon salt
Two tablespoons minced onion
One cup grated American cheese
Cooking time: Until the cheese is melted
Six hard-cooked eggs, cut into halves, lengthwise
One cup cooked, diced celery
One-fourth cup slivered green or stuffed olives
One-third cup buttered bread crumbs
Oven temperature: 325 degrees
Baking time: Twenty minutes
Servings: Six

In the top of a double boiler, melt the butter; stir in the Ac'cent and flour. Add the milk slowly, stirring constantly until smooth and thick. Add the salt, onion and cheese. Cook, stirring constantly until the cheese is melted. Arrange in a well-

buttered casserole half of the sliced eggs; sprinkle the celery and olives over the eggs, then half of the cheese sauce. Repeat the layers, sprinkling the buttered crumbs over the top. Bake in a moderately slow oven until the crumbs are lightly browned. Serve hot from the casserole.

ISABEL R. TINSLEY, *New York, N.Y.*

A FAVORITE RECIPE
Potato Eggs

Four hard-cooked eggs, separated
One can (4 oz.) minced ham
One-fourth teaspoon salt
One-eighth teaspoon pepper
Four medium-sized potatoes, peeled, cooked, drained, mashed and seasoned
One tablespoon flour
One egg, beaten light
Two tablespoons browned crumbs
Deep fat for frying
Frying temperature: 365 degrees
Frying time: Three minutes
Servings: Four

Cut the hard-cooked eggs into halves lengthwise. Remove the yolks to a bowl; add the minced ham, salt and pepper, blending well. Refill the egg whites, pressing the halves together. Divide the potatoes into four parts; flatten each part into a circle; place an egg in the center of each, folding the mashed potatoes around the egg, making sure the egg is well covered. Dip into the flour, then into beaten egg and the browned crumbs. Heat the fat in a deep kettle. Cook the eggs, drain and serve hot.

MRS. VIOLET TESKEY, *Bronx, N.Y.*

Cheese

Asparagus Ham Swiss Rarebit

Twenty stalks asparagus
Two cups boiling water
One teaspoon salt
Cooking time: Twelve minutes, or more
Four slices boiled ham
Twelve toasted bread triangles
Three tablespoons flour
One-half teaspoon salt
One-half teaspoon dry mustard
One-fourth teaspoon pepper
One-half pound grated Swiss cheese
One and three-fourths cups warm milk
One tablespoon steak sauce
Six drops Angostura bitters
Cooking time: Five minutes, or more
Serves: Four

Break off each stalk of asparagus as far down as it snaps easily. Wash very thoroughly under a stream of water. Remove any loose scales. With soft cord, tie five stalks together for each bundle. Cook, covered in one inch of boiling salted water until stalk can be easily pierced with fork. Remove cord. Wrap each bundle in a slice of ham and place on a piece of toast in a warm serving dish. Keep warm. Meanwhile, blend the dry ingredients with the Swiss cheese. Pour milk into chafing dish or electric skillet; heat until bubbly. Add the coated Swiss cheese, only in small amounts, stirring each time until cheese is melted. Add the steak sauce and bitters. Pour over the asparagus and ham in the serving dish. Garnish with remaining toast triangles. Serve immediately.

A FAVORITE RECIPE

Cheese Custard-Frankfurters

Three slices bread, buttered, cubed
One-half pound sharp cheese, cut in thin slices
Six frankfurters, cut into one-inch pieces
Three eggs
Two cups milk
One teaspoon salt
One-fourth teaspoon pepper
Oven temperature: 350 degrees
Baking time: Fifty minutes, about
Serves: Four

In a well buttered casserole (1½ qts.) place layers of the cubed bread, cheese and frankfurters. Beat the eggs, milk and seasonings in a bowl; pour over top. Bake in a moderate oven until firm. Serve hot.

ROSE JOSEPH, *Glens Falls, N.Y.*

Pizza Omelet

Six eggs
One-third cup milk
One teaspoon salt
One-eighth teaspoon pepper
One-half cup diced cooked ham (four
    slices boiled ham)
One-fourth cup ripe olive pieces
One cup grated cheddar cheese
One tablespoon butter or margarine
Cook: Five minutes, or more
Broiler temperature: 500 degrees
Broil: Three to five minutes
Serves: Four

In a bowl beat the eggs, blend in the milk, salt and pepper. Dice cooked ham, cut ripe olives and grated cheddar. In a large heavy skillet melt the butter or margarine. When heated pour in the eggs. Cook, lifting edge of omelet with a spatula so uncooked portion may run underneath. When eggs are almost set, scatter ham, olives and finally the cheese over the omelet and slip under the broiler just long enough to melt the cheese. Cut into portions and serve at once.

Omelet with Cheese Sauce

Sauce
Two tablespoons butter or margarine
Two and one-half tablespoons flour
One and one-fourth cups milk
Cook: Ten minutes, about
One-half cup grated cheddar cheese
One-half teaspoon salt
One-sixteenth teaspoon pepper
Two teaspoons steak sauce
One-fourth cup chopped nuts
Omelet
Six eggs
One-third cup milk
One-half teaspoon salt
One-sixteenth teaspoon pepper
Two tablespoons butter or margarine
Cook: Five to eight minutes
Serves: Four

In the upper half of a double boiler melt the first measure of butter or margarine. Stir in the flour and gradually blend in the milk. Cook, stirring constantly until the sauce thickens. Add the cheese, salt, pepper, steak sauce and chopped nuts and stir over low heat until the cheese is melted. Place over hot water to keep warm while preparing the omelet. In a bowl beat the eggs, add the milk, salt and pepper. Melt the two tablespoons of butter or margarine in an omelet pan or large heavy skillet. (Use large pan if single omelet is to be cooked, a six-inch pan for four individual omelets.)

Heat butter to bubbling point and pour in the egg mixture. Cook over low heat, lifting the cooked portion with a spatula to allow the uncooked portion to run underneath. When creamy increase the heat slightly to brown the under surface of the omelet lightly. Remove from the heat. Fold over and remove to platter or plates. Spoon sauce over individual servings.

A FAVORITE RECIPE
Crab Meat and Cheese Fondue

One can (No. 8) crab meat
One cup minced celery
One tablespoon prepared mustard
One-fourth teaspoon salt
Three tablespoons mayonnaise or a
    favorite salad dressing
Eight thin slices white bread
Three-fourths pound sliced American
    cheese
Two eggs, beaten with
One cup milk
One teaspoon Worcestershire sauce
Oven temperature: 325 degrees
Baking time: Forty-five minutes
Servings: Four

Remove all cartilage from the crab meat. In a bowl, mix with the celery, mustard, salt and enough salad dressing to make a spreading consistency. Spread the mixture over the bread, making sandwiches. Cut into halves or three strips. Place in a casserole, making alternate layers of the sandwiches and cheese. Beat the eggs and milk in a bowl, add the Worcestershire sauce. Pour over the cheese and sandwiches. Bake in a moderately slow oven. Serve hot.

MRS. ELLEN MARSHALL, *Portland, Maine*

A FAVORITE RECIPE
Pancakes au Gratin

Three tablespoons butter
Two tablespoons flour
One cup milk
Cooking time: Ten minutes in a double
    boiler
Three-fourths cup grated American cheese
Seasonings to taste
One cup diced (¼ in.) cooked chicken

Batter

One egg, beaten light
One and one-half cups milk
One and one-fourth cups pancake mix
Two tablespoons melted butter
Frying time: Five minutes
One-fourth cup grated cheese
Oven temperature: 350 degrees
Baking time: Until cheese is melted
Yield: Eight cakes

In the top of a double boiler, blend the butter and flour; add the milk, stirring until smooth. Stir in the cheese, stirring until melted; add seasonings and the chicken. For the batter: Beat the egg in a bowl, add the milk, mix. Stir in the pancake mix, stir until well blended; stir in the melted butter. Fry in a hot heavy skillet, well greased, or a pancake griddle, using two tablespoonfuls for each cake. While still hot, spread the cakes with the creamed chicken; roll as for jelly roll, binding with toothpicks. Sprinkle with the grated cheese. Place in a long serving oven dish. Bake in a moderate oven until the cheese is melted. Serve hot.

MRS. HARRY FRANK, *Bronx, N.Y.*

A FAVORITE RECIPE
Asparagus Rarebit

One tablespoon butter or margarine,
    melted
Two cups grated sharp cheddar cheese
Cooking time: Until cheese is melted in
    a double boiler
One-half teaspoon dry mustard
One teaspoon Worcestershire sauce
Three-fourths cup warm milk
One dash tabasco
One egg, well beaten
Cooking time: Until thickened
One package frozen asparagus, thawed
    and cooked, or one pound fresh, cooked
One-half teaspoon salt
One-eighth teaspoon pepper
Eight toast triangles
Servings: Four

In the top of a double boiler, melt the butter; add the grated cheese, stirring until the cheese is melted. Stir in the mustard, Worcestershire sauce, milk and tabasco; until well blended. Beat the egg in a small bowl, add several tablespoons of the hot cheese mixture, mix well and return to the cheese mixture. Cook until the mixture thickens. Cook the asparagus with salt and pepper as directed on package. Drain thoroughly. Arrange the asparagus over the toast; cover with cheese sauce.

MRS. FRANK DORST, *Freeport, L.I.*

Cheese Soup

One-fourth cup butter or margarine
Two tablespoons finely chopped onion
Sauté: Until tender
One-half teaspoon dry mustard
One-fourth teaspoon paprika
Three cups milk
One pound aged cheddar, cubed
Heat: Just until cheese melts
Toasted bread cubes
Serves: Four, or more

In the top of a large double boiler or in a very heavy saucepan or skillet melt the butter or margarine. Add the finely chopped onion and sauté until tender. Stir in the dry mustard and paprika. Add the milk and cubed cheddar cheese. Heat carefully just until the cheese melts, stirring occasionally; do not permit to boil. Serve in soup bowls with cubes of toasted wheat or rye bread tossed on top.

Onion Cheese Soufflé

Three tablespoons butter or margarine
Three medium-sized onions, chopped
Sauté: Till golden
Three tablespoons flour
One tablespoon prepared mustard
One teaspoon salt
One-eighth teaspoon cayenne pepper
One and one-fourth cups milk
Cook: Till thickened
One-half cup grated sharp cheddar cheese
Four egg yolks
Four egg whites
Oven temperature: 375 degrees
Bake: Thirty-five minutes
Serves: Four

In a heavy skillet or saucepan melt the butter or margarine. Add the chopped onion and sauté until golden. Stir in the flour, prepared mustard, salt, pepper and gradually blend in the milk, stirring smooth. Cook, stirring, until thickened. Add the cheese and stir until melted, remove from heat. In a small bowl beat the egg yolks, stir into the sauce. In a large bowl beat the egg whites until they hold soft peaks. Fold the sauce into the beaten whites. Transfer to an ungreased baking dish (1½ qts.) and bake in a moderately hot oven for thirty-five minutes. Serve at once.

Hot Cheese Tartlets

Two cups finely grated Swiss cheese
Two teaspoons flour
One egg, beaten
One-half cup evaporated milk or cream
One-half teaspoon salt
One-eighth teaspoon dry mustard
One-eighth teaspoon pepper
One-half recipe pastry
Oven temperature: 425 degrees
Baking time: Seventeen minutes (about)
Yield: Forty-eight

Mix the cheese and flour. Combine the egg, milk and seasonings. Set both aside. Roll out pastry (⅛ in. thick or less); cut into rounds (1½ in.). Fit into small muffin pans (1½ in.). Bake for five minutes to a light brown in a hot oven. Remove from the oven. At once put one-fourth teaspoon floured cheese over each tartlet and pour one teaspoon egg mixture over the cheese. Return to the oven. Bake until golden brown for 12 minutes. Sprinkle with paprika. Serve hot, or cool and reheat.

Cheese Rice Timbales

Two tablespoons butter or margarine
One-fourth cup finely chopped green pepper
One tablespoon finely chopped onion
Sauté: Five to eight minutes
One tablespoon flour
Three-fourths cup milk
Cook: Five minutes, or more
One-half teaspoon salt
One-half teaspoon dry mustard
One cup grated cheddar cheese
Two beaten eggs
One cup cooked rice
Oven temperature: 350 degrees
Bake: Twenty-five minutes, about
Serves: Four

In a heavy skillet melt the butter or margarine. Add the finely chopped green pepper and onion and sauté until tender. Stir in the flour and gradually blend in the milk, stirring the while. Cook over moderate heat, stirring constantly, until the sauce thickens. Stir in the salt and dry mustard. Remove from heat and stir in the grated cheese. Blend in the beaten eggs and cooked rice. Mix well. Spoon into four greased custard cups and bake in a moderate oven until firm. Unmold and serve at once.

Cheese Timbales

One and one-half tablespoons butter or margarine
Three tablespoons flour
Three-fourths cup undiluted evaporated milk
Three-fourths cup beer (room temperature)
Cooking time: Fifteen minutes or more in a double boiler
Three cups grated American cheddar cheese (¾ lb.)
Two eggs, beaten
Two teaspoons grated onion
One-half cup dry bread crumbs
One-half teaspoon dry mustard
One-half teaspoon salt
One-eighth teaspoon pepper
Oven temperature: 350 degrees
Baking time: Thirty minutes, or until firm
Serves: Six

Make a white sauce of the butter, flour, mixed evaporated milk and beer in a double boiler, stirring until thickened. Then cover and cook 10 minutes longer; stir occasionally. Take from the hot water; stir in the cheese. Slowly add the hot mixture to the beaten eggs in a bowl, stirring the while. Add the onion, dry bread crumbs and seasonings. Place in greased timbale molds or custard cups and set them in a pan containing hot water. Bake in a moderate oven until firm in the center like custard. Take from the hot water; let stand five minutes. Unmold upon a heated platter and serve with tomato sauce.

Swiss Cheese Tarts

Two cups sifted flour
One teaspoon salt
Two-thirds cup shortening
Five or six tablespoons cold water
Two eggs
One cup milk
Pinch dry mustard
Pinch cayenne
One-fourth teaspoon Worcestershire sauce
One-fourth teaspoon salt
Two cups grated Swiss cheese
Oven temperature: 400 degrees
Bake: Fifteen minutes
Yield: Eight (3½ inch)

Sift the flour and salt together into a bowl. Cut in half the shortening until as fine as corn meal, cut in second half until the size of small peas. Stir in enough cold water to bind the crumbs together. When dough follows fork around the bowl, turn it out on a floured board. Divide into eight pieces with a knife and roll each piece out to line an individual tart shell or a custard cup. Trim and flute the edge. In a bowl beat the eggs, add the milk, mustard, cayenne, Worcestershire sauce, salt and grated Swiss cheese. Mix well and spoon into the tart shells. Bake in a quick oven for fifteen minutes or until pastry is crisp and browned and filling set. Serve at once.

Roquefort Asparagus Soufflé

One-fourth cup butter or margarine
One-fourth cup flour
One cup milk
Cook: Five minutes
One-third cup crumbled packed Roquefort cheese
Four egg yolks
One cup sliced, cooked asparagus
Four egg whites
One-fourth teaspoon cream of tartar
Oven temperature: 350 degrees
Bake: One hour
Servings: Four

In a saucepan, melt the butter or margarine, stir in the flour. Gradually blend in the milk, stirring smooth. Cook, stirring constantly, until the sauce thickens. Add the crumbled Roquefort cheese and cook and stir until cheese is melted. In a bowl, beat the egg yolks until thick and lemon colored. Add a little of the cooked mixture to the yolks; return combination to the saucepan and mix well. Fold in the sliced cooked asparagus. In a large bowl, beat the egg whites until foamy. Add the cream of tartar and beat until stiff but not dry. Add the cheese and vegetable mixture and fold carefully into the beaten whites. Transfer to a baking dish (1½ qts.) and bake in a moderate oven for one hour or until set and well browned. Serve at once from the baking dish.

Onion Cheese Custard Pie

One-fourth cup butter or margarine
One large onion, thinly sliced
Sauté: Five to ten minutes
Four eggs
One-half cup heavy cream
One-fourth cup dry white wine
Two teaspoons steak sauce
One teaspoon salt
One-eighth teaspoon pepper
One-half cup grated cheddar cheese
One unbaked pastry shell (9 in.)
Oven temperature: 350 degrees
Bake: Thirty minutes
Serves: Six

In a large heavy skillet melt the butter or margarine, add the thinly sliced onion and sauté until just golden in color. Remove from the heat. In a bowl beat the eggs, blend in the cream, dry white wine, steak sauce, salt, pepper and grated cheese. Mix with the sautéed onion and pour combination into the unbaked pastry shell. Bake in a moderate oven for thirty minutes or until the custard is set and filling is nicely browned on top. Cut into wedges and serve at once.

American Cheddar Cheese

It is a hard cheese ranging in color from nearly white to orange and ripening anywhere from two months to two years. The flavor becomes sharper and richer, as well as more expensive as it ages.

Armenian Bread: Solid, fine-grained, crusty bread, slashed and topped with a few sesame seeds.

American Chianti Wine: Has a fragrant flavor, pleasant even when slightly chilled.

The American Cheddar Cheese, because of its sharpness, is served with a pungent American red wine and a simple Armenian bread.

Finnish Swiss Cheese

It is one of the most difficult cheeses to make and requires a skilled cheese maker. Three species of bacteria are needed as starters. The cheese is cured from six to ten months and has a pronounced flavor.

Swiss Bread: Called St. Gall bread, is crusty and reminds one of the old-fashioned close textured homemade kind.

California or French Rosé Wine: Is dry, light, delicate in color and flavor. Serve it slightly chilled.

The Finnish Swiss Cheese is mild and complements the delicate flavor and firm texture of the St. Gall bread. The very dry and light chilled Rosé wine makes a perfect "marriage."

Swiss Appenzeller

Named after the Canton of Appenzell, it is made of whole cow's milk. The cheese is put for a week into cider or white wine to which spices have been added. The flavor is delicate and the eyes of the cheese are small and sparsely distributed.

American Bread: It is white, enriched and toasted.

Neuchatel Swiss Wine: It is a young wine and is light, refreshing and sparkling. Usually served in a small (5 oz.) glass.

The delicate flavor and solid texture of the cheese go well with the bland soft-textured warm toast. Neuchatel wine adds a touch of lightness.

Canadian Smoked Cheese

It is a Swiss cheese, cut into small portions, wrapped loosely in parchment and smoked where sturgeon is smoked. The flavor is nutty.

Swedish Bread: Slightly sweet and spicy dark bread.

Alsatian Gewurztraminer Wine: A light white wine, delightfully fruity and is served well chilled.

The smoky taste of the Canadian cheese is well balanced by the lightly sweetish flavor of the Swedish bread and the fruitiness and freshness of the Alsatian Riesling wine.

Stilton Cheese in Port Wine

It is a rich creamy color with a tinge of greenish-yellow, its veins wide-branching and its texture somewhat flaky. Port wine is worked into the Stilton cheese to a spreading consistency. It is marketed in crockery jars.

Syrian Bread: An over-sized crusty English muffin without the in-between breadiness.

Spanish Sherry Wine: Blended in a unique way by mixing aged mellow sherry with the newer wine. It ranges from extremely dry to very sweet.

Crusty bread is selected because of its crispness and mildness and tastes wonderful with the highly flavored sharp Stilton Port spread. The Spanish dry sherry has a round oak flavor which goes well with the cheese spread. This combination is ideal for a cocktail party.

St. Paulin Cheese

A French cheese which comes from the French district of the Alps, it's somewhat pungent, orange in color, superb in flavor and semi-soft.

Italian Bread: Called Montagha, it is shaped like a priest's biretta, mild-flavored, soft and crusty.

Red Bordeaux Wine of Medoc: It is full-bodied, dry, superb in bouquet and delicate in flavor. To drink it at its best, uncork the bottle one hour before serving.

The Montagha Italian bread is chosen because of its mild flavor, crustiness and soft texture to go with the St. Paulin cheese which is rather pungent. Both bring out the delicate flavor of the Red Bordeaux Wine of Medoc.

Danish Tilsit With Caraway Seed

It is forthright in flavor, semi-soft, light creamy in color and with many small holes to give it texture.

Russian Rye Bread: Very dark and coarse in texture.

French Chablis Wine: Light, very dry, has a characteristic flinty flavor. It is served very cold.

The Danish Tilsit with caraway seeds is excellent with the coarse textured, extremely dark bread. Serve a French Chablis wine, for it is very dry, and has a "clean" taste which does not interfere with the pungent seedy cheese or bread.

Dredge the cheese in flour. Pour the white wine into an earthenware dish, chafing dish or electric frying pan. Set the dish over very low heat, cook to the point that air bubbles rise to the surface (never allow it to boil). Add the cheese by handfuls, each handful to be completely dissolved before another one is added, stirring constantly. When mixture starts to bubble slightly, add a few grains of freshly ground pepper. Finally stir in the Kirschwasser, thoroughly. (If it becomes too thick add hot wine to mixture.) Cut the bread into bite-size pieces. Each one spears a piece of bread with a fork; then swirls it in the fondue and eats it. Towards the end some of the melted cheese forms a brown crust at the bottom of the utensil. Remove with a fork. This morsel is considered a special delicacy.

A FAVORITE RECIPE
Cheese Dumplings

One pound pot cheese
One white bread roll (5 in.) soaked in water, squeezed dry
Two egg yolks, beaten light
One tablespoon flour
Two tablespoons bread crumbs
One-half teaspoon salt
Chilling time: One hour
Two tablespoons flour, seasoned
Three quarts, boiling water
Simmering time: Five minutes
Servings: Four

In a bowl, mix the cheese, bread roll, egg yolks, flour, bread crumbs and salt. Chill. Form into dumplings (1½ in.); dust with flour; have the salted water boiling; drop in the dumplings, reduce the heat, simmer. Remove carefully from the water with a perforated spoon. Serve sprinkled with sugar and cinnamon and hot melted butter, or plain with meat.

MRS. A. STACKMAN, *Bronx, N.Y.*

Asparagus Pizza-Type Specialty

One recipe (2 cups) pastry
Oven temperature: 425 degrees
Baking time: Twenty minutes
One-half pound sliced boiled ham
One can (10½ oz.) condensed cream of asparagus soup
One can (4 oz.) sliced mushrooms
One and one-half cups grated Switzerland Swiss cheese
Two tablespoons Spanish sherry wine
One teaspoon salt
One-fourth teaspoon pepper
One-fourth teaspoon sage
One tablespoon minced onion flakes
One and one-half pounds asparagus, cooked
Baking time: Fifteen minutes
Serves: Four

On a floured board roll out the pastry to fit a pizza pan (12 in.). Flute edge and prick side and bottom of pastry. Chill in refrigerator about one-half hour; then bake in a hot oven until golden. Remove to rack. Set aside four slices of ham. Chop the remaining slices; scatter over the bottom of the cooled baked pastry shell. Combine the asparagus soup, sliced mushrooms and liquid, grated Switzerland Swiss cheese, sherry wine, salt, pepper, sage and onion flakes; pour over the ham. Roll each slice of reserved ham around 3 stalks of cooked asparagus into a cornucopia. Arrange over the sauce. Then place remaining stalks in a pinwheel fashion between the cornucopias. Bake in a very hot oven for 15 minutes. Serve immediately in wedges.

Switzerland Swiss Cheese Fondue

One pound Switzerland Swiss cheese, finely grated
Three tablespoons flour
Two cups Neuchatel wine, or any dry white Rhine or Chablis type
Few grains pepper
Cooking time: Fifteen minutes
One-fourth cup Kirschwasser
Six long thin hard rolls or one loaf French bread
Serves: Six

A FAVORITE RECIPE
Potato Cheese Casserole

Five medium-sized potatoes, peeled,
  sliced very thin
One medium-sized onion, sliced thin
One-fourth pound American cheese,
  shredded
One-half cup grated Parmesan cheese
One teaspoon salt
One-fourth teaspoon pepper
One-fourth teaspoon garlic salt
One can (10½ oz.) condensed cream of
  mushroom soup
One cup milk
Two tablespoons bread crumbs
Three tablespoons butter, melted
Oven temperature: 325 degrees
Baking time: One and one-half hours
Servings: Six

Wash, peel and slice the potatoes,
wafer thin. Line the bottom of a casserole
(1½ qt.) with a layer of the potatoes,
onion and shredded cheese, season with
the Parmesan, salt, pepper and garlic salt.
Repeat the layers until all ingredients are
used. Pour the mushroom soup mixed
with the milk over the top. Sprinkle the
bread crumbs over the top and dot with
butter. Bake in a moderately slow oven
until a golden brown. Serve from the casserole.

MRS. JOHN J. MICELI, *New London, Conn.*

Cheese Scallop of Okra and Corn

Two tablespoons butter or margarine
One can (No. 2) cut okra, drained
Sauté: Ten minutes
One can (No. 2) whole kernel corn or
  red kidney beans, drained
Two tablespoons butter or margarine
Two tablespoons flour
One-fourth teaspoon salt
One cup milk
Cook: Five to eight minutes
One-fourth pound cheddar cheese, grated
Two tablespoons fine dry bread crumbs
Oven temperature: 350 degrees
Bake: Thirty minutes
Serves: Six

Melt the two tablespoons of butter or
margarine in a heavy skillet, add the
drained okra and sauté briefly. Place the
drained corn or kidney beans in a greased
casserole, top with sautéed okra. In a
heavy bottomed saucepan melt the two
tablespoons of butter or margarine, stir
in the flour and salt, gradually blend in
the milk. Cook, stirring constantly, over
moderate heat until the sauce thickens.
Add the grated cheese and stir until
melted. Pour sauce over the vegetables
in the casserole. Sprinkle fine dry bread
crumbs over the top and bake in a moderate oven until the crumbs are lightly
browned.

Eggplant Stacked with Mozzarella

Two tablespoons olive oil
One medium-sized onion, finely chopped
One large clove garlic, crushed
Sauté: Ten minutes
Two cans (6 oz. each) tomato sauce
One-half cup water
Two bouillon cubes
One-eighth teaspoon salt
Simmer: Fifteen minutes
One eggplant (1½ lbs.)
Two eggs, beaten
Three-fourths cup fine dry bread crumbs
One-fourth cup grated Parmesan cheese
Shortening for frying
Sauté: Five minutes, about
One-half pound mozzarella cheese
One-half teaspoon oregano
Oven temperature: 350 degrees
Bake: Thirty minutes
Servings: Four to six

In a heavy, skillet heat the olive oil.
Add the chopped onion and crushed garlic and sauté until golden. Add the tomato sauce, water, bouillon cubes and
salt. Simmer. Wash the eggplant; cut off
the stem and blossom ends and slice into
one-fourth inch slices. (If the vegetable
is young you need not peel unless you
prefer.) Dip the slices in the slightly
beaten eggs, then in the combined fine
dry bread crumbs and grated Parmesan
cheese. Heat shortening in the large
heavy skillet to a depth of about one-
fourth inch. Add the prepared eggplant
slices a few at a time and sauté until
browned on both sides. Remove to absorbent paper. When all the slices are
fried arrange in stacks in a greased shallow baking dish with thin slices of the
mozzarella between eggplant slices; end
with slice of cheese on top. Each stack
is an individual portion. Pour the tomato
sauce over and around these individual
servings. Sprinkle the oregano over top.
Bake in a moderate oven for thirty minutes. Serve piping hot.

Eggplant Parmesan

Four cups diced fresh tomatoes
Two tablespoons olive or salad oil
Two tablespoons tomato paste
One teaspoon sugar
One and three-fourths teaspoons salt
One-fourth teaspoon pepper
One clove garlic, crushed
Simmer: Fifteen minutes
One medium-sized eggplant
One-half cup olive or salad oil, about
Two cups soft bread crumbs
Two tablespoons finely chopped parsley
One-half cup grated Parmesan cheese
One-fourth pound Mozzarella cheese
  (optional)
Oven temperature: 350 degrees
Bake: Thirty minutes
Servings: Four

In a saucepan combine the tomatoes,
two tablespoons olive oil, tomato paste,
sugar, salt, pepper and crushed garlic.
Simmer over low heat for 15 minutes or
until thick. In the meantime, wash, peel
and cut the eggplant into half-inch crosswise slices. Heat the olive or salad oil as

needed in a large heavy skillet and add
a few slices of eggplant at a time to
brown well on both sides. Place half the
browned slices in a baking pan (12 x 7
x 2 in.) or two pie plates. In a bowl
combine the bread crumbs with the parsley and grated Parmesan cheese. Spoon
half the tomato sauce over the eggplant
and top with half the crumbs. Add remaining eggplant, sauce and crumbs in
second layering. Top with thinly sliced
Mozzarella if desired. Bake in a moderate
oven for 30 minutes. Serve piping hot.

A FAVORITE RECIPE
Stuffed Eggplant

One-fourth cup olive oil
Three large onions, chopped
One large green pepper, chopped
Cooking time: Five minutes
Pulp from two eggplants (1 lb. each)
One cup drained canned tomatoes
One-third cup chopped parsley
Three tablespoons grated Parmesan
  cheese
One teaspoon salt
One-half teaspoon pepper
Four slices mozzarella cheese
One-fourth teaspoon paprika
Oven temperature: 350 degrees
Baking time: Fifty minutes
Servings: Four

Heat the oil in a skillet; sauté the
onions and peppers in the oil. Wash the
eggplants. With a sharp knife cut the
eggplants into halves, lengthwise. Scoop
out the pulp. Add the pulp to the onion
mixture, tomatoes, parsley, cheese, salt
and pepper. Fill the eggplant shells with
the mixture. Top each with a slice of
mozzarella cheese. Dust with paprika. Arrange the filled shells in a baking dish
(12 in.); add hot water to depth of one-
inch. Bake in a moderate oven. Serve hot.

MRS. H. KRAUSE, *New York, N.Y.*

Cheesed Asparagus on Deviled
Ham Toast

Three tablespoons butter
Three tablespoons flour
One-fourth teaspoon salt
One cup milk
Cook: Five minutes, or more
One-half cup grated cheddar cheese
Fresh, frozen or canned asparagus spears
  (about sixteen)
One can (3 oz.) ham spread or deviled ham
Four slices crisp hot toast
Serves: Four

In a saucepan melt the butter. Stir in
the flour and salt. Gradually blend in
the milk. Cook, stirring constantly, until
the sauce thickens. Add the grated cheddar cheese and stir until blended into
sauce. Cook fresh or frozen asparagus
spears or heat the canned. Spread the
ham spread or deviled ham over the four
slices of crisp hot toast and place on
serving plates. Arrange hot drained asparagus on toast and top off with the
cheese sauce. Serve at once.

Lamb Hash au Gratin

One cup finely diced potatoes
One-third cup minced onion
One-third cup minced green pepper
Two cups boiling water
Blanching time: Five minutes
Three tablespoons diced pimiento
Two cups cubed (¼ in.) cold lamb
One cup leftover gravy
One-third cup tomato puree
One-half teaspoon salt
One-eighth teaspoon pepper
One-eighth teaspoon paprika
One teaspoon Worcestershire sauce
Two tablespoons margarine
One-half cup grated cheddar cheese
Oven temperature: 350 degrees
Baking time: Twenty-five minutes
Serves: Four

In a saucepan blanch the potatoes, onions and green peppers in the boiling salted water. Drain. Combine the pimiento, lamb, gravy, tomato puree, salt, pepper, paprika, Worcestershire sauce and one tablespoon of butter. Pour into a greased shallow baking dish (2 qts.). Sprinkle with cheese and dot with the remaining butter. Bake in a moderate oven until lightly browned. Remove; serve.

Tri-Cheese Lasagna

Three tablespoons olive oil
One cup finely chopped onion
One clove garlic, crushed
Sauté: Five to ten minutes
One can (No. 2) tomatoes
Two tablespoons chopped parsley
Two cans (6 oz. each) tomato paste
One teaspoon sugar
One teaspoon salt
One-eighth teaspoon pepper
One cup water
Simmer: Thirty minutes
One-half pound lasagna noodles
Boiling salted water
Cook: Until tender
One-half pound cheddar cheese, sliced
Two cups creamed cottage cheese
One-third cup grated Parmesan cheese
Oven temperature: 350 degrees
Bake: Thirty-five minutes
Serves: Six

In a large skillet or saucepan heat the olive oil. Add the finely chopped onion and garlic and sauté until soft but not browned. Add the tomatoes, parsley, tomato paste, sugar, salt, pepper and water. Stir together thoroughly. Bring to a boil, lower heat and simmer for thirty minutes. In the meantime cook the lasagna noodles in boiling salted water according to package directions. Do not overcook. Drain. Pour about two-thirds cup of sauce in the bottom of a rectangular baking dish. Arrange a layer of lasagna noodles, one-third of the sliced cheddar, one-third of the cottage cheese, a sprinkling of Parmesan and two-thirds cup of tomato sauce. Repeat twice. Top with a layer of noodles, remaining sauce and Parmesan cheese. Bake in a moderate oven for thirty-five minutes. Remove from oven and let stand five to ten minutes before serving.

Tomato Cheese Pie

Two cups sifted flour
Four teaspoons baking powder
Three-fourths teaspoon salt
One-fourth cup shortening
Two-thirds cup milk
Three large tomatoes
One cup grated cheddar cheese
Two tablespoons finely chopped onion
One-half cup mayonnaise
Oven temperature: 375 degrees
Bake: Forty-five minutes
Servings: Six

Sift the flour, baking powder and salt together in a bowl. Cut in the shortening until mixture resembles coarse meal. Stir in the milk to form a soft dough. Turn dough out on floured board, kneading briefly. Roll out to fit a pie plate (10 in.). Trim and flute edge. Peel tomatoes by dipping briefly in boiling water or holding over gas flame to loosen skin. Cut into wedges and arrange in layer over crust. In a bowl mix the grated cheese with the chopped onion and mayonnaise. Spread over the tomatoes. Press pastry down to level of filling. Bake in a moderately hot oven for 45 minutes or until pie is nicely browned and crust crisp. Remove from oven, let stand five to 10 minutes and serve cut in wedges.

Cheese Refrigerator Pie

Two cups fine corn flake crumbs
One-fourth cup sugar
One tablespoon flour
One-half cup butter or margarine, melted
Oven temperature: 350 degrees
Bake: Ten to twelve minutes
One tablespoon unflavored gelatin
One-half cup water
Three egg yolks
One-half cup sugar
Three-fourths teaspoon salt
One cup milk
Cook: Five to eight minutes
Two cups creamed cottage cheese
Grated rind of one lemon
One-fourth cup lemon juice
Chill: Until beginning to set
Three egg whites
Chill: Until set
Servings: Eight

In a bowl stir the corn flake crumbs, one-fourth cup of sugar and tablespoon of flour together. Blend in the melted butter or margarine, mixing well. Set aside one-half cup of the crumbs and pack the remainder firmly against the bottom and sides of a pie plate (10 in.). Bake in a moderate oven for ten to twelve minutes. Remove from oven and cool in pie pan on a rack. Sprinkle the unflavored gelatin over one-half cup of cold water in a small bowl. In the upper half of a double boiler beat the three egg yolks with the half cup of sugar and salt. Blend in the milk gradually. Place over hot water and cook, stirring constantly until mixture coats a metal spoon. Remove from heat and stir in the softened gelatin. Rub the cottage cheese through a sieve and add to the custard mixture with the grated lemon rind and lemon juice. Chill until the mixture just begins to set. In a bowl beat the egg whites until stiff; fold into the chilled cheese mixture. Transfer to the baked corn flakes shell and scatter the reserved crumb mixture over the top. Chill several hours until set before serving.

Strawberries and Sour Cream on Cream Cheese Shortcakes

Two cups sifted flour
Three teaspoons baking powder
Three-fourths teaspoon salt
One-fourth cup sugar
One pkg. (3 oz.) cream cheese
Two tablespoons butter
One egg
Milk
One tablespoon butter
Oven temperature: 450 degrees
Bake: Ten to twelve minutes
One quart ripe strawberries
One-third cup sugar
One cup dairy sour cream
Two tablespoons sugar
Serves: Eight

Sift the flour, baking powder, salt and fourth cup of sugar into a bowl. Cut in the cream cheese and two tablespoons of butter, using two knives or a pastry blender, until the mixture resembles coarse meal. Beat the egg with a fork in a measuring cup. Add enough milk to measure three-fourths cup. Stir into the dry ingredients. Turn out on floured board and knead briefly. Roll out to a little less than one-half inch in thickness. Cut three-inch and two-inch rounds of dough. Lay large rings on baking sheet, brush with melted butter and top with small ring. Brush with butter and bake in a very hot oven for 10 to 12 minutes. Wash, hull and slice strawberries into a bowl. Stir in the third cup of sugar and let stand in the refrigerator. Sweeten sour cream with remaining sugar. At serving time layer individual shortcakes with strawberries and sour cream. Serve at once.

Refrigerator Cheese Cookies

One-fourth pound butter
One-fourth pound cream cheese
One-half cup sugar
One and one-half cups sifted flour
Two teaspoons baking powder
One teaspoon salt
One teaspoon cinnamon
Chill: Until firm
Oven temperature: 400 degrees
Bake: Ten minutes, about
Yield: Four dozen, or more

In bowl cream the butter, blend in the cream cheese. Beat in the sugar. Sift together the flour, baking powder, salt and cinnamon and gradually work into the creamed mixture, beating smooth. Form dough into two rolls about two inches in diameter and wrap in waxed paper. Chill until firm enough to slice. Cut into slices about one-fourth inch thick and bake on an ungreased baking sheet for 10 minutes or until lightly browned. Store in a tightly covered container.

Quiche Lorraine

One unbaked (9 in.) pastry shell, or
  10 (3¼ in.) pastry shells, chilled
One-half pound bacon, fried crisp, or
  one cup sliced cooked ham
One-half pound Swiss cheese, sliced
  paper-thin
Three eggs, slightly beaten
Two cups milk or light cream
One tablespoon flour
One-half teaspoon salt or onion salt
One-eighth teaspoon pepper
Few grains cayenne
Few grains nutmeg
One tablespoon melted butter,
  slightly browned
Oven temperature: 400 degrees
Baking time: Thirty minutes (about)
Serves: Four, or more

In the bottom of the pastry shell crumble the bacon; cover with slices of Swiss cheese. In a bowl beat the eggs slightly, add the milk, flour and seasonings, blending well. In a pan melt the butter and brown slightly; add to the mixture. Pour over the cheese. Bake in a quick oven for 30 minutes. The center will appear somewhat soft. Cool on rack for 10 minutes. Serve hot in wedges.

Mushroom Rarebit

Two cans (12 oz. each) cream of
  mushroom soup
One teaspoon Worcestershire sauce
Few drops tabasco sauce
One-half teaspoon salt
One and one-half cups sliced mushrooms,
  fresh or canned
Cook: Ten minutes
One-half pound grated cheddar cheese
Cook: Until cheese melts
Two tablespoons Spanish sherry
Toasted hamburger buns or rusks
Six slices baked ham, halved
Twelve slices chicken
Serves: Six

In a heavy saucepan cook the cream of mushroom soup, Worcestershire sauce, tabasco, salt and sliced mushrooms until hot and bubbly. Gradually add the grated cheese, stirring until the cheese is melted. Remove. Add sherry. On a platter arrange toasted hamburger buns topped with a slice of ham and chicken. Ladle mushroom rarebit over each bun. Garnish with parsley.

Switzerland Emmentaler Fondue

One pound Switzerland Emmentaler
  cheese finely grated
Three tablespoons flour
Garlic
Two cups Neuchatel wine, or any dry
  white Rhine or Chablis type
Heat: Until bubbly
Cook at low temperature (about fifteen
  minutes)
Four sprigs dill
Salt and pepper
One-fourth cup Kirschwasser
One crusty loaf dark bread, cut into
  chunks
One pound cooked, cleaned shrimp
Serves: Six

Mix the cheese thoroughly with the flour. Rub the chafing dish with garlic. Pour the wine into the dish. Heat until bubbly, just under boiling. Reduce heat to a very low temperature. Add a half cupful of cheese at a time, stirring stedily in one direction until completely dissolved. Slowly repeat procedure until all cheese is dissolved. Place over a heating element. Add the dill. Season with salt and pepper. Add Kirschwasser. To eat: Spear a piece of crusty bread or shrimp and swirl in the fondue and then eat it. Repeat until all fondue is eaten.

Sardine Dip

Two cans (3¾ oz. each) sardines
Two packages (3 oz. each) cream cheese
Two tablespoons lime or lemon juice
One tablespoon minced onion
One teaspoon salt
One-fourth teaspoon dill salt or tarragon
Two tablespoons milk
Yield: Two cups

With fork mash the sardines and oil in a bowl. Blend in the cheese and other ingredients. Pile in a serving bowl. To serve: Dip potato chips or small crackers into the mixture.

Appetizers

A FAVORITE RECIPE

Pick 'n' Dip

Two frozen lobster tails (12 oz. each)
    cooked as directed on package
One cup mayonnaise
One tablespoon anchovy paste
One-half tespoon dry mustard
One-half teaspoon tabasco
One-fourth teaspoon garlic salt
Two tablespoons vinegar
Two hard cooked eggs, chopped
Three tablespoons minced stuffed olives
Three tablespoons minced sweet pickles
One tablespoon chopped parsley
One teaspoon minced onion
Servings: Six

Cook the lobster as directed. Remove the meat from the shell. Chill. Cut into 24 cubes. Save and rinse one lobster shell. Combine in a small bowl the mayonnaise, anchovy paste, mustard, tabasco, garlic salt, vinegar, chopped eggs, olives, pickles, parsley and onion. Mix to a paste. Turn into the reserved lobster shell. Stick a toothpick into each cube of lobster. Place the shell containing the sauce paste in the center of a round platter; surround with the lobster cubes.

CLARA BERMAN, *Brooklyn, N.Y.*

A FAVORITE RECIPE

Curry Olive Spread

One package (3 oz.) cream cheese
Three tablespoons butter
One-fourth teaspoon curry powder
One-fourth teaspoon chopped ripe olives
Four tablespoons flaked coconut
Yield: One cup

In a bowl cream the cheese, with the butter, having both at room temperature. Add the curry powder, mix. Stir in the ripe olives and coconut. Chill and serve as a spread for crackers or toast wedges.

MARY T. FREE, *Jersey City, N.J.*

California Dip

One-fourth cup olive oil
Two tablespoons lemon juice
One-fourth teaspoon salt
One-sixteenth teaspoon pepper
One-fourth teaspoon prepared mustard
One large avocado, peeled and sieved
One-fourth cup chopped pecans
One tomato, peeled and sieved
Yield: One cup

Place all the ingredients in a mixing bowl. Beat till smooth and blended. Chill. Garnish with pecans and sliced tomato.

Chiffonade Dip

One-fourth cup minced pimiento
One-fourth cup minced onion
One-fourth cup minced parsley
One-fourth cup minced green pepper
One-eighth teaspoon tabasco
Two chopped hard-cooked eggs
One-fourth cup salad dressing
One-fourth teaspoon salt
One-half teaspoon garlic salt
Yield: Two cups (about)

Combine all the ingredients in a bowl. Chill till needed. Garnish with chopped parsley.

Cheese Olive Dip

Three packages (3 oz. each) cream cheese
One-half cup minced stuffed olives
One tablespoon minced onion or chives
One-half teaspoon salt
One-fourth teaspoon angostura bitters
One-eighth teaspoon pepper
One-third cup milk (about)
Yield: One and one-half cups

Combine all the ingredients in a bowl. Add more milk if necessary to make a dipping consistency. Chill. Garnish with sliced stuffed green olives.

Liver Pate Dip

Two cans (4½ oz. each) liver paté
One-half cup minced watercress
One-half cup crisp crumbled bacon
Two tablespoons chili sauce
One-fourth cup mayonnaise
One teaspoon angostura bitters
Yield: Two cups

Combine all ingredients in a bowl. Serve immediately. Garnish with crumbled crisp bacon and a dill pickle fan.

Salmon Loaf — Curry Sauce

One can (1 lb.) salmon
Three-fourths cup milk
One and one-half cups rolled oats
Two eggs, slightly beaten
One-fourth cup finely chopped celery
Two tablespoons minced parsley
Two tablespoons grated onion
One teaspoon lemon juice
One teaspoon salt
One-fourth teaspoon tabasco sauce
One-half teaspoon dry mustard
One-half teaspoon curry powder
Oven temperature: 350 degrees
Baking time: Forty-five minutes
Two cups white sauce
Two tablespoons curry powder, or less
Servings: Six

Drain the oil from the salmon into a cup; add enough milk to make one cup. Flake the salmon into a bowl. Add the rolled oats, eggs, celery, parsley, onion, lemon juice, salt, tabasco sauce, mustard and curry powder. Mix. Pack into a well-greased loaf pan (9 in.), having bottom of pan lined with waxed paper. Bake in a moderate oven. Serve with curry sauce, made by adding the curry powder to the white sauce.

Celery Root Relish

One bunch knob celery (three or four
  knobs)
One-fourth cup mayonnaise, or more
One tablespoon vinegar
Chill: Thoroughly
Yield: Two cups, about

Trim the tops from the knob celery.
Scrub the roots with a brush. Peel carefully. Cut the roots into slender julienne
strips like matchsticks or grate coarsely.
Blend in the mayonnaise and vinegar and
chill thoroughly. If this is offered as an
appetizer you might like to garnish with
a little finely cut parsley or green pepper.

Mexicana Dip

Combine one can (10½ oz.) condensed
bean with bacon or black bean soup with
one-third cup chili sauce, one teaspoon
lime juice, two tablespoons sherry, two
teaspoons chili powder, one clove pureed
garlic, and one-half pound whipped cream
cheese. Chill. Dip with crackers or fritos.

Scandinavian Dip

Combine two tablespoons lemon juice,
one jar (8 oz.) marinated herring in sour
cream, two teaspoons dill seed, or powder, one teaspoon caraway seed and one-
half pound whipped cream cheese. Serve
with crackers, rye wafers, or fingers of
pumpernickel bread.

Roquefort and Cottage Cheese Dip

Two ounces Roquefort cheese
One-half pound creamed cottage cheese
One teaspoon onion juice
One-third cup dairy sour cream
Milk
Chill: Thoroughly
Finely chopped parsley
Yield: One and one-half cups

Crumble the Roquefort cheese very
fine in a bowl. Stir in the creamed cottage
cheese, onion juice and dairy sour cream,
mixing thoroughly. Add enough milk to
give dipping consistency. (This may be
added after chilling if you wish.) Chill
well. Serve in a bowl with generous sprinkling of finely chopped parsley over the
top.

Bacon Cheese Onion Dip

One jar (5 oz.) cheese spread with bacon
One-half cup dairy sour cream
Two tablespoons instant minced onion
One-half teaspoon barbecue seasoning or
One-eighth teaspoon chili powder
Yield: One and one-half cups

In a bowl blend the softened cheese
spread with the dairy sour cream, instant
minced onion and seasoning. Mix thoroughly; chill well. Blend in a little milk
just before serving to restore fluffy quality.
Serve with potato chips or crisp crackers
for dipping.

Vegetable Cheese Dip

One package (3 oz.) cream cheese
One-half pint dairy sour cream
One tablespoon grated onion
One-half cup grated cucumber
One-fourth cup grated radish
One-fourth cup grated carrot
Two tablespoons chopped parsley
One-half teaspoon salt
One-fourth teaspoon tabasco sauce
Chill: Thoroughly
Yield: Two cups

In a bowl cream the cheese well and
gradually blend in the dairy sour cream.
Add the grated onion, cucumber, radish,
carrot and chopped parsley. Add the salt
and tabasco sauce, mix well and chill thoroughly before using. Good with crackers,
potato chips or vegetable sticks.

Ripe Olives Stuffed with Water Chestnuts

Marinate slivers of well drained canned
water chestnuts in French or Italian type
dressing overnight. Stuff into pitted black
olives and chill thoroughly.

A FAVORITE RECIPE
Curry Olive Spread

One package (3 oz.) cream cheese
Three tablespoons butter
One-fourth teaspoon curry powder
One-fourth teaspoon chopped ripe olives
Four tablespoons flaked coconut
Yield: One cup

In a bowl cream the cheese, with the
butter, having both at room temperature.
Add the curry powder, mix. Stir in the
ripe olives and coconut. Chill and serve
as a spread for crackers or toast wedges.

MARY T. FREE, *Jersey City, N.J.*

A FAVORITE RECIPE
Cheese for Snacks

Two packages (3 oz. each) cream cheese
  (at room temperature)
One-fourth cup butter
One teaspoon capers
One teaspoon paprika
Two anchovies, finely minced
One small green onion, minced
One-half teaspoon salt
One-half teaspoon caraway seed
Chilling time: Three hours
Yield: One cup

In a bowl cream the cheese; add the
butter, capers, paprika, anchovies, onion,
salt and caraway seed. Form into a roll
and wrap in waxed paper. Chill. Serve
sliced on round crackers.

MRS. JOHN F. WADE, *Westport, Conn.*

Cheese Straws

One cup sifted flour
One and one-half teaspoons baking powder
One-half teaspoon salt
Two tablespoons shortening
One-half cup finely grated cheddar cheese
One-third cup milk
Paprika
Oven temperature: 425 degrees
Baking time: Five to seven minutes
Yield: Eight dozen small, four dozen large

Sift the flour, baking powder and salt
into a bowl. Using a pastry blender or
two knives, cut the shortening and finely
grated cheese into the dry ingredients
until the mixture resembles coarse meal.
Stir in the milk and mix well. Turn dough
out on a floured board and roll to a thickness of one-eighth inch. Cut into strips
one-third by three inches or one-half by
six inches. Sprinkle generously with paprika. Transfer small sticks to a greased
baking sheet flat, twist the larger ones
into a spiral. Bake in a hot oven for five
to seven minutes, taking care not to burn.
Remove to racks to cool thoroughly; store
in a tightly covered tin.

Coconut Curry Cheese Balls

One package (8 oz.) cream cheese
One and one-half tablespoons finely
  chopped chutney
One teaspoon curry powder
One-sixteenth teaspoon salt
Chill: Thoroughly
One can (3½ oz.) flaked coconut
Chill: Well
Yield: Three dozen, about

Blend the softened cream cheese in a
bowl with the finely chopped chutney,
curry powder and salt. Mix thoroughly
together. Chill to firmness then form into
small balls. These may be easily made
uniform by using a rounded half measuring teaspoonful of the mixture and releasing it with a narrow rubber spatula. Roll
these in the flaked coconut; chill until
serving time.

Sauerkraut Cheese Balls

Eight ounces cream cheese, softened
One tablespoon milk
One cup sauerkraut, drained and chopped
One-fourth teaspoon paprika
Chill: Thoroughly
One cup finely chopped parsley, about
Chill: Thoroughly
Yield: Three dozen, or more

In a bowl cream the softened cheese
with the milk, chopped sauerkraut and
paprika until well blended. Chill thoroughly. Form into small balls using a
leveled teaspoonful with rubber spatula
for uniformity of size. Roll balls in finely
chopped parsley and chill well. Serve on
cocktail picks.

A FAVORITE RECIPE
Cheese Balls

One package (8 oz.) cream cheese,
　room temperature
One snappy cheese (3 oz.)
One package (3 oz.) blue cheese
One tablespoon finely minced onion
Two drops Worcestershire sauce
One-half cup finely chopped pecans
One-fourth cup finely minced parsley
Chilling time: Three hours
Servings: Eight

Have the cheeses at room temperature. Turn into a bowl; mash and beat until well blended and smooth. Add the onion, Worcestershire sauce and pecans, mix. Form into two small or one large ball. Roll in parsley. Place on a serving plate; chill until serving time. Serve with crackers or party rye bread.

MRS. ELSIE PROVAN, *New York, N.Y.*

Bacon Cheese Puffs

Six pieces thin sliced bread
Twelve slices bacon
One cup grated cheese (Swiss or cheddar)
Oven temperature: 400 degrees
Bake: Twenty minutes
Yield: Twenty-four

Trim the crusts from the bread and cut each slice into four squares. Cut bacon slices in two (each piece will be about three inches long). Lay a piece of bread in the middle of each piece of bacon, sprinkle with grated cheese and roll up. Secure with a wooden pick and place on a rack in a shallow pan. Scatter remaining cheese over top. Bake in a quick oven for twenty minutes or until lightly browned. Serve at once. These may be prepared ahead and baked when needed.

Almond Cheesed Sprouts

Two packages (10 oz. each) frozen
　Brussels sprouts
Three ounces cream cheese
One-half teaspoon mayonnaise
One tablespoon milk
One-eighth teaspoon nutmeg
One-sixteenth teaspoon salt
One-half cup finely chopped blanched
　almonds
Chill: Thoroughly
Yield: Approximately sixty

Cook the frozen Brussels sprouts according to package directions. Drain and chill thoroughly. In a bowl blend the softened creamed cheese with the mayonnaise, milk, nutmeg and salt; mix thoroughly. Dip chilled sprouts into soft cheese mixture then in finely chopped almonds to coat the tops. Place on tray and chill thoroughly before serving.

Stuffed Mushrooms

One pound mushrooms (1½ inch)
Two tablespoons butter
Two tablespoons finely chopped onion
One-third cup finely chopped parsley
Sauté: Five minutes
One-third cup lemon juice
One-half teaspoon salt
Two cups fine soft bread crumbs
One-half cup milk, about
Oven temperature: 400 degrees
Bake: Twenty minutes
Yield: Thirty to forty

Wash, dry and peel the mushrooms if necessary. Chop the stems very fine and place in a heavy skillet with the butter, chopped onion and two-thirds of parsley. Sauté until tender. Remove from the heat and stir in the lemon juice, salt and fine bread crumbs. Stuff the mushroom caps with this mixture and place them in a single layer in a shallow tray or baking dishes. Pour milk around caps to depth of one-eighth inch and cover with foil. Bake in a hot oven for twenty minutes. Remove foil and keep hot in a slow oven until needed. Sprinkle with remaining chopped parsley when served.

Stuffed Mushroom Appetizers

Eighteen mushrooms (one and one-half
　inch size)
One-third cup butter or margarine
Two tablespoons finely chopped onion
Sauté: Five minutes, about
Eight ounces chicken livers, cooked and
　finely chopped
One cup packaged prepared stuffing
One cup chicken broth
One-fourth cup finely chopped parsley
Two tablespoons lemon juice
One teaspoon salt
Oven temperature: 375 degrees
Bake: Twenty minutes
Yield: Eighteen

Wash and trim the mushrooms. Snap off the stems, setting the caps aside. Chop the stems very fine and sauté in butter in a skillet with the chopped onion. Remove from heat and stir in the finely chopped cooked chicken livers, the packaged prepared stuffing, chicken broth, finely chopped parsley, lemon juice and salt. Mix well. Spoon into the mushroom caps and place in a greased shallow baking pan. Bake in a moderately hot oven for twenty minutes. Serve piping hot.

Liverwurst Spread

One-half cup liverwurst, mashed
Three tablespoons chili sauce
One-fourth cup chopped green olives
One-fourth teaspoon onion juice
Yield: Three-fourths cup (about)

Mix the chili sauce, olives and onion juice with the mashed liverwurst. Good on buttered pumpernickel bread.

Chicken Liver Pate

One-half pound chicken livers
Two tablespoons butter
Saute: Five minutes
One-fourth cup chopped onion
One small clove garlic, sliced
Cook: Two minutes
One-fourth cup water or chicken broth
One-half teaspoon salt
One-eighth teaspoon pepper
One-fourth teaspoon poultry seasoning
Blend: Three minutes
Chill: Until firm
Yield: One and one-fourth cups

Cut livers into coarse pieces; saute in butter until done, about five minutes. Add onion and garlic; cook another two minutes. Put water into glass container; add livers, onion, garlic and seasonings. Blend until smooth in the blender, stopping to stir when necessary. Chill and serve over crackers or melba toast.

Baked Liver Paté

Three slices stale white bread with crusts
Two-thirds cup milk
One pound pork liver
One-half pound calves' liver
One large onion
Six anchovy fillets, drained
One and one-half teaspoons salt
One-sixteenth teaspoon each of pepper,
　allspice, thyme
One teaspoon flour
Two eggs, beaten
Two-thirds cup heavy cream
Oven temperature: 350 degrees
Bake: One hour
Yield: Two loaves

Break bread into pieces in a bowl and pour on the milk. Cut liver in pieces (removing tough membrane) and run through a food grinder. Put ground liver through grinder a second time with the softened bread, onion and anchovy fillets. Add the salt, seasonings, flour and beaten eggs. Mix well. Blend in the heavy cream and pour into two small loaf pans (7¼ x 3½ x 2 in.). (A five cup mold may be used.) Place in a pan of hot water and bake for one hour or until set in the center like a custard. Remove from oven and cool loaves in pans on racks. Chill thoroughly. Cold paté may be decorated with sliced stuffed olives and a layer of jellied aspic or consomme.

Pickle Cocktail Franks in Blanket

Wrap a double strip of pastry around each tiny cocktail frankfurter and small or split gherkin. Press pastry to seal on under side. Place on baking sheet and brush with slightly beaten egg white. Sprinkle with grated Parmesan cheese and bake in a hot oven (425 degrees) for ten to fifteen minutes, until lightly browned. Serve at once.

Hot Cheese Tartlets

Two cups finely grated Swiss cheese
Two teaspoons flour
One egg, beaten
One-half cup evaporated milk or cream
One-half teaspoon salt
One-eighth teaspoon dry mustard
One-eighth teaspoon pepper
One-half recipe pastry
Oven temperature: 425 degrees
Baking time: Seventeen minutes (about)
Yield: Forty-eight

Mix the cheese and flour. Combine the egg, milk and seasonings. Set both aside. Roll out pastry (⅛ in. thick or less); cut into rounds (1½ in.). Fit into small muffin pans (1½ in.). Bake for five minutes to a light brown in a hot oven. Remove from the oven. At once put one-fourth teaspoon floured cheese over each tartlet and pour one teaspoon egg mixture over the cheese. Return to the oven. Bake until golden brown for 12 minutes. Sprinkle with paprika. Serve hot, or cool and reheat.

Chicken Liver Pate

Two cups cooked chopped chicken livers
Two tablespoons chicken fat or butter
One teaspoon finely minced onion
One teaspoon minced parsley
One-fourth teaspoon prepared mustard
One-eighth teaspoon ground sage
One teaspoon sherry or brandy
Chilling time: Overnight
Yield: Two cups

Put the livers through the grinder, using the finest blade. Add the remaining ingredients, blending thoroughly. Pack into a jar; cover. Chill. To serve: Spread on hot crackers or small toast squares. Garnish with sieved egg yolks and parsley.

A FAVORITE RECIPE

Ham Puffs

One egg white
One small can (2½ oz.) deviled ham
One tablespoon (or less) prepared
    mustard
Twelve toast rounds, or round crackers
Broiler oven temperature: 375 degrees
Broiling time: Two or three minutes
Servings: Four

In a bowl beat the egg white until stiff; beat in the ham and mustard. Spread on toast or cracker rounds; broil in a preheated broiler. Serve with soup or drinks.

MRS. JANE F. DUNHAM, *Silver Springs, Md.*

Bordeaux Pate

Three-fourths pound ground calves' liver
One-half pound ground pork
One teaspoon salt
One-half teaspoon thyme
One bay leaf, crushed
One-fourth teaspoon marjoram
One clove garlic, crushed
Few grains nutmeg
Few grains cayenne
One-fourth cup dry Bordeaux wine
One pound pork, cut in finger lengths
    (3 x ½ x ½ in.)
One-half pound bacon
Oven temperature: 350 degrees
Baking time: Two hours
Serves: Twelve

Rub ground liver through a fine sieve.

Add ground pork, salt, thyme, bay leaf, marjoram, garlic, nutmeg, cayenne and wine, blending thoroughly with an electric blendor or beater. Cut pork into finger lengths (3 x ½ x ½ in.). Line a loaf pan (8 x 5 x 3 in.) with strips of bacon. Spoon a layer of the ground liver mixture over bottom of bacon-lined pan. Arrange two rows of pork finger lengths over the mixture. Repeat procedure ending with a layer of ground mixture. Cover with foil. Place in pan containing one inch of water. Bake in a moderate oven two hours. Remove from oven onto a rack. Cool. Place in refrigerator overnight. Unmold. Slice and serve on crackers.

Bordeaux pate keeps two weeks in refrigerator.

Cheese Caraway Spread

Two packages (1¼ oz. each) camembert
   cheese
One-half pound cream cheese
Two tablespoons milk
Two tablespoons chopped parsley
One teaspoon grated onion
Two tablespoons white wine
One teaspoon caraway seed
Yield: One and one-half cups

Beat all ingredients in a bowl; blending thoroughly. Chill. Spread on crackers.

Zesty Dip Sauce

One cup real mayonnaise
One teaspoon curry powder
One teaspoon prepared mustard
One teaspoon angostura bitters
One-half teaspoon salt
One-half teaspoon paprika
Crisp vegetables, cooked shrimp
Yield: One cup

Mix all ingredients in a bowl. Chill.
Use sauce to dip raw vegetables or
cooked shrimp into mixture.

Red Devil Spread

Two large cans (4½ oz. each) deviled ham
One hard-cooked egg, sieved
One tablespoon horseradish sauce
Two teaspoons Worcestershire sauce
One-fourth cup dairy sour cream
One teaspoon prepared mustard
One teaspoon salt
Few drops tabasco
Yield: One and one-half cups

Blend all ingredients in a bowl. Chill.
Spread on crackers.

Liver Spread

One package (8 oz.) frozen chicken livers,
   thawed
Two tablespoons minced onion
One-half cup Bordeaux wine or water
Cooking time: Five minutes
Two cans (4½ oz. each) liver paté
One-half cup heavy cream or evaporated
   milk
One teaspoon Worcestershire sauce
One teaspoon salt
Yield: Two cups

In a saucepan cook the chicken livers,
onion and wine or water for 5 minutes.
Put through a sieve, or puree. With an
electric beater or blendor, beat in remaining ingredients. Chill, Spread on
crackers.

Chicken Cheese Spread

One package (1¼ oz.) Roquefort cheese
One package (3 oz.) cream cheese
Four tablespoons dairy sour cream
Few drops tabasco
One-fourth teaspoon salt
Few grains cayenne
One jar (3½ oz.) chicken, finely chopped
Yield: One cup

Mix in a bowl the cheeses, sour cream
and seasonings together until thoroughly
blended. Add the finely chopped chicken.
Serve on crackers.

Cream Cheese Spread

Six ounces cream cheese
One tablespoon sour cream or milk
Three radishes, minced
One teaspoon minced onion
One tablespoon minced green pepper
One-half teaspoon salt
One-eighth teaspoon pepper
Yield: One cup

Mix three-fourths of the cheese and
the other ingredients. Spread on squares
(2 in.) of buttered bread. Pipe the edges
with the remaining cheese, tinted pale
green. Garnish each with a radish slice.

Chopped Egg Spread

Four hard-cooked eggs, chopped
One-fourth cup mayonnaise
One teaspoon milk
One teaspoon minced parsley
One-fourth teaspoon salt
One-eighth teaspoon pepper
Yield: One cup

Combine lightly the ingredients.
Spread on heart-shaped pieces of buttered bread. In the center of each put a
rolled anchovy; garnish with a bit of
pimiento.

Danish Meat Balls

One-half pound chopped round steak
One pork chop, boned
One teaspoon minced onion
Two rusks, soaked in
One-fourth cup milk
One egg, slightly beaten
Three-fourths teaspoon salt
One-eighth teaspoon pepper
Two tablespoons flour
Four tablespoons butter
One-fourth cup hot water
Cooking time: Fifteen minutes
Yield: Sixteen

Put the meats and onion through the
food chopper three times, using the fine
blade. Combine with the soaked rusks,
egg and seasonings. Shape into small
balls (1 in.); flour lightly. Brown on all
sides in the butter in a heavy skillet. Add
the water; cover; simmer until firm. When
cold, slice thin. Arrange on triangles of
buttered pumpernickel; edge with parsley butter.

Pickled Cauliflower with Ham

Wrap a strip of ham around small pickled caulifloweret. Secure with wooden pick and chill thoroughly.

Midget Meat Balls

One egg
One pound round steak, ground
Two tablespoons prepared mustard
One tablespoon prepared horseradish
One teaspoon salt
One-fourth teaspoon pepper
Two tablespoons grated onion
One-fourth cup fine dry bread crumbs
Salad oil
Frying time: Five minutes
Yield: Sixty or more

In a bowl beat the egg. Blend in the ground round steak, prepared mustard, horseradish, salt, pepper, grated onion and fine dry bread crumbs. Mix thoroughly together. Form into small marble-sized balls. Measuring teaspoon may be used to assure uniformity of size. Heat one-fourth inch of salad oil in a large heavy skillet. Add the meat balls and sauté quickly until browned. Spear with wooden picks and serve as soon as possible.

Herbed Stuffed Eggs

Six hard-cooked eggs
Two tablespoons soft blue cheese
One teaspoon prepared mustard
One teaspoon freshly snipped chives
One-half teaspoon crumbled dried
   rosemary
Two tablespoons mayonnaise
Salt and pepper
Paprika
Chill: Well
Yield: Twelve halves

Cut eggs in half and remove the yolks to a bowl. Mash yolks well with a fork and stir in the soft blue cheese, prepared mustard, snipped chives, dried rosemary and mayonnaise. Mix well and add salt and pepper to taste. Spoon into the egg whites and sprinkle top with paprika. Chill well before serving.

Anchovy Beef Balls

One egg
One pound ground beef
One-half cup soft white bread crumbs
One-third cup milk
Two cans (2 oz. each) rolled anchovies
Two to three tablespoons butter or
   margarine
Sauté: Five to ten minutes
Yield: Three dozen, about

In a bowl beat the egg, blend in the ground beef, soft white bread crumbs and milk. Mix thoroughly together. Drain the rolled anchovies on absorbent paper and cut into two pieces if large. Portion out level measuring tablespoonfuls of the meat mixture and form each into a ball over the piece of rolled anchovy. Heat the butter or margarine in a large heavy skillet, add the meat balls and sauté until browned on all sides. Spear with wooden picks and serve at once. These may be kept hot on an oven proof tray for about 45 minutes in an oven set at 250 degrees without becoming hard.

Pickled Shrimp

One pound small or medium-sized shrimp
Boiling water
One teaspoon salt
One stalk celery
One onion, sliced
Cook: Six minutes
One-half cup salad oil
One-half cup vinegar
Juice of two lemons
One tablespoon sugar
Three bay leaves
One-half teaspoon crushed peppercorns
One-half teaspoon dill seed
One-fourth teaspoon crumbled tarragon
One-half teaspoon celery salt
One-half teaspoon dry mustard
Dash of cayenne pepper
Simmer: Ten minutes
Simmer: Three minutes
Two medium-sized onions, thinly sliced
Marinate: One or two days
Serves: Six

Clean and devein the shrimp leaving tails intact. To a saucepan of boiling water add teaspoon of salt, cut stalk of celery and sliced onion. Add shrimp and cook just until pink, about six minutes. In a saucepan combine the salad oil, vinegar, lemon juice, sugar, bay leaves, peppercorns, dill seed, tarragon, celery salt, dry mustard and cayenne pepper. Bring to a boil, lower heat and simmer for 10 minutes. Add the drained cooked shrimp and simmer three minutes more. Remove from heat and layer shrimp with sliced onion in a casserole or bowl. Pour hot spiced mixture over top, cover and let marinate in the refrigerator for one or two days. Arrange shrimp with tails up for taking hold on a platter with small pieces of buttered rye or pumpernickel bread.

Shrimp Olive Canapé Spread

One-half pound fresh shrimp, cooked
   and cleaned
One teaspoon grated onion
One teaspoon prepared horseradish
One-third cup chopped olives
One-fourth cup finely chopped celery
One-fourth cup mayonnaise
One-eighth teaspoon garlic salt
Chill: Thoroughly
Yield: One and one-half cups

Chop the cooked shrimp fairly fine and combine in a bowl with the grated onion, horseradish, chopped stuffed olives, chopped celery, mayonnaise and garlic salt. Mix well and chill thoroughly. Serve in center of a large platter with a ring of round melba toast so each person may spread his own.

A FAVORITE RECIPE
Crab Cheese Canapes

One-fourth pound butter, melted or
   softened
Four tablespoons flour
One cup milk
One-fourth pound soft yellow cheese
Cooking time: Ten minutes in a double
   boiler
One-half pound fresh crab meat
One-half teaspoon salt
One-fourth teaspoon pepper
Chilling time: Until serving time
Crackers or rounds or bread (toasted on
   one side)
Broiler temperature: 375 degrees
Broil: Five minutes
Yield: Thirty, or more canapes

In the top of a double boiler blend the melted butter and flour; add the milk and cheese, cooking until smooth and thickened. Remove all cartilage from the crab meat, add to the creamed mixture, seasoning with salt and pepper. Cool. Remove to a bowl, cover and chill until serving time. Spread on crackers or rounds of bread toasted on one side. Place on a baking sheet and brown lightly. Serve hot.

E. L. FORTUNE, *Bolivar, Ohio*

Stuffed Shrimp Appetizers

One-half pound fresh lean pork, ground
Three scallions, finely chopped
Two tablespoons finely chopped celery
One-half teaspoon salt
One pound medium or small fresh
   shrimp (20-30)
Steam: Thirty minutes
Mustard sauce
Yield: Twenty

In a bowl combine the ground pork with the finely chopped scallions, celery and salt. Shell and devein the shrimp leaving the tiny tails attached. Split shrimp almost through, opening flat like a book. Spoon a little of the pork mixture on each, then fold over from the wide end toward the tail, skewering together with a wooden pick. Place shrimp on a rack arranged in a shallow pan or kettle over an inch of gently boiling water. Cover pan and steam for twenty minutes or until pork is thoroughly cooked. Serve hot dipped into mustard sauce.

Shrimp Canapes

Two tablespoons butter
Two teaspoons lemon juice
Twenty-four toast rounds (1½-2 in.)
Twenty-four canned shrimp, cleaned
Yield: Twenty-four canapes

Cream the butter and lemon juice; spread on the toast rounds. Top each with a whole shrimp; garnish with parsley.

Sliced Cucumber and Onion Pickle

Three pounds firm cucumbers
Two pounds small white onions
One-third cup salt
Standing time: Overnight
Four cups cider vinegar
Three-fourths cup water
Three-fourths cup sugar
Two and one-half teaspoons whole celery seed
One and one-half tablespoons whole mustard seed
Two and one-half teaspoons ground turmeric
Four large sweet red peppers
Simmer: Ten to fifteen minutes
Yield: Ten (half-pint) jars

Wash and slice the cucumbers one-fourth inch thick. Peel onions and slice one-fourth inch thick. Place both in a large bowl with the salt, mixing well. Let stand overnight. Drain into colander and place under running water to wash out salt. Drain well. Measure the vinegar, water, sugar, celery seed, mustard seed and turmeric into a large saucepan or kettle. Bring to a boil. Add the cucumbers, onions, and coarsely diced peppers. Simmer uncovered for 10 to 15 minutes or until cucumbers and onions are transparent and peppers not quite so bright in color. Pack into hot sterilized jars. Seal. Store in a cool place for six weeks before using for maximum development of flavor.

A FAVORITE RECIPE
Hot Relish

Five pounds tomatoes
Two cups chopped celery
Three sweet red peppers
Three sweet green peppers
One cup sweet onions, peeled, chopped
One jar (4 oz.) horseradish
One-half cup white mustard seed
Two tablespoons mixed pickling spice
One-half cup salt
Three cups sugar
Cooking time: Thirty minutes
Yield: Five pints

Scald and peel tomatoes, removing stem end (¼ in.); chop. Chop the celery, including several green leaves; wash, seed and clean peppers, chop into small pieces. Peel and chop onions. In a large kettle combine all ingredients. Add the horseradish, mustard seed, pickling spice, salt and sugar. Bring to a boil, stirring until well blended. Cook, stirring frequently. Pour into hot sterilized jars; seal. Store in a dark place.

MRS. L. B. HULSLANDER, *Norman, Oklahoma*

Raisin Rhubarb Conserve

Two pounds rhubarb, trimmed
One orange
One cup seedless raisins
Two cups sugar
Standing time: Two hours
Cooking time: One hour or until thickened
Yield: Three to four cups

Trim the tops and root ends from the rhubarb stalks. Wash but do not peel. Cut into dice (½ inch) and measure into a heavy kettle. There will be five cups of diced rhubarb. Peel the orange; dice the pulp and cut the peel very fine and add to the rhubarb with the raisins. Mix in the sugar; cover; let stand. Slowly bring the mixture to a boil, stirring until the sugar dissolves. Then boil over moderate heat until thickened, stirring often. Store in hot sterilized glasses; cover with paraffin at once. When cold store in a cool place.

Chow Chow

Twenty-four small cucumbers, cut
Two heads cauliflower, cut
Six green peppers, cut
One quart pickling onions, peeled
Two quarts chopped green tomatoes
One pint diced celery
One-half pound salt, dissolved in four quarts of water
Standing time: Twenty-four hours
Cooking time: Ten minutes, or more
Three quarts vinegar
Two cups sugar
One-half cup dry mustard
One cup flour
One-half ounce turmeric
One and one-half cups cold vinegar or water
Boiling time: Three to five minutes
Yield: Six quarts, about

Place the prepared cucumbers, cauliflower, peppers, onions, green tomatoes and celery in a large kettle. Dissolve the salt in the four quarts of water and add. Cover and let stand for 24 hours. Slowly bring the vegetables to a boil in the kettle, then drain into a colander. Measure the vinegar into the kettle and heat to boiling. Add the sugar. Make a smooth paste of the dry mustard, flour, turmeric and cold vinegar or water. Add to the vinegar and sugar and cook, stirring constantly, until thickened. Add the vegetables and take from the heat. Fill hot sterilized jars; seal as for canned fruit.

Cranberry Conserve

One pound cranberries
One cup water
Cook: Ten minutes, about
Two cups diced peeled apple
One cup diced peeled orange
One-half cup seedless raisins
Three and one-half cups sugar
Cook: Twenty-five minutes
One-half cup chopped walnuts
Yield: Five cups

Wash and pick over the fresh cranberries. Place in a saucepan with the water and cook until skins burst. Add the diced apple, orange, raisins and sugar. Cook, stirring frequently, until the mixture thickens, about twenty-five minutes. Add the nuts. Pour into hot sterilized glasses and top with melted paraffin. If you prefer, this may be kept in a bowl in the refrigerator instead. Serve with hot or cold meats or breads.

Preserves

Chili Sauce

Three pounds ripe tomatoes
One large green pepper
Three medium-sized onions
Cook: Thirty minutes, or more
One-half cup sugar
One and one-third cups vinegar
One teaspoon salt
One-half teaspoon cinnamon
One-half teaspoon allspice
One teaspoon nutmeg
One-fourth teaspoon cloves
One-half teaspoon mustard seed
Cook: Twenty minutes
Yield: One quart

Wash and dry the fully ripened tomatoes. Peel and chop. Chop the green pepper and onions fairly fine and combine with the chopped tomato in a large heavy skillet or saucepan. Cook, stirring occasionally until all vegetables are tender. Add the sugar, vinegar, salt, cinnamon, allspice, nutmeg, cloves and mustard seed and continue cooking for twenty minutes, stirring occasionally. Spoon into sterilized jars and seal at once.

Fruit Chile Sauce

Fifteen large ripe tomatoes, peeled
Three large peaches, peeled
Three large apples, peeled, cored
Three onions
One small hot pepper
One pint vinegar
Two cups sugar
Two tablespoons salt, or less
One and one-fourth teaspoons cinnamon
One-fourth teaspoon cloves
Cooking time: One and one-half hours
Yield: Twelve half pint jars

Prepare the vegetables and fruit and run through food chopper. Place in a deep kettle. Mix the vinegar, sugar, salt and spices. Add fruit and vegetable mixture. Bring to a boil, reduce heat, simmer. Stir frequently. Pour into hot sterilized jars, seal. Store in a dark place until needed.

Plum or Prune Conserve

Six cups quartered plums or prunes
Three oranges
Cooking time: Ten minutes
Four cups sugar
Cooking time: Forty minutes, or more
One cup broken walnut meats
Yield: Six glasses (about)

Measure the fresh plums or prunes into a saucepan; add the juice of 3 oranges and the grated rind of 1 orange; cook slowly for ten minutes, stirring. Add the sugar; place an asbestos mat under the pan. Cook until thickened, stirring often. Five minutes before taking from the flame, add the walnuts. Stir until thoroughly heated. Store in hot, sterilized glasses; paraffin at once.

Corn Relish

Six ears corn
One-half pound cucumbers
One-half pound white onions
One and one-half pounds tomatoes
Two green peppers
Two sweet red peppers
Three small hot red peppers
One small bunch celery
One teaspoon turmeric
One quart vinegar
Two and one-half tablespoons salt
Two cups sugar
Five tablespoons whole light mustard seed
Boiling time: One hour
Yield: Five pints

In the preparation of all vegetables for the relish use a knife, not a food chopper. Cut corn from the cob, without scraping. Peel and coarsely dice the cucumbers, onions and tomatoes. Remove seeds and white portion from the green and red peppers; cut fine. Cut celery into small pieces. Combine turmeric with small amount of vinegar in a large bowl, then add the remaining vinegar with salt and sugar; stir until dissolved. In a large kettle, place the corn, cucumbers, onions, tomatoes, peppers, celery and mustard seed. Add the vinegar mixture and stir well. Boil one hour, stirring frequently. Pack into five hot sterilized pint jars. Seal.

Pepper Relish

Five and one-half cups (about 12)
    green peppers
Five and one-half cups (about 12)
    sweet red peppers
Two cups (about 12) white onions, chopped
Standing time: Ten minutes
One pint vinegar
One and one-half cups sugar
Three tablespoons salt
Boiling time: Five minutes
Yield: Five pints (about)

Wash the peppers and remove the seeds and white portion; peel the onions. Chop the peppers and onions fine with a knife. Place chopped vegetables in a kettle, cover with boiling water; let stand ten minutes, then drain.

Mix together in a large bowl the vinegar, sugar and salt; add this to the drained pepper and onion combination. Bring to a boil; boil gently for five minutes. Pour into hot sterilized jars. Seal.

Orange Honey Marmalade

One medium-sized orange
One medium-sized lemon
One-half cup honey
One-half cup water
One-sixteenth teaspoon soda
Simmering time: Thirty minutes
Two and one-half cups honey
Boiling time: One minute
One-half bottle (½ cup) fruit pectin
Stirring time: Five minutes
Yield: Six glasses (6 oz.)

Remove the rind from the fruit in sections; reserve the fruit. Lay the rind flat; shave off and discard half the white part; shred the remaining rind very fine with a sharp knife. Place in a saucepan with the honey, water and soda; bring to a boil. Cover; simmer 10 minutes, stirring occasionally. Add the diced fruit, freed of membrane and seeds. Again bring to boil; reduce the heat; cover; simmer 20 minutes. Measure; there should be one and one-half cups. If not, add water to make up the difference. Turn into a large kettle. Add the remaining honey. Bring to a full rolling boil, stirring. Boil hard one minute. Take from the heat; stir in the fruit pectin. Then stir and skim by turns for five minutes, to cool slightly and prevent floating fruit. Quickly pour into hot sterilized glasses; paraffin at once.

Preserved Kumquats

Two pounds kumquats (2 qts.)
Two tablespoons soda
Two quarts boiling water
Standing time: One hour
Six cups boiling water
Cooking time: Ten minutes
Two cups white corn syrup
Two cups sugar
Three and one-third cups water
Boiling time: Ten minutes
Cooking temperature: 226 degrees
Cooking time: Fifteen minutes (about)
Standing time: Overnight
Yield: Three pints

Remove stems and leaves from kumquats. Wash well; drain. Place in deep kettle. Sprinkle with baking soda; cover with boiling water; let stand till cool. Rinse three times in fresh cold water. Drain. With a sharp knife cut two slits (¼ in. deep) at right angles across both stem and blossom ends. Drop kumquats, one at a time, into rapidly boiling water to cover. Cook until tender, about ten minutes.

Meanwhile prepare syrup by boiling together corn syrup, sugar and water for ten minutes. Add drained kumquats. Boil slowly, stirring occasionally until fruit is clear and syrup thickens (226 degrees) or about fifteen minutes. Remove from heat; let stand overnight. Next day reheat and pack the kumquats into hot sterilized jars. Bring the syrup to a boil and pour over the fruit to within ½ inch from the top. Seal immediately according to type lid and jar.

Citrus Marmalade

One cup grapefruit juice (one grapefruit)
One and three-fourths cups orange juice
    (four oranges)
One-third cup lemon juice (one lemon)
Peel of one-half grapefruit
Peel of one orange
Peel of one lemon
One quart cold water
Simmer: Thirty minutes
Three cups boiling water
Three cups sugar
Boil: Twenty minutes
Simmer: One hour, about
Yield: Four or five glasses (6 oz.)

Wash the fruit and extract the juice; set juice aside. Remove membrane from inside of the peels to be used; cut peels into very thin strips an inch to inch and a half long. Place cut peel and cold water in a saucepan, cover and simmer until peel is tender, about thirty minutes. Drain off liquid and add boiling water and sugar to the peel. Boil rapidly for twenty minutes, uncovered. Add the fruit juices and cook again, stirring frequently until somewhat reduced and slightly thickened. Remove from heat and skim and stir for five minutes. Ladle into hot sterilized jelly glasses and seal.

A FAVORITE RECIPE
Cranberry Pear Relish

One pound raw cranberries, ground
Three large pears, cut in eighths,
    unpeeled, ground
One cup broken pecan meats
Two cups sugar
One-fourth teaspoon salt
Yield: Four cups, about

Grind the cranberries and pears in the food chopper. Turn into a bowl; add the pecans, sugar and salt. Mix well. Turn into jars; cover and store in the refrigerator until needed.

MRS. MAY KEMMERLING, *New Harmony, Ind.*

Fresh Pineapple Rhubarb Jam

Two pounds fresh rhubarb, cut (four cups)
Two cups finely diced fresh pineapple
Six cups sugar
Cook: One hour, about
Yield: Six cups

Trim the leaves and root ends of the fresh rhubarb but do not peel the stalks. Cut into half inch slices. The two pounds will give about four cups of the cut fruit. Combine the rhubarb in a heavy kettle with the finely diced fresh pineapple and the sugar. Bring to a boil over low heat, stirring constantly until the sugar dissolves. Cook gently, stirring occasionally, until fruit is tender and the juice jells slightly. Remove from heat and ladle into hot sterilized glasses. Cover with hot paraffin. Store on a cool dark shelf if possible.

Golden Jam

One and one-half cups shredded carrots
    (3 or 4)
One and one-half cups boiling water
One-eighth teaspoon salt
Boiling time: Five minutes
One and one-half cups shredded ripe
    pineapple
One cup diced orange pulp
Cooking time: Fifteen minutes, or until
    tender
Three cups sugar
Cooking time: One hour, or until
    thickened
One tablespoon lemon juice
Yield: Three cups (about)

Pack the shredded carrots firmly in the cup when measuring. Cook in the boiling salted water in a heavy saucepan. Add the pineapple and orange pulp; cover. Cook until the carrots and pineapple are tender but not broken. Stir in the sugar. Cook steadily until the syrup thickens, stirring often to prevent sticking. Remove from the heat; stir in the lemon juice. Ladle into hot sterile glasses (8 oz.); paraffin at once. When cold store in a cool dry place.

Strawberry Jam

One quart strawberries
Boiling water
Standing time: Three minutes
One cup sugar
Boiling time: Five minutes
Two cups sugar
Boiling time: Ten minutes
Yield: Two cups

Wash and hull the strawberries, place in a large saucepan. Pour boiling water to cover over the berries. Let stand for three minutes, drain. Add one cup of sugar and bring to a boil; boil for five minutes. Remove from heat and add two cups of sugar. Bring to a boil again and boil for 10 minutes. Pour into a large bowl, cover and let stand overnight. Stir occasionally. Pour into hot sterilized jelly glasses and paraffin.

We especially enjoy the combination of strawberries and rhubarb. A small amount of each will provide you with a nice array for your preserve shelf.

Spiced Prune Jam

Three pounds Italian fresh prunes
Four and one-half cups sugar
One-half teaspoon cinnamon
One-fourth teaspoon cloves
One-fourth teaspoon allspice
One-fourth teaspoon dry mustard
One-eighth teaspoon ginger
One-fourth cup vinegar
Simmer: One hour, about
Yield: Three pints, about

Wash, dry, halve and pit the fresh prunes. Place in a large kettle with the sugar, cinnamon, cloves, allspice, dry mustard, ginger and vinegar. Bring

slowly to a boil, stirring constantly, until thick, about one hour. Pour into hot sterilized jars and seal immediately.

Strawberry-Rhubarb Preserve

Two cups rhubarb, cut small
Four cups sugar
Standing time: Twelve hours
Cook: To boiling point
One quart strawberries
Boiling time: Fifteen minutes
Yield: Five cups

In a large saucepan, combine the cut rhubarb and sugar. Allow to stand 12 hours or overnight. Wash and hull the strawberries. Bring rhubarb and sugar to boil, add strawberries; boil until thick. Spoon into hot sterilized jelly glasses and top with paraffin.

A FAVORITE RECIPE
Grape Orange Conserve

Two pounds Concord grapes, pulp and
    skins separated
Cooking time: Until pulp is soft
Two tablespoons grated orange rind
Sliced pulp two seeded oranges
Four cups sugar
Cooking time: Twenty minutes
One cup chopped pecans
Cooking time: Three minutes
Yield: Six jars (½ pint)

Wash and separate the pulp of grapes from the skins. In a saucepan boil the pulp until soft. When cool, press through a sieve to remove seeds. In a saucepan mix the pulp, skins, orange rind and sliced orange pulp with the sugar. Cook until as thick as desired. Add the pecans, blending well. Cook. Turn into hot sterilized jars. Seal.

MRS. G. B. HARRISON, *Huntington, W. Va.*

Prune and Orange Conserve

One seedless orange
Two cups water
Simmer: Twenty minutes
Two pounds Italian fresh prunes
One-half cup seedless raisins
One package (2½ oz.) powdered fruit
    pectin
Heat: To boiling
Seven cups sugar
Cook: At hard boil two minutes
One-half cup walnut or pecan meats
Yield: Four to five pints

Chop the whole orange very fine. Place in a kettle or large saucepan with the water and simmer covered for 20 minutes. In the meantime, wash, dry, halve and pit the fresh prunes. Add the prunes and raisins to the orange and place over high heat. Add the powdered pectin. Heat to boiling. Add the sugar all at once and heat, stirring constantly, to boiling again. Boil hard for two minutes, stirring the while. Remove from heat and add the nuts. Skim the top and spoon into hot sterilized jars. Seal as for canned fruit.

Cauliflower Mustard Pickle

Two tablespoons flour
One teaspoon dry mustard
One-fourth teaspoon turmeric
One cup cold water
Cook: Until thickened
One-fourth cup brown sugar
One-third cup cider vinegar
One and one-half teaspoons salt
One-half teaspoon celery seed
One-eighth teaspoon garlic powder
One teaspoon whole mustard seed
Two cups small raw cauliflower clusters
One-half cup sliced onion rings
Cook: Two minutes
One-fourth cup thinly sliced green pepper
Yield: One pint

In a saucepan stir together the flour, dry mustard and turmeric, gradually blend in the water. Cook, stirring constantly, until thickened. Add the sugar, vinegar, salt, celery seed, garlic powder and whole mustard seed; mix well. Add the small pieces of raw cauliflower (measuring about one by one-half inches) and the onion rings. Cook for two minutes, cauliflower should remain somewhat crisp. Stir in the green pepper, spoon into hot sterilized jars and seal.

Sweet Pickle Relish

One green pepper
One large tomato
Six medium-sized cucumbers
One onion
Two tablespoons salt
Standing time: Twenty-four hours
One cup vinegar
One-half cup water
Heat: To boiling point
One cup sugar
One-half teaspoon cinnamon
One-half teaspoon turmeric
One-fourth teaspoon cloves
One-fourth teaspoon allspice
One and one-half tablespoons mixed
  pickling spice
One cup vinegar
Boiling time: Twenty minutes
Yield: Three pints (about)

Remove the seeds and membranes from the pepper. Cut tomato into quarters and cucumbers into one-inch chunks. Cut onion into thick slices. Put vegetables through grinder with coarse blade. Combine in a bowl with the salt and let stand for 24 hours. Drain. Combine in a large saucepan with one cup of vinegar and one-half cup water. Bring to a boil and drain. Add the sugar, cinnamon, turmeric, cloves, allspice, mixed pickling spice (tied in a piece of cheesecloth) and vinegar. Bring to a boil and cook gently for 20 minutes. Stir frequently. Pour into hot sterilized jars and seal immediately.

Cranberry Sauce

Two cups sugar
Two cups water
Boil: Five minutes
One pound (four cups) cranberries
Boil: Five minutes
Yield: Three cups sauce

Place the sugar and water in a saucepan; boil for five minutes. Add the cranberries and boil without stirring until all the berries pop open. Remove from the heat and allow the sauce to remain in the saucepan until cool. Serve with turkey or chicken.

Cranberry Orange Relish

One pound (four cups) cranberries
Two whole oranges
One and one-half to two cups sugar
Chill: Thoroughly
Yield: Four cups, approx.

Put the raw cranberries and oranges (cut into sixths with skin on) through the food grinder. Add sugar to taste and chill thoroughly.

Pepper Relish

Twelve sweet green peppers
Twelve sweet red peppers
Twelve medium-sized onions, peeled
Six ribs of celery
Boiling water to cover
Standing time: Five minutes
One cup sugar
Two tablespoons salt
One-eighth teaspoon cayenne pepper
One tablespoon celery seed
Vinegar to cover (3-4 cups)
Simmering time: Ten minutes
Yield: Eight pints

Wash and dry the peppers, onions and celery. Trim stem and core from peppers, removing seeds and white membrane. Run the cut peppers, onions and celery through a food chopper using the coarse knife. Turn into a kettle; cover with boiling water; let stand. Pour into a colander to drain thoroughly. Return to the kettle; add the sugar, salt, cayenne, celery seed and vinegar to cover. Slowly bring to a boil, stirring; reduce the heat and simmer. Place in hot sterilized jars; seal as for canned fruit. Store in a dark place. Ready to eat in a week.

Fruit and Vegetable Relish

Twelve fresh Italian prunes
Three Bartlett pears
Three ripe tomatoes
Two green peppers
Three medium-sized onions
Two and one-half cups sugar
One pint vinegar
One tablespoon salt
One tablespoon pickling spice
One stick cinnamon
Cook: Until thick
Yield: Six half-pint jars

Wash the fruit, tomatoes and peppers; peel the onions, pit the prunes and peel and core the pears. Finely chop the fruit and vegetables and combine in a large saucepan or kettle with the sugar, vinegar, salt, pickling spice and cinnamon. Boil until thick, stirring occasionally. Spoon into hot sterilized jars and top immediately with the melted paraffin for long keeping.

Spiced Apple Relish

One cup sugar
One tablespoon prepared mustard
One-third cup cider vinegar
Two-thirds cup water
Four whole allspice
One stick cinnamon
One piece crystallized ginger
Simmer: Ten minutes
Four green apples
Simmer: Five to ten minutes
One-half cup seedless raisins
One-fourth cup chopped walnuts
Yield: One quart

In a saucepan or large heavy skillet blend the sugar and mustard together. Stir in the cider vinegar and water. Add the allspice, stick cinnamon and piece of crystallized ginger and bring to a boil. Lower heat and simmer gently for ten minutes. Remove spices from liquid. Pare and core the apples. Cut each into eight wedges. Quarter each wedge crosswise for sizable chunks. Add to the simmered liquid and cook, stirring to turn pieces over carefully, until apple is just tender. Do not overcook. A large skillet will permit a single layer of fruit and thus speed the cooking. Rinse raisins with hot water and drain. Add to the apples with the nuts and remove from heat. Chill thoroughly before serving.

Spiced Cranberries

One pound (four cups) cranberries
Two-thirds cup vinegar
One-third cup water
Three cups sugar
One tablespoon cinnamon
One and one-half teaspoons ground cloves
One and one-half teaspoons ground
  allspice
Simmer: Forty-five minutes
Yield: Four cups

Rinse and pick over the cranberries. Place in a large saucepan or kettle and add the vinegar, water, sugar and spices. Bring to a boil, lower the heat and simmer gently for forty-five minutes. Remove from the heat and chill before serving.

Cherry Preserves

One and one-third cups cherry juice
  plus water
Four cups sugar
Boiling time: Five minutes
Four cups pitted sour cherries, drained
Boiling time: Fifteen minutes
Standing time: Twelve hours
Boiling time syrup: Ten minutes
Yield: Two pints

Drain juice from pitted cherries; measure, adding hot water to make 1 1/3 cups liquid. Mix with the sugar in a large saucepan; stir until boiling begins; boil hard. Add drained cherries; bring to a boil; stirring often. Turn into an earthen bowl; when cool, cover; let stand. Next day return to saucepan; bring to a mad boil; skim cherries into hot, sterile jars. Boil syrup until thickened; pour over cherries; seal as for canned fruit.

French Café au Lait: Pour strong, hot freshly brewed coffee and hot, rich milk simultaneously into a large cup. Serve with fruit and croissants, brioches, toast or toasted rolls for a Continental breakfast.

Vienna Coffee: Brew extra strength coffee, sweeten to taste, mix with light cream and top with schlagobers (whipped cream). Pictured is a spread for a Kaffee Klatsch using Blue Onion China.

American coffee: measure into filter of coffeemaker; keep pouring boiling water over it until coffee reaches the proper level. Remove filter. Serve with cream and sugar.

Irish Coffee: Pour jugger of Irish whiskey into stemmed wine glass; fill almost to brim with hot, strong coffee, sweeten and top with whipped cream. Do not stir after cream has been added.

Turkish Coffee: Bring to a boil one and one-half cups of water combined with four teaspoons of sugar and one-fourth of a cup of pulverized coffee. Allow to froth up three times; pour into cups.

Caffe Cappuccini: In macchinetta water boils; steam passes through coffee; condenses into caffe espresso. Stir in hot milk and dust the top with cinnamon.

Wonderful World of Wine

Starting from center back and moving clockwise we see a fine variety of wines served in proper wine glasses: Rhine Wine, Brandy, Cognac, Pink Champagne, White Champagne, Creme de Menthe, White Burgundy Wine, Red Burgundy Wine, White Bordeaux Wine, Red Bordeaux Wine and Alsatian Wine.

A SIMPLE WINE GUIDE

SELECTIONS		RED	WHITE	ROSE	CHAMPAGNE
BEEF		 🍷			
VEAL		 🍷	 🍷		
LAMB		 🍷	 🍷		
PORK		 🍷	 🍷		
GAME		 🍷			
POULTRY		 🍷	 🍷		
FISH AND SHELLFISH			 🍷		
CHEESE		 🍷	 🍷	(red usually best)	
DESSERT			 🍷		
WITH ALL KINDS OF FOOD				 🍷	 🍸

BUYING CHAMPAGNE

BRUT—Driest

EXTRA DRY—Fairly dry

DEMI-SEC—Very sweet

SEC—Sweet

Percolator, drip and vacuum are the three most popular methods of preparation in this country with an increasing interest in the many special makers devised in Europe.

But regardless of the type of pot, the cardinal rule for good coffee seems to be to make it by accurate measurement. Enjoy fewer cups of fine brew in preference to more cups of lesser quality, if necessary. Economy will give you nothing but a poorer cup of coffee because the beans are graded by the number of imperfections per bag and thus priced. The imperfections are leaves, broken beans and the like and add nothing to the flavor.

Coffee may seem like an oilless fluid, but it isn't so. This substance is deposited in the pot and takes real scouring to remove. Accumulations over a period of time can really spoil the flavor of a freshly ground, top quality blend. So keep the inside of your coffee maker spotlessly clean.

Heat cold water from the tap and scald the container first unless it is electric. Standard procedure specifies two tablespoons of coffee for each three-fourths cup measure of water.

Yes; it takes a certain amount of heat to make coffee, but never, never boil it. Reheating spoils the flavor too because coffee is one of the timely delights; to be at its best it must be freshly brewed. To sum up then, use good quality coffee, use enough and time well.

Mocha Cream Whip

One cup heavy cream
One-half teaspoon almond extract
One quart brewed coffee, chilled
One quart chocolate ice cream
One-eighth teaspoon salt
Ground nutmeg
Serves: Twelve

Add the heavy cream and almond extract to the chilled brewed coffee. Add the chocolate ice cream and salt and use a whisk or egg beater to blend thoroughly. Serve in glasses or punch cups with a dusting of ground nutmeg.

Hot Chocolate

Two squares (2 oz.) unsweetened
  chocolate
One cup water
Three tablespoons sugar
Dash of salt
Boiling time: Three minutes
Three cups milk
Heating time: Ten minutes
Servings: Six

In the upper half of a double boiler melt the chocolate with the water, over low heat. Add the sugar and salt and boil three minutes stirring constantly. Place pan over boiling water. Add milk gradually stirring constantly. Heat. Before serving beat with rotary beater until light and frothy.

Nutmeg Cocoa

Two tablespoons cocoa
Three tablespoons sugar
One-fourth teaspoon nutmeg
One-sixteenth teaspoon salt
One-half cup water
Boil: One minute
Three and one-half cups milk
Heat: Five to ten minutes
Marshmallows
Serves: Six

In a saucepan mix the cocoa, sugar, nutmeg and salt. Gradually stir in the water blending smooth. Bring to a boil; boil one minute, stirring constantly. Add the milk; heat thoroughly. Before serving beat with a rotary beater until light and frothy. Top each serving with a marshmallow if desired.

Tea Making

One reason tea is enjoying an increasing popularity is the fact that 200 cups can be made from one pound. This makes tea a most economical beverage. Tea should not be judged by color alone as many infusions are almost colorless. For best flavor:

1. Always use a teapot; 2. Allow one teaspoon of tea or one tea bag per cup; 3. Use fresh BOILING water; 4. Let the tea brew 3 to 5 minutes.

The briskly boiling water is emphasized as is the importance of rinsing out the teapot with boiling water before brewing. Should you prefer weak tea brew it the prescribed way and dilute with hot water afterward.

Iced Tea

One quart water
Heat: To rolling boil
One-third cup loose tea or fifteen tea bags
Brewing time: Five minutes
One quart cold water
Ice cubes
Serves: Ten to twelve

Bring the water to a full rolling boil in a saucepan. Remove from the heat. Immediately add the tea. Brew for five minutes. Stir. Strain into a pitcher containing the quart of cold water. Serve in tall iced tea glasses filled with ice cubes. Pass sugar and lemon.

Pink Lemonade

Six lemons
One and one-half cups sugar
Two trays ice cubes
Six cups cold water
One bottle (10 oz.) maraschino cherries
Servings: Sixteen

With a sharp knife cut the lemons in thin slices; discard the seeds. Put the slices in a large bowl; add the sugar. Press hard with a wooden spoon until the sugar is dissolved. Add the ice, water and cherry juice. Strain into glasses; garnish with cherries. Serve with gay colored sippers.

Fruit Punch

Two cups water
One tablespoon loose tea
Brew: Five minutes
One quart grape juice
Two cups grapefruit juice
One can (6 oz.) frozen orange juice
  concentrate
One can (6 oz.) lemon-limeade concentrate
One-half cup rum
Three or four quarts ginger ale or
  sparkling water
Yield: Thirty to forty punch-cup servings

In a saucepan heat the water to rolling boil. Add loose tea, remove from heat and let brew for five minutes. Strain into a large bowl. Add the fruit juices and concentrates with rum. Chill thoroughly. Serve in a chilled punch bowl over a block of ice or several trays of ice cubes adding the chilled ginger ale or sparkling water at the last moment.

Spiced Fruit Punch Rose

One and one-half cups sugar
Three-fourths cup water
Simmer: Five minutes
Two cups orange juice
One-third cup lemon juice
One cup fresh pineapple wedges
Whole cloves
One bottle New York State rose wine
Chill: Thoroughly
One quart carbonated water
Two trays ice cubes
One lime, thinly sliced
Yield: Three quarts

Place the sugar and water in a saucepan and bring to a boil. Simmer gently for five minutes. Remove from heat and cool. Add the orange juice and lemon juice. Cut fresh pineapple into half inch slices, peel and cut the fruit into small wedges. Press a clove into each piece of pineapple and add to the fruit juices with the rose wine. At serving time pour into punch bowl with the carbonated water and ice cubes. Stir to blend. Add thinly sliced lime for color.

Whiskey Sour Punch

Four cups orange juice, chilled
Four cups lemon juice, chilled
One-fourth cup grenadine syrup
One quart whiskey or bourbon, chilled
Three quarts sparkling water, chilled
Sugar to taste
Maraschino cherries, orange slices
Servings: Thirty-six

Combine the orange and lemon juice, grenadine syrup, whiskey and sparkling water. Add sugar to taste, stirring until dissolved. Pour over ice in a punch bowl. Garnish with cherries and orange slices. Ladle into cold punch cups.

Alsace Punch

Two cups diced pineapple
One cup sugar
Four whole allspice
One-half cup orange juice
One-fourth cup lemon juice
Two bottles (4/5 qts. each) Alsace
  riesling wine
Refrigerate: One hour
Two quarts sparkling water
Servings: Twenty-four

In a bowl mix the pineapple, sugar, allspice, orange juice, lemon juice and wine until the sugar is dissolved. Let stand in refrigerator for 1 hour. Strain into a punch bowl. Add sparkling water. Ladle into punch cups.

Ginger Apple Punch

One cup sugar
One-half cup water
Cooking time: Three minutes
One quart apple juice, chilled
One-half cup lemon juice, chilled
Green food coloring
One quart ginger ale, chilled
Lemon slices
Yield: Two quarts

In a saucepan combine the sugar and water; boil three minutes. Cool. Add the combined juices and coloring. When ready to serve, add the ginger ale. Pour over ice cubes. Garnish with thinly sliced lemon. Serve immediately.

Bordeaux Punch

Six medium-sized apples, sliced
Six lemons, thinly sliced
Two and one-fourth cups sugar
Six cloves
Four large bottles red Bordeaux wine
Two quarts sparkling water
Ice, sliced fruit, fresh mint leaves
Servings: Twenty-four

In a bowl combine the apples, lemons, sugar, cloves and wine. Let stand in refrigerator for two hours. Strain. Pour over ice in a large punch bowl. Add sparkling water. Stir. Garnish with sliced fruit and mint leaves.

Tea Punch

Three and one-half cups sugar
Three cups water
Boiling time: Five minutes
Six cups strong brewed tea
One cup lemon juice
One cup orange juice
Four cups cranberry juice
Chilling time: Three hours
Two quarts ginger ale, chilled
Lemon and orange slices for garnish
Servings: Twenty-four

Boil the sugar and water together and combine with the tea. Add the fruit juices; chill. Add the ginger ale. Pour over ice cubes in a punch bowl; garnish with lemon and orange slices. Serve in small cups.

Accurate measuring of the ingredients and careful blending of flavors make for a perfect punch. Estimate about one-third cup per serving and allow two or three servings per person or one quart of punch for five or six guests.

Bordeaux Wine Punch

One bottle Rosé wine, chilled
One bottle Bordeaux Sauternes wine, chilled
One-fourth cup cognac brandy
*Block of ice
One large bottle sparkling water
Lime or orange slices
Serves: Twenty-four approximately

Chill rosé and sauternes wines. Combine with cognac. Pour over a block of ice in a punch bowl. Stir in sparkling water. Serve immediately. Garnish with lime slices.

*Instead of block of ice: arrange orange sections and cherries in a mold. Add a small amount of water at a time and freeze. Repeat until mold is filled. Freeze. When ready to serve remove from freezer; let stand a few minutes before placing in punch bowl.

A FAVORITE RECIPE
Fruity Tea

Peel and juice of three lemons
One cup boiling water
Standing time: Until cool
One cup sugar
One quart cold strong tea
Three small oranges, sliced
One bottle (5 oz.) cherries, chopped
One can (8 oz.) apricots, chopped
Ice cubes
Servings: Six

Squeeze the juice from the lemons; place the rinds in a pitcher; cover with the boiling water; let cool. Drain into a two quart pitcher (or larger). Combine with the sugar and lemon juice, stirring until sugar is dissolved. Add the tea, orange slices, juice from the cherries and the apricots. Chop the cherries and apricots. When serving add the chopped fruit. Pour fruity tea over ice cubes.

MRS. NICHOLAS SCALLION, *Easton, Pa.*

A FAVORITE RECIPE
Hot-Weather Punch

Four teaspoons black tea
Four cups boiling water
Steeping time: Five minutes
One cup sugar, or less
One-third cup lemon juice
One and one-half cups orange juice
Chilling time: Until serving time
One quart ginger ale
Ice cubes
Yield: Two quarts, about

Place the tea in a pot or saucepan; pour fresh boiling water over the tea. Steep. Strain. Add the sugar, stirring until dissolved. Add the fruit juices. Chill until ready to serve. Add the ginger ale last. Place ice cubes in glasses, pour in the tea mixture.

MRS. IRENE YOUNG, *Honesdale, Pa.*

A FAVORITE RECIPE
Frosty Fruit Punch

One cup sugar
Two cups water
Cooking time: Five minutes
Six whole cloves
One-half teaspoon nutmeg
One-half teaspoon cinnamon
Cooling time: Ten minutes
One cup pineapple juice
Three tablespoons lime juice
One and one-half teaspoons grated lime rind
Ice cubes
Three pints ginger ale
Yield: Eleven cups, about

In a saucepan cook the sugar and water. Add the spices. Cool. Stir in the pineapple juice, lime juice and grated lime rind. When ready to serve add the ice cubes and pour in the ginger ale.

MRS. W. C. JERVIS, *Somerville, Mass.*

Chocolate Milk Honey Nog

Three eggs
Five tablespoons honey
One quart chocolate milk
One cup heavy cream, whipped
Servings: Four

Break the eggs into a medium-sized bowl. Add honey and beat until frothy with a whisk or rotary beater. Beat in the chocolate milk. Fold in the whipped cream and serve at once.

A FAVORITE RECIPE
Orange Blossom Punch

Three cups sugar
Three cups water
Cooking time: Five minutes
Six cups grapefruit juice
Six cups orange juice
One and one-half quarts ginger ale
Ice cubes
Servings: Ten

In a saucepan mix the sugar and water; cook and stir until the sugar is dissolved. Bring to a boil and cook for five minutes without stirring. Cool and chill. Add the fruit juices and ginger ale at serving time. Serve over ice cubes.

MRS. LORETTA COLES, *Brooklyn, N.Y.*

Banana Nog

One egg
One tablespoon sugar
One-half teaspoon vanilla
One cup milk
One-third banana, mashed
Serves: One

Break the egg into a small bowl. Add sugar and vanilla and beat with whisk or rotary beater until frothy. Beat in the milk and stir in the mashed banana. Serve at once.

Sparkling Fruit Punch

One can (6 oz.) frozen lemonade
 concentrate
One can (6 oz.) frozen orange juice
 concentrate
One can (6 oz.) frozen pineapple juice
 concentrate
Two cans (12 oz. each) apricot whole
 fruit nectar
One-fourth cup kirsch or brandy, or more
One and one-half quarts cold water
Two cups California muscatel wine
Chill
One quart sparkling water
One cup sliced strawberries
One cup diced fresh or drained crushed
 canned pineapple
Yield: Approx. one gallon

In a large bowl combine the frozen concentrates with the apricot whole fruit nectar, kirsch, cold water and muscatel. Chill. When ready to serve pour into a chilled punch bowl and add the sparkling water, strawberries, pineapple and two trays of ice cubes.

Fresh Fruit Punch

Four cups water
Three tablespoons tea
Brew: Five minutes
One and one-half cups sugar
One cup lemon juice
Two cups orange juice
One can (No. 2) pineapple juice
Two quarts cold water
One orange, thinly sliced and quartered
Mint leaves
Yield: Approx. one gallon

Heat the water in a saucepan to the rolling boil. Remove from heat and add tea. Allow to brew for five minutes then stir and strain into a large bowl. Add the sugar and stir to dissolve. Add the lemon, orange and pineapple juice and the cold water. Chill thoroughly. To serve pour over ice cubes in a punch bowl and toss in thin slices of orange and mint leaves pulled from the coarse stems. Note: Added sparkle may be given this punch by added chilled ginger ale or sparkling water.

Spiced Fruit Punch

Three-fourths cup sugar
One and one-half cups water
Three sticks cinnamon
Three-fourths teaspoon whole cloves
One-half teaspoon whole allspice
Six roots whole ginger
Boil: Three minutes
Three-fourths cup lemon juice
Chill: Thoroughly
Three cups chilled pineapple juice
Three cups chilled grape juice
One and one-half cups chilled apricot
 nectar
Ice
Lemon slices stuck with whole cloves
Yield: Two and one-half quarts

In a saucepan bring the sugar, water, cinnamon sticks, whole cloves, allspice and ginger to a boil. Boil three minutes and strain into a bowl. Add the lemon juice and chill thoroughly. At serving time combine with the chilled pineapple juice, grape juice and apricot nectar in a large punch bowl. Add ice cubes or a block of ice and garnish with lemon slices stuck with whole cloves. Ladle into punch cups or glasses to serve.

Cranberry Fruit Punch

One and one-half cups sugar
Three cups water
Heat: To melt sugar
Three pints cranberry juice cocktail
Three cups orange juice
One cup lemon juice
One can (No. 2) pineapple juice
Yield: Four quarts

In a saucepan heat the sugar and water together until sugar is completely dissolved. Add to the cranberry juice cocktail with the orange, lemon and pineapple juice. Chill and serve over cracked ice.

Mint Jelly Punch

One quart water
One-third cup loose tea
Brew: Three to five minutes
One cup mint jelly
One-half cup strained lemon juice
Cool: One hour or more
Two cups pineapple juice
One can (6 oz.) frozen orange juice
 concentrate
One bottle (12 oz.) sparkling water
Few drops green food coloring
Yield: Three quarts

Bring water to a full rolling boil in a saucepan. Remove from the heat; immediately add the tea. Brew three to five minutes. Stir and strain into a large bowl; add the mint jelly and stir to dissolve. Add the lemon juice and permit to cool gradually. At serving time, combine the tea mixture with the pineapple juice, frozen orange juice concentrate and sparkling water in a punch bowl. Add ice cubes and a few drops of green food coloring.

Cognac Cider Punch

One cup orange juice
One cup lemon juice
One cup canned pineapple juice
One cup cognac
One-fourth cup maraschino liqueur
Two quarts cider
Ice
Thin lemon and orange slices
Yield: Twenty-four four-ounce servings

In a large punch bowl combine the orange juice, lemon juice, pineapple juice, cognac, maraschino liqueur and cider. Stir well together. At serving time add a block of ice or trays of cubes and the thin slices of lemon and orange for garnish. Serve very cold.

Hot Buttered Cider

One gallon apple cider
Heat: To boiling
One cup dark brown sugar
One-half cup butter
Two sticks cinnamon
Simmer: Five minutes
Cinnamon
Yield: One gallon

In a kettle heat the cider to boiling. Add the sugar, butter and stick cinnamon and simmer just until the sugar is dissolved. Ladle into mugs and sprinkle the top with cinnamon.

Champagne Punch

Four cups boiling water
Three tablespoons tea
Brew: Three minutes
Two tablespoons brandy
Six tablespoons lemon juice
Two cups sugar
One cup water
Boil: Five minutes
Chill: Two hours
Two bottles New York state
 champagne, chilled
Block of ice
Serves: Twenty-five

Bring the four cups of water to a full rolling boil. Remove from heat. Add the tea; brew 3 minutes. Stir and strain. Add brandy and lemon juice. Cool at room temperature. Cook the sugar and water for 5 minutes. Cool and chill. When ready to serve, pour the tea mixture, chilled syrup and champagne over the block of ice. Ladle into punch cups.

Eggnog

One egg
One tablespoon sugar
One-half teaspoon vanilla
One cup milk
Serves: One

Break the egg into a small bowl. Add sugar and vanilla and beat with whisk or rotary beater until frothy. Beat in the milk and serve at once. Dust top with grated nutmeg if desired.

A FAVORITE RECIPE
Cream Cheese Spread

One package (8 oz.) cream cheese
Three tablespoons butter
One small onion, minced
One-fourth teaspoon salt
One-sixteenth teaspoon pepper
One tablespoon or less paprika
Three tablespoons beer
Rye bread for sandwiches
Servings: Four

Have the cheese at room temperature. Mash in a glass bowl; add the butter, onion, salt, pepper and paprika; mix. Beat in the beer. Use as a spread for sandwiches or on crackers.

MRS. HELEN BARONE, *Jackson Heights, N.Y.*

Waffle Cheese Sandwiches

One package frozen waffle sections
  (six small)
Horseradish mustard
Sliced tomato
Six slices cheddar cheese
Oven temperature: 400 degrees
Baking time: Ten minutes
Paprika
Servings: Three

Spread the frozen waffles with horseradish mustard and place on baking sheet. Lay one or two tomato slices on each and top with sliced cheddar cheese. Bake in a quick oven for 10 minutes or until the cheese has melted. Dust with a shake of paprika and serve at once.

Cottage and Cheddar Blend

Two cups cottage cheese
One cup grated cheddar cheese
Two tablespoons prepared horseradish
Two tablespoons grated onion
Two tablespoons chopped green pepper
Three tablespoons mayonnaise
One-fourth teaspoon salt
One-fourth teaspoon pepper
Yield: Three cups

Blend cottage cheese with the grated cheddar, horseradish, onion, green pepper, mayonnaise, salt and pepper. Mix well and chill thoroughly several hours or overnight to develop full flavor.

Rolled Tea Sandwiches

You need fresh, close textured bread. Use a very sharp knife to remove the crusts from an unsliced loaf. Cut thin lengthwise slices about one-eighth to one-fourth inch thick. Spread with soft sandwich filling and roll up. Wrap each roll in waxed paper and chill thoroughly. Slice into one-fourth inch pinwheels at serving time.

Bacon Cheese Spread

One cup grated cheddar cheese
Four slices crisp, cooked bacon, crumbled
One tablespoon finely chopped green onion
One-fourth cup mayonnaise
One-eighth teaspoon Worcestershire sauce
Yield: One cup, about

Blend the grated cheddar cheese with the crumbled bacon, chopped onion, mayonnaise and steak sauce. Mix thoroughly. Serve as a spread for sandwiches or on crackers. Particularly delicious for hot broiled open-face sandwiches or appetizers. (Broil until bubbly.)

Kipper Cheese Cress Sandwiches

One package (3 oz.) softened cream cheese
Four slices toasted bread
One tomato, thinly sliced
One-half cup coarsely cut water cress
One can (3¼ oz.) Norway kippers, flaked
One tablespoon finely chopped pecans
Servings: Two

Spread the softened cream cheese over the four slices of toasted bread. Trim off the crusts if desired. Top cheese with thin slices of tomato, a layer of coarsely cut water cress and the flaked Norway kippers. Sprinkle with the finely chopped pecans. Serve open-face with each slice cut into fourths.

Olive and Chipped Beef Spread

One-half cup ripe olives
One jar (2½ oz.) chipped beef
One cup finely chopped celery
One-third cup mayonnaise
Yield: One and one-half cups

Cut the olives into small pieces and mix in a bowl with the well-chopped chipped beef, chopped celery and mayonnaise.

Cottage Cheese and Bacon Sandwich Filling

One cup creamed cottage cheese
One cup grated carrot
One-third cup sweet pickle relish
Two tablespoons real mayonnaise
One-half teaspoon salt
One-eighth teaspoon pepper
Four slices crisp cooked bacon, crumbled
Yield: Filling for four sandwiches

In a bowl blend the creamed cottage cheese, grated carrot, sweet pickle relish, mayonnaise, salt and pepper together. Spread over buttered slices of bread. Sprinkle with crumbled bacon and top with additional slices of buttered bread.

Broiled Corned Beef and Kraut Sandwiches

One loaf French bread (15 inch)
Softened butter or margarine
Two cups drained sauerkraut
One can (12 oz.) corned beef
One-half pound Mozzarella cheese
One tablespoon brown sugar
One teaspoon onion salt
One-half teaspoon dry mustard
One-fourth teaspoon garlic powder
One-half teaspoon chili powder
One-fourth teaspoon pepper
One-half cup chili sauce
Broiler temperature: 500 degrees
Broil: Five to seven minutes
Serves: Four to six

With a sharp knife split the loaf of French bread from end to end. Spread with the softened butter or margarine and lay on a shallow pan. Spoon the drained kraut over the bread and cover with thin slices of corned beef. Top with sliced Mozzarella cheese. In a cup stir together the brown sugar, salt, dry mustard, garlic powder, chili powder and pepper; blend in the chili sauce. Spoon over the cheese. Broil the sandwich about five inches from the heat until cheese is melted. Cut into five-inch lengths to serve.

Baked Ham and Cheese Sandwiches

Eight slices bread
One cup cubed cooked ham
One-fourth pound grated cheddar cheese
Two eggs
One and one-fourth cups milk
One-sixteenth teaspoon cayenne pepper
Oven temperature: 350 degrees
Baking time: Forty minutes
Servings: Four

Remove the crusts from the slices of bread and place four in the bottom of a greased baking pan (8 x 8 x 2 in.). Sprinkle half of the ham and cheese over the bread. Cover with remaining slices of bread, then the remainder of the ham and cheese. In a bowl, beat the eggs, add the milk and cayenne and pour over the bread, ham and cheese in the baking dish. Bake in a moderate oven for forty minutes; serve at once.

Submarine Sandwich

One small loaf French bread
Butter, mayonnaise, mustard
Two or three slices Swiss cheese
Four or five slices salami
One small onion, thinly sliced
Two tablespoons sweet pickle relish
One tomato, thinly sliced
Two or three lettuce leaves
Servings: Two

Split the loaf of French bread through. Butter both pieces. Spread one side with mayonnaise, one with mustard. Lay the cheese on the mustard side, top with salami, onion, relish, tomato and lettuce. Top with other piece of bread. Cut into two or four pieces.

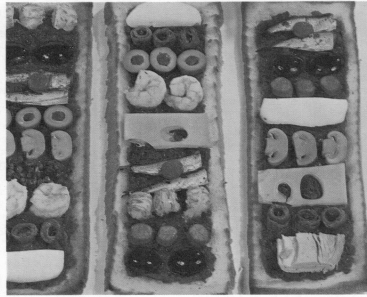

Open Broiled Cheese Sandwich

One loaf French bread
Two cans (3 oz.) deviled ham spread
Eight slices (½ lb.) cheddar cheese
One tomato, quartered
Four green pepper strips
One-fourth cup melted margarine
One clove garlic, crushed
One can (3 oz.) anchovies
Oven temperature: 500 degrees
Broiling time: Six minutes (about)
Servings: Four

Cut diagonal gashes in the bread (1½ in. apart). Scoop out alternate gashed sections of the loaf almost to the bottom to form shell. Cover the inside of the shell with the ham spread. Arrange a slice of cheese, tomato wedge, green pepper strip and a second slice of cheese in each shell. Brush the combined margarine and garlic over the entire loaf. Set on a baking sheet. Place four inches from the broiler unit; broil until the cheese melts. Garnish with rolled anchovies. Cut into four servings and place on heated plate. Serve.

Club Chef Sandwich

Twelve slices bread, toasted
Four slices Swiss cheese
Four slices cooked tongue
One-half cup mayonnaise
Four large slices tomatoes
Four slices chicken
Four lettuce leaves
Servings: Four

Place four slices of warm toast on a board. Arrange a slice of cheese and tongue on each slice of toast; spread with mayonnaise. Add a second slice of toast and on it arrange a slice of tomato, chicken and a lettuce leaf; spread with mayonnaise. Finish with a third slice of toast. Fasten each sandwich with toothpicks, placed at opposite corners; cut into triangles with a sharp knife. Arrange each sandwich on a plate; garnish with a stuffed olive and gherkin. Serve at once with hot coffee.

Hero Pizza Sandwiches

One loaf unsliced sandwich bread
Two jars (6 oz. each) barbecue relish
One tablespoon parlsey, chopped
One tablespoon chives, chopped
One-fourth teaspoon pepper
One can (3¾ oz.) Norway sardines
One can (4 oz.) sliced mushrooms
One bottle (3¼ oz.) capers
One package (6 oz.) mozzarella cheese, sliced
One package (6 oz.) Switzerland Swiss cheese
Six stuffed olives, sliced
Six black olives, sliced
One can (7 oz.) tuna fish
One package (12 oz.) Chilean lobster tails
One can (2 oz.) rolled anchovies
One can (4½ oz.) shrimp
One can (4 oz.) Vienna sausages, sliced
Oven temperature: 375 degrees
Baking time: Fifteen minutes
Yield: Seven

With a sharp knife slice the loaf lengthwise into seven rectangular pieces. Toast one side of the bread. Remove to board. Spread the combined barbecue relish, parsley, chives and pepper on the untoasted side. Arrange the Norway sardines, mushrooms, capers, mozzarella and Switzerland Swiss cheese, stuffed and black olives, tuna fish, Chilean lobster tails, anchovies, shrimp and Vienna sausages over the sauce. Place on cookie sheets. Bake in a moderately hot oven until edges are browned and cheese melted. Serve immediately.

Peanut Butter Bacon Sandwiches

One-half cup peanut butter
Eight crisp bacon slices
One egg, beaten slightly
One-half cup milk
Four tablespoons butter or margarine
Browning time: Five minutes
Servings: Four

Spread the peanut butter on four slices of bread; place two strips of bacon on

top. Cover each with a slice of bread. Combine the egg and milk. Pour into a shallow plate. Dip both sides of the sandwiches in the egg mixture. Brown in the butter or margarine in a skillet, turning once. Remove to a hot plate. Serve with honey or jelly.

Skyscraper Sandwiches

One large loaf unsliced sandwich bread
One-half cup softened butter
One can (1 lb.) salmon, flaked
One small cucumber, peeled and minced
One-fourth cup minced parsley
One tablespoon lemon juice
Salt and pepper
Mayonnaise
One-half pound cream cheese
One-half cup chopped stuffed olives
Milk
Four hard-cooked eggs, sliced
Eight rolled anchovies
Eight pimiento strips
Yield: Eight sandwiches

Slice the bread thin; toast. For each sandwich cut four rounds of toast varying in diameter from 5 to 2 inches. Spread the rounds with softened butter. In a bowl mix the salmon, cucumber, parsley and lemon juice. Season with salt and pepper. Moisten with enough mayonnaise to make a spreading consistency. Cover the 5-in. rounds with salmon mixture.

Spread the 4-in. rounds with the combined cream cheese and chopped stuffed olives moistened with enough milk to make a spreading consistency. Place over the salmon mixture. Cover the 3-in. rounds with sliced eggs; center on top of cream cheese mixture. On the 2-in. rounds place a rolled anchovy surrounded with a strip of pimiento. Top the sandwich with this. Place on a platter.

Unusual Sandwiches

Salad Stuffed Rolls

Mix equal portions of ground boiled ham and Swiss cheese with chopped celery and minced India chutney. Fill hollowed out rolls; replace top. Serve in salad greens and garnish with black olives.

Rag-Rug Canapes

Butter a round slice of rye or pumpernickel bread. Spread the center with a mixture of deviled ham and India relish. Around the edge of the ham mixture arrange a row of parsley. Spread the remaining bread with a combination of finely grated cheddar cheese and real mayonnaise. Garnish with a stuffed olive. Cut into triangles. Place on a tray; serve.

Grilled Ham and Cheese

On each toasted and buttered English muffin place a slice of tomato, boiled ham and cheddar cheese. Grill until cheese melts. Garnish with sliced olives.

Ham and Swiss Cheese

A slice of ham and Swiss cheese, with prepared mustard and lettuce is placed between buttered sliced pumpernickel bread. Place a dill pickle slice on top.

Salty Rye Snacks

Mix equal portions of ground ham and Swiss cheese together, season to taste, and add enough real mayonnaise to make mixture of spreading consistency. Then spread on slices of buttered, salted rye snack bread; garnish with parsley and olives.

Pinwheel

Mix equal portions of ground boiled ham and cream cheese; season to taste and add enough boiled salad dressing to make mixture of spreading consistency. Spread on a crustless long rectangular slice of fresh bread which is lying on a damp cloth. Then roll as for jelly roll. Seal edges with butter. Wrap in foil. Chill. When ready to serve, slice (¼ in. thick). Garnish.

Hero

Between buttered French bread sliced lengthwise, place slices of ham, Swiss cheese, tomatoes and hard-cooked eggs, green pepper rings and lettuce. Serve.

Hot Turkey Sandwiches

Three tablespoons butter or margarine
Three tablespoons flour
Three-fourths teaspoon salt
One-fourth teaspoon dry mustard
Pinch of cayenne pepper
Two cups milk
Cooking time: Eight to ten minutes
Two cups grated cheddar cheese
Six slices toast
Sliced turkey for six portions
Paprika
Oven temperature: 450 degrees
Baking time: Ten minutes
Twelve slices crisp bacon
Sliced tomatoes and stuffed olives
   (optional)
Servings: Six

In a saucepan, melt the butter or margarine. Stir in the flour, salt, dry mustard and cayenne pepper. Gradually blend in the milk and cook over moderate heat until the sauce is smooth and thickened. Add the grated cheddar cheese and heat until melted, stirring all the while. Arrange the slices of toast in a shallow baking dish or on a heat-proof platter and top with the slices of turkey. Pour on the cheese sauce, dust with paprika and bake in the oven until bubbling hot. Serve each portion with the crisp bacon, adding sliced tomatoes and stuffed olives if desired.

Hot Ham and Cheese Sandwiches

Eight slices bread
Eight teaspoons diablo mustard
Four slices boiled ham
Eight thin slices Switzerland Swiss cheese
Four tablespoons butter or margarine
Saute: Three minutes
Yield: Four

Spread one side of bread with the diablo mustard. Trim the ham and cheese to fit the bread. Put a slice of cheese on four slices of bread; cover with a piece of ham and then another slice of cheese. Top with bread. In a heavy skillet, heat half the butter until it is hot, not brown. Brown sandwiches on one side; add remaining butter and brown other side. Serve immediately.

Fried Shrimp Sandwich

Two cups cooked shrimp, finely minced
One teaspoon salt
One-eighth teaspoon pepper
One teaspoon sherry wine
Six parsley leaves, minced
Two egg whites, beaten stiff
Eight thin slices white bread,
   crusts removed
Salad oil
Frying temperature: 370 degrees
Fry: Three minutes
Yield: Sixteen sandwiches

In a bowl, combine the cooked shrimp, salt, pepper, sherry wine and parsley. Mix in the stiffly beaten egg whites. Spread mixture firmly (¼ in. thick) on the bread. Cut each lengthwise. Pour salad oil into a heavy skillet to the depth of 1 inch. When oil has reached frying temperature, place the sandwiches, bread side up, in the oil; fry a few seconds; turn and brown the bread side. Drain on absorbent paper. Serve immediately.

Oyster Club Sandwiches

One pint oysters
Twelve slices bacon
Cook: Ten minutes
One cup flour
One cup seasoned bread crumbs
One egg, beaten
Two tablespoons milk
One-half teaspoon salt
One-eighth teaspoon pepper
One-eighth teaspoon paprika
Cook: Five minutes
One-third cup real mayonnaise
Eight slices buttered toast
Six crisp lettuce leaves
Six slices tomatoes
Serves: Six

Drain oysters. Remove any pieces of shell from oysters. Fry bacon in a skillet until crisp. Drain on absorbent paper. Combine flour and seasoned crumbs. Combine the egg, milk and seasonings. Roll oysters in flour and crumb mixture. Fry in the hot bacon fat. Brown both sides. Drain on absorbent paper. Spread the mayonnaise on 6 slices of toast. Arrange lettuce and tomato on top. Cover each with a slice of toast. Arrange bacon and oysters on top. Cover with remaining slices of toast. Secure with toothpicks. Cut into triangles. Serve immediately.

Carrot Sandwich Filling

One cup grated carrot
One-fourth cup finely chopped green
   pepper
One-fourth cup finely chopped celery
Four strips bacon, cooked and crumbled
Two tablespoons chili sauce
One tablespoon mayonnaise
One-eighth teaspoon onion salt
Yield: One cup, approx.

In a bowl stir together the grated carrot, chopped green pepper and celery, crumbled bacon, chili sauce, mayonnaise and onion salt. Mix well and chill. Use as sandwich filling. For the lunch box sandwich, spread the bread with butter or margarine to prevent juicy filling from soaking in.

Creamy Nutted Tuna

Eight ounces cream cheese
Two tablespoons lemon juice
One-half cup mayonnaise
One-half cup ripe olives, finely chopped
One cup flaked tuna (one 7 oz. can)
One-fourth teaspoon Ac'cent
Twelve slices white bread
Six slices whole wheat bread
Butter or margarine
One cup salted pecan tidbits
Yield: Six sandwiches

In a bowl blend together the cream cheese, lemon juice and mayonnaise. Fold in the chopped ripe olives and tuna fish. Season. Spread all slices of bread with butter or margarine. Spread six slices of white bread with tuna filling; cover with whole wheat slices. Spread with tuna filling and top with remaining slices of white bread. Trim crusts and cut in four triangles. Spread inside cut edges with filling remaining and dip in the salted pecans. Serve with sweet pickle sticks and potato chips.

Festive Sandwich Loaf

One loaf (1 lb.) unsliced bread
*Egg salad filling
*Parsley butter filling
*Chicken salad filling
*Cream cheese filling
Chilling time: One hour
Serves: Six, or more

Trim the crusts from the bread and cut into four lengthwise slices. Spread the bottom slice with egg salad filling. Cover with a second slice, spread with parsley butter filling. Cover with a third slice, spread with chicken salad filling. Cover with the last slice and spread top and sides with cream cheese frosting. Chill in refrigerator. Garnish with pimiento. Surround with crisp relishes.

*Egg Salad Filling

Remove the yolks from two hard-cooked eggs; sieve. Blend with a tablespoon of rich prepared mustard and a tablespoon of soft butter. Finely chop the egg whites: add these together with three tablespoons of minced celery and two tablespoons of minced onion.

*Parsley Butter Filling

Cream one-fourth cup butter with two tablespoons of minced parsley and one-half teaspoon paprika.

*Chicken Salad Filling

Combine one cup minced cooked chicken with one-fourth cup minced celery. Moisten with two tablespoons mayonnaise. Add two tablespoons sour cream, one teaspoon rich prepared mustard, one half teaspoon salt and one-eighth teaspoon pepper.

*Cream Cheese Frosting

Blend three tablespoons milk into one-half pound of cream cheese. Blend in one tablespoon grated onion, one-fourth teaspoon salt and two drops of tabasco.

Cookies and Candies

Peanut Butter Cookies

One-half cup margarine or butter
One-half cup peanut butter
Three-fourths cup sugar
One egg
One teaspoon vanilla
One and one-fourths cups sifted flour
One-fourth teaspoon baking powder
One-half teaspoon salt
Shelled peanuts
Oven temperature: 350 degrees
Bake: Ten to twelve minutes
Yield: Five dozen

In a bowl cream the margarine or butter until fluffy. Blend in the peanut butter and gradually beat in the sugar, egg and vanilla. Sift the flour, baking powder and salt together and beat into the creamed mixture. Drop by measuring teaspoonfuls on ungreased baking sheets. Flatten with a fork dipped in cold water and press one or more peanuts into each cooky. Bake in a moderate oven for ten or twelve minutes. Remove to racks to cool. Store in jar or tightly covered tin.

Spiced Coconut Biscuit

Three tablespoons butter or margarine
One and one-half cups sugar
Two eggs
One and one-half cups sifted flour
Three teaspoons baking powder
One teaspoon allspice
One-half teaspoon ginger
One-half teaspoon salt
Two cups flaked coconut
Oven temperature: 400 degrees
Bake: Eight minutes
Yield: Six dozen

In a bowl cream the butter or margarine. Beat in the sugar and eggs. Sift together the flour, baking powder, allspice, ginger and salt. Gradually blend into the sugar mixture. Add the flaked coconut and mix well. Drop batter by teaspoonfuls on greased baking sheets. Bake in a quick oven until lightly browned around the edge. Cool on racks. Store in tightly covered container.

Coconut Almond Cookies

One cup shortening
One and one-half cups sugar
One egg
One tablespoon water
One teaspoon almond extract
Two and one-half cups sifted flour
One-half teaspoon salt
Three-fourths teaspoon baking powder
One-half cup flaked coconut
One-fourth cup blanched almonds, split
Oven temperature: 400 degrees
Bake: Ten to twelve minutes
Yield: Four dozen, about

In a bowl, cream the shortening. Blend in the sugar gradually. Beat in the egg, water and almond extract. Sift together the flour, salt and baking powder. Blend into the creamed mixture. Add the flaked coconut, mixing well. Form dough into balls using rounded measuring teaspoonfuls and rolling smooth between the palms of hands. Place on ungreased baking sheet. Flatten with bottom of a glass to ⅜ inch in thickness. Press almond half in center of each. Bake in a quick oven for ten to twelve minutes, or until lightly browned. Remove to racks to cool thoroughly. Store in tightly covered tin.

Nut Fudge Balls

One package (6 oz.) semi-sweet chocolate pieces
Heat: To melt
Three tablespoons corn syrup
One teaspoon vanilla
One cup finely chopped nuts
One-half cup undiluted evaporated milk
One-half cup confectioners' sugar
Two and one-half cups vanilla wafer crumbs (8 oz.)
Standing time: Thirty minutes
Three-fourths cup chopped nuts
One-half cup chocolate decorettes
Chill: Thirty minutes
Yield: Two pounds, approx.

Melt the semi-sweet chocolate pieces in the upper half of a double boiler over hot, not boiling water, stirring occasionally. Remove from heat and stir in the corn syrup, vanilla and finely chopped nuts. Gradually blend in the evaporated milk, confectioners' sugar and wafer crumbs. Mix thoroughly. Let stand for 30 minutes. Roll teaspoonfuls into balls with the fingers then coat with chopped nuts or chocolate decorettes. Chill for 30 minutes before serving.

Chocolate Fudge

Two ounces unsweetened chocolate
Three-fourths cup milk
Two cups sugar
One-sixteenth teaspoon salt
Cook: To softball stage (238 degrees)
Two tablespoons butter
One teaspoon vanilla
Cool: To lukewarm (110 degrees)
Yield: One pound (approx.)

In a saucepan melt the chocolate in the milk over low heat. Cook until smooth and well mixed, stirring the while. Add sugar and salt and stir until completely dissolved and to the boiling point. Continue to boil without stirring until the temperature of the mixture registers 238 degrees on a candy thermometer or forms a soft ball in cold water. Remove from the heat. Add butter and vanilla. Cool to lukewarm (110 degrees). Beat until the mixture is thick and loses its gloss. Pour into a greased pan (8 x 4 in.). When firm cut into squares.

Marshmallow Fudge

Two-thirds cup undiluted evaporated milk
One and two-thirds cups sugar
One-half teaspoon salt
Cook: Five minutes
Sixteen marshmallows, cut up (one and one-half cups marshmallow pieces)
One and one-half cups semi-sweet chocolate pieces (nine ounces)
One teaspoon vanilla
Yield: Two pounds, about

Measure the evaporated milk, sugar and salt into a saucepan. Place over low heat and bring to the boiling point, stirring constantly. Cook, stirring, for five minutes. Remove from heat and add the cut up marshmallows, semi-sweet chocolate pieces and vanilla. Stir until chocolate and marshmallows are blended in. Pour into a buttered square pan (9 x 9 x 2 in.).

Chocolate Ripple Divinity

Three cups sugar
One-half cup water
One-half cup white corn syrup
Cook: To 240 degrees
Two egg whites
One-eighth teaspoon salt
Cook: To 265 degrees
One teaspoon vanilla
One pkg. (6 oz.) semi-sweet chocolate bits
Yield: Four dozen

In a two-quart saucepan combine the sugar, water and white corn syrup. Heat to boiling, stirring occasionally. Add a candy thermometer and cook to 240 degrees or the softball stage. In a large bowl beat the egg whites with salt until stiff. Slowly pour one-third of the syrup into the egg whites, beating constantly. Cook the remaining syrup to 265 degrees or the hard crack stage. Gradually add this to the candy mixture, beating with a wooden spoon. Continue beating until mixture will hold its shape when dropped from a spoon. Stir in vanilla and fold in the chocolate bits. These will melt slightly for the ripple effect. Drop from teaspoon onto waxed paper.

Penuche

Two cups brown sugar (one pound)
Two-thirds cup milk
Cook: To softball stage (238 degrees)
One tablespoon butter
One teaspoon vanilla
Cool: To lukewarm (110 degrees)
One cup nuts
Yield: One pound (approx.)

In a saucepan, combine the sugar and milk. Cook, stirring constantly until the mixture reaches the softball stage when a small amount is dropped into cold water or until the temperature of the mixture reaches 238 degrees on a candy thermometer. Remove from the heat, add the butter and vanilla and set aside to cool, without stirring. When lukewarm (110 degrees) beat until thick and creamy. Add the nuts and mix thoroughly. Pour into a greased pan to cool.

Easy Cookies

Two tablespoons margarine
Two eggs, beaten slightly
One teaspoon vanilla
One cup brown sugar (packed)
One-third cup sifted flour
One-eighth teaspoon baking soda
One cup chopped nuts
Oven temperature: 350 degrees
Baking time: Twenty-five minutes
Yield: Sixteen squares

Assemble all the ingredients. Melt the margarine in a square pan (8 in.) over low heat. Remove from the fire. Beat the eggs slightly in a bowl; add the vanilla. Combine the sugar, flour, soda and nuts and add to the eggs; mixing thoroughly. Spoon the cooky dough over the margarine in the pan. Don't stir. Bake in a moderate oven until firm to the touch. Remove from the oven; let stand until cool; turn upside down on a board. Sprinkle the top with confectioners' sugar. Cut into squares (2 in.).

Quick Molasses Cookies

One cup sifted flour
One teaspoon baking soda
One-half teaspoon salt
One-half teaspoon allspice
One-half teaspoon cinnamon
One-half cup shortening
One-half cup sugar
One-half cup molasses
One egg
One cup rolled oats
One cup seedless raisins
Oven temperature: 325 degrees
Baking time: Seventeen minutes
Yield: Thirty-six

Assemble all ingredients. Sift the flour with the soda, salt, allspice and cinnamon; set aside. In a large bowl beat the shortening, sugar and molasses until fluffy. Stir in the egg, oats and raisins. Blend in flour mixture. Drop by tablespoonfuls onto greased baking sheets, having the cookies three inches apart. Bake in a moderately slow oven until firm. Remove; let stand a minute before removing from the sheets.

Gingerbread Cookies

Two-thirds cup brown sugar
Two-thirds cup dark molasses
One teaspoon ginger
Three-fourths teaspoon cinnamon
One-half teaspoon cloves
Heat: To the boiling point
Two teaspoons baking soda
Two-thirds cup butter or margarine
One egg
Five cups sifted flour
Oven temperature: 325 degrees
Bake: Eight to ten minutes
Yield: One hundred

Heat the sugar, molasses and spices to the boiling point. Stir in soda; pour mixture over butter in a bowl. Stir until butter melts. Beat in the egg. Add the sifted flour; blend thoroughly. Knead on board until well blended. Roll out on cookie sheets and cut with fancy cutters. Remove excess dough. Bake in a moderately slow oven until firm. Remove to racks to cool. Decorate as desired with confectioners' icing.

Macaroons

One and one-third cups blanched ground
  almonds
One and one-half cups confectioners'
  sugar
Two egg whites
Oven temperature: 325 degrees
Bake: Thirty minutes
Whole almonds, halved
Yield: Three dozen

Chop almonds very very fine, or use a blender. Mix in sugar and egg whites. Drop by teaspoonfuls on cookie sheets. Top with halved almonds. Bake in a moderately slow oven until light brown. With a spatula remove cookies to racks to cool. If desired, decorate with candied cherries.

Lebkuchen

One-half cup honey
One-half cup molasses
Three-fourths cup brown sugar
Heat: To a boil
One egg, slightly beaten
One tablespoon grated lemon rind
One tablespoon grated orange rind
One tablespoon lemon juice
Two and three-fourths cups sifted flour
One-half teaspoon soda
One teaspoon each cinnamon, nutmeg
  and cloves
One-eighth teaspoon salt
One-half cup finely chopped almonds
One-fourth cup each finely chopped
  candied orange and lemon rind
One-fourth cup finely chopped citron
Oven temperature: 400 degrees
Bake: Fifteen minutes
Confectioners' icing — candied cherries
  and angelica
Yield: Twelve dozen

In a saucepan bring the honey, molasses and brown sugar to a boil. Cool slightly. Beat the egg, rinds and juice into the honey mixture. Add the sifted flour, soda, cinnamon, nutmeg, cloves, salt, almonds, candied rinds and citron. Spread in a greased and floured shallow pan (10 x 15 x ½ in.). Bake in a quick oven until a cake tester inserted in the center comes away clean. Remove to a rack; cut immediately into inch squares. Brush a confectioners' icing over the top. Decorate with candied cherries and angelica.

Viennese Bars

One and one-half cups shelled filberts
Three ounces sweet chocolate
Two egg whites, unbeaten
Two cups confectioners' sugar (about)
Standing time: Over-night
One-half cup semisweet chocolate bits
One-half cup heavy cream, heated
Cooking time: Two minutes
Chilling time: Overnight
Yield: Twenty-four bars

Both the cookies and icing must stand overnight. Grind the filberts and chocolate, using the fine blade. Blend in the egg whites and sugar. Pat out on waxed paper into a square (¼ in. thick). Let stand at room temperature to dry.

For the icing: Melt the chocolate bits in the cream in a heavy saucepan and cook, stirring constantly. Cool. Beat until bubbles appear. Chill. Next day ice the cooky square; cut into bars or any desired shape.

Mincemeat Cookies

One cup butter or margarine
One and one-half cups sugar
Three eggs
One package (9 oz.) mincemeat, crumbled
Three and one-fourth cups sifted flour
One teaspoon soda
One-half teaspoon salt
Oven temperature: 400 degrees
Baking time: Ten minutes
Yield: Forty-eight cookies

In a bowl cream the butter; gradually add the sugar beating until light and fluffy. Add the eggs one at a time, beating well after each addition. Beat in the crumbled mincemeat. Add the sifted flour, soda and salt. Drop from a tablespoon onto a cooky sheet two-inches apart. Bake in a quick oven until firm. Remove to racks.

Snow Cap Cookies

One-half cup butter or margarine
One and two-thirds cups sugar
Two eggs
Two squares (2 oz.) unsweetened chocolate, melted
Two cups sifted flour
Two teaspoons baking powder
One-half teaspoon salt
One-third cup milk
Two teaspoons vanilla
Chill: Overnight
Two-thirds cup confectioners' sugar
Oven temperature: 350 degrees
Baking time: Fifteen minutes
Yield: Forty-eight

Cream the butter in a bowl; add the sugar gradually beating until light and fluffy. Add the eggs one at a time, beating well after each addition. Add the melted chocolate. Beat in the sifted flour, baking powder and salt alternately with the combined milk and vanilla. Cover bowl. Chill. Shape into balls (1 in.); roll into confectioners' sugar quickly. Place on baking sheets three-inches apart. Bake in a moderate oven until firm. Remove from cooky sheets onto racks.

Belgian Trees

Two-thirds cup strained honey
One-half cup butter
Two tablespoons orange juice
One teaspoon grated orange rind
One teaspoon grated lemon rind
One cup cut blanched almonds, ground
Five cups sifted flour
One cup sugar
One teaspoon nutmeg
One-half teaspoon cloves
One-half teaspoon cinnamon
Two teaspoons baking powder
Chilling time: Eight hours
Oven temperature: 325 degrees
Baking time: Ten minutes
Yield: Eight dozen trees

Blend the honey and butter in a mixing bowl over hot water. Remove from the water. Add the fruit juice, rinds and almonds. Mix in the sifted dry ingredients. Chill. Roll very thin on a lightly floured board; cut with a tree cutter. Bake on greased baking sheets in a moderately slow oven to a light brown. Decorate with confectioners' icing and cinnamon drops.

Oatmeal Almond Drops

Two-thirds cup butter or margarine
One-half cup sugar
One beaten egg
One teaspoon almond extract
Three cups rolled oats
Oven temperature: 400 degrees
Bake: Ten minutes
Yield: Four dozen

In a bowl cream the butter or margarine, blend in the sugar, beaten egg and almond extract. Stir in the rolled oats and mix thoroughly together. Drop mixture by level measuring teaspoonfuls onto a baking sheet. Flatten slightly and bake in a quick oven for 10 minutes or until lightly browned. Remove to rack to cool. Store in a tightly covered container.

Chocolate Cereal Drops

One cup semi-sweet chocolate pieces
One-fourth cup light corn syrup
One-fourth teaspoon salt
Two tablespoons butter or margarine
Heat: Until melted
Two cups corn flakes
Yield: Thirty pieces

In the upper half of a double boiler combine the semi-sweet chocolate pieces, corn syrup, salt and butter or margarine. Place over boiling water and heat until melted. Stir smooth and remove from heat. Add the corn flakes and stir until all are well coated. Drop teaspoonfuls upon waxed paper. Chill until firm.

Gumdrop Oatmeal Cookies

One-half cup shortening
One-half cup granulated sugar
One-half cup brown sugar
One egg
One teaspoon vanilla
Two tablespoons milk
One cup sifted flour
One-half teaspoon soda
One-half teaspoon salt
One and one-half cups rolled oats
Three-fourths cup finely cut mixed spiced gumdrops
Oven temperature: 375 degrees
Bake: Twelve minutes, about
Yield: Three and one-half dozen

In a bowl cream the shortening, gradually blend in the granulated sugar and the brown sugar. Beat in the egg, vanilla and milk. Sift the flour with the soda and salt into a bowl, stir in the rolled oats. Add to the creamed mixture with the finely cut mixed spiced gumdrops. Mix thoroughly. Drop by rounded measuring teaspoonfuls on a greased baking sheet allowing two inches between. Decorate tops with bits of cut red and green gumdrops if desired. Bake in a moderately hot oven for twelve minutes or until lightly browned. Remove to racks to cool. Store in tightly covered tin.

Apple Sauce Cookies

One-half cup butter or shortening
One cup sugar
One egg, beaten
One and three-fourths cups sifted flour
One-half teaspoon baking powder
One teaspoon soda
One-half teaspoon salt
One teaspoon cinnamon
One-half teaspoon cloves
One-half teaspoon nutmeg
One cup apple sauce
One-half cup seedless raisins
One cup rolled oats
Oven temperature: 375 degrees
Bake: Ten minutes
Yield: Four dozen, approx.

Cream the butter or shortening in a mixing bowl, gradually add the sugar then the beaten egg. Sift together the flour, baking powder, soda, salt, cinnamon, cloves and nutmeg; add to the creamed mixture alternately with the apple sauce. Stir in the raisins and rolled oats. Mix well. Drop by measuring teaspoonfuls on greased baking sheet. Bake in a moderately hot oven until golden brown. Remove to rack to cool thoroughly before storing in a tightly covered tin.

Apple Cookies

One-half cup shortening
One cup brown sugar
Two eggs
One-half cup rolled oats
One cup rinsed raisins
One and one-half cups diced unpeeled Delicious apple
One teaspoon grated lemon rind
Two cups sifted flour
One-half teaspoon salt
One-half teaspoon baking powder
One-half teaspoon baking soda
One-half teaspoon cinnamon
Oven temperature: 375 degrees
Bake: Ten minutes
Yield: Four to five dozen

In a bowl cream the shortening, gradually blend in the brown sugar, beat in the eggs. Add the rolled oats, raisins, diced apple and lemon rind. Sift together the flour, salt, baking powder, baking soda and cinnamon and blend into the creamed mixture. Drop by rounded measuring teaspoonfuls on a greased baking sheet. Bake ten minutes or until lightly browned. Remove to racks to cool. Frost with confectioners' sugar frosting if desired (confectioners' sugar with milk and lemon juice to form a thin glaze).

Creme Fudge Crispies

One cup marshmallow creme
One-fourth cup sugar
Two tablespoons butter or margarine
One pkg. (6 oz.) semi-sweet chocolate bits
Cooking time: Five to ten minutes
Two cups rice krispies
Yield: Three to four dozen

In the upper half of a double boiler combine the marshmallow creme with the sugar, butter or margarine and chocolate bits. Place over hot water and cook and stir until chocolate is melted and mixture is smoothly blended. Stir in the rice krispies and drop by teaspoonfuls on waxed paper or aluminum foil.

Orange Oatmeal Cookies

Two cups sifted flour
Two cups sugar
Four teaspoons baking powder
One teaspoon salt
One teaspoon nutmeg
One cup soft shortening
Two eggs
Two tablespoons orange juice
Grated rind of one orange (one tablespoon)
Three cups rolled oats
Oven temperature: 375 degrees
Baking time: Twelve to fifteen minutes
Yield: Four to five dozen

Sift together into a mixing bowl the flour, sugar, baking powder, salt and nutmeg. Add the shortening, eggs and orange juice and beat until smooth. Stir in the grated rind and rolled oats. Mix thoroughly. Drop dough by level measuring tablespoonfuls on a greased baking sheet allowing two or three inches between. Bake in a moderately hot oven until lightly browned. Cool on racks. Store in tightly covered container.

Maraschino Cherry Honey Drops

One-half cup butter or margarine
One-half cup honey
One egg
One teaspoon vanilla
One cup sifted flour
One teaspoon baking powder
One-fourth teaspoon salt
One-half cup rolled oats
One-half cup chopped walnuts
One-half cup seedless raisins
One-half cup chopped maraschino cherries
Oven temperature: 375 degrees
Baking time: Fifteen minutes, or more
Yield: Three dozen, about

In a bowl, cream the butter or margarine, blend in the honey. Beat in the egg and vanilla. Sift together the flour, baking powder and salt and work into the creamed mixture with the rolled oats, chopped walnuts, raisins and chopped maraschino cherries. Mix well. Drop by rounded teaspoonfuls on a lightly greased baking sheet. Bake in a moderately hot oven for fifteen to twenty minutes or until edges are browned. Remove to rack to cool. Store in a tightly covered tin.

A FAVORITE RECIPE
Pecan Fingers

One cup sifted all-purpose flour
One-half cup butter
Oven temperature: 350 degrees
Baking time: Twelve minutes
Two eggs, beaten light
One and one-half cups brown sugar
One and one-half cups chopped pecans
Two tablespoons flour
One-half teaspoon baking powder
One-half teaspoon salt
One teaspoon vanilla
Oven temperature: 350 degrees
Baking time: Twenty-five minutes
One cup confectioners' sugar, mixed with
Juice of one lemon, about
Yield: 36 fingers (2 x 2½ in.)

In a bowl, cream the flour and butter to a smooth paste. Spread the mixture in a pan (8 x 11 in.) pressing down to cover pan completely. Bake in a moderate oven. Have the mixture of eggs, brown sugar, pecans, flour, baking powder, salt and vanilla prepared. Spread over the hot cake; return to the oven, bake. When cool, spread with the icing made by mixing in a bowl the confectioners' sugar with enough lemon juice to make a thin icing. Cut into fingers (2 x 2½ in.) when cool.

MRS. F. C. CHANDLER, *Bridgeport, Conn.*

Butter Nut Coconut Bars

One-third cup butter or margarine
Three-fourths cup light brown sugar
One egg
One teaspoon vanilla
Two-thirds cup sifted flour
One teaspoon baking powder
One-half teaspoon salt
Three-fourths cup flaked coconut
One-half cup chopped walnuts
Oven temperature: 350 degrees
Baking time: Thirty minutes
Yield: Twenty-four

In a saucepan melt the butter or margarine. Remove from heat. Stir in the sugar. Beat in the egg and vanilla, then the flour, baking powder and salt. When smooth add the flaked coconut and walnuts. Spread in a greased baking pan (8 x 8 x 2 in.) and bake in a moderate oven for 30 minutes. Cool in the pan. Cut into small bars before removing to tightly covered container to store.

Brown Sugar Brownies

Two eggs
One and one-third cups brown sugar
Cook: Ten minutes, about
Three tablespoons butter or margarine
One cup sifted flour
One teaspoon baking powder
One teaspoon ginger
One-fourth teaspoon salt
One cup chopped nuts
Oven temperature: 300 degrees
Baking time: Thirty-five minutes
Yield: Twenty

Beat the eggs in the upper half of a double boiler. Add the sugar and cook over boiling water, stirring constantly until the sugar is thoroughly dissolved. Remove from heat, stir in the butter or margarine. Sift together the flour, baking powder, ginger and salt and add gradually to the egg and sugar mixture. Blend in thoroughly. Add the chopped nuts and pour into a greased square pan (8 x 8 x 2 in.). Bake in a slow oven for thirty-five minutes. Cool thoroughly before cutting into bars or squares.

A FAVORITE RECIPE
Cherry Bars

One-half cup butter
One-fourth cup brown sugar
One cup flour, sifted with
One-half teaspoon salt
One-half teaspoon baking powder
Oven temperature: 350 degrees
Baking time: Ten minutes
One package (6 oz.) candied cherries, cut into thirds
Two egg whites, beaten stiff
One-half teaspoon cream of tartar
One-fourth teaspoon baking powder
One cup light brown sugar
Oven temperature: 350 degrees
Baking time: Until lightly browned
Yield: One pan (8 x 8 in.) cut into bars

In a bowl cream the butter and sugar. Add the sifted flour, salt and baking powder. Pat into a well greased pan (8 x 8 in.). Bake in a moderate oven for 10 minutes; remove from oven. Place the cherries on top of the baked mixture. Beat the egg whites, with cream of tartar and the baking powder. Gradually beat in brown sugar. Spread over the cherries. Bake until browned in a moderate oven. Cut into bars. Cool. Store in a tight container.

MRS. G. A. GOGO, *Montreal, P.Q., Canada*

Sesame Seed Sugar Bars

One-fourth cup sesame seed
Oven temperature: 350 degrees
Toast: Twenty-five minutes
One egg
Three-fourths cup light brown sugar
Three tablespoons butter, melted
One-half cup sifted flour
One-fourth teaspoon salt
One-fourth teaspoon soda
One-half teaspoon cinnamon
One-fourth teaspoon allspice
One-fourth teaspoon mace
Oven temperature: 350 degrees
Bake: Thirty minutes
Yield: Eighteen

Scatter the sesame seed over a shallow baking pan and toast in a moderate oven for twenty-five minutes or until lightly browned. In a bowl beat the egg, beat in the sugar and melted butter. Sift together the flour, salt, soda, cinnamon, allspice and mace and blend into the egg mixture. Sprinkle half the toasted sesame seed over the bottom of a greased pan (8 x 8 x 2 in.), spoon in the batter and scatter remaining seed over the top. Bake in a moderate oven for thirty minutes. Cool thoroughly in the pan. Cut into bars to serve.

Tiny Almond Logs

One-half cup butter or margarine
One egg yolk
One cup sifted flour
Three tablespoons confectioners' sugar
One-fourth teaspoon salt
One-fourth teaspoon baking powder
Two tablespoons milk or cream
One-fourth teaspoon vanilla
Drop of almond extract
Chill: Thoroughly
One cup blanched almonds
One egg white, beaten until foamy
One-fourth cup sugar
One-eighth teaspoon salt
One-half teaspoon vanilla
Oven temperature: 400 degrees
Bake: Ten to twelve minutes
Yield: Three dozen

Cream the butter or margarine thoroughly. Beat in the egg yolk. Sift together the flour, three tablespoons of confectioners' sugar, salt and baking powder. Blend into the butter with the milk or cream, vanilla and almond extract. Mix thoroughly. Chill thoroughly. Chop blanched almonds very fine or reduce to powder in electric blender. Mix with beaten egg white, sugar, salt and vanilla in a bowl. Dust board and rolling pin generously with confectioners' sugar. Cut thoroughly chilled dough into four parts and roll each out into a seven and a half inch square. With a knife cut into nine two and one-half inch squares. Handle dough quickly and gingerly, returning to the refrigerator to chill again should it become too soft to handle. Spread a little of the almond filling across the center of each small square. Use a knife or spatula to fold one-third of the square of dough over the filling from two sides forming a small roll. Transfer rolls to ungreased baking sheet with spatula, turning over so open edge is underneath. Bake in a quick oven for ten to twelve minutes, until lightly browned. Remove to racks to cool. Dust with confectioners' sugar.

Divinity

Three cups sugar
One-half cup light corn syrup
One cup water
Cook: To 260 degrees (hard ball stage)
Two egg whites, beaten
One-half cup chopped nuts
One-half cup chopped candied cherries
One-half teaspoon vanilla
Yield: Nine pieces, or more

In a heavy saucepan, cook the combined sugar, corn syrup and water until thermometer reaches 260 degrees or a few drops of mixture tried in cold water forms a hard ball. Pour syrup in a thin stream into the beaten egg whites, beating constantly with a rotary beater. When mixture forms a peak add remaining ingredients. Pour into a buttered square pan (8 in.). Cut into squares; garnish with cherries.

Ginger Coconut Creams

Two cups sugar
One cup brown sugar
Three-fourths cup milk
Two tablespoons light corn syrup
Cook: To 238 degrees (soft ball stage)
Two tablespoons butter
Two tablespoons crystallized ginger, cut fine
One-half cup flaked coconut
One-half teaspoon vanilla
Yield: Sixteen, or more

In a heavy saucepan combine the sugars, milk and syrup. Cook to 238 degrees or until a drop of the mixture tried in cold water forms a soft ball. Add butter, ginger, half the coconut and vanilla (do not stir). Allow to cool to lukewarm.

Beat until creamy. Pour into a buttered square pan (8 in.). Sprinkle top with remaining coconut. Cut into squares. Top each square of candy with a nut half.

Sesame Seed Peanut Brittle

Two cups sugar
One-fourth teaspoon cream of tartar
One-half cup water
Cook: To 280 degrees (crack stage)
Two tablespoons molasses
Two tablespoons butter
One-half teaspoon salt
Cook: To 300 degrees (brittle stage)
One cup salted peanuts
One-half teaspoon soda
One-half cup sesame seeds
Yield: Fifty pieces

In a heavy skillet combine the sugar, cream of tartar and water; cook without stirring to 280 degrees or until a drop of the mixture tried in cold water cracks. Stir in the molasses, butter and salt, continue to cook to 300 degrees or until a drop of mixture tried in cold water becomes brittle. Remove. Add nuts and soda. Pour into a buttered shallow pan (8x12x½ in.); sprinkle with half the sesame seeds; spread as thin as possible. Sprinkle remaining sesame seeds on top. When cold, break in pieces.

Easy Chocolate Drops

Cook in a heavy saucepan over low heat, two cups of semi-sweet chocolate bits with one cup sweetened condensed milk, stirring until smooth and well blended. Remove. Drop by teaspoonfuls onto waxed paper. Press a pecan into each piece. Yield: 24.

Five Minute Fudge

Two-thirds cup (small can) undiluted evaporated milk
One and two-thirds cups sugar
One-half teaspoon salt
Cook: Five minutes
Sixteen diced marshmallows
One and one-half cups semi-sweet chocolate pieces
One teaspoon vanilla
One-half cup chopped nuts (optional)
Yield: One and one-half pounds (approx.)

In a saucepan combine the evaporated milk, sugar and salt. Heat to boiling, stirring. Cook for five minutes, stirring constantly. Remove from heat and add the diced marshmallows, semi-sweet chocolate pieces, vanilla and nuts. Stir until thoroughly blended and pour into a buttered pan. Let the thickness of the fudge you prefer determine the size of the pan. Cut into squares to serve.

Caramel Fudge Drops

Two-thirds cup undiluted evaporated milk
One cup brown sugar
Two-thirds cup granulated sugar
One-half teaspoon salt
Cook: Five minutes
One and one-half cups diced marshmallows
One package (6 oz.) caramel chips
One teaspoon vanilla
One-half cup chopped nuts
Yield: Two pounds, approx.

In a saucepan combine the evaporated milk, brown sugar, granulated sugar and salt. Stir while heating to the boiling point. Lower heat and cook, stirring constantly for five minutes. Remove from heat and stir in the marshmallows, caramel chips, vanilla and nuts. Stir just until marshmallows melt. Drop mixture by teaspoonfuls on waxed paper.

A FAVORITE RECIPE

Red Jelly Apples

Eight wooden skewers
Eight medium-sized apples, wash, dry, stem removed
Three cups granulated sugar
One-half cup white corn syrup
One-half cup water
Cooking time: Until hard when tested in cold water
One drop oil of cinnamon
One teaspoon liquid red coloring
Chilling time: One hour
Yield: Eight

Insert the wooden skewers into the stem end of apples. In a large heavy saucepan mix the sugar, syrup and water. Cook over a medium heat, stirring constantly until the mixture boils. Continue cooking without stirring until the mixture separates into hard threads, but not brittle. Remove from heat; add the cinnamon and food coloring, stirring only enough to blend well. Twist the apples in the syrup until well coated. Place apples on a lightly buttered cookie sheet. Let harden in refrigerator.

TERRY ANN HAWKINS, *E. Meadow, L.I., N.Y.*

Felix The Cat Cookies

One-half cup butter or margarine
One-half cup peanut butter
One cup sugar
One egg
Four cups sifted flour
One-half teaspoon soda
One teaspoon salt
One-fourth teaspoon nutmeg
One-half cup milk
One-half cup uncooked oatmeal
Four squares (1 oz. each) unsweetened
    chocolate, melted
Oven temperature: 400 degrees
Baking time: Five minutes
One can (12 oz.) uncooked chocolate
    frosting mix
Candies, angelica
Yield: Eight dozen

In a bowl cream the butter, peanut butter and sugar until light and fluffy. Beat in the egg. Add the sifted dry ingredients alternately with the milk. Add the oatmeal and melted chocolate, mixing thoroughly. Out of heavy cardboard cut a cat-face to use as a pattern. Roll out the dough on a floured cookie sheet. Place pattern on dough and with a sharp knife cut around the pattern. Remove excess dough. Bake in a quick oven until firm to the touch. Remove. Follow the directions on the can to make frosting. While cookies are still warm, frost the cookies. With candies and strips of angelica make the faces on the chocolate covered cookies.

Molasses Taffy

Two cups light or dark molasses
One-half cup sugar
One tablespoon vinegar
Cooking time: To 265 degrees
One-half tablespoon butter
One-fourth teaspoon soda
One teaspoon cold water
Yield: Fifty pieces

Combine the molasses, sugar and vinegar in a heavy saucepan (3 qts.); bring to a boil, stirring. Cook over low heat until the syrup dropped in very cold water separates into threads which are hard but not brittle. Stir during the last of the cooking; boil slowly to prevent sticking. Remove from the heat; add the remaining ingredients, stirring only until mixed. Pour onto a greased platter. As the edges cool, fold toward the center or they will harden before the center is ready to pull. Do not disturb that part of the candy which has not cooled or it will stick to the platter. Shape into a ball. When the candy is cool enough to handle, pull with lightly buttered fingers until yellow and rather firm. Stretch into a long rope. Twist slightly. Cut with the scissors into inch pieces, turning the rope half over after each piece is cut. Wrap in waxed paper.

Mr. Jolly Jacks

Cut a slice off the top of each orange. Reserve the tops. Cut out a face; remove

pulp. Fill with any prepared fruit flavored gelatin. With toothpicks, secure pieces of angelica to the tops of the oranges. Then place on the oranges.

Chewy Popcorn Balls

Ten cups freshly popped corn
Two cups brown sugar (packed)
Three tablespoons light corn syrup
One-third cup butter or margarine
Boiling time: To 270 degrees
One-eighth teaspoon soda
Yield: Six

Place the popcorn in a buttered large bowl; keep warm. Combine the sugar, syrup and butter in a saucepan (2 qts.). Boil until a few drops tried in cold water become almost brittle. Cook slowly toward the last to keep the candy from scorching. Remove from the stove; add the soda. Pour the candy over popcorn, stirring with a wooden spoon to mix the candy and popcorn. With lightly buttered hands shape into balls. To make the Goblin Heads, use candy fruit rings and gumdrops for the face and cut licorice whip for the hair.

Jewel Cookies

One-half cup butter or shortening
One cup sugar
Two eggs, beaten
Two tablespoons milk
One tablespoon vanilla
Three and one-fourth cups sifted flour
Two teaspoons baking powder
One-half teaspoon salt
Chill: Until firm
Oven temperature: 375 degrees
Bake: Eight minutes, about
Raspberry or apricot jam
One-half cup confectioners' sugar
Juice of half a lemon
Yield: Two and a half to eight and a half
    dozen double cookies

In a bowl cream the butter or shorten-ing, gradually beat in the sugar, eggs, milk and vanilla. Sift together the flour, baking powder and salt and blend into the creamed mixture. Wrap dough in waxed paper and chill for easier han-dling. Dust a board and rolling pin with confectioners' sugar and roll out portions of the chilled dough to a thickness of about one-fourth inch or slightly less. You need two circular cutters, one small-er than the other. Cut circles of dough with the large cutter and place half of these on a greased baking sheet. Use smaller cutter to remove centers of other circles of dough. Place these rings on greased baking sheet, too. Bake in a moderately hot oven for eight minutes or slightly more until very lightly browned. Remove from oven and run a spatula rapidly under all the baked pieces. (If this is not quickly done they may continue to bake and may break in re-moving.) Transfer to racks to cool. Spread the cookies with raspberry or apricot jam and top with the cookie rings. Press together and store in a tightly covered tin. If desired brush the tops with a simple frosting made by placing the confectioners' sugar in a cup and stirring in enough lemon juice and water for a thin frosting. This will give a glaze to the top.

King Sized Soft Molasses Cookies

One-half cup butter or margarine
One cup dark molasses
One cup sugar
Two eggs, beaten
Four cups flour
One teaspoon salt
One teaspoon soda
Two and one-fourth teaspoons cinnamon
One teaspoon ginger
Three-fourths cup milk
Oven temperature: 350 degrees
Bake: Twelve to fourteen minutes
Yield: Three dozen, or more

In a large saucepan melt the butter or margarine with the dark molasses. Stir over low heat until blended. Re-move from heat and add the sugar and beaten eggs. Sift together the flour, salt, soda, cinnamon and ginger. Add to the molasses mixture alternately with the milk, beating well after each addition.

Beat smooth. Drop rounded measuring tablespoonfuls on a greased baking sheet, allowing ample room between for they will spread. These will be about four inches in diameter. Bake in a moderate oven for 12 to 14 minutes. Remove to racks with spatula to cool thoroughly. Store in tightly covered tin. For ice cream sandwiches put two cookies to-gether with vanilla ice cream (soft or sliced). Wrap in aluminum foil and place in the freezing section of the re-frigerator until ready to use.

Chocolate Spice Cookies

One-half cup shortening
One cup brown sugar
One egg
Two squares unsweetened chocolate,
    melted
One-half cup buttermilk
One and one-fourth cups sifted flour
One-fourth teaspoon salt
One-fourth teaspoon soda
One-half teaspoon cloves
One-half teaspoon allspice
One-half teaspoon cinnamon
One cup chopped walnuts
Oven temperature: 350 degrees
Bake: Twelve minutes
Yield: Three dozen, or more

In a bowl cream the shortening. Grad-ually beat in the brown sugar. Beat in the egg. Add the melted chocolate and buttermilk, beating smooth. Sift together the flour, salt, soda and spices and blend into the chocolate mixture. Add the chopped walnuts. Drop mixture by rounded measuring teaspoonfuls on an ungreased baking sheet. Bake for about twelve minutes or until firm when touched with a finger. Remove with spat-ula to a rack and frost while still warm with the Lemon Butter Frosting.

Lemon Butter Frosting

One-fourth cup butter or margarine
Two cups sifted confectioners' sugar
One tablespoon lemon juice
One tablespoon milk
One-half teaspoon finely grated lemon rind

Cream the butter or margarine until fluffy in a bowl. Blend in the confection-ers' sugar with the lemon juice and milk gradually until the right consistency, adding more liquid if necessary. Stir in the grated lemon rind.

Soft Chocolate Cookies

One cup shortening
Two cups brown sugar
Two eggs
Three squares unsweetened chocolate,
    melted
Two teaspoons vanilla
Two and one-half cups sifted flour
One teaspoon soda
One teaspoon salt
One cup sour milk
One cup chopped nuts
Oven temperature: 375 degrees
Baking time: Twelve to fifteen minutes
Yield: Thirty to thirty-six cookies (3 in.)

In a bowl, cream the shortening with the brown sugar. Beat in the eggs, melted chocolate and vanilla. Sift to-gether the flour, soda and salt and add alternately to the creamed mixture with the sour milk. Beat until smooth. Stir in the chopped nuts and drop by table-spoonfuls on a greased baking sheet al-lowing ample room for cookies to spread. Bake in a moderately hot oven for twelve to fifteen minutes. Remove to rack to cool.

Toll House Cookies

One-half cup butter or margarine
One-third cup sugar
One-third cup brown sugar
One egg
One cup plus two tablespoons sifted flour
One-half teaspoon salt
One-half teaspoon soda
One teaspoon hot water
One-half teaspoon vanilla
One package (6 oz.) semi-sweet
    chocolate pieces
One-half cup chopped nuts
Chill: Until firm
Oven temperature: 375 degrees
Baking time: Ten to twelve minutes
Yield: Fifty

In a bowl cream the butter or mar-garine with the sugars. Beat in the egg. Sift together the flour, salt and soda and beat into the creamed mixture. Add the hot water, vanilla, semi-sweet chocolate pieces and chopped nuts. Mix thorough-ly together and chill batter until firm. Spoon measuring teaspoonfuls of the chilled batter onto baking sheets about two inches apart. Flatten slightly with the finger tips. Bake in a moderately hot oven for ten minutes or until well browned. Remove from oven to racks to cool. Store in tightly covered tin.

Spritz Cookies

One cup butter or margarine
Three-fourths cup sugar
One teaspoon vanilla
One egg
Two and one-half cups sifted flour
One-half teaspoon baking powder
One-eighth teaspoon salt
Oven temperature: 400 degrees
Baking time: Eight to ten minutes
Yield: Five dozen, about

In a bowl, cream the butter or mar-garine thoroughly. Gradually blend in the sugar and beat in the vanilla and egg. Sift together the flour, baking powder and salt and add to the creamed mixture in three parts, beating well after each addition. Force this soft dough through a cooky press upon ungreased baking sheets about two inches apart. If desired, decorate some of the cookies with bits of candied cherries, citron or nuts. Bake to a delicate brown in a quick oven. Re-move from the baking sheets to a rack to cool. Store in a tightly covered tin.

Chocolate Thumb Print Cookies

One-half cup butter or margarine
One-half cup brown sugar
One teaspoon vanilla
One and one-half cups sifted flour
One-half teaspoon salt
One-fourth cup semi-sweet chocolate
    pieces, chopped fine
Oven temperature: 375 degrees
Bake: Twelve minutes
Three-fourths cup semi-sweet chocolate
    pieces
One tablespoon butter
Heat: Until blended
Two tablespoons light corn syrup
One tablespoon water
One teaspoon vanilla
Cool: Ten minutes or more
Yield: Three dozen

In a bowl cream the butter. Beat in the brown sugar gradually, add the vanilla. Work in the flour, salt and finely chopped fourth cup of semi-sweet chocolate pieces. Using a rubber spatula and measuring teaspoon, form small balls of dough on an ungreased baking sheet. Make a depression in the center of each with thumb or spoon. Bake in a moderately hot oven for 12 minutes. Remove to racks to cool. Melt the three-fourths cup of chocolate pieces with the tablespoon of butter in double boiler over hot water. When smooth add the light corn syrup, water and vanilla. Remove from heat and let cool for 10 minutes or more. Spoon about a half teaspoon of chocolate mixture into the center depression of each thoroughly cooled cooky. Note: The cookies, while still warm, may be rolled in confectioners' sugar two or three times for a snowy effect before they are thoroughly cooled and filled with the chocolate.

A FAVORITE RECIPE
Tutti-Frutti Drops

Three-fourths cup shortening
One and one-half cups brown sugar
Three teaspoons vanilla
Two well-beaten eggs
Four cups sifted flour, sifted with
Four teaspoons baking powder
One-half teaspoon salt
Three-fourths cup milk
One-half cup tutti-frutti
Oven temperature: 400 degrees
Baking time: Twelve to fifteen minutes
Yield: Six dozen about

In a bowl, cream the shortening, sugar and vanilla until fluffy. Add the beaten eggs, continue beating until well blended. Add the sifted dry ingredients alternately with the milk. Fold in the tutti-frutti, mixing well. Drop upon a greased baking sheet from a teaspoon, two inches apart. Bake in a quick oven until a golden brown. Cool; store in a tight container.

MRS. HENRY TOMASELLO, *Ft. Lauderdale, Fla.*

Easy Ginger Snaps

One-half cup molasses
One-half cup shortening
Heating time: Three minutes
One-half cup sugar
Two and one-fourth cups sifted flour
One and one-half teaspoons ginger
One-half teaspoon salt
One-half teaspoon soda, dissolved in
One tablespoon warm water
Oven temperature: 350 degrees
Baking time: Ten to twelve minutes
Yield: Three and one-half dozen

In a small saucepan, heat the molasses and shortening to the boiling point, stirring until well blended. Remove from heat and add to the sugar in a bowl. Sift together the flour, ginger and salt and blend into the molasses mixture. Lastly, stir in the soda and water. Form the stiff dough into balls the size of a walnut, using the hands. Place balls on ungreased baking sheets about an inch and one-half apart. Bake in a moderate oven for ten to twelve minutes. Remove to rack with spatula to cool. Store in tightly covered container.

Lemon Snaps

Two-thirds cup butter or margarine
One and one-half cups sugar
One egg
One tablespoon grated lemon rind
Three tablespoons lemon juice
Three cups sifted flour
Six teaspoons baking powder
Three-fourths teaspoon salt
Oven temperature: 400 degrees
Baking time: Ten minutes
Yield: Five dozen

In a bowl, cream the butter or margarine; gradually blend in the sugar. Beat in the egg, grated lemon rind and lemon juice. Sift together the flour, baking powder and salt. Stir dry ingredients into the creamed mixture well. Batter should be very stiff. Form the dough into balls the size of a walnut, using the hands. Place balls one and one-half inches apart upon ungreased baking sheets. Bake in a quick oven until delicately browned. Remove to rack with spatula to cool. Store in a tightly covered container.

Cinnamon Almond Lace Cookies

One cup brown sugar
Three-fourths cup sifted flour
One teaspoon cinnamon
One-third cup butter or margarine
One-fourth cup cold water
One cup coarsely chopped blanched
    almonds
Oven temperature: 400 degrees
Bake: Eight to ten minutes
Yield: Four dozen

In a bowl blend together the brown sugar, flour and cinnamon. Using two knives or a pastry blender cut in the

butter or margarine. Stir in the water and the chopped almonds. Drop by level measuring teaspoonfuls onto a baking sheet. Bake in a quick oven for eight to 10 minutes. Remove from oven and let stand a minute or so to firm slightly before removing with a spatula to a rack to cool completely. If somewhat oily transfer to absorbent paper briefly before placing in a tightly covered tin to store.

Coconut Orange Jumbles

Three-fourths cup shortening
One and one-fourth cups sugar
Two beaten egg yolks
One cup flaked coconut
Two and one-half cups flour
One-half teaspoon baking soda
One-fourth teaspoon salt
One-third cup orange juice
Oven temperature: 400 degrees
Bake: Ten to twelve minutes
Yield: Four to five dozen

In a bowl, cream the shortening, blend in the sugar. Beat in the egg yolks and flaked coconut. Sift together the flour, baking soda and salt and add to the creamed mixture alternately with the orange juice. Mix thoroughly. Drop mixture from a teaspoon onto an ungreased baking sheet. Bake in a quick oven until lightly browned. Remove to racks to cool thoroughly. Store in tightly covered tin.

Orange Spice Cookies

One cup butter or margarine
One and one-half cups sugar
One tablespoon grated orange rind
One egg
Three tablespoons orange juice
Three cups sifted flour
One teaspoon baking powder
Three-fourths teaspoon nutmeg
One-half teaspoon salt
One-half teaspoon allspice
Chill: Thoroughly
Candied orange peel
Oven temperature: 400 degrees
Bake: Eight minutes, about
Yield: Eight to ten dozen

In a bowl cream the butter or margarine. Beat in the sugar gradually. Add the grated orange rind, egg and orange juice. Sift together the flour, baking powder, nutmeg, salt and allspice. Add to the creamed ingredients gradually and mix thoroughly together. Chill the dough until firm for ease of handling in rolling out. Divide dough into fourths, rolling out one portion while remainder is kept in refrigerator. Roll out on floured board to about one-eighth inch in thickness. A pretty cooky may be made by cutting dough into two inch diamonds and pressing the longest points together in the center with a small piece of candied orange peel.

Bake on ungreased baking sheets in quick oven until lightly browned around edge. Remove to racks to cool. Store in tightly covered container.

Toffee Squares

Three-fourths cup shortening
One cup brown sugar
One egg
One teaspoon vanilla
Two cups sifted flour
One-half teaspoon salt
Oven temperature: 350 degrees
Bake: Twenty minutes
One package (6 oz.) semi-sweet chocolate
   pieces
Bake: Five minutes
One-half cup chopped walnuts
One-half cup flaked coconut
Yield: Forty-eight

In a bowl cream the shortening. Gradually beat in the brown sugar. Beat in the egg and vanilla. Sift together the flour and salt and blend thoroughly into the creamed mixture. Spread mixture in an ungreased baking pan (jelly roll pan 10 x 15 x ½ in.). Bake in a moderate oven for twenty minutes. Remove from oven and scatter semi-sweet chocolate pieces over top. Return to oven and spread the softened chocolate over top evenly. Scatter chopped walnuts, then flaked coconut over chocolate. Mark into squares while still warm.

Viennese Chocolate Squares

One-half cup butter or margarine
One-half cup brown sugar
One egg yolk
One cup semi-sweet chocolate pieces,
   chopped
Grated rind of one lemon
One teaspoon vanilla
One-fourth cup water
One cup sifted flour
One egg white
Oven temperature: 375 degrees
Bake: Thirty minutes
Confectioners' sugar
Yield: Sixteen

In a bowl cream the butter, gradually blend in the brown sugar. Beat in the egg yolk, coarsely chopped chocolate, grated lemon rind, vanilla and water. Blend in the sifted flour. In a small bowl beat the egg white until stiff but not dry and fold into the chocolate mixture. Spread in a greased baking pan (8 x 8 x 2 in.) and bake in a moderately hot oven for thirty minutes. Cool in the pan. Cut into squares. Sprinkle with confectioners' sugar.

Date Nut Bars

One-third cup shortening
One-half cup sugar
One egg
One teaspoon vanilla
One cup sifted flour
One-half teaspoon baking powder
One teaspoon salt
Two-thirds cup undiluted evaporated milk
One cup chopped walnuts
One pkg. (7½ oz.) pitted dates, sliced
Oven temperature: 350 degrees
Bake: Thirty minutes, about
Yield: Twenty-four bars

In a bowl cream the shortening, gradually blend in the sugar, beat in the egg and vanilla. Sift the flour, baking powder and salt together; add to the creamed mixture alternately with the undiluted evaporated milk. Beat until smooth and fold in the chopped walnuts and sliced pitted dates. Spread batter in a greased pan (8 x 8 x 2 in.) and bake in a moderate oven for thirty minutes or until the cake leaves the sides of the pan slightly and springs back at the touch of a finger. Remove from oven and cool in pan. Sprinkle with confectioners' sugar and cut into bars to serve.

Date Filled Cookies

One cup sugar
One cup water
Two cups chopped dates
One cup chopped nuts
Cooking time: Five to ten minutes
Two tablespoons lemon juice
One cup shortening
Two cups brown sugar
Two eggs
Four cups sifted flour
One teaspoon salt
One-half teaspoon soda
One-fourth cup milk
Oven temperature: 375 degrees
Bake: Twelve minutes
Yield: Fifty-four large cookies

To make the filling, combine in a saucepan the sugar, water, dates and nuts. Cook over medium heat until the sugar dissolves and the mixture begins to thicken. Remove from heat; add lemon juice and set aside. Prepare the cooky dough by creaming the shortening in a bowl; gradually add the sugar then the eggs; beat well. Sift the flour, soda and salt together and add to the creamed mixture alternately with the milk. Blend thoroughly. Chill. Roll out to about one-fourth inch thickness and cut into circles or squares. Place a quantity of the filling on each piece and top with another circle of dough. Press edges together with a fork. Bake on a cooky sheet in a moderately hot oven until golden. Remove to rack and cool.

Date Drops

One-fourth cup shortening
Three-fourths cup brown sugar
One egg
One and one-fourth cups sifted flour
One-half teaspoon baking powder
One-half teaspoon soda
One-fourth teaspoon salt
One-half cup dairy sour cream
Two cups pitted dates
One-half cup pecan halves
Oven temperature: 400 degrees
Bake: Ten minutes
Yield: Approx. five dozen

In a bowl cream the shortening with the sugar. Beat in the egg. Sift together the flour, baking powder, soda and salt. Add to the creamed mixture alternately with the dairy sour cream. Stuff each pitted date with a pecan half. Add to the batter, coating well. Spoon coated stuffed dates onto a greased baking sheet. Bake in a quick oven for about ten minutes. Remove cookies from oven to rack to cool thoroughly before storing in a covered tin.

Walnut Horns

One-half pound butter or margarine
One-half pound creamed cottage cheese
One and one-half cups sifted flour
Chill: Until firm
Three-fourths cup sugar
One teaspoon cinnamon
One and one-half cups finely chopped
   walnuts
One egg yolk, beaten
Oven temperature: 350 degrees
Bake: Fifteen to twenty minutes
Yield: Thirty

In a bowl cream the butter or margarine, blend in the creamed cottage cheese and the sifted flour. Mix thoroughly. Chill dough until firm. Combine the sugar, cinnamon and finely cut nuts. Roll out the dough on a floured board. Roll fairly thin. Cut into squares (4 in.) and top with a rounded teaspoonful of the sugar and nut mixture. Roll from one corner to the opposite; shape into crescents. Place on ungreased baking sheets. Brush with beaten egg yolk. Bake to a delicate brown in a moderate oven. Remove to rack to cool.

Raisin Nut Molasses Drop Cookies

One cup shortening
One cup sugar
One cup molasses
Two eggs
Four and one-half cups sifted flour
Three teaspoons baking powder
One and one-half teaspoons baking soda
One teaspoon salt
One cup milk
One and one-half cups chopped nuts
One and one-half cups raisins
Oven temperature: 375 degrees
Bake: Ten minutes
Yield: Seven to eight dozen

In a bowl cream the shortening with the sugar. Beat in the molasses and eggs. Sift together the flour, baking powder, baking soda and salt and add to the creamed mixture alternately with the milk. Mix thoroughly. Stir in the chopped nuts and raisins. Drop mixture by tablespoonfuls on an ungreased baking sheet allowing two inches between cookies. Bake in a moderately hot oven for ten minutes. Remove to racks to cool. Store in a tightly covered container.

Fish

Planked Fish Dinner

One whitefish (3 lbs.), cleaned
Salt and pepper
Broiling temperature: 500 degrees
Broiling time: Fifteen minutes (about)
Two eggs, slightly beaten

Four cups hot seasoned mashed potatoes
Two cups cooked seasoned peas
One bunch cooked broccoli
Serves: Four

Clean and wash the fish; salt and pepper the inside. Place on a wooden plank (16 in.) or broiler platter. Place in a preheated broiler compartment. Broil for five minutes. Meanwhile, beat the eggs into the seasoned mashed potatoes. Press the potatoes through a pastry bag into the shape of four nests around the broiled fish. Return to broiler; broil until the potatoes are a golden brown. Remove. Fill nests with hot cooked peas and arrange cooked seasoned broccoli around the potatoes. Garnish with lemon slices. Serve immediately.

A FAVORITE RECIPE
Butterfish-Sour Cream

Two pounds butterfish
One teaspoon salt
One-fourth teaspoon pepper
One egg, beaten
One-half cup milk
Three-fourths cup sifted flour
One tablespoon melted butter
Fat for deep frying, heated
Frying time: Until a golden brown

Sauce

One cup dairy sour cream
One-half teaspoon salt
One tablespoon minced parsley
One tablespoon minced green onion
Juice one lemon
One-sixteenth teaspoon cayenne
Heating time: Until warm
Servings: Four

Have the fish prepared for cooking at the market; wash; dry; sprinkle with salt and pepper. In a bowl, beat the egg, add the milk, flour and melted butter; beat until smooth. Dip the fish in the butter; fry in the deep fat until a golden brown. For the sauce: combine the sour cream, salt, parsley, minced onion, lemon juice and cayenne. Serve the fish on a hot platter. Serve with the warm sauce.

CEIL TRAVERS, *North Bergen, N.J.*

Codfish Balls

One pound dried codfish
Water
Standing time: Overnight
Boiling water
Standing time: Twenty minutes
Boiling water
Standing time: Twenty minutes
Four cups diced peeled potatoes
Cook: Fifteen to twenty minutes
Two tablespoons butter or margarine
Two eggs
One-half teaspoon salt
One-half teaspoon dry mustard
One-half teaspoon celery salt
One-eighth teaspoon pepper
One-sixteenth teaspoon garlic powder
Fine dry bread crumbs
Shortening or oil for frying
Frying time: Five to ten minutes
Yield: Sixteen patties or more

Place the dried codfish in a bowl, cover with cold water and let stand overnight. Drain, cover with boiling water and let stand twenty minutes. Drain, cover with boiling water a second time and let stand twenty minutes. Drain and shred with a fork. Place shredded fish and diced peeled potatoes in a large saucepan with an inch or so of water. Cover and cook until potatoes are very tender. Drain and mash. Stir in the butter or margarine. In a large bowl beat the eggs with the salt, dry mustard, celery salt, pepper and garlic powder. Beat in the mashed potatoes. Blend thoroughly together. Chill mixture until firm enough to form into balls or flat cakes. Roll in fine dry bread crumbs and fry

to a golden brown in the hot shortening or oil. Drain on absorbent paper and serve at once. Note: If you form small one-inch balls of the chilled mixture as many as five dozen cocktail appetizers to be served on toothpicks may be made.

A FAVORITE RECIPE
Deviled Cod Fillets

Eight small codfish fillets, (3 x 7 in.)
One-half teaspoon dry mustard
One-half teaspoon oregano
One tablespoon anchovy paste
One-half cup salad oil
Two teaspoons lemon juice
Standing time: One hour in refrigerator
One-half cup flour
One egg, beaten lightly
Four tablespoons shortening, heated
Frying time: Until browned lightly on both sides
One lemon, cut into wedges
Eight sprigs parsley
Servings: Four

Wash and dry the fillets. In a bowl mix the mustard, oregano, anchovy paste, salad oil and lemon juice. Spread the mixture on one side of the fish; place on a platter; let marinate in refrigerator. Roll each fillet; fasten with toothpicks. Dip into the flour, roll, then dip into the egg. Heat the fat in a heavy skillet. Fry the fish, turning until all sides are browned. Remove the toothpicks and serve on a hot platter, garnished with the lemon and parsley.

MRS. JOSEPH ALIANO, *N. Arlington, N.J.*

Creamed Smoked Cod

One pound smoked cod fillets
Boiling water
Simmer: Ten to fifteen minutes
Three tablespoons butter or margarine
Three green onions
Sauté: Five minutes, about
One-fourth cup flour
One teaspoon salt
Two cups milk
Cook: Five minutes, about
One-third cup dry white wine
One-fourth teaspoon grated lemon rind
One tablespoon lemon juice
Two tablespoons chopped pimiento
Two tablespoons chopped parsley
Heat: Five to ten minutes
Four slices hot toast
Servings: Four

Place the smoked cod fillets in a skillet and pour boiling water around them to depth of one-half inch. Cover tightly and simmer until fish flakes easily. Drain and flake fish. In a saucepan melt the butter or margarine. Add the thinly sliced onions and sauté until soft. Stir in the flour and salt and gradually blend in the milk, stirring smooth. Cook, stirring constantly, until sauce thickens. Add the dry white wine, grated lemon rind, lemon juice, chopped pimiento, parsley and flaked cod. Heat to piping hot and serve over crisp toast triangles.

Baked Codfish Cakes

One pound salt codfish
Cold water
Soaking: Overnight
Six medium-sized potatoes
One tablespoon grated onion
Four tablespoons butter
One-eighth teaspoon pepper
Two eggs
Oven temperature: 350 degrees
Bake: Thirty-five minutes
Servings: Six or more

Cover the codfish with cold water and let soak overnight. Drain and cover fish with boiling water. After 20 minutes repeat. Drain after a second 20-minute stand. Flake the fish with a fork. In the meantime cook the potatoes until soft; drain and mash. Add the flaked fish, grated onion, butter, pepper and unbeaten eggs. Beat all together. Shape into eighteen small flat cakes and place on a greased baking sheet. Bake in a moderate oven until flecked with gold. If you prefer the cakes may be pan fried in hot fat. We like these with stewed tomatoes and buttered green beans.

A FAVORITE RECIPE
Tangy Mackerel

Two large onions, sliced thin
Juice one and one-half lemons
Four cups water
One cup sugar
One teaspoon salt, or more
Cooking time: Twenty-five minutes
Four mackerel (1 lb. each) split
One large carrot sliced
Cooking time: Forty-five minutes
Chilling time: Six hours
Servings: Eight

In a heavy saucepan, cook the onions, lemon juice, water, sugar and salt (to taste); bring the mixture to a boil, reduce the heat and simmer. Add the split, cleaned mackerel and sliced carrot. Cook. Remove the fish to a serving dish; surround with the carrots. Strain the cooked sauce over the fish. Chill until serving time. Serve sliced on lettuce.

MRS. F. SILVER, *Brooklyn, N.Y.*

Baked Swordfish Steaks

One and one-half pounds swordfish steak (cut ¾ inch thick)
One tablespoon flour
One cup dairy sour cream
One tablespoon grated onion
One tablespoon lemon juice
Oven temperature: 400 degrees
Bake: Thirty minutes
Servings: Four, or more

Have the swordfish sliced into steaks three-fourths of an inch thick. Portion into individual servings, trim off the skin. Lay in a greased shallow baking dish. Measure the flour into a small bowl, gradually blend in the dairy sour cream.

Add the grated onion and lemon juice and spoon over the swordfish. Bake in a quick oven until the fish flakes easily with a fork.

Red Snapper Baked with Vegetables

One-fourth cup butter or margarine
One-fourth cup finely chopped onion
Two cups soft bread crumbs
One-half teaspoon salt
One-sixteenth teaspoon pepper
One teaspoon poultry seasoning
One red snapper (four pounds)
Four medium-sized potatoes
Four medium-sized carrots
One-half teaspoon salt
One-eighth teaspoon pepper
Two cups milk
Two tablespoons butter or margarine
Oven temperature: 400 degrees
Bake: Twenty-five minutes
One pkg. (10 oz.) frozen peas
Bake: Twenty-five minutes
Serves: Six

In a skillet melt the butter or margarine. Add the chopped onion and sauté until soft. Stir in the soft bread crumbs, half teaspoon of salt, pepper and poultry seasoning. Fill into the fish cavity; close opening with skewers. Lay fish in a large greased baking pan. Peel the potatoes and carrots; cut potatoes into one-inch dice, the carrots into half-inch dice. Arrange around the fish. Stir salt and pepper into the milk and pour over the vegetables. Dot fish with bits of butter. Bake in a quick oven for 25 minutes. Scatter frozen peas amongst the vegetables and continue baking until fish and vegetables are thoroughly cooked.

A FAVORITE RECIPE
Oriental Swordfish Steaks

Two pounds swordfish, cut into serving pieces

Sauce

One-fourth cup soy sauce
One-fourth cup orange juice
Two tablespoons salad oil
Two tablespoons catsup
Two tablespoons minced parsley
One teaspoon lemon juice
One-half teaspoon oregano
One-half teaspoon pepper
One clove garlic, minced
Marinating time: Three hours
Broiler temperature: 375 degrees
Broiling time: Fifteen minutes
Servings: Four, or more

Wipe the cut steaks with a damp cloth. Place in a saucepan. For the marinating sauce: Mix the soy sauce, orange juice, salad oil, catsup, parsley, lemon juice, oregano, pepper and garlic. Pour over the fish; place in refrigerator, turning the fish several times while marinating. Drain the fish, place on a rack over a shallow pan, broil, browning lightly on each side. Serve hot with mashed potatoes and creamed broccoli.

W. E. CLEGG, *Salem, Mass.*

Swordfish Supreme with Grapes

Two pounds swordfish steak (1 inch thick)
Salt
Flour
Three tablespoons butter
Browning time: Five to ten minutes
Cook: Five minutes, about
One and one-half tablespoons flour
One-half teaspoon salt
One-eighth teaspoon pepper
One-half cup heavy cream
One cup dry white wine
One cup green grapes, split
Serves: Six

Cut the inch thick swordfish steak into six portions. Sprinkle each piece lightly with salt, dredge in flour. Heat the butter in a large heavy skillet, add the floured fish and brown well on both sides. This will take about 10 minutes. Cover the skillet and cook another 5 minutes or until the fish flakes easily with a fork but is not dried out. Remove steaks to a hot platter and keep warm. Stir the flour, salt and pepper into the drippings in the pan and gradually blend in the cream and wine, stirring smooth. Cook over moderate heat, stirring constantly, until the sauce thickens. Add the grapes and correct seasoning to taste. Spoon sauce over the portions of steak and serve.

Herb Broiled Swordfish

Two pounds swordfish steak (one inch thick)
Four teaspoons lemon juice
Two teaspoons thyme, crumbled
Black pepper
Two tablespoons dry white wine
Broiling temperature: 500 degrees
Broil: Fifteen minutes, about
Two tablespoons finely chopped parsley
Lemon wedges
Serves: Four or five

Cut the swordfish steak into individual portions. Lay on lightly greased shallow broiling pan. Spoon on the lemon juice. Sprinkle with the crumbled thyme, black pepper and dry white wine. Place in a pre-heated broiler and broil for fifteen minutes or until fish flakes easily with a fork. Remove from broiler, sprinkle with finely chopped parsley and serve with lemon wedges.

Pan-Fried Swordfish

One and one-half pounds swordfish steak (cut ¾ inch thick)
Flour
Salt and pepper
One egg
One-third cup milk
One cup fine dry bread crumbs
Three tablespoons oil or shortening
Sauté: Four to five minutes on each side
Lemon wedges
Water cress
Servings: Four, or more

Cut the swordfish steak into individual servings. Dust with flour. Sprinkle with salt and pepper on each side. In a shallow dish beat the egg; stir in the milk. Dip the floured pieces of fish into the egg mixture then coat with fine dry bread

crumbs. Heat the oil or shortening in a heavy skillet. Add the coated fish and cook for four or five minutes on each side. The fish will be flaky and an opaque white after this time if broken with a fork. Only exceptionally thick pieces will take longer. Serve with lemon wedges and a generous garnish of water cress. Frozen swordfish needs only the surface glaze of frost removed before cooking.

Shad Roe Manhattan

Two shad roes (about one and one-half pounds)
One teaspoon salt
One tablespoon vinegar
Two or three cups hot water
Parboil: Five to ten minutes
Cold water to cover
Blanch: Five minutes
Three tablespoons butter
Broiler temperature: 500 degrees
Broil: Ten minutes
One teaspoon dry mustard
One-third cup heavy cream
One tablespoon lemon juice
Salt and pepper
Serves: Four

Rinse the shad roe under cold water and lay in a shallow skillet. Sprinkle with salt and vinegar. Pour on enough hot water to cover. Cook very gently for five to ten minutes, until it firms slightly. Drain and cover with cold water. Let stand for five minutes, drain and dry on paper toweling. Melt butter in small saucepan and use some to oil a piece of aluminum foil. Lay roe on foil and brush melted butter over it. Broil for five minutes, turn and brush with butter and broil until nicely browned. Stir the dry mustard into the remaining melted butter, add cream. Heat slightly. Add lemon juice, salt and pepper to taste and serve over the browned roe.

A FAVORITE RECIPE
Sweet and Sour Fish

Two tablespoons salt
One large onion, sliced thin
One carrot, sliced
One-half cup cider vinegar
One-half cup brown sugar
Ten gingersnaps, crumbled
One-fourth cup seedless raisins
One lemon, sliced thin
Twelve peppercorns
Three bay leaves
Cooking time: Thirty minutes
Three pounds pike or white fish, sliced (½ in.)
Simmering time: Thirty minutes
Two lemons cut into wedges
Servings: Six

In a large saucepan mix the salt, onion, carrot, vinegar, sugar, gingersnaps, raisins, lemon slices, peppercorns and bay leaves. Cover; cook. Reduce the heat, add the sliced fish a few slices at a time to the mixture. Simmer. Cool in the liquid. Remove fish to a platter. Strain the sauce; pour over the fish. Garnish with the lemon wedges. If preferred, chill before serving.

RUTH ROTH, *New Hyde Park, L.I., N.Y.*

Danish Trout Tartar

After the Danish trout has been cooked on both sides, spoon a mixture of one-third cup condensed cream of celery soup, one-third cup real mayonnaise and one-half cup minced dill pickle. Brown under the broiler until golden and bubbling hot. Serve immediately.

Cold Planked Salmon Meal

One quart water
One cup dry white wine
One onion
Two whole cloves
One stalk celery
Few sprigs parsley
Ten whole black peppers
One tablespoon salt
Five pounds salmon
Sliced green pepper
Simmer: Forty minutes (8 min. to pound)
One package unflavored gelatin, dissolved
    in one cup cold salmon stock
Eight cups potato salad
Four cups peas, marinated in French
    dressing
Tomato wedges, parsley, carrot strips,
    lemon wedges and slices
Refrigerate: Two hours
Serves: Eight, or more

Put the water, wine, onion, cloves, celery, parsley, whole black peppers and salt in a kettle. Bring to a boil. Put in salmon; cover; simmer for 40 minutes. Turn off heat. Let stand until cold. Place salmon in center of wooden plank and garnish with green pepper. Sprinkle gelatin in one cup cold stock in which the salmon was cooked. Heat until gelatin is dissolved; cool until it starts to gel. Brush over garnished salmon. Arrange a border of potato salad along edge of plank. Fill space with marinated peas. Garnish with tomato wedges, parsley, carrot strips, lemon wedges and slices. Place in refrigerator until ready to serve. Serve with Lemon Lime Dressing or Mayonnaise.

Danish Trout
With Anchovy Sherry Sauce

Four frozen Danish trout, defrosted
Four tablespoons olive oil
One can (2 oz.) anchovy fillets, minced
One-fourth cup lemon juice
Few grains cayenne
Three tablespoons flour
Cook: Ten minutes
One cup Spanish sherry wine
Cook: Three minutes
Serves: Four

Rinse the Danish trout; dry with absorbent paper. In a skillet heat the olive oil with the anchovies, lemon juice and cayenne. Place the trout which has been dusted lightly with flour, into the hot skillet. Brown the trout five minutes on one side, turn and brown five minutes on the other side. Add the sherry; cook another three minutes. Serve on a hot platter with lemon wedges. Pour the sauce from the skillet into a bowl. Serve immediately.

Piquant Danish Trout

After the Danish trout has been cooked on both sides, brush each side of the trout with a mixture of two tablespoons soft butter or margarine, and one and one-half teaspoons prepared mustard, one teaspoon each lemon juice, onion juice and Worcestershire sauce. Broil until the skin is crisp and brown. Serve immediately.

Lemon Lime Salad Dressing

Combine one tablespoon each lemon and lime juice, two tablespoons sugar and three-fourths cup mayonnaise. Whip one-half cup cream slightly; fold in. Makes 2 cups.

Steamed Salmon Steaks

Two pounds salmon steaks
Boiling water
Steaming time: Ten minutes, about
Servings: Four to six

Contrive a rack in a large kettle or skillet with one-half to one inch of boiling water in the bottom. Lay the steaks in a single layer on the rack above the water, cover the pan and steam for 10 minutes or until the fish flakes easily with a fork. Remove to a plate and strip off the skin and bones. Serve at once with salt, pepper and lemon wedges.

Stuffed Swordfish Steaks

One package (11 oz.) frozen chopped
    spinach
Boiling water
Two tablespoons butter or margarine
Two large fresh mushrooms, sliced
Sauteing time: Five minutes
One-fourth cup water
Two tablespoons fine bread crumbs
One-fourth cup dairy sour cream
One teaspoon prepared mustard
One-half teaspoon salt
One-eighth teaspoon pepper
Two packages (12 oz. each) frozen
    swordfish steaks, defrosted
One tablespoon salad oil
One-half teaspoon brown bouquet sauce
Oven temperature: 350 degrees
Baking time: Twenty minutes
Serves: Four, or more

Cook spinach in boiling water according to directions on the package. In a skillet melt the butter; add the mushrooms. Saute briefly. When light brown add water. Stir and cook for 1 minute. In a bowl combine the cooked, drained spinach with the crumbs, sour cream, mustard, salt and pepper. Split the defrosted swordfish in half lengthwise. Spoon spinach mixture on half the fish steaks. Top with sliced steaks. Place in a greased shallow baking dish. In a cup combine the salad oil and the bouquet sauce; brush over the steaks. Pour sauteed mushrooms around steaks. Cover and bake in moderate oven till fish flakes with a fork. Serve immediately.

Poached Salmon

One piece salmon (3 lbs.)
Four cups boiling water
One carrot, scraped
Two sprigs parsley
One stalk celery
Four peppercorns
One bay leaf
One-fourth teaspoon tarragon
Poaching time: Thirty to forty minutes
Servings: Four, or more

Tie the salmon in a piece of cheesecloth. Place the salmon on a rack in a kettle containing one and one-half to two inches of boiling water. Add the remaining ingredients. Cover. Steam very slowly until the fish flakes. Lift from the stock. Reserve one cup of the fish stock for the sauce. Remove the cheesecloth. Discard the skin and center bone if it can be readily lifted out. Place the fish on a hot platter; garnish as desired. Serve with egg sauce.

Egg Sauce

Two tablespoons butter
Three tablespoons flour
One-half teaspoon salt
One-fourth teaspoon dry mustard
One cup strained fish stock or milk
One-half cup thin cream or evaporated
    milk
Two teaspoons lemon juice
Two hard-cooked eggs, chopped
Cooking time: Five minutes
Yield: Two cups (about)

Blend the butter, flour and seasonings in a saucepan. Add the stock or milk, stirring until thickened over low heat.

Slowly stir in the cream and lemon juice. Add the chopped eggs. Pour into a sauceboat; serve with poached salmon.

Stuffed Fish Fillets

One package (11 oz.) frozen chopped
    spinach
Boiling water
Two tablespoons butter
Two large fresh mushrooms sliced
Sautéing time: Five minutes
One-fourth cup water
Two tablespoons fine dry bread crumbs
One-fourth cup dairy sour cream
One-half teaspoon salt
One-eighth teaspoon pepper
One teaspoon prepared mustard
Four flounder or other flat fish fillets (1½
    pounds)
Salt
One tablespoon salad oil
One-half teaspoon brown bouquet sauce
Oven temperature: 350 degrees
Baking time: Twenty minutes
Servings: Four

Cook the frozen chopped spinach in
the boiling water according to directions
on the package. Melt the butter in a skillet; add the sliced mushrooms and sauté
briefly. When lightly browned, add the
fourth cup of water. Stir and cook for a
minute to dissolve the pan brownings.
In a bowl, combine the cooked, drained
spinach with the bread crumbs, sour
cream, salt, pepper and mustard. Sprinkle the fillets with salt. Divide the spinach mixture between the four pieces of
fish, rolling up and fastening with a
toothpick. Place in a greased shallow
baking dish or pie plate. In a cup, combine the salad oil and the brown bouquet
sauce; brush over the fillets. Pour sautéed
mushrooms and pan gravy around the
fillets. Cover and bake in a moderate
oven until the fish flakes with a fork.
Serve at once.

Baked Stuffed Fillets

Two pounds flounder (or other fish) fillets
Three tablespoons butter
Two tablespoons finely chopped onion
One-third cup finely chopped celery
Sauté: Until soft
One-half teaspoon salt
One-eighth teaspoon pepper
One-half teaspoon thyme or savory
Dash of tabasco
Two cups soft bread crumbs
One-fourth cup butter, melted
Oven temperature: 350 degrees
Bake: Thirty to forty minutes
Servings: Four

Use fresh or frozen fillets, defrosting
the latter. Lay half the fillets in a buttered shallow baking dish or pan. Prepare
the stuffing by melting the three tablespoons of butter in a skillet, adding the
finely chopped onion and celery and
sautéing until soft. Stir in the salt, pepper, thyme or savory, dash of tabasco
and soft bread crumbs. Mix thoroughly.
Spoon over the fish in the baking pan
and cover with remaining fillets. Pour
melted butter over the top and bake in
a moderate oven for thirty to forty minutes or until the fish is snowy white and
flakes easily when tested with a fork.
Portion fish in pan, cutting down through
both layers. Serve with broad spatula.

A FAVORITE RECIPE
Stuffed Haddock-Fillet

Four slices fillet, haddock, or any other
    kind of fish
One-fourth teaspoon allspice
One-half teaspoon salt
One-fourth teaspoon pepper
One cup white vinegar
Marinating time: Overnight in refrigerator
One can (8 oz.) cream style corn
Two tablespoons butter
Oven temperature: 350 degrees
Baking time: Forty minutes
Servings: Four

Wash the fillets; dry. Season with the
allspice, salt and pepper. Place in a
shallow dish. Pour the vinegar over the
fish. Marinate. Pour off the vinegar, dry
the fish. Over each fillet, place a tablespoonful of the corn; fold over and fasten
the fish with toothpicks. Butter a baking
dish well. Place the stuffed fish in dish.
Bake in a moderate oven until the fish is
lightly browned.

MRS. SELMA WEISS, *New York, N.Y.*

A FAVORITE RECIPE
Stuffed Fish

One-half cup butter, melted
Two and one-half cups minced celery
Three tablespoons chopped onion
Three tablespoons chopped parsley
Cooking time: Ten minutes
Two and three-fourths cups soft bread
    crumbs
One-fourth teaspoon sage
Cooking time: Until lightly browned
One-half cup light cream
One egg, beaten slightly
Two tablespoons chopped pimiento-stuffed
    olives
One teaspoon salt
One-half teaspoon pepper
Two pounds boneless fish fillets
One-fourth cup butter, melted
One-fourth cup lemon juice
One-half cup sliced pimiento-stuffed olives
Oven temperature: 350 degrees
Baking time: Thirty minutes
Servings: Six

Melt the butter in a deep skillet; add
the celery, onion and parsley; cook, stirring frequently. Stir in the bread crumbs
and sage, blend and cook until browned.
Remove from the heat; add the cream,
egg, chopped olives, salt and pepper.
Wipe the fillets with a damp cloth; spread
the bread mixture over half of the fillets.
Top with the remaining fillets. Place in
a well greased shallow pan. For the sauce:
Combine the melted butter, lemon juice
and sliced olives. Spread over the fillets.
Bake in a moderate oven until a golden
brown. Serve with a green vegetable and
coleslaw.

MRS. MURL AUCHMOODY, *Newburgh, N.Y.*

Pan-Fried Fillets

Two pounds fish fillets (perch, sole,
    flounder)
One egg
One tablespoon milk
One teaspoon salt
One-eighth teaspoon pepper
One cup dry bread crumbs or cornmeal
Fat for frying
Frying time: Ten minutes, about
Servings: Six

If the fillets are large, cut them into
serving portions. Beat the egg in a shallow dish; add the milk, salt and pepper.
Dip pieces of fish in the egg then in the
fine dry bread crumbs or cornmeal. Heat
fat or oil for frying to depth of one-
eighth inch, in a heavy skillet, add the
coated fish and cook over moderate heat
until fish is nicely browned. Turn and
brown other side. Drain on absorbent
paper. Serve with tartar sauce.

A FAVORITE RECIPE
Stuffed Fillet of Sole

Two pounds cooked, well drained, chopped
    spinach
One teaspoon salt
One-eighth teaspoon pepper
One-third cup white cooking wine
One-fourth cup bread crumbs
Two pounds fillet of flounder
One-half cup minced onion
Two tablespoons minced parsley
One-fourth cup cooking wine
Two tablespoons butter
One cup sliced mushrooms
Two medium-sized tomatoes, peeled,
    quartered
Oven temperature: 500 degrees
Baking time: Fifteen minutes
Two tablespons flour, blended with
One-half cup cold water
Simmering time: Three minutes
One-fourth cup heavy cream, whipped
One tablespoon lemon juice
Broiler oven temperature: 375 degrees
Browning time: Five minutes
Servings: Six

Season the well drained spinach with
salt and pepper; in a bowl mix with ⅓
cup of wine and bread crumbs. Place a
mound of the mixture on one end of each
fillet, fold the other end over the spinach.
Bind with toothpicks. Place the fish in a
well greased baking dish. Add the onion,
parsley, ¼ cup of wine and butter to the
fish. Arrange the mushrooms and tomatoes over the top. Cover with parchment
paper and bake in a hot oven. Remove
the fish to very hot platter; thicken the
pan drippings with the flour and water
mixture. Simmer, stirring constantly; remove from the heat, fold in the whipped
cream and lemon juice. Pour over the
fish; brown lightly in broiler. Serve with
peas and a tossed salad.

LINDA DUNCAN, *Corona, N.Y.*

A FAVORITE RECIPE
Halibut Surprise

One pound halibut (one piece)
One small onion, sliced
Salted boiling water to cover
Cooking time: Fifteen minutes
One tablespoon mayonnaise
Two tablespoons sour cream
One tablespoon horseradish
One-half teaspoon salt
One-sixteenth teaspoon pepper
One head crisp lettuce
Two tomatoes, cut into wedges
Two hard-cooked eggs, cut into wedges
Servings: Four

Place the halibut in a heavy saucepan with onion on top; cover with the boiling salted water; bring to a boil; reduce heat; cook until the fish is flaky. When cool, flake. Mix the mayonnaise, sour cream, horseradish, salt and pepper in a bowl. Fold in the flaked fish, mixing well. Serve on salad plates covered with crisp lettuce. Garnish with the tomato and egg wedges.

MRS. D. PASAMANEK, *New York, N.Y.*

Broiled Halibut Steak

Two pounds halibut steak (1 in. thick)
Two tablespoons butter or margarine
One-half teaspoon salt
One-half teaspoon paprika
Dash of pepper
Broiler temperature: 500 degrees
Broil: Ten minutes, about
Servings: Four

For four servings you need two pounds of sliced halibut steak. This will be one or two slices when cut one inch thick. It may be broiled as is, or may be simply trimmed of skin and bone with a small sharp knife. Run knife close to the center bony structure that divides the steaks into four parts and just under the outer skin. Lay strips of bone-free fish on a greased shallow pan or tray. Combine the melted butter with the salt, paprika and dash of pepper. Brush over the fish. Broil about three inches from the source of heat in a preheated broiler for ten minutes or until fish flakes easily when tested with a fork. It will be snowy white on the inside but still moist when cooked. Transfer to serving plates and spoon on a little of the Ripe Olive Sauce.

Ripe Olive Sauce

One-fourth cup butter or margarine
One-fourth cup pitted ripe olives, sliced
One tablespoon lemon juice
Heat: Briefly
Two tablespoons finely chopped parsley
Yield: One-half cup, about

Place the butter or margarine, sliced ripe olives and lemon juice in a small saucepan and heat briefly to blend. Stir in the finely chopped parsley and serve over the broiled strips of halibut.

A FAVORITE RECIPE
Crab Stuffed Halibut
Stuffing

Two tablespoons butter, heated
One tablespoon minced onion
One tablespoon minced parsley
One tablespoon minced celery
Sauté: Ten minutes
One-half cup cracker crumbs
One can (6½ oz.) crab meat (all cartilage removed)
One egg
One-half teaspoon salt
One-eighth teaspoon pepper
Four halibut steaks (cut ½ in. thick)
Three tablespoons butter, melted
Oven temperature: 375 degrees
Baking time: Thirty minutes
Serves: Four

Heat the butter in a small skillet. Sauté the onion, parsley and celery in the butter. Remove from the heat, add the cracker crumbs, crab meat, egg, salt and pepper, mixing thoroughly. Cut the halibut steaks into halves. Spread half the steaks with the stuffing, cover with remaining halves of halibut. Brush with the melted butter. Place in a shallow pan; bake in a moderately hot oven, basting with melted butter, during the baking period. Serve with mashed potatoes and stewed tomatoes.

MR. WILLIAM SMITH, *New York, N.Y.*

A FAVORITE RECIPE
Poached Halibut

Two packages frozen halibut, partially thawed, cut into six servings
One teaspoon salt
One-eighth teaspoon pepper
One-fourth cup olive oil, heated
Two white onions, chopped fine
Two tablespoons minced parsley
Cooking time: Ten minutes
One cup water
Simmering time: Fifteen minutes
Two tablespoons butter, melted
One-fourth cup minced almonds
Sauté: Five minutes
Two tablespoons bread crumbs
Sauté: Until browned
Stock drained from cooked fish
Cooking time: To boiling point
One-half teaspoon paprika
Serves: Six

Thaw and cut the halibut into serving pieces. Season with salt and pepper. Heat the olive oil in a large skillet; add the onions and parsley; cook until onions are soft. Arrange the fish on top; add water; cover, simmer. Melt the butter in a saucepan; sauté the almonds. Add the bread crumbs, mix and brown lightly. Pour the stock off the cooked fish over the bread crumbs and almonds. Bring the mixture to a boil. Place the halibut on a hot platter; pour sauce over the fish. Garnish with paprika.

MRS. JULIA KISH, *Mt. Clemens, Mich.*

Tartar Sauce

One-half cup mayonnaise
One tablespoon finely chopped onion
One tablespoon finely chopped pickle
One tablespoon finely chopped parsley
One tablespoon finely chopped stuffed olives
Chill: Thoroughly
Yield: Three-fourths cup

Measure the mayonnaise into a small bowl or jar. Add the finely chopped onion, pickle, parsley and olives and chill thoroughly before serving with the cooked fish.

A FAVORITE RECIPE
Fish with Sauce

One-fourth cup salad oil, heated
Two onions, chopped
Two tablespoons minced parsley
Cooking time: Until onion is soft
One cup hot water
Simmering time: Fifteen minutes
Two packages frozen halibut, cod or haddock cut into six pieces
One cup water
One teaspoon salt
One-eighth teaspoon pepper
Cooking time: Fifteen minutes

Sauce

Two tablespoons margarine, melted
Sauté: Five minutes
One-fourth cup chopped almonds
Two tablespoons bread crumbs or wheat germ
One-fourth cup fish stock
One-half cup white wine
Heat: To boiling point
One teaspoon minced parsley
Servings: Six

Heat the oil in a large shallow pan; add the onions and parsley. Cook until onions are soft. Arrange the fish over onions, add water, salt and pepper. Simmer. For the sauce: Melt the margarine in a saucepan; sauté the almonds and bread crumbs. Pour the ¼ cup of liquid from the cooked fish and wine into the almond mixture; heat to boiling point. Serve the fish on a hot platter, pouring the sauce over the top. Garnish with parsley.

RUTH W. REHNS, *New York, N.Y.*

A FAVORITE RECIPE
Broiled Haddock Fillets-Sauce

Two packages (lb.) frozen haddock fillets,
    partially thawed
One-fourth cup melted butter or margarine
One teaspoon salt
One-fourth teaspoon pepper
Broiling oven temperature: 350 degrees
Broiling time: Twenty minutes, about

Sauce

Four tablespoons butter, or margarine,
    melted
One teaspoon vinegar
One-half teaspoon grated onion
One-fourth teaspoon salt
One-eighth teaspoon pepper
Few drops tabasco
Three tablespoons grated cucumber
One tablespoon chopped parsley
Heating time: To boiling point
Serves: Six

Brush the partially thawed fillets with
the melted butter; sprinkle with salt and
pepper. Place the fish on a broiler rack,
broiling on each side until lightly browned
on each side. While broiling the fish, prepare the sauce: Melt the butter in a small
saucepan, add the vinegar, onion, salt,
pepper, tabasco, grated cucumber and
parsley. Heat, stirring constantly until
it comes to boiling point. Place the hot
fish on a heated platter. Pour over the
hot sauce. Garnish with raw onion rings
and serve.

MRS. HOWARD F. SNAY, *Haven, Kansas*

Baked Stuffed Fish

One (5 lb.) mackerel, boned
Two cups soft bread crumbs
Two tablespoons chopped celery and
    leaves
Two tablespoons grated onion
One cup chopped stuffed green olives
One-fourth teaspoon pepper
One teaspoon tarragon
One-fourth cup melted butter or margarine
Oven temperature: 400 degrees
Bake: Twenty-five minutes to the pound
Lemon wedges
Serves: Six

Have the fish man bone the mackerel;
remove the tail, head and fins (will
weigh about 3 lb.). Partially split the
mackerel. Lightly mix together the
crumbs, celery, onion, half of the stuffed
olives, pepper, tarragon and butter. Fill
one half of the fish with the stuffing;
fold over the other half. Skewer and tie
with a string to hold the stuffing intact.
Put into a shallow pan. Sprinkle the remaining stuffed olives around the edge.
Bake in a quick oven until a fork will
flake the fish (1 hour and 15 minutes).
Remove from oven. Remove skewers and
string. Garnish with lemon wedges.
Serve.

Baked Fish Fillets

One and one-half pounds fish fillets
One teaspoon salt
One-eighth teaspoon pepper
One-eighth teaspoon tarragon
One bay leaf
Three whole cloves
One-half cup milk
Two tablespoons margarine, melted
Oven temperature: 400 degrees
Baking time: Thirty minutes
Servings: Four to Six

Place the fish in a shallow baking dish
(10 in.). Sprinkle with salt and pepper.
Pour the combined remaining ingredients
over the fish. Bake in a quick oven with
the vegetables until done. Serve immediately.

Easy Potatoes: Combine three cups
diced boiled potatoes, one-half teaspoon
salt, one-fourth teaspoon pepper, one-
fourth cup minced parsley and one can
(10½ oz.) condensed mushroom soup.
Place in a greased casserole (1 qt.). Bake
until the soup is absorbed.

Glazed Carrots: Place ten halved whole
cooked carrots in a shallow baking dish
(9 in.). Sprinkle over the top two tablespoons melted margarine, four tablespoons sugar and one teaspoon lemon
juice. Bake until glazed.

Sardine and Egg Roll

Two cans (3¼ oz. each) Norway sardines
Six hard-cooked eggs
Three-fourths cup minced celery
Two tablespoons minced parsley
One tablespoon minced onion
One-half teaspoon salt
Two teaspoons lemon juice
One tablespoon mustard sauce
One-fourth cup real mayonnaise
Three cups sifted flour
Four teaspoons baking powder
One-half teaspoon salt
Six tablespoons shortening
One egg
One-half cup milk
Oven temperature: 425 degrees
Baking time: Thirty minutes
Serves: Six

Reserve four whole sardines and one hard-cooked egg for garnish. In a bowl chop and combine the remaining sardines and eggs. Add the celery, parsley, onion, salt, lemon juice, mustard and mayonnaise. Reserve. In a second bowl sift the flour, baking powder and salt. Blend in the shortening with two knives or blender to the consistency of cornmeal. Add the combined egg and milk. Turn out on a floured board; knead four times (about). Roll out into a rectangle (⅛ in. thick). Spread the sardine mixture on dough. Roll up jelly-roll fashion. Place on a baking sheet. Bake in a hot oven until a golden brown. Garnish with egg slices and sardines. Serve with a cheese sauce.

Norway Sardine Egg Strudel

Four tablespoons butter or margarine
One-fourth cup grated onion
Cook: Three minutes
Three tablespoons flour
One cup milk
Cook: Five minutes
Three tablespoons minced parsley
One teaspoon salt
One-fourth teaspoon pepper
One-fourth teaspoon tarragon
Three tablespoons lemon juice
Five pastry leaves (14x10 in.) or one recipe
    baking powder biscuit dough (2 cups)
Melted butter
Two cans (3¾ oz. each) Norway sardines,
    drained
Six hard-cooked eggs
Oven temperature: 400 degrees
Bake: Thirty minutes
Pimiento
Serves: Six

In a skillet melt the butter. Add the onion; cook until straw-colored. Blend in the flour. Gradually add the milk and cook until thickened. Add the parsley, salt, pepper, tarragon and lemon juice. Set aside. Cover a cooky sheet with foil. Place a piece of tissue-like pastry on the foil. Brush with melted butter. Reserve a few sardines and egg slices for garnish. Chop the remaining hard-cooked eggs,

coarsely. Take half the sardines and chopped eggs and place over the pastry. Spoon and spread half the cream mixture over the sardines and eggs. Repeat the procedure. Cover with another layer of tissue-pastry; brush with melted butter. Fold in the short ends of the pastry. Lift the foil and roll as for jelly roll. Remove the foil. Carefully shape the roll into a crescent. Brush the top with butter. Tuck another of the pastry sheets around the crescent. Brush again with butter. Bake in a quick oven until golden on top. Remove to a rack. Serve on a hot platter. Garnish with pimiento, sliced hard-cooked eggs and sardines. Serve in wedges with a mustard sauce.

Mustard Sauce

One tablespoon minced onion
Three tablespoons butter
Cook: Two minutes
Two tablespoons vinegar
Simmer: Five minutes
Two teaspoons dry mustard
One tablespoon water
One cup milk
Simmer: Two minutes
Yield: One and one-fourth cups

Saute the onion in the butter until straw-colored. Add the vinegar; simmer. Blend the mustard with the water. Stir into the vinegar mixture. Gradually add the milk and simmer for 5 minutes.

Supreme of Tuna

One-third cup butter or margarine
One-third cup flour
One teaspoon salt
One-fourth teaspoon pepper
One teaspoon paprika
One-fourth teaspoon sage
Three cups milk
Cook: Ten minutes
Two cans (7 oz. each) tuna
Two cups cooked white onions (one
    No. 303 can)
One-half cup cut pieces of ripe olives
Cook: Ten minutes
Serves: Six

In a large heavy skillet melt the butter, blend in the flour, salt and seasonings. Gradually stir in the milk. Cook over low heat, stirring constantly until the sauce is smooth and thickened. Add the flaked tuna, cooked white onions and cut ripe olive pieces. Cook to heat thoroughly. Serve over parsley rice.

Parsley Rice

One and one-third cups pre-cooked rice
One and one-third cups boiling water
One-half teaspoon salt
Three tablespoons chopped parsley
Two tablespoons finely chopped onion
Standing time: Five minutes
Two tablespoons butter or margarine
Serves: Six

In a saucepan combine the pre-cooked rice, boiling water, salt, chopped parsley and onion. Cover tightly and let stand for five minutes. When moisture is absorbed and rice is fluffy, stir in the butter or margarine. Serve at once.

A FAVORITE RECIPE
Vegetable Tuna Pie

One package mixed frozen vegetables
    (cooked as directed on package)
One can (10½ oz.) condensed cream of
    mushroom soup (undiluted)
One teaspoon mustard
One-half teaspoon Worcestershire sauce
One-half cup milk
One can (6½ oz.) tuna, flaked
Two cups prepared biscuit mix (mixed as
    directed on package)
One teaspoon minced parsley
Oven temperature: 425 degrees
Bake: Fifteen minutes, or more
Serves: Four

In a saucepan cook the vegetables; drain. Add the soup, mustard, Worcestershire sauce, milk and flaked tuna. Turn into a baking dish (8 in.). In a bowl prepare the biscuit mix for drop biscuits, adding the parsley to the dry mix. Drop one-half the mixture by spoonfuls over the hot tuna mixture. Drop the remaining biscuit dough by spoonfuls onto baking sheet. Bake in a hot oven. Serve tuna hot with a green salad and hot biscuits.

MR. ELMER WHITTAKER, *Taunton, Mass.*

Creole Tuna

Two tablespoons salad oil
Two large onions, chopped
Two cloves garlic, crushed
One medium-sized green pepper, chopped
Sauté: Ten minutes, about
One-half teaspoon thyme
One teaspoon salt
One-eighth teaspoon pepper
One tablespoon flour
One can (1 lb.) stewed tomatoes
Simmer: Ten minutes
Two tablespoons chopped parsley
Three cups seasoned mashed potatoes
Two cans (7 oz. each) tuna
Oven temperature: 375 degrees
Baking time: Twenty minutes
Serves: Six

Heat the salad oil in a heavy skillet or saucepan. Add the chopped onion, crushed garlic, and green pepper and sauté until soft. Add the thyme, salt, pepper and flour. Blend in the canned stewed tomatoes and simmer ten minutes, until slightly thickened. Add the chopped parsley. Spread the mashed potatoes in a greased baking pan (9 x 9 x 2 in.). Flake the drained tuna over the potatoes and spoon sauce over all. Bake in a moderately hot oven for twenty minutes.

A FAVORITE RECIPE
Tuna Pancakes

Two eggs, beaten light with
One-half cup milk
One-half cup sifted flour
One-fourth teaspoon coarse ground
    black pepper
One-half teaspoon parsley flakes
One-eighth teaspoon paprika
One can (7½ oz.) tuna fish
Fat for frying, heated
Frying time: Until browned on each side
Servings: Four

In a bowl beat the eggs and milk. Add the flour gradually, beating until smooth. Season with pepper and parsley flakes and paprika. Break and stir in the tuna; stir until well blended. Drop by tablespoonfuls into the hot fat (⅛ in. deep). Fry, browning on each side.

KATHERINE ECKERD, *Harrisburg, Pa.*

Tuna Souffle

One-fourth cup butter or margarine
One-fourth cup flour
One-half teaspoon salt
Dash of pepper
One cup milk
Cook: Five minutes, about
One teaspoon Worcestershire sauce
One-half cup grated cheddar cheese
One can (7 oz.) tuna
Six egg yolks
Six egg whites
Oven temperature: 350 degrees
Bake: Forty-five to fifty minutes
Serves: Six

In a saucepan melt the butter or margarine. Stir in the flour, salt and pepper. Gradually blend in the milk, stirring smooth. Cook, stirring constantly, until sauce is thickened and smooth. Add the Worcestershire sauce, grated cheddar and flaked, drained tuna. In a bowl beat the egg yolks until light. Add a little of the cooked mixture to the yolks, return combination to the saucepan. In a bowl beat the egg whites until they hold soft peaks. Fold tuna cheese mixture into the egg whites. Pour into a well greased casserole (2 qts.) and bake in a moderate oven for forty-five to fifty minutes or until the souffle is high, well browned and firm in the center. Serve at once.

A FAVORITE RECIPE
Salmon Rolls

Three tablespoons flour
Two tablespoons butter
One-half teaspoon salt
One cup evaporated milk
Cook: Ten minutes
One egg, slightly beaten
Two cups (No. 2 can) well-drained flaked
    salmon
One tablespoon grated onion
One-third cup fine cracker crumbs
Two tablespoons lemon juice
Oven temperature: 350 degrees
Bake: Forty minutes (about)
Serves: Four

In a double boiler blend the flour, butter and salt; add the milk, stirring until smooth. Cook until thickened. Stir in the egg, salmon (all bones and heavy skin removed), onion, crumbs and lemon juice. Cool. Shape into rolls (4 x 1 in.); place on a greased baking sheet. Bake in a moderate oven until a golden brown. Serve with a tomato or mushroom sauce. Tuna or any cooked seafood may be used in place of the salmon.

MRS. A. F. TEMPLE, *Rosendale, N.Y.*

Salmon Tetrazzini

Eight ounces fine spaghetti
Boiling salted water
Cook: Until tender
Two tablespoons butter or margarine
One can (4 oz.) sliced mushrooms, drained
Sauté: Five minutes
Two tablespoons flour
One-half teaspoon salt
One-eighth teaspoon pepper
One-eighth teaspoon nutmeg
One can (one pound) salmon
Milk
Cook: Five minutes
Two tablespoons fine dry bread crumbs
Two tablespoons grated Parmesan cheese
Oven temperature: 350 degrees
Bake: Thirty minutes
Servings: Six

Cook the fine spaghetti in boiling salted water until tender. Drain and set aside. Melt the butter or margarine in a large heavy saucepan or skillet, add the drained sliced mushrooms and sauté until lightly browned. Stir in the flour, salt, pepper and nutmeg. Drain the liquid from the canned salmon and add enough milk to measure two cups. Gradually blend into the sautéed mushrooms and cook, stirring until thickened and smooth. Add the flaked salmon and drained spaghetti, mixing well. Transfer to a greased shallow baking pan or two pie plates (10 in.). Sprinkle with combined fine dry bread crumbs and grated Parmesan cheese. Bake in a moderate oven until lightly browned and piping hot.

A FAVORITE RECIPE
Upside Down Salmon

Two hard-cooked eggs, sliced
One can (1 lb.) salmon
One cup American cheese, diced
Two cups bread crumbs
One-fourth cup crushed pineapple
Three-fourths cup milk
One-fourth cup melted butter
One egg, beaten lightly
One tablespoon lemon juice
One-half teaspoon salt
One-eighth teaspoon pepper
Oven temperature: 350 degrees
Baking time: Thirty minutes
Servings: Six

Place the hard-cooked egg slices over the bottom of a well greased loaf pan (8 x 4 in.); spread one-half of the salmon (with heavy skin and bones removed) over the eggs. Mix the cheese, bread crumbs and pineapple in a bowl; add the milk, butter, egg, lemon juice and seasonings. Pour the mixture over the eggs; spread with the remaining salmon, over the top. Bake in a moderate oven until firm. Unmold upon a hot platter, garnish with parsley and lemon wedges. Serve sliced, plain or with a tomato or cream sauce.

ANNIE JAMES, *Burlington, N.C.*

Salmon Turnovers

Pastry for two-crust pie
One can (7 oz.) salmon
One-half can (10½ oz.) condensed celery soup
One tablespoon chopped parsley
One-fourth teaspoon salt
One tablespoon lemon juice
Pinch of dill
One egg yolk
Oven temperature: 375 degrees
Baking time: Twenty minutes
Yield: Six turnovers

Roll out the pastry and cut into six squares (6x6 in.). In a bowl flake the canned salmon, removing large bones and skin. Add the celery soup, parsley, salt, lemon juice and dill to the salmon; mix well. Place a tablespoon of this mixture upon each square of pastry. Fold dough over to make triangle; use fork to press edges together. Beat the egg yolk slightly in a cup with a fork. Brush over the turnovers; prick each with fork. Bake in a moderately hot oven until crisp and light brown. Serve hot.

A FAVORITE RECIPE
Salmon Steaks — Olive Sauce

Four medium-sized salmon steaks
Broiling temperature: 375 degrees
Broil: Ten minutes
One cup dairy sour cream
One-third cup sliced stuffed olives
One-third cup chopped cucumber
One tablespoon prepared horseradish
One-half teaspoon salt
One-fourth teaspoon pepper
Broil: Five minutes
Servings: Four

On a broiler pan place the salmon steaks. Broil the steaks in a moderately hot oven. Turn. Mix the sour cream in a bowl with the sliced olives, cucumber, horseradish, salt and pepper. Pour one-half of the mixture over the unbroiled side of the salmon. Broil for five minutes. Heat the remaining half of the olive sauce in a saucepan. Serve hot with the salmon steaks.

AMELIA FLEMMING, *Madison, Wisconsin*

Salmon Loaf

One can salmon (1 lb.)
Two-thirds cup evaporated milk
Two cups soft bread crumbs
One egg, beaten
One tablespoon minced parsley
Two tablespoons minced onion
One-half teaspoon salt
One-fourth teaspoon poultry seasoning
One-fourth teaspoon tabasco sauce
Oven temperature: 375 degrees
Baking time: Forty minutes
Servings: Four

In a bowl, combine the canned salmon and liquid with the evaporated milk and bread crumbs. Mix with a fork until well blended. Add beaten egg, parsley, onion, salt, poultry seasoning and tabasco. Mix well. Transfer to a greased loaf pan (9 x 4 x 3 in.). Bake in a moderately hot oven until loaf is firm in the center.

Barbecued Salmon Steaks

Four one inch salmon steaks (1½ to 2 pounds)
Two tablespoons butter or margarine
One-fourth cup chopped onion
Two tablespoons finely chopped green pepper
One clove garlic, crushed
Sauté: Five minutes, about
One cup tomato juice
Two tablespoons lemon juice
Two teaspoons sugar
One tablespoon Worcestershire sauce
Two teaspoons salt
One-fourth teaspoon pepper
Simmer: Five minutes
Broiler temperature: 500 degrees
Broil: Ten minutes, about
Serves: Four

Use fresh or defrosted frozen salmon steaks. In a saucepan melt the butter or margarine. Add the chopped onion, green pepper and crushed garlic. Sauté until soft. Add the tomato juice, lemon juice, sugar, Worcestershire sauce, salt and pepper and simmer together for five minutes. Lay the salmon steaks in a shallow pan and pour the sauce over top. Broil for about ten minutes or until the fish may be flaked easily with a fork. Serve at once.

A FAVORITE RECIPE
Boiled Salmon

Three pounds salmon steaks, cut (½ in.) thick
Cheesecloth for wrapping
One cup chopped carrots
One cup chopped onions
One cup chopped celery
One-half clove garlic, minced
Two tablespoons melted butter
Two quarts water
Three peppercorns
One bay leaf
One-fourth teaspoon salt
One teaspoon vinegar
One-sixteenth teaspoon ginger
Boiling time: Ten minutes
Cook: Ten minutes
One cup fish stock
One tablespoon butter
One tablespoon flour
Yolk one egg
Cooking time: One minute
Servings: Six

Wrap the salmon steaks in cheesecloth, tie securely. In a bowl, chop the carrots, onion, celery and garlic. Add the melted butter. Place in a deep kettle. Cover with the water. Add the peppercorns, bay leaf, salt, vinegar and ginger. Boil. Add the wrapped salmon steaks, cook. Unwrap the salmon. Place on a hot platter, keep hot. Take one cup of the fish stock, add the butter blending with the flour; add the stock with the beaten yolk of an egg, stir and cook. Serve over the salmon and serve at once with wild rice.

MRS. BEA MOLLOY, *Brooklyn, N.Y.*

Codfish Balls

One box (4 oz.) codfish
Three medium-sized potatoes, peeled and
   quartered
Boiling water
Cook: Fifteen minutes
One tablespoon butter
One egg, separated
One-fourth teaspoon pepper
Deep fat
Frying temperature: 350 degrees
Frying time: Three minutes
Serves: Four

Follow the directions on package to
freshen the codfish. Peel and quarter
the potatoes; cook in boiling water until
tender. Drain. Rice or force potatoes
through a sieve into a bowl. Beat in the
butter, egg yolk and pepper. Mix in the
codfish. Fold in the slightly beaten egg
white. Drop by rounded tablespoonfuls
into hot fat; fry until brown on all sides.
Serve immediately.

Baked Scallops in Shells

One cup milk
Six soda crackers, crumbled
Soaking time: Ten minutes
Two cups chopped par-boiled scallops
Two tablespoons melted butter
Three hard-cooked eggs, chopped
One-half teaspoon salt
One-eighth teaspoon pepper
One-eighth teaspoon tarragon
One-half cup buttered crumbs
Oven temperature: 400 degrees
Baking time: Twenty minutes
Parsley, pimiento strips
Servings: Four

Pour the milk over the crackers; let
stand. Add the scallops, butter, eggs and
seasonings. Heap in buttered scallop
shells; top with crumbs. Place the shells
in a shallow oven dish two-thirds full of
rock salt. Bake in a quick oven until
brown. Garnish with parsley and pimiento strips. Serve with lemon wedges.

Sea Food Dinner Azzurra

Four striped bass fillets (2 in. thick)
Four hard-shell clams (optional)
Four mussels (optional)
Twelve shrimp
One-half cup finely chopped onion
Two tablespoons olive oil
Cooking time: Three minutes
One cup clam broth
Four tablespoons butter
One-fourth cup finely minced parsley
One-half teaspoon salt
One-fourth teaspoon pepper
Cooking time: Seventeen minutes (about)
Four tablespoons lemon juice
Serves: Four

Have the striped bass cleaned and
sliced at the market into 2 inch fillets.
Scrub and wash the clams and mussels;
soak in water. With a scissors cut off the
beard (vegetation on the shell) from the
mussels. Shell and devein the shrimp
leaving tails intact. In an electric or
heavy skillet cook the onions in the oil
until straw-colored. Pour off excess oil.
Add the clam broth, butter, parsley, salt
and pepper. Place the clams and bass
(cut side down) in the skillet. Cover
tightly; cook 10 minutes. Put in mussels
and shrimp, cover and continue cooking
7 minutes longer. Sprinkle with lemon
juice. Serve from the skillet.

Stuffed Shrimp

Twelve large raw shrimp
One can (4 oz.) sliced mushrooms and
  liquid
One-fourth cup melted butter
One teaspoon instant flaked onion
Three-fourths cup dry bread crumbs
One tablespoon minced parsley
One-half teaspoon salt
Few grains cayenne
One-eighth teaspoon tarragon
One cup Bordeaux white wine
Oven temperature: 350 degrees
Baking time: Twenty-five minutes
Serves: Four, or more

Wash shrimp; remove shell, leaving the shell on tail intact. Devein. From the underside of the shrimp, with a sharp knife split the shrimp almost through. Place between two layers of waxed paper and mash flat with a rolling pin. Score the shrimp. This is necessary to prevent the shrimp from curling. Sandwich pairs of shrimp together with the mushroom filling. To make the filling: Combine the mushrooms and liquid, melted butter, flaked onion, bread crumbs, parsley, salt, cayenne and tarragon. Place the shrimp in a shallow baking dish. Pour in the wine. Bake in a moderate oven until the shrimp is tender and pink; baste occasionally. Serve on a hot platter with lemon wedges.

Horseradish Dressing

One-half cup heavy cream, whipped
One-half teaspoon salt
Four tablespoon grated horseradish
Three tablespoons real mayonnaise
Yield: One and one-half cups

Beat the cream in a bowl until stiff. Stir in salt, horseradish, mayonnaise.

Stuffed Fillets
With Shrimp Sauce

Two tablespoons butter or margarine
Two tablespoons flour
One teaspoon salt
One-fourth teaspoon pepper
One-eighth teaspoon tarragon
One-half cup milk
Cooking time: Ten minutes
One pound cooked shrimp, deveined, halved
Six fillets (sole or haddock)
One cup cooked seasoned spinach,
  well drained
One tablespoon lemon juice
Two teaspoons brown bouquet sauce
One cup white wine
Steaming time: Ten minutes
Serves: Six

In a heavy saucepan melt the butter; blend in the flour and seasonings. Add the milk; cook, stir until thick and smooth. Add the shrimp; set aside; keep warm. Place the fillets on a flat surface. Spread some of the combined spinach and lemon juice over each fillet. Roll up; secure with toothpicks. Brush sides with bouquet sauce. Place in heavy skillet. Pour wine

over fillets. Cover; simmer gently 10 minutes. Remove fillets to hot serving dish.

Stir the shrimp mixture into the liquid in the pan. Reheat until thoroughly heated.

A FAVORITE RECIPE
Fish Steak in Milk

Two pounds fish steaks, cut into serving
  pieces
One-fourth cup flour
One teaspoon salt
One-eighth teaspoon pepper
One small onion, chopped
One and one-half cups milk
Oven temperature: 350 degrees
Baking time: Twenty minutes
Three tablespoons butter or six strips
  bacon
Baking time: Fifteen minutes
Servings: Four

Dredge the prepared fish in the flour
with seasonings. Place in a baking dish;
add the onion and pour the milk over the
top. Bake for 20 minutes in a moderate
oven. Baste with the butter or spread
the bacon over the fish. Serve on a hot
platter, garnished with minced parsley.

MRS. ETHEL THOMAS, *Dover, N.J.*

Pan Fried Trout

Four one-pound trout, cleaned
One-fourth cup flour
One teaspoon salt, or less
One-eighth teaspoon freshly ground pepper
Three tablespoons olive oil
Two tablespoons butter
Cooking time: Ten minutes, about
One-half cup dry white wine
Four anchovy fillets, finely dropped
Two tablespoons finely chopped parsley
One tablespoon finely chopped mint
  (optional)
Two tablespoons lemon juice
Cooking time: Three minutes
Servings: Four

Rinse the cleaned fish thoroughly and
dry well. (The frozen fish need not be
thoroughly defrosted.) Combine the flour
with the salt and freshly ground pepper.
Dredge the fish in the seasoned flour.
Heat the olive oil and butter together
in a large heavy skillet. Add the fish and
cook and brown well, about five minutes
each side. When fish is cooked remove
to platter and keep hot. Add the wine to
the skillet drippings with the chopped
anchovy fillets, parsley, mint and lemon
juice and heat together briefly. Spoon
sauce over each fish as served.

Oven Fried Fish

One pound fish fillets
One-half cup milk
One and one-half teaspoons salt
One-half cup fine dry bread crumbs, or
  more
Two tablespoons butter or fat, melted
Oven temperature: 500 degrees
Baking time: Twelve to fifteen minutes
Servings: Four

Cut the fish into serving portions and
dip each piece into the milk that has
been seasoned with salt. Dip in the fine
dry bread crumbs and place on a greased
shallow baking pan. Sprinkle each piece
with the melted butter or fat and bake
in a very hot oven for twelve to fifteen
minutes or until crisply browned. The
fish will flake easily with a fork when
completely cooked.

A FAVORITE RECIPE
Apple Creole Baked Fish

One white fish (5 lbs.) cleaned, boned
One tablespoon salt
Three cups bread crumbs
Two tablespoons chopped onion
Two tablespoons melted butter
One-fourth teaspoon salt
One-half teaspoon poultry seasoning
One-sixteenth teaspoon pepper
Five tablespoons apple sauce
Three tablespoons margarine (melted
  for basting)
Three tablespoons butter
One-half cup minced green pepper
One-half cup chopped onion
One clove garlic
Two tomatoes, peeled, cut into eighths
Simmering time: Ten minutes
One teaspoon sugar
One small bay leaf
One teaspoon salt
One-fourth teaspoon pepper
One and one-half cups apple sauce
Oven temperature: 400 degrees
Bake: Ten minutes to pound
Serves: Six

Have the fish cleaned and boned at
the market. Rub the inside and out with
salt. In a bowl combine for the dressing,
the bread crumbs, onion, butter, salt,
poultry seasoning, pepper and apple
sauce. Fill the cavity of the fish with the
dressing; sew edges together. Brush with
the melted margarine. For sauce: Heat
the butter in a saucepan, add the minced
green pepper, onion, garlic and tomatoes;
simmer. Add the sugar, bay leaf, salt,
pepper and the remaining apple sauce;
pour over the fish. Bake in a quick oven.
Baste frequently with the sauce. Serve
hot with the sauce; garnish with parsley.

MRS. CAROLE HAEUSSLER, *Miami, Florida*

Sherry-Baked Fish Fillets

Four flounder fillets or other fresh fish (one
  and one-half pounds or more)
Salt and pepper
Four large mushrooms
Four tablespoons butter
Four tablespoons dry sherry
Bake: Twenty minutes, about
Serves: Four

Cut sizable double thicknesses of foil.
Lay a fish fillet on each and sprinkle with
salt and pepper. Slice a mushroom over
each fillet and top with a tablespoon butter. Fold up the sides of foil for each
package and add the tablespoon of dry
sherry to each. Wrap each package

securely and lay in hot ashes of a charcoal fire for about 20 minutes, turning
once. Good served with chilled dry
sherry.

Fish Fillets a la Marguery

One pound fish fillets (eight small)
One tablespoon melted butter
Salt and pepper
Two tablespoons finely chopped onion
Oven temperature: 450 degrees
Bake: Twelve minutes
Two tablespoons butter
Two tablespoons flour
Two-thirds cup milk
One-third cup light cream
Cook: Five to eight minutes
One tablespoon lemon juice
One tablespoon sherry wine
One-half teaspoon salt
One tablespoon grated Parmesan cheese
Dash of pepper
Heat: Five minutes
Two beaten egg yolks
Brown: Three to five minutes
Serves: Four

In a large shallow baking dish arrange
the fillets in pairs, one on top of the
other. Brush with one tablespoon of butter and sprinkle lightly with salt and pepper. Scatter the chopped onion over top
and bake in a very hot oven until fish
flakes easily with fork.
Meanwhile melt the two tablespoons
of butter in the upper half of a double
boiler, blend in the flour; gradually add
the milk and cream. Place over hot
water and cook until the mixture thickens, stirring constantly. Add the lemon
juice, sherry, salt, grated cheese and pepper and heat thoroughly. Just before serving pour sauce over the well beaten egg
yolks in a bowl, stirring while adding.
Pour sauce over fish and brown under
broiler. Garnish with water cress or parsley and serve at once.

A FAVORITE RECIPE
Pickled Herring

Two large salt herrings, skin and bones
  removed
One-half cup vinegar
One-half cup water
One large onion, sliced very thin
Two teaspoons peppercorns
One-half teaspoon sugar
Three or four bay leaves
Standing time: Overnight in the
  refrigerator
Servings: Four

Remove the heavy skin and bones from
the fish. Cut the herring into pieces (1½
in.). Rinse the fish in cold water, drain
thoroughly. Combine the vinegar, water,
onion, peppercorns, sugar and bay leaves
in a bowl. Place the herring in a jar with
cap, pour the vinegar mixture over all.
Shake. Let stand in refrigerator until
needed.

MRS. CHARLES O. SELVIG, *New York, N.Y.*

Poached Scallops with Green Sauce

One pound sea scallops
One-half cup dry white wine
One small onion, chopped
Sprig of parsley
One teaspoon salt
One-eighth teaspoon pepper
One-half cup water
Simmer: Seven minutes
Three-fourths cup mayonnaise
Three-fourths cup finely chopped washed
   spinach
One-fourth cup finely chopped parsley
One-fourth cup finely chopped green onion
One tablespoon finely chopped fresh dill or
One-half teaspoon dried dill
Yield: One cup sauce
Serves: Four

Place the scallops in a saucepan and add the dry white wine, chopped onion, sprig of parsley, teaspoon of salt, pepper and half cup of water. Bring to a boil, lower heat and simmer gently for seven minutes or until tender. Prepare the green sauce by combining the mayonnaise with the finely chopped raw spinach, parsley, green onion and dill. Mix well. Serve with the cooked and drained scallops at once or when both are well chilled.

A FAVORITE RECIPE
Scallops and Rice

One and one-half pounds scallops, sliced
   crosswise (¼ in. thick)
One-fourth cup butter, melted
Cooking time: Three minutes
One can (4 oz.) pimiento, cut into strips
One cucumber (7 in.) cut lengthwise into
   strips (ten)
One teaspoon salt
Simmering time: Three minutes
One cup catsup
One and one-half cups milk
One and one-half teaspoons cornstarch
Two tablespoons sherry
Cooking time: Three minutes
Servings: Six

Wash and slice the scallops. Dry. Heat the butter in a skillet; cook the scallops, turning several times. Add the pimiento, cucumber and salt; cover. Simmer. Stir in the catsup and one cup of the milk, mixing thoroughly. Add the cornstarch to the remaining milk, stirring in a cup until smooth. Add the mixture to the scallops stirring until well blended. Blend in the sherry. Serve hot with hot fluffy rice.

MRS. A. DONATO, *Rochester, N.Y.*

Tangy Broiled Scallops

Two pounds scallops, fresh or frozen
One-fourth cup butter or margarine
One-fourth cup grated onion and juice
Two teaspoons dry mustard
Two tablespoons lemon juice
One-fourth cup brown sugar
One-half teaspoon salt
One-eighth teaspoon pepper
Broiler temperature: 500 degrees
Broil: Fifteen minutes
Servings: Four, or more

Rinse the scallops and drain on absorbent paper. Defrost frozen if used. Cut very large scallops in half, aiming at uniformity of size. Arrange scallops in a greased shallow baking pan or tray. In a small saucepan melt the butter or margarine. Stir in the grated onion and juice, dry mustard, lemon juice, brown sugar, salt and pepper. Mix well. Spoon combination over the scallops. Broil about three inches from the source of heat for fifteen minutes about, basting with the sauce every five minutes. Broil until nicely browned on top. Serve at once.

A FAVORITE RECIPE
Holiday Scalloped Oysters

One pint small oysters or two containers
   (8 oz. each) drained
Two and one-half cups soda crackers
   coarsely broken
One-half teaspoon salt
One-eighth teaspoon pepper
One-third cup melted butter
One-half teaspoon Worcestershire sauce
One cup liquid (oyster liquid and milk)
Oven temperature: 350 degrees
Bake: Thirty minutes
Serves: Four

Drain the oysters reserving liquid. In a bowl mix the cracker crumbs with the salt, pepper and butter, tossing until the crumbs are well coated with butter. Spread one-third of the mixture over bottom of casserole (1½ qts.); cover with a layer of oysters. Repeat the layers. Add the Worcestershire sauce to the milk and oyster liquid. Pour ⅔ of milk mixture over contents of casserole. Sprinkle the remaining cracker crumbs over top. Sprinkle remaining milk and oyster liquid over all. Bake in a moderate oven until the top is lightly browned. Serve with a mixed green salad.

MRS. D. KINSELLA, *Waterloo, N.Y.*

California Oyster Bake

Four tablespoons butter or margarine
Three tablespoons flour
One-half teaspoon salt
One-fourth teaspoon cayenne pepper
One and one-third cups milk
Cook: Five to eight minutes
One teaspoon grated onion
Two tablespoons lemon juice
One teaspoon Worcestershire sauce
One pint oysters, drained
Two or three slices buttered toast, cut in
   strips
Oven temperature: 350 degrees
Bake: Fifteen minutes
Servings: Three or four

In a saucepan, melt the butter or margarine. Stir in the flour, salt and pepper. Gradually blend in the milk. Cook, stirring constantly, until thickened. Remove from heat and add the grated onion, lemon juice and Worcestershire. Fold in the oysters. Pour into a shallow baking

dish or individual ramekins and top with narrow strips of toast, buttered side up. Bake in a moderate oven for fifteen minutes. Serve piping hot.

A FAVORITE RECIPE
Scalloped Scallops

One-fourth cup butter, melted
Four cups soft bread crumbs
One teaspoon grated onion
One teaspoon finely minced parsley
One teaspoon minced chives
One tablespoon lemon juice
One and one-fourth teaspoons salt
Cook: Five minutes
One and one-half pounds scallops
Oven temperature: 400 degrees
Bake: Twenty minutes, about
Serves: Six

In a deep skillet melt the butter. Add the bread crumbs, onion, parsley, chives, lemon juice and salt. Toss together while cooking. In a well buttered casserole arrange layers of the bread crumb mixture and scallops (if the scallops are large cut into quarters) having the top layer of bread crumb mixture. Bake in a quick oven until a golden brown. Serve hot from the casserole.

MRS. ARTHUR NEWMAN, *St. Petersburg, Fla.*

Poached Halibut with
Shrimp Sauce

Two pound piece of halibut, cut two
   inches thick
One cup milk
One cup water
One-half teaspoon salt
Simmer: Thirty minutes, about
One can (4½ oz.) tiny Pacific shrimp
Two tablespoons butter or margarine
Two tablespoons flour
One-half cup shrimp liquid
Three-fourths cup milk broth
Salt if necessary
Cook: Five minutes
Serves: Four to six

Wipe the fish with a damp cloth, then wrap in a piece of cheesecloth leaving tabs of several inches on each end to simplify its removal from pan after poaching. Combine the milk, water and salt in a saucepan and heat to the boiling point. Add the fish, cover and simmer gently until the fish flakes with a fork. (If liquid does not cover fish, turn it once during the simmering time.) When cooked, place upon a cutting board; unwrap. Remove skin and bones, cutting fish into serving portions. Set aside and keep warm. To make the sauce: Drain the liquid from the canned shrimp. In a saucepan melt the butter or margarine. Stir in the flour and gradually add the shrimp liquid. Add the three-fourths cup of milk broth in which fish was poached, stirring to keep smooth. Add shrimp and cook, stirring constantly until the sauce thickens slightly. Taste to see if salt is needed. Serve sauce hot over portions of fish. Garnish with parsley.

Deviled Stuffed Lobster Tails

One package (1½ lbs.) frozen South
 African rock lobster tails, cooked
 according to package directions
Two tablespoons butter or margarine
One-fourth cup minced onions
One can (3 oz.) sliced mushrooms
One-fourth cup minced green pepper
Sauté: Five minutes
Two tablespoons flour
One-fourth teaspoon salt
One-eighth teaspoon pepper
One-half teaspoon dry mustard
One tablespoon Worcestershire sauce
Few drops of tabasco sauce
One cup milk or cream
One cup clam broth
Cook: Ten minutes
Two egg yolks, slightly beaten
One-fourth cup Spanish sherry
Oven temperature: 400 degrees
Bake: Fifteen minutes
Serves: Six

Cook the rock lobster tails according
to package directions. Remove the lobster
meat; cut into chunks. Reserve the lobster tails. In a heavy skillet melt the butter; add the onion, mushrooms and green
pepper. Sauté until the onions are straw-
colored. Stir in the flour, salt, pepper,
mustard, Worcestershire and tabasco
sauce. Gradually stir in the milk and
clam broth; cook until slightly thickened.
Stir some of the sauce into the egg yolks;
then add to the sauce in the skillet. Add
the lobster meat and sherry. Spoon the
mixture into the lobster tails. Bake in a
quick oven until the top is golden. Serve
with lemon wedges.

A FAVORITE RECIPE
Continental Lobster

One-half cup olive oil
Two cloves garlic, minced
Sautéing time: Until lightly browned
One-half cup diced (¼ in.) celery
One-half cup diced (¼ in.) carróts
Three-fourths cup diced onion
One and one-half cups sliced mushrooms
One-half teaspoon pepper
Two teaspoons salt
Simmer: Twenty-five minutes
Three cups partially drained tomatoes
One-half teaspoon curry powder
One-half teaspoon basil
Simmering time: Fifteen minutes
One-half cup butter, heated
One and one-half pounds lobster (cut
 in 1½ in. pieces)
Sauté: Ten minutes
One teaspoon minced parsley
One-half cup light rum
Cooking time: Five minutes
Serves: Six

In a heavy skillet heat the olive oil;
sauté the garlic. Add the vegetables,
mushrooms, and seasonings. Simmer. Add
tomatoes, curry and basil. Simmer. Heat
the butter in a skillet, sauté the lobster.
Add to the tomato mixture with the parsley and rum. Cook. Serve at once with
hot rolls.

MRS. MARTIN VAN HAASTEREN, *Miami, Fla.*

Rock Lobster Tails — Butterfly Style

Six South African rock lobster tails, frozen
 (3 to 5 oz. each) defrosted
Two eggs, slightly beaten
One-half cup flour
One-half teaspoon salt
One-eighth teaspoon curry powder
One-half cup water
One teaspoon soy sauce
Fat for frying
Frying temperature: 365 degrees
Frying time: Three minutes
Serves: Four

Defrost the South African lobster tails.
With a sharp knife split the tail in half
lengthwise. Carefully remove the shell,
leaving the shell-end of the tail intact.
In a bowl beat the eggs slightly. Add
the flour, salt, curry, water and soy sauce.
Beat until smooth. Dip the white meat
of the lobster into the batter. Fry in deep
fat until golden. Remove to absorbent
paper. Keep warm. Repeat procedure
with the remaining tails. Serve immediately with a tartar sauce.

Broiled Rock Lobster Tails

With a sharp knife cut down through
the middle of the hard shell and solid
meat of four (3 to 5 oz. each) frozen
South African lobster tails. Grasp tail in
both hands and open flat. Spread with
butter and place 4 inches below heating
unit in preheated broiler. Broil 8 to 10
minutes. Serve with drawn butter or
browned butter sauce.

Baked Stuffed Lobster

Four boiled lobsters (1-½lbs. each)
Four tablespoons butter or margarine
One-third cup flour
One teaspoon salt
One teaspoon paprika
One-half teaspoon tarragon
Three cups milk
One cup grated cheddar cheese
One-fourth cup sherry
One-half cup soft bread crumbs, mixed
    with
One tablespoon melted butter
Oven temperature: 350 degrees
Baking time: Twenty minutes
Serves: Four

Lobster to be good must be fresh. Select dark green, lively lobsters. Cook in briskly boiling water 15 to 20 minutes, then plunge into cold water.

Partially split lobsters from head to tail. Remove the meat; discard inedible contents of the body. Cut meat into large chunks. Reserve. In a saucepan melt the butter. Blend in the flour and seasonings. Gradually add the milk; cook, stirring until thick and smooth. Remove; add cheese, stirring until melted. Add the sherry. Add lobster pieces. Fill and heap each shell with mixture; cover with soft buttered bread crumbs. Lay filled shell in shallow baking pan allowing the tails to curl around slightly on edge of pan. Bake in a moderate oven until brown. Garnish with paprika. Serve immediately.

How To Tackle That Lobster

1. Lift out tail meat in one piece with oyster fork. Cut, and dip in drawn butter; then eat.

2. Remove small claws from body with twisting motion of hand. Then press them between teeth to release sweet meat and juices.

3. Break arms of lobster from body, then break claws from the arms. Using oyster fork, remove meat from arms, dip in butter and eat.

4. Crack hard shell at the base of each claw with stout nutcracker. This makes it easier to extract meat.

5. Remove meat from each claw in one piece. Cut, and with oyster fork dip meat in drawn butter and eat.

A FAVORITE RECIPE

Baked Stuffed Lobster Tails

Six frozen lobster tails, thawed, cut
    lengthwise
One-half pound cooked, peeled shrimp,
    cut into small pieces
One cup soft bread crumbs
One-half teaspoon salt
One-half teaspoon pepper
One-half teaspoon minced parsley
One-half cup olive oil
Oven temperature: 375 degrees
Baking time: Thirty minutes
Servings: Six

Cut the thawed lobster tails into halves with a sharp knife. For the stuffing: In a bowl mix the cut shrimp, bread crumbs, salt, pepper, parsley and one-half the oil. Stuff the lobster tails with the mixture. Pour the remaining oil in a shallow baking pan. Place the lobsters in the pan. Bake in a moderately hot oven. Serve hot.

MRS. PETER CORRADI, *Brooklyn, N.Y.*

Mussels in Tomato Sauce

Two quarts mussels, scrubbed
Two cloves garlic, crushed
Two tablespoons olive oil
Sauté: Until golden
One can (No. 2½) tomatoes, drained
One-half teaspoon sugar
One-half teaspoon salt
One-fourth teaspoon crumbled oregano
One-fourth teaspoon basil leaves
Simmer: Fifteen minutes
Steam: Six to eight minutes
Serves: Four

Scrub the mussels under running water; trim off the beards. In a heavy kettle, combine the garlic with the olive oil. Sauté until golden. Add the drained tomatoes, sugar, salt, oregano and basil. Simmer for 15 minutes then press mixture through a coarse sieve. Return to the kettle, add the scrubbed mussels, cover and steam for six to eight minutes, or until the shells open. Serve the sauce or broth with the mussels. Dip the mussels in the sauce, drink what remains.

A FAVORITE RECIPE
Shrimp Special

Five tablespoons butter, heated
Four, or less, cloves garlic, minced
Two tablespoons minced parsley
One-half teaspoon salt
One-eighth teaspoon pepper
One teaspoon soy sauce
One teaspoon Worcestershire sauce
Three-fourths pound jumbo shrimp,
    washed, cleaned, deveined
One-half teaspoon paprika
Broiler oven temperature: 450 degrees
Broiling time: Six minutes
Cooking time: Two minutes
Two tablespoons sherry
Cooking time: One minute
One cup brown rice, cooked
Servings: Three

Mix in a heavy skillet, the butter, garlic, parsley, salt, pepper, soy and Worcestershire sauce. Arrange the prepared shrimp on top of the butter sauce. Sprinkle the paprika over the top. Place the skillet in a broiler 450 degrees, having the skillet five inches from the heat. Broil. Remove the skillet to stove, cook for two minutes over a low flame. Sprinkle with the sherry cooking for another minute. Serve on hot plates with the browned rice and a green cooked vegetable.

MRS. ELEANOR A. LAUFFER, *Brooklyn, N.Y.*

Mussels in Wine

Two quarts mussels, scrubbed
One cup white wine
One medium-sized onion, chopped
Three tablespoons chopped parsley
Steam: Six to eight minutes
One-fourth cup butter
Servings: Four

Scrub the mussels under running water; trim off the beards. In a heavy kettle combine the wine, chopped onion and parsley. Add the mussels; cover and steam for six to eight minutes or until the shells open. Remove mussels and keep warm. Increase the heat under the broth to reduce to one-half the volume. Stir in the butter and serve the sauce or broth with the mussels, dipping each in the broth and drinking what remains.

Deviled Clams

One-fourth cup butter or other fat
One-fourth cup finely chopped onion
One clove garlic, crushed
One-half cup finely chopped celery
Sauté: Ten minutes, about
One tablespoon flour
One tablespoon chili sauce
Three-fourths teaspoon salt
One-fourth teaspoon pepper
One-fourth teaspoon thyme
Dash of tabasco
Two cans (7½ oz. each) minced clams
    and juice
One beaten egg
One-half cup cracker meal
Two tablespoons chopped parsley
Two tablespoons butter, melted
One-half cup fine dry bread crumbs
Oven temperature: 400 degrees
Bake: Ten minutes, about
Servings: Six

Melt the butter or fat in a large heavy skillet. Add the finely chopped onion, garlic and celery. Sauté over low heat until tender. Stir in the flour, chili sauce, salt, pepper, thyme, tabasco, minced clams and juice. Mix well. Add the beaten egg and stir in the cracker meal and chopped parsley. Spoon into greased scallop shells or small ramekins. Melt the two tablespoons of butter and stir in the fine dry bread crumbs. Scatter the buttered crumbs over the clam mixture in the shells. Place in a quick oven for ten minutes or until browned and piping hot. Serve at once.

A FAVORITE RECIPE
Shrimp Supreme

Two tablespoons butter, melted in a
    double boiler
Two tablespoons flour
Two cups milk
Cooking time: Fifteen minutes
One tablespoon Worcestershire sauce
One-half teaspoon salt
One-sixteenth teaspoon paprika
One can (8½ oz.) peas, drained
One pound large cooked shrimp
Cooking time: Five minutes
Four slices hot buttered toast
Servings: Four

Melt the butter in the top of a double boiler; add the flour, mixing until smooth. Pour the milk in slowly, stirring constantly and cooking until thick. Add the Worcestershire sauce, salt and paprika. When the sauce is cooked, add the drained peas and shrimp. Heat thoroughly, stirring until well mixed. Serve on hot buttered toast.

MRS. FLORENCE ARMSTRONG, *Brooklyn, N.Y.*

Scampi

Two pounds jumbo shrimp
Two or more cloves garlic, crushed
Two teaspoons salt
One teaspoon dry mustard
One-fourth teaspoon pepper
Four tablespoons finely chopped parsley
    (two tablespoons dried parsley flakes)
Six tablespoons lemon juice
One-half cup olive oil
Marinate: Two hours
Broiler temperature: 500 degrees
Broil: Six to eight minutes
Serves: Four to six

Shell and devein shrimp leaving tails intact. With a sharp knife split shrimp almost through for two-thirds of length from inner arc leaving the two halves connected at tail end. Flatten split portion. Tail will curl in broiling. In a bowl combine crushed or finely chopped garlic with the salt, mustard and pepper. Add the finely chopped parsley, lemon juice and olive oil.

Pour over the prepared shrimp, cover and let marinate for two hours. To broil arrange shrimp in a shallow pan and spoon on the marinade. Broil about four inches from the source of heat until shrimp are pink and white and lightly browned. Don't overcook. Note: Many restaurants prepare shrimp in the shell. They are split and deveined and broiled in the shell.

A FAVORITE RECIPE
Lobster Tails

Four rock lobster tails (thawed if frozen)
Boiling water to cover
Cooking time: Ten minutes
One can (10½ oz.) frozen condensed
    cream of shrimp soup
One-fourth cup light cream
One tablespoon lemon juice
One tablespoon sherry wine
One tablespoon, or less, minced parsley
One-half teaspoon dry mustard
One tablespoon, or more, grated Parmesan
    cheese
Broiling oven temperature: 375 degrees
Broiling time: Ten minutes (until brown)
Serves: Four

Place the lobster tails in a deep kettle; cover with boiling water; cook. With a sharp knife, or kitchen scissors remove the meat from the shells, keeping the shells intact. Cut the meat into pieces (½ in.). In a saucepan combine the soup, cream, lemon juice, sherry, parsley and mustard. Heat, stirring until well blended. Add the lobster meat. Spoon into the lobster shells, sprinkling with Parmesan or another cheese. Broil four to five inches from the flame until the cheese is lightly browned.

MRS. JAMES MC GUIGAN, *Elmhurst, N.Y.*

Seafood Trio with Rice

One cup raw rice
One-half cup chopped onion
One clove garlic, crushed
One-fourth cup chopped green pepper
One-fourth cup butter or margarine
Sauté: Five minutes, about
Two tablespoons flour
One can (No. 2½) tomatoes
One and one-half teaspoons salt
One-half teaspoon chili powder
One-half teaspoon sugar
One-eighth teaspoon pepper
One-eighth teaspoon cayenne
Two tablespoons grated Parmesan cheese
One-half pound scallops, bay or cut small
One can (5 oz.) lobster meat
One pint oysters
Oven temperature: 350 degrees
Bake: Twenty minutes, about
Servings: Six

Cook the cup of raw rice according to package directions. In the meantime sauté the onion, garlic and green pepper in the butter or margarine until very lightly browned. Stir in the flour. Blend in the canned tomatoes, using a spoon to break up the large pieces, add the salt, chili powder, sugar, pepper, cayenne and grated Parmesan cheese. Cook until thickened slightly. Add the scallops and flaked lobster meat. Arrange the cooked rice over the bottom of a greased shallow casserole or baking dish (9 x 9 x 2 in.). Lay oysters over rice. Stir oyster liquid into the sauce and pour over all. Bake in a moderate oven for about twenty minutes, until thoroughly heated through. Oysters and scallops will cook in that time.

Crab Supreme

Two tablespoons butter
Two tablespoons flour
One cup hot milk
Cooking time: Ten minutes in a double boiler
Three egg yolks, beaten light
One-half cup mayonnaise
One can (9 oz.) crabmeat (all cartilage removed) flaked
One-half teaspoon salt
One-eighth teaspoon pepper
One dash cayenne
Three egg whites, beaten stiff
One-sixteenth teaspoon paprika
Oven temperature: 400 degrees
Baking time: Twenty-five minutes, about
Servings: Six

In the top of a double boiler, melt the butter, stir in the flour. Add the milk, cook, stirring until smooth and thick. Fold in the egg yolks, mixed with the mayonnaise, blending thoroughly. Add the flaked crabmeat and seasonings. Beat the egg whites in a bowl until stiff, fold in the crabmeat mixture. Turn into a well buttered casserole (10 in.). Sprinkle with paprika. Bake in a hot oven until puffed and lightly browned. Serve from the casserole.

MRS. R. L. ROSENTRETER, *Rye, N.Y.*

A FAVORITE RECIPE
Deviled Crab Meat-Mushrooms

One package mushroom soup mix
Two cups milk
Two tablespoons minced parsley
One-half teaspoon horseradish
Two teaspoons lemon juice
One teaspoon prepared mustard
Cooking time: Until thick
Two cups crab meat, flaked, cartilage removed
Three-fourths cup buttered soft bread crumbs
Oven temperature: 350 degrees
Baking time: Thirty minutes
Servings: Six

In a saucepan mix the mushroom soup mix with the milk. Add the parsley, horseradish, lemon juice and mustard. Cook, stirring until thick. Stir in the prepared crab meat. Fill individual casserole dishes with the mixture. Sprinkle buttered bread crumbs over the top. Bake in a moderate oven until lightly browned.

MRS. THOMAS DEL VERDE, *Wanaque, N.J.*

Pan Roast of Oysters

Four tablespoons butter or margarine
Two tablespoons finely chopped onion
Sauté: Five minutes
One pint oysters, drained
Cook: Until edges curl
One tablespoon Worcestershire sauce
Two teaspoons paprika
One-half teaspoon salt
Two cups milk
Heat: Thoroughly
Two cups heavy cream
Heat: Thoroughly
Four slices crisp toast
Servings: Four

In a saucepan, melt the butter or margarine. Add the onion and sauté until soft. Add the oysters and cook just until the edges curl. Add the Worcestershire sauce, paprika, salt and milk. Heat rapidly. Blend in the heavy cream and heat, do not boil. Serve over slices of toast in soup plates permitting some of the oysters to ride atop the toast.

A FAVORITE RECIPE
Baked Crabmeat

One-half cup heavy cream
Two teaspoons minced onion
One and one-half teaspoons prepared mustard
One and one-half teaspoons salt
Three tablespoons flour
Two cups milk
Cook: Until thick
Two egg yolks, well beaten
Two teaspoons Worcestershire sauce
One pound crabmeat, fresh or canned
Two egg whites, beaten stiff
Oven temperature: 375 degrees
Bake: Forty-five minutes
Serves: Six, or more

In a heavy saucepan combine the heavy cream, onion, mustard and salt. Stir in the flour, adding the milk gradually. Cook, stirring constantly until thick. Stir in the well beaten egg yolks, Worcestershire sauce and crabmeat (with all cartilage removed). Fold in the stiffly beaten egg whites. Turn into a well greased casserole (10 in.). Place in a pan of hot water. Bake in a moderately hot oven until firm in the center. Serve hot from the casserole.

MRS. LILLIAN HOLMES, *Baltimore, Maryland*

Oyster Potato Chip Scallop

One-half cup butter or margarine
One-half cup cracker crumbs
One-half cup finely crumbled potato chips
One cup crumbled stale bread
One pint oysters
Salt and pepper
One-third cup heavy cream
One-fourth teaspoon celery seed
One-eighth teaspoon pepper
One-eighth teaspoon mace
Oven temperature: 350 degrees
Bake: Forty minutes
Serves: Four

In a saucepan melt the butter or margarine. Stir in the cracker crumbs, finely crumbled potato chips and crumbled stale bread. Mix well. Spread half the crumbs over the bottom of a shallow baking dish (9 or 10 in.) and lay drained oysters over crumbs. Season lightly with salt and pepper. Scatter remaining crumbs over oysters. Stir cream, celery seed, pepper and mace together. Spoon over the top layer of crumbs. Bake in a moderate oven until crisp and well browned. Mark into four parts and use a broad spatula to serve.

Lobster Sauce

Three tablespoons butter or margarine
Two tablespoons flour
One teaspoon salt
One-eighth teaspoon pepper
One cup milk
One cup heavy cream
Cook: Five minutes, about
Two egg yolks
Cook: Two minutes
One cup lobster meat (one 5 oz. can)
One tablespoon lemon juice
Heat: Five minutes, or more
Yield: Three cups

In a saucepan melt the butter or margarine. Stir in the flour, salt and pepper. Gradually blend in the milk and heavy cream. Cook, stirring constantly until sauce thickens. In a small bowl beat the egg yolks. Add a little of the cooked mixture to the yolks and return combination to the saucepan. Cook for two minutes, stirring. Add the lobster meat (cartilage removed), lemon juice and heat through.

cracked ice in a soup plate. Imbed a small cocktail glass of the sauce in the ice in the center of the plate. To make the sauce, combine the remaining ingredients. Serve with lemon, oyster crackers, tabasco sauce and horseradish.

Oysters Rockefeller

Two dozen oysters on the half-shell
One-half cup cooked spinach, sieved
One tablespoon minced onion
One tablespoon minced parsley
One-fourth teaspoon celery salt
Dash of cayenne
Four tablespoons butter
Cooking time: Three minutes
Six tablespoons fine bread crumbs
Oven temperature: 450 degrees
Baking time: Twelve minutes
Servings: Four

For each portion, arrange six oysters on the deep half of their shell and set in rock salt in a baking dish or pie plate (9 in.). Cook the spinach, onion, seasonings and butter until well blended. Add the crumbs. Spread the mixture over the oysters. Bake in a very hot oven until the oysters are piping hot. Garnish with sliced lemon and serve.

Seafood Platters

*Two (1½ lbs. each) cooked lobsters
**Sixteen cooked shrimp
***Sixteen steamed clams
Three-fourths pound cooked crabmeat, chilled
Eight slices tomato
Chilling time: Two hours
One cup coleslaw
Two lemons, sliced thin
One hard-cooked egg, sliced
Four sprigs parsley
One cup mayonnaise
One cup thick French salad dressing
Serves: Four

Using a sharp heavy knife split the lobster from end to end starting at the head. Remove stomach and intestinal vein. Crack the claws. Set on a platter; cover. Remove the shell and vein from the shrimp. Place in a bowl; cover. Remove half the clam shell from the clams. Place on platter; cover. Chill all seafood in the refrigerator. On each cold platter arrange one-half of a cold lobster, four shrimp, four clams, a lettuce cup of crabmeat and slices of tomato on a bed of coleslaw. Garnish with lemon and egg slices and parsley. Serve with a pitcher of mayonnaise or a thick French salad dressing.
Note: *Cook lobster 5 minutes to each pound.
   **Cook shrimp 7 minutes.
   ***Steam clams in ½ inch boiling, salted water about 8 minutes.

Oysters on the Half-Shell

Two dozen oysters on the half-shell
Three-fourths cup tomato catsup
Two tablespoons minced celery hearts
One tablespoon lemon juice or vinegar
One tablespoon horseradish sauce
One-fourth teaspoon salt
One-half tablespoon Worcestershire sauce
Four drops tabasco sauce
Servings: Four

For each portion, arrange six oysters on the deep half of their shell and set in

Meat

A FAVORITE RECIPE
Stuffed London Broil

One tablespoon butter, melted
One-half pound chicken livers, cut into
 pieces (¼ in.)
One onion, chopped
One-fourth pound mushrooms, sliced thin
Cook: Five minutes
One-eighth teaspoon basil
Three tablespoons minced parsley
Three-fourths teaspoon salt
One-fourth teaspoon pepper
One cup bread crumbs
One-fourth cup consomme
Cook: Five minutes
One flank steak (2 to 3 lbs.)
One teaspoon salt
One-half teaspoon pepper
One-half taspoon oil (for pan)
Browning time: Fifteen minutes
One-half cup chili sauce
One-half cup tomato juice
Oven temperature: 300 degrees
Baking time: One and one-half hours
Serves: Six

In a skillet melt the butter; add the
chicken livers, onion and mushrooms;
cook, stirring frequently. Stir in the seasonings, bread crumbs and consomme.
Cook. Have the butcher score the steak.
Season with salt and pepper; spread the
cooked dressing over the steak. Roll carefully, binding with skewers or tie with
thread. Oil a Dutch oven or heavy skillet;
brown the steak roll on all sides. Add the
chili sauce and tomato juice. Cover and
bake in a very slow oven until tender;
baste frequently, adding hot water to pan
if needed. Serve on a hot platter with
green vegetable.

MRS. JEAN URASHKA, *Ansonia, Conn.*

Swiss Steak

Two pounds round steak (cut one and
 one-half inches thick)
Flour
One tablespoon salad oil
Browning time: Five to ten minutes
One large onion, thinly sliced
One tablespoon sugar
One-half-teaspoon dry mustard
One-fourth teaspoon chili powder
Two teaspoons salt
One-fourth cup vinegar
One cup tomato juice
One cup tomato sauce
Simmer: Two hours, about
Serves: Six

Cut the round steak into six pieces.
Place on a board and sprinkle with flour.
Pound flour into meat with the edge of
a heavy saucer or a meat hammer. Heat
the salad oil in a heavy skillet. Add the
meat to the hot fat and brown quickly on
both sides. Add the sliced onion. In a
bowl stir together the sugar, dry mustard, chili powder and salt. Blend in the
vinegar, tomato juice and tomato sauce.
Pour over the meat and onions. Cover
tightly and simmer very slowly until
meat is very tender. Serve with the pan
gravy. Should the gravy become too
thick stir in enough water and bring to
a boil for the consistency preferred.

Beef Birds

One and one-half pounds round steak (cut
 one-half inch thick)
Two tablespoons butter or margarine
One medium-sized onion, chopped
One-half cup chopped celery and leaves
Sautéing time: Five to ten minutes
Two cups soft bread crumbs
One-half teaspoon salt, or more
One-eighth teaspoon pepper
One-fourth teaspoon savory
Two tablespoons butter or margarine
Browning time: Ten to fifteen minutes
One-fourth cup water
Simmering time: One and one-fourth hours
Servings: Four

Cut the round steak into strips approximately three by four inches and
pound with mallet or the edge of a
heavy plate upon a board to flatten and
tenderize on both sides. In a skillet melt
the butter or margarine. Add the
chopped onion and celery and sauté until tender. Remove from the heat, stir in
the soft bread crumbs, salt, pepper and
savory. Divide the bread crumb mixture
between the strips of pounded meat.
Fold meat over stuffing and skewer in
place with a toothpick. Melt the second
measure of butter or margarine in the
skillet. Add the meat rolls and brown
quickly on all sides. Add the water;
cover tightly. Simmer gently until the
meat is very tender.

Stuffed Braised Flank Steak

Two cups mashed potatoes
Two tablespoons butter or margarine
One-half cup fine dry bread crumbs
One beaten egg
One teaspoon salt
One-fourth teaspoon onion salt
One-eighth teaspoon pepper
One flank steak (two pounds approx.)
Two teaspoons brown bouquet sauce
Two tablespoons fat or oil
Browning time: Five to ten minutes
Two stalks celery, thinly sliced
Two medium-sized onions, thinly sliced
One-half cup water
Simmer: Two hours, about
Servings: Five

Cook and mash fresh potatoes to
measure two cups or reconstitute the instant variety with water and milk. Stir
in the butter or margarine, bread crumbs,
beaten egg, salt, onion salt and pepper.
Mix well. Trim any excessive fat from
the flank steak. Brush one side with the
brown bouquet sauce. Turn over and
spread with the mashed potatoes, leaving a margin of an inch around edge of
steak. Roll up and skewer overlapping
edges together. Heat the fat or oil in a
heavy kettle or deep skillet and brown
roll of meat carefully on all sides. Add
the thinly sliced celery and onions. Pour
on the water and cover tightly. Simmer
very gently for two hours, checking to
see if additional water is needed from
time to time. When meat is tender remove to a board to slice. Serve with the
vegetables and pan liquid.

Daube Bordelaise

Two pounds beef rump
One-fourth cup salad or olive oil
Browning time: Ten minutes
One-half pound mushrooms, sliced
Sautéing time: Five minutes
Eight peeled white onions
Browning time: Five minutes
Two tablespoons flour
One cup red Bordeaux wine
One-fourth cup water
One can (No. 303) tomatoes
One clove garlic, crushed
Two tablespoons chopped parsley
One teaspoon salt
One-eighth teaspoon pepper
One carrot, sliced
Simmering time: Two hours, or more
Servings: Four

Slice the beef rump into four equal
slices. In a large heavy skillet or Dutch
oven, heat the salad or olive oil. Add the
meat and brown on both sides. Remove
from the pan. Add the mushrooms and
sauté briefly; remove. Add the onions
and cook until brown, allowing onions to
pick up the pan brownings. Stir in the
flour. Gradually blend in the wine and
water, stirring constantly until smooth.
Return the meat and mushrooms to the
pan with tomatoes, garlic, parsley, salt,
pepper and sliced carrot. Cover and
simmer gently for two hours or more, until the meat is very tender.

Sauerbraten

Four pounds beef rump, round or chuck
Two tablespoons salt
Two tablespoons sugar
Two cups vinegar
Two cups water
Two medium-sized onions, sliced
One lemon, sliced
Three bay leaves
Ten peppercorns
Ten whole cloves
Marinating time: Thirty-six hours, or more
Two tablespoons flour
Two tablespoons fat
Browning time: Twenty minutes, about
Simmering time: Three hours
Servings: Eight, or more

Rub the beef with the salt. Measure
the sugar into a large bowl. Add the vinegar, water, sliced onions and lemon,
bay leaves, peppercorns, and cloves. Stir
to dissolve the sugar. Place the piece of
beef in the bowl, spooning marinade
over top. Cover and refrigerate. Let
marinate for 36 hours or more, turning
the meat over two or three times. To
cook, remove meat from the liquid and
dry with paper towels. Coat beef with
flour. Heat the fat in a large heavy skillet or kettle, add the meat and brown
well on all sides. Add one and one-half
cups of the strained marinade to the
meat, cover and simmer gently until meat
is very tender. Fifteen minutes before
serving add the potato dumplings if desired. Note: Liquid in pan may be thickened for a sharp gravy with crumbled
gingersnaps, a little flour and possibly
some dairy sour cream.

Beef Pot Roast with Olives

One piece chuck beef (3-4 pounds)
One-fourth cup flour
One teaspoon salt
One-fourth teaspoon pepper
One-fourth cup salad oil
Browning time: Fifteen to twenty minutes
One teaspoon dried tarragon
Juice and grated rind of one lemon
One can (10½ oz.) condensed beef
    bouillon
Simmer: Two and one-half hours, about
One-half cup sliced pimiento stuffed olives
Cook: Ten minutes
Medium egg noodles
Boiling salted water
Cook: Ten minutes
Servings: Six, or more

Select a piece of beef for pot roasting at least two inches in thickness. Stir the flour, salt and pepper together and dredge meat with the combination on all sides. Heat the salad oil in a large heavy skillet or kettle and add the floured meat. Brown well on all sides. Add the dried tarragon, juice and grated rind of one lemon, can of condensed beef bouillon. Cover tightly and simmer gently until meat is tender, add water if necessary during cooking. Two and one-half to three hours will be needed for three to four pound roast. Skim fat from pan liquid just before serving and add the sliced stuffed olives. Let simmer ten minutes more. Cook the medium egg noodles in boiling salted water until tender. Drain. Serve meat with the noodles, spooning pan liquid with olives over the noodles.

Creole Beef Stew

Two pounds stewing beef
One-third cup flour
Three teaspoons salt
One-half teaspoon black pepper
Two tablespoons shortening
Browning time: Twenty minutes, about
One cup hot water
Simmer: Two hours
One cup sliced onion rings
One cup sliced fresh okra or
One can (No. 303) okra, drained
One cup fresh corn, cut from cob
Two cups diced fresh tomatoes
Two cups diced potatoes
Simmer: Thirty minutes
Servings: Six

Have beef cut into one and one-half inch cubes. Trim off excess fat. In a cup stir the flour, salt and black pepper together. Dredge beef in seasoned flour. Heat the shortening in a large heavy skillet; add the coated beef and brown well on all sides. Add the hot water. Cover tightly and simmer gently for two hours or until beef is tender. Add the sliced onion rings, sliced fresh or drained canned okra, cut fresh corn, diced tomatoes and potatoes. Cover tightly and simmer until potatoes are tender. Serve piping hot.

Burgundian Pot Roast

Three to five pound pot roast (rump or
    chuck)
Flour
One-fourth cup shortening
Browning time: Ten minutes, about
Two teaspoons salt
One-fourth teaspoon pepper
One cup Burgundy wine
Simmering time: Two hours
Six small potatoes, peeled
Twelve small onions, peeled
Six medium-sized carrots, peeled and
    quartered
Cooking time: Forty-five minutes, about
One-half cup Burgundy wine
One-half cup water
Two tablespoons flour
Simmering time: Five to eight minutes
One-fourth cup finely chopped parsley
Servings: Six or more

Coat the roast with flour on all sides. Melt the shortening in a heavy skillet or kettle; add the floured meat and brown quickly on all sides. Sprinkle with salt and pepper, add one cup of the Burgundy wine, cover and simmer gently until the meat is almost tender, about two hours. Add the vegetables and continue cooking until both meat and vegetables are tender. Remove roast and vegetables to a serving platter. Stir remaining wine into the stock in the pan. In a cup, blend the water into the flour until smooth. Gradually stir into the stock. Cook, stirring constantly until the mixture thickens, about five minutes. Stir in the finely chopped parsley and pour into a serving bowl. Spoon over the individual portions of the roast and vegetables.

Spicy Brown Beef Stew

One-third cup flour
Two pounds beef stew meat, two inch
    cubes
Three tablespoons fat
Browning time: Ten minutes, about
One and one-half teaspoons salt
One-half teaspoon celery salt
One-fourth teaspoon thyme
One clove garlic, crushed
Two cups water
Cook: Until thickened
Two teaspoons Worcestershire sauce
Two tablespoons chili sauce
Simmer: One and one-half hours
Four to six potatoes
One can (one pound) boiled white onions
Twelve whole cloves
Simmer: Forty-five minutes
One pkg. (10 oz.) frozen peas and carrots
Simmer: Fifteen minutes
Servings: Six

Use flour to coat cubes of meat. Reserve remaining flour. Heat the fat in a large skillet or kettle, add the floured meat and brown well on all sides. Remove meat to a plate and stir in salt, celery salt, thyme, garlic and remaining flour into pan drippings. Gradually blend in the water and cook, stirring until thick-

ened and smooth. Add the Worcestershire sauce and chili sauce with the meat. Cover tightly and simmer gently for one hour and a half. Add the peeled and quartered potatoes and boiled white onions with liquid. Stick a whole clove into twelve of the onions. Cook until potatoes are almost tender, about forty-five minutes. Add the frozen peas and carrots and cook fifteen minutes. Serve piping hot with hot biscuits.

Beef Pot Pie

Three tablespoons shortening
Two pounds of stew meat (one inch cubes)
Two large onions, sliced
Browning time: Ten minutes, about
Two teaspoons salt
One-fourth teaspoon pepper
One teaspoon Worcestershire sauce
One-fourth teaspoon basil
One-fourth teaspoon thyme
Three cups bouillon or hot water
Simmer: One hour
One can (No. 2) tomatoes
Four medium-sized carrots, sliced
Four medium-sized potatoes, diced
One teaspoon salt
Simmer: Forty-five minutes
One-fourth cup flour
One-fourth cup cold water
One cup sifted flour
One-half teaspoon salt
One-third cup shortening
Three tablespoons cold water
Oven temperature: 425 degrees
Bake: Twenty minutes, about
Servings: Six

Heat the three tablespoons of shortening in a large heavy skillet. Add the cubes of stewing beef and sliced onions and brown quickly on all sides. Add the two tablespoons of salt, pepper, Worcestershire sauce, basil, thyme and bouillon or hot water. Cover tightly and simmer gently for one hour. Add the canned tomatoes, sliced carrots and diced potatoes with one teaspoon of salt. Continue cooking until both meat and vegetables are tender. Using a slotted spoon transfer the meat and vegetables to six individual casseroles (5 inch). Blend one-fourth cup of flour with one-fourth cup of cold water in a small bowl. Add a little of the pan liquid to the combination then return to the skillet. Cook, stirring until smooth and thickened. Spoon over the meat and vegetables in the casseroles. Sift the cup of flour into a bowl with the half teaspoon of salt. Cut in the shortening until mixture resembles coarse meal. Stir in enough cold water with a fork to hold mixture together. Transfer to a floured board and divide into six parts. Roll each out into circles a little smaller than the casserole tops and lay over the contents for a floating crust. Bake in a hot oven long enough to lightly brown the pastry topping. Serve at once.

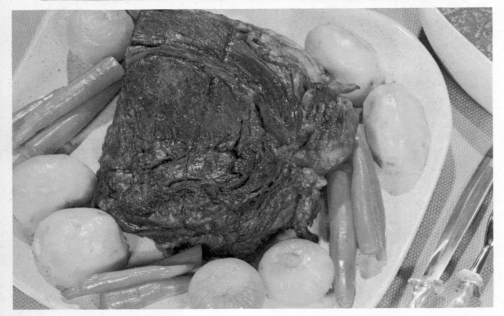

Roast Beef

Place roast, fat side up, on a rack in an open, low-sided pan. Do not add water. Do not cover. Insert a roast meat thermometer into the center or the thickest part of the meat, not touching bone.

Meat is roasted from refrigerator temperature in an open pan in a slow oven (325 degrees). When finished roasting allow the roast to stand at least 20 minutes to retain the juices.

Roasting Timetable for Beef

(Roasting temperature 325 degrees)

Weight	Roasting Temperature Per Pound	Degrees of Doneness	By Meat Thermometer
3-5 lbs.	18-20 minutes	rare	140 degrees
3-5 lbs.	22-25 minutes	medium	160 degrees
3-5 lbs.	27-30 minutes	well-done	170 degrees
6-8 lbs.	15-18 minutes	rare	140 degrees
6-8 lbs.	20-22 minutes	medium	160 degrees
6-8 lbs.	27-30 minutes	well-done	170 degrees

Pot Roast

Five pounds rump, round or chuck beef
Two tablespoons flour
One teaspoon salt
One-fourth teaspoon pepper
Two tablespoons of dripping or shortening
Browning time: Five minutes
One-half cup Bordeaux red wine, tomato
    juice or water
Four carrots
Four large potatoes, halved
Four onions
Simmering time: Four hours (about)
Two tablespoons flour, mixed with
One cup water
Cook: Five minutes
Serves: Four

Wipe the meat. Rub seasoned flour on all sides. In a heavy saucepan or Dutch oven heat the drippings or shortening until very hot. Quickly brown the meat on all sides. Add the wine and cover tightly. Cook over very low heat for 4 hours, or until meat is tender (it should simmer so gently that it will just barely bubble). Turn during cooking. Add more wine if necessary. The last 30 minutes of cooking, the carrots, potatoes and onions are placed around the roast. Cover and cook. Remove the meat and vegetables to a hot platter. Stir in the flour which has been mixed with the water, scraping the bottom and sides of the pan. Cook until slightly thickened. Serve.

Baked Chuck Roast

One chuck beef roast (4 lbs.)
Unseasoned meat tenderizer
One package dry onion soup mix
Oven temperature: 325 degrees
Bake: Two and one-half hours
Serves: Six

Apply the meat tenderizer on the chuck roast as directed on bottle. After the tenderizing period, place meat on a rack in a roasting pan. Sprinkle the onion soup mix on top of roast. Bake in a moderately slow oven until tender, basting occasionally with the drippings. Serve on a hot platter. Serve with diced French-fried potatoes and baked mushrooms.

Swiss Steak

One and one-half cups flour
One teaspoon salt
One-half teaspoon pepper
Three pounds round steak (in one piece
 1½ inches thick)
Suet or three tablespoons fat
Brown: Fifteen minutes
One can (No. 2) whole tomatoes, sieved
Simmering time: One and one-half hours
Six carrots, peeled
Nine onions, peeled
Serves: Six, or more

Mix the flour, salt and pepper together. Generously cover one side of the meat with some of the flour mixture. With a heavy-edged saucer pound the seasoned flour into the meat. Turn; generously cover the meat with some of the seasoned flour. Pound again. Repeat procedure until all the seasoned flour has been pounded into the steak. This part of the preparation is tedious. In an electric skillet or heavy saucepan fry out the suet. Brown the meat on all sides in the hot fat. Add the sieved tomatoes. Cover the skillet tightly, lower the heat to simmer and cook one and one-half hours or until tender. During the last 30 minutes of cooking add the carrots and onions. Serve from the skillet.

London Broil

One flank steak (2-2½ lbs.)
Salt and pepper
Broiling temperature: 500 degrees
Broiling time: Twelve minutes (about)
Serves: Four, or more

With a sharp knife lightly score the steak crosswise on both sides. Place the broiler pan and rack four inches from source of heat. Preheat broiler compartment five minutes. Place steak on broiler rack; broil seven minutes. Turn and broil five minutes on the other side. Season with salt and pepper. When serving, slice diagonally against the grain (on the bias). Serve immediately.

Broiled Steak Dinner

One porterhouse or sirloin steak (1½ in.
 thick), trimmed
One cup cooked lima beans
Two cups canned whole kernel corn
Three tomatoes, halved and oiled
Broiling temperature: 550 degrees
Broiling time: Twenty minutes (about)
Servings: Four

Wipe the steak with a damp cloth. Preheat the broiling compartment and pan ten minutes. Lift the rack; put the combined limas and corn in the broiling pan, replacing the rack. Lay the steak on the rack; slide under the broiler so the surface of the meat is one inch from the heat. Broil ten minutes. Turn. Add the tomatoes. Broil ten minutes for medium rare. Transfer to hot platter; let rest five minutes; garnish with watercress. Arrange the tomatoes in a serving dish; sprinkle with scallion rings. Place the limas and corn in a bowl with a few pieces of pimiento over the top. Serve at once.

Individual Meat Pies

One and one-half to two pounds beef
    for stew, cubed
Two tablespoons fat
Browning time: Ten minutes
Two medium-sized onions, diced
One small clove garlic, crushed
One bay leaf
One-half teaspoon marjoram
Two cups boiling water
Simmering time: One and one-half hours
One and one-half teaspoons salt
One teaspoon paprika
One-eighth teaspoon pepper
Two bouillon cubes
Four medium-sized carrots, cut
Twelve small peeled onions
Three medium-sized potatoes, peeled
    and quartered
Boiling water, if necessary
Simmering time: Thirty minutes, about
Three tablespoons flour
One-half cup cold water
Boiling time: Three to five minutes
One cup cooked green peas
Pastry for the top (one cup flour)
Oven temperature: 425 degrees
Baking time: Twenty minutes
Servings: Six

Brown the cubed beef in the fat in a
heavy kettle. Add the onion, garlic, bay
leaf and marjoram; cover with boiling
water. Cover tightly and simmer gently
for one and one-half hours. Add salt,
paprika, pepper, bouillon cubes, carrots,
onions and potatoes. Cover and simmer
until all is tender. Add more boiling
water if necessary. In a cup mix the flour
and cold water to form a paste. Add
to the kettle, stirring until thickened.
Take from the heat and divide the meat
and vegetables among six individual casseroles. Spoon cooked green peas over
top of each. Cover with pastry, fluting
the edge with thumb and finger and
pressing the pastry against the rim of
the dish. Cut several slits in the center
of each to permit steam to escape. Bake
in a hot oven until the pastry is brown
and crisp. Serve hot.

Dried Beef Casserole

One-fourth pound sliced dried beef
Boiling water
One cup finely diced celery
One can (8½ oz.) peas
One can (10½ oz.) condensed cream of
    chicken soup
One can (10½ oz.) condensed cream of
    mushroom soup
One-sixteenth teaspoon pepper
One can (5 oz.) crisp chow mein noodles
Oven temperature: 375 degrees
Bake: Thirty minutes
Serves: Four or five

Tear the dried beef into bite-sized
pieces and cover with boiling water.
Drain at once and combine with the
diced celery, canned peas and liquid,
condensed soups and pepper. Mix thoroughly together. Spoon mixture into a
baking dish (1½ qts.) layering with the
chow mein noodles and finishing off with
the noodles. Bake in a moderately hot
oven for 30 minutes or until piping hot.
Serve at once.

Beef Stroganoff

Two tablespoons butter or margarine
One-half pound mushrooms, sliced
Sauté: Five minutes
Three tablespoons butter or margarine
One-half cup chopped onion
Sauté: Five minutes
One and one-half pounds round steak (cut
    two inches thick)
Flour
Brown: Five to ten minutes
One can (No. 2) tomatoes, drained
One teaspoon salt
Simmer: One hour
One-half pint dairy sour cream
Serves: Four

In a large heavy skillet, melt the two
tablespoons of butter or margarine, add
the sliced mushrooms and sauté briefly.
Remove mushrooms to a bowl. Add three
tablespoons of butter to the skillet with
the chopped onion and sauté. Cut steak
in finger size strips an eighth of an inch
thick. Dredge the strips of steak in the
flour, add to the skillet and brown quickly. Add the drained tomatoes (breaking
up with a spoon), salt and sautéed mushrooms. Cover; simmer slowly until meat
is tender. Just before serving stir in the
dairy sour cream. Do not use high heat
after adding cream. Stroganoff may be
served over rice or noodles if you wish.

A FAVORITE RECIPE
Sweet and Sour Short Ribs

Fat cut from short ribs, rendered in a
    Dutch oven
Two pounds short ribs, cut into serving
    pieces
One teaspoon salt, or more
One-sixteenth teaspoon pepper
One-third cup flour
One cup water
Cook: Forty-five minutes
Ten small onions, cleaned
One cup dried prunes
One cup dried apricots
One green pepper, cleaned, cut into inch
    pieces
One-half cup sugar
One-fourth teaspoon cinnamon
One-fourth teaspoon allspice
One-fourth teaspoon ground cloves
Three tablespoons vinegar
Cook: One hour and fifteen minutes
Serves: Four

Cut the fat from the short ribs and
render in a deep heavy skillet or Dutch
oven. Coat the cut short ribs in the seasoned flour. Drain off most of the fat in
the skillet; place the short ribs in the
skillet; add water; cover; cook. Add the
onions, prunes, apricots and green pepper. Season with the sugar, spices and
vinegar. Cover and simmer until meat is
very tender. Serve with noodles.

BETTY TOLES, *Colorado Springs, Colo.*

A FAVORITE RECIPE
Short Ribs-Sauerbraten

Three pounds short ribs of beef, cut into
    serving pieces
One cup catsup
One cup water
One tablespoon sugar
One tablespoon horseradish
One bay leaf
One tablespoon dry mustard
One tablespoon vinegar
One teaspoon salt
One-fourth teaspoon pepper
Two onions, sliced thin
One tablespoon Worcestershire sauce
Marinating time: Overnight in the
    refrigerator
One cup flour
Three tablespoons fat
Frying time: Until a golden brown
Marinating sauce
Simmering time: One hour
Servings: Five

Have the butcher cut the ribs into
serving pieces. Wash and dry. Place in
a deep bowl. In a saucepan mix the
catsup, water, sugar, horseradish, bay
leaf, mustard, vinegar, salt, pepper,
onions, and Worcestershire sauce. Pour
over the ribs, mixing well. Place in the
refrigerator to marinate, tossing the ribs
several times. Drain the ribs thoroughly,
reserving the sauce; roll in the flour. In
a heavy skillet melt the fat. Brown the
ribs in the fat. Add the reserved marinating sauce. Cover; simmer until the meat
is tender (this may also be cooked in
pressure cooker, taking one-half the time).
Serve on a hot platter with mashed potatoes and a tossed green salad.

MRS. HOWARD MURNS, *Kings Park, L.I.*

Quick Skillet Beef

Two tablespoons butter or margarine
One-half pound fresh mushrooms, sliced
One-half cup chopped onion
Sauté: Ten minutes
One pound ground beef
Brown: Five to eight minutes
One bouillon cube
One cup boiling water
One-half teaspoon salt
One-eighth teaspoon pepper
One-fourth teaspoon nutmeg
Simmer: Fifteen minutes
One-fourth cup dairy sour cream
Crisp fried noodles
Serves: Four

In a large heavy skillet melt the butter
or margarine. Add the sliced mushrooms
and chopped onion, sauté until tender.
Add the ground beef and continue cooking and stirring until the meat is thoroughly browned. Dissolve the bouillon
cube in the cup of boiling water and add
to the browned meat. Add the salt, pepper and nutmeg. Cover and simmer gently
for 15 minutes. Stir in the dairy sour
cream just before serving over the crisp
noodles.

Biscuit Topped Hamburgers

One pound ground beef
One-half cup rolled oats
One-half teaspoon onion salt
One-half teaspoon garlic salt
One-eighth teaspoon pepper
Two-thirds cup tomato juice
Three tablespoons shortening
Brown: Five minutes, about
One cup thinly sliced onion
One-fourth cup flour
Two bouillon cubes
Two cups boiling water
One cup sifted flour
One-half teaspoon salt
One and one-half teaspoons baking powder
Three tablespoons shortening
One-fourth cup grated Parmesan cheese
One-third cup milk, or more
Oven temperature: 425 degrees
Bake: Fifteen minutes
Servings: Six

In a bowl combine the ground beef with the oats, onion salt, garlic salt, pepper and tomato juice. Mix well. Shape into six patties. Heat the three tablespoons of shortening in a heavy skillet, add the patties and brown on both sides. Arrange hamburgers in a single layer in a shallow baking dish. Add the onion to the drippings in the skillet and brown lightly. Stir in the fourth cup of flour. Dissolve the bouillon cubes in the boiling water and gradually blend into the onions, stirring smooth. Cook over low heat until thickened. Pour over the hamburgers. In a bowl sift together the flour, salt and baking powder. Cut in the three tablespoons of shortening using a pastry blender or two knives. Stir in the grated Parmesan cheese and enough milk to hold the mixture together. Turn out upon a floured board and knead briefly. Roll out and cut into six large biscuits that are placed over the hamburgers. Bake in a hot oven for 15 minutes or until the biscuits are baked and nicely browned. Serve at once.

Meat Ball Skillet Stew

One egg
One and one-half pounds ground chuck
One small onion, chopped
One-fourth cup soft bread crumbs
One and one-half teaspoons salt
One teaspoon dry mustard
One-fourth teaspoon chili powder
One-half cup milk
Two tablespoons fat
Browning time: Ten minutes, about
Six small potatoes
Two medium-sized onions, sliced
Two stalks celery, sliced
One teaspoon salt
One and one-half cups tomato juice
Simmer: Thirty minutes, about
Servings: Six

In a large bowl beat the egg. Add the ground chuck, chopped onion, soft bread crumbs, salt, mustard, chili and milk. Mix well together. Form into small balls.

Heat the fat in a large heavy skillet, add the balls of meat and brown well. Add the peeled potatoes, sliced onions and celery and sprinkle with the teaspoon of salt. Add the tomato juice and cover tightly. Simmer gently until vegetables are tender.

Ginger Cheese Meat Balls

One pound ground beef
One small onion, chopped
One and one-half teaspoons salt
One-sixteenth teaspoon pepper
One-eighth teaspoon garlic powder
One-fourth cup fine dry bread crumbs
One-half cup grated cheddar cheese
One teaspoon ground ginger
Two tablespoons shortening
Browning time: Ten minutes
One can (8 oz.) tomato sauce
One-fourth teaspoon oregano
One-fourth teaspoon dried tarragon
One-eighth teaspoon ginger
One-fourth cup water
Simmering time: Twenty-five minutes
Servings: Four

In a bowl combine the ground beef with the chopped onion, salt, pepper, garlic powder and dried bread crumbs. Mix well. Divide into eight portions. In a small bowl blend the grated cheese with the ginger. Form into eight small cheese balls. Shape the portions of meat mixture around the cheese balls. In a heavy skillet melt the shortening. Add the meat balls and brown on all sides. In a bowl mix the canned tomato sauce with the oregano, tarragon, ginger and water. Pour over the browned meat balls. Cover tightly and simmer for 25 minutes. Serve meat balls piping hot with sauce spooned over top.

A FAVORITE RECIPE
Apple Sauce Meat Balls

Two cups corn flakes, crushed slightly
Three tablespoons minced onion
One and one-half pounds ground beef
One and one-half teaspoons salt
One-eighth teaspoon pepper
One-fourth teaspoon sage (optional)
One egg, slightly beaten
Two-thirds cup thick apple sauce
One can (10½ oz.) condensed tomato
  soup
One-half cup water
Oven temperature: 350 degrees
Baking time: Forty-five minutes
Serves: Six

Crush the corn flakes slightly. In a bowl mix the flakes with the onion, beef, seasonings, egg and apple sauce. Shape into balls (1¾ in.). Place in a shallow baking pan. Combine the soup and water; pour over the meat balls. Bake in a moderate oven. Serve hot with a green salad.

MRS. R. F. TURNER, *Charleston Heights, S.C.*

Meat Balls in Sour Cream Gravy

Two cups corn flakes
One pound ground beef
One-half cup milk
One teaspoon salt
One-eighth teaspoon pepper
One-half cup chopped onion
Ten stuffed green olives
Two tablespoons shortening
Browning time: Five minutes
One and one-half tablespoons flour
One-fourth cup water
Cooking time: Five minutes
One cup dairy sour cream
One-half teaspoon dill salt
One-eighth teaspoon salt
Simmering time: Fifteen minutes
Servings: Five

Crush the corn flakes into fine crumbs and combine in a large bowl with the ground beef, milk, salt, pepper and chopped onion. Shape the meat balls around the stuffed olives. Melt the shortening in a heavy skillet, add the meat balls and brown on all sides. Remove the meat balls to plate. Blend the flour into the drippings, add the water, stirring to keep smooth. Cook, stirring constantly, until thickened. Add the dairy sour cream, dill salt and salt. Mix well. Add the meat balls and cover. Cook slowly for fifteen minutes. Serve over hot buttered noodles if desired.

Oven Baked Beef Stew

Two pounds beef for stew
Two medium-sized onions, sliced
One-half cup chopped green pepper
Three-fourths cup chili sauce
Three-fourths cup water
One and one-half teaspoons salt
One-eighth teaspoon pepper
Oven temperature: 350 degrees
Bake: Two hours
One pkg. (10 oz.) frozen baby limas
Bake: Forty-five minutes
Three tablespoons flour
One-third cup cold water
Cook: Until thickened
Heat: Briefly
Serves: Six

Cut the beef for stew into two-inch cubes. Place in a large heavy kettle or casserole dish. Arrange the sliced onions and chopped green pepper over the meat and pour on the combined chili sauce and three-fourths cup of water. Cover kettle or casserole and bake in a moderate oven for two hours, or until the meat is tender. Add the frozen limas, breaking apart with a fork. Cover and continue cooking for forty-five minutes more. Measure the flour into a large skillet and gradually blend in the cold water. Drain the liquid from the oven stew and gradually blend into the flour and water. Cook, stirring, until the gravy thickens and is smooth. Add the meat and vegetables and heat briefly before serving.

Beef Roulades

One cup seasoned mashed potatoes
   (not soft)
One-half cup minced cooked ham
One can (3¾ oz.) sliced mushrooms,
   drained
One cup chopped hard-cooked eggs
One-fourth chopped parsley
One-half teaspoon celery salt
One-eighth teaspoon pepper
Eight slices round steak (3x5x¼ in.)
Three tablespoons flour
One teaspoon salt
One-fourth teaspoon pepper
One-half teaspoon paprika
Six tablespoons butter or margarine
Brown: Ten minutes
One bouillon cube, dissolved in
One-half cup hot water
One cup red Bordeaux wine
Simmer: One hour, or more
One cup dairy sour cream
Serves: Four, or more

In a bowl mix the mashed potatoes, ham, mushrooms, eggs, parsley, celery salt, and pepper. Place equal amounts of the mixture on each slice of steak. Roll jelly roll fashion; secure ends and top with toothpicks. Roll in seasoned flour. In a large skillet heat the butter; brown the rolls on all sides. Mix the dissolved bouillon cubes and wine together; add to the rolls. Cover; simmer gently until the meat is tender. Remove meat to a hot platter.

Add the dairy sour cream to the skillet. Stir and scrape bottom and sides of pan. Reheat (do not boil). Pour into gravy boat and serve with meat.

Hungarian Goulash

One tablespoon shortening, or oil
Two pounds onions, chopped
Cooking time: Fifteen minutes
Four pounds chuck steak (1½ in. cubes)
Browning time: Ten minutes
One tablespoon salt
One and one-half teaspoons paprika
One-fourth teaspoon black pepper
One-fourth teaspoon marjoram
One-fourth teaspoon caraway seed
Two bay leaves
One-half cup water
One-half cup red wine
Simmering time: One and one-half hours
Serves: Six

In a heavy skillet or Dutch oven melt the shortening. Add the onion. Cook over high heat scraping sides and bottom of pan with a wooden spoon until the onions are straw-colored and glazed. Remove to a bowl. Add meat (do not remove fat or gristle). Brown on all sides. Add the remaining ingredients and onions. Cover tightly; cook until meat is tender. Carefully remove the meat, scraping off the onions. Rub the onions and remaining liquid through a sieve into the skillet. If a reddish color gravy is desired stir in one teaspoon of paprika. Add the meat and reheat. Serve on a hot platter with noodles.

Dilled Carrots

One bunch carrots, scraped and quartered
One cup boiling water, salted
Cooking time: Twenty minutes
One teaspoon ground dill seed, or one
   tablespoon chopped fresh dill
Two tablespoons melted butter
Serves: Four

In a saucepan cook the carrots in boiling salted water. Drain. Add the combined dill and butter. Pour into a vegetable dish. Serve.

A FAVORITE RECIPE
Neapolitan Rolled Meat

One and one-half pounds round steak,
  cut (¼ in. thick)
One-half pound ground beef
One teaspoon salt
One-fourth teaspoon pepper
One-half pound sliced boiled ham
Five hard-cooked eggs (do not slice) shelled
One-fourth cup cooking oil, heated
Browning time: Fifteen minutes
One can (8 oz.) tomato sauce
Simmering time: One hour
Servings: Six

Have steak cut and flattened by the butcher. Mix the ground beef and seasonings. Spread over the steak, spread the sliced ham over the top. Place the hard-cooked eggs down the center. Form into a large roll, binding with string. Heat the oil in a large skillet or Dutch oven, brown the roll on all sides. Reduce the heat; add the tomato sauce; cover; simmer, adding hot water if sauce has evaporated. Serve on a hot platter.

DOROTHY FURMAN, *Brooklyn, N.Y.*

Beef Bourguignon

Two and one-half pounds beef chuck,
  cubed (1½ in.)
One-fourth cup flour
Two tablespoons each butter and salad oil
Browning time: Fifteen minutes
One-fourth cup cognac
One-fourth pound salt pork, minced
Two cloves garlic, minced
Two carrots, sliced (1 in. pieces)
Two medium-sized onions, sliced
Two tablespoons minced parsley
Cook: Until lightly browned
Two bay leaves
One-half teaspoon thyme
Two teaspoons salt
One-fourth teaspoon pepper
Two cups Burgundy wine
Oven temperature: 350 degrees
Bake: Two and one-half hours
One pound small white onions, peeled
Two tablespoons salad oil
One teaspoon sugar
Cook: Five minutes
One can (3¾ oz.) sliced mushrooms, heated
Minced parsley
Serves: Six

Dust the cubes of meat lightly in flour. In a heavy skillet brown only six cubes at a time over low heat in the butter and salad oil (too many cubes in pan makes the meat steam rather than brown). Add the cognac to meat and ignite. Transfer meat to a casserole (2 qts.). To the skillet add the salt pork, garlic, carrots, onions and parsley, cooking salt pork and vegetables until lightly browned. Put vegetable mixture over meat; add bay leaves, thyme, salt, pepper and wine. Cover; bake in a moderate oven until the meat is tender. Meanwhile brown the white onions in the salad oil with a sprinkling of sugar. Add to the meat mixture during the last half hour of cooking. Serve garnished with mushrooms and parsley.

May be simmered on top stove.

Stuffed Flank Steak

One flank steak
One-half cup chopped black olives
One-half cup chopped green olives
One-half cup chopped mushrooms
One-half cup chopped onions
One-half cup chopped pimiento
One-half cup slivered salami
One clove garlic, puréed
Brown: Five minutes
One cup red Bordeaux wine
Simmer: Two hours (about)
One tablespoon flour
One-fourth cup water
Cook: Five minutes
Serves: Four

Split the flank steak lengthwise almost all the way through. Then spread open the steak so it is flat. In a bowl mix the olives, mushrooms, onions, pimiento, salami and garlic. Spread over steak. Roll lengthwise; skewer or tie together. In a skillet brown the steak in its own fat. Pour one half the wine over the meat. Cover. Simmer until tender. Baste frequently with the remaining wine. When tender, remove to a board. Remove skewers. Cut into slices (2 in.). Place on a hot platter. Stir the combined flour and water into drippings; cook until slightly thickened.

Swedish Meat Balls

One pound ground chuck beef
One-fourth pound ground shoulder pork
One-half cup soft bread crumbs
One-half cup milk
One egg, beaten
Two tablespoons minced onion
Three tablespoons fat or drippings
Cooking time: Two to three minutes
One and one-fourth teaspoons salt
One-fourth teaspoon allspice or nutmeg
One-eighth teaspoon pepper
Browning time: Ten to fifteen minutes
Three tablespoons flour
One and one-half cups water
One-half cup milk
Cooking time: Forty minutes, or until tender
Servings: Six

Combine the ground meats in a large bowl. Blend the crumbs, milk and beaten egg into the meat. Sauté the onion in the fat in a heavy kettle until tender. Skim out the onion and add to the meat with salt, spice and pepper. Form into small balls with two teaspoons and drop into the hot fat remaining in the kettle. Brown the balls on all sides; remove them to a plate. Stir the flour into the fat in the kettle; add the water and cook until thickened. Add the milk; reheat. Return the balls to the sauce; cover. Simmer over low heat until very tender. Serve hot.

A FAVORITE RECIPE
Polish Cabbage Rolls

One firm head cabbage (core removed)
Boiling water to cover
Cooking time: Until boiling
One-fourth pound ground pork
One-fourth pound ground beef
One teaspoon salt
One-fourth teaspoon pepper
One onion, minced
Frying time: Until meat is cooked
One and one-half cups cooked rice
Cooking time: Until heated
Four strips bacon
One can (10½ oz.) condensed tomato soup
Oven temperature: 325 degrees
Baking time: Thirty minutes
Servings: Four

With a sharp knife remove the core from the cabbage. Place in a deep kettle; cover with boiling water. Bring to a boil. Remove cabbage, draining thoroughly. Separate the leaves. Mix in a bowl the pork and beef, seasonings and onion; fry until the meat is cooked (not browned); add the rice, stirring until well blended and heated. Place two tablespoons of the mixture on each cabbage leaf, rolling tightly and binding with toothpicks. Place in an oven dish, spread the bacon over the rolls. Pour the tomato soup over all. Bake in a slow oven, basting several times with the soup.

DEBORAH MANDEN, *Bronx, N.Y.*

Pippin Meat Balls

One pound ground beef
One-half cup applesauce
One-half cup soft bread crumbs
One egg
One teaspoon salt
One-eighth teaspoon pepper
Flour
Two tablespoons butter or shortening
Browning time: Ten minutes (about)
One stalk celery, finely chopped
One carrot, thinly sliced
One small onion, thinly sliced
One teaspoon salt
One cup tomato juice
Simmering time: Thirty minutes
Servings: Four

In a bowl mix the ground beef with the applesauce, bread crumbs, egg, salt and pepper. Form into 12 balls and roll in flour. Melt the butter or shortening in a heavy skillet. Add the floured meat balls and brown on all sides. Scatter the chopped celery, sliced carrot and onion over the meat balls. Stir the salt into the tomato juice; pour over the browned meat balls. Cover tightly and simmer for 30 minutes. Serve piping hot.

Belgian Meat Balls

One cup bread cubes (½ inch)
One-fourth cup milk
One tablespoon shortening
One green onion, finely chopped
Sauté: Five minutes
One pound ground beef
One teaspoon salt
One-eighth teaspoon pepper
One-eighth teaspoon nutmeg
One egg
Flour
Two tablespoons shortening
Browning time: Five to ten minutes
Two cups bouillon
Twelve small white onions
Eight small potatoes
One sprig parsley
Small clove garlic, sliced
One-fourth teaspoon thyme
Five peppercorns
Simmer: One hour, about
One-fourth cup finely chopped parsley
Servings: Four

Place the bread cubes in a large bowl and pour on the milk. In a large heavy skillet melt the tablespoon of shortening and sauté the chopped green onion until soft. Add onion to the bread cubes with the ground beef, salt, pepper, nutmeg and egg, mixing well together. Form into one-inch balls and roll in flour. Add remaining shortening to skillet and heat. Add meat balls and brown well on all sides. Add the bouillon, onions and potatoes. Prepare a bouquet garni by tying the parsley, garlic, thyme and peppercorns into a piece of cheesecloth, adding to the skillet. Cover, simmer gently for one hour or until potatoes and onions are tender. Discard the bouquet

garni and serve meat balls and vegetables with a sprinkling of the finely chopped parsley.

Scandinavian Meat Balls

Two eggs
One pound ground beef
One-half cup soft bread crumbs
One cup grated carrots
One-fourth cup finely chopped onion
One and one-half teaspoons salt
One-eighth teaspoon pepper
One-fourth teaspoon thyme
Flour
Two tablespoons salad oil
Brown: Ten minutes
One-half cup bouillon
One-half cup cream
Simmer: Thirty minutes
Serves: Four or five

In a bowl beat the eggs. Add the ground beef, soft bread crumbs, grated carrots, finely chopped onion, salt, pepper and thyme. Mix thoroughly together and form into small balls. We like to portion the mixture off in one-fourth measuring cups and divide each into two. Roll into balls. This will make about 20. Roll balls of meat mixture in the flour to coat and brown on all sides in the heated salad oil in a large heavy skillet. Add the combined bouillon and cream, lower heat, cover and simmer gently until meat balls are thoroughly cooked. Serve meat balls with pan gravy.

A FAVORITE RECIPE
Sauerkraut-Meat Balls

One-half pound ground veal
One-half pound ground beef
One-half pound ground pork
One small onion, minced
One teaspoon salt
One-fourth teaspoon pepper
One small clove garlic, minced
One egg, beaten light
Two tablespoons bread crumbs
One-fourth cup uncooked rice
One-half cup water
Two tablespoons fat, heated
Browning time: Twenty minutes
One can (No. 2½) sauerkraut
One can (10½ oz.) condensed tomato soup
Simmering time: Two hours
Serves: Six

In a bowl combine the veal, beef and pork; add onion, salt, pepper, garlic, egg, bread crumbs, rice and water. Form into small balls (1 in.). Heat the fat in a Dutch oven or a deep heavy skillet; brown the meat balls. Add the sauerkraut and pour the tomato soup over all. Cover and simmer, stirring frequently. Serve hot with corn bread.

MRS. WILLIAM MILLER, *Manitowoc, Wisc.*

A FAVORITE RECIPE
Sour Spiced Tongue

One tongue (4-5 lbs.)
Hot water to cover
One tablespoon salt
Cooking time: Four hours
One-half cup vinegar
One-half cup corn syrup
One-fourth teaspoon allspice
One-fourth teaspoon cinnamon
One-fourth teaspoon cloves
One-half cup seedless raisins
Simmering time: Forty-five minutes
Servings: Eight

Scrub the tongue with a stiff brush. Place in a deep kettle, add water to cover and salt. Bring to a boil; reduce the heat; simmer. While the tongue is still hot remove skin and root ends. Return to the kettle and let cool in the liquid. Place the tongue in a baking pan. Make a sauce by mixing the vinegar, syrup, spices and raisins together. Pour over the tongue. Simmer on top of the stove; baste frequently with the liquid. Slice and serve on a hot platter with the sauce.

MRS. HEDWIG KREUSCHER, *Brooklyn, N.Y.*

Bacon Wrapped Sweetbreads

One pound sweetbreads
Boiling water
One tablespoon lemon juice or vinegar
One teaspoon salt
Simmer: Thirty minutes
One egg
One-third cup fine dry bread crumbs
Ten slices bacon, about
Oven temperature: 425 degrees
Bake: Twenty minutes
Servings: Four

Place the sweetbreads in boiling water to cover with the lemon juice or vinegar and salt. Simmer gently for thirty minutes. Drain and cover with cold water. Trim off any membrane and cut dark veins or connective tissue. Cut into chunks the size of a walnut. Beat egg in small shallow bowl. Place crumbs in a second bowl. Cut each slice of bacon into three pieces. Dip chunks of sweetbread in egg and crumbs and wrap in bacon. Skewer bacon on small wooden pick. Place on shallow tray or baking pan and bake in a hot oven until bacon is crisp. Serve at once.

Sweetbreads en Brochette

Two pairs veal sweetbreads (approx. two pounds)
Boiling water
One teaspoon salt
Simmering time: Thirty minutes
Two tablespoons salad oil
Two tablespoons lemon juice
One teaspoon salt
Four slices bacon
Eight medium-sized mushrooms
Broiling temperature: 500 degrees
Broiling time: Ten minutes
Servings: Four

In a saucepan, cover the sweetbreads with boiling water, add salt. Cover and simmer gently for 30 minutes. Let cold water run over the cooked sweetbreads, slip off the membrane and cut away tubes and veins. Separate into pieces about an inch and a half square. In a small bowl, mix the salad oil, lemon juice and salt. Coat the cubes of meat with the combination. Fill four skewers with the cubes alternated with squares of bacon using a mushroom cap at either end. Broil turning frequently until the bacon is cooked. Serve at once.

Creamed Sweetbreads with Ham and Almonds

One pair sweetbreads
Four cups boiling water
Two tablespoons lemon juice
Simmering time: Twenty minutes
One-fourth cup butter
One-fourth cup flour
One cup chicken broth
One cup light cream
Cooking time: Ten to twelve minutes
One teaspoon steak sauce
One cup diced cooked ham
One-third cup blanched, toasted almonds
Salt to taste
Heating time: Ten to fifteen minutes
One recipe pastry, baked into triangles
Servings: Four

Soak the sweetbreads one hour in cold water. Drain. Place in a saucepan with the four cups of water and lemon juice. Bring to a boil, lower heat and simmer for 20 minutes. Drain and remove membrane and tubes. Separate into segments. In the upper half of a double boiler melt the butter. Stir in the flour and gradually blend in the chicken broth and light cream. Cook, stirring constantly, until thickened. Place over hot water and add the steak sauce, cook diced ham, sweetbreads and almonds. Taste and add salt if necessary. Heat briefly but thoroughly. Serve over crisp baked pastry triangles.

A FAVORITE RECIPE
Stuffed Veal Hearts

Two veal hearts, cleaned, pocket cut
Three tablespoons fat, heated
Two tablespoons chopped onion
Browning time: Five minutes
One and one-half cups cracker crumbs
Three-fourths teaspoon salt
One-fourth teaspoon pepper
One-fourth teaspoon celery salt
One-fourth cup water
Two tablespoons flour
Three tablespoons fat
Browning time: Ten minutes
One can condensed consomme
Two whole cloves
Three whole black peppers
One bay leaf
Simmering time: One and one-half hours
Servings: Four

Remove veins and arteries from the hearts. Rinse pocket and dry with a cloth. Set aside. In a heavy skillet, heat the fat, add onion, cook. Add the cracker crumbs, seasonings and water, mix. Stuff the hearts with the mixture, fasten the opening with skewers. Roll in the flour. Heat the fat in a skillet, brown the hearts on all sides. Add the consomme, cloves, whole peppers and bay leaf. Cover tightly. Simmer until hearts are very tender. Serve on a hot platter, sliced.

MRS. ROSE HOLOWINSKI, *So. Hackensack, N.J.*

A FAVORITE RECIPE
Baked Stuffed Heart

Two slices (3 in.) salt pork, diced
Frying time: Until crisp
Two cups bread crumbs
Two tablespoons minced onion
One teaspoon powdered sage
One beef heart (4-5 lbs.) pocket cut
One-fourth cup flour
Three tablespoons melted butter
Browning time: Fifteen minutes
One-half teaspoon salt
One-fourth teaspoon pepper
One-half cup water
One tablespoon Worcestershire sauce
Oven temperature: 350 degrees
Baking time: Two hours
Servings: Six

In a skillet, fry the salt pork until crisp. Combine with the bread crumbs, onion and sage. Fill the cavity in the heart with the dressing. Bind with skewers or twine. Roll in the flour until the heart is well coated. Heat the butter in a skillet. Brown the heart on all sides. Season with salt and pepper to taste. Add the water and Worcestershire sauce. Bake in a moderate oven, turning the heart several times. Serve sliced on a hot platter with stewed tomatoes and a salad.

MRS. GEORGE EBSEN, *Superior, Nebr.*

A FAVORITE RECIPE
Kidneys — St. Albons

Twelve lamb kidneys, skinned, sliced (½ in.)
Water to cover
Standing time: Three hours in refrigerator
Two tablespoons butter, melted
One large green pepper, cleaned, minced
One large onion, diced
Cooking time: Two minutes
Two large tomatoes, peeled, seeded, chopped fine
Cooking time: Two minutes
One can (4 oz.) cut mushrooms with liquid
Simmering time: One hour
One cup rice, cooked
Servings: Four

Wash and remove skin and membrane from the kidneys. Slice crosswise (⅛ in.). Place in a bowl, cover with water, let stand. Heat the butter in a saucepan; add the green pepper and onion, cook. Add the chopped tomatoes, cook. Add the mushrooms and liquid, stirring until well blended. Add the drained kidneys, season to taste, cover, simmer. Serve over hot rice or noodles.

MRS. MATHILDE RADLAUER, *Brooklyn, N.Y.*

New England Boiled Dinner

One piece of corned beef (5 to 6 lbs.)
Cold water
Simmer: Four to five hours
Six potatoes, peeled
Six onions, peeled
Four carrots, peeled
One small yellow turnip, peeled, cut
 into wedges
Simmer: Thirty minutes
One head cabbage, quartered and cored
Cook: Ten minutes
Mustard or Horseradish sauce
Serves: Four, or more

Put the beef in a kettle. Cover with cold water. Bring slowly to boiling point. Remove scum. Cover; simmer until tender. Skim off excess fat. Add the potatoes, onions, carrots and turnip. Simmer until vegetables are tender. During the last ten minutes of cooking add wedges of cabbage. Arrange beef on a platter with the vegetables. Serve with mustard or horseradish sauce.

Corned Beef Oven Hash with Peaches

Four tablespoons butter or margarine
One-third cup finely chopped onion
One-third cup finely chopped green pepper
Sauté: Five to ten minutes
Two cans (12 oz. each) corned beef
One cup dairy sour cream
Oven temperature: 400 degrees
Bake: Twenty minutes
Six large canned peach halves
Two teaspoons prepared mustard
Bake: Ten minutes
Servings: Six

In a large heavy skillet melt the butter or margarine. Add the finely chopped onion and green pepper and sauté until soft. Stir in the crumbled corned beef and dairy sour cream, mixing well. Spread in a large shallow baking dish or pie plate (10 in.). Bake in a quick oven for 20 minutes to heat through. Top with the drained peach halves brushed with the prepared mustard. Continue baking for ten minutes and serve piping hot.

Western Hash Casserole

Two tablespoons shortening
Two-thirds cup chopped onion
Sauté: Until lightly browned
One can (8 oz.) tomato sauce
One tablespoon Worcestershire sauce
One teaspoon prepared mustard
One-fourth teaspoon salt
Two cans (1 pound each) corned beef hash
One cup grated sharp cheddar cheese
Oven temperature: 325 degrees
Bake: Thirty minutes
Serves: Six

In a heavy skillet heat the shortening. Add the chopped onion and sauté until lightly browned. Stir in the tomato sauce, Worcestershire sauce, prepared mustard and salt. Layer the canned corned beef hash with the grated cheese and seasoned sauce in a greased casserole (1½ qts.) repeating the series of layers twice. Bake in a moderately slow oven for thirty minutes before serving.

Corned Beef

Four pounds corned brisket of beef
Cold water to cover
Standing time: Four hours, or more
Two cups hot water
One slice onion
One clove garlic
One bay leaf
Pressure cooking time: Forty minutes
Servings: Six

To freshen the corned beef: Cover with cold water; let stand, changing the water twice. Drain. Place the meat on the rack in the pressure cooker. Add the hot water, onion, garlic and bay leaf. Cover. Place over high heat. When the steam escapes in a steady flow, place the weight over the vent pipe; then follow the instructions for regulating the pressure as given in the manufacturer's recipe booklet. Cook under steady pressure 40 minutes. Reduce the pressure immediately by placing the cooker in a pan of cold water. As soon as the pressure is down, remove the cover. Serve immediately with whipped potatoes, crumbed onions and broccoli.

Old-Fashioned Beef Stew

Two pounds chuck or round steak,
    cubed (1½ in.)
One teaspoon salt
One-fourth teaspoon pepper
Three tablespoons flour
Four tablespoons drippings or bacon fat
One clove garlic, minced
Brown: Fifteen minutes
One onion, sliced
Few sprigs parsley
Few sprigs celery leaves
One bay leaf
Three bouillon cubes, dissolved in
Three cups boiling water
One cup Bordeaux red wine
Simmer: Three hours, or until tender
Six peeled white onions
Six peeled carrots, halved crosswise
Six peeled potatoes, quartered
Two tablespoons flour, mixed with
One-fourth cup water
Simmer: Five minutes
Serves: Four, or more

Wipe the cubed meat; dust with seasoned flour. In a heavy kettle heat the drippings until hot. Add garlic. Brown a few pieces of meat at a time. Add the onion, parsley, celery leaves, bay leaf, dissolved bouillon cubes and wine. Cover very tightly. Bring to a boil; turn down the heat and simmer very gently until the meat is tender. Add the onions, carrots and potatoes 45 minutes before the final cooking period. Stir in the mixed flour and water and cook until slightly thickened. Serve.

A FAVORITE RECIPE
Oxtail Ragout

Two pounds oxtail, cut into serving pieces
One teaspoon salt
One-fourth teaspoon pepper
One-fourth teaspoon paprika
Three tablespoons butter, heated with
Three tablespoons cooking oil
One large carrot, cleaned, chopped fine
One large onion, chopped fine
One cup chopped celery
One-half cup chopped parsley
One small clove garlic, minced (optional)
Browning time: Fifteen minutes
One cup red wine or soup stock
One cup tomato juice
Simmering time: Two hours
Two tablespoons flour
Stock for gravy
Servings: Four

Have the oxtail cut in the market. Season with salt, pepper and paprika. Heat the butter and oil in a Dutch oven; add the oxtail and vegetables, browning well and turning several times. Add the wine or stock and tomato juice; cover; simmer, stirring frequently. For the gravy: Remove the meat and vegetables to a hot platter. Add the flour to the remaining liquid in pan, stirring until smooth, adding more stock to the mixture. Serve hot over the oxtails.

MRS. G. STEINMEYER, *Brattleboro, Vermont*

Greek Beef Stew

Three to four tablespoons olive oil
Two pounds cubed (1 in.) beef
One cup red wine
One can (8 oz.) tomato sauce
Three tablespoons vinegar
One tablespoon salt
One-half teaspoon black pepper
One stick cinnamon
Four whole cloves
Two pounds whole white onions, peeled
Simmering time: Two and one-half hours
Serves: Four, or more

Heat the oil in a Dutch oven or heavy skillet over low heat; brown the meat on all sides. Add the wine, tomato sauce, vinegar, salt, pepper and cinnamon stick. Stud one of the onions with whole cloves; add. Cover; simmer until the meat is almost tender (2 hours). Add the onions and continue cooking for another half hour. Remove the onion with the cloves. Serve with rice or groats.

Bacon Kidney Rolls

Six lamb or two veal kidneys
One-half teaspoon salt
One-fourth teaspoon pepper
One cup soft bread crumbs
One tablespoon finely chopped onion
One tablespoon finely chopped parsley
One tablespoon lemon juice
Eight to ten slices bacon
Oven temperature: 425 degrees
Bake: Twenty to thirty minutes
Serves: Four

Trim fat and membrane from rinsed kidneys and cut into sixteen to twenty sections, removing tubes and tough muscle. Sprinkle pieces with combined salt and pepper. In a bowl, combine the soft bread crumbs, chopped onion, parsley and lemon juice; mix well. Cut the bacon slices in half and sprinkle each with some of the bread crumb mixture. Lay a portion of kidney on each piece of bacon; roll up and secure with a wooden toothpick. Stand rolls on end in a greased shallow pan or two pie plates. Bake in a hot oven until the kidney is cooked and the bacon brown. To test the kidney, cut into a roll to see if red color has gone. Serve with parsley garnish.

Steak and Kidney Pies

One beef kidney (12 ounces)
Soak: Thirty minutes
One pound round steak (¾ inch thick)
One-fourth cup shortening
Two medium-sized onions, chopped
Browning time: Ten to fifteen minutes
One and one-half teaspoons salt
One-eighth teaspoon pepper
One teaspoon Worcestershire sauce
One cup water
Simmer: One and one-fourth hours
Two medium-sized potatoes
Cook: Ten minutes
Two cups sifted flour
One teaspoon salt
Two-thirds cup shortening
Four or more tablespoons ice water
Two tablespoons flour
Three-fourths cup water
Cook: Five minutes
Oven temperature: 425 degrees
Bake: Thirty minutes
Servings: Six

Split the kidney lengthwise into halves. Remove all fat and heavy white veins. Place in a bowl and cover with cold water. Let stand for thirty minutes. Drain well and cut into one inch cubes. Cut round steak into one inch cubes. Heat the shortening in a heavy kettle or skillet, add the cut steak, kidney and chopped onion. Brown quickly over high heat, stirring to brown evenly. Add salt, pepper, Worcestershire sauce and water. Cover tightly and cook over low heat until the steak is tender, about an hour and a quarter. Wash, peel and dice the potatoes into three-fourth inch cubes. Cook in salted water until almost tender; about ten minutes. Drain and set aside. Prepare the pastry by sifting flour and salt into a mixing bowl. Cut in half the shortening until as fine as cornmeal; cut in remaining shortening until the size of small peas. Stir in enough of the ice water with a fork to bind crumbs together. Roll out pastry on a floured board to line six small pie pans (5 inch). Roll out circles of dough to cover pies. When meat is tender blend two tablespoons of flour with the three-fourths cup of water in a small bowl and stir into the cooked meat mixture. Cook and stir until thickened, adding a little more water if too thick. Cook for five minutes; add the cooked potatoes. Spoon into the pastry lined pie pans. Cut slits in the circles of pastry and lay over the filling. Crimp edges together with a fork. Bake in a hot oven for thirty minutes. If you wish these unbaked pies may be refrigerated and baked as needed adding about ten minutes more to the baking time.

Sherried Kidneys on Toast

Six lamb kidneys
Two tablespoons bacon drippings
Sauté: Three minutes
One-fourth pound mushrooms
Two tablespoons finely chopped parsley
One-fourth cup sherry wine
Simmer: Six minutes
One-half cup heavy cream
One package (10 oz.) frozen peas, cooked and drained
Simmer: Five minutes
Hot buttered toast points
Servings: Four

Trim fat and membrane from rinsed kidneys and cut into thin slices, removing tubes and tough muscle. Heat the bacon drippings in a large heavy skillet, add the sliced kidneys and sauté until lightly browned. Add the cleaned, sliced mushrooms, chopped parsley and sherry wine and simmer for six minutes. Add the heavy cream with the cooked and drained peas and simmer carefully to heat through. Do not allow to boil. Serve on hot buttered toast points.

Crisp Broiled Tripe

One and one-half pounds fresh honeycomb tripe, cooked
Cracker meal
Oil
Broiling time: Six minutes
Salt
Pepper
One-fourth cup finely minced parsley
Servings: Four

Cut the cooked tripe, that has been simmered very tender in boiling salted water for about three hours, into two or three inch squares. Dry well on absorbent paper. Dip squares in cracker meal, then in oil and again in cracker meal. Place on foil in the heated broiler. Broil until crumbs are brown, about three minutes. Turn and brown other side. To serve sprinkle with salt and pepper and finely minced parsley.

Tripe Creole

One and one-half pounds fresh honeycomb tripe, cooked
Two tablespoons butter or margarine
Browning time: Five minutes, about
Two tablespoons butter or margarine
One tablespoon minced onion
One tablespoon minced green pepper
Four medium-sized mushrooms, sliced
Sautéing time: Five minutes, about
One tablespoon flour
One cup canned tomato sauce
One cup bouillon
Cooking time: Five minutes, or more
Three cups hot fluffy rice
Servings: Four, or more

Cut the cooked tripe, that has been simmered very tender in boiling salted water for about three hours, into julienne strips about two by one-half inch. Melt the two tablespoons of butter or margarine in a large heavy skillet, add the cut tripe and brown quickly on both sides. In a second skillet, melt the second measure of butter or margarine. Add the minced onion, green pepper and sliced mushrooms. Sauté until just tender. Stir the flour into the onion mixture and gradually blend in the tomato sauce and bouillon. Add the browned tripe and cook until the sauce thickens slightly, stirring to keep smooth. When piping hot serve over hot cooked rice.

Liver with Apples, Onion

Four slices bacon, diced
Pan-fry: Briefly
One pound beef liver
One-fourth cup flour
One teaspoon salt
One-half teaspoon thyme
One-sixteenth teaspoon pepper
Browning time: Five to ten minutes
One large red skinned apple, diced
One tablespoon lemon juice
One medium-sized onion, sliced
Cook: Five to ten minutes
One tablespoon finely chopped parsley
Servings: Four

Place the diced bacon in a heavy skillet and pan-fry until partially cooked. Trim skin and membrane from the sliced beef liver (one-fourth inch slices) and dip in the combined flour, salt, thyme and pepper. Add dredged liver to the bacon and brown quickly on both sides. Combine diced apple with lemon juice and add to the skillet with the thinly sliced onion. Cover tightly and cook for five to ten minutes, until fruit and onion are tender. Serve liver with apple, onion and bacon spooned over top. Sprinkle with finely chopped parsley.

Liver with Sour Cream

One pound beef liver
Three tablespoons bacon drippings or shortening
Two tablespoons chopped onion
Browning time: Five minutes
Cook: Ten minutes
One teaspoon salt
One-fourth teaspoon pepper
Two tablespoons flour
Two cans (3 oz. each) mushroom pieces
One bouillon cube
One-third cup boiling water
Heat: Five minutes
One-half cup dairy sour cream
Heat: Briefly
Four slices crisp toast
Servings: Four

Trim any skin or membrane from the liver; cut into half inch cubes. Heat the bacon drippings or shortening in a large heavy skillet. Add the chopped onion and cubed liver and brown quickly. Lower heat and cook for ten minutes. Sprinkle with salt, pepper and flour. Stir in the liquid from the canned mushrooms and the bouillon cube dissolved in boiling water. Heat, stirring smooth. Add the mushroom pieces, and dairy sour cream and heat briefly. Serve over crisp toast triangles.

Liver with Gravy

One and one-half pounds sliced calf or beef liver
One-fourth cup flour
One-fourth teaspoon salt
One-eighth teaspoon pepper
Three tablespoons shortening
Browning time: Five minutes, about
One tablespoon flour
One and one-half cups chicken bouillon
Cook: Five minutes
Serves: Four

Using a sharp knife, trim off any skin or membrane that might be found on the sliced liver. Dredge in the combined flour, salt and pepper. Heat the shortening in a heavy skillet, add the liver and brown quickly on both sides. Remove to a warm serving platter and cover to keep warm. Stir the flour into the pan drippings using a wooden spoon to scrape up browned bits in the pan. Gradually blend in the chicken bouillon cubes (made from chicken bouillon cubes and water). Cook and stir until thickened and smooth. Taste to check seasoning. Serve a spoonful of the gravy over each portion of liver.

A FAVORITE RECIPE
Liver and Wine

Two tablespoons butter or margarine
Three medium-sized onions, chopped
Sautéing time: Five minutes
One and one-half pounds liver (one piece)
Browning time: Ten minutes
One-half cup white wine
One-half teaspoon salt
Simmering time: Twenty minutes
Two teaspoons cornstarch, mixed with
One-fourth cup water
Cooking time: Until as thick as desired
One-third cup sour cream
Cooking time: Until heated thoroughly
One cup rice, cooked
Servings: Six

In a heavy skillet (9 in.), heat the butter. Sauté the onions. Add the liver, patted dry with a cloth. Brown on each side. Add the wine, stirring well. Season with salt. Cover; simmer, until the liver is cooked through. Remove the liver from the pan; cut into thin strips. Thicken the pan liquid with the cornstarch mixed with the water. Place the strips of liver back into the pan; add sour cream, heat thoroughly and blend well with onion sauce. Serve hot with the rice and a green tossed salad.

DELCINA BOBB, *Bronx, N.Y.*

Rice Casserole with Liver

Two tablespoons salad oil or bacon drippings
One-half cup chopped celery
One-fourth cup chopped green pepper
One medium-sized onion, chopped
One pound sliced beef liver
Browning time: Ten minutes, about
One can (8 oz.) tomato sauce
One can (No. 303) tomatoes
One and one-half teaspoons salt
One-fourth teaspoon pepper
One-fourth teaspoon thyme
Three cups cooked rice
Simmer: Fifteen minutes
One-third cup grated cheddar cheese
Serves: Six

Heat the salad oil or bacon drippings in a large heavy skillet. Add the chopped celery, green pepper and onion. Trim skin and membrane from the liver and cut into inch squares. Add to the skillet and cook until liver is browned. Add the tomato sauce, tomatoes, salt, pepper, thyme and cooked rice. Simmer for fifteen minutes before serving piping hot with the grated cheddar sprinkled over the top. If preferred transfer combination to greased casserole (2 qts.) before simmering, sprinkle with the grated cheese and bake in a moderate oven (350 degrees) for thirty minutes.

Deviled Liver Saute

One pound sliced beef liver (one-half inch)
One and one-half teaspoons salt
One teaspoon dry mustard
One-eighth teaspoon pepper
One-eighth teaspoon paprika
Three tablespoons melted butter or margarine
Two teaspoons vinegar
Two teaspoons Worcestershire sauce
Two egg yolks
Two-thirds cup fine dry bread crumbs or cornflake crumbs
One-fourth cup salad oil or bacon drippings
Sauté: Ten to fifteen minutes
Serves: Four

Trim the skin and membrane from sliced liver. Cut into serving portions. Stir together the salt, mustard, pepper, paprika, melted butter, vinegar, Worcestershire sauce and egg yolks. Mix thoroughly. Dip pieces of liver in the seasoning mixture and then in crumbs. Heat the salad oil or bacon drippings in a heavy skillet. Add the liver and brown well on both sides, turning as necessary. Do not overcook the liver or it will become dry and hard.

Quick Liver Dish

One pound calf or beef liver, sliced
One medium-sized onion
Six sprigs parsley
One egg
One-half teaspoon salt
One-fourth teaspoon pepper
Six strips bacon
Saute: Ten minutes
Serves: Four

Remove skin from liver. Cut into chunks (1 in.). Chop onion and parsley together. Put egg, salt and pepper into blender with some of the liver, onion and parsley. (Add a little at a time so as not to overtax the blender.) In a heavy (10 in.) skillet fry the bacon until crisp. Remove excess bacon fat from pan. Pour liver batter evenly into a medium hot pan forming a large omelet. Saute 5 minutes on medium heat. Then cut into 6 or 8 pie slices. Turn each piece over and saute another 5 minutes. Serve with mashed potatoes and pickled beets.

Savory Beef Tongue

One smoked, cured beef tongue (3 lbs.)
Two cups water
One tablespoon salt
One bay leaf
Three peppercorns
Three cloves
One onion, quartered
Pressure cooking time: Forty-five minutes
Servings: Six, or more

Wash the tongue; place upon a rack in the pressure cooker saucepan. Add the water, salt, bay leaf, peppercorns, cloves and onion. Place the cover on the cooker. Set over high heat. When the steam escapes in a steady flow, place the indicator weight on the vent pipe; then follow the instructions for regulating the pressure as given in the manufacturer's recipe booklet. Cook under steady pressure 45 minutes. When the cooking is completed, reduce the pressure instantly by placing the cooker in a pan of cold water. As soon as the pressure is down, take off the cover. Remove the tongue to a board; skin. Keep the tongue in the liquid until ready to serve with a sour cream cucumber sauce.

Piquant Liver

One cup tomato juice or sauce
Four slices beef liver (1½ in. thick)
One clove garlic, split
Chilling time: Four hours
One teaspoon salt
One-eighth teaspoon pepper
One-fourth teaspoon basil
Three tablespoons flour
Four tablespoons bacon drippings
Cooking time: Four minutes (about)
Servings: Four

Pour the tomato juice over the liver in a shallow pan; add the garlic. Chill. Drain, reserve the liquid. Coat each slice lightly with seasoned flour. Heat the drippings in a heavy skillet; brown the liver under low heat on both sides. Pierce the liver with a fork so it cooks quickly. Use the reserved tomato juice to make the gravy. Serve at once.

Kidney Stew

Eight lamb kidneys
Soaking time: Fifteen minutes
Two tablespoons bacon fat or drippings
Sautéing time: Three minutes
Three tablespoons butter or margarine
One-half cup sliced mushrooms
One medium-sized onion, cut into rings
One green pepper, cut into strips
Cooking time: Five minutes
Two tablespoons flour
One cup bouillon
One teaspoon salt
One-eighth teaspoon pepper
One-fourth teaspoon savory
Cooking time: Ten minutes
Two tablespoons sherry wine
Serves: Four

Remove the fat from kidneys; skin. Cut each into quarters. Remove tubes; soak in water to cover. Drain; dry thoroughly. In a heavy skillet heat drippings until they are very hot. Add kidneys; sauté very quickly (about 3 minutes). Drain. Put butter into skillet; add mushrooms, onion and green pepper; cook 5 minutes. Stir in flour. Add bouillon, salt, pepper and savory. Cook, stirring until thickened. Add kidneys and wine; bring to a boil but do not allow it to boil. Serve in a ring of mashed potatoes garnished with parsleyed potato balls.

Veal Roulees

Three-fourths pound mushrooms, grated
One-half cup chopped green olives
One-fourth cup butter or margarine
One can (No. 2) whole tomatoes, strained
Cook: Twelve minutes, or longer
Five slices veal, scaloppine style
   (7 x 5 in.)
Five teaspoons prepared mustard
Five thin slices boiled ham
One-fourth cup flour
One teaspoon salt
One-fourth teaspoon pepper
One tablespoon paprika
Six tablespoons butter or margarine
Browning time: Ten minutes
One cup light Bordeaux dry wine
Oven temperature: 350 degrees
Baking time: One hour
Stuffed olives
Yield: Five

In a saucepan cook the grated mushrooms and green olives with the butter or margarine for five minutes. Strain the tomatoes into the mixture; cook, stirring until the mixture has absorbed all the liquid. Place the thin slices of veal on a board. Spread a teaspoonful of prepared mustard over each slice. Place a ham slice on top. Spread the mushroom mixture over each ham slice. Fold the edge of ham lengthwise (⅛ of an inch). Roll the veal as for jelly roll. Secure with toothpicks. Dust each well in the combined flour, salt, pepper and paprika. In a heavy skillet melt the butter. Brown the rolls on all sides. Place in a deep casserole. Pour the wine into the skillet, removing all the brownings from the pan. Pour over the veal. Cover; bake for 45 minutes in a moderate oven; remove cover and continue baking 15 minutes longer. Serve over buttered noodles. Garnish with sliced stuffed olives.

Veal Birds

Four-medium sized onions, chopped
Six tablespoons butter or margarine
Cooking time: Ten minutes
Two cups soft bread crumbs, packed
Four tablespoons minced parsley
Two teaspoons salt
One teaspoon pepper
One-fourth cup heavy cream or evaporated
   milk
Eight slices boiled ham
Eight slices veal (pounded paper-thin)
One-fourth cup flour
One-half teaspoon salt
One-eighth teaspoon pepper
Four tablespoons melted butter
Browning time: Ten minutes
Four carrots, thinly sliced
One cup chicken stock or bouillon
Oven temperature: 350 degrees
Braising time: One hour (about)
Serves: Six

Cook the onion in the butter, in a saucepan until golden. Add the bread crumbs, parsley, salt, pepper and heavy cream, mixing lightly. Place a slice of ham on each piece of veal and a portion of dressing; skewer or tie securely. Roll each in seasoned flour. Brown the meat in the melted butter. Remove to a casserole. Add the carrots and stock. Cover; braise in a moderate oven until the meat is tender. Serve the meat on buttered, cooked fine noodles. Pour the liquid from the casserole over the meat and noodles. Garnish with carrot strips. Serve immediately.

Veal Paprika

One and one-half pounds veal steak
One egg
Three teaspoons salt
One tablespoon water
One cup packaged corn flake crumbs (four
    cups corn flakes, finely crumbled)
Three tablespoons shortening
One clove garlic, sliced
Sauté: Five minutes
Browning time: Five to ten minutes
One-half cup water
Simmer: One hour
One cup sour cream
One tablespoon paprika
Simmer: Fifteen minutes
Serves: Four to six

Portion the veal steak. Beat the egg in a bowl and stir in the salt and tablespoon of water. Dip pieces of veal in egg then in the corn flake crumbs. Heat the shortening in a large heavy skillet and add the sliced clove of garlic. When garlic is lightly browned, remove and discard. Add prepared veal pieces and brown quickly on both sides. Lower heat, add water, cover and simmer gently until veal is tender. Spoon the sour cream over the veal pieces but do not stir into pan liquid. Sprinkle with paprika and continue simmering for fifteen minutes. Good served on drained hot noodles.

Veal with Green Peppers

One and one-half pounds veal cutlets
One teaspoon salt
One teaspoon paprika
One-half teaspoon sugar
One-fourth teaspoon nutmeg
One teaspoon prepared mustard
Two tablespoons lemon juice
One-half cup salad oil
One clove garlic
Marinate: Fifteen minutes
Flour
One-fourth cup salad oil
Browning time: Ten minutes, or more
One medium-sized onion, thinly sliced
One green pepper, cut in strips
One cup chicken bouillon
Simmering time: Thirty minutes
Servings: Four

Cut the veal cutlets into serving portions and place in a large shallow baking dish. In a bowl combine the salt, paprika, sugar, nutmeg, mustard, lemon juice and half cup of salad oil. Stir together. Add clove garlic. Pour over the veal and allow to stand for fifteen minutes. Lift meat from the marinade and dry with paper toweling. Dredge in flour. Heat the fourth cup of salad oil in a skillet; add the floured cutlets and brown slowly on both sides. Add the thinly sliced onion and green pepper strips. Add the bouillon to the marinade, removing garlic and pour over the contents of the skillet. Cover and simmer gently until veal is very tender, about thirty minutes.

A FAVORITE RECIPE
Veal and Squash

Two pounds lean veal, cut from shin or
    shoulder
Two tablespoons fat
Browning time: Five minutes
One large onion, diced
Sautéing time: Five minutes
Three zucchini squash (7 in.) sliced
Four green peppers, cleaned, cut into
    strips
Simmering time: Ten minutes
One and one-half cups, fresh or canned
    tomatoes
One-sixteenth teaspoon oregano
One teaspoon salt
One-fourth teaspoon pepper
Simmering time: One hour
One-fourth cup sherry or water (optional)
Simmering time: Five minutes
Servings: Four, or more

Have the butcher cut the veal into pieces (1 in.). Heat the fat in a deep kettle; brown the veal, turning frequently. Add the onion, sauté in the fat. Add the zucchini and peppers; simmer. Pour in the tomatoes, mixing well. Season with oregano, salt and pepper; cover; simmer, turning several times. Add either the sherry or water. Continue to cook, stirring well until the meat and vegetables are tender. Serve hot with rice and salad.

ADRIENNE LEONE, *Bronx, N.Y.*

A FAVORITE RECIPE
Veal Cutlets-Wine Sauce

Two tablespoons olive or salad oil, heated
Two pounds Italian cut, veal cutlets
One teaspoon salt
One-fourth teaspoon pepper
Frying time: Until browned on both sides
One-fourth cup chopped onion
Three-fourths cup canned sliced
    mushrooms, drained
One tablespoon minced parsley
Cooking time: Three minutes
Two tablespoons flour
Browning time: Five minutes
One and one-half cups stock or water
One-fourth cup cooking sherry
Two tablespoons lemon juice
Oven temperature: 325 degrees
Baking time: One hour
Servings: Six

Heat the oil in a large heavy skillet. Season the cutlets with salt and pepper. Brown in the oil on both sides. Place the cutlets in a casserole (10 in.). Add the onion, mushrooms and parsley. Cook, stirring well. Add the flour, blending well, cooking until lightly browned. Add the stock, sherry and lemon juice, cook, stirring until smooth. Pour over the cutlets. Bake in a moderately slow oven. Serve from the casserole with rice.

MRS. STANLEY WEINER, *Yonkers, N.Y.*

A FAVORITE RECIPE
Scaloppine in Wine

One and one-half pounds veal
One-fourth cup flour
One teaspoon salt
One-fourth teaspoon pepper
Four tablespoons butter, heated
Four tablespoons oil, heated
Two cups sliced mushrooms
Cooking time: Ten minutes
Juice one lemon
One-half cup sherry
Cooking time: Five minutes
Servings: Four

Have the butcher cut the meat from the leg, into slices about ⅛ inch thick; have it flattened with a wooden mallet. Mix the flour, salt and pepper. Dip each slice of veal in the flour mixture. Heat the butter and oil in a heavy skillet. Brown the veal on each side. Add the mushrooms, cook. Add the lemon juice and sherry, stirring well; cover and cook. Serve on a hot platter with stewed tomatoes and a green salad.

MARY RUFALINO, *Pittston, Penna.*

Veal Sauté over Rice

One pound thinly sliced veal steak
Two tablespoons butter or margarine
Cook: Two to three minutes
Two tablespoons finely chopped onion
One and one-half tablespoons flour
One-half teaspoon salt
One-eighth teaspoon pepper
One-fourth teaspoon crumbled marjoram
Two chicken bouillon cubes
One cup water
Cook: Two to three minutes
Simmer: Twenty minutes
One cup raw rice
Two cups cold water
One teaspoon salt
One tablespoon butter or margarine
Simmer: Fifteen minutes
One-fourth cup finely chopped parsley
Servings: Four

With a sharp knife cut the veal into julienne strips about two inches by one-fourth inch. Heat the two tablespoons of butter or margarine in a large heavy skillet, add the veal and cook, stirring until all pink color disappears. Remove meat to plate with slotted spoon. Add the finely chopped onion to the pan liquid, blend in the flour, salt, pepper, crumbled marjoram and bouillon cubes. Gradually stir in the water. Cook, stirring, until thickened and smooth. Add meat, cover tightly and simmer gently for twenty minutes. In the meantime place the raw rice, cold water, salt and tablespoon of butter or margarine in a saucepan. Bring to a boil, stir once, cover tightly and cook over low heat until moisture is absorbed. This will take about fifteen minutes. Serve veal in sauce over cooked rice with a sprinkling of finely chopped parsley over top.

Veal in Lemon Sauce

Two pounds boneless veal (2 inch cubes)
One carrot
One medium-sized onion
One clove garlic
One bay leaf
Two whole cloves
Two teaspoons salt
One-eighth teaspoon pepper
One-eighth teaspoon nutmeg
Several sprigs parsley
Four cups water
Simmer: One and one-half hours
Two tablespoons butter
Two tablespoons flour
Cook: Two or three minutes
Two egg yolks
Juice of one lemon
Heat: Briefly
Hot cooked rice
Servings: Four or five

Place the cubed veal in a large saucepan or kettle. Add the peeled and sliced carrot, onion, whole clove of garlic, bay leaf, cloves, salt, pepper and nutmeg. Lay sprigs of parsley over top and pour on the water. Cover tightly and simmer until meat is tender. Remove meat from broth, discard parsley, bay leaf, garlic and cloves. Rub cooked carrot and onion through a sieve with broth into a bowl. Melt the butter in the saucepan and stir in the flour. Gradually stir in the puree. Cook and stir until thickened. In a bowl beat the egg yolks with the lemon juice. Gradually blend about half the cooked mixture into the yolks, return combination to the saucepan. Add the veal and heat gently. Serve over the hot cooked rice.

Bernese Veal

One and one-half pounds veal cutlet (12 thin pieces prepared for scaloppine)
Salt and pepper
Six pieces Swiss cheese
One-fourth cup flour
Two beaten eggs
Three-fourths cup fine dry bread crumbs or corn flake crumbs
One-third cup olive oil, or more
Sauté: Ten minutes, about
Serves: Six

You need 12 thin pieces of veal for six servings. They will be sizable when pounded thin. Sprinkle both sides lightly with salt and pepper. Lay pieces of Swiss cheese over half the veal pieces and trim slightly smaller than the meat. Top with remaining meat pieces and press together around the edges. Dust each serving in flour, dip in the beaten egg then into the crumbs. Heat the olive or other salad oil in a large heavy skillet and add the crumbed servings of meat. Sauté for four or five minutes on each side. Drain on absorbent paper and serve at once. Excellent with baked potato, creoled zucchini and crisp water cress.

Veal Chops with Lemon

Four loin or rib veal chops (one inch thick)
Two tablespoons flour
One teaspoon salt
One-fourth teaspoon pepper
One-eighth teaspoon thyme
Two or more tablespoons shortening
Browning time: Five to ten minutes
One lemon
One teaspoon Worcestershire sauce
One-half cup water
Simmer: Forty-five minutes, or more
Serves: Four

Coat the chops with the combined flour, salt, pepper and thyme. Heat the shortening in a large heavy skillet, add the chops and brown well on both sides. Cut the lemon into quarter-inch slices and arrange over the chops. Stir the Worcestershire sauce into the water and pour over the chops. Cover tightly and simmer gently for forty-five minutes or more until chops are very tender. Discard the lemon slices and serve chops with some of the pan liquor spooned over top.

Breast of Veal in Mustard Sauce

Two pounds breast of veal, cut in small pieces
One quart water
Two teaspoons salt
Heat: To boiling
Six cloves
One large onion
Three carrots, halved
One bay leaf
One-half cup finely chopped celery
One-eighth teaspoon crumbled thyme
Simmering time: One hour
Eight small white onions
Simmering time: One-half hour
Three tablespoons butter or margarine
Three tablespoons flour
Two tablespoons prepared mustard
Two and one-half cups meat broth
Cooking time: Five minutes, or more
Servings: Four, or more

Have the butcher cut the breast of veal into pieces (about 2 inch). Place meat in a kettle with the water and salt and heat to boiling point. Stick the cloves into the large peeled onion and add to the kettle with the scraped carrots, bay leaf, celery and thyme. Cover tightly and simmer gently for about one hour. Add the peeled small white onions and continue to simmer until the meat and onions are tender.

Drain off broth and reserve adding enough water if necessary to make two and one-half cups. In a saucepan, melt the butter or margarine and blend in the flour and prepared mustard. Gradually blend in the broth, stirring smooth. Cook over moderate heat, stirring constantly until the sauce thickens. Combine with the cooked meat and vegetables and serve with cooked rice or noodles if desired. Note: Peeled halved potatoes could be added with the onions for the last half hour of cooking if preferred.

Veal Chops in Cream

Three tablespoons fat or oil
Four veal chops
Browning time: Five minutes, about
One clove garlic, crushed
One-fourth pound mushrooms, sliced
Sautéing time: Five minutes
Three tablespoons flour
One cup water
One-half cup cream
One teaspoon salt
One-fourth teaspoon pepper
One-fourth teaspoon crumbled thyme
Simmering time: One hour, about
Servings: Four

Heat the fat or oil in a large heavy skillet. Add the chops and brown quickly on both sides. Remove meat to a plate, add the crushed garlic and sliced mushrooms to the drippings and sauté briefly. Stir in the flour, gradually blend in the water, stirring smooth. Add the cream, salt, pepper and thyme, stirring smooth. Return meat to the skillet, cover and simmer gently for about one hour or until the meat is tender.

A FAVORITE RECIPE
Stuffed Breast of Veal

One veal breast (4-5 lbs.) pocket cut

Dressing

One pound chopped veal
One hard-cooked egg, chopped
One raw egg
One cup grated sharp cheese
Two tablespoons bread crumbs
One small onion, minced
One can (8 oz.) tomato sauce, (less two tablespoonfuls)
One teaspoon salt (or more)
One-fourth teaspoon pepper
One-half teaspoon minced parsley
Two tablespoons oil heated
Cooking time: Ten minutes
Six medium-sized potatoes
Six small carrots
Oven temperature: 400-350 degrees
Baking time: One and one-half hours
Servings: Six

Have the butcher prepare the veal breast with pocket. For the dressing: In a bowl, mix the chopped veal with the chopped egg, raw egg, cheese, crumbs, onion and tomato sauce. Season with salt and pepper. Stir in the parsley; mix. Heat the oil in a heavy skillet. Turn the mixture into the skillet, cook, turning several times. Stuff the pocket in the breast, binding with skewers, or twine. Place in a shallow baking pan, spread the reserved two tablespoons of tomato sauce over the veal. Bake in a quick oven for one hour. Reduce the heat to moderate and add peeled potatoes and carrots to pan. Bake for another 30 minutes. Serve the veal on a hot platter with the vegetables and dressing.

MRS. CONNIE RAZIANO, *Brooklyn, N.Y.*

Veal Stew

Four tablespoons salad oil
Two pounds cubed veal for stew
One teaspoon salt
One-fourth teaspoon pepper
Two tablespoons flour
Twelve small white onions, peeled
Browning time: Fifteen minutes
One clove garlic, pureed
One and one-half cups chicken broth
One-half cup sherry wine
One cup canned tomato pulp, sieved, or
    bouillon
One bouquet garni (stalk celery, bay leaf,
    sprig parsley, carrot slice)
Simmer: Forty-five minutes
Twelve mushrooms, peeled
Eight small potatoes, peeled
Simmer: Thirty minutes
Fried rounds of bread
Serves: Four, or more

Heat the oil in a heavy kettle or iron casserole until hot. Dredge meat in seasoned flour; add and brown on all sides. Remove the meat. Then brown the onions on all sides. Add the garlic, chicken broth, sherry wine, sieved tomato pulp and bouquet garni. Add meat. Cover; simmer over low heat for 45 minutes. Add mushrooms and potatoes. Recover; simmer again until potatoes are tender. Remove the bouquet garni. Garnish casserole with rounds of bread fried in oil.

Veal Stew with Parsley Dumplings

Two pounds veal stew (1 in. cubes)
Flour
One-fourth cup olive oil
Brown: Ten minutes
One teaspoon paprika
One teaspoon thyme
Two cups chicken broth
One cup dry white Bordeaux wine
Simmer: Forty minutes
Twelve pearl onions, peeled
Four carrots, peeled and sliced
Two stalks celery, sliced
Two teaspoons salt
Simmer: Fifteen minutes

Parsley Dumplings

One and one-half cups sifted flour
Three teaspoons baking powder
One-half teaspoon salt
Two tablespoons shortening
One-fourth cup minced parsley
Three-fourths cup milk
Simmer: Twenty minutes
Serves: Four

Dust the veal with flour. In a heavy skillet heat the olive oil. Add the veal; brown on all sides. Sprinkle the paprika and thyme over the meat. Add the chicken broth and dry white Bordeaux wine. Cover; simmer gently for 40 minutes. Add the onions, carrots, celery and salt. Cover; simmer 15 minutes. Meanwhile in a bowl sift the flour, baking powder and salt; blend in the shortening. Add the parsley; toss. Add the milk all at once; stirring just enough to moisten the dry ingredients. Drop by large spoonfuls over stew (makes 12 dumplings). Cover and simmer 20 minutes. Serve immediately.

Mushroom Veal Pie

Two pounds lean veal, cubed
One teaspoon salt
One-fourth teaspoon pepper
One-fourth cup flour
One-fourth cup butter or margarine
Brown: Fifteen minutes
One cup vermouth or white wine
Simmer: Forty minutes
Twelve small onions, peeled
Six carrots, peeled, cut into strips
Eight small new potatoes, halved
One cup hot water
Simmer: Thirty minutes
One cup cooked peas
One recipe (2 cups) pastry mix
One cup chopped fresh mushrooms
Ice water
Oven temperature: 425 degrees
Bake: Twenty minutes
Sautéed mushrooms, pimiento strips
Serves: Four, or more

Dust the veal in the seasoned flour. In a heavy skillet or kettle, brown the meat over low heat in the butter. Add the vermouth. Cover tightly; simmer gently for forty minutes, stirring occasionally. Add the onions, carrot strips, halved potatoes and hot water. Cover; simmer until the vegetables are tender. Add the peas. To the pastry mix blend in the chopped mushrooms. Add enough ice water, a tablespoon at a time (about 5), to hold the mix together. Roll out on a floured board. Fit into shallow baking dish. Chill. Bake in a hot oven for 20 minutes. Pour in hot veal mixture. Arrange sautéed mushrooms around edge of crust with pimiento strips. Allow to re-heat in the oven. Serve immediately.

Braised Veal Shanks
(Osso Buco)

One-half cup salad oil
One clove garlic, pureed or finely chopped
Three veal shanks
Three tablespoons flour
Browning time: Fifteen minutes
One onion, finely chopped
Two small carrots, finely chopped
One stalk celery, finely chopped
One can (No. 2½) whole tomatoes
Two bay leaves
One cup Chablis or Sauterne wine
Cooking time: One and one-half to two hours
Two tablespoons finely chopped parsley
One tablespoon finely grated lemon rind
Salt and pepper
Serves: Four, or more

In a heavy kettle heat the salad oil and garlic. Add the shanks dusted lightly in

flour; brown on all sides. Add the onion, carrots, celery, tomatoes, bay leaves and wine. Cover and cook very slowly until tender. Add the parsley and grated lemon rind. Season to taste with salt and pepper. Serve on a hot platter with saffron rice. Be sure to remove and eat the marrow from the shanks.

Lamb Stew

One and one-half pounds lamb stew
  meat, diced
One-fourth cup flour
Two tablespoons shortening
Browning time: Ten minutes, or more
One teaspoon salt, or more
One-eighth teaspoon pepper
Two cups water
Simmering time: One and one-half hours
One cup sliced onion
One cup inch cuts of celery
Two tablespoons finely chopped parsley
Simmering time: Thirty minutes
Servings: Four

Cut the stewing lamb into cubes, one or two inches. Dredge in flour and brown in the hot shortening in a large heavy skillet. Add the salt, pepper, remaining flour and water. Cover and simmer gently for one and one-half hours or until the meat is very tender. Add more water if necessary with the sliced onion, celery and parsley and continue cooking over low heat for 30 minutes more. If desired add dumplings for the last 20 minutes.

Parsley Dumplings

One cup sifted flour
One and one-half teaspoons baking powder
Three-fourths teaspoon salt
One egg
One-third cup milk
Two tablespoons salad oil
Two tablespoons finely chopped parsley
Yield: Eight medium-sized dumplings

Sift together in a bowl the flour, baking powder and salt. In a small bowl beat the eggs, add the milk and salad oil. Stir into the dry ingredients with the chopped parsley, stirring only until all flour is moistened. Drop by spoonfuls over the bubbling contents of the skillet. Cover pan tightly and simmer till tender and fluffy in about 20 mnutes.

Scotch Stew

One tablespoon shortening
Two pounds lamb shanks
Browning time: Ten to fifteen minutes
Two quarts water
One-fourth cup barley
One large onion, thinly sliced
Two tablespoons finely chopped parsley
One cup sliced celery with leaves
Two teaspoons salt
Simmer: One and one-half hours
Four medium-sized potatoes, peeled
Simmer: Forty-five minutes
Servings: Four, or more

Melt the shortening in a large heavy skillet or kettle. Add the lamb shanks and brown well in the shortening. Add the water, barley, thinly sliced onion, chopped parsley, celery and salt. Cover, bring to a boil, reduce the heat and simmer for an hour and a half. Cut the peeled potatoes into quarters and add. Continue cooking until potatoes are tender. Remove shanks and strip meat from bones. Return meat to the stew and serve hot.

Crown Roast of Lamb

One crown roast of lamb (made from two
  or three racks of rib chops)
Oven temperature: 325 degrees
Roasting time: Two hours, about (172
  degrees)
Servings: Allow two or three ribs for each

The butcher will skewer and tie the racks of rib chops (six to nine ribs in a rack) into the crown roast for you. Have him cut off the backbone to make carving easy. He will grind lamb trimmed from rib bones and this can be used for the stuffing. Place roast, rib bones down, on a rack in a shallow roasting pan and roast in a moderately slow oven for about two hours. Insert a meat thermometer in the thickest part of the meat and roast until it registers 172 degrees for lamb with the pink tinge. Cook to 182 degrees for well done. One-half hour before serving turn the roast right side up and fill with the stuffing that has baked in foil for an hour and a half. Continue roasting for last thirty minutes before transfering stuffed crown roast to heated serving platter. Serve at once, using a sharp knife to slice down between the ribs.

Spinach Lamb Stuffing

Two packages (10 oz. each) frozen chopped
  spinach
Eight cups half-inch bread cubes
One-half cup butter or margarine
One cup finely chopped onion
One clove garlic, crushed
Sauté: Until golden
One pound raw lamb, ground
Browning time: Five minutes, about
One teaspoon salt
One-half teaspoon allspice
One-fourth teaspoon pepper
One-third cup grated Parmesan cheese
Oven temperature: 325 degrees
Bake: One and one-half hours

Cook the frozen chopped spinach according to package directions, drain well and place in a large bowl. Add the bread cubes. Melt the butter or margarine in a large heavy skillet and add the chopped onion and crushed garlic. Sauté until golden. Lift the sautéed onions from the butter and add to the spinach and bread cubes. Add the ground lamb to the skillet and brown quickly. Add lamb to stuffing mixture with the salt, allspice, pepper and Parmesan cheese. Mix thoroughly. Place in the center of a large piece of heavy foil and fold edges in carefully to make a snug package. Place in the moderately slow oven with the crown roast of lamb for an hour and a half.

Easy Lamb Chops with Vegetables

Two tablespoons butter or margarine
Four shoulder lamb chops (one-inch thick)
Browning time: Ten minutes, about
One cup bouillon
Simmer: Thirty minutes
Two teaspoons cornstarch
Two teaspoons water
Cook: Until thickened
One can (1 lb.) whole onions, drained
One can (1 lb.) julienned carrots, drained
One cup canned whole kernel corn
Salt and pepper
Heat: Ten minutes
Servings: Four

Melt the butter or margarine in a large heavy skillet. Add the shoulder lamb chops browning well on both sides. Add the bouillon, cover tightly and cook over low heat for thirty minutes, or until lamb is tender. Remove chops from pan. In a small bowl blend the cornstarch with the two teaspoons of water. Gradually blend in the liquid from the skillet; return combination to skillet and cook over low heat until slightly thickened. Add the drained vegetables and the chops. Cover and cook until all is piping hot before serving.

Savory Breast of Lamb with Vegetables

Two pounds breast of lamb
One-fourth cup flour
One teaspoon paprika
One teaspoon salt
One-fourth teaspoon pepper
Three tablespoons salad oil
Browning time: Fifteen minutes, or more
One envelope (1½ oz.) dehydrated onion
  soup mix
Three cups boiling water
Cook: One and one-half hours
Four carrots
Four medium-sized potatoes
One pound fresh green beans
Cook: Twenty minutes, or more
Servings: Four

Cut the breast of lamb into riblet strips between the bones. Mix the flour, paprika, salt and pepper together and use to coat the pieces of lamb. Reserve the unused seasoned flour. Heat the salad oil in a heavy skillet, add the coated lamb and brown well on all sides. Drain off the drippings. Combine the onion soup mix and water and add to the lamb. Cover tightly and cook over low heat for an hour and a half. Wash and scrape the carrots and potatoes. Slice carrots and dice potatoes. Trim tips from washed beans and cut through to French. Add vegetables to the cooked lamb and continue cooking for twenty minutes or until vegetables are tender. Add additional water if needed. Spoon some of the pan liquid into the reserved seasoned flour and return combination to the skillet to thicken the stew. Cook brefly. Serve piping hot.

Lamb with Carrots and Onions

Two and one-half pounds shoulder lamb
  chops (one piece)
One clove garlic, sliced
One teaspoon salt or more
One-eighth teaspoon pepper
Two tablespoons shortening
Browning time: Twenty minutes
Two cups carrot slices
Two cups small peeled onions (one pound
  approx.)
Several sprigs parsley
One-half cup water
One teaspoon salt
Oven temperature: 350 degrees
Baking time: One and one-half hours, or
  until tender
Servings: Four

Have most of the fat removed from
the piece of lamb, also part of the bone
if desired. Make small cuts into the meat
with a sharp knife. Insert slices of garlic.
Sprinkle with salt and pepper. Melt the
shortening in a heavy kettle. Brown the
meat on all sides. Add the carrots, onions, sprigs of parsley, water and salt.
Cover tightly. Bake in a moderate oven
until the meat is tender. Remove meat
and vegetables to platter to serve. Garnish with fresh parsley.

Lamb Stew with Spinach

Two pounds lean lamb for stew
Browning time: Five to ten minutes
Two large onions, thinly sliced
Cooking time: Ten minutes
Two cups boiling water
Simmer time: One hour
One package frozen chopped spinach
Two cups fresh diced tomatoes
One-fourth pound fresh diced mushrooms,
  chopped
One and one-half teaspoons salt
One-eighth teaspoon pepper
Cooking time: Fifteen minutes
Three tablespoons cold water
Three tablespoons flour
Simmering time: Two minutes, about
Servings: Six

Cut excess fat from the lamb and melt
some of it in a large heavy skillet. Add
the cubes of lamb and brown quickly
over brisk heat. Add the onions and cook
over low heat for about ten minutes.
Pour on the boiling water, cover tightly
and simmer for about one hour or until
the meat is tender. If there is not a good
half inch of liquid in the pan add water
with the frozen spinach, chopped tomatoes and cut mushrooms. Add the salt
and pepper. Cook until spinach is completely thawed. Taste and correct seasoning as desired. In a cup blend the cold
water into the flour. Stir into the stew.
Cook and stir until the stew thickens
slightly. Serve at once.

Shoulder Lamb Skillet Dinner

One-fourth cup salad oil
One clove garlic, split
Four shoulder lamb chops (one inch thick)
Browning time: Ten minutes, about
One-half cup dry white wine
One-half cup boiling water
One bouillon cube
Four small peeled onions
Four medium-sized peeled potatoes
Six carrots, peeled and quartered
Simmer: Fifty minutes, about
Serves: Four

In a large heavy skillet heat the salad
oil. Add the split clove of garlic and the
shoulder lamb chops. Brown chops well
on both sides. Add the dry white wine,
boiling water and bouillon cube. Add the
peeled onions, halved or quartered potatoes and carrot pieces. Cover tightly
and simmer gently until all is tender.
Serve from the skillet, using pan liquid as
gravy. This may be thickened if desired.

A FAVORITE RECIPE
Veal or Lamb on Skewers

Twelve small slices veal or lamb cutlet
One teaspoon salt
One-fourth teaspoon pepper
Three tablespoons lemon juice
Twelve thin slices, Swiss cheese
Twelve thin slices, Italian ham
One-half teaspoon grated Parmesan
  cheese
Twelve squares (2 x 2 in.) bread, crust
  removed
One-third cup melted butter
Oven temperature: 450 degrees
Baking time: Fifteen minutes
Servings: Eight

Pound the veal or lamb until very flat;
season with salt and pepper; sprinkle with
lemon juice. Place a slice of Swiss cheese
over it, a slice of ham and sprinkle with
Parmesan cheese. Roll up, binding well.
Cut the bread into squares; place the rolls
alternately with the bread on skewers.
Bake in a hot oven, brushing and basting
several times with the melted butter.
Serve hot with a salad.

LOUISE PUGLIA, *Ridgewood, N.J.*

Broiled Bacon Lamburgers

One pound ground lamb
One-half teaspoon salt
One-fourth teaspoon cinnamon
One-eighth teaspoon cloves
One-eighth teaspoon allspice
Four slices bacon
Broiling temperature: 500 degrees
Broil: Ten minutes
Servings: Four

In a bowl combine the ground lamb
lightly with the salt, cinnamon, cloves
and allspice; mixing well. Form into four
cakes. Wrap each with a slice of bacon.
Secure with a wooden pick or two. Broil
about three inches from source of heat
in pre-heated broiler for five minutes.
Turn and broil five minutes more.

Shish Kabob

Two teaspoons salt
One-eighth teaspoon pepper
Three-fourths teaspoon crumbled rosemary
One-fourth teaspoon dry mustard
One clove garlic, crushed
One medium-sized onion, finely chopped
One-third cup salad oil
One-fourth cup lemon juice
One cup dry red wine
Three pounds shoulder or leg of lamb
  meat (2-inch cubes)
Marinating time: Five hours or overnight
Two or three green peppers, cut in inch
  squares
Four large tomatoes, cut in wedges
Four to six medium-sized potatoes,
  quartered, cooked
Sixteen small onions, cooked
Sixteen small fresh mushrooms
Grill: Fifteen minutes, about
Serves: Eight

In a bowl blend the salt, pepper,
crumbled rosemary and dry mustard together. Add the crushed garlic and finely
chopped onion. Stir in the salad oil,
lemon juice and red wine. Pour mixture
over the cubed lamb in a bowl. Press
meat down in the liquid so it is covered.
Cover bowl and allow meat to marinate
in the refrigerator several hours or overnight. Turn meat in the marinade once
or twice. Prepare the vegetables. At
mealtime arrange four or more cubes of
meat on long skewers alternately with
two pieces each of green pepper, tomato, potato and two onions and use the
mushrooms as terminals for each portion. Lay skewers on the grill over glowing coals and grill about fifteen minutes,
turning occasionally and basting with the
marinade. When well cooked and nicely
browned serve a skewer to each diner to
enjoy at once. Note: Those preferring
may broil the filled skewers in the kitchen
with broiler set at 500 degrees, basting
occasionally for about the same length
of time. A time and effort-saver is the
use of canned onions and potatoes. We
prefer the fresh to the canned mushrooms.

A FAVORITE RECIPE
Stuffed Leg of Lamb

One leg lamb (6-7 lbs.) boned Dressing
One cup bread crumbs
One-half teaspoon thyme
One-fourth teaspoon marjoram
One-fourth teaspoon grated nutmeg
One-fourth teaspoon grated lemon rind
One-half teaspoon salt
One-eighth teaspoon pepper
One teaspoon capers, chopped
Four anchovies, chopped
Four hard-cooked eggs, chopped
One-half cup butter, melted
Oven temperature: 325 degrees
Roasting time: Three hours
One cup white wine for basting
Servings: Eight

Have the butcher remove the bone from the lamb. For the stuffing: In a bowl, mix the bread crumbs, thyme, marjoram, nutmeg, lemon rind, salt, pepper, capers, anchovies, eggs and melted butter. Stuff the leg with the mixture, binding with skewers and twine. Place in a roasting pan and roast in a moderately slow oven. Thirty minutes before the meat is done, pour in the wine; baste frequently with wine until the meat is done. Serve on a hot platter with stewed tomatoes and a salad.

MRS. PEGGY IROLLA, *New York, N.Y.*

Crown Roast of Lamb

Have butcher prepare a crown roast of lamb, grinding the trimmings and mixing them with ground pork. Fill center with this mixture. Pieces of salt pork may be set on each rib bone at the market, or pieces of raw potato placed on rib bones at home. This prevents rib bones from burning. Wipe roast with a damp cloth. Rub with salt and pepper. Place ribs upright in uncovered roaster. Roast for 1½ hours to 2 hours. Allow 2 ribs per serving.

Allow 25 minutes per pound for roasts under 6 lbs., and 22 minutes per pound for roasts over 6 lbs.

Garnish rib bones with preserved kumquats and cooked cauliflowerets.

Shoulder Lamb Chop Casserole

One tablespoon drippings
Five shoulder lamb chops
Brown: Ten minutes
One clove garlic, minced
Cooking time: Three minutes
One can (14½ oz.) evaporated milk
One-half cup French vermouth
Two tablespoons paprika
Two teaspoons salt
One-fourth teaspoon pepper
One-half teaspoon tarragon
Oven temperature: 325 degrees
Baking time: Two hours
Four medium-sized potatoes, peeled
Six white onions, peeled
One pound Frenched green beans
One can (6 oz.) button mushrooms
Serves: Four

In a heavy skillet heat the drippings; slowly brown the shoulder lamb chops on both sides. Remove to a deep casserole (3 qts.). In the drippings cook the garlic until golden. Add the evaporated milk, vermouth, paprika, half the measure of salt, pepper and tarragon; blend well scraping the sides of the pan. Pour over the chops. Cover and bake in the oven for one hour. Place the potatoes, onions, Frenched green beans and mushrooms in with the chops; sprinkle remaining measure of salt on vegetables. Cover; bake in the oven for another hour. Remove. Serve immediately.

Lamb Casserole

Four tablespoons butter or margarine
One clove garlic, split
Two pounds lean lamb stew
Brown: Ten minutes, or longer
Four cups potato balls
Six medium-sized onions, sliced
One bay leaf, crushed
One and one-half teaspoons salt
One-half teaspoon pepper
One-half teaspoon marjoram
One and one-half cups bouillon or
   chicken stock
Oven temperature: 350 degrees
Bake: One and one-half hours
One-fourth cup seasoned bread crumbs
*One cup Mexican pepitas
Serves: Four, or more

In a heavy skillet heat the butter and garlic. Add the lamb; brown on both sides. Remove garlic. Add the potato balls, thinly sliced onion, crushed bay leaf, salt, pepper, marjoram, bouillon and mix thoroughly. Put into one large or six small casseroles. Cover. Bake in a moderate oven until meat is tender. Last 15 minutes of baking remove cover and sprinkle bread crumbs and pepitas on top. Serve. Garnish as desired.

Lamb and Noodle Loaf

One package (8 oz.) wide noodles
Two cups cooked ground lamb, packed
Two tablespoons grated onion
Two tablespoons chopped parsley
One teaspoon salt
One-fourth teaspoon pepper
One-fourth teaspoon rosemary
Two whole pimientos
Two cups milk
Two eggs, slightly beaten
Oven temperature: 350 degrees
Baking time: Thirty minutes
Green pepper slices
One can (8 oz.) tomato sauce
Serves: Four

Cook the noodles according to package directions. Drain. Combine with the lamb, onion, parsley, salt, pepper and rosemary. Chop one pimiento; add. Combine the milk and eggs; add. Pack into greased and floured loaf pan (9 x 5 x 3 in.). Bake in a moderate oven until firm. Unmold on platter. Garnish with pimiento and green pepper. Serve with hot tomato sauce.

Shepherd's Pie

Two tablespoons fat
One-fourth cup chopped onion
Cooking time: Three minutes
Two tablespoons flour
One teaspoon salt
One-eighth teaspoon pepper
One-eighth teaspoon marjoram
Two bouillon cubes dissolved in
Two cups boiling water
Two cups cooked cubed lamb
One cup cooked or canned peas
One cup cooked diced celery
One tablespoon capers
Simmering time: Five minutes
Two cups hot mashed potatoes
Oven temperature: 375 degrees
Baking time: Thirty minutes
Serves: Four

Melt the fat in a heavy skillet. Add the onion; cook until straw-colored. Blend in the flour and seasonings. Add the dissolved bouillon cubes, meat, peas, celery and capers; simmer. Pour into a baking dish (2 qts.). Place spoonfuls of potatoes around the edge of the meat mixture. Bake in a moderately hot oven until potatoes are brown. Remove. Serve immediately.

A FAVORITE RECIPE
Mock Chicken Legs

One-half pound lean veal, ground
One-half pound lean pork, ground
Two teaspoons salt
One-fourth teaspoon paprika
Two tablespoons minced green pepper
One-half cup drained crushed pineapple
One egg, beaten with
One tablespoon water
One cup corn flakes, crushed fine
Three tablespoons fat
Browning time: Ten minutes
One-half cup water
Simmering time: One hour, about
One-half cup sweet or sour cream
Heating time: To boiling point
Servings: Four

In a bowl combine the veal, pork, salt, paprika, green pepper and pineapple. Shape like chicken legs around wooden skewers. Beat the egg and water together in a bowl, dip each piece into egg and then in the crushed corn flakes. Heat the fat in a heavy skillet; brown the legs in the fat, turning several times. Add the water; cover and let simmer. Remove to a hot platter. Make a gravy by adding the cream to pan drippings. Season and serve hot.

MRS. LOUIS ZALEWSKI, *Baltimore, Md.*

Veal Chops Tarragon

Four veal chops (one inch thick)
One-fourth cup flour
One teaspoon salt
One-eighth teaspoon pepper
One tablespoon paprika
Two tablespoons shortening
Two medium-sized onions, thinly sliced
Browning time: Ten minutes, about
One teaspoon dried tarragon
One cup water
One tablespoon lemon juice
Simmer: One hour
Serves: Four

Dredge the veal chops in the combined flour, salt, pepper and paprika. Heat the shortening in a large heavy skillet, add the chops and brown well. Add the thinly sliced onions and brown. Sprinkle with the dried tarragon and add water and lemon juice. Cover tightly and simmer gently until meat is tender, about one hour. Serve chops with onions and pan gravy spooned over top.

A FAVORITE RECIPE
Jellied Veal

Three pounds lean veal, cut into pieces
One large onion, minced
Two stalks celery, chopped
One tablespoon butter
One teaspoon salt
One-fourth teaspoon pepper
Water to cover
Cooking time: Two hours
One envelope unflavored gelatin
One-half cup cold water
Standing time: Five minutes
Chilling time: Three hours, or longer
Servings: Eight, or more

In a deep kettle place the veal, onion, celery, butter, salt and pepper. Cover with water. Bring to a boil, reduce the heat, simmer until the meat is very tender and the water is reduced to two cups. Cool. Strain the stock and reserve. Grind the veal. Soak the gelatin in cold water; add to the hot reserved stock, stirring until the gelatin is dissolved. Turn the veal into a loaf pan (9 in.); pour the hot gelatin over the meat. Cool; chill until serving time.

MRS. MARGARET BEDELL, *Bronx, N.Y.*

A FAVORITE RECIPE
Minced Veal and Eggs

Two tablespoons butter or margarine
One teaspoon flour
One teaspoon lemon juice
One cup stock, or water
Salt and pepper to taste
Cooking time: To the boiling point
Two pounds cooked veal, coarsely chopped
Cooking time: Ten minutes
Six slices buttered toast
Six eggs, poached
Servings: Six

In a heavy skillet, heat the butter; stir in the flour. Add the lemon juice and stock (made with bouillon cube), salt, pepper to taste, stirring and cooking until smooth. Fold in the chopped veal. Serve hot on buttered toast. Place a poached egg in the center of each serving. Garnish with parsley.

MRS. ANNA V. MURPHY, *Tarrytown, N.Y.*

A FAVORITE RECIPE
Veal and Ham Patties-Apricots

One-fourth pound ground raw veal
One-fourth pound ground smoked ham
One tablespoon chopped onion
One tablespoon minced parsley
One-sixteenth teaspoon sage
One teaspoon salt
One-fourth teaspoon paprika
One-sixteenth teaspoon thyme
One-fourth cup sifted bread crumbs
Hot water to moisten
Broiling oven temperature: 350 degrees
   (preheated)
Two teaspoons melted butter
Broiling time: Eight minutes, or longer
Four canned apricots, halved, drained
Broiling time: Five minutes
Servings: Four

In a bowl, mix the veal, ham, onion, parsley, seasonings and crumbs. Add enough hot water to bind the mixture into four patties. Preheat the broiling oven for 10 minutes. Place the patties on the broiler rack, three inches from the heat. Broil, baste with butter. Turn the patties, place apricot halves on each pattie. Broil for five minutes. Serve hot.

RUTH PEDERSON, *The Springs, E. Hamp., N.Y.*

Baked Eggplant with Veal

One medium-sized eggplant (1½ to 2 lbs.)
Three-fourths cup flour
One and one-half teaspoons salt
One-fourth teaspoon pepper
One egg
One tablespoon milk
Three tablespoons salad or olive oil
Fry: Until browned
Three tablespoons salad or olive oil
One-half pound ground veal
One cup chopped fresh mushrooms
   (three large)
One-fourth cup finely chopped onion
Cook: Ten minutes, about
One egg
One-half cup stale bread crumbs
Two tablespoons grated Parmesan cheese
One teaspoon salt
One-eighth teaspoon pepper
Oven temperature: 350 degrees
Bake: Twenty minutes
Two or three large tomatoes
Bake: Fifteen minutes
Two tablespoons finely chopped parsley
Serves: Six

Cut the stem and blossom end from the washed eggplant. Cut into three-quarter-inch slices. Peeling is unnecessary. Combine the flour, salt and pepper and scatter over a sheet of waxed paper. Beat the egg in a shallow dish, adding the tablespoon of milk. Dip slices of eggplant in seasoned flour, in the egg and in the seasoned flour again. In a large skillet heat three tablespoons of the oil. Brown all the eggplant slices in the hot oil on both sides. Arrange in a single layer in shallow baking dishes or pie plates. When the eggplant is browned add the additional oil to the skillet with the ground veal, chopped mushrooms and onion and cook until the meat is lightly browned. In a bowl beat the egg, add the bread crumbs, grated Parmesan, salt and pepper. Add to the meat mixture in the skillet, mixing thoroughly. Spoon meat mixture on top of each slice of eggplant. Cover dishes with foil and bake in a moderate oven for 20 minutes. Remove from oven and top with half inch slices of tomato. Cover and bake 15 minutes longer. Serve hot from the oven with a sprinkling of finely chopped parsley over top.

Veal Scallops with Cream

Three tablespoons flour
One teaspoon salt
One-fourth teaspoon pepper
One teaspoon paprika
Eight veal scallops
Six tablespoons butter or margarine
Brown: Ten minutes
Cook: Five minutes
One-half cup light cream
Cook: Three minutes
Serves: Four

Mix the flour, salt, pepper and paprika. Dredge the scallops in the mixture. Brown them on both sides in the hot butter. Cover and cook slowly until meat is tender. Add the cream and let cook over low heat for another three minutes.

Baked ham will be the main item on many a dinner table this Sunday and a fine choice it is. With a large group to serve, you will rightly choose a whole or half ham. The small family can gain the same pleasure from a thick slice.

Most hams these days are of the pre-cooked variety, requiring thorough heating more than real cooking. This heating takes time, however, especially when a large ham is involved. It is important for the best development of flavor. If you use a meat thermometer insert it at the thickest part, away from the bone and roast at 325 degrees until it registers an internal temperature of 150 degrees. It will take about twenty minutes to the pound, a little longer per pound for the smaller cuts of ham.

When the internal temperature is reached remove the ham from the oven and increase the oven setting to 400 degrees to ready it for glazing. Pour off the drippings, remove any skin and score the top of the ham. Leave about a fourth inch of fat on top for the scoring. Press in whole cloves if you like, following the scoring or in free form pattern. Sift brown sugar over the scored surface, adding a tablespoon of dry mustard or flour to a cup of sugar. Sprinkle on a little pineapple juice if you like (do not pour or you wash off the brown sugar).

Return to the hot oven and continue roasting to form a glaze. It will take from fifteen to twenty-five minutes.

For ease of carving you'll want that glazed ham to rest for fifteen minutes after leaving the oven. Fine time for getting vegetables into serving dishes, heating plates and putting on the coffee.

If you choose to serve a center cut slice of ham, make it one and one-half to two-inches in thickness. Give it about a half hour to the pound in a moderately hot oven, 375 degrees. Brush with mustard and top off for the last twenty minutes with drained crushed pineapple if you wish. There is so little waste with this cut that two pounds will generously serve six.

Baked potatoes and almost any green vegetable are appropriate with ham, many like to offer a tomato juice appetizer. Keep the salad simple so you can graduate to a special dessert — is strawberry shortcake welcome at your house?

Ham Steak with Cheesed Limas

One center ham slice (one inch thick)
Broiling temperature: 500 degrees
Broil: Fifteen minutes
One pkg. (10 oz.) frozen baby lima beans, cooked (two cups)
One tablespoon prepared mustard
One cup coarsely grated cheddar cheese
Broil: Two minutes, about
Servings: Four

Place the ham slice in preheated broiler and broil ten minutes. Turn and broil for five minutes. Frozen limas may be cooked in this time. Spread the top side of the ham with the prepared mustard, top with drained limas and a generous sprinkling of the grated cheese. Return to broiler for one or two minutes, just long enough to melt the cheese. Carve into portions and serve at once.

Baked Ham Steak with Kraut

One can (No. 303) sauerkraut
One-fourth teaspoon celery seed
Two medium-sized apples
One ham steak (one inch thick)
One-third cup molasses
One teaspoon dry mustard
Oven temperature: 350 degrees
Bake: One hour, or more
Servings: Four or five

Mix the undrained sauerkraut with the celery seed and arrange in the bottom of a greased shallow baking dish. Peel, core and slice the apples thin. Arrange slices of apple over the sauerkraut evenly. Lay on the ham steak. Stir the molasses into the dry mustard in a cup and spread over the ham. Bake in a moderate oven for one hour or until the apples are tender. Cut ham steak into individual portions and serve with the kraut and apples.

Pineapple Glazed Ham Steak

One ham steak, cut one inch thick (1½ lbs. approx.)
One-half teaspoon brown bouquet sauce
One tablespoon fat
Browning time: Five minutes
One tablespoon cornstarch
One-fourth cup brown sugar
One-sixteenth teaspoon ginger
One cup crushed pineapple and juice
One tablespoon lemon juice
One-fourth cup sherry
Cooking time: Five minutes, about
Oven temperature: 375 degrees
Baking time: Forty-five minutes
Servings: Four

Brush the ham steak on both sides with the brown bouquet sauce. In a heavy skillet melt the fat. Add the ham steak and brown quickly on both sides. In a small saucepan mix the cornstarch, brown sugar and ginger. Stir in the crushed pineapple, lemon juice and sherry. Heat, stirring constantly, until the sauce is hot and thickened. Place the browned ham in a shallow baking dish. Spread fruit mixture over the top. Bake in a moderately hot oven until the ham is lightly browned.

Eggplant Ham Specials

One tablespoon butter or margarine
One medium-sized onion, chopped
Sauté: Until soft
One can (4 oz.) mushroom pieces
Two tablespoons chopped parsley
One teaspoon Worcestershire sauce
One-half teaspoon salt
One-eighth teaspoon pepper
One teaspoon lemon juice
One cup soft bread crumbs
Three tablespoons butter or margarine
Four slices eggplant (one inch thick)
Flour
Browning time: Ten minutes, or more
Four thick individual sliced cooked ham
One tablespoon butter or margarine
One-half cup soft bread crumbs
One-fourth cup grated Parmesan cheese
One-half teaspoon paprika
Oven temperature: 400 degrees
Bake: Fifteen minutes
Serves: Four

Melt the tablespoon of butter or margarine in a heavy skillet. Add the chopped onion and sauté until soft. Stir in the canned mushroom pieces, chopped parsley, Worcestershire sauce, salt, pepper, lemon juice and one cup of soft bread crumbs. Mix well and remove to a plate. Melt the three tablespoons of butter or margarine in the skillet. Dredge the thick slices of peeled eggplant in the flour and brown well on both sides in the butter or margarine. Place slices of cooked ham in greased baking pan. Spoon crumb mixture over ham and top with browned eggplant slices. Melt the remaining tablespoon of butter or margarine and stir in the half cup of soft bread crumbs, grated Parmesan cheese and paprika. Scatter over the eggplant and bake in a quick oven until piping hot and nicely browned.

A FAVORITE RECIPE
Ham Cubes-Green Beans

Two tablespoons butter
Two medium-sized onions, sliced thin
One clove garlic, minced
Two tablespoons minced green pepper
Sautéing time: Five minutes
One can (8 oz.) tomato sauce
Simmering time: Five minutes
One pound green beans washed, cut into pieces (1 in.)
One and one-half cups cubed ham
One-third cup white wine
One teaspoon salt
One-fourth teaspoon pepper
Few grains cayenne
Simmering time: Forty-five minutes
Servings: Six

In a large heavy skillet, heat the butter; add the onion, garlic and green pepper, sauté until the onions are transparent. Stir in the tomato sauce, heat and simmer. Add the green beans, ham, wine and seasonings. Bring to a boil; reduce the heat. Cover; simmer until the beans are tender. Serve in a casserole with hot biscuits.

JULIANNA KELEMEN, *New York, N.Y.*

Pour the vermouth over the lamb; let stand. In a heavy skillet melt the butter; add the onion; cook until straw-colored. Stir in the flour and seasonings. Gradually stir in the milk. Cook until slightly thickened. Add meat and vermouth; stir until hot and bubbly. Add the mushrooms, hard-cooked eggs, pimiento and peas. Pour into a hot dish.

Lamb with Dill Sauce

Two and one-half pounds shoulder or
   breast of lamb (2 in. cubes)
Five cups water
One tablespoon salt
Four peppercorns
One bay leaf
Few sprigs fresh dill
Simmer: One hour
Ten to twelve new potatoes
Two cups lima beans
One bunch carrots, peeled
Steam: One-half hour
Serves: Four

Lamb Supper Dish

One-fourth cup French vermouth
Two cups chopped cooked lamb
Marinate: Fifteen minutes
Two tablespoons butter or margarine
One medium-sized onion, chopped
Browning time: Three minutes
One tablespoon flour
One teaspoon salt

One-half teaspoon basil
One tablespoon Worcestershire sauce
One cup milk
Cook: Five minutes
One can (3¼ oz.) mushrooms, drained,
   sliced
Two hard-cooked eggs, quartered
One pimiento, chopped
One cup cooked peas
Serves: Four

Dill Sauce

Two tablespoons butter or margarine
Three tablespoons flour
Two cups stock (from boiled lamb)
Cook: Ten minutes
Two tablespoons dill (minced)
One and one-half tablespoons vinegar
One teaspoon sugar
One teaspoon salt
Yield: Two cups

In the bottom of a Swedish aluminum cooker (3 qts.) place the meat. Add the water. Bring to a boil. Skim. Add the salt, peppercorns, bay leaf and dill. Cover; simmer over low heat for 1 hour. Place the top of the steamer over the cooker. On one side place the new potatoes which have been peeled down the center. Put lima beans on the other side and place the carrots on top. Cover. Increase the heat until the lid of kettle will spin when turned. Then reduce heat to simmer; cook until vegetables are tender. Remove vegetables and meat to a hot platter. Then use stock to make the dill sauce: In a heavy saucepan melt the butter, add the flour, stirring until blended. Gradually stir in stock from the lamb; cook until thickened. Add dill, vinegar, sugar and salt. Serve in a bowl.

broil the kebabs three inches from the heat unit, turning to broil on all sides. Remove. Serve on the plank with a dish of hot fluffy rice.

Roast Leg of Lamb A La Boulangere

One leg of lamb (5 lbs.)
Oven temperature: 325 degrees
Roasting time: Two and one-half hours
Six potatoes, pared, sliced (¼ in. thick)
One onion, chopped
One teaspoon chopped parsley
One teaspoon salt
One-fourth teaspoon pepper
Two cups boiling water or stock
Two tablespoons butter, melted
Three tablespoons mint jelly, melted
Serves: Four, or more

Place the leg of lamb in a shallow pan. Roast in a moderately slow oven for one hour. Remove the lamb. Place the sliced potatoes in the roasting pan. Pour the combined onion, parsley, salt, pepper and boiling water over the potatoes. Dot with butter. Place partially roasted lamb on top. Continue roasting for about 1½ hours. Remove roast onto a piece of foil. Brush surface of roast with mint jelly. Place in oven to glaze (about 5 minutes). Place potatoes on a hot platter. Meanwhile make gravy. Place glazed roast in center of platter with potatoes on both sides of roast. Serve.

A FAVORITE RECIPE

Lamb Chops Montblanc

Eight double-cut lamb chops rubbed with
One-half clove garlic
Six tablespoons olive oil, heated
Sauté Ten minutes
Four green peppers, cleaned, cut into
  halves
One small can pearl onions, cut into halves
Four tomatoes, peeled, cut into halves
Eight mushroom caps, cleaned
One teaspoon salt
One-half teaspoon pepper
One-eighth teaspoon rosemary
One-half glass sherry wine
Oven temperature: 400 degrees
Baking time: Forty-five minutes
Two cups cooked rice
Servings: Six

Rub the chops with garlic on both sides. Heat the olive oil in a large skillet. Brown the chops on both sides. Cut eight pieces of foil large enough to fully cover the chops and vegetables. Place a chop on each piece of foil; arrange a piece of pepper, onion, tomato and mushroom on each chop; season each with salt, pepper and rosemary. Add a spoonful of wine over all. Fold the foil and place the bundle on a baking pan. Bake in a quick oven. No water is needed. Serve with hot rice.

MRS. EDWIN C. CAREY, *New Castle, Pa.*

Shish Kebab

Two pounds lamb, cut into squares
  (1½ in.)
Three tablespoons lemon juice
Four tablespoons olive oil
One tablespoon grated onion
Two teaspoons salt
One-eighth teaspoon pepper
Two bay leaves
Marinating time: Five hours
Four tomatoes, sliced
Four onions, sliced
Eight green pepper squares (1½ in.)
Eight mushroom caps
Broiling temperature: 550 degrees
Broiling time: Twenty minutes (about)
Serves: Four

Meat from the leg of lamb is the preferred cut to use for this dish. Rub into the meat squares a mixture of lemon juice, two tablespoons olive oil, grated onion, salt and pepper. Place in a bowl; add the bay leaves. Cover; let marinate in refrigerator. Remove. Run the marinated meat onto skewers, alternating lamb with slices of tomato, green pepper, onion and mushroom caps, and an occasional bay leaf. Arrange on a plank. Brush with the remaining olive oil. In a pre-heated broiler compartment quickly

Ham and Swiss Rolls

Three tablespoons butter or margarine
Three tablespoons flour
One teaspoon salt
One-eighth teaspoon pepper
One and one-half cups milk
Cooking time: Ten minutes, about
One egg yolk
One-half cup grated Swiss cheese
Cooling time: Five to ten minutes
One-half cup diced Swiss cheese
Six thick slices boiled ham (approx. one pound)
One package frozen asparagus spears, cooked
One can (8 oz.) seasoned tomato sauce
One-fourth cup heavy cream
Oven temperature: 375 degrees
Baking time: Fifteen minutes
Broiling time: Two minutes
Servings: Six

In a saucepan melt the butter or margarine. Stir in the flour, salt and pepper, gradually add the milk, stirring constantly. Cook over moderate heat, stirring constantly until the sauce thickens. Remove from the heat and beat in the egg yolk and the grated cheese. Let cool slightly and stir in the diced cheese. Spread some of the sauce generously over each slice of ham, top with cooked asparagus, roll up and skewer with toothpicks. Pour the canned seasoned tomato sauce into a greased baking dish (12 x 7½ x 2 in.). Lay in the ham rolls. Stir the heavy cream into the remaining cheese sauce and pour over the ham rolls. Bake in a moderately hot oven for 15 minutes then place under the direct broiler heat to brown quickly. Serve at once. Note: Endive, split through and braised tender in butter and lemon juice may be substituted for the asparagus spears.

A FAVORITE RECIPE
Ham Pineapple Yams

Two cups ground cooked ham
One-fourth cup fine bread crumbs
Three tablespoons pineapple juice
One-sixteenth teaspoon cloves
Four slices pineapple
Two cups cooked, mashed yams
Three-fourths cup dry bread crumbs
One-half teaspoon salt
One tablespoon pineapple juice
One egg yolk, beaten
Oven temperature: 350 degrees
Bake: Thirty minutes
Serves: Four

In a bowl mix the ham, bread crumbs, pineapple juice and cloves. Shape into four patties; place in a well-greased shallow baking pan. Top the patties with slices of pineapple. Mix the yams, bread crumbs, salt, pineapple juice and egg yolk; form into patties and place over the pineapple. Bake in a moderate oven. Serve hot with a fresh green salad.

MRS. SARA GRAY, *Ponca, Nebr.*

Easy Ham Loaf

Three cups ground cooked ham
One-half cup fine dry bread crumbs
One-fourth cup finely chopped onion
Two tablespoons finely chopped green pepper
One-half teaspoon dry mustard
One-eighth teaspoon allspice
One-eighth teaspoon cloves
Two beaten eggs
One-half cup milk
Oven temperature: 350 degrees
Baking time: Forty-five minutes
Servings: Six

In a bowl combine the ground cooked ham with the fine dry bread crumbs, chopped onion, green pepper, mustard, allspice and cloves. Blend thoroughly together. Stir in the beaten eggs and milk. Pack into one quart loaf pan and bake in a moderate oven for 45 minutes. Unmold on a platter and serve at once.

Ham and Corn Fritters

Three eggs
One cup ground cooked ham
One can (one pound) whole kernel corn, drained
One-half cup sifted flour
Two teaspoons baking powder
One-eighth teaspoon pepper
Four tablespoons shortening, or more
Frying time: Ten minutes, about
Yield: Twelve fritters

In a bowl beat the eggs; stir in the ground ham, drained canned corn, flour, baking powder and pepper. Mix well. In a large heavy skillet melt the shortening. Drop spoonfuls of the mixture into the hot fat and brown well on both sides. Drain on absorbent paper and serve hot.

Sweet and Sour Ham

Two tablespoons shortening
Three cups cubed cooked ham
Two-thirds cup chopped green pepper
Brown: Five to ten minutes
Two tablespoons cornstarch
Two tablespoons brown sugar
Two tablespoons vinegar
One teaspoon prepared mustard
One-eighth teaspoon pepper
One and one-half cups pineapple syrup and water
Cook: Ten minutes
One cup drained pineapple tidbits
Hot cooked rice
Serves: Six

In a large heavy skillet melt the shortening. Add the cubed ham and chopped green pepper and brown lightly. Stir in the cornstarch, brown sugar, vinegar, mustard and pepper. Gradually blend in the pineapple syrup with water if needed. Cook, stirring constantly, until thickened and clear. Stir in the pineapple and continue cooking long enough to heat through. Serve over hot cooked rice.

A FAVORITE RECIPE
Ham Loaf

One and one-half pounds ground ham
One-half pound ground pork
One cup crushed corn flakes
One egg
Two-thirds cup milk
One teaspoon dry mustard
One-sixteenth teaspoon powdered cloves
One-half teaspoon Worcestershire sauce
One tablespoon minced onion
Oven temperature: 350 degrees
Baking time: One hour
Two pounds sweet potatoes, cooked, peeled, mashed
One-fourth cup melted butter
Broiling temperature: 375 degrees
Broiling time: Until lightly browned
Serves: Four

In a bowl mix the ground ham and pork with the corn flakes, egg, milk, mustard, cloves, Worcestershire sauce and onion. Form into a loaf; pack into a well buttered bread pan. Bake in a moderate oven. Boil, mash and season the sweet potatoes. Remove meat loaf from oven. Invert on oven proof serving dish. Cover the loaf with the mashed sweet potatoes, brush with the melted butter. Broil in a moderately hot oven until brown. Serve with a green tossed salad.

MRS. GRACE C. PETERSON, *Kenora, Ont., Can.*

A FAVORITE RECIPE
Spicy Ham Cubes

Three tablespoons butter, heated
Two cups cubed (¼ in.) cooked ham
Frying time: Five minutes
One-third cup minced green pepper
One-third cup minced leafy celery
One-fourth cup minced scallions
One-third cup minced onion
Sauté: Ten minutes
One-eighth teaspoon curry powder
One-fourth teaspoon salt
One-fourth teaspoon dry mustard
One-fourth teaspoon cayenne pepper
One-eighth teaspoon black pepper
Cooking time: One minute
Four tablespoons catsup
One tablespoon Worcestershire sauce
Cooking time: One minute
One beef bouillon cube, dissolved in
One and one-half cups hot water
Simmer: Twenty minutes
Servings: Four

In a large heavy skillet, heat the butter; fry the ham. Add the vegetables, sauté. Add the seasonings, mix, cook. Stir in the catsup and Worcestershire sauce. Cook. Dissolve the bouillon cube in the hot water. Add the ham mixture, stirring well until blended. Simmer until the bouillon is completely absorbed. Serve hot on rice with a tomato salad.

JAMES MC CASLAND, *Forest Hills, N.Y.*

A FAVORITE RECIPE
Pork Chops Supreme

Six medium-sized pork chops
One teaspoon salt
One-fourth teaspoon pepper
Browning time: Fifteen minutes
One can (1 lb.) tomatoes
One can (1 lb.) white kidney beans
One-fourth cup sliced thin onions
One teaspoon salt
One-fourth teaspoon pepper
Oven temperature: 350 degrees
Baking time: One hour
Servings: Six

Wipe the chops with a damp cloth. Season with salt and pepper. Brown in a heavy skillet, turning chops to brown on both sides. Place the chops in a shallow casserole. Add the tomatoes and beans. Spread the onions over the beans, season with salt and pepper. Bake in a moderate oven. Serve from the oven dish with a green salad.

MRS. E. J. VISIOLI, *Denville, N.J.*

Nut Stuffed Pork Chops

Two tablespoons fat or drippings
One-third cup minced onion
Sauté: Five minutes
One cup fine dry bread crumbs
Four tablespoons minced parsley
One-half cup chopped walnuts
One teaspoon salt
One-eighth teaspoon pepper
One-fourth teaspoon nutmeg
Three-fourths cup evaporated milk
Six double or twelve single pork chops
One-fourth cup flour seasoned with salt
    and pepper
Browning time: Five to eight minutes
One-half cup evaporated milk
One-half cup water
Oven temperature: 350 degrees
Bake: One hour
Serves: Six

In a large heavy iron skillet melt the fat or drippings. Add the minced onion and sauté until soft. Remove onion from fat and add to the fine dry bread crumbs in a bowl. Add the minced parsley, chopped nuts, salt, pepper and nutmeg. Moisten the stuffing with three-fourths cup of undiluted evaporated milk. Cut pockets in the double pork chops and fill with stuffing, or skewer pairs of chops together with stuffing between. Dredge chops in the seasoned flour and brown in the fat in which the onion was cooked, adding more if necessary. Combine the half cup of evaporated milk with the half cup of water and pour over the chops. Bake in a moderate oven for one hour, until tender and well done.

Casseroled Pork Chops

Four one inch pork chops
Browning time: Ten to fifteen minutes
One-half can (one pound size) whole
    cranberry sauce
Three tablespoons honey
One-half teaspoon cloves
Oven temperature: 350 degrees
Bake: One hour
Serves: Four

Cut any excess fat from the pork chops. Place a small amount in a large heavy skillet to melt. Brown chops well on both sides in this hot fat. Transfer the chops to a shallow baking dish or large pie plate. Combine the half can of whole cranberry sauce with the honey and cloves and spoon over the chops. Cover with lid or foil and bake in a moderate oven for one hour or until very tender.

A FAVORITE RECIPE
Pork Chops-Kraut

Six pork chops
Browning time: Fifteen minutes
Two apples, sliced crosswise
Frying time: Five minutes
One can (No. 2½) sauerkraut
Two tablespoons brown sugar,
One-fourth cup hot water
Oven temperature: 350-300 degrees
Baking time: One and one-half hours
Servings: Four, or more

In a skillet, brown the chops on both sides; add the apples; cook. Place the chops and apples in a casserole (10 in.). Pour the hot water into the skillet, stir well. Place the kraut over the chops, sprinkle with the brown sugar. Pour the water from skillet over the kraut. Bake in a moderate oven until pork chops are tender. Serve with mashed potatoes.

MRS. W. J. KERBER, *Princess Bay, S.I., N.Y.*

Skillet Barbecued Pork Chops

Eight thin pork chops
One-fourth cup flour
Browning time: Ten minutes, or more
One-fourth cup vinegar
One-half teaspoon salt
One-half teaspoon dry mustard
One teaspoon celery seed
One tablespoon chili sauce
One-half cup catsup
Two tablespoons brown sugar
Two tablespoons paprika
One-eighth teaspoon pepper
Simmer: Thirty minutes, about
Serves: Four

Trim the pork chops of any excess fat and melt some in a heavy skillet. Dredge chops in flour to coat well, add to the hot fat and brown well on both sides. In a small bowl stir together the vinegar, salt, dry mustard, celery seed, chili sauce, catsup, brown sugar, paprika and pepper. Pour over the chops, cover tightly and simmer over very low heat until chops are thoroughly cooked. Serve piping hot.

A FAVORITE RECIPE
Pork and Mushroom Bake

Six pork chops, bone removed and
    pounded flat
One egg, beaten light, with
One tablespoon water
One-half cup cracker crumbs
One-half cup cooking oil or shortening
Browning time: Five minutes, about
Two tablespoons butter, heated
One cup chopped almonds
One onion, minced
One-half pound fresh mushrooms, cleaned,
    sliced
Sauté: Ten minutes
One can (10½ oz.) cream of chicken soup
One-half cup cooking sherry
Simmering time: Fifteen minutes
Oven temperature: 425 degrees
Baking time: Forty-five minutes
Servings: Six

Have the chops cut ¾ inch thick; remove bone; pound flat. Dip into egg and water beaten in a bowl, then into the cracker crumbs. Heat the oil in a heavy skillet, brown cutlets on both sides. Remove from the skillet, place in baking dish (10 in.). Add the butter to drippings in the skillet, add almonds, onion and mushrooms; sauté, stirring several times. Add the chicken soup and sherry. Simmer, stirring occasionally. Pour the soup mixture over the pork cutlets. Bake in a hot oven. Serve from oven dish with hot rice.

JANE L. HOSKOVEC, *Bayside, L.I., N.Y.*

Currant Glazed
Pork Shoulder Steaks

Four pork shoulder steaks (one inch thick)
Two tablespoons flour, about
One and one-half tablespoons salad oil
Browning time: Ten minutes, about
One teaspoon salt
One-eighth teaspoon pepper
One-third cup water
Simmer: Forty-five minutes
One-third cup currant jelly
One-eighth teaspoon allspice
Broiling temperature: 500 degrees
Broil: Three minutes on each side
Serves: Four

Dredge the pork shoulder steaks in flour. Heat the salad oil in a large heavy skillet, add the floured steaks and brown well on both sides. Sprinkle with salt and pepper and pour on the water. Cover tightly and simmer gently until meat is very tender, adding additional water if necessary. Whip currant jelly and allspice together with a fork. Arrange steaks in shallow pan and brush with spiced jelly. Broil three minutes. Turn, brush other sides with jelly and broil a second three minutes or just long enough to glaze. Serve at once.

Sweet and Sour Stuffed Ham

Two cups shredded cabbage
Two tablespoons wine or cider vinegar
One-fourth cup water
Three-fourths cup currant jelly
One-half teaspoon salt
Three cloves
Two tablespoons butter or margarine
One cup sliced tart apples
Cooking time: Ten minutes
Two (¾ in. thick) ham steak slices
Oven temperature: 325 degrees
Baking time: One hour
Serves: Six, or more

In a skillet combine the first eight ingredients and cook over low heat 10 minutes, stirring constantly. Spread the filling between the ham slices. Place on a rack in a shallow pan. Bake in a moderately slow oven for one hour. Place on a platter. Serve with marshmallow sweet potato rosettes.

Ham Sauerkraut Dinner

Two cans (No. 2) sauerkraut
One large onion, thinly sliced
Three tart apples, sliced
One tablespoon caraway seed
Four large potatoes, peeled and halved
Six carrots
One teaspoon salt
Four cups water
Four slices ham
Cooking time: Thirty minutes
Serves: Six, or more

In a deep heavy kettle place the sauerkraut, onion, sliced apples, caraway seed, potatoes, carrots, salt and water. Place the ham slices on top. Cover; cook 30 minutes or until the vegetables are tender. Arrange on hot platter with ham slices on top. Serve.

A FAVORITE RECIPE
Ham and Pineapple Loaf

One pound ground cured ham
One pound ground pork
One egg, beaten
One tablespoon minced celery
One-fourth teaspoon celery seed
One teaspoon minced onion
One-fourth teaspoon poultry seasonings
One-sixteenth teaspoon paprika
Oven temperature: 375 degrees
Baking time: Forty-five minutes
One-fourth cup brown sugar
One cup crushed pineapple
Oven temperature: 350 degrees
Baking time: Thirty minutes
Servings: Six

In a bowl, blend the ham, pork, egg, celery, celery seed, minced onion, poultry seasoning and paprika. Turn into a loaf pan (9 in.); press into loaf shape. Bake in a moderately hot oven for 45 minutes. Cover the loaf with the brown sugar mixed with the crushed pineapple. Continue baking for another 30 minutes. Serve sliced on a hot platter with sweet potatoes and creamed spinach.

MRS. HOWARD D. STEVENS, *Ridgefield, Conn.*

Family Cook Book

Roast Fresh Ham

One fresh ham (8 to 10 lbs.), skin and
part of fat removed
One cup cider vinegar
Two cups water
Five peppercorns
Two bay leaves
One-half teaspoon cloves
One clove garlic, crushed
One-half teaspoon sage
One tablespoon salt
Cook: To the boiling point
One cup cranberry juice
One-fourth cup apple jack (optional)
Standing time: Two days in refrigerator
One-half cup apricot jam
Oven temperature: 325 degrees
Bake: Five hours (about)
One-fourth cup flour
One teaspoon salt
One-fourth teaspoon pepper
Three cups milk
Serves, Eight, or more

Wipe ham with a damp cloth. Place
meat in shallow roasting pan. In a saucepan bring to a boil the vinegar, water,
peppercorns, bay leaves, cloves, garlic,
sage and salt. Cool; add the cranberry
juice and apple jack. Pour mixture over
ham. Let stand in refrigerator two days,
turning the meat occasionally. Remove
meat; pour off marinade and reserve.
Place meat back in roasting pan on a
rack. Roast in a moderately slow oven
basting frequently with the reserved
marinade. Roast until no trace of pink
remains around center of bone and meat
is well done (about 5 hours). Pour off
the fat. Spread jam over ham. Return to
oven and roast until glazed; about 15
minutes longer. Plan on 15 minutes rest
period out of oven on hot platter before
carving. Then make gravy. Heat about
four tablespoons of pork fat in the roasting pan. Stir in flour, salt and pepper,
scraping down the brown bits on sides
and bottom of pan and blending thoroughly. Stir in the milk; cook until
slightly thickened. Pour into gravy bowl;
serve.

Pre-Carved Baked Ham

One hickory smoked canned ham
(11 lbs. 8 oz.) sliced
One-eighth cup honey or corn syrup
One cup brown sugar
One-eighth cup orange or apple juice
One bottle (8 oz.) maraschino cherries
Two tablespoons prepared mustard
One-fourth teaspoon powdered cloves
Oven temperature: 325 degrees
Baking time: One and one-half hours
Serves: Twenty, or more

Have the butcher remove the ham
from the can. Then allow him to slice it
on the meat slicer, to desired thickness
(about ¼ in.). Let him tie three rows of
soft cord around side of ham to keep slices
intact. Place the ham on a large piece of
heavy aluminum foil. Spread the combined honey, brown sugar, orange juice,

maraschino cherry juice, mustard and
cloves over top and sides of ham. Fold the
foil over the prepared ham in a drug store
fold. Place in a shallow pan. Bake in a
moderately slow oven. Remove to hot
platter; remove the foil — cut the cord.
Garnish with the maraschino cherries and
parsley. Serve immediately.

Shoulder Pork With Fresh Vegetables

Two pounds pork shoulder
Browning time: Ten minutes
One cup bouillon
Simmering time: Fifteen minutes
One cup sliced onion
Two cups sliced celery
Two cups shredded cabbage
One-half cup chopped green pepper
One can (18 oz.) Italian plum tomatoes
One and one-half teaspoons salt
One-eighth teaspoon pepper
Two and one-half tablespoons cornstarch
Simmering time: Thirty minutes, or more
Servings: Four

Trim off the fat which may be considerable and cut the meat into strips approximately one by one-half by three inches. Use some of the pork fat for drippings in a large heavy skillet. Try out then add the strips of meat and brown quickly. Discard fat and add three-fourths of the cup of bouillon. Cover and simmer for 15 minutes. Add the sliced onion and celery, shredded cabbage, chopped green pepper, Italian plum tomatoes, salt and pepper, stirring well together. Add the remaining fourth cup of bouillon gradually to the cornstarch in a cup. Stir into the contents of the skillet. Cover and let simmer for 30 minutes or until the meat is very tender. Serve with mashed potatoes or fluffy rice.

A FAVORITE RECIPE
Apple Stuffed Pork Shoulder

One pork shoulder (8-12 lbs.) boned, pocket cut in
Salt and pepper
One-fourth cup butter or margarine
One medium-sized onion, chopped
Cooking time: Five minutes
One-sixteenth teaspoon pepper
One teaspoon salt
One-fourth teaspoon oregano
Two and one-half cups bread crumbs
One and three-fourths cups chopped apples
One-half cup boiling water
Oven temperature: 350 degrees
Bake: Forty minutes to the pound
Serves: Eight, or more

Wipe the prepared shoulder with a damp cloth. Season with salt and pepper inside and out. For the dressing: Heat the butter or margarine in a large skillet and cook the onion. Add seasonings. Fold in the bread crumbs and apples. Stir in the boiling water. Fill the pocket of shoulder with the dressing, fasten with skewers laced together with twine. Place the shoulder on a rack in an open roasting pan. Roast, allowing 40 minutes to the pound.

MRS. I. HACKBERG, *Bronx, N.Y.*

A FAVORITE RECIPE
Sweet Sour Pork

One cup (cut 1 in. pieces) loin of pork
One-half teaspoon salt
Two tablespoons cornstarch
One tablespoon water
Fat for deep frying
Frying time: Five minutes (until a golden brown)
One tablespoon cooking oil, heated
One green pepper, cut into pieces (½ in.)
Six pieces (1 in. long) scallions
Sauté: Three minutes

Sauce

Two tablespoons vinegar
Two tablespoons sugar, or more
One teaspoon salt
One tablespoon hot water
One tablespoon Worcestershire sauce
One tablespoon cornstarch
One-half teaspoon ginger
Cooking time: Five minutes
Servings: Four

Cut the pork loin into one inch pieces; season with salt. Rub the cornstarch into the pork, add water, adding more cornstarch if meat is not well coated. Heat the fat in a kettle, deep fry the pork in hot (not boiling) fat, until a golden brown. Remove and drain. Heat the oil in a skillet, fry the green peppers and scallions. Make a sauce with the vinegar, sugar, salt and hot water, Worcestershire sauce, cornstarch and ginger. Mix well. Add to the peppers and scallions with the browned pork. Heat thoroughly and serve with hot rice.

MRS. EARL E. BENNETTS, *L.I. City, N.Y.*

Sweet and Pungent Pork

Two tablespoons salad oil
One teaspoon salt
One clove garlic, crushed
One pound lean pork
Browning time: Five to ten minutes
One cup chicken consomme
One cup canned pineapple tidbits, drained
Two cups thinly sliced celery
One green pepper, cut into strips
Simmer: Fifteen minutes
Two tablespoons cornstarch
One-fourth cup sugar
Two teaspoons soy sauce
One-third cup vinegar
Cook: Five minutes
One cup raw rice, cooked
Serves: Four

Heat the salad oil in a large heavy skillet with the salt and crushed clove of garlic. Cut the lean pork into half-inch cubes and brown quickly in the hot oil. Add one-third cup of consomme with the drained pineapple, sliced celery and green pepper. Cover and simmer gently for fifteen minutes. In a small bowl stir cornstarch and sugar together, add the soy sauce, vinegar and remaining consomme. Add to the cooked mixture and stir until it thickens slightly. Serve piping hot over hot cooked rice.

Little Pork Pies

One and one-half pounds ground shoulder pork
One can (10½ oz.) condensed beef bouillon
Six slices bread, cubed (½ in.)
One-half teaspoon salt
One-fourth teaspoon nutmeg
One tablespoon Worcestershire sauce
Simmer: Thirty minutes
Two cups flour
One teaspoon salt
Two-thirds cup shortening
Six tablespoons cold water, or more
Oven temperature: 450 degrees
Bake: Thirty minutes
Serves: Six, or more

In a saucepan stir together the ground pork and condensed beef bouillon. Add the cubed bread, salt, nutmeg and Worcestershire sauce. Simmer over low heat, stirring frequently, for 30 minutes. Taste and add more salt if necessary. Cool slightly, spooning away from fat into a bowl. Prepare the pastry by sifting flour and salt into a bowl. Cut in half the shortening until the mixture resembles fine meal. Cut in second half of shortening until the size of small peas.

Stir in enough cold water for dough to hold together and follow a fork around the bowl. Turn out on floured board and roll out pastry. It should be quite thin. Cut circles of pastry to fit in muffin pans extending up about an inch at top. Spoon meat in the pastry. Cut slightly smaller circles of dough to lay over top. Crimp edges together. Prick tops of pies with fork for escape of steam. Bake in a very hot oven until nicely browned. Ten or 12 muffin size pies may be made. If preferred, shape turnovers instead.

A FAVORITE RECIPE
Baked Ham and Pork Loaf

One pound lean ham
Two pounds shoulder pork
One-half cup milk
One cup bread crumbs
Two eggs, beaten slightly
One can (10½ oz.) condensed tomato soup
One tablespoon minced onion
One teaspoon salt (or more)
One-fourth teaspoon pepper
Oven temperature: 350 degrees
Baking time: Two hours
Servings: Six or more

In a bowl combine the ham, pork, milk, bread crumbs, eggs, soup and onion. Season with salt and pepper. Pack into a well greased loaf pan (10 in.). Bake in a moderate oven. Serve with apple sauce, mashed potatoes and buttered spinach.

MRS. ARTHUR L. GARBER, *Brooklyn, N.Y.*

A FAVORITE RECIPE
Pork Casserole

One tablespoon melted butter or bacon fat
Four pork chops
One teaspoon salt
One-fourth teaspoon pepper
Two tablespoons flour
Two apples, peeled, cored, sliced
Two onions, sliced thin
Seasonings to taste
Four potatoes, peeled, sliced thin
One tablespoon flour
Three tablespoons butter
One cup hot water
Oven temperature: 350 degrees
Baking time: One hour
Servings: Four

In a deep oven dish (10 in.) put the melted butter or fat. Season the chops with salt and pepper, dredge in flour. Place in the pan. Spread the apples over the chops, onions over the apples. Season to taste. Spread the sliced potatoes over the top, season, sprinkle with flour and dot with butter. Pour in the hot water. Cover; bake until the potatoes are tender. Serve from the oven dish with coleslaw.

MRS. VERA C. MORROW, *Crescent City, Fla.*

Pork Chops with Milk Gravy

Four shoulder pork chops (round bone or blade)
Four tablespoons flour
One and one-half teaspoons salt
One-fourth teaspoon pepper
Browning time: Ten minutes
One cup hot water (optional)
Cooking time: Twenty minutes, or until well done
One cup milk
Cooking time: Five minutes
Spiced prunes or applesauce
Servings: Four

The shoulder pork chops, or steaks as often called, should be cut two-thirds inch thick. Score the edges to keep them flat during cooking. Trim off a little fat and fry it out in a heavy skillet. Dredge the chops with the mixed flour and seasonings, reserving the excess to thicken the gravy. Brown the chops slowly on both sides in the hot fat in the skillet. Cover; reduce the heat and cook slowly until the meat is well done, adding the water as needed or omitting it if the chops are moist. Transfer the chops to a hot platter. Stir the reserved flour mixture into the skillet fat, scraping any crisp bits from the bottom and sides. When blended add the milk; cook, stirring constantly, until smooth and thickened. Correct the seasoning. Serve with the chops, passing spiced prunes or applesauce.

Curried Baked Limas with Pork Chops

One cup large dry lima beans
Two and one-half cups water
Boil: Two minutes
Standing time: One hour
One teaspoon salt
Simmer: Thirty minutes
Four pork chops (cut one inch thick)
Salt, pepper, flour
Browning time: Ten minutes
One-fourth cup catsup
One-half teaspoon curry powder
Oven temperature: 350 degrees
Bake: One hour
Serves: Four

Place the large dry limas and water in a saucepan, bring to a boil and boil for two minutes. Remove from heat, cover and let stand for one hour. Return to the heat adding salt and simmer gently 30 minutes. Cut excess fat from the pork chops and melt some in a large heavy skillet. Dust the chops on both sides with salt, pepper and flour and brown well on both sides in the hot fat in the skillet. Place beans in a casserole (1½ qts.) and mix with the catsup and curry powder. Arrange chops on top. Pour pan drippings over all adding a little water to the skillet if necessary. Cover and bake in a moderate oven for one hour.

A FAVORITE RECIPE
Orange Pork Loaf

One-half cup orange juice
One tablespoon lemon juice
One and one-half cups soft bread crumbs
One pound ground ham
One pound ground fresh pork
One-fourth cup minced onion
Two tablespoons minced parsley
Two eggs, beaten light
One-fourth cup brown sugar, packed firmly
One-half teaspoon dry mustard
One teaspoon flour
Five slices, seedless orange, unpeeled
Oven temperature: 350 degrees
Baking time: One hour and fifteen minutes
Servings: Six

In a cup combine the orange and lemon juice. Place the bread crumbs in a bowl; pour the orange juice over crumbs, mix. Add the ground ham, pork, onion and parsley, mix. Stir in the eggs. In a cup mix the brown sugar, mustard and flour. Sprinkle over the bottom of a well greased baking loaf pan (9½ x 5¼ in.); overlap the orange slices over sugar mixture. Spoon in the meat mixture pressing firmly into the sugar. Bake in a moderate oven. Unmold on a hot platter having sugar mixture and orange slices on top. Good hot or cold.

MRS. MILDRED RODEVITZ, *Garfield, N.J.*

Curried Pork Casserole

One and one-half pounds boneless pork
Two tablespoons shortening
One-half cup coarsely chopped walnuts
One and one-half cups finely diced celery
Sauté: Ten minutes, or more
Two tablespoons butter or margarine
Two tablespoons flour
One teaspoon salt
Two teaspoons curry powder
One-half cup milk
One-half cup dry white wine
Cook: Until thickened
One tablespoon butter or margarine
Three tablespoons fine dry bread crumbs
Oven temperature: 350 degrees
Bake: One hour
Servings: Four

Cut the boneless pork into half inch cubes. Heat the shortening in a heavy skillet, add the diced pork, chopped walnuts and celery and sauté until pork is nicely browned. In a saucepan melt the two tablespoons of butter or margarine, stir in the flour, salt and curry powder, gradually blend in the milk and wine, stirring smooth. Cook, stirring, until sauce thickens. Add the sautéed pork, nuts and celery and transfer to a greased casserole (1½ qts.). Melt the tablespoon of butter or margarine and blend with the fine dry bread crumbs. Scatter over the sauced pork and bake in a moderate oven for one hour. Serve hot with a green vegetable.

Pork Apple Balls with Kraut

One egg
One pound ground pork
One-half teaspoon salt
One-fourth teaspoon nutmeg
One-fourth teaspoon cinnamon
One medium-sized apple, pared and cored
One-fourth cup yellow corn meal
Two tablespoons butter or margarine
Browning time: Ten minutes
Simmer: Thirty minutes
Two cups sauerkraut
Heat: Ten minutes
One cup dairy sour cream
Heat: Three to five minutes
Serves: Four

In a bowl beat the egg, blend in the ground pork, salt, nutmeg and cinnamon. Grate the apple into the meat mixture, mixing well. Form into two inch balls and roll in the corn meal. Heat the butter or margarine in a large heavy skillet. Add the meat balls and brown well on all sides. Reduce heat to low, cover and cook slowly for thirty minutes, until pork is thoroughly cooked. Heat the kraut in a saucepan until piping hot. Stir the dairy sour cream into the cooked pork balls and heat briefly to blend with pan drippings. Do not allow to boil. Spoon pork balls in cream over the drained hot kraut.

Sweet and Sour Canadian Bacon

Eight slices Canadian bacon (¼ inch thick)
Six cooked sweet potatoes, or yams, halved
Two medium-sized onions, thinly sliced
One can (No. 2) pineapple chunks
One-half cup water
One-fourth cup vinegar
One-fourth cup brown sugar
Two tablespoons lemon juice
Two tablespoons prepared mustard
Two tablespoons Worcestershire sauce
One teaspoon salt
One-eighth teaspoon pepper
One-eighth teaspoon ginger
Two tablespoons cornstarch
Cook: Three minutes
Oven temperature: 350 degrees
Bake: One hour
One green pepper, sliced
Serves: Six

In a shallow casserole arrange the Canadian bacon and sweet potatoes pinwheel fashion. Scatter onions on top. Drain the pineapple juice from chunks, reserving the chunks. To the pineapple juice add water, vinegar, brown sugar, lemon juice, mustard, Worcestershire sauce, salt, pepper, ginger and cornstarch. Stir until smooth. Cook until slightly thickened, stirring constantly. Pour sauce over the meat and sweet potatoes. Cover; bake in an oven for 30 minutes. Uncover and put in green peppers and reserved pineapple chunks. Bake for another 30 minutes.

Pork Chop Casserole
(Zuitzi)

One-fourth pound butter
One large onion, sliced
Cooking time: Five minutes
Two large potatoes, thinly sliced
One and one-half tablespoons salt
One and one-half tablespoons paprika
Three large tomatoes, peeled and sliced
One pound raw rice, washed
Two green peppers, sliced
Six loin pork chops (1 in. thick)
Browning time: Five minutes
Four cups water
Oven temperature: 350 degrees
Baking Time: Two and one-half hours
Serves: Six

In a skillet melt the butter; add the onion, cooking until straw-colored. Place the onion in the bottom of a casserole (4 qts.). Arrange the sliced potatoes over the onion. Sprinkle with a little salt and paprika. Repeat same procedure using tomatoes, then rice and ending with a layer of green pepper rings and season each layer with a little salt and paprika. Brown the chops on both sides in the skillet. Arrange on top of peppers. Add enough water (about 4 cups) to reach the top of the green peppers. Place casserole in a moderate oven until meat is tender. Add more water if necessary. Remove. Garnish with spiced crabapples.

A FAVORITE RECIPE
Spiced Pork Chops — Prunes

Two tablespoons Worcestershire sauce
One-half teaspoon mustard
Three-fourths teaspoon salt
Five pork chops (cut one inch thick)
Three teaspoons fat, heated
Browning time: Twenty minutes
One cup soft prunes
One-fourth teaspoon cinnamon
Five whole cloves
Two and one-half teaspoons vinegar,
    or lemon juice
One-half cup water
Two tablespoons sugar
Simmering time: Ten minutes
Simmering time: Forty minutes
Servings: Five

In a bowl mix the Worcestershire sauce, mustard and salt. Rub each pork chop on both sides with the mixture. Heat the fat in a heavy skillet, brown the chops on each side. Simmer the prunes, cinnamon, cloves, vinegar, water and sugar in a saucepan for 10 minutes. Pour over the chops. Cover. Simmer until the chops are tender. Serve hot with browned potatoes.

MRS. S. MOLE, *Brooklyn, N.Y.*

Crown Roast of Spareribs

Three racks of spareribs
One-fourth cup chopped onion
One tablespoon butter or margarine
Cooking time: Three minutes
One and one-fourth cups bread crumbs
Four cups hot mashed potatoes
One teaspoon poultry seasoning
One teaspoon salt
One-eighth teaspoon pepper
One-half cup water
Oven temperature: 325 degrees
Roasting time: Ninety minutes
Two tablespoons flour
Two cups hot water
Cooking time: Five minutes
Servings: Six, or more

Have the butcher crack the ribs. Wipe the meat with a damp cloth. Shape the ribs into a crown; skewer together. Place upright on a piece of aluminum foil (this holds the stuffing within the crown). Set on a rack in a shallow roasting pan. Melt the butter in a skillet. Cook the onion in the butter until straw-colored. In a bowl mix the bread crumbs, hot mashed potatoes and seasonings. Add the onions. Stuff the center of the crown with the dressing. Pour the water into the bottom of the roasting pan. Roast in a moderately slow oven until crisp and brown. Remove to a hot platter; garnish with cooked prunes and kumquats. Pour off all the fat except two tablespoons. Stir in the flour. Add the hot water. Cook until slightly thickened. Serve in a gravy bowl.

Pork and Veal Goulash With Sauerkraut

Three medium-sized onions
Four tablespoons butter or margarine
Cooking time: Five minutes
Two pounds pork shoulder, (1½ in. cubes)
One pound veal (1½ in. cubes)
Browning time: Fifteen minutes
Two tablespoons vinegar
One tablespoon paprika
Two teaspoons salt
One-eighth teaspoon pepper
Two teaspoons caraway seed
One bouillon cube, dissolved in
One cup boiling water
Simmering time: One hour
One can (No. 2½) sauerkraut
One cup dairy sour cream
One tablespoon tomato purée
Cooking time: Ten minutes
Serves: Six, or more

In heavy skillet, cook the onion in the butter or margarine until straw-colored. Add the meat; brown on all sides. Add the vinegar, spices, seeds and stock. Cover; simmer one hour; add the sauerkraut, sour cream and tomato purée. Cover and cook 10 minutes. Serve with boiled potatoes.

Stuffed Pork Chops

One cup soft bread crumbs
One-half cup minced raw apple
Two tablespoons shredded raisins
One tablespoon minced onion
One teaspoon salt
One-eighth teaspoon pepper
One tablespoon soft margarine
One tablespoon grated lemon rind
One tablespoon lemon juice
Four double pork chops, trimmed
Two tablespoons fat
Browning time: Ten minutes
Oven temperature: 350 degrees
Baking time: One hour
Servings: Four

Combine the first 9 ingredients for the stuffing. Beginning at the bone, cut a pocket through the center of each chop. Fill with the stuffing, pressing the edge of the pocket firmly together. Brown quickly on both sides in the hot fat in a skillet. Transfer to a baking dish. Bake in a moderate oven until tender. Spoon a tablespoon apple jelly over each chop; bake 5 minutes. Place a thin slice of lemon topped with raisins, in the center of each chop. Serve.

A FAVORITE RECIPE
Molasses Spareribs

Three pounds spareribs, cut into serving
  pieces
One teaspoon salt
One lemon, sliced very thin
One medium-sized onion, chopped
Oven temperature: 350 degrees
Cooking time: Thirty minutes

Sauce

One-fourth cup molasses
One teaspoon chili powder
One tablespoon celery seed
One-fourth cup vinegar
One-fourth cup Worcestershire sauce
One cup catsup
One-half teaspoon tabasco
Two cups water
Broiling temperature: 300 degrees
Broiling (or grilling) time: One hour
Serves: Four

Wipe the ribs with a damp cloth. Place
in a baking pan, meat side up. Sprinkle
with salt; top with the lemon slices and
chopped onion. Bake in a moderate oven.
For the sauce: In a small bowl mix the
molasses, chili, celery seed, vinegar,
Worcestershire sauce, catsup, tabasco and
water. Place the ribs under a slow broiler,
cover with some of the sauce; broil; baste
with remaining sauce while the ribs broil
to a deep brown. Serve hot with mashed
potatoes and stewed tomatoes.

LOUISE WILLIAMS, *Richmond, Va.*

Soy Sauced Spareribs with Limas

One and one-half cups large dried limas
Three cups boiling water
Boil: Ten minutes
One medium-sized onion, chopped
One tablespoon salad oil
Sauté: Ten minutes, about
One-fourth teaspoon crumbled thyme
One teaspoon salt
Oven temperature: 300 degrees
Two to three pounds spareribs
One-fourth cup soy sauce
Two tablespoons honey
Bake: Two hours
Bake: Thirty minutes
Servings: Four

Place the dried limas in a sieve, rinse
and add to the boiling water. Boil for ten
minutes. In the meantime add the
chopped onion to the salad oil in a skillet
and sauté until soft. Stir onion into the
boiled limas with the thyme and salt and
transfer to a shallow baking dish (possibly a 9 x 14 x 2 in.). Cover and place
in a slow oven. Cut the spareribs into
serving pieces and lay on a shallow baking tray. Mix the soy sauce and honey
and brush a little over the ribs. Bake
limas and ribs for two hours. Uncover
the limas, add a little water if dry, top
with spareribs. Pour remaining sauce
honey mixture over ribs and limas and
continue baking uncovered for thirty
minutes more.

Barbecued Spareribs

Two pounds spareribs
Oven temperature: 500 degrees
Baking time: Fifteen minutes
One tablespoon prepared mustard
Two tablespoons sugar
Two tablespoons steak sauce
Three-fourths cup vinegar
One-third cup catsup
One teaspoon salt
One teaspoon paprika
One-eighth teaspoon pepper
One clove garlic, crushed
Simmering time: Fifteen minutes
Oven temperature: 325 degrees
Baking time: One and one-half hours
Servings: Four

Place the spareribs on a rack in a baking pan and set in a very hot oven for 15
minutes. In the meantime, blend the prepared mustard with the sugar in a small
saucepan. Add the steak sauce, vinegar,
catsup, salt, paprika, pepper and crushed
clove of garlic. Simmer for 15 minutes
over moderate heat. Remove the ribs
from the oven, drain off the drippings
and lay the ribs in the bottom of the pan,
rounded side up, without the rack. Baste
both sides with the sauce. Return to a
moderately slow oven and bake (basting two or three times with the remaining sauce) until the meat is very tender.
Separate ribs into four servings with
sharp knife or shears.

A FAVORITE RECIPE
Jellied Pig Knuckles

Three fresh pig knuckles
Water to cover
One tablespoon salt
Cooking time: To boiling point
One-half cup vinegar
Two small onions, sliced
Two cloves garlic, cut
Two bay leaves
Simmering time: Three hours
Two hard-cooked eggs, sliced
Six large stuffed olives, sliced
Chilling time: Overnight
Servings: Six, or more

Place the washed knuckles into a deep
kettle; cover completely with water; add
the salt. Bring to a boil; reduce the heat
and skim off the top. Add the vinegar,
onion, garlic and bay leaves. Cover; simmer until the meat starts to fall from the
bones. Remove the knuckles. Cool. Cut
the meat into small pieces. Line a loaf
pan (9 in.) with the hard cooked sliced
eggs and olives. Place the meat on top.
Strain the liquid and pour over all. Cool.
Place in refrigerator to gel. Serve on a
platter, garnished with water cress.

MRS. MICHAEL PAWLOFF, *Sarasota, Florida*

Pork Hocks with Carrot Sauce

Four fresh pork hocks
Water to cover
Two teaspoons salt
Simmering time: Two hours or more
Four tablespoons butter or margarine
One small onion, finely chopped
One medium-sized carrot, grated
Four whole cloves
Sautéing time: Ten minutes
One-fourth cup flour
Two cups meat broth
Salt and pepper to taste
Cooking time: Five to ten minutes
Servings: Four

Place the fresh pork hocks in a kettle.
Add water to cover, with salt. Cover and
simmer gently for two hours or until tender. Drain, reserving two cups of cooking broth. Skin hocks and place in a
serving dish to keep warm. In a heavy
skillet, melt the butter or margarine; add
the chopped onion, grated carrot and
whole cloves. Sauté until tender and
lightly browned. Stir in the flour. Gradually add the meat broth, stirring to keep
smooth. Add salt and pepper to taste
and cook, stirring constantly until sauce
thickens. Discard cloves and serve sauce
over the hot cooked hocks.

Braised Pork Hocks

Four fresh pork hocks
Browning time: Ten minutes, about
One and one-half teaspoons salt
One-eighth teaspoon pepper
Three cups boiling water
Simmering time: Two hours
Four small carrots
Eight small onions, peeled
Four medium-sized potatoes, peeled
Simmering time: Thirty minutes
Servings: Four

Remove the skin and some of the fat
from the pork hocks using a sharp knife.
In a Dutch oven, brown the pieces of
meat in their own fat. Add the salt, pepper and boiling water; cover. Simmer
until the meat is almost tender. Put the
prepared vegetables around the hocks.
Cover; simmer until the vegetables and
meat are done. Arrange on platter to
serve.

A FAVORITE RECIPE
Meat and Apple Patties

One pound ground pork
One-half pound ground beef
One egg
One-half teaspoon salt, or more
Six slices apple, cut (¼ in.) thick, peeled,
  cored
Oven temperature: 350 degrees
Baking time: Forty minutes
Servings: Four

In a bowl combine the pork, beef, egg
and salt. Shape into twelve patties. Place
a slice of apple on six of the patties. Cover
with another meat pattie. Arrange in a
baking dish. Bake in a moderate oven.
Serve hot with a tossed green salad and
crisp rolls.

MRS. JOHN W. REED, *Jersey Shore, Penna.*

Noodle Sausage Skillet Supper

Three cups noodles (plain or spinach)
Boiling salted water
Cook: Until tender
Sixteen link sausages (one pound)
Cook: Thoroughly
One-third cup chopped onion
One clove garlic, crushed
Sauté: Until golden
Two teaspoons chili powder
One teaspoon salt
One tablespoon cornstarch
One can (No. 2) tomato juice
Cook: Until thickened
One-half cup ripe olive pieces
Heat: Five minutes, about
One-half cup grated cheddar cheese
Serves: Four to six

Cook the noodles in boiling salted water until tender. Drain. In a large heavy skillet cook the sausages until browned and thoroughly cooked. Remove from the skillet and drain off all but two tablespoons of the drippings. Add the onion and garlic and sauté until golden. Stir in the chili powder, salt and cornstarch. Gradually blend in the tomato juice, stirring smooth. Cook and stir until mixture boils and thickens slightly. Add the olives and sausages cut in one inch pieces. Mix lightly with cooked, drained noodles and heat briefly until piping hot. Serve with the grated cheddar sprinkled over each portion.

Barbecued Sausage

Two pounds small link sausages
Cooking time: Fifteen to twenty minutes
Two tablespoons sausage drippings
One-third cup chopped celery
One-third cup chopped onion
Sautéing time: Ten minutes
One-half cup catsup
One-fourth cup vinegar
One-third cup water
One and one-half tablespoons brown sugar
One and one-half tablespoons prepared mustard
One tablespoon steak sauce
One-eighth teaspoon salt
Simmering time: Fifteen minutes
Servings: Six

Place the sausages in a large cold skillet. Cook over moderate heat, turning as necessary until the sausages are evenly browned. Remove to platter. Drain off all but two tablespoons of the sausage drippings. Add the chopped celery and onion and sauté until tender. Add the catsup, vinegar, water, brown sugar, mustard, steak sauce and salt to the sautéed celery and onion; blend thoroughly. Add the sausage and simmer for about 15 minutes.

Creole Sausage Skillet Meal

One package (8 oz.) brown and serve sausage
Browning time: Ten minutes, or less
One can (1 lb.) Frenched green beans, drained
One-half cup packaged pre-cooked rice
One can (1 lb.) tomatoes
One-fourth teaspoon salt
Simmer: Twenty minutes
One-half cup grated cheddar cheese
Heat: Five minutes
Serves: Three or four

Place the sausage in a large heavy skillet and brown well on all sides. Remove to a plate and add the drained green beans to the skillet. Sprinkle the packaged pre-cooked rice over the beans and top with the canned tomatoes, broken up with a spoon if need be. Sprinkle with salt. Cover and simmer for 20 minutes or until rice is cooked. Place sausages over tomatoes in skillet and sprinkle with grated cheese. Cover and heat for five minutes or until cheese has melted. Serve at once.

A FAVORITE RECIPE
Acorn Squash-Sausage

Two acorn squash, cut into halves, seeds and part of pulp scooped out
Boiling salted water to cover
Boiling time: Five minutes
Two tart apples, peeled, cored, chopped fine
One-half pound loose sausage meat
One-eighth teaspoon pepper
One-half teaspoon salt
Water to cover bottom of pan
Oven temperature: 375 degrees
Baking time: Thirty-five minutes
Servings: Four

In a heavy saucepan boil the squash, draining thoroughly. Mix the squash with the apples, sausage and seasonings. Fill the cavities in squash with the mixture. Place in a large casserole. Bake in a moderately hot oven. Serve hot with snap beans and a salad.

MRS. T. C. DARLING, *West Hartford, Conn.*

Quick Cassoulet

One-half pound link sausage
Sauté: Until brown
One pound veal, cut in inch cubes
One cup chopped onion
One clove garlic, crushed
Browning time: Five to eight minutes
One teaspoon salt
One teaspoon crushed rosemary
One-half teaspoon paprika
One-fourth teaspoon pepper
One cup tomato juice
Simmer: Thirty minutes
Two cans (No. 303) red kidney beans
Oven temperature: 350 degrees
Bake: One hour
Serves: Six

Cut the sausage links in half and sauté until browned in a large heavy skillet. Remove sausage from the pan and pour off the drippings. Return one-fourth cup of drippings to the pan, add the cubed veal, chopped onion and garlic and sauté until lightly browned. Add the salt, rosemary, paprika, pepper and tomato juice. Cover, and simmer for thirty minutes. Transfer to a casserole, stir in the beans and bake in a moderate oven for one hour. Serve piping hot with plain or garlic buttered hot French bread.

A FAVORITE RECIPE
Sausage Shell Rice Pie

One pound bulk pork sausage
One cup fine cracker crumbs
One-fourth cup fine minced onion
One-half cup minced green pepper
One-half teaspoon salt
One-half cup condensed tomato soup

Filling

Three cups cooked rice
One-half cup condensed tomato soup
One-half teaspoon salt
One cup grated cheddar cheese
One-fourth teaspoon black pepper
Oven temperature: 350 degrees
Bake: One hour
Parsley for garnish
Serves: Four

In a bowl mix the sausage, cracker crumbs, onion, green pepper, salt and half of the tomato soup. Pat the mixture into a pie plate (10 in.). In another bowl mix the rice, remaining tomato soup, salt, cheese and black pepper. Turn into the sausage shell. Bake in a moderate oven. Serve hot; cut into wedges, garnish with parsley.

MRS. WILTON KAY, *Greenville, S.C.*

Corn and Sausage Casserole

One pound sausage meat
Frying time: Fifteen minutes, about
One can (10½ oz.) condensed green pea soup
One-half can milk
Two and one-half cups crumbled non-sweet crackers
One can (12 oz.) whole kernel corn
Oven temperature: 350 degrees
Bake: Forty-five minutes
Serves: Four, or more

In a heavy skillet cook the sausage meat over low heat until well browned. Blend the condensed green pea soup with the milk in a small bowl; add the crumbled crackers. Layer the cracker mixture, canned corn and sausage meat in a one quart casserole finishing with layer of sausage meat. Bake in a moderate oven for forty-five minutes or until nicely browned on top. Serve piping hot.

Poultry

Chicken Dinner

One roasting chicken (4 lbs.)
One-third cup shortening
Browning time: Ten minutes
Four medium-sized onions
Six carrots, scraped
Four medium-sized potatoes
Two teaspoons salt

One-eighth teaspoon pepper
One-fourth teaspoon savory
One-half cup hot water
Cooking time: One and one-half hours
Servings: Four

Remove the pin feathers from the chicken. Singe. Rinse; wipe dry. Brown the chicken in the hot shortening in a Dutch oven type of kettle. Add the onions, carrots, potatoes, seasonings and hot water. Cover tightly. Cook over low heat until tender, adding more water if necessary. Romove to a hot platter. Serve immediately with combination salad.

Crown of Chicken

One-half cup flour
One teaspoon salt
One-fourth teaspoon pepper
One-fourth teaspoon savory
Two fryers (2 lbs. each), cut into serving
    pieces
Eight tablespoons butter or margarine
Brown: Fifteen minutes
Two-thirds cup chicken broth
Cook: Forty-five minutes
Cooked broccoli
Two egg yolks
One cup light cream
Serves: Six, or more

In a paper bag put the flour, salt, pepper and savory. Add a few pieces of chicken at a time, shaking the bag. Remove chicken; continue until all chicken is lightly dusted with seasoned flour. In a large heavy skillet, heat half the butter. Brown a few pieces of chicken at a time, adding more butter when necessary. Arrange chicken in pan. Add the chicken broth, cover; cook over low heat until chicken is tender. Remove; arrange chicken around garnished rice mold. Put frills on the chicken legs. Tuck cooked broccoli around the crown. For the gravy: Stir in some of the liquid from the skillet into the blended egg yolks and cream. Then stir into skillet scraping sides and bottom of pan. Heat over low heat (do not boil) until thoroughly hot and blended.

Rice Mold

Pack six cups of hot cooked rice into an oiled mold. Unmold onto a platter. Decorate with cranberries, grapes, dragees, fancy cutouts of green pepper, skin of cucumber and carrots.

Roasted Capon

One capon (7 lbs.)
One-half cup butter or margarine
One-half cup chopped onion
One cup minced celery
One-fourth cup minced parsley
Cook: Three minutes
One tablespoon poultry seasoning
One package (8 oz.) bread stuffing
One cup chicken broth
One-fourth cup melted butter
Oven temperature: 325 degrees
Roast: Four hours
Six medium-sized onions, washed
    (leave skins on)
Six medium-sized potatoes, peeled
Six medium-sized carrots, peeled
Serves: Four, or more

Wash the capon; dry with absorbent paper. Meanwhile melt the butter in a skillet, add onion, celery and parsley. Cook until onion is transparent. Add the poultry seasoning and bread stuffing, blending thoroughly. Add the chicken broth. Stuff; truss the capon. Brush with melted butter. Place on a rack in a shallow pan. Roast in a moderately slow oven, basting occasionally. The last hour of cooking arrange the onions, potatoes and carrots around the capon. To determine if capon is done insert a fork in the thickest part of breast and second joint. If juice is not red the capon is done.

Pot Roasted Chickens

One-fourth cup butter or margarine
One-third cup chopped onion
One-third cup chopped celery
Sautéing time: Five to eight minutes
Five cups soft bread crumbs
One-half teaspoon salt
One teaspoon poultry seasoning
Two tablespoons chopped parsley
Two frying chickens (2-3 pounds each)
Salt and pepper
Two tablespoons shortening
Browning time: Twenty minutes
One teaspoon salt
One-half cup water
Simmering time: One hour
Carrots, potatoes, onions
Simmering time: Thirty minutes
Servings: Six

In a large heavy skillet melt the butter or margarine, add the chopped onion and celery and sauté until tender. Remove from heat and stir in the soft bread crumbs, salt, poultry seasoning and chopped parsley. Mix well. Sprinkle the insides of the chickens with salt and pepper; stuff lightly with the seasoned bread crumbs. Skewer or sew up the birds; truss with string. Melt shortening in the skillet.

Add the birds and brown thoroughly on all sides. Add one-half cup of water, cover tightly and simmer for one hour. Add small whole carrots, potatoes and onions that have been peeled. Sprinkle with salt and add a second half cup of water if necessary. Simmer until vegetables are tender.

Noodle Fruit Stuffed Roast Chicken

Eight ounces fine egg noodles
Three quarts boiling water
One tablespoon salt
Cooking time: Ten minutes, about
One-fourth cup butter or margarine
One medium-sized onion, chopped
One medium-sized apple, chopped
Sautéing time: Five to eight minutes
One cup cooked prunes, pitted and
   chopped
One-fourth cup chopped parsley
One teaspoon salt
One teaspoon poultry seasoning
One roasting chicken (5 lbs.)
Salt
Melted fat
Oven temperature: 325 degrees
Roasting time: Two hours, or more
Servings: Six

Cook the egg noodles in the boiling water with salt until tender. Drain in colander. In a large skillet melt the butter or margarine, add the onion and apple and sauté until tender. Add noodles, prunes, parsley, teaspoon of salt and poultry seasoning; mix well. Rub the body and neck cavities of the chicken with salt and stuff with the noodle mixture. Fasten with skewers. Place on a rack in a shallow roasting pan. Brush with fat. Roast in a moderately slow oven for two hours or more until the chicken is browned and its meat well cooked. Baste occasionally with fat.

A FAVORITE RECIPE
Peasant Style Chicken

Two frying chickens (3½ lb.) disjointed
One teaspoon salt
One-half teaspoon black pepper
One-half cup peanut oil
Browning time: Until slightly browned
Two tablespoons chopped fresh parsley
One teaspoon garlic salt
One teaspoon oregano
Simmering time: Forty-five minutes
Six ounces sauterne wine
Simmering time: One hour
Servings: Six

Season the disjointed chicken with the salt and pepper. Heat the peanut oil in a large heavy skillet. Brown the chicken, turning until both sides are browned. Add the parsley, garlic salt and oregano. Cover; simmer. Add the wine, cover and simmer. Serve with browned potatoes and cream coleslaw.

MRS. JOHN PICHIONE, *New York, N.Y.*

A FAVORITE RECIPE
Chicken Venetian

Four chicken breasts, cut into halves
Four tablespoons flour
One teaspoon salt
One-fourth teaspoon pepper
Four tablespoons butter, heated
Browning time: Fifteen minutes
One-half teaspoon garlic salt
Two tablespoons minced onion
Two tablespoons diced celery
Two tablespoons minced parsley
Cooking time: Until vegetables are tender
Liquid drained from one can (No. 2) peas
Simmering time: Twenty-five minutes
One can (No. 2) drained peas
Two egg yolks, beaten with
One and one-half tablespoons lemon juice
Servings: Four

Have the chicken breasts cut into halves in the market. Dredge in the flour, salt and pepper. Heat the butter in a large heavy skillet. Brown the chicken in the butter, with the skin side down; turn and season with the garlic salt, brown the other side. Add the onion, celery and parsley. Cook covered until onion and celery are tender. Add the liquid drained from the peas, stir, cover and cook until the chicken is tender. Add the drained peas, heat thoroughly. Remove the chicken breasts to a hot platter, stir in the egg yolks, mixed with the lemon juice. Pour over the breasts. Serve at once.

JEAN SCHWARTZ, *Flushing, N.Y.*

Individual Chicken Roasts

One cup raw rice
One-half cup butter or margarine
One cup blanched, slivered almonds
Sauté: Two minutes, about
One small onion, finely chopped
One-half pound mushrooms, sliced
Sauté: Five to eight minutes
Three tablespoons diced pimiento
One-half teaspoon salt
One-fourth teaspoon pepper
Six chicken breasts
Salt
Pepper
Marjoram
Tarragon
Oven temperature: 400 degrees
Bake: Forty-five minutes
Servings: Six

Cook the rice according to package directions. In a skillet melt three tablespoons of the butter, add the slivered almonds and sauté until lightly browned. Remove almonds to a plate, add three more tablespoons of butter and sauté the chopped onion and sliced mushrooms until tender. Add the pimiento, salt, pepper, almonds and cooked rice. Mix well. Taste and correct the seasoning if necessary. Rinse and dry the pieces of chicken. Use a small sharp knife and carefully bone each piece. Sprinkle each piece lightly on both sides with salt, pepper, crumbled marjoram and tarragon. Mound the rice mixture in six portions in a greased shallow baking pan. Arrange seasoned chicken on top, skin side up. Melt remaining butter and brush over chicken. Pour just enough water into pan to glaze the surface, about one-eighth inch. Bake in a quick oven for forty-five minutes until chicken is nicely browned. Run a broad spatula under each portion to serve the chicken topped stuffing.

A FAVORITE RECIPE
Cashew Chicken

Four tablespoons oil or fat, heated
Two slices ginger
Browning time: Three minutes
Two chicken breasts, diced (¼ in.)
Two teaspoons cornstarch
One tablespoon white wine
One-fourth teaspoon pepper
Cooking time: Until the chicken is half
   cooked
Two tablespoons soy sauce
One-half teaspoon sugar
One-half teaspoon salt
Cooking time: Five minutes
One-half cup broken cashew nuts
Servings: Four

In a skillet heat the fat; brown the ginger. Add the diced chicken rolled in the cornstarch, wine and pepper. Cook stirring frequently until the chicken is half cooked. Add the soy sauce, sugar and salt; mix well and cook, stirring constantly. Fold in the cashew nuts and serve at once.

MISS FRANCES DEE, *Rydal, Jenkintown, Pa.*

Honey Wine Broiled Chicken

One-half cup salad oil
One-half cup honey
One-half cup Rhine type wine
One-fourth cup lemon juice
One-half teaspoon crumbled rosemary
One tablespoon prepared mustard
Two teaspoons salt
One-fourth teaspoon pepper
One teaspoon Worcestershire sauce
Two quartered broiling chickens
Marinate: Several hours or overnight
Broiling temperature: 500 degrees
Broil: Thirty to forty minutes
Servings: Four to six

Combine the salad oil, honey, Rhine wine and lemon juice. Gradually stir into the blended crumbled rosemary, prepared mustard, salt, pepper and Worcestershire sauce. Place chicken pieces in this mixture in a shallow dish and allow to marinate in the refrigerator for several hours or overnight if possible, turning once or twice. To cook: Place the chicken pieces skin side down in a heated broiler six inches or as far from the source of heat as possible. Turn after fifteen minutes and baste with the marinade. Continue broiling until the thickest part of the leg may be pricked with a fork and colorless juices come forth. If you wish to grill marinated chicken out of doors, place over glowing coals (coals covered with a gray ash, no flames) at a distance of four to six inches and turn and baste frequently. Marinade left may be heated and served as a sauce to the chicken or may be reserved for future use.

A FAVORITE RECIPE
Baked Chicken and Mushrooms

Two chickens (broilers) 2½ lbs. each, disjointed
Two teaspoons salt, or less
One-half teaspoon pepper
One-fourth teaspoon paparika
Fat for frying
Browning time: Twenty minutes
Oven temperature: 350 degrees
Baking time: One hour
Three tablespoons fat
Two cans (4 oz. each) button mushrooms
One cup sliced onion
Sauté: Until a golden brown
Two cans (10½ oz. each) condensed cream of mushroom soup
Cooking time: Ten minutes
One and one-half cups milk
Cooking time: To the boiling point
One cup sliced black olives
Oven temperature: 325 degrees
Baking time: Thirty minutes
Servings: Six

Season the chicken with the salt, pepper and paprika. Heat the fat in a large heavy skillet. Brown the chicken on each side. Remove the chicken to an oven pan. Bake in a moderate oven. In the fat, brown the mushrooms and onion slightly.

Add the mushroom soup, a little at a time, stirring constantly. Add the milk slowly mixing thoroughly. Heat to boiling point (do not boil). Add the sliced olives. Pour the mixture over the chicken. Cover. Bake in a moderately slow oven. Serve with hot biscuits.

MRS. PETER D. DAVIDSON, *Novoto, Calif.*

A FAVORITE RECIPE
Poultry Stuffing

One pound pork sausage meat
Six chicken livers, finely chopped
Cooking time: Ten minutes
Six slices whole wheat bread, diced
Six dried apricots, finely chopped
One cup water
Cooking time: Until lightly browned
One and one-half teaspoons poultry seasoning
Three teaspoons sherry
One-half cup chopped walnuts
Yield: Stuffing for turkey (10-12 lbs.)

In a large heavy skillet break up the sausage meat with a fork over a low heat; add the chopped chicken livers, cook, stirring constantly. Add the diced bread and apricots, mix, stirring until browned. Add the water slowly, stirring well. Stir in the poultry seasoning and sherry while still in the skillet. Remove from heat, stir in the chopped walnuts. Stuff turkey (10-12 lbs.) or two large chickens and roast.

MRS. LAWRENCE BLANEY, *Woodside, N.Y.*

Chicken Parisian with Asparagus

One broiler-fryer (2½ pounds)
One-half teaspoon salt
Boiling water
Simmer: One hour
One bunch (2½ pounds) asparagus
Boiling salted water
Cook: Twenty minutes
One-fourth cup butter or margarine
One-fourth cup flour
One teaspoon salt
One-eighth teaspoon pepper
One-fourth teaspoon nutmeg
Two cups milk
Cook: Five minutes, about
One tablespoon lemon juice
One-fourth cup heavy cream
Two tablespoons grated Parmesan cheese
Broiler temperature: 500 degrees
Broil: Five minutes, about
Servings: Four

Place the cut-up broiler fryer in a deep saucepan or kettle. Add the half teaspoon of salt and cover with boiling water. Cover and simmer gently until chicken is very tender. Cool slightly. Snap off the white tough ends of asparagus, wash well and cook in boiling, salted water until tender. Drain and arrange asparagus in bottom of a greased shallow baking dish or oven proof platter (two pie plates may be used). Take chicken meat from the bones, discarding skin. Leave meat in fairly large pieces.

Arrange meat over asparagus. Prepare the sauce by melting the butter or margarine in a saucepan, stir in the flour, salt, pepper and nutmeg. Gradually blend in the milk. Cook, stirring constantly, until sauce is thickened and smooth. Blend in the lemon juice. Pour sauce over chicken. Spoon on the heavy cream and sprinkle with the grated Parmesan cheese. Place under the broiler until nicely browned. Serve at once. May be offered in individual ramekins.

Mushroom Olive Stuffed Chicken

One-half cup butter or margarine
One medium-sized onion, chopped
One-fourth pound mushrooms, chopped
Sautéing time: Ten minutes, about
Four cups soft bread crumbs
One-third cup sliced stuffed green olives
One-half teaspoon poultry seasoning
One-fourth teaspoon thyme
One-half teaspoon salt
One roasting chicken (4-5 pounds) cleaned
One tablespoon melted butter or margarine
Oven temperature: 325 degrees
Roasting time: Two hours, or more
Servings: Four, or more

In a large heavy skillet, melt the butter or margarine. Add the chopped onion and mushrooms and sauté until tender. Stir in the soft bread crumbs, sliced olives, poultry seasoning, thyme and salt. Mix well. Fill lightly into the cleaned roasting chicken. Fasten opening with skewers and cord. Truss and place on a rack in roasting pan. Brush with melted butter or margarine. Roast in a moderately slow oven until well browned and tender.

A FAVORITE RECIPE
Chicken with Sherry

One frying chicken (2½ lbs.) disjointed
Three tablespoons fat or oil, heated
One-half teaspoon pepper
One-half teaspoon garlic salt
Browning time: Twenty minutes
One and one-half cups sherry wine
Cooking time: To the boiling point
Two large onions, sliced thin
Two teaspoons rosemary, or less
Simmering time: Forty minutes
One cup rice, cooked
Servings: Four

Have the chicken disjointed in the market. Heat the oil in a heavy skillet. Season the chicken with pepper and garlic salt. Brown the chicken. Remove the chicken to a plate. Remove some of the fat. Add the wine, when it starts to boil add the onions and rosemary. Simmer, covered. Serve on a hot platter with rice.

MRS. WILLIAM R. VELEZ, *Hillsdale, N.J.*

Sweet and Pungent Chicken

One fryer (3-3½ lbs.), cut up
Four tablespoons flour
One teaspoon salt
Four tablespoons butter or margarine
Browning time: Fifteen minutes
One-half cup hot water (about)
Simmering time: Forty-five minutes
One green pepper, diced and blanched
Four slices pineapple
One cup white vinegar
One cup sugar
One tablespoon cornstarch, mixed with
One-half cup water
One teaspoon soy sauce
One-eighth teaspoon pepper
Cooking time: Five minutes
Oven temperature: 350 degrees
Baking time: Fifteen minutes
Servings: Four

Dust the chicken lightly with seasoned flour. Brown in the fat in a heavy saucepan on all sides; add the water. Cover tight; simmer until tender. Arrange the chicken, green pepper and pineapple in a shallow casserole. Bring the vinegar and sugar to the boiling point, stirring. Blend in the cornstarch paste and seasoning; cook, stirring until thickened. Pour over the chicken. Bake in a moderate oven until glazed. Remove from oven. Into three cups cooked green noodles mix two tablespoons each butter and diced toasted almonds, and one teaspoon poppy seed. Place around the edge of the casserole.

Chicken in Red Wine

One-fourth pound salt pork, diced
Two frying chickens, cut fricassee style
One-fourth cup flour
Two teaspoons salt
One teaspoon paprika
One-eighth teaspoon pepper
Few grains nutmeg
One-fourth cup butter or margarine
Two cloves garlic, crushed
Browning time: Fifteen minutes
Twenty-four pearl onions
Cooking time: 10 minutes
Twelve whole small mushrooms
One teaspoon sugar
Two sprigs celery tops tied with
Six sprigs parsley
One bay leaf
Two cups Burgundy wine
Oven temperature: 375 degrees
Baking time: One hour
Two tablespoons flour mixed with
One-fourth cup Burgundy wine
Servings: Eight

In a heavy skillet cook the salt pork over low heat until crisp. Remove the salt pork; reserve. Dust the chicken portions in the combined flour, salt, paprika, pepper and nutmeg.

Add the butter and garlic in the skillet Brown the chicken over low heat on all sides. Remove to a casserole (4 qts.). Cook the onions in the skillet until straw-colored. Add the onions, mushrooms, sugar and bay leaf. Lay the bundle of celery and parsley on top. Heat the wine in the skillet to boiling. Pour over the chicken. Add salt pork. Cover. Bake in a moderately hot oven until the chicken is tender. Remove from oven. Discard the tied celery bundle. Blend in the paste (wine and flour) thoroughly. Cover; let stand for five minutes. Serve in the casserole.

Deviled Chicken

Two frying chickens (3½ lbs. ea.), cut
    fricassee style
Two teaspoons salt
Chilling time: Six hours
One cup flour
One-fourth cup shortening
One-fourth cup butter or margarine
Browning time: Fifteen minutes
One and one-half teaspoons dry mustard
Two tablespoons flour
One cup hot water or soup stock
Cooking time: Five minutes
One tablespoon Worcestershire sauce
One tablespoon catsup
Simmering time: One hour
Servings: Eight, or more

Remove the pin feathers from the
chicken; singe; wash quickly in lukewarm water. Drain; wipe dry; rub with
salt. Place in a shallow pan; cover lightly
with waxed paper; chill. Drop into a sack
containing the flour; shake to coat each
piece evenly. In a heavy skillet heat the
shortening and butter; brown the chicken
on all sides; remove to a dish. Stir the
combined mustard and remaining flour
into the fat; add the hot water or stock.
Cook until the mixture thickens, stirring
constantly; add the remaining ingredients. Place the chicken in the sauce;
cover tightly. Simmer gently until tender.
Uncover; cook ten minutes. Serve hot or
cold.

Chicken Kiev

Three chicken breasts
Six tablespoons butter
Salt and pepper
One-half cup flour
Two eggs, mixed with
One-fourth cup water
Two cups fine bread crumbs
Shortening for deep fat frying
Frying temperature: 365 degrees
Cooking time: Seven minutes (about)
Serves: Six

Split the chicken breasts in half; pull
off the skin. With a sharp knife bone the
chicken. This is done by cutting closely
along the bone structure. Leave the wing
joint attached to the breast but scrape
the meat from the bone. There remain
two pieces of chicken from each breast —
a solid triangular piece of white meat
with the wing bone attached and a long
narrow piece of white meat. Place these
two pieces of meat between waxed paper.
With a rolling pin, flatten the meat very
thin. Wrap a hard piece of butter the
size of a marble in the small piece of
meat, placing it in the widest part of the
other piece of meat. Roll into funnel

shape. Dust each lightly with seasoned
flour, dip into egg mixture and crumbs;
place on a platter. Repeat procedure.
Place in the refrigerator for several hours.
In a skillet, melt the shortening to 365

degrees or when a cube of bread browns
quickly in the hot fat. Place the chicken
rolls in the hot fat until they brown, about
7 minutes. Remove to absorbent paper.
Place on platter; serve immediately.

Glazed Roast Chicken

One roasting chicken (4-4½ lbs.)
Two teaspoons salt
One-fourth teaspoon pepper
One-half cup butter or margarine
One-fourth cup minced onion
One-fourth cup minced parsley
One-half cup minced celery
Cook: Five minutes
Six cups soft bread crumbs
One-fourth teaspoon sage
One and one-half cups apricot nectar
One cup chicken broth, or more
Oven temperature: 350 degrees
Roast: Two hours or until tender
Serves: Four, or more

To provide the broth for basting the chicken, cook the neck and giblets in four cups of water until giblets are tender. Sprinkle the cavity of the chicken with half the salt and pepper. Cook the minced vegetables slowly in the butter in a covered saucepan. Mix in the crumbs, sage and remaining salt and pepper. Remove from heat. Add one-half cup of the apricot nectar. Stir; stuff the cavity. Skewer the opening and lace edges together with soft cord. Place the chicken on a rack in a shallow roasting pan. Roast in a moderate oven. After 30 minutes baste with some of the remaining apricot nectar. Cover the bottom of pan with a little of the broth. Roast until tender.

Baste occasionally with nectar and, when that is gone, with the pan liquid. Add broth to pan to keep the nectar from scorching. Place chicken on hot platter. Serve with gravy made from pan liquid, chopped giblets and remaining broth, thickened slightly (one tablespoon flour for each cup of liquid).

Fruit Dressing

One-fourth cup chopped onion
One-fourth cup butter
One-fourth cup margarine
Saute: Five minutes
Six cups cubed white bread
Oven temperature: 325 degrees
Toast: Ten minutes
Two cups chicken broth
One teaspoon salt
One-fourth teaspoon pepper
One teaspoon poultry seasoning
Two cups diced apples or prunes
One cup chopped walnuts
Yield: Enough to stuff shoulder of veal
    or pork

In a skillet, saute the onion in the butter and margarine. Add bread; blend thoroughly. Scatter the bread on a large shallow pan. Bake in moderately slow oven until golden. Put into a bowl; moisten with broth, seasonings, apples and nuts. Stuff shoulder of veal or pork.

Western Chicken Pie

One small onion
One stalk celery
One-fourth cup butter or margarine
Sauté: Until soft
One-half cup flour
One teaspoon salt
One-eighth teaspoon crumbled rosemary
Two cups milk
One cup chicken bouillon or broth
Cook: Until thickened
Two cups large pieces cooked chicken
One-half cup yellow cornmeal
One-half cup sifted flour
One tablespoon sugar
One and one-half teaspoons baking powder
One-half teaspoon salt
One egg
Two-thirds cup milk
Three tablespoons salad oil
Oven temperature: 425 degrees
Bake: Twenty minutes
Serves: Six

In a saucepan cook the finely chopped onion and celery in the fourth cup of melted butter or margarine until soft. Blend in the flour, salt and crumbled rosemary. Gradually stir in the two cups of milk and the chicken bouillon, stirring smooth. Cook, stirring until sauce thickens. Add the chicken. Transfer to a baking pan or shallow casserole (7 x 12 x 2 in.). Prepare the cornbread crust by sifting the cornmeal, flour, sugar, baking powder and salt together into a bowl. In a second bowl beat the egg, stir in the milk and salad oil; beat into the sifted dry ingredients. Pour over the creamed chicken and bake in a hot oven for twenty minutes or until nicely browned on top. Serve at once. Bake in individual ramekins or baking dishes if preferred.

Chicken Specialty

Two broilers (2 lbs. each) quartered
One teaspoon salt
One-fourth teaspoon pepper
One-fourth cup flour
One-half cup pure vegetable oil
Browning time: Twenty minutes
Three large onions, sliced
One clove garlic, minced
One green pepper, cut into strips
Saute: Five minutes
One can (8 oz.) tomato sauce
One can beer
One teaspoon salt
Simmer: One hour
One-fourth cup seedless raisins
Cook: Ten minutes
Four cups cooked rice
Serves: Six, or more

Singe, rinse and dry the broilers. Dust each quarter of broiler in seasonal flour. In a heavy skillet heat half the vegetable oil. Brown four pieces of the chicken. Remove. Add the rest of oil; brown the remaining quarters. Remove. Add the onions, garlic, green pepper strips; saute for 5 minutes. Stir in the tomato sauce, beer and salt; blending thoroughly. Add the browned chicken. Cover; simmer until chicken is tender. Uncover; add raisins; reheat. Serve with hot rice.

Chicken and Veal with Duchess Potatoes

Two cups cooked chicken
Two cups diced cooked veal (1 lb.)
One cup heavy cream
Heat: Ten minutes
Two tablespoons butter or margarine
Two tablespoons flour
One teaspoon salt
One-fourth teaspoon pepper
One-fourth teaspoon savory
*Two cups Duchess potatoes
Oven temperature: 400 degrees
Bake: Thirty minutes
Serves: Four, or more

In the top of a double boiler, put in the chicken, veal and heavy cream. Cook over boiling water till the cream is absorbed in the chicken and veal. In a saucepan heat the butter; blend in the flour, salt, pepper and savory. Add the chicken mixture and half the cheese. Pour into a casserole (1½ qts.). Spoon the Duchess potatoes around the edge of the casserole. Sprinkle the remaining cheese on top. Bake in a quick oven until potatoes are golden.

*Two cups mashed potatoes beaten with two eggs yolks.

Brunswick Stew

Three slices bacon
Fry: Crisp
Two large onions, thinly sliced
Cook: Until tender
One frying chicken, cut up
Browning time: Ten to fifteen minutes
Two quarts cold water
One tablespoon salt
Simmer: Two to three hours
One package (10 oz.) frozen lima beans
One package (10 oz.) frozen cut corn
One package (10 oz.) frozen okra
One teaspoon salt or more
One-fourth teaspoon pepper
Bay leaf (optional)
Simmer: Thirty minutes
Servings: Six

In a large heavy kettle fry the bacon until crisp. Remove and set aside. Add the thinly sliced onions and sauté until tender. Remove. Add the chicken pieces cut to similar size and brown quickly on all sides, adding oil or shortening to the kettle if necessary. Crumble bacon over the browned chicken, add the onion and pour on the two quarts of cold water. Add the salt and cover. Bring to a boil and simmer gently for two to three hours, until the meat will slip easily from the bones. Remove chicken from pan, discard skin and bones and return meat to pan. Add the frozen limas, cut corn and okra and additional salt and pepper to taste. Simmer 30 minutes more. Serve in deep soup plates.

Baked Chicken and Corn Casserole

Three tablespoons butter or margarine
Four tablespoons flour
One teaspoon salt
One-fourth teaspoon pepper
One-fourth teaspoon thyme
Two cups rich chicken stock
Cook: Ten minutes
One can (1 lb.) whole kernel corn, drained
One can (4 oz.) mushrooms
One tablespoon parsley flakes
One pimiento, chopped
One-half cup seasoned bread crumbs
Four tablespoons melted butter or
　margarine
Oven temperature: 350 degrees
Bake: Twenty-five minutes
Serves: Four, or more

In a saucepan, melt the butter; stir in the flour, salt, pepper and thyme. Gradually stir in the chicken stock, cooking until smooth and thickened. Add the whole kernel corn, mushrooms, parsley flakes, pimiento and chicken. Blend. Pour into a casserole (1½ qts.). Mix the bread crumbs with the butter. Sprinkle over the top of the chicken. Bake in a moderate oven until hot and bubbly.

Baked Chicken with Rosemary

One frying chicken (2½-3 lbs.), cut up
Paprika
Garlic salt
Flour
One-third cup salad oil
Frying time: Fifteen minutes, about
One can (10½ oz.) condensed cream of
　chicken soup
One-third cup light cream
One-third cup white wine
One teaspoon crushed rosemary
Oven temperature: 350 degrees
Baking time: Forty-five minutes
Servings: Four

Rinse and dry thoroughly the pieces of chicken. Lay on a board or platter and sprinkle generously with paprika, garlic salt and flour on both sides. Heat the salad oil in a large heavy skillet, add the seasoned chicken pieces and brown well on both sides. In a bowl place the condensed cream of chicken soup. Beat smooth with a fork and stir in the light cream and white wine. Transfer the browned chicken to a casserole (2 qts.) and sprinkle with the crushed rosemary. Pour on the soup mixture. Cover tightly and bake in a moderate oven for forty-five minutes. Serve hot from the casserole.

Baked Chicken Salad

Two cups diced cooked chicken
One cup chopped celery
One-third cup chopped green pepper
One-half teaspoon salt
One-eighth teaspoon pepper
One tablespoon finely chopped onion
One tablespoon prepared mustard
One-third cup mayonnaise, or more
One-half cup crushed potato chips
Cranberry sauce (optional)
Servings: Four to six

In a bowl mix the diced cooked chicken, chopped celery, green pepper, salt, pepper, onion, prepared mustard and mayonnaise. Add more mayonnaise if desired. Mix well. Transfer to a shallow baking dish or pie plate (9 in.) and top with the crushed potato chips. Decorate top with spoonfuls of cranberry sauce if desired. Bake in a quick oven for 20 minutes or until piping hot and browned.

Baked Chicken Americana

Four cups cooked, diced chicken
Two cups soft bread crumbs
One cup cooked rice
One and one-half teaspoons salt
One-fourth teaspoon paprika
One and one-half cups chicken stock
One and one-half cups light cream
Four eggs, well beaten
Oven temperature: 325 degrees
Bake: One hour
Serves: Six to eight

Mix the chicken, bread crumbs, rice, salt, paprika and chicken stock. Beat the light cream and eggs together. Blend into the chicken mixture. Pour into a greased ring mold (2 qts.). Bake in a moderately slow oven for one hour or until firm. Unmold and serve with Mushroom Sauce.

Mushroom Sauce

In a saucepan blend four tablespoons each of melted butter and flour. Gradually stir in two cups chicken stock and one-fourth cup light cream. Add one can (4¾ oz.) prepared sauteed mushrooms, one-fourth teaspoon paprika, one tablespoon minced parsley and one-fourth teaspoon lemon juice. Cook 10 minutes. Serve.

Oven Fried Spiced Chicken

One tablespoon mixed pickling spice
One teaspoon poultry seasoning
One-half teaspoon salt
One can (10½ oz.) beef bouillon
One teaspoon curry powder
One and one-half tablespoons lemon juice
One frying chicken (3½ lbs.) cut up
Marinate: Overnight
Oven temperature: 425 degrees
Bake: Thirty-five minutes, about
Serves: Four

In a saucepan combine the mixed pickling spice, poultry seasoning, salt beef bouillon, curry powder and lemon juice. Heat to the boiling point. Arrange the cut-up chicken in a bowl and pour marinade over. Cover and let stand in the refrigerator several hours or overnight if possible. To cook arrange the marinated pieces of chicken in a shallow pan skin side down. Pour half a cup of the marinade over top and bake in a hot oven for 20 minutes. Turn the pieces of chicken, pour on more of the marinade and continue baking for 15 minutes or until well browned, adding marinade as surface of the chicken seems dry.

Chicken with Tarragon

Two broiler-fryers (2½ to 3 lbs. each),
　cut up
Tarragon salt or salt and pepper
One-third cup bacon drippings or butter
Browning time: Fifteen minutes, about
One-half teaspoon dried tarragon, or more
One-third cup Bordeaux white wine
Simmering time: Forty minutes, or less
One-third cup Bordeaux white wine
Cooking time: One to two minutes
Servings: Four to six

Wash and dry the chicken pieces; dust lightly with tarragon salt or salt and pepper. In a large heavy skillet, melt the bacon drippings or butter. When hot, add the chicken pieces and brown quickly on all sides. Sprinkle with the dried tarragon and pour on the wine. Cover tightly and simmer gently over low heat until the chicken is very tender. Remove chicken to serving platter and keep warm. Add additional wine to skillet, bringing to a quick boil and stirring to dissolve pan brownings. Spoon sauce over individual portions of chicken.

A FAVORITE RECIPE
Paprika Chicken

One broiler (3 lbs.) disjointed
Two or more tablespoons fat, heated
Browning time: Twenty minutes
One cup chopped onion
Cooking time: Five minutes
Two teaspoons paprika
One clove garlic, crushed
One-half cup warm water
Two green peppers, cleaned, cut into
　thin rings
Two tomatoes, peeled, quartered
Simmering time: One hour
One tablespoon flour mixed with
One cup thick sour cream
Cooking time: To the boiling point
One package noodles, cooked as directed,
　drained
Servings: Four, or more

Have the chicken disjointed. Season to taste. Heat the fat in a large heavy skillet. Brown the chicken, turning each piece until all sides are browned. Add the onion, cook, stirring several times. Add the paprika, garlic and water. Arrange the green pepper rings and tomatoes on top. Cover. Simmer until tender. Mix the flour with three tablespoons of cream, add to the remaining cream; pour over the chicken. Bring to the boiling point, do not boil. Serve at once with hot, well drained noodles.

MRS. W. A. JAMIESON, *Mars Hill, Maine*

Chicken Paprika

Two chicken fryers (3 lbs. each) quartered
One teaspoon salt
One-fourth teaspoon pepper
One-fourth cup flour
One clove garlic, pureed
Six tablespoons butter
Browning time: Fifteen minutes
One can (16 oz.) chicken broth
Four tablespoons paprika
Simmer: Forty-five minutes
One cup Spanish sherry wine
Oven temperature: 400 degrees
Baking time: Fifteen minutes
One-half cup dairy sour cream
Serves: Six, or more

Dredge the chicken in the seasoned flour. In a heavy skillet brown the chicken and garlic in the butter. Add the chicken broth and paprika. Cover and cook 45 minutes. Place chicken in large shallow pan. Add 1 cup sherry to liquid in skillet, stirring until well blended. Pour over chicken. Place in quick oven for 15 minutes, basting occasionally. Serve on hot platter. Stir in dairy sour cream to liquid in pan; pour into gravy boat. Serve.

Chicken Fricassee

One fowl (5 lbs.) cut into serving pieces
One-fourth cup flour
Four tablespoons butter or margarine
Brown: Fifteen minutes
One small onion, halved
One carrot, peeled
One teaspoon salt
Four peppercorns
Four cups chicken broth or water
Simmering time: One and one-half hours,
    or longer
Let stand: Overnight
One-third cup flour
One cup heavy cream
One tablespoon lemon juice
Heat: To the boiling point
Chopped parsley
Serves: Six

Singe, wash and dry the chicken. Dust the chicken with the flour. In a deep kettle melt the butter. Brown the chicken on all sides. Add the onion, carrot, salt, peppercorns and broth or water. Cover and simmer over low heat until the chicken is tender. Take out the onion and carrot. Let stand overnight (Do not store in refrigerator until it is cold, otherwise it will turn sour). Skim off the fat. Stir in the combined flour and cream, blending thoroughly; add the lemon juice. Heat to the boiling point, stirring constantly. Correct the seasoning. Garnish with chopped parsley.

Chicken Supreme

Four chicken breasts
One teaspoon salt
One-fourth teaspoon pepper
Two tablespoons flour
Four tablespoons butter or margarine
Browning time: Ten minutes
One-half cup water
Cooking time: Thirty minutes
Two slices ready-to-eat smoked ham
    (¼ in. thick) cut in half
One-fourth cup Bordeaux white wine
Serves: Four

Dust the chicken breasts in seasoned flour. In a large heavy skillet melt the butter; add the chicken, browning on all sides. Pour in the water. Cover; simmer for 30 minutes. Place a slice of ham under each breast of chicken; add wine. Cover; simmer for 15 minutes. Remove to a hot platter. Serve immediately.

Chicken a la King

Four tablespoons butter or margarine
One cup canned or cooked mushrooms,
    sliced
One-fourth green pepper, cut in strips
Cooking time: Five minutes
Three tablespoons flour
One teaspoon salt
One-fourth teaspoon pepper
One and one-half cups milk
Cooking time: Ten minutes
One-half cup heavy cream, mixed with
Two egg yolks, slightly beaten
Two cups chicken (1 in. pieces)
One pimiento, chopped
Reheat: Until hot
Three tablespoons sherry
Patty shells, or toast triangles
Serves: Six

In the top of a double boiler over low
heat melt the butter. Cook the mushrooms
and green pepper five minutes. Stir in
the flour and seasonings. Place over hot
water. Gradually add the milk, stirring
constantly until mixture thickens. Mix
the cream with the slightly beaten egg
yolks. Stir into sauce (never allow it to
boil). Add chicken and pimiento; reheat
until thoroughly hot. Stir in sherry. Serve
in patty shells or on toast triangles.

Chiffon Chicken Pie

One-third cup butter or margarine
One and one-half cups cracker crumbs
Cook: Five minutes (or until toasted)
One envelope unflavored gelatin
One-fourth cup cold water
Two cups boiling chicken broth
Chill: Until it becomes the consistency
    of unbeaten egg white
Four cups chopped, cooked chicken
One-fourth cup minced celery
Two pimientos, sliced
One teaspoon salt
One teaspoon pepper
One tablespoon prepared mustard or
    mustard sauce
One cup heavy cream, whipped
Cooked peas, pimiento, halved crackers
Chill: Until firm
Serves: Four, or more

Melt the butter in a heavy skillet over
low heat; blend in the cracker crumbs,
tossing until toasted. Cool. Coat the sides
and bottom of a slightly buttered pie pan
(10 in.) with the crumbs. In a cup soften
the gelatin in the cold water. Stir into
the boiling chicken broth until dissolved.
Place in refrigerator until it becomes the
consistency of unbeaten egg white. Beat
until light and airy. Fold in chicken,
celery, pimientos, salt, pepper, prepared
mustard and whipped heavy cream. Pour
into crumb shell. Garnish with peas and
pimientos. Around rim of pie garnish with
halved crackers. Chill until firm. Serve in
wedges.

Chicken Mousse

One and one-half tablespoons unflavored gelatin
One-fourth cup cold chicken broth
One-half cup hot chicken broth
Three egg yolks
One and one-half cups milk
Cooking time: Ten minutes, or more
Two cups finely cut cooked chicken
One teaspoon salt
One-eighth teaspoon pepper
One-fourth teaspoon paprika
Two tablespoons finely chopped parsley
Chill: Until slightly thickened
One cup heavy cream, whipped
Chill: Until firm
One head crisp lettuce
Servings: Eight

Sprinkle the unflavored gelatin in the fourth cup of cold chicken broth in a bowl. Let stand to soften. Add the hot chicken broth and stir to dissolve. In the upper half of a double boiler beat the egg yolks. Add the milk and place over hot water to cook, stirring constantly, until smooth and slightly thickened. Add to gelatin mixture. Cool and add the diced, cooked chicken, salt, pepper, paprika and finely chopped parsley. Chill until the mixture starts to thicken then fold in the whipped cream. Pour into a four cup mold and chill until firm. Unmold upon a platter and slice into eight portions to serve on generous amounts of crisp lettuce. Garnish plates with gherkins or olives. Melba toast is a good accompaniment.

A FAVORITE RECIPE
Orange-Dipped Chicken

Two tablespoons butter, heated
One frying chicken (4-5 lbs.) disjointed
Browning time: Fifteen minutes, or longer
Two tablespoons flour
One-half teaspoon salt
Browning time: Three minutes
One tablespoon brown sugar
One tablespoon white sugar
Two cups orange juice
One-half cup water
Cooking time: Until thick
Sliced orange
Simmering time: Forty-five minutes
Servings: Four

Heat the butter in a heavy skillet. Dry the chicken; brown in the butter, turning until all sides are browned. Remove the chicken to a casserole (with cover); add the flour and salt to the butter in skillet, brown the flour slightly; add the brown and white sugar; stir into the flour until smooth.

Add the orange juice and water. Simmer, stirring constantly until the sauce is smooth and thick. Pour over the chicken; place the sliced orange (from which juice was squeezed) over the chicken. Cover tightly. Simmer until the chicken is tender, basting frequently with the sauce. Serve hot with the vegetables.

DR. ESTHER P. ROTHMAN, *New York, N.Y.*

Chicken with Lemon and Rosemary

One frying chicken, cut up (2½ lbs.)
Salt and pepper
One-third cup shortening
Browning time: Twenty minutes
One clove garlic, crushed
One-half teaspoon salt
One-third cup lemon juice
One-fourth cup olive oil
One small onion, finely chopped
One-eighth teaspoon pepper
One-half teaspoon crushed rosemary
Simmering time: Forty minutes, about
Servings: Four

Rinse off the chicken, dry thoroughly. Sprinkle with salt and pepper. In a large heavy skillet heat the shortening. Add the chicken pieces and brown evenly on all sides. In a small bowl combine the crushed garlic, salt, lemon juice, olive oil, chopped onion, pepper and rosemary. Pour over the browned chicken pieces. Cover the skillet tightly and simmer gently over very low heat until the chicken is very tender. Spoon sauce over chicken when served.

A FAVORITE RECIPE
Spiced Chicken

One cup orange juice
One and one-half cups sliced canned or frozen peaches (thawed)
Two tablespoons brown sugar
Two tablespoons vinegar
One teaspoon mace or nutmeg
One teaspoon basil
One clove garlic, minced
Simmering time: Ten minutes
One-half cup flour
One teaspoon salt
One-sixteenth teaspoon pepper
Six chicken (fryer) legs and thighs
One-fourth cup cooking oil or fat, heated
Cooking time: Forty minutes
Servings: Four

In a saucepan combine the orange juice, peaches, brown sugar, vinegar, spices and garlic. Simmer. Mix the flour, salt and pepper in a paper bag; dredge the chicken in the mixture coating each piece well. Heat the oil or fat in a heavy skillet; fry the chicken, turning until each piece is well browned. Pour the orange juice mixture over the chicken; reduce the heat, simmer, stirring and turning the chicken frequently. Serve with any sauce left in pan poured over the chicken.

MRS. A. MAYER, *Richmond, Va.*

Chicken in Wine Saute

One broiler-fryer chicken (quartered)
Two tablespoons flour
Salt and pepper
Three tablespoons salad oil
One medium-sized onion, finely chopped
Sautéing time: Five minutes
Browning time: Ten minutes
One-fourth cup finely chopped parsley
One-third cup finely chopped celery leaves
One-half cup chablis or other dry white wine
Simmering time: Thirty minutes, or more
Servings: Four

Rinse off the chicken and dry thoroughly. Dust on all sides with the flour. Sprinkle with salt and pepper on both sides. In a large heavy skillet heat the oil. Add the finely chopped onion and sauté only until transparent. Skim off onion to a small plate and reserve. Add the floured chicken to the skillet and brown carefully on both sides. Sprinkle sautéed onion, chopped parsley and chopped celery leaves over the chicken and pour on the dry white wine. Cover skillet tightly and simmer gently until chicken is tender, about thirty minutes. Spoon slightly thickened pan drippings over the portions of chicken as served.

A FAVORITE RECIPE
Floating Chicken

One-third cup enriched flour
Two teaspoons salt
One and one-half teaspoons ground sage
One teaspoon pepper
One frying chicken (2½-3 lbs.) disjointed
One-fourth cup fat, heated
Browning time: Twenty minutes
One cup flour, sifted with
One teaspoon baking powder
One teaspoon salt
Three eggs, well beaten
One and one-half cups milk
One-half cup butter, melted
One-fourth cup chopped parsley (optional)
Oven temperature: 350 degrees
Baking time: One hour
Servings: Four

In a pan, mix the flour, salt, sage and pepper. Coat each piece of the chicken with the mixture. Heat the fat in a large, heavy skillet. Fry the chicken, browning on all sides. Into a bowl sift the flour, baking powder and salt. Add the combined beaten eggs, milk, melted butter and parsley, beating until smooth. Place the fried chicken in an oven dish (11½ x 7½ x 1½ in.). Pour the egg mixture over the chicken. Bake in a moderate oven until browned. Serve from the oven dish.

MRS. ARTHUR HUEBSCH, *East Paterson, N.J.*

Lemon Broiled Chicken

One chicken (2½ to 3 pounds), quartered
One tablespoon butter, melted
One tablespoon lemon juice
Broiler temperature: 500 degrees
Broil: Thirty minutes, about
Serves: Four

Rinse, dry and examine the quartered chicken for pinfeathers. Trim off any excess fat. Combine the melted butter and lemon juice. Place the chicken skin side down on rack in broiling pan and brush with lemon butter. Broil six inches from source of heat or as far from heat as space will permit in a shallow broiler. Broil twenty minutes, turn chicken pieces over, brush with lemon butter and broil ten minutes more or until chicken is well browned and thoroughly cooked. Serve at once.

A FAVORITE RECIPE
Chicken Loaf

One cup soft bread crumbs
Two cups milk
Two eggs, beaten light
One-half teaspoon salt
One-fourth teaspoon paprika
Three cups cooked chicken, diced (¼ in.)
One-half cup cooked peas
One-fourth cup chopped pimiento
Oven temperature: 325 degrees
Baking time: Forty minutes
One can (10½ oz.) condensed cream of
    mushroom soup for sauce
Servings: Six

In a bowl blend the bread crumbs, milk, eggs, salt and paprika. Stir in the chicken, peas and pimiento. Turn into a well greased loaf pan (9 in.). Bake in a moderately slow oven until firm. Serve with the mushroom sauce made from the canned soup.

MRS. JAMES I. HARRIS, *New York, N.Y.*

Chicken Noodle Supreme

Four ounces fine egg noodles
Two quarts boiling water
Two teaspoons salt
Cooking time: Ten minutes, about
Three tablespoons butter or margarine
Three tablespoons flour
Two cups chicken broth or bouillon
One teaspoon salt
One-eighth teaspoon pepper
One cup heavy cream
Two cups diced cooked chicken
One can (6 oz.) sliced mushrooms
One-third cup shredded blanched almonds
One-fourth cup grated Parmesan cheese
Oven temperature: 375 degrees
Baking time: Thirty minutes
Servings: Four to six

Cook the egg noodles in the boiling water with salt until tender. Drain in colander. In a saucepan melt the butter or margarine and blend in the flour. Gradually add the chicken broth or bouillon and cook, stirring constantly until the mixture thickens. Season with salt and pepper. Remove from the heat and blend in the heavy cream. Add half of this sauce to the drained noodles and spread them in a shallow baking dish (2 qts.) or in the bottom of individual casseroles (2 cup). Add the diced chicken to the remaining sauce with the mushrooms and shredded almonds. Spoon over the noodles in the baking dish and sprinkle with the Parmesan cheese. Bake in a moderately hot oven for 30 minutes or until lightly browned. If necessary place briefly under the broiler heat to brown before serving.

Chicken Tetrazzini

Three tablespoons butter
Three tablespoons flour
One teaspoon salt
One-eighth teaspoon pepper
Two cups chicken broth or bouillon
Two cups diced cooked chicken
Cook: Five to eight minutes
One cup heavy cream
Eight ounces fine spaghetti
Boiling salted water
Cook: Ten minutes
Two tablespoons butter
Two tablespoons lemon juice
One-fourth pound fresh mushrooms
Sauté: Five to eight minutes
One-fourth cup grated Parmesan cheese
Oven temperature: 400 degrees
Bake: Twenty minutes
Serves: Four to six

In a large saucepan or skillet melt the three tablespoons of butter. Stir in the flour, salt and pepper, gradually blend in the chicken broth or bouillon. Add the diced chicken and cook and stir until the sauce thickens. Blend in the heavy cream carefully and keep warm over low heat. Cook the fine spaghetti in the boiling salted water.

In a skillet melt the two tablespoons of butter with the lemon juice. Add the thinly sliced fresh mushrooms (cut from top to bottom through cap and stem) and sauté until lightly browned and golden. Drain the cooked spaghetti and combine with the creamed chicken. Add about two-thirds of the sautéed mushrooms, saving rest for garnish. Transfer to shallow individual ramekins or a shallow baking dish or pie plate. Garnish with the reserved sautéed mushrooms and sprinkle with the grated Parmesan cheese. Bake in a quick oven until piping hot and lightly browned. Serve at once.

Chicken Cacciatore

One broiler-fryer (2½-3 pounds) cut up
One-half cup olive oil
Browning time: Fifteen minutes, or more
One large onion, thinly sliced
Cook: Five minutes, about
One can (No. 2½) tomatoes
One clove garlic
One and one-half teaspoons salt
One-fourth teaspoon pepper
Simmer: Thirty minutes
One-half cup dry white wine
Simmer: Five minutes
Servings: Four

Rinse and dry the chicken pieces. Heat the olive oil in a large heavy skillet. Add the chicken and brown slowly on all sides. Add the thinly sliced onion and cook until onion is golden. Add the canned tomatoes, whole clove of garlic, salt and pepper. Cover tightly and simmer gently until chicken is tender. Add the dry white wine and cook briefly. Remove garlic clove and serve chicken pieces with vegetables spooned over top.

Chicken Marengo

One-fourth cup olive oil
One frying chicken (2-3 lbs.) cut up
Browning time: Ten minutes, or more
Cook: Ten minutes
One-half pound fresh mushrooms, sliced
One clove garlic, crushed
Two medium-sized onions, sliced
Browning time: Five to ten minutes
One can (No. 2) tomatoes
Four sprigs parsley
Two stalks celery with leaves, sliced
One teaspoon salt
Cook: Thirty to forty minutes
Servings: Four

In a large, heavy skillet or kettle, heat the olive oil, add the chicken pieces and brown on all sides. Cover the pan and cook for 10 minutes. Remove chicken to platter. Add mushrooms, garlic and sliced onions to the drippings, brown lightly. Add the canned tomatoes, parsley, celery and salt with the chicken. Cover and continue cooking 30 minutes or more, until the chicken is tender. Taste and correct seasoning if necessary. Serve with fluffy rice.

Note: One-half cup of dry white wine may be added during the final cooking period.

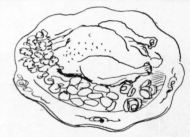

Browned Fricassee of Chicken

One-third cup flour
One teaspoon paprika
One broiler-fryer chicken (2½ pounds),
    quartered
One-third cup shortening
Frying time: Fifteen to twenty minutes
One and one-half cups water
One-half cup dry white wine
One-fourth cup instant minced onion (one
    cup finely chopped fresh onion)
One teaspoon salt
One-eighth teaspoon pepper
Simmer: Thirty-five minutes
One stalk celery, finely chopped
One carrot, finely chopped
Simmer: Twenty minutes
Serves: Four

Stir the flour and paprika together. Wash and dry the chicken pieces and dredge in the seasoned flour. Heat the shortening in a large heavy skillet. Add the floured chicken and brown well on all sides. Drain off any excess fat. Combine the water, dry white wine, instant or fresh onion, salt and pepper. Pour over the chicken and cover tightly. Cook over low heat for thirty-five minutes. Add the finely chopped celery and carrot, cover and continue cooking over low heat for twenty minutes more. Serve chicken with vegetable sauce spooned over top.

Oven Barbecued Duckling

One duckling (5 to 6 lbs.) quartered
Oven temperature: 325-375 degrees
Roasting time: Two hours (about)
One-half cup lemon juice
One-third cup wine vinegar
One-third cup tomato catsup
One-fourth cup water
One tablespoon honey or brown sugar
One teaspoon salt
One teaspoon powdered mustard
One teaspoon paprika
One-half teaspoon ground black pepper
One-fourth teaspoon cayenne
One-half teaspoon onion salt
One-eighth teaspoon garlic salt
One teaspoon tabasco sauce
Two tablespoons butter or margarine
Heat: To the boiling point
Serves: Four

Place the duckling skin side up on a rack in a shallow roasting pan. Roast uncovered in a slow oven until tender (about 90 minutes). Meanwhile, combine all the remaining ingredients in a saucepan heating only to the boiling point. Set aside. Drain the fat from pan, remove rack. Brush duckling all over with the sauce. Return to a moderately hot oven and continue roasting. At 10 minute intervals, for 30 minutes, brush the duckling with the barbecue sauce. Serve immediately.

Ducklings With Green Grapes

Two ducklings (5 lbs. each) quartered
Oven temperature: 400 degrees
Roast: Thirty minutes
Four tablespoons drippings
Two teaspoons flour
One cup chicken broth
One cup dry white Bordeaux wine
One teaspoon salt
One-fourth teaspoon pepper
Cook: Five minutes
One bay leaf
Pinch of thyme
One teaspoon dried parsley
One cup green grapes
Simmer: One hour
Serves: Six, or more

Prick the ducks with a fork; place on a rack in a roasting pan. Roast in the oven until brown. Put four tablespoons drippings into a heavy kettle. Stir in the flour and brown the flour slightly. Blend in the chicken broth, wine, salt and pepper; cook until slightly thickened. Place the browned ducklings into the kettle. Add bay leaf, thyme and parsley. Cover tightly; simmer gently until ducklings are tender. The last five minutes of cooking add the grapes. Remove ducklings to a hot platter; serve.

Best Roast Duckling

One Long Island duckling (4 to 5 pounds)
Oven temperature: 450 degrees
Roast: Thirty minutes
Oven temperature: 350 degrees
Roast: Thirty minutes
Oven temperature: 300 degrees
Roast: Forty-five minutes
Servings: Four

It's best to defrost frozen duckling before roasting. This will take several hours at room temperature or overnight on a lower shelf of the refrigerator. Use a kitchen shears to quarter the duck. Trim off the backbone. With a very sharp knife score the skin at one inch intervals. Place pieces of duck skin side up on rack in roasting pan and roast in a very hot oven for thirty minutes. Reduce heat to moderate and roast a second half hour. Reduce heat to slow and roast until tender, thirty to forty-five minutes. Serve while very hot and crisp.

Oven-Fried Turkey

One frozen fryer turkey (3 to 6 lbs. ready-to-cook weight)
Thawing time: Six to eight hours
Two teaspoons salt
One-half teaspoon pepper
One-half cup flour
One-fourth cup shortening
One-fourth cup butter
Browning time: Ten minutes
One-half cup water
Oven temperature: 325 degrees
Baking time: Ninety minutes (about)
Oven temperature: 450 degrees
Browning time: Fifteen minutes
Servings: Ten, or more

Thaw the turkey at room temperature. Cut into 10 to 12 serving portions and coat evenly with seasoned flour. Heat the shortening and butter in heavy skillet; brown the turkey delicately on all sides, beginning with the choice parts. When browned transfer the turkey and drippings to a roasting pan; add half the water. Cover. Bake in a moderately slow oven until tender, adding the rest of the water at intervals. The turkey is done when the thigh is easily pierced with a fork. Then increase the oven temperature to very hot and bake uncovered until the turkey is golden brown. Serve upon a hot platter. Make gravy from the pan drippings.

Giblet Gravy

One-fourth cup any fat
One-fourth cup flour
Two and one-half cups water
Three chicken bouillon cubes
One-half teaspoon salt (about)
One-sixteenth teaspoon pepper
Boiling time: Three minutes
Chopped cooked giblets
Yield: Three cups

Brown the fat and flour lightly. Stir in the water, bouillon cubes and seasonings. Cook, stirring, until thickened. Add the giblets; reheat gently.

Rock Cornish Hen
With Olive Wine Sauce

Six Rock Cornish hens (¾ lb. each)
One clove garlic, split
Two tablespoons chopped onion
Four tablespoons olive oil
Sauteing time: Three minutes
One cup pimiento stuffed green olives, sliced
One-fourth cup lemon juice
One-fourth cup chili sauce
One cup New York sherry wine
One tablespoon mushroom powder
One teaspoon rosemary
One teaspoon salt
One-fourth teaspoon pepper
Cooking time: Five minutes
Oven temperature: 325 degrees
Roasting time: Seventy-five minutes (about)
Serves: Six

Wash and wipe the Cornish hens. Tie the legs with soft cord. Place on a rack

in a shallow roasting pan. In a saucepan cook the garlic and onion in the olive oil until straw-colored. Remove garlic. Add olives, lemon juice, chili sauce, wine, mushroom powder, rosemary, salt and pepper; cook 5 minutes. Brush the hens with half of the olive wine sauce. Roast in a moderately slow oven for seventy-five minutes, basting occasionally with the remaining sauce. Remove from oven. Remove cord. Bank the hens in the center of a hot platter; garnish center with water cress. Serve with wine sauce from roasting pan.

Spicy Sauced Turkey Curry

One-fourth cup butter or margarine
One small onion, finely chopped
One tart apple, finely chopped
Sautéing time: Five to eight minutes
One-fourth cup flour
One to two teaspoons curry
One teaspoon salt
One-fourth teaspoon ginger
One cup turkey or chicken broth or
   bouillon
One cup milk
Cooking time: Five to ten minutes
Three cups diced turkey or chicken
One tablespoon lemon juice
Heating time: Ten minutes
One cup rice, cooked
Pineapple chunks, apricot halves, fresh
   grapes
Servings: Four

In a large heavy skillet, melt the butter or margarine, add the chopped onion and apple and sauté until tender. In a cup combine the flour, curry, salt and ginger and stir in the sautéed onion and apple. Gradually stir in the broth or bouillon and milk, stirring the while to keep the sauce smooth. Cook, stirring constantly, until the mixture thickens slightly. Add the diced turkey or chicken and lemon juice; permit to heat through thoroughly. Serve over hot cooked rice with fresh or canned fruit accompaniments.

Turkey Macaroni Skillet Meal

Two medium-sized onions, sliced
Two green peppers, sliced
One-third cup olive oil or salad oil
Cooking time: Ten minutes
One can (No. 2½) tomatoes
One can (6½ oz.) tomato paste
One can (6 oz.) mushrooms, undrained
One-half pound uncooked thin macaroni
Cooking time: Twenty minutes
Two cups cooked diced turkey
Salt and pepper to taste
Heating time: Ten minutes
Grated Parmesan cheese
Servings: Four

In a deep kettle or Dutch oven cook the sliced onions and green pepper in the oil until tender. Add the canned tomatoes, tomato paste, undrained mushrooms and thin macaroni. Cover and cook gently until the macaroni is tender, stirring occasionally. Add the diced cooked turkey and salt and pepper to taste. Heat through for about 10 minutes. Serve with a generous sprinkling of grated Parmesan cheese.

Turkey Turnovers

Pastry for two crust pie
Two cups diced cooked turkey
One-half can (10½ oz.) condensed celery
   soup
One tablespoon chopped parsley
One-fourth teaspoon salt
One egg yolk
Two tablespoons milk
Oven temperature: 375 degrees
Bake: Twenty minutes
Serves: Six

Roll out the pastry and cut into six squares (6 x 6 in.). In a bowl mix the diced turkey with the condensed celery soup, parsley and salt. Mix well. Divide the mixture between the six squares of pastry. Fold dough over to make a triangle; use fork to press edges together. Beat the egg yolk and two tablespoons of milk slightly in a cup with a fork. Brush over the turnovers; prick each with fork. Bake in a moderately hot oven until crisp and light brown. Serve with turkey gravy if desired.

Turkey Supreme

Four tablespoons butter or margarine
One-half pound mushrooms, sliced
One-fourth cup diced green pepper
Sautéing time: Five to ten minutes
One-fourth cup flour
One-half cup milk or light cream
One cup turkey stock or chicken bouillon
One teaspoon salt
One-fourth teaspoon pepper
Cooking time: Ten minutes, about
Two cups diced cooked turkey
Two tablespoons minced pimiento
One-fourth to one-half teaspoon marjoram
One-fourth cup white wine
Heating time: Ten minutes
Four patty shells or slices of toast
Servings: Four

In a large heavy skillet melt the butter or margarine; add the sliced mushrooms and diced pepper and sauté briefly. Sprinkle with the flour, stir and mix. Gradually add the milk or cream and the stock or bouillon, stirring to keep smooth. Cook over low heat until thickened slightly, stirring the while. Add the diced turkey, pimiento, marjoram and white wine. Heat thoroughly and serve in patty shells or over toast.

Turkey Tetrazzini

Two tablespoons butter
One tablespoon flour
One can (10½ oz.) condensed cream of
   mushroom soup
Mushroom liquid from four ounce can
   sliced mushrooms
Three-fourths cup light cream
One-fourth teaspoon salt
One tablespoon prepared mustard
Cook: Ten minutes
Two cups diced cooked turkey
One-half pound thin spaghetti, cooked
One-fourth cup grated Parmesan cheese
Oven temperature: 400 degrees
Bake: Twenty minutes
Serves: Four

In a saucepan melt the butter. Stir in the flour, mushroom soup, liquid from canned mushrooms, cream, salt and mustard. Cook, stirring constantly, until thickened. Mix half the sauce with the diced turkey and mushrooms. Arrange cooked, drained spaghetti in a greased casserole or baking dish (2 qts.) or individual ramekins, making a well in the center. Fill the well with the creamed turkey mixture; pour remaining sauce around edge of spaghetti ring. Top with grated cheese. Bake in a quick oven un-

til lightly browned on top. Serve at once from the single casserole or place individual baking dishes on serving plates.

Turkey Hash with Cream

Two tablespoons butter or margarine
Two tablespoons chopped onion
Two tablespoons chopped green pepper
Sauté: Five minutes, about
Two tablespoons chopped pimiento
One and one-half cups chopped cooked
   turkey
Heat: Thoroughly
Four slices crisp toast, cubed
One-half cup heavy cream
Heat: Five minutes, about
Servings: Five

Melt the butter or margarine in a heavy skillet. Add the chopped onion and green pepper and sauté until tender. Add the chopped pimiento and chopped cooked turkey. Heat thoroughly until piping hot, stirring constantly. Stir in the cubes of crisp toast. Pour cream over mixture and cook over gentle heat until the cream is absorbed. Serve hot.

Turkey Divan

Two packages (10 oz. each) frozen
   broccoli spears
Boiling salted water
Four tablespoons butter or margarine
One-fourth cup flour
One cup turkey or chicken broth or bouillon
One cup milk
Cook: Five minutes or more
One cup grated cheddar cheese
One-half teaspoon salt
One-eighth teaspoon pepper
Six portions of cooked sliced turkey
Oven temperature: 400 degrees
Baking time: Twenty minutes
Servings: Six

Cook the frozen broccoli spears in the boiling salted water according to package directions. Drain and lay in a shallow baking dish (7 x 12 x 2 in.) or in two pie plates. In a saucepan, melt the butter or margarine. Stir in the flour and gradually blend in the broth or bouillon. Add the milk and cook and stir until the sauce thickens. Add the grated cheese, stirring until melted. Season to taste with the salt and pepper. Lay the sliced cooked turkey meat over the broccoli and pour the cheesed sauce over all. Place in a quick oven to heat through thoroughly and to slightly brown the top.

Turkey Patties

Two eggs
Two cups finely chopped cooked turkey
Two cups soft bread crumbs
One cup chopped ripe olive pieces
One-half teaspoon salt
One-eighth teaspoon pepper
Two tablespoons milk, or more
Flour
Salad oil for frying
Frying time: Five to ten minutes
Servings: Four

In a bowl, beat the eggs. Add the finely chopped cooked turkey, the soft bread crumbs, chopped olives, salt, pepper and chopped onion. Mix well. Add enough milk to hold the mixture together. Use a third-cup measure to portion out the mixture and shape into patties with the hands. Dust with flour. Heat salad oil in a large heavy skillet, add the floured patties and brown quickly on both sides. Serve at once with a green vegetable, salad and cranberry sauce.

A FAVORITE RECIPE
Turkey Casserole

Three tablespoons butter or shortening, heated
One-half cup minced onion
Two tablespoons diced green pepper
Two-thirds cup sliced celery
Cooking time: Twenty minutes
One and one-half cups canned tomatoes
One-half teaspoon celery salt
One-half teaspoon sugar
One cup finely chopped turkey
One-half cup cooked peas
One and one-fourth cups cooked rice
One teaspoon salt
One-fourth teaspoon pepper
Cooking time: Until thoroughly heated
Servings: Four

Heat the butter in a deep heavy skillet; add the onion, green pepper and celery. Cover. Cook until tender. Add the tomatoes, celery salt and sugar. Mix. Fold in the turkey, peas and rice. Add the seasonings. Heat thoroughly. Serve on hot plates.

MRS. ANN ROSEN, *Hewlett, L.I., N.Y.*

Barbecued Duckling

One Long Island duckling
Oven temperature: 350 degrees
Roast: One and one-half hours
Two tablespoons salad oil
One-third cup finely chopped onion
One clove garlic, crushed
Sauté: Five minutes
One-half cup honey
One-half cup tomato catsup
One-half cup red wine vinegar
One-fourth cup Worcestershire sauce
One teaspoon brown bouquet sauce
One and one-half teaspoons dry mustard
One and one-half teaspoons salt
One-fourth teaspoon marjoram
One-fourth teaspoon pepper
One-sixteenth teaspoon rosemary
Simmer: Five minutes
Oven temperature: 375 degrees
Roast: Thirty to forty minutes
Servings: Four

Using poultry shears or heavy scissors, remove wing tips and neck from the duck and cut through skin, flesh and bone from vent to neck. Turn duckling and cut upward through back at side of backbone. Cut down other side of backbone and discard. Cut across each half just above the thigh. Lay pieces, skin side up, on a rack in a roasting pan and roast in a moderate oven for one and one-half hours. To prepare the barbecue sauce, heat the oil in a saucepan with onion and garlic. Sauté until onion is soft.

Add the honey, catsup, vinegar, Worcestershire sauce, brown bouquet sauce, dry mustard, salt, marjoram, pepper and rosemary. Bring to a boil, reduce the heat and simmer gently for five minutes. After the hour and a half of roasting, pour the fat from the pan and place pieces of duck in bottom of pan without rack. Brush pieces all over with barbecue sauce and return to a moderately hot oven for thirty to forty minutes, basting with barbecue sauce two or three times in all. Leave duck in oven ten minutes after last basting.

Sweet and Sour Duckling

One (5 lb.) duckling, cleaned, quartered
Two tablespoons fat
Browning time: Fifteen minutes
Two cups canned sauerkraut
One can (6 oz.) orange juice concentrate
One-fourth cup water
One-half teaspoon caraway seeds
Simmering time: One hour, about
Servings: Four

Skin the quartered duckling using a sharp knife. Melt the fat in a large heavy bottomed skillet and brown the skinned pieces of duckling. Scatter the sauerkraut over the browned meat. In a bowl combine the undiluted orange juice concentrate, water and caraway seeds; pour over the sauerkraut. Cover the skillet and cook gently until the duckling is tender; about an hour. Serve with fluffy mashed potatoes and a green vegetable.

Duckling in Wine

One (5 lb.) duckling, cleaned, quartered
Three cups water
One teaspoon salt
Simmering time: Forty minutes
Two tablespoons duck fat
Browning time: Fifteen minutes
One-half clove garlic, finely chopped
Sautéing time: Five minutes
Two tablespoons flour
Two cups dry red wine
Eight medium-sized mushrooms, sliced
Two tablespoons chopped parsley
One bay leaf
Pinch of thyme
One teaspoon salt
Cooking time: Ten to twelve minutes
Eight small white onions, peeled
Eight small carrots, scraped
Oven temperature: 350 degrees
Baking time: One and one-half hours
Servings: Four

Remove the skin and fat from the quartered duckling using a sharp knife. Place skin and fat in a saucepan with water, salt, giblets, neck and wing tips. Cook, covered, over moderate heat until tender. Pour off broth into bowl. Allow fat to rise to the top and skim two tablespoons off into a large heavy skillet. Add the sections of duckling and brown over moderate heat. Remove duckling to a baking dish (3 qts.). Add the garlic to the fat and sauté briefly. Stir in the flour; gradually blend in the wine, stirring the while to make a smooth sauce. Add the

mushrooms, parsley, bay leaf, thyme and salt. Bring to a boil, stirring constantly, until the sauce thickens. Place peeled onions, carrots and giblets in casserole with duck. Pour sauce over all. Cover tightly. Bake in a moderate oven until the duckling and vegetables are tender.

Flared Duckling

One-fourth cup currant jelly, melted
One cup orange juice
One tablespoon lemon juice
One teaspoon dry mustard
One teaspoon paprika
One-half teaspoon ground ginger
One-half cup cognac
One hot roasted duckling, quartered
Serves: Four

In a saucepan melt the currant jelly over low heat. Mix in the juices and seasonings. Add all but one tablespoon of the cognac. Pour over quartered roasted duckling in a chafing dish or heat-proof dish. Warm over heating unit or candle warmer until thoroughly hot. Warm remaining cognac in a ladle over a match or candle; ignite it and spoon over the duckling. (This is safer and better than lighting the flame in the dish.) Serve immediately.

Roast Duck

One duckling (4½ to 5 lbs. ready-to-cook weight)
One and one-half teaspoons salt
One-fourth teaspoon pepper
One and one-half cups bread crumbs
One-half cup chopped celery
One-half cup chopped cooked apricots
One egg, beaten slightly
One-fourth teaspoon salt, or more
One-fourth teaspoon thyme
One-half cup apricot liquid
Oven temperature: 350-450 degrees
Roasting time: Two hours, or until tender and brown
Serves: Four

Prepare the duckling for roasting. If a quick-frozen bird is used, let it thaw at room temperature, about three hours. The giblets may be simmered in one quart water until tender and reserved with the broth for soup. Wipe the prepared duck with a cloth; sprinkle inside and out with the mixed salt and pepper. For the dressing: Mix the crumbs, celery, drained apricots, egg, remaining salt, and the thyme in a bowl. Moisten with two tablespoons apricot liquid, or use more for a moister dressing. Stuff the duck; close the cavity. Arrange, breast up, on a rack in an open roasting pan. Do not add water or cover the pan.

Roast in a moderate oven until tender, allowing 25 minutes to the pound. Increase the oven temperature to very hot and bake 20 minutes, basting once with the remaining apricot liquid. When done, the flesh will be very tender and the skin brown and crisp. Serve hot.

A FAVORITE RECIPE
Baked Oranges

Four thin skinned seedless oranges
Three cups boiling water
Cook: Until tender
Two cups sugar
One cup water (in which oranges were
   cooked)

Cook: Five minutes
Butter
Oven temperature: 375 degrees
Bake: One hour
Serves: Four

Place oranges in a deep kettle; cover with boiling water. Cook until skin is tender when tried with a fork. Remove from water. Cool; cut into halves. In a

saucepan cook the sugar in one cup of water drained from the cooked oranges, for five minutes. Place the orange halves in a glass dish; pour over the syrup and dot the butter. Cover and bake in a moderately hot oven for one hour. Serve with roast duck.

ELLEN D. SMITH, *Norfolk, Va.*

Duckling
With Purple Plum Sauce

Two frozen ducklings (5 to 6 lbs. each),
   thawed
Oven temperature: 350 degrees
Baking time: Two hours, or more
Four tablespoons butter or margarine
One medium-sized onion, chopped
Two cloves garlic, minced
Cooking time: Five minutes
One can (1 lb. 14 oz.) purple plums,
   pureed

One can (6 oz.) frozen concentrate
One-fourth cup chili sauce
One-fourth cup soy sauce
One tablespoon Worcestershire sauce
One teaspoon ginger
One teaspoon dry mustard
Few drops tabasco
Cooking time: Fifteen minutes
Two large oranges, sliced
Serves: Six, or more

Allow the ducklings to thaw completely. Place on rack in a shallow pan. Roast in a moderate oven until tender. At inter-

vals, drain off fat in pan. Meanwhile melt the butter in a heavy skillet. Cook the onion and garlic until straw-colored. Add the plum puree and remaining ingredients. Simmer 15 minutes. The last half hour of roasting pour off the remaining fat from the ducklings. Brush the ducklings with the purple plum sauce. Return to oven and keep basting the ducklings until tender. Garnish with orange slices. Pour remaining plum sauce in a bowl and serve with the duckling.

Casserole and Easy Dishes

Double Cheese Macaroni Casserole

One package (8 oz.) macaroni (large quills) cooked according to directions on package

Three tablespoons butter or margarine

Three tablespoons flour

Two cups milk

One teaspoon salt

One-fourth teaspoon pepper

One-half teaspoon basil

Cook: Five minutes

Two cups grated Cheddar cheese

One-half pound Swiss cheese, sliced

Three tomatoes, thinly sliced

Five rolled anchovies

Oven temperature: 350 degrees

Bake: Thirty-five minutes, about

Serves: Four, or more

Cook the macaroni, large quills, according to the directions on the package. In a saucepan melt the butter; blend in the flour. Gradually stir in the milk; add the salt, pepper and basil. Cook until smooth and thickened. Remove. Stir in Cheddar cheese until melted. In a greased casserole arrange a layer of quills, sliced Swiss cheese and tomatoes. Pour on a third of the cheese sauce. Repeat procedure. Arrange anchovies on top. Bake in a moderate oven until golden on top. Serve from casserole.

A FAVORITE RECIPE
Crabmeat Souffle

One tablespoon butter
One tablespoon flour
One cup milk
One-half teaspoon salt
One-eighth teaspoon pepper
Cooking time: Ten minutes in a double
  boiler
Two eggs, beaten separately
One pound crabmeat (all cartilage
  removed)
One-fourth cup buttered bread crumbs
Oven temperature: 350 degrees
Baking time: Forty-five minutes
Servings: Six

In the top of a double boiler, melt the butter. Blend in the flour. Add the milk and seasonings. Cook, stirring until thick and smooth. Cool; stir in the beaten egg yolks. Fold in the beaten egg whites and the crabmeat. Pour into a well greased casserole. Top with buttered bread crumbs. Place the casserole in a pan of hot water. Bake in a moderate oven. Serve with a tossed mixed green salad.

MRS. FLORENCE STONE, *Schenectady, N.Y.*

Shrimp and Eggplant Parmigiana

One-fourth cup olive oil
One clove garlic, crushed
One medium-sized onion, finely chopped
One-half cup finely chopped celery
Sauté: Until tender
One can (No. 303) plum tomatoes
One can (6 oz.) tomato paste
Three-fourths cup water
One teaspoon salt
One-half teaspoon oregano
One-fourth teaspoon basil
One-fourth teaspoon Worcestershire sauce
Simmer: Forty-five minutes
One pound shrimp
One large eggplant
Two eggs, beaten
Three-fourths cup fine dry bread crumbs
Oil for frying
Fry: Five minutes
One-half cup grated Parmesan cheese
Eight ounces Mozzarella cheese, sliced
Oven temperature: 375 degrees
Bake: Twenty-five minutes, about
Serves: Six

In a saucepan or skillet heat the fourth cup of olive oil. Add the crushed garlic, chopped onion and celery and sauté until tender. Add the canned tomatoes, tomato paste, water, salt, oregano, basil and Worcestershire sauce and simmer to thicken and develop flavor. Add the shelled and deveined shrimp and cook just until shrimp turn pink. Peel and cut the eggplant into slices one-half inch thick. Dip slices in beaten egg and fine dry bread crumbs. Heat oil for frying in a large heavy skillet and brown eggplant slices on both sides. Remove to absorbent paper to drain. In a large shallow baking dish (9 x 15 x 2 in.) lay half the eggplant slices. Spoon on half the shrimp sauce, sprinkle with half the grated Parmesan cheese, top with half the sliced mozzarella. Repeat layers. Bake in a moderately hot oven until

cheese is melted and lightly browned and contents bubbling hot.

A FAVORITE RECIPE
Party Hot Sea Food Salad

Two and three-fourth cups cooked shell
  macaroni
One cup cooked cleaned shrimp, cut into
  pieces
One cup crab meat (fresh or canned)
One cup tuna
One green pepper, minced
One pimiento, minced
One small onion, minced
Two hard-cooked eggs, chopped
Two cups mayonnaise
Oven temperature: 350 degrees
Baking time: Thirty minutes
Servings: Ten

Cook and thoroughly drain the macaroni as directed on the package. Cool. In a bowl mix the shrimp (fresh or canned), crab meat and tuna. Add the green pepper, pimiento, onion and eggs. Toss with the sea food until well mixed. Fold in mayonnaise. Turn into a casserole (2 qts.); bake in a moderate oven. Serve hot or cold with crisp rolls.

MRS. ED. KOESTER, *Vancouver, Wash.*

A FAVORITE RECIPE
Pompeian Shrimp Casserole

One green pepper, cleaned, minced
One medium-sized onion, chopped
One cup minced celery
One can (6½ oz.) crab meat, flaked
One can (7 oz.) shrimp, cut into
  small pieces
One-half teaspoon salt
One-sixteenth teaspoon pepper
One teaspoon Worcestershire sauce
One cup mayonnaise
One cup finely grated buttered bread
  crumbs
Oven temperature: 350 degrees
Baking time: Thirty minutes
Servings: Four

In a bowl mix the green pepper, onion and celery. Flake the crab meat, removing all cartilage; mix with the cut shrimp; add to the vegetable mixture. Season with salt and pepper. Add the Worcestershire sauce and mayonnaise. Turn into four well-greased individual casseroles; sprinkle with the buttered crumbs. Bake in a moderate oven until the crumbs are lightly browned. Serve hot.

MRS. ROBERT J. RAMSBOTTOM, *Hamilton, Ohio*

Baked Macaroni with Sardines

Eight ounces elbow macaroni
Boiling salted water
Cook: Ten minutes
One can (No. 2) tomatoes
One-fourth pound sliced cheddar cheese
Two cans (3¼ oz. each) sardines
One cup milk
Two tablespoons butter
Oven temperature: 350 degrees
Bake: Thirty minutes
Serves: Four

Cook the macaroni in the boiling salted water until tender. Drain and rinse. Place

a layer of the macaroni in a buttered casserole (2 qts.). Cover with half the canned tomatoes, half the sliced cheese and half the sardines. Repeat the layers. Pour the milk over all, dot with butter and bake in a moderate oven until lightly browned. Serve hot from the casserole.

A FAVORITE RECIPE
Shrimp-Buffet Style

Two cups minced cooked shrimp
One cup mayonnaise
One cup dry bread crumbs
One-half cup minced green pepper
One-half cup minced onion
One-half teaspoon salt
One-fourth teaspoon pepper
One-half cup flour
One egg, slightly beaten with
Two tablespoons water
One cup sifted dry bread crumbs
One-fourth cup margarine
Cooking time: Twenty minutes

Sauce

One can (8 oz.) tomato sauce
One-fourth cup water
Oven temperature: 350 degrees
Baking time: Twenty minutes
Servings: Six

In a bowl, blend the shrimp, mayonnaise, bread crumbs, green pepper, onion, salt and pepper. Form into balls (1 inch). Dip into the flour, then into egg beaten with the water, then roll in the bread crumbs until well coated. In a heavy skillet melt the margarine, add the shrimp balls, browning slowly on all sides. While cooking the balls, heat in a saucepan the tomato sauce and water. Place the balls in a serving casserole, pour the sauce over all. Bake in a moderate oven. Serve with cole slaw.

MISS KERSEY, *Wilmington, Del.*

California Spaghetti

One cup ripe olive pieces
One-third cup butter or margarine
Two-thirds cup chopped onion
Sauté: Until soft
Two tablespoons chopped pimiento
Two teaspoons prepared mustard
One cup milk
Two cups grated cheddar cheese
Salt and pepper to taste
One pound thin spaghetti
Boiling salted water
Cook: Until tender
Simmer: Five minutes
Serves: Four

Cut ripe olives from pits to measure one cup. In a large heavy skillet melt the butter or margarine. Add the chopped onion and sauté until soft. Add the chopped pimiento, mustard, milk and grated cheddar cheese. Stir until smooth and blended over low heat. Season with salt and pepper to taste. Add the cut olives and keep warm. Cook the thin spaghetti in boiling salted water until tender. Drain well and add to the cheese and olive sauce, mixing well. Simmer for five minutes or until piping hot. Serve at once.

Special Baked
Macaroni and Cheese

Two cups elbow macaroni
Boiling salted water
Cook: Ten minutes, or more
Two tablespoons butter or margarine
One-fourth cup finely chopped onion
Sauté: Five minutes, about
Two tablespoons flour
One teaspoon salt
Two cups milk
One teaspoon Worcestershire sauce
One teaspoon prepared mustard
Dash of Tabasco sauce
Two cups grated cheddar cheese
Four tablespoons butter or margarine
One-fourth teaspoon paprika
Two cups soft bread cubes (one-fourth inch)
Oven temperature: 350 degrees
Bake: Thirty minutes
Serves: Four to six

Cook the macaroni in boiling salted water until tender. Drain. In a saucepan melt the two tablespoons of butter or margarine, add the chopped onion and sauté until tender, blend in the flour and salt, gradually stir in the milk. Add the Worcestershire sauce, mustard and Tabasco. Cook, stirring constantly, until the sauce is thickened and smooth. Remove from the heat and stir in the cheese. Combine with the cooked macaroni and transfer to a baking dish (8 x 9 x 2 in.). In a saucepan melt the four tablespoons of butter or margarine and add the paprika. Add the small cubes of bread and toss to coat well. Scatter over the macaroni and cheese in the baking dish and bake in a moderate oven for thirty minutes.

Olive, Cheese and Noodle Casserole

Four ounces noodles
Boiling salted water
Cook: Ten minutes
Two tablespoons butter or margarine
Two tablespoons flour
One teaspoon salt
One-sixteenth teaspoon pepper
One and one-half cups milk
Two-thirds cup grated cheddar cheese
One cup canned tomatoes
One-half cup ripe olives
Oven temperature: 350 degrees
Bake: Thirty minutes
Serves: Four or five

Cook the noodles in the boiling salted water until tender. Drain. In a saucepan melt the butter or margarine. Stir in the flour, salt and pepper and gradually blend in the milk. Cook, stirring constantly, until the sauce thickens. Add the grated cheese and stir until it melts. Add the canned tomatoes and pieces of ripe olives cut from pits. Combine with the drained noodles and transfer to a greased casserole (1½ qts.). Bake in a moderate oven for 30 minutes. Serve piping hot.

Smoky Macaroni and Cheese

Eight ounces elbow macaroni
Boiling salted water
Cook: Ten minutes
One-fourth cup butter or margarine
One-fourth cup chopped onion
One-fourth cup chopped celery
Sauté: Five to ten minutes
Three tablespoons flour
One-half teaspoon salt
One and one-half cups milk
Cook: Five minutes or more
Four ounces rindless smoked cheddar, grated
One-third cup fine dry bread crumbs
One tablespoon melted butter or margarine
Oven temperature: 350 degrees
Bake: Twenty-five minutes
Serves: Four, or more

Cook the macaroni in the boiling salted water in a large kettle until tender. Drain and rinse. In a large skillet, melt the butter or margarine. Add the onion and celery; sauté until lightly browned. Stir in the flour and salt. Add the milk gradually, stirring the while. Cook, stirring constantly, until sauce thickens. Add the grated cheese, stirring until well blended. Remove from the heat and stir in the drained macaroni. Pour into a greased casserole (2 qts.) and top with the combined crumbs and melted butter or margarine. Bake in a moderate oven until lightly browned on top. Serve from the casserole.

Quick Macaroni and Cheese

Eight ounces elbow macaroni
Boiling salted water
Eight ounces cream cheese
Three-fourths cup milk
One-half teaspoon salt
One-half teaspoon garlic salt
One-half cup grated Parmesan cheese
Two tablespoons finely chopped parsley
Servings: Four to six

Cook the elbow macaroni in the boiling salted water until tender. In the meantime, cream the cheese in the upper half of a double boiler. Gradually blend in the milk then the salts. Add one-half of the grated Parmesan cheese and the chopped parsley. Heat thoroughly over hot water. When macaroni is tender, drain well and mix with the sauce. Transfer to serving dish and sprinkle remaining grated Parmesan cheese over the top.

Spring Garden Skillet Macaroni

One-half pound elbow macaroni
Boiling salted water
Cook: Until tender
One-fourth cup butter or margarine
One-fourth cup flour
One teaspoon salt
One teaspoon prepared mustard
Two cups milk
One and one-half cups finely cubed cheddar
One-half cup finely grated raw carrot
One-fourth cup finely chopped green onion
Serves: Six

Cook the elbow macaroni in the boiling salted water until tender. In the meantime melt the butter or margarine in a large saucepan or skillet. Stir in the flour, salt and prepared mustard, gradually blend in the milk. Cook and stir until thickened and smooth. Add the drained macaroni, cubed cheddar, grated carrot and green onion. Stir well to mix thoroughly, heat and serve.

Cucumber Cheese Macaroni

One-half pound elbow macaroni
Boiling salted water
Cook: Until tender
One can (14½ oz.) evaporated milk
One-half teaspoon salt
One teaspoon dry mustard
One tablespoon Worcestershire sauce
Heat: To boiling point
Two cups grated cheddar
One-third cup chopped cucumber
Serves: Four to six

Cook the elbow macaroni in the boiling salted water until tender. In the meantime in a saucepan heat the undiluted evaporated milk, salt, dry mustard and Worcestershire to the boiling point, stirring smooth. Add the grated cheddar and heat and stir until melted. Add cucumber and drained macaroni. Mix well.

Curried Eggs on Parslied Noodles

Six eggs
Four ounces broad noodles
Boiling salted water
Cook: Ten minutes, about
Three tablespoons butter or margarine
One-fourth cup flour
One teaspoon salt
One-eighth teaspoon pepper
One teaspoon curry powder
Two and one-half cups milk
Cook: Five minutes, about
Three tablespoons butter or margarine
One-fourth cup finely chopped parsley
Paprika
Servings: Three or four

Put the eggs on to hard-cook in cold water. This will take about 15 minutes. Cook the noodles in boiling salted water according to directions on package. In the meantime melt three tablespoons of butter or margarine in a saucepan and stir in the flour, salt, pepper and curry powder. Gradually blend in the milk, stirring smooth and cook, stirring constantly until the sauce thickens. Shell and slice the hard-cooked eggs and add to the sauce. Keep hot. Drain the cooked noodles. Toss well to coat with butter or margarine and the chopped parsley. Serve noodles at once with the curried eggs spooned over top. Garnish with a sprinkling of paprika.

Party Hamburger Casserole

Three tablespoons butter or margarine
*One pound chopped round steak
Cooking time: Five minutes
One teaspoon salt
One-fourth teaspoon pepper
One-fourth teaspoon basil
*Two cans (8 oz. each) tomato sauce
One package (8 oz.) broad noodles, cooked
   according to directions on package
One-half pint creamy cottage cheese
One-half pound cream cheese
One-half cup dairy sour cream
One tablespoon poppy seed
One-third cup chopped onions or chives
One-third cup chopped green pepper
Cooking time: Five minutes
Oven temperature: 350 degrees
Baking time: Twenty minutes
Servings: Six

In a heavy skillet melt one tablespoon of butter over low heat. Add the meat; cook until redness disappears. Mix in the seasonings and tomato sauce. Remove; set aside. In a bowl combine the drained cooked noodles, cottage cheese, cream cheese, sour cream and poppy seed. In a saucepan cook the onions and green pepper in the remaining butter until soft. Add to the noodle mixture, blending thoroughly. In the bottom of a buttered casserole (2 qts.) arrange the noodle mixture. Spread the meat mixture over the noodles. Bake in a moderate oven until brown on top. Garnish with pimiento and green pepper. Serve immediately.

*Note: Cooked pieces of chicken and chicken broth may be substituted for the meat and tomato sauce.

Skilletburger Dinner

One-third cup chopped onion
One tablespoon chopped parsley
One tablespoon butter or margarine
Cooking time: Three minutes
Two slices bread, crusts removed
One cup dairy sour cream
One and one-half pounds chopped beef
One egg
One tablespoon steak sauce
One teaspoon salt
One-fourth teaspoon pepper
One-fourth teaspoon dry mustard
Few drops Angostura bitters
Three tablespoons flour
One-fourth cup butter or margarine
One-half cup hot water
Cooking time: Twenty minutes
One small onion, thinly sliced
One-fourth cup chopped green pepper
Two cans (1 lb. each) whole kernel corn
One can (No. 1) lima beans
Cooking time: Ten minutes
Serves: Four, or more

In a skillet cook the onion and parsley in the butter until onion is soft. In a large bowl soak the bread in three tablespoons sour cream. Reserve the remaining sour cream. Then add the onion mixture, beef, egg, steak sauce, salt, pepper, mustard and bitters, blending well. Shape into balls (2 in. in diam.). Dust lightly in flour. In the skillet brown the meat balls in the butter. Add the water. Cover; cook 20 minutes. Remove meat balls to a warm platter. Add the onion and green pepper; cook 3 minutes. Mix in the corn, lima beans and sour cream. Cook until thoroughly heated; add the meat balls. Reheat. Serve.

A FAVORITE RECIPE
Moussaka

One pound ground lean beef
One teaspoon salt
One-fourth teaspoon pepper
One eggplant (1½ lbs.) peeled, sliced
   (¼ in.)
One can (No. 2) plum tomatoes, drained
Two tablespoons olive oil
One-half cup bread crumbs
Two tablespoons butter
Oven temperature: 350 degrees
Baking time: Forty-five minutes
One-half cup grated Parmesan cheese
Servings: Four

In a bowl, mix the meat with salt and pepper. Press into the bottom of a well greased casserole. Spread the sliced, seasoned-to-taste eggplant over the meat. Drain and pour the tomatoes over the top. Pour olive oil over all. Sprinkle the top with the bread crumbs. Dot with butter. Cover; bake for 30 minutes; uncover, bake for 15 minutes. Serve with the Parmesan cheese.

MRS. ESTHER ZURRO, *Bronx, N.Y.*

Meat Loaf with Rice Stuffing

One medium-sized onion, minced
Four tablespoons butter or margarine
Cook: Three minutes
One pound chopped beef
One pound chopped veal
One-fourth pound chopped pork
One cup fine soft bread crumbs, packed
Three eggs, slightly beaten
One cup milk
One tablespoon horseradish sauce
One tablespoon salt
One-fourth teaspoon pepper
One teaspoon savory

Rice Stuffing

Three cups cooked rice
One-fourth cup melted butter or margarine
One teaspoon salt
One-fourth teaspoon pepper
One tablespoon poultry seasoning
One-fourth cup minced parsley
One cup chopped nuts
Oven temperature: 350 degrees
Bake: Seventy-five minutes
One-half cup tomato sauce
Three strips bacon
Serves: Eight, or more

In a heavy skillet cook the onions over low heat in the butter until straw-colored. In a bowl blend the beef, veal, pork and onions. Mix the bread crumbs, eggs, milk, horseradish sauce, salt, pepper and savory; blend in thoroughly with the meat mixture. Pat out in a rectangle (11 x 14 in.) on aluminum foil. In a bowl mix the rice, butter, salt, pepper, poultry season-ing, parsley and nuts. Spread rice mixture over the meat. Roll up the meat like a jelly roll. Carefully place in an oiled shallow pan. Bake in a moderate oven for 75 minutes. During the last fifteen minutes brush top with tomato sauce and lay strips of bacon on top. Place on a hot platter. Serve.

Danish Meat Balls

One pound chopped round steak or
   chuck
One-fourth pound veal, chopped
One loin pork chop, chopped
One cup light cream
Three egg yolks
One-half cup fine bread crumbs
Standing time: Twenty minutes
One medium-sized onion, finely chopped
One teaspoon salt
One-fourth teaspoon pepper
One-fourth cup flour
One-fourth cup butter or margarine
One-half cup hot water
Cooking time: Thirty minutes
Three-fourths cup dairy sour cream
Serves: Six

Have the butcher grind the beef, veal and meat from the pork chop. In a large bowl beat the light cream and egg yolks until well blended. Add the crumbs; let stand. Add the meat, onion, salt and pepper. With the hands mix thoroughly. Shape into 18 balls (1½ inches). Dust lightly in flour. In a heavy skillet melt the butter. Brown the balls on all sides. Add the hot water; cover tightly. Cook over low heat until meat is done. Shake the pan occasionally. Place meat balls in a chafing dish. Blend in the sour cream with the drippings in the skillet. Pour over the meat balls. Cover; keep warm and serve.

A FAVORITE RECIPE
Spaghetti-Bologna Casserole

Two tablespoons salad oil or bacon
    drippings
One large onion, chopped
Sautéing time: Five minutes
One pound veal bologna, cut into cubes
    (½ in.)
Browning time: Five minutes
Two cans (12 oz. each) whole kernel corn
Two cans (15¼ oz. each) spaghetti in
    tomato sauce
Three-fourths cup grated sharp cheddar
    cheese
Oven temperature: 350 degrees
Baking time: Twenty minutes
Serves: Six

Heat the oil or drippings in a large skillet; sauté the onion. Add the bologna browning lightly. Stir in the well drained corn with the spaghetti. Turn into a casserole (1½ qts.); sprinkle the grated cheese over the top. Bake in a moderate oven until the cheese melts. Serve with Italian bread sticks and a tossed green salad.

MRS. CARL REYNOLDS, *Bristol, Tenn.*

Ham Creamed Noodles

Four ounces medium noodles
Boiling salted water
Cook: Ten minutes, about
Three tablespoons butter or margarine
One-fourth cup finely chopped parsley
Two tablespoons finely chopped onion
Sauté: Five minutes
Two tablespoons flour
One-half teaspoon salt
One-eighth teaspoon pepper
Three-fourths cup water
Cook: Three to five minutes
One cup dairy sour cream
One can (4½ oz.) deviled ham
One tablespoon butter or margarine
Three tablespoons fine dry bread crumbs
Oven temperature: 350 degrees
Bake: Thirty minutes
Servings: Four, or more

Cook the medium noodles in boiling, salted water until tender; drain. In a saucepan heat the three tablespoons of butter or margarine, add the finely chopped parsley and onion and sauté briefly. Stir in the flour, salt and pepper; gradually blend in the water. Cook, stirring, until thickened and smooth. Remove from heat and blend in the dairy sour cream and deviled ham. Add the drained noodles and mix well. Transfer to a greased casserole (1½ qts.). Melt the tablespoon of butter or margarine, stir in the fine dry bread crumbs and scatter over the casserole contents. Bake in a moderate oven until thoroughly heated through and lightly browned on top.

Baked Macaroni with Ham

Eight ounces elbow macaroni
Boiling salted water
Cook: Ten minutes
One-fourth cup butter or margarine
One-fourth cup chopped onion
One-fourth cup chopped celery
Sauté: Five to ten minutes
Three tablespoons flour
One teaspoon salt
Dash of paprika
One and one-half cups milk
Cook: Ten minutes
One and one-half cups grated cheddar
    cheese
One teaspoon prepared mustard
Two cups cubed cooked ham
One-third cup fine dry bread crumbs
One tablespoons melted butter or
    margarine
Oven temperature: 350 degrees
Bake: Twenty-five minutes
Serves: Four, or more

Cook the macaroni in the boiling salted water in a large kettle until tender. Drain and rinse. In a large skillet melt the butter and sauté the onion and celery until lightly browned. Stir in the flour, salt and paprika. Add the milk gradually and cook until thickened, stirring constantly. Add the grated cheese and mustard, stirring until well blended. Fold in the macaroni and cubed ham. Pour into a casserole (2 qts.) and top with the bread crumbs that have been mixed with the melted butter or margarine. Bake in a moderate oven until lightly browned on top.

Eggs Tetrazzini

One-fourth cup butter or margarine
Two tablespoons finely chopped onion
One-fourth cup chopped parsley
Two-thirds cup finely diced celery
One can (3 oz.) mushrooms, sliced
Sauté: Five minutes, about
One tablespoon flour
One cup milk
Cook: Five minutes
One-half cup grated cheddar cheese
One-half teaspoon salt
Two teaspoons Worcestershire sauce
Six hard-cooked eggs, cut in eighths
Six to eight ounces fine spaghetti
Boiling salted water
Serves: Six

In a skillet or saucepan melt the fourth cup of butter or margarine. Add the finely chopped onion, parsley, diced celery and sliced drained mushrooms. Sauté until onion is soft. Stir in the flour and gradually blend in the milk, stirring smooth. Cook, stirring until thickened. Add the cheddar cheese and stir until melted into sauce. Add salt and Worcestershire and cut eggs. Cook the fine spaghetti in boiling salted water until tender. Drain and serve with the hot egg sauce.

A FAVORITE RECIPE
Spaghetti Loaf

Two and one-half cups light cream
One-half cup butter
Heating time: Until scalded
Two and one-half cups bread crumbs
One and two-thirds tablespoons salt
Two-thirds teaspoon thyme
Standing time: Ten minutes
One and one-fourth cups grated cheddar
    cheese
One-third cup minced onion
Five tablespoons minced green pepper
Two and one-half pimientos, slivered
Two and one-half tablespoons minced
    parsley
Seven eggs, well beaten
One and one-fourth cups cooked spaghetti
Oven temperature: 350 degrees
Baking time: One and one-half hours
Three cups mushroom or cheese sauce
Servings: Eight

In a saucepan scald the cream and butter. In a bowl place the bread crumbs; pour hot cream over crumbs. Add the salt and thyme. Mix. Let stand. Stir in the cheese, onion, green pepper, pimientos and parsley. Mix. Add the beaten eggs and spaghetti, tossing until well mixed. Turn into a well-greased loaf pan (10 in.). Place in a pan ½ full of hot water; bake in a moderate oven until firm. Remove from the oven, let stand for three minutes. Unmold on a hot platter. Slice and serve with a mushroom or cheese sauce.

MRS. A. MARTINEZ, *Bronx, N.Y.*

Eggs in Creoled Rice

Two tablespoons shortening
One-fourth cup chopped onion
One-fourth cup chopped green pepper
Sauté: Until tender
One can (No. 303) tomatoes
Two cups water
Heat: To boiling
One cup raw rice
Cook: Twenty minutes, about
Salt and pepper
Four eggs
Simmer: Ten minutes
Serves: Four

In a large heavy skillet melt the shortening. Add the chopped onion and green pepper and sauté until tender. Add the canned tomatoes, breaking them up with a spoon if necessary, with the water. Heat to boiling and add the rice. Cover tightly and cook gently until the rice is tender. Season to taste with salt and pepper. Make four depressions in the cooked rice with the back of a spoon and break an egg into each. Cover skillet and cook gently until the eggs are set. Serve at once.

A FAVORITE RECIPE
Creole of Rice

One large onion, chopped
Two slices boiled ham, chopped
One tablespoon butter, melted
One cup cooked rice
One can (1 lb.) tomatoes, mashed
Twelve almonds, chopped
One-fourth cup buttered bread crumbs
Oven temperature: 375 degrees
Baking time: Fifteen minutes
Servings: Four

In a saucepan mix the onion, ham, butter, rice and tomatoes. Turn into a well buttered casserole (9 in.); sprinkle the top with the almonds and then the buttered bread crumbs. Bake in a moderately hot oven. Serve from the casserole over hot toast.

MRS. GAMBALE, *West Haverstraw, N.Y.*

Spinach Rice Casserole

One package (10 oz.) frozen chopped
    spinach
Three egg yolks
One-fourth cup finely chopped onion
Two cups cooked rice
One cup grated cheddar cheese
One-fourth cup dry white wine
Two tablespoons salad oil
One-half teaspoon salt
One-fourth teaspoon nutmeg
Three egg whites
One-half cup grated cheddar cheese
Oven temperature: 350 degrees
Bake: Forty minutes
Serves: Six

Cook the frozen chopped spinach according to directions on package; drain. In a bowl beat the egg yolks. Add the cooked spinach, chopped onion, cooked rice, one cup of grated cheddar, dry white wine, salad oil, salt and nutmeg. Mix well. In a bowl beat the egg whites until they hold soft peaks; fold into the spinach mixture. Transfer to a one-quart baking dish and scatter remaining grated cheese over the top. Bake in a moderate oven for 40 minutes. Serve at once.

A FAVORITE RECIPE
Green Rice

Two cups cooked rice
One cup, or less, minced fresh parsley
One-half cup minced green onion
One cup grated Parmesan cheese
Three eggs, beaten until fluffy
Four tablespoons milk
One teaspoon salt
One-eighth teaspoon pepper
Oven temperature: 350 degrees
Baking time: Thirty minutes
Servings: Four

Cook the rice as directed on package. Drain. In a bowl mix the rice, parsley, onion and cheese. Fold in the beaten eggs, milk and seasonings. Turn into a well buttered casserole. Place in a pan of hot water. Bake until firm. Serve hot from the casserole.

MRS. JOHN R. GIBSON, *Saco, Maine*

Easy Spanish Rice

Three tablespoons butter or margarine
One cup raw rice
One teaspoon salt
One clove garlic, crushed
Browning time: Five minutes, or more
Two cups water
One-half cup diced green pepper
Simmering time: Fifteen minutes
Standing time: Ten minutes
Two tablespoons butter or margarine
One pound ground beef
One clove garlic, crushed
Browning time: Five minutes, or more
One-half teaspoon salt
One-eighth teaspoon pepper
One-fourth teaspoon oregano
One-third cup catsup
One can (8 oz.) tomato sauce
One cup grated cheddar cheese
Servings: Six

In a two-quart saucepan melt the three tablespoons of butter or margarine. Add the raw rice, teaspoon of salt and crushed clove of garlic. Cook, stirring constantly until the rice begins to brown. Slowly stir in the water. Add the diced green pepper, cover and bring to a vigorous boil. Reduce the heat and simmer gently for 15 minutes. Remove from heat and let stand 10 minutes. In the meantime melt the two tablespoons of butter or margarine in a large heavy skillet. Add the ground beef and crushed clove of garlic. Cook, stirring constantly, until the meat is browned. Add salt, pepper and oregano. Stir in the catsup and tomato sauce and heat briefly. Combine with the cooked rice and grated cheese and serve at once.

Olive Rice Casserole

Two tablespoons salad oil
One pound ground lean beef
Browning time: Five to ten minutes
Two tablespoons salad oil
One-half cup chopped onion
One cup sliced celery
One-fourth cup chopped green pepper
One cup raw rice
Browning time: Five minutes, or more
One can (No. 2) tomatoes
One cup water
Two teaspoons salt
One teaspoon chili powder
One-fourth teaspoon pepper
One-half teaspoon Worcestershire sauce
One cup ripe olives
Oven temperature: 325 degrees
Bake: One hour
Servings: Four, or more

Heat the salad oil in a large heavy skillet. Add the ground beef and brown quickly, stirring with a fork. Remove meat to a plate and add more oil with the chopped onion, sliced celery, chopped pepper and raw rice. Cook, stirring until lightly browned. Add canned tomatoes, water, salt, chili powder, pepper and Worcestershire sauce. Cut the olives from the pits into large pieces and add. Add meat. Mix well and transfer to a casserole (2 qts.). Cover with lid or aluminum foil and bake in a moderately slow oven for one hour, stirring up the contents of the casserole two or three times. Serve piping hot with crisp crusted bread or rolls.

Olive Rice Loaf

One cup ripe olives
Three eggs
One teaspoon salt
One-eighth teaspoon pepper
One-fourth cup chopped parsley
One-fourth cup finely chopped onion
One cup grated cheddar cheese
One-fourth cup melted butter or margarine
Three cups hot cooked rice
Oven temperature: 350 degrees
Bake: One hour
Serves: Six

Cut the ripe olives from the pits in large pieces. In a bowl beat the eggs. Add the salt, pepper, chopped parsley, onion, grated cheese, melted butter or margarine and hot cooked rice. Add the olive pieces and mix well. Transfer to a greased loaf pan (9 x 5 x 2½ in.) and set in a pan of hot water. Bake in a moderate oven until the loaf is set. Remove from oven, loosen edges and turn loaf out on platter. Slice to serve.

A FAVORITE RECIPE
Deviled Peas

One can (10½ oz.) small peas
One cup chopped celery
One green pepper, chopped
One can (10½ oz.) condensed tomato soup
One cup grated cheese
Six hard-cooked eggs, sliced
One and one-half cups white sauce
One-half cup buttered bread crumbs
Oven temperature: 350 degrees
Baking time: Forty minutes, about
Serves: Six

In a bowl mix the peas, celery and green pepper. Make a layer of the pea mixture in a baking dish (10 x 10 in.). Pour over half of the combined tomato soup and cheese. Make a layer of the sliced eggs. Make a second layer of peas, soup mixture and eggs. Pour the white sauce over all and top with the buttered crumbs. Bake in a moderate oven until crumbs are a golden brown.

MRS. TOLIVER BUSH, *Wetumpka, Ala.*

Pick over the beans; wash; turn into a bowl containing the water; cover. Let stand. Do not drain. Coat the oxtail joints with seasoned flour; brown well on all sides in the drippings in the pressure cooker. Place the rack under the meat; add the kidney beans and water with the remaining ingredients. Cover. Place over high heat; when the steam escapes in a steady flow, place the weight over the vent pipe; then follow the instructions for regulating the pressure as given in the manufacturer's recipe booklet. Cook under steady pressure 40 minutes. When the cooking is completed, reduce the pressure instantly by placing the cooker in a pan of cold water. As soon as the pressure is down, remove the cover; serve immediately.

Hamburger Bean Medley

Two tablespoons butter or margarine
One pound chopped beef
Cook: Five minutes
Two cans (No. 2 each) baked beans, drained
Two cans (No. 2 each) kidney beans, drained
Two cups cooked frozen lima beans
One can (13 oz.) French onion soup
One teaspoon Worcestershire sauce
One teaspoon salt
One tablespoon chili powder
One teaspoon dry mustard
One-fourth teaspoon pepper
Oven temperature: 375 degrees
Bake: Twenty minutes
Pimiento and green pepper strips
Two cans crisp noodles
Serves: Eight

In a skillet, melt the butter. Add the beef; cook until it changes color. Add the remaining ingredients. Pour into a large casserole. Bake in a moderately hot oven until hot. Remove. Garnish with pimiento strips and green pepper. Sprinkle hot crisp noodles around the edge of the casserole. Serve immediately.

Oxtails and Kidney Beans

One box (1 lb.) red kidney beans
Six cups boiling water
Soaking time: Two hours
One large oxtail, disjointed
Two tablespoons flour
One teaspoon salt
One-fourth teaspoon pepper
Two tablespoons drippings
Browning time: Fifteen minutes
One onion, sliced
One-half cup sliced celery
One bay leaf
One teaspoon grated lemon rind
Two tablespoons lemon juice
One teaspoon salt
Pressure cooking time: Forty minutes
Servings: Six

A FAVORITE RECIPE
Boston Baked Beans

Three cups pea beans, soaked overnight in water to cover
Three tablespoons molasses
Three tablespoons brown sugar
One-half teaspoon dry mustard
One-half pound salt pork, cut into pieces (1 inch)
Two small onions, peeled, minced
Water to cover
Oven temperature: 300 degrees
Baking time: Six hours, or longer
Servings: Ten

Wash and pick over the beans. Place in a pan; cover with water; let soak overnight. Drain. Place the beans in a bean pot or heavy oven dish (2 qts.). Mix the molasses, sugar and mustard. Stir into the beans. Cut the salt pork, placing the pieces with the onion through the beans. Pour enough water over the beans to cover. Bake in a slow oven. Serve hot.

ISABEL R. TINSLEY, *New York, N.Y.*

A FAVORITE RECIPE
Hot Bean Salad

Four strips bacon, cut in pieces (½ in.)
One-half small onion, cut into thin slices
Browning time: Five minutes
One-third cup minced celery
One-third cup tomato catsup
Two tablespoons vinegar
Two tablespoons water
Two tablespoons prepared mustard
Two cans (10½ oz. each) baked beans (any style)
Simmering time: Twenty minutes
Servings: Six

In a saucepan, brown the bacon and onion. Add the celery, catsup, vinegar, water and mustard; mix. Stir in the baked beans, simmer, stirring frequently until thickened. Serve hot with brown bread and a crisp green salad.

MILDRED M. KENNEDY, *Trenton, N.J.*

Easy Bean Casserole

One-half pound ham, cut into strips
One clove garlic, minced
One medium-sized onion, chopped
Two tablespoons drippings
Cooking time: Three minutes (about)
One can (1 lb.) baked beans
One can (1 lb.) green lima beans
One can (1 lb.) kidney beans
One tablespoon brown sugar
One teaspoon dry mustard
One-half cup catsup
One tablespoon Burgundy wine or vinegar
One teaspoon salt
One-eighth teaspoon pepper
One small onion, cut into rings
Oven temperature: 375 degrees
Baking time: Thirty minutes
Servings: Six

In a heavy skillet brown the ham, garlic and onions in the drippings. Mix in the beans, sugar, mustard, catsup, wine, salt and pepper. Turn into a casserole (3 qts.); top with the onion rings. Bake in a moderately hot oven until bubbly. Serve immediately.

Homemade Baked Beans

One pint navy (pea) beans, washed
Six cups boiling water (about)
Standing time: Three or four hours
Simmering time: One hour
One-fourth pound salt pork, slashed
One onion, peeled and quartered
One clove garlic (optional)
Simmering time: One hour, or until tender
One-fourth cup molasses
One-half teaspoon dry mustard
One teaspoon salt, or more
One-eighth teaspoon pepper, or one-fourth
    teaspoon chili powder
Oven temperature: 350 degrees
Baking time: Two hours or until brown
Servings: Six to eight

Look over the beans before washing them well. Place in a saucepan and pour in the boiling water; cover. Let stand to soften and absorb water. Do not drain. Bring the beans and water slowly to a boil; reduce the heat; cover; simmer. Cut the piece of salt pork into squares but do not cut through the rind. Add the pork to the beans with the onion and garlic. Cover, Simmer until the beans are thoroughly tender but not broken. Gentle cooking keeps the beans whole. Drain, reserving the liquid. Discard the garlic.

Turn the beans, onion and salt pork into a greased shallow casserole or baking dish (2 qts.). Mix the molasses, mustard, salt, pepper or chili powder with one cup of the reserved bean liquid. Pour over the beans. Cover. Bake in a moderate oven one hour, adding reserved bean liquid or boiling water to keep the beans moist. Uncover; bake until brown. Serve hot or cold.

A FAVORITE RECIPE
Cabbage Stew and Cornbread

One large head cabbage, cut into four
  or six wedges
Four medium-sized potatoes, peeled,
  quartered
One large onion, quartered
Four carrots, scraped and cut into
  two-inch pieces
One pound Polish or Italian sausages,
  cut into one inch pieces
One teaspoon salt
One-fourth teaspoon pepper
Two bay leaves
Water to cover
Simmering time: Forty minutes, about
Servings: Four

Wash and prepare the vegetables and
sausage. Place the vegetables in a roasting pan, cover with the sausage. Season
with salt, pepper and bay leaves. Add
enough hot water to cover. Bring to a
boil; reduce the heat; simmer until the
vegetables are tender. Serve with hot
cornbread squares. The cornbread may
be made with a prepared mix.

MRS. CALVIN CAMPBELL, *New Rochelle, N.Y.*

A FAVORITE RECIPE
Cabbage Caraway

One medium-sized head cabbage (3 lbs.),
  shredded
One teaspoon salt
One teaspoon caraway seed
Two cups ground ham
One cup water
One-half red chili pepper or a dash of
  tabasco sauce
Cooking time: Fifteen minutes
Two cups small boiled potatoes, (canned
  may be used)
One-sixteenth teaspoon white pepper
Cooking time: Five minutes
Servings: Four

Wash and shred the green and white
leaves of cabbage. Place in a large saucepan; add salt, caraway seed, ham, water
and chili pepper. Cover tightly; cook over
medium heat. Add the potatoes and pepper; reduce the heat; cook for five minutes, tightly covered. Serve with rye
bread.

MARY L. HILL, *New York, N.Y.*

Eggplant Casserole

One medium-sized eggplant (six cups
  diced)
Two quarts boiling salted water
Boil: Five minutes
Six slices bacon
Fry: Crisp
One tablespoon chopped onion
Sauté: Five minutes
One can (No. 2½) tomatoes, well drained
One-fourth pound cheddar cheese, cubed
One-half teaspoon salt
Oven temperature: 375 degrees
Bake: Thirty minutes
Serves: Four

Peel the eggplant and dice. Add to the
salted boiling water in a saucepan and
cook briefly until almost tender. Drain
and transfer to a shallow baking dish or
large pie plate (10 or 12 in.). In a heavy
skillet fry the bacon until crisp; remove
from pan and drain on absorbent paper.
Crumble coarsely. Pour off all but a
tablespoon of the bacon fat. Add the
chopped onion to the skillet and sauté
until soft. Add bacon, well drained
canned tomatoes, cheese and salt. Mix
well. Spoon over the eggplant in the
baking dish. Bake in a moderately hot
oven. Serve from the baking dish.

Tamale Casserole

Two tablespoons olive oil
One-half cup chopped onion
One-fourth cup chopped green pepper
Sautéing time: Ten minutes, about
One can (No. 303) tomatoes
One can (No. 303) whole kernel corn
One teaspoon salt
One and one-half teaspoons chili powder
Simmer: Five minutes
One cup milk
One-half cup corn meal
Two eggs
One cup chopped ripe olives
Three-fourths cup grated cheddar cheese
Oven temperature: 350 degrees
Baking time: Forty-five minutes
Servings: Six

In a large heavy skillet heat the olive
oil. Add the chopped onion and green
pepper and sauté until transparent. Stir
in the canned tomatoes and drained
whole kernel corn with the salt and chili
powder. Simmer briefly. In the meantime heat the milk in a small saucepan
to scalding, gradually stir in the corn
meal. Cook and stir until thick. Add to
the vegetable mixture. In a bowl beat
the eggs, gradually stir in part of the
vegetable mixture then return combination to the skillet. Add the chopped ripe
olive pieces and mix well. Pour into a
shallow baking pan (8 x 8 x 2 in.). Scatter the grated cheese over the top. Bake
in a moderate oven for 45 minutes or
until set in the center. Serve spooned hot
from the baking pan.

Cottage Casserole with Broccoli

One pkg. (10 oz.) frozen chopped broccoli
One and one-half cups (12 oz.) creamed
  cottage cheese
Six eggs
Four tablespoons butter or margarine
One small onion, finely chopped
Sauté: Five minutes
One-fourth cup flour
One teaspoon salt
One and one-half cups milk
Cook: Five minutes, about
One cup grated cheddar cheese
Fine dry bread crumbs
Oven temperature: 325 degrees
Bake: One hour
Serves: Six

Cook the frozen chopped broccoli according to directions on package. Drain
and place in the bottom of a casserole
(1½ qts.). Measure the cottage cheese
into a bowl and beat with a rotary beater.
Beat in the eggs, one at a time. Melt the
butter or margarine in a saucepan, add
the onion and sauté briefly. Stir in the
flour and salt. Add the milk, stirring
smooth and cook and stir until the sauce
thickens. Add three-fourths of the grated
cheese and stir until melted. Fold sauce
into the cottage cheese and egg mixture.
Pour over the broccoli in the casserole.
Sprinkle with fine dry bread crumbs and
the remaining grated cheese. Bake in a
moderately slow oven for one hour or
until nicely browned on top and set in
the center. Serve from the casserole.

Creamy Vegetable Casserole

Four cups sliced celery (one inch)
One cup sliced carrots (¼ inch)
One-half green pepper, sliced
Boiling salted water
Cook: Fifteen minutes, about
One-third cup butter or margarine
One-fourth cup flour
One teaspoon salt
Two cups milk
One-half cup grated cheddar
Cook: Five to ten minutes
One tablespoon butter or margarine
Two tablespoons fine dry bread crumbs
Oven temperature: 400 degrees
Bake: Thirty minutes
Servings: Six

Place the sliced celery, carrots and
green pepper in a saucepan with about
an inch and a half of boiling salted
water. Cover tightly and cook until just
tender. Drain and place in a casserole
(2 qts.). In a saucepan melt the one-third
cup of butter or margarine; stir in the
flour and salt; gradually blend in the two
cups of milk. Add the grated cheese.
Cook, stirring constantly, until sauce
thickens and is smooth. Pour over the
vegetables in the casserole. Melt the
tablespoon of butter or margarine, stir
in the fine dry bread crumbs and scatter
over the sauced vegetables. Bake in a
quick oven until bubbling hot and crumbs
are browned.

Rigoletti and Cheese

One-half package (8 oz.) rigoletti pasta,
  cooked as directed on package
One-half pound sharp American cheddar
  cheese (½ in. cubes)
Three-fourths teaspoon salt
One-fourth teaspoon pepper
Two cups milk
One teaspoon paprika
Oven temperature: 350 degrees
Bake: Forty minutes
Serves: Six

Place in alternating layers the cooked
rigoletti, cheese, seasonings and milk in
a buttered baking dish (1½ qts.). Bake
in a moderate oven until golden.

Spicy Baked Beans

One pound navy beans
Water
Soak: Overnight
Water
Simmer: One hour
One cup dark brown sugar
One tablespoon salt
One-half teaspoon dry mustard
One-fourth teaspoon ground cloves
One medium-sized onion
One-third pound salt pork
Oven temperature: 300 degrees
Bake: Six hours
Water
Bake: One hour
Yield: Twelve servings, or more

Place the navy beans in a large saucepan and cover with water. Let stand overnight. Drain, cover with fresh water and bring to a boil. Simmer one hour. Combine the brown sugar, salt, dry mustard and ground cloves and stir into the beans. Transfer to a bean pot or large casserole (2½ qts.). Bury the peeled onion and piece of salt pork in the beans and cover. Bake in a slow oven for six hours, adding water occasionally to cover beans as necessary. Remove cover and bake for one hour without the cover.

A FAVORITE RECIPE
Baked Beanie Frankfurter

Two cups cooked navy beans
Eight frankfurters, split lengthwise
One medium-sized onion, sliced thin
One can (10½ oz.) condensed tomato
    soup
One-half teaspoon salt
One-fourth teaspoon pepper
One-fourth teaspoon dry mustard
One teaspoon Worcestershire sauce
Oven temperature: 350 degrees
Baking time: Forty-five minutes
Servings: Four

Place in layers in a well greased casserole the beans, frankfurters and sliced onion. Add the soup with salt, pepper, mustard and Worcestershire sauce stirred into the soup. Cover the casserole; bake in a moderate oven. Serve hot from the casserole.

MISS GRACE GOODBODY, *Brooklyn, N.Y.*

Easy Barbecued Beans

Two cans (1 lb. each) red kidney beans
One-half cup dry red wine
One tablespoon instant minced onion
One tablespoon cornstarch
One teaspoon chili powder
One-half teaspoon seasoning salt (optional)
One-fourth cup catsup
Simmer: Five minutes
Heat: Until piping hot
Serves: Six

Drain the liquid from the canned red kidney beans into a saucepan. Add the dry red wine (Burgundy type) and instant minced onion. In a cup stir together the cornstarch, chili powder and seasoning salt. Blend in the catsup. Add to the contents of the saucepan. Cook stirring constantly until sauce thickens slightly. Add the beans and keep over low heat until piping hot and ready to serve.

Sauerkraut Frankfurter Casserole

Four medium-sized potatoes
Boiling salted water
Cook: Until tender
Two tablespoons butter or margarine
One pound frankfurters
Sauté: Five minutes, or more
One-fourth cup vinegar
One-fourth cup salad oil
One teaspoon salt
One can (No. 2½) sauerkraut, drained
One teaspoon dill seed
Oven temperature: 350 degrees
Bake: Thirty minutes
Servings: Six

Cook the peeled and halved potatoes in boiling salted water until tender. In the meantime melt the butter or margarine in a heavy skillet, add the sliced frankfurters and sauté until browned on all sides. Stir the vinegar, salad oil and salt together in a cup and pour over the sliced, cooked potatoes, tossing lightly to mix well. Drain the sauerkraut and arrange half over the bottom of a greased casserole (2½ qts.). Sprinkle with half the dill seed. Arrange half the frankfurter slices over the kraut and top with potatoes. Finish off with remaining kraut, dill seed and frankfurters. Bake in a moderate oven for thirty minutes.

Frankfurter Rice Bake

Four tablespoons butter or margarine
One-half cup fine dry bread crumbs
Two tablespoons flour
One teaspoon salt
One-fourth teaspoon dry mustard
One and one-half cups milk
Cook: Five to eight minutes
One cup grated cheddar cheese
Four sliced frankfurters
Two cups fluffy cooked rice
Two pimientos, diced
One cup ripe olives, quartered
Oven temperature: 350 degrees
Bake: Thirty minutes
Servings: Four or five

In a saucepan melt the four tablespoons of butter. Stir half into the fine dry bread crumbs, mixing well. Blend flour, salt and dry mustard into the remaining melted butter and gradually stir in the milk. Cook, stirring, until the sauce thickens. Add the grated cheese and stir until melted. Add sliced frankfurters, cooked rice, diced pimientos and cut olives. Mix well and transfer to a shallow baking dish or large pie plate. Scatter the buttered crumbs over top and bake in a moderate oven for thirty minutes or until bubbling hot and nicely browned.

Noodle Frankfurter Casserole

Four ounces egg noodles
Boiling salted water
Cook: Ten minutes
Two tablespoons butter or margarine
Four frankfurters, sliced
Browning time: Five minutes
One-fourth cup chopped onion
One-fourth cup chopped green pepper
Sauté: Five minutes
One can (10½ oz.) condensed cream of
    mushroom soup
One cup warm water
Two tablespoons butter or margarine
One cup soft bread crumbs
One tablespoon grated Parmesan cheese
Oven temperature: 350 degrees
Bake: Thirty minutes
Serves: Four

Cook the egg noodles in boiling salted water until tender; drain. Heat the two tablespoons of butter or margarine in a large heavy skillet. Add the sliced frankfurters and brown on all sides. Add the chopped onion and green pepper and sauté briefly. Stir in the condensed cream of mushroom soup and gradually add the warm water, blending smooth. Add the drained noodles and transfer to a greased baking dish (1½ qts.). Melt the two tablespoons of butter or margarine and stir in the soft bread crumbs. Add the grated Parmesan cheese and scatter over the top of the noodle mixture in the baking dish. Bake in a moderate oven for 30 minutes; serve at once.

Bohemian Stew

One-third cup salad oil
Two medium-sized onions, thinly sliced
One clove garlic, crushed
Sauté: Five to ten minutes
One pound frankfurters
Sauté: Until browned
One can (No. 303) kidney beans and liquid
One can (No. 303) drained hominy
One and one-half teaspoons chili powder
Two cups tomato juice
One-half cup sliced stuffed olives
Heat: To boiling
One-half cup diced (½ in.) cheddar cheese
Buttered slices of French bread
Oven temperature: 400 degrees
Bake: Fifteen to twenty minutes
Serves: Six

In a large heavy skillet heat the salad oil. Add the sliced onions and crushed garlic and sauté until soft. Add the frankfurters that have been sliced into half-inch lengths and sauté until browned. Add the canned kidney beans with liquid, drained hominy, chili powder, tomato juice and sliced stuffed olives. Add salt if necessary. Heat to the boiling point, add the diced cheese and remove from heat. Pour into a shallow baking dish (12 x 7½ x 2 in.). Arrange buttered slices of French bread over top and bake in a quick oven for 15 to 20 minutes or until the bread is lightly browned. Serve at once.

Frankfurter Casserole

One can (No. 2) red kidney beans
One can (8 oz.) tomato sauce
One can (12 oz.) chili con carne
One tablespoon prepared mustard
One jar (8 oz.) frankfurters
Oven temperature: 375 degrees
Baking time: Thirty minutes
Servings: Six

Combine the beans, tomato sauce, chili and mustard; pour half into a greased casserole (2 qts.). Tuck in half of the frankfurters; add the rest of the mixture. Top with the remaining frankfurters. Bake in a moderately hot oven until piping hot. Serve with hard rolls and coleslaw.

Lemon Barbecued Frankfurters

Two tablespoons butter or margarine
One small onion, finely chopped
Sauté: Five minutes
One cup water
Two tablespoons lemon juice
Two tablespoons vinegar
Three tablespoons Worcestershire sauce
Two tablespoons brown sugar
One teaspoon salt
One-fourth teaspoon pepper
One-fourth teaspoon paprika
One-fourth teaspoon dry mustard
Simmer: Ten minutes
One pound frankfurters
Simmer: Ten minutes
Serves: Four

In a saucepan or skillet melt the butter or margarine. Add the finely chopped onion and sauté briefly. Add the water, lemon juice, vinegar, Worcestershire sauce, brown sugar, salt, pepper, paprika and dry mustard. Cover and simmer over low heat for ten minutes. Cut several diagonal slashes in each frankfurter and add to the sauce. Heat for ten minutes and serve piping hot.

Cheesed Franks with Hominy

Two tablespoons butter or margarine
Two tablespoons flour
One-eighth teaspoon pepper
One and one-third cups milk
Two-thirds cup sauerkraut juice
Cook: Five minutes, about
Two cans (No. 303) cooked hominy
One pound frankfurters
One cup grated cheddar cheese
Broiling temperature: 500 degrees
Broil: Ten minutes, about
Serves: Four

In a saucepan melt the butter or margarine. Stir in the flour and pepper and gradually blend in the milk, stirring smooth. Gradually blend in the sauerkraut juice. Cook, stirring constantly until the sauce thickens. Drain the canned hominy and place in the bottom of a shallow baking dish or large pie plate. Pour sauce over top. Split the frankfurters lengthwise and crosswise. Arrange cut side up over the hominy. Sprinkle with the grated cheddar and broil until cheese is melted and lightly browned. Serve at once.

Sweet and Pungent Frankfurters

Four teaspoons cornstarch
One cup vinegar
One teaspoon soy sauce
One cup brown sugar
One teaspoon salt
Eight frankfurters
One large green pepper, cut into triangles
Four slices pineapple
One carrot, peeled
Cooking time: Ten minutes
Serves: Four

In a saucepan mix the cornstarch and vinegar until smooth. Add the soy sauce, brown sugar and salt, blending thoroughly. Cut the frankfurters into thirds. Clean and cut each green pepper into triangles and the pineapple into eight pieces. Peel carrot, cut into thin lengthwise strips (3 in.). Add the frankfurters, green pepper, pineapple and carrots to the cornstarch mixture. Under low heat cook until the sauce thickens and is transparent. Serve with crisp noodles and rice.

Vegetables in Meat Shell

One and one-half pounds chopped lean beef chuck
Three-fourths cup uncooked oatmeal
One cup tomato juice or milk
One small onion, minced
One egg, slightly beaten
Two teaspoons salt (about)
One-fourth teaspoon pepper
Four drops tabasco
Oven temperature: 350 degrees
Baking time: Fifteen minutes
One-fourth cup soft margarine
One-half cup grated cheddar cheese
One-fourth cup flour
One-fourth cup minced parsley
Two cups diced potatoes, cooked
One cup shelled peas, cooked
One-half cup diced carrots, cooked
One-half cup sliced celery, cooked
Six tiny onions, cooked
Baking time: Fifteen minutes (about)
Servings: Six

In a bowl mix the beef, oatmeal, tomato juice, onion, egg and seasonings. Press the mixture evenly over the bottom and sides of a pie plate (9 in.). Bake in a moderate oven until almost firm. Meanwhile blend the margarine, cheese, flour and parsley. Combine with the drained, mixed hot vegetables. Remove the meat shell from the oven; fill with the vegetable mixture. Place cheese diamonds over the top; garnish with sliced cooked carrots. Then bake until piping hot at the center. Serve with quick mushroom sauce.

Creamed Chipped Beef with Egg

Four tablespoons butter or margarine
Four or five ounces dried chipped beef
Fry: Crisp
Four tablespoons flour
Two cups milk
Cook: Five minutes, about
Three hard-cooked eggs
One-eighth teaspoon pepper
Six slices crisp toast, halved
Servings: Four

In a large heavy skillet melt the butter or margarine. Add the dried chipped beef that has been coarsely torn and fry crisp. Stir in the flour and gradually blend in the milk. Cook, stirring until the mixture boils and thickens. Rub the yolks of the hard-cooked eggs through a sieve and coarsely chop the whites. Add the whites to the creamed beef with pepper. Add salt if necessary. Heat well and serve over the crisp toast. Sprinkle sieved yolk over the top of each portion.

Hash in Peppers

Three tablespoons chopped onion
Three tablespoons drippings
Cooking time: Three minutes
One can (12 oz.) corned beef
Two cups diced cooked potatoes
One-fourth cup milk
One teaspoon salt
One-eighth teaspoon pepper
One-eighth teaspoon dry mustard
Six green peppers, parboiled
Oven temperature: 375 degrees
Baking time: Thirty minutes
Servings: Four to six

Insert fork in stem end of tomato. Place over flame until the skin bursts. Peel. Cut a slice from top of each tomato. Scoop out center part (use for scrambled eggs). Turn upside down. Drain. Chill. In a bowl mix the eggs, celery, green pepper, onion, mayonnaise, mustard, salt and pepper. Chill. When ready to serve fill each tomato; set in a lettuce cup. Garnish with anchovies and scallions.

A FAVORITE RECIPE
Stuffed Bell Peppers

Eight medium-sized green peppers, seeds removed, rinsed
Four slices crisp fried bacon, finely chopped
Three tablespoons bacon fat
One large onion, chopped fine
One tablespoon paprika
One pound ground pork
One pound ground beef
One-half cup raw rice, parboiled
One teaspoon salt
One-fourth teaspoon pepper
One clove garlic, minced

Sauce

Two cans (10½ oz. each) condensed tomato soup
One can (6 oz.) tomato paste
Four cans (10½ oz. each) water
One-half teaspoon salt
One-eighth teaspoon pepper
Simmering time: Two hours
Servings: Six, or more

Wash the peppers, cut a slice (¼ in.) from the stem end; remove seeds, rinse. In a skillet fry the bacon until crisp; set aside. In three tablespoons of the bacon fat, sauté the onion. Remove skillet from the heat; stir in the paprika. Add the pork and beef; well-drained rice, seasonings and garlic. Mix thoroughly. Fill the peppers with the mixture. Arrange the filled peppers standing in a deep kettle. For the sauce: In a saucepan mix the tomato soup and paste, water and seasonings. Pour over the filled peppers, making sure the sauce reaches the top of peppers. Bring to a boil, reduce heat, cover and simmer until the peppers are soft. Serve hot.

MRS. JOHN H. KOLEK, *Lakeland, Fla.*

Cheese and Rice Stuffed Peppers

Four medium-sized green peppers
Boiling salted water
Cooking time: Five minutes
Two tablespoons butter or margarine
One-fourth cup chopped celery
One cup cooked rice
One-half cup grated cheddar cheese
One-fourth teaspoon salt
Two tablespoons fine dry bread crumbs
One tablespoon melted butter or margarine
Oven temperature: 350 degrees
Baking time: Thirty minutes
Servings: Four

Slice the stem ends from the peppers, remove seeds and white membrane from the inside. Place in the boiling salted water and cook for five minutes. Drain. In a small skillet, melt the two tablespoons of butter or margarine, add the chopped celery and sauté until tender. Remove from heat and stir in the cooked rice, grated cheese and salt. Fill the parboiled peppers with this mixture and top with the bread crumbs that have been mixed with the tablespoon of melted butter or margarine. Place peppers in a baking dish that has a half inch of hot water in the bottom and bake in a moderate oven until the peppers are tender and the crumbs are browned.

A FAVORITE RECIPE
Potato Meat Loaf

One pound ground beef
One cup bread crumbs
One tablespoon chopped parsley
Two eggs
One small onion, chopped
One-half cup Parmesan cheese
One teaspoon salt
One-half teaspoon pepper
Four tablespoons olive oil
Two tablespoons bread crumbs
Two cups mashed potatoes
One-half pound mozzarella cheese, sliced
Oven temperature: 375 degrees
Baking time: Thirty minutes
Servings: Four

In a bowl blend the ground beef, bread crumbs, parsley, eggs, onion, Parmesan cheese, salt and pepper. Brush a baking dish (10 in.) with one tablespoon of bread crumbs over the oil. Place ½ of the meat mixture over the crumbs; add a layer of mashed potatoes, a layer of mozzarella cheese. Top with the remaining meat. Close the edges firmly to keep the potatoes and cheese from coming out. Brush the mixture with the remaining oil. Bake in a moderate hot oven until a golden brown.

MRS. JULIA FERRARA, *Amsterdam, N.Y.*

A FAVORITE RECIPE
Meat and Spinach Loaf

One and one-half pounds ground chuck beef
One-fourth pound ground pork
One-half cup, or more, bread crumbs
Three-fourths cup chopped, cooked, drained spinach
One-fourth cup grated cheese
Two tablespoons minced onion
One egg
One-half teaspoon oregano
One teaspoon salt
One-fourth teaspoon pepper
One-half cup tomato sauce
Oven temperature: 325 degrees
Baking time: One hour
Servings: Six

In a bowl, blend the beef, pork, bread crumbs, chopped spinach, cheese, onion, egg and seasoning. Turn into a lightly greased loaf pan (9 in.); pour the tomato sauce over the top. Bake in a moderately slow oven. Serve on a hot platter with mashed potatoes and coleslaw.

MRS. PAUL V. GUNNING, *Elmhurst, N.Y.*

A FAVORITE RECIPE
Picadillo

One tablespoon olive oil, heated
One clove garlic, crushed
One teaspoon salt
One teaspoon chili powder
One medium-sized onion, minced
Cooking time: Until lightly browned
One pound pork shoulder, ground
Cooking time: Until browned
One cup canned tomatoes
Simmering time: Thirty minutes
One package (12 oz.) frozen corn
Seasoning to taste
Cooking time: Until thoroughly heated
One cup rice, cooked
Servings: Four

In a heavy skillet, heat the olive oil; add the crushed garlic, salt, chili powder and the onion; brown slightly. Add the pork, brown. Add the tomatoes, cover; simmer, stirring several times. Add the corn, mix, heating thoroughly. If desired add more chili powder. Serve with the hot rice.

ELEANOR L. DODGE, *New York, N.Y.*

A FAVORITE RECIPE
Beef and Eggplant Casserole

Six tablespoons olive oil
Two pounds beef, cubed (½ in.)
Browning time: Twenty minutes
One eggplant (2½ lbs.) peeled, sliced thin
Two onions, sliced thin
Four tomatoes, peeled, chopped
Two green peppers, cleaned, sliced into thin rings
Two and one-half teaspoons salt
One-fourth teaspoon pepper
Oven temperature: 325-350 degrees
Baking time: One hour and fifteen minutes
Servings: Six

In a heavy skillet, heat the oil; add the cubed beef. Cook, turning often to brown on all sides. In a casserole place layers of the eggplant, beef, onions, tomatoes and green peppers. Pour the oil and drippings from the skillet into casserole. Season with salt and pepper. Cover; bake in a moderately slow oven for one hour. Remove cover and increase heat to moderate. Bake for 15 minutes. Serve from the casserole with hot cornbread.

PEARL E. MANNE, *Bayside, N.Y.*

Baked Stuffed Eggplant

One large eggplant
One-fourth cup salad oil or shortening
One pound ground beef
One medium-sized onion, chopped
Sauté: Ten minutes, about
One cup soft bread crumbs
One teaspoon salt
One-eighth teaspoon pepper
One-third cup finely chopped parsley
Oven temperature: 350 degrees
Bake: One hour and fifteen minutes
Servings: Four to six

Wash and dry the eggplant. With a sharp knife split through into two halves. Carve out the centers of each leaving a shell about a half inch thick. Dice the eggplant removed from the shells into pieces one-half inch. In a large heavy skillet heat the oil or shortening. Add the ground beef, chopped onion and diced eggplant and sauté until meat loses pink color and eggplant shrinks down somewhat. Remove from heat and stir in the soft bread crumbs, salt, pepper and chopped parsley. Spoon into the eggplant shells and place in a baking pan. Pour hot water to the depth of an inch and a half to two inches around the stuffed eggplant and bake in a moderate oven for one hour or until the shells are fairly soft when tested with a fork. Cut stuffed eggplant into portion sized servings.

A FAVORITE RECIPE
Cornmeal Scrapple

One and one-half cups boiling water
One teaspoon salt
One-fourth teaspoon white pepper
One-half teaspoon poultry seasonings
One cup minced onion
One cup chopped ham
Two-thirds cup cornmeal
Cooking time: Thirty minutes in a double boiler
Standing time: Until firm
Butter or fat for frying, heated
Frying time: Until browned on both sides
One can (10½ oz.) condensed cream of mushroom soup for gravy
Servings: Four

In the top of a double boiler bring the water, salt, pepper, poultry seasonings, onion and ham to a boil; add the cornmeal, stirring until smooth. Cook over hot water in the double boiler. Turn into a buttered loaf pan (8 in.); let stand until firm. Heat the butter in a skillet; fry the sliced scrapple in hot butter, browning lightly on both sides. Serve with a gravy made with the heated mushroom soup. If served as a breakfast dish, serve with syrup.

HELEN REIGSTAD, *Lake Mohawk, Sparta, N.J.*

A FAVORITE RECIPE
Ham Souffle-Asparagus Sauce

One and one-third cups evaporated milk
One-fourth cup flour
One-half teaspoon salt
One-fourth teaspoon pepper
One-half teaspoon dry mustard
Cooking time: Five minutes in a double boiler
One and one-third cups ground, cooked ham
Cooking time: Ten minutes
Four egg yolks, well beaten
Four egg whites, beaten stiff
Oven temperature: 325 degrees
Baking time: One hour

Sauce

One can (10½ oz.) condensed cream of asparagus soup
One-third cup milk
One-fourth teaspoon curry powder
Cooking time: Ten minutes
Servings: Four

In the top of a double boiler, cook the evaporated milk and flour, seasoned with salt, pepper and mustard, stirring until smooth and slightly thickened. Add the ham, stirring frequently while cooking. Stir in the egg yolks. Beat the whites until stiff; fold into the ham mixture. Turn into an ungreased casserole (1½ qts.). Bake in a moderately slow oven. For the sauce, combine the condensed soup with the milk and curry powder, heating slowly and stirring until smooth. Serve over the souffle.

MRS. CLAIRE HARTMAN, *Fort Lee, N.J.*

Sherried Ham Casserole

Three cups ground cooked ham
Two tablespoons finely chopped onion
Two tablespoons finely chopped green pepper
Two eggs, beaten
One-half cup heavy cream
Two canned tomatoes, drained, chopped
One teaspoon dry mustard
One teaspoon Worcestershire sauce
One-half cup dry sherry
Two cups cooked rice
One tablespoon butter or margarine
Two tablespoons fine dry bread crumbs
Oven temperature: 350 degrees
Bake: Forty-five minutes
Servings: Six

In a large bowl combine the ground cooked ham, chopped onion, green pepper, beaten eggs, heavy cream, chopped tomatoes, mustard, Worcestershire sauce, sherry and cooked rice. Mix thoroughly together and transfer to a greased baking dish (2 qts.). Melt the butter or margarine in a small saucepan, stir in the fine dry bread crumbs. Scatter over the top of the casserole. Bake in a moderate oven for 45 minutes or until thoroughly heated and lightly browned on top.

A FAVORITE RECIPE
Ham and Potato Scallop

Six medium-sized potatoes, peeled, sliced (⅛ in.)
Boiling salted water to cover
Cooking time: Ten minutes
One cup diced (¼ in.) cooked ham
Two hard-cooked eggs, sliced
One-eighth teaspoon salt
One-sixteenth teaspoon pepper
Two cups thin white sauce
Oven temperature: 325 degrees
Baking time: Twenty-five minutes
Servings: Six

Cook the sliced potatoes in the boiling salted water; drain thoroughly. Arrange a layer of potatoes, ham and sliced eggs in a casserole (2 qts.). Season with salt and pepper. Make a thin white sauce, pouring over the top. Bake in a moderately slow oven. Serve from the casserole with cole slaw.

MRS. HARRY KRUITHOF, *Goshen, N.Y.*

A FAVORITE RECIPE
Macaroni-Sausage Bake

One pound bulk sausage
One cup finely chopped onion
Cooking time: Fifteen minutes
One-half package (3 oz.) macaroni, cooked as directed, drained
One can (10½ oz.) condensed cream of celery soup
Two-thirds cup milk
Two eggs, slightly beaten
One-half pound processed American cheese, shredded (2 cups)
Two cups corn flakes, crushed
One tablespoon butter, melted
Oven temperature: 350 degrees
Baking time: Forty-five minutes
Servings: Six

In a heavy skillet cook the sausage and onion, breaking the meat with a fork and cooking until lightly browned. Place the mixture in the bottom of an ungreased baking dish (8 x 8 x 2 in.). Drain the cooked macaroni thoroughly; place over the meat. Combine the soup and milk in a saucepan; heat. Remove. Beat in the eggs slowly, then the shredded cheese, stirring well. Pour over the macaroni. Mix the crushed corn flakes with the butter and sprinkle over the top of the dish. Bake in a moderate oven. Serve hot from the oven dish with a green tossed salad.

MRS. L. W. PRAIRIE, *St. Petersburg, Fla.*

Ham and Spinach Souffle

Two pkgs. (10 oz. each) frozen chopped spinach
One-third cup butter or margarine
One-third cup flour
One and one-half teaspoons salt
One-eighth teaspoon pepper
One and one-half cups milk
Cook: Until thickened
Four egg yolks
Two cups ground cooked ham (6 to 8 oz. sliced boiled ham, diced, may be used)
Two tablespoons lemon juice
Four egg whites
Oven temperature: 350 degrees
Bake: One hour, about
Serves: Four or five

Cook the frozen chopped spinach according to package directions. Drain, reserving one-fourth cup of the spinach water. In a saucepan melt the butter or margarine. Stir in the flour, salt and pepper and gradually blend in the milk and spinach liquid. Cook, stirring until the sauce thickens. In a bowl beat the egg yolks. Add the drained spinach, ground or diced ham, lemon juice and cooked sauce, mixing well. In a bowl beat the egg whites until they hold peaks, fold carefully into the spinach and ham mixture. Transfer to a greased souffle or casserole dish (2½ qts.) and bake in a moderate oven for one hour or until well browned on top and set. Serve at once.

Tuna Supper Dish

Two cans (10½ oz. each) condensed
    chicken soup
Three-fourths cup milk
Two cans (7½ oz. each) tuna fish
One teaspoon tarragon
One teaspoon salt
One-fourth teaspoon pepper
Oven temperature: 375 degrees
Baking time: Twenty minutes
One recipe (2 cups) hot, baked baking
    powder biscuits (1 in. wide)
Twenty-four hot, cooked pearl onions
Two cups hot, cooked peas
One pimiento
Serves: Six, or more

In a bowl combine the first six ingredients. Pour into a greased shallow baking dish (2 qts.). Bake in a moderately
hot oven for twenty minutes. Remove to
rack. Arrange hot baked biscuits around
the edge of the dish, then a ring of hot
cooked pearl onions, and last, a ring of
hot cooked peas. Garnish with pimiento.
Serve immediately.

Deviled Norway Sardines

Two cans (3¾ oz. each) Norway sardines,
    drained
Five slices white bread, crust removed
    and crumbled
Two tablespoons minced parsley
Two tablespoons minced green pepper
One teaspoon onion juice
Three-fourths cup condensed cream of
    celery soup
One-half teaspoon salt
Few drops tabasco
One teaspoon prepared mustard
One tablespoon lime or lemon juice
One-fourth cup real mayonnaise
Oven temperature: 400 degrees
Bake: Thirty minutes
Pimiento strips
Reserve six sardines for garnish
Serves: Four

Blend together the sardines, crumbled
bread, parsley, green pepper, onion juice,
celery soup, salt, tabasco, prepared mustard and lime juice. Spoon into six scallop
shells or casseroles. Spread a little mayonnaise on top. Bake in a quick oven for 30
minutes or until top is browned. Garnish
with pimiento strips and sardines.

A FAVORITE RECIPE

Finnish Fish Pie

Two cups flaked cooked fish
Three tablespoons minced green peppers
One-half cup fried onions
One cup cooked green peas
One teaspoon salt
One-fourth teaspoon pepper
One-eighth teaspoon sage (optional)
One cup medium white sauce
Two cups mashed, seasoned, potatoes
Oven temperature: 450 degrees
Baking time: Twenty minutes
Servings: Four

In a bowl mix the flaked cooked fish,
green pepper, fried onions, peas and
seasonings. Add the white sauce. Cook
and mash the potatoes, adding seasonings
to taste. Pour the fish mixture into a
casserole (10 in.). Cover top with mashed
potatoes. Bake in a very hot oven until
brown. Serve hot with tomato salad.

FAYE MARIE BULLOCK, *Somerville, N.J.*

Frogs' Legs Supreme

Four tablespoons butter or margarine
One onion, chopped
One small clove garlic, minced
Cooking time: Five minutes
Two packages (8 oz. each) frozen frogs'
　legs, thawed
One-fourth cup flour
Cooking time: Five minutes
One can (4 oz.) sliced mushrooms
One can (10½ oz.) condensed cream of
　celery soup
One-third cup Bordeaux white wine
One teaspoon salt
One-fourth teaspoon pepper
One teaspoon paprika
Cooking time: Five minutes
Serves: Four

In an electric skillet over medium heat melt the butter. Add the onions and garlic. Cook until onion is straw-colored. Dredge the thawed frogs' legs in flour. (Be sure to remove rubber bands from legs). Brown the frogs' legs. Add the remaining ingredients and cook for five minutes. Garnish with parsley. Serve.

A FAVORITE RECIPE

Seaman's Pie

One package (6 oz.) noodles
Cooked as directed on package
One can (7 oz.) tuna fish, flaked
One-fourth cup minced onion
Two hard-cooked eggs chopped
One can (10½ oz.) condensed cream of
　mushroom soup
One teaspoon Worcestershire sauce
One-half teaspoon salt
One-sixteenth teaspoon pepper
One-fourth cup grated American cheese
Oven temperature: 350 degrees
Baking time: Thirty minutes
Servings: Four

Cook the noodles in boiling salted water; drain. Arrange a border of the noodles in a well greased baking dish (8 x 8 x 2 in.). Place the tuna in the center. Sprinkle the onion and eggs over the tuna. Blend the soup with the Worcestershire sauce, salt and pepper; pour over tuna. Sprinkle the top with the grated cheese.

MRS. GERTRUDE ECK, *Hasbrouck Hgts, N.J.*

Potato-Oyster-Mushroom Pie

Six medium-sized potatoes
One-half cup butter or margarine
One large onion, chopped
One-half pound mushrooms, sliced
One cup chopped celery
One-fourth cup chopped parsley
One teaspoon paprika
Pastry for pie (3 cups)
Salt and pepper
Sixteen oysters and liquor
Oven temperature: 425 degrees
Baking time: One hour and fifteen
　minutes (about)
One cup heavy cream or evaporated milk
Standing time: Fifteen minutes
Serves: Four, or more

Peel the potatoes; slice paper-thin. Cover potatoes with ice water. In a skillet melt 4 tablespoons butter. Cook the onions and mushrooms until onions are straw-colored. Add the celery, parsley and paprika. Line a casserole with pastry. Drain potatoes; dry thoroughly. Arrange half the potatoes over the pastry. Season with salt and pepper; dot with half the remaining butter. Pour the oysters and liquor over the potatoes. Spread the mushroom mixture over the oysters. Top with remaining layer of potatoes. Season with salt and pepper; dot with remaining butter. Cover with pastry; do not slit the top. Bake in a hot oven until brown. Remove from oven to rack. Cut a small opening on top. Test with a knife to make certain potatoes are done. Then pour cream into hot pie through the opening. Let potatoes absorb cream for 15 minutes. Serve.

Favorite Tuna Casserole

Two cans (7 oz. each) tuna
One tablespoon finely chopped onion
One tablespoon lemon juice
Two tablespoons finely chopped parsley
One-eighth teaspoon instant garlic or
One-half teaspoon garlic salt
One-fourth cup butter or margarine
One-fourth cup flour
One-half teaspoon salt
Dash of cayenne pepper
Two cups milk
Cooking time: Ten minutes, about
One cup soft bread cubes
One-half cup crushed potato chips
Oven temperature: 400 degrees
Baking time: Fifteen minutes, or more
Servings: Four to six

Drain the oil from the tuna and flake into a bowl. Add the onion, lemon juice, parsley and instant garlic or garlic salt. Mix well. In a saucepan melt the butter or margarine. Stir in the flour, salt and cayenne, then gradually blend in the milk, stirring to keep smooth. Cook over moderate heat, stirring constantly until the sauce thickens. Add to the flaked seasoned tuna with the bread cubes. Transfer to a greased casserole (1½ qts.) and top with the crushed potato chips. Bake in a quick oven for fifteen minutes to heat thoroughly and slightly brown. Serve at once from the casserole.

Tuna Cheese Loaf

Two cans (7 oz. each) tuna fish
One cup grated American cheddar cheese
One cup cracker or bread crumbs
One tablespoon onion flakes
One-half teaspoon salt
One-half teaspoon celery salt
One-fourth teaspoon pepper
One egg, beaten
Two-thirds cup milk
Two tablespoons melted butter or
   margarine
Oven temperature: 350 degrees
Bake: Thirty minutes
One can (10½ oz.) condensed cream
   of celery soup
One-fourth cup milk
One-fourth cup sliced olives (stuffed)
Serves: Six

Drain tuna fish; flake. Add the other ingredients; blend well. Shape into a loaf. Place on a greased shallow pan, brush with butter. Bake in a moderate oven until lightly browned. Serve hot with olive sauce made by combining the heated condensed celery soup, milk and olives.

Cottage Cheese Tuna Bake

One egg
Two cups creamed cottage cheese (one
   pound)
One can (7 oz.) tuna, drained and flaked
One teaspoon salt
One and one-half teaspoons Worcestershire
   sauce
One-fourth teaspoon paprika
One-half cup fine cracker meal
Oven temperature: 350 degrees
Bake: Thirty minutes
Serves: Four

In a bowl beat the egg. Blend in the creamed cottage cheese, flaked and drained tuna, salt, Worcestershire sauce and paprika. Add half the cracker meal and mix well. Spread in a greased pie plate (10 in.) and top with remaining cracker meal. Bake in a moderate oven for 30 minutes. Serve piping hot.

Tuna Terrific

One-fourth pound spaghetti or elbow
   macaroni
Boiling salted water
Cook: Ten minutes, about
One-half cup grated cheddar cheese
One tablespoon poppy seed
One cup dairy sour cream
One can tuna (7 oz.)
One-half teaspoon salt
One-eighth teaspoon pepper
One tablespoon finely chopped onion
One tablespoon lemon juice
One tablespoon finely chopped parsley
Oven temperature: 375 degrees
Bake: Twenty minutes
Servings: Four

Cook the fine spaghetti or elbow macaroni in the boiling, salted water until tender. Drain. Add the grated cheese to the spaghetti with the poppy seed, sour cream and oil drained from the canned tuna. Add the salt and pepper and toss well to blend thoroughly. Arrange in a shallow baking dish or pie plate (9 in.). Break tuna into chunks with a fork and arrange over the spaghetti. Scatter finely chopped onion, lemon juice and chopped parsley over tuna. Bake in a moderately hot oven for twenty minutes. Use a broad spatula for serving.

Shrimp and Macaroni Shell Casserole

Three cups macaroni shells
Two quarts boiling water
Two teaspoons salt
Boiling time: Thirty minutes
Two cups cooked shrimp
One cup diced celery
One cup grated cheddar cheese
Two eggs, slightly beaten
Two cups milk
One-half teaspoon salt
One-eighth teaspoon pepper
One-eighth teaspoon tarragon
One tablespoon butter
Oven temperature: 350 degrees
Baking time: One hour
Serves: Four, or more

Cook the shells in a large kettle in the boiling salted water until just tender. Drain. Place a third of the shells in the bottom of a greased casserole (2 qts.). Add a layer of shrimp and celery. Sprinkle on some of the cheese. Repeat layers and finish with layer of shells. Pour the combined eggs, milk and seasonings over the shells. Dot the top of the casserole with butter. Set the casserole in a pan of hot water. Bake in a moderate oven until firm. Remove. Serve immediately.

A FAVORITE RECIPE
Macaroni Salmon Casserole

Two tablespoons butter or margarine
Two tablespoons flour
One and one-fourth teaspoons salt
One-half teaspoon dry mustard
One and one-half cups liquid (use the
   liquid drained from salmon and peas
   with milk)
Cooking time: Ten minutes in a double
   boiler
One egg beaten lightly
Two tablespoons lemon juice
One can (8 oz.) salmon
One can (8 oz.) peas
One-half cup minced celery
Two tablespoons chopped pimiento
One package (4 oz.) shell macaroni,
   cooked as directed on package, drained
One-fourth cup buttered bread crumbs
Oven temperature: 350 degrees
Baking time: Forty minutes, about
Servings: Four

Blend the butter and flour in the top of a double boiler, add salt, mustard and the liquid. Stir until smooth and thick. Pour the sauce into a bowl with the beaten egg. Add lemon juice, salmon, peas, celery and pimiento. Mix. Fold in the cooked, well drained macaroni. Pour into a well greased casserole (2 qts.); sprinkle buttered bread crumbs over the top. Bake in a moderate oven until the cheese is lightly browned. Serve with a mixed green salad.

DONA SCHWAB, *Baldwin, L.I., N.Y.*

A FAVORITE RECIPE
Salmon Baked in Potato Shells

One can (1 lb.) salmon, all bones and skin
   removed
Eight medium-sized potatoes, baked,
   split lengthwise
One-half cup milk
One small onion, minced
One teaspoon salt
One-fourth teaspoon pepper
One cup bread crumbs
Two tablespoons butter or margarine
Oven temperature: 400 degrees
Baking time: Twenty-five minutes
Servings: Six

Flake the salmon, removing skin and bones. Bake the potatoes. Slice off the top of potatoes, scoop out the pulp, mashing thoroughly. In a bowl, add milk, onion, salt and pepper. Stir in the flaked salmon, mixing lightly. Refill the potato shells. Cover with the bread crumbs and dot with butter. Bake in a quick oven. Serve with a green vegetable and coleslaw.

FRANCES LENORE WARREN, *Bronx, N.Y.*

Salmon Gumbo

Two tablespoons butter or margarine
Two medium-sized onions, sliced
Two cloves garlic, minced
Cook: Five minutes
One tablespoon flour
Four cups water
Simmer: Ten minutes
One medium-sized green pepper, chopped
One cup chopped celery
Two tablespoons chopped parsley
One-half teaspoon thyme
One bay leaf
One-half teaspoon salt
One-eighth teaspoon hot pepper flakes
One-eighth teaspoon file powder (optional)
One can (1 lb.) whole tomatoes
One package (10 oz.) frozen okra
Simmer: Ten minutes
One can (1 lb.) salmon, flaked
One can (7-oz.) crab meat
One cup cooked or canned shrimp
Reheat: Five minutes
Serves: Six

Over low heat in a deep kettle, melt the butter or margarine; cook the onion and garlic until straw-colored. Stir in the flour. Add half the water; simmer for 10 minutes. Add remaining water, green pepper, celery, parsley, thyme, bay leaf, salt, hot pepper flakes, file power, tomatoes and okra. Simmer for 15 minutes. Add the liquid from canned salmon, flaked salmon, crab meat and shrimp. Reheat for 5 minutes. Serve over cooked rice.

Salmon Stuffed Peppers

Four medium-sized green peppers
One teaspoon salt
One cup water
Boil: Five minutes
One can (7¾ oz.) salmon
Two tablespoons flour
One can evaporated milk (1⅔ cups)
Cook: Five minutes, about
One-half teaspoon salt
One-eighth teaspoon pepper
One-fourth teaspoon celery salt
One tablespoon minced onion
Two tablespoons lemon juice
One and one-half cups soft bread crumbs
One tablespoon butter
One-half cup soft bread crumbs
Two tablespoons grated Parmesan cheese
Oven temperature: 350 degrees
Bake: Twenty-five minutes
Serves: Four

Wash the green peppers. Cut through into halves from top to bottom. Remove seeds and membrane and place halves in a large saucepan. Sprinkle with the teaspoon of salt and pour on the water. Cover and bring to a boil. Boil five minutes. Drain. In a saucepan blend the liquid drained from the canned salmon with the flour. Gradually blend in the evaporated milk. Cook, stirring constantly, until thickened. Remove from heat and stir in the salt, pepper, celery salt, minced onion, lemon juice and one and one-half cups soft bread crumbs and flaked salmon. Arrange pepper halves in a greased baking pan and fill with the salmon mixture. Melt the tablespoon of butter in a small saucepan, stir in the half cup of soft bread crumbs and the grated Parmesan cheese. Scatter over the filled pepper halves and bake in a moderate oven until piping hot and nicely browned on top.

A FAVORITE RECIPE
Salmon Confetti Casserole

One package (8 oz.) elbow macaroni, cooked as directed on package
One cup grated cheese
One can (1 lb.) salmon, bones and heavy skin removed, flaked
Two cups hot cooked peas
One can (10½ oz.) cream of celery soup
One-half cup milk
One tablespoon chopped pimiento
Oven temperature: 350 degrees
Baking time: Thirty-five minutes
Servings: Four or more

Cook the macaroni; drain thoroughly. Combine in a bowl with the cheese, salmon, peas, celery soup, milk and pimiento. Turn into a well-greased casserole (10 in.). Bake in a moderate oven. Serve from the casserole with a lettuce and tomato salad.

MRS. ADELE MC GUIGAN, *Elmhurst, N.Y.*

Clam and Eggplant Casserole

One large eggplant
Boiling salted water
Cook: Until tender
One tablespoon instant minced onion or
One-fourth cup finely chopped fresh onion
One-fourth cup chopped celery
One-fourth cup butter or margarine
Sauté: Five to ten minutes
One-fourth cup flour
One-half teaspoon salt
One-half cup milk
One can (7 oz.) minced clams and liquid
Cook: Until thickened
One beaten egg
Two tablespoons butter or margarine
One cup soft bread crumbs
Two tablespoons grated Parmesan cheese
Oven temperature: 375 degrees
Bake: Thirty minutes
Servings: Four or five

Wash and peel the eggplant. Cut into one inch cubes. Cook in boiling, salted water until tender. Drain and place in a shallow casserole (1½ qt.). Soften the instant minced onion, if used, with a tablespoon of water. In a saucepan melt the fourth cup of butter or margarine, add the instant or fresh chopped onion and the chopped celery and sauté until soft. Stir in the flour and salt, gradually blend in the milk and undrained clams. Cook, stirring until mixture thickens. Add a little to the beaten egg, blending thoroughly, return combination to the saucepan. Spoon over the eggplant. Melt the remaining butter or margarine in a small saucepan, stir in the soft bread crumbs and grated Parmesan cheese. Mix well and scatter over the sauced eggplant. Bake in a moderately hot oven until piping hot and well browned.

A FAVORITE RECIPE
Oyster Pie

One-half cup diced carrots
One-fourth cup diced (¼ in.) celery
One teaspoon minced parsley
One cup diced potatoes
One large onion, diced
Water to cover
Cooking time: Until tender
Two dozen oysters
Cooking time: Until edges curl
One teaspoon salt
One-fourth teaspoon pepper
Pie crust to cover bottom, sides and top
Oven temperature: 400 degrees
Baking time: Until crust browns
Serves: Six

In a saucepan place the vegetables. Cover with water; bring to a slow boil; cook until tender. Add the oysters, cooking until the oysters curl. Season with salt and pepper. Line a casserole (10 in.) with pie crust; pour in the vegetables and oyster mixture. Cover with pie pastry, making slits in top for steam to escape. Bake in a hot oven until crust is a golden brown. Serve hot from the casserole with cole slaw.

MRS. GRACE L. MORAVEK, *Summit Hill, Penna.*

A FAVORITE RECIPE
Oysters and Macaroni

One-half cup butter, melted
One tablespoon chopped onion
Cook: Five minutes
One-half cup flour
One-half teaspoon salt
One-eighth teaspoon pepper
Cook: Two minutes
Three cups milk
Cook: Ten minutes in a double boiler
One cup grated American cheese
Four cups broken cooked macaroni
One and one-half dozen oysters
One cup fine bread crumbs
Oven temperature: 375 degrees
Bake: Thirty minutes, about
Serves: Six

In the top of a double boiler, melt the butter; add the onion, cooking until tender. Stir in the flour, salt and pepper. When the mixture bubbles, add the milk gradually, stirring until smooth and thickened. Place over hot water; add the grated cheese, stirring until melted and smooth. Arrange in a well greased casserole, two cups of cooked macaroni; pour one-half of the cream sauce over the macaroni; make another layer of macaroni and cheese sauce. Roll the drained oysters in the fine bread crumbs. Place around the edge of casserole. Cover center with buttered bread crumbs. Bake in a moderately hot oven until a golden brown. Serve hot from the casserole with a mixed green salad.

MRS. JULIA M. AUER, *Brooklyn, N.Y.*

A FAVORITE RECIPE
Capri Spaghetti Buffet

Eight ounces spaghetti (cooked as directed on package), drained
Two cans (7 oz. each) tuna fish, drained
One-fourth cup sliced pimiento stuffed olives
One-half pound processed Swiss cheese, sliced
Two and one-half cups 3 minute cheese sauce

3 Minute Cheese Sauce

One large can evaporated milk
One-half teaspoon salt
One teaspoon dry mustard
One tablespoon horseradish
Simmering time: Until hot (not boiling)
Two cups (½ lb.) grated processed American cheese
Cooking time: Until the cheese melts
Oven temperature: 350 degrees
Baking time: Thirty minutes
Servings: Six

Cook the spaghetti in boiling salted water as directed on package; drain thoroughly. Place the spaghetti in a well buttered casserole (2½ qts.); spread the tuna and olives over the spaghetti. Arrange the cheese over the top and around the sides of the dish. Make the sauce by mixing the milk, salt, mustard and horseradish in a saucepan; heat to near boiling over a low heat. Add the grated cheese, stirring until melted and smooth. Pour the mixture over the spaghetti and bake in a moderate oven until firm. Serve hot with a tossed salad.

MRS. JAMES F. NUGENT, *Staten Island, N.Y.*

Alaska King Crab Meat Tetrazzini

Four tablespoons butter or margarine
One-half pound mushrooms, thinly sliced
Cook: Ten minutes
Five tablespoons flour
Two cups milk
One cup light cream, or evaporated milk
One-half teaspoon salt
One teaspoon prepared mustard
One teaspoon chopped parsley
One teaspoon Worcestershire sauce
Few grains cayenne
Cook: Ten minutes
Two frozen packages (6 oz. each) Alaska king crab meat, defrosted
One-half pound thin spaghetti, cooked
One-fourth cup grated Parmesan cheese
Oven temperature: 400 degrees
Bake: Twenty minutes
Serves: Four

In a skillet melt the butter. Add the sliced mushrooms; cook until golden. Reserve four mushrooms for garnish. Sprinkle the flour over the mushrooms stirring until blended. Gradually add the milk and light cream. Add the salt, prepared mustard, parsley, Worcestershire sauce and cayenne. Cook, stirring until thickened. Reserve a few pieces of crab meat for garnish. Mix half the sauce with the Alaska king crab meat. Arrange the cooked spaghetti in a greased casserole (2 qts.) making a well in the center. Fill the well with the creamed crab meat. Pour the remaining sauce over the spaghetti. Sprinkle the Parmesan cheese on top. Bake in a quick oven until brown on top. Garnish with crab meat and mushrooms. Serve from casserole.

Shrimp Green Noodle Casserole

Two cans (10½ oz. each) condensed cream of chicken soup
One cup milk
Three cups cooked shrimp
Four cups cooked green noodles
One-half cup slivered almonds, toasted
One-fourth cup chopped pimiento
One teaspoon salt
One-fourth teaspoon pepper
Oven temperature: 350 degrees
Baking time: Thirty minutes
Servings: Six

In a large bowl blend the soup and milk. Add the shrimp, noodles, almonds, pimiento, salt and pepper; mix thoroughly. Pour into a greased casserole (3 qts.). Bake in a moderate oven until lightly browned on top. Remove and serve at once.

French Artichokes

Four medium-sized artichokes
Two teaspoons salt
Two quarts boiling water
One clove garlic, split
Cooking time: Twenty-five minutes
Four tablespoons melted butter
Servings: Four

Rinse the artichokes; remove any imperfect outer leaves and trim the leaves and cut stem. Cook the artichokes in boiling salted water with the garlic in a covered kettle until pierceable at the stem. Drain upside down. Gently open the leaves; scoop out the fuzzy choke with a spoon and discard. Close the leaves. Serve with individual dishes of melted butter. To eat: Pull off the leaves one at a time, and dip the fleshy end in the butter, or sauce. Draw gently between the teeth and pull off the tender part. Eat the heart and stem with a fork.

Easy Hollandaise

Four tablespoons butter
Two egg yolks
One-eighth teaspoon salt
Dash of cayenne
One tablespoon lemon juice
One-third cup boiling water
Cooking time: Seven to eight minutes
     over hot water
Yield: Three-fourths cup

Melt the butter in a double boiler, having one inch of hot water in the lower compartment. Remove the top from the water. Blend in the egg yolks, one at a time; add the seasonings and lemon juice. Slowly stir in the boiling water. Place over hot, not boiling, water and stir constantly to the consistency of custard. Serve at once as sauce with artichokes or other green vegetables.

Vinaigrette Sauce

Six tablespoons olive oil
Two tablespoons lemon juice
One-fourth teaspoon salt
One-eighth teaspoon pepper
One teaspoon minced onion
One teaspoon minced sweet pickle
One teaspoon minced parsley
One hard-cooked egg, chopped
Yield: Two-thirds cup

Mix all the ingredients. Serve with hot or cold artichokes.

Stuffed Baked Artichokes

Four medium-sized artichokes
Boiling salted water
Cook: Twenty minutes
Two cans (5 ozs. each) lobster meat
Three-fourths cup condensed cream of
     mushroom soup
Four tablespoons grated Parmesan cheese
One-half teaspoon salt
One-eighth teaspoon pepper
One-fourth teaspoon tarragon
Four tablespoons bread crumbs, mixed
     with
One tablespoon butter or margarine
One-half cup water
Two tablespoons oil
Oven temperature: 400 degrees
Bake: Twenty minutes
Serves: Four

Vegetables

Break off artichoke stems; trim. Cut about one-half inch from top of leaves. Put in boiling salted water; cook until almost tender. Rinse in cold water. Drain. Gently spread leaves apart and pull out center leaves and with a teaspoon remove the choke. Remove cartilage from lobster meat. Reserve a few pieces for garnish. Fill the artichoke with the combined cream of mushroom soup, lobster meat, grated cheese and seasonings. Top with crumbs. Place in a deep baking dish with one-half cup water and two tablespoons oil in the bottom of the baking dish. Bake in a quick oven for 20 minutes. Remove. Serve immediately garnished with the reserved lobster meat. The filling and the heart of the artichoke are eaten with a fork and the leaves with the fingers.

Asparagus Baked in Cheese Sauce

One bunch (2½ pounds) asparagus
Cook: Fifteen minutes, about
One can (4 oz.) pimientos, slivered
One-half cup milk
One pkg. (3 oz.) cream cheese
One-fourth cup crumbled blue cheese
Heat: Until blended
One tablespoon butter or margarine
Three tablespoons fine dry bread crumbs
Oven temperature: 325 degrees
Bake: Thirty minutes
Servings: Four

Snap off the white woody stems of the fresh asparagus and discard. Wash the green tips well and cook in boiling salted water until almost tender. Drain and arrange in greased shallow baking pan or pie plate. Scatter the slivered pimientos over the asparagus. In a small saucepan place the milk, cream cheese and crumbled blue cheese. Heat, stirring until blended smooth. Pour over the asparagus. Melt the butter or margarine and blend with the fine dry bread crumbs. Scatter over the sauced asparagus. Bake in a moderately slow oven for thirty minutes or until crumbs are nicely browned and all is piping hot.

Asparagus Soufflé

One-fourth cup butter or margarine
One-fourth cup flour
One and one-third cups milk
Cooking time: Five to ten minutes, about
One-half cup grated cheddar cheese
Five eggs
One teaspoon salt
One pound fresh or one package frozen
  asparagus, cooked and chopped
Oven temperature: 350 degrees
Baking time: One hour
Servings: Four to six

In a saucepan, melt the butter or margarine. Stir in the flour. Gradually add the milk. Cook over moderate heat, stirring constantly, until the mixture thickens. Add the grated cheese; stir until melted; remove from the heat. Using two bowls, separate the egg whites from the yolks. Beat the yolks with half of the salt; stir into the cheese mixture. Beat the egg whites and remaining salt with a rotary beater until they hold soft peaks. Fold into the cheese mixture with the chopped asparagus. Pour into a greased baking dish (2½ qts.) and bake in a pan containing hot water in a moderate oven for one hour. Serve at once.

Asparagus Polonaise

Two pounds fresh asparagus
One teaspoon salt
Boiling water
Cook: Ten to twelve minutes
One-fourth cup butter or margarine
One-third cup soft bread crumbs
Sauté: Five minutes, about
Serves: Four

Snap the less tender ends from each spear of asparagus where the stalk naturally gives when pressed between the fingers. Trim and wash thoroughly. Tie enough stalks for each portion together with soft string. Place asparagus bundles upright in the lower half of a double boiler. Add salt and enough boiling water to measure two inches. Cover with the inverted upper part of the double boiler. Cook until the asparagus is tender, about 10 minutes. In the meantime melt the butter or margarine in a small skillet or saucepan, add the soft bread crumbs and sauté until lightly browned. Spoon crumbs and melted butter over each portion of cooked, drained asparagus.

A FAVORITE RECIPE
Asparagus Pudding

One-half cup butter
One cup flour
One cup liquid, drained from asparagus
One-half cup milk
Cooking time: Fifteen minutes in a
  double boiler
Six eggs (whole)
Six egg yolks
One teaspoon salt
One can (10½ oz.) asparagus tips (16
  tips, about)
Steaming time: Two hours
Six sprigs parsley
One cup drawn butter
Servings: Four

For this pudding it is necessary to have a tightly covered mold. In a bowl, cream the butter and flour. Add the asparagus liquid and milk slowly, beating to a smooth paste. Cook in a double boiler, stirring constantly. Remove from heat, add the eggs and egg yolks, one at a time beating constantly. Add salt, mix. Butter the mold generously. Press the asparagus lightly against the buttered sides of the mold. Pour the batter over all. Cover tightly. Place the mold in a pan of hot water, covering the mold ¾ to top. Steam. Unmold. Slice and serve with hot butter.

MRS. MATHEW PODESYWA, *Staten Island, N.Y.*

Asparagus with Lemon Butter Sauce

One bunch asparagus (2½ pounds)
One quart boiling water
One teaspoon salt
One teaspoon sugar
Boiling time: Fifteen or twenty minutes

Sauce

Two egg yolks
One-half cup light cream or evaporated
  milk
Cooking time: Four to six minutes
Three tablespoons butter
One tablespoon lemon juice
One-fourth teaspoon salt
Servings: Four

Snap the tough end from each spear of asparagus with the fingers. Wash carefully. Trim the stalks the same length (four to five inches) cut the remainder of the stalk into inch pieces. Tie the trimmed stalks into two bunches with soft cord.

Stand the bunches of asparagus upright in the lower part of a double boiler containing the boiling water, salt and sugar. Add the loose pieces of asparagus. Cover, using the top of the double boiler as a lid. Bring to a boil and boil gently until the ends of the stalks are tender. The tips cook more quickly than the stalks although not immersed in water.

For the sauce: Combine the egg yolks and cream or evaporated milk in the upper half of a double boiler. Cook over hot water, stirring constantly, until thickened. Remove from the heat. Gradually stir in the butter, cut into bits, the lemon juice and salt.

Drain the bunches of asparagus, discard the cord and serve with the hot sauce. Continue cooking tougher pieces, using them and the liquid in a cream of asparagus soup.

Spiced Artichokes

Six medium-sized artichokes
One stick cinnamon
Twelve whole cloves
One tablespoon olive oil
One tablespoon vinegar
Two tablespoons salt
Water
Boil: Forty-five minutes
Servings: Six

Wash the artichokes. Trim off most of the stem and pull off the outer leaves. Trim off the top inch and a half of the artichoke with a sharp knife. Place in a large kettle with the cinnamon, cloves, olive oil, vinegar, salt and water to cover the artichokes. Bring to a boil and boil gently for forty-five minutes. Turn upside down to drain. Serve warm or thoroughly chilled.

Ravigote Sauce

Two-thirds cup salad or olive oil
One-third cup vinegar
One-half teaspoon salt
One-fourth teaspoon pepper
Two tablespoons capers, chopped
One tablespoon finely chopped onion
One tablespoon finely chopped parsley
One-half teaspoon dried tarragon
Yield: One cup approx.

Combine the ingredients in a jar with a screw top. Cover tightly and shake until thoroughly blended together. Serve with cooked artichokes as a dip for the leaves.

Ten Minute Beets

One bunch beets
One tablespoon butter
One tablespoon vinegar
One teaspoon salt
One-eighth teaspoon pepper
Two tablespoons boiling water
Simmer: Ten minutes
Serves: Four

Wash, peel and grate the fresh beets medium fine. Place in a saucepan with the butter, vinegar, salt, pepper and boiling water. Cover tightly and place over high heat until mixture comes to a boil. Reduce heat and simmer for ten minutes. If necessary a small additional amount of water may be added. These are delicious hot or good chilled for salad.

A FAVORITE RECIPE
Spicy Pickled Beets

Twelve medium-sized beets, washed
Water to cover
Cook: Until tender
One cup beet liquid
Three and one-half cups vinegar
One-half cup lemon juice
Two cups thinly sliced onions
One-third teaspoon dry mustard
Two tablespoons brown sugar
One-third cup pickling spices
Cooking time: To the boiling point
Boiling time: Five minutes
Yield: Three pints, about

Wash and remove the tops from the beets, leaving 1¼ inch of stems on the beets. Place in a kettle, add water to cover. Cook until tender. Drain, reserving one cup of the liquid. Peel and slice the beets. Add the vinegar to the beet liquid, lemon juice, onions, mustard, sugar and spices. Bring to a boil. Add the sliced beets, boil. Turn into sterilized jars, seal and store in a dark place.

MRS. JULIA FOLEY, *Oakdale, Conn.*

Blueberry Hill Beets

Four tablespoons butter
Two tablespoons flour
Two tablespoons light brown sugar
One cup orange juice
One tablespoon lemon juice
One-half teaspoon salt
Peel of one-half navel orange
One can (No. 2½) julienne beets
Servings: Four, or more

Melt the butter in a saucepan, stir in flour, making a smooth paste. Add the brown sugar and gradually blend in the orange juice, lemon juice and salt. Cook, stirring constantly, until thickened. Cut the orange peel into thin slivers and place in one-half cup of salted water in a saucepan. Bring to a boil and boil two minutes. Drain and add peel to sauce. Drain canned beets and stir into the orange juice, heat briefly.

Burgundy Beets

One can (No. 303) sliced beets
Two teaspoons cornstarch
One tablespoon brown sugar
One tablespoon lemon juice
One-eighth teaspoon allspice
One-third cup beet liquid
One-third cup Burgundy wine
Cooking time: Five minutes
One tablespoon butter
Heating time: Five minutes, about
Servings: Four

Drain the liquid from the canned beets reserving one-third cup. In a saucepan blend the cornstarch with the brown sugar; add the lemon juice, allspice, beet liquid and red wine gradually, stirring to keep smooth. Cook over moderate heat, stirring constantly, until thickened and clear. Remove from the heat and add the butter and sliced beets. Return to heat and cook until thoroughly heated.

Broccoli on Toast

One bunch fresh broccoli
Boiling salted water
Cook: Twenty minutes, about
One-half pound processed cheddar cheese
One-third cup milk
Four slices crisp toast
One can (2¼ oz.) deviled ham
Paprika
Servings: Four

Wash and trim the fresh broccoli. Cut through thick stems so all will cook at same rate of speed. Cover with boiling salted water and cook until tender crisp. Drain. In the upper half of a double boiler place the processed cheddar cheese, cut coarsely and the milk. Set over hot water and heat until combined. Spread hot toast with the deviled ham and arrange cooked broccoli on top. Spoon cheese sauce over all and dust lightly with paprika. Serve at once.

Spanish Broccoli

One bunch fresh or two boxes (10 oz.) frozen broccoli
Boiling salted water
Cook: Until tender
Three tablespoons olive oil
One clove garlic, crushed
Two chopped anchovy fillets
One-third cup chopped olives
Cook: Two or three minutes
One tablespoon lemon juice
Serves: Six

Cook the fresh or frozen broccoli in boiling salted water until tender. Drain well. In a skillet heat the olive oil with the crushed clove of garlic, chopped anchovy fillets and olives, cook briefly. Add the lemon juice and spoon over the drained hot broccoli. Serve at once or chill thoroughly.

Golden Broccoli

One bunch broccoli
Boiling salted water
Cook: Twenty minutes, about
One tablespoon lemon juice
One-half can (10½ oz.) condensed cream of chicken soup
One-fourth cup grated cheddar cheese
Broiler temperature: 500 degrees
Broil: Five minutes, about
Serves: Four or six

Wash the fresh broccoli very well, trimming off any withered leaves and some of the very thick portions of stem. Cut thick pieces into uniform slenderness for even cooking. Add to boiling, salted water in a large saucepan or kettle, cover and cook until fork tender. Drain. Transfer to a large shallow baking dish or pie plate and sprinkle with the lemon juice. Beat the half can of condensed cream of chicken soup smooth with a fork. Spoon over the broccoli. Scatter the grated cheddar over the top. Broil just long enough to melt the cheese and lightly brown. Serve at once. Note: Two packages of the frozen broccoli may be cooked according to package directions and finished off in the broiler this way.

A FAVORITE RECIPE
Red Cabbage-Apple Sauce

One-fourth cup margarine, heated
One-half cup sliced onions
Sauté: Five minutes
One head (3 lbs.) red cabbage, (outer leaves removed) shredded
Two cups applesauce
One-half teaspoon salt
Simmering time: Thirty minutes
Servings: Six

Heat the margarine in a heavy skillet; add the onions, sauté. Add the shredded cabbage, (rinsed in cold water and drained) applesauce and salt. Stir until well blended; cover. Simmer, stirring frequently. Serve hot with pork roast or chicken.

MRS. S. KELTING, *Brooklyn, N.Y.*

Red Cabbage in Bouillon

One medium-sized red cabbage (1½ lbs.)
One can (10½ oz.) condensed beef broth (bouillon)
Four whole cloves
One small onion, thinly sliced
Cook: Ten minutes, about
Two tablespoons butter or margarine
One-eighth teaspoon nutmeg
One-eighth teaspoon pepper
One tablespoon vinegar
Servings: Six

Wash and slice the cabbage very fine. Place in a large heavy skillet or saucepan and pour on the condensed beef broth. Add the cloves and thinly sliced onion. Cover tightly and cook until tender crisp, about ten minutes. Remove cover and stir in the butter, nutmeg, pepper and vinegar. Serve hot.

The Uncommon Vegetables

Chinese Cabbage

Is a pale green long-leaved vegetable of delicate flavor. Prepare it like cabbage for salads or cut it in wedges and braise in chicken stock.

Horseradish

Is a white root having a pungent flavor. Use it as a condiment, ground or grated and mixed with vinegar. Excellent when shaved and served with roast beef.

Butternut Squash

Is a buff-colored, orange-fleshed vegetable. To prepare for cooking, cut open, remove fibers and seeds; then cook it like any other type of squash.

Finocchi

Or Italian fennel is a bulbous licorice flavored vegetable that pulls apart like celery. Treated and served like celery hearts or cut into slices, simmered and buttered.

Celeriac

Or celery knobs. One pound serves three. This root vegetable with a flavor of celery is served either raw in salads or cooked and dressed with a savory sauce.

Jerusalem Artichoke

Is a vegetable low in starch, looking like a knobby potato. Easy to fix; pare, dice and boil. Nice with browned butter or a tangy sauce.

Shallot

Is a member of the onion family and grows in clusters somewhat like garlic. Peeled and boiled, then served with butter. Shallot butter is wonderful for broiled meats.

Zucchini

Or Italian squash is a striped dark green vegetable resembling a cucumber. It is mild in flavor. Good cut into slices and fried in butter or steamed.

Vegetable Plate No. 1

Poached Eggs over Potato Patties
With Quick Hollandaise Sauce
Buttered Corn
Frenched Green Beans
Crisp Radishes
Baked Acorn Squash with
Peas — Piquant Sauce

Vegetable Plate No. 2

Volcano Potatoes
Asparagus
Spicy Beets
Baby Carrots — Mint Sauce
Broccoli — Colbert Sauce

Piquant Sauce

In a saucepan combine three tablespoons brown sugar, one tablespoon butter, one-fourth cup catsup, one-fourth teaspoon nutmeg and one teaspoon dry mustard. Heat to the boiling point. Use over tomatoes, squash or onions.

Quick Hollandaise Sauce

Place three-fourths cup of butter or margarine in the top of a double boiler. Beat until creamy with a rotary beater. Add one-fourth teaspoon salt and a dash of cayenne. Add one and one-half tablespoons lemon juice, a few drops at a time, beating constantly. Add three egg yolks, one at a time; continue beating until light and fluffy. Place over hot, not boiling water, beating constantly until glossy. Remove. Use over green vegetables.

Note: Water should not touch bottom of the top of the double boiler.

Colbert Sauce

In a saucepan dissolve one tablespoon of beef extract in one cup of boiling water. Boil two minutes. Remove. Add one-fourth cup of butter a teaspoonful at a time, beating constantly with a rotary beater. Beat in two tablespoons each of lemon juice and sherry. Add one teaspoon minced parsley. Use over any green vegetable.

Mint Sauce

Dissolve one tablespoon super-fine sugar in one-half cup cider vinegar. Pour the mixture over two tablespoons finely chopped mint. Let stand 30 minutes. Heat to boiling. Use over carrots.

Acorn Squash with Spinach

Two acorn squash, split
One cup hot water
Oven temperature: 375 degrees
Baking time: Forty minutes (about)
Three tablespoons margarine
One teaspoon salt
One-eighth teaspoon nutmeg
Two cups cooked spinach, drained
One-half cup thick seasoned cream sauce
Heating time: Three minutes
Servings: Four

Cut the squash into halves lengthwise; discard the seeds. Place cut side down, in a large baking dish. Pour in the hot water. Bake 20 minutes in a moderately hot oven. Turn; brush the centers with margarine and sprinkle with seasonings. Bake until the squash is pierceable. Remove. Fill the centers with spinach and cream sauce; reheat. Serve.

Sweet and Sour Brussels Sprouts

One quart fresh Brussels sprouts
One quart boiling water
One and one-half teaspoons salt
Boiling time: Ten minutes (about)
Three tablespoons brown sugar
Two tablespoons lemon juice
One tablespoon butter
Cooking time: One minute
Servings: Four

Trim the stems of the sprouts and make a gash in stem end of each. Wash. Let stand 10 minutes in a bowl of salted water; examine for insects. Drain. Cook, in a covered saucepan containing the boiling water and salt, until pierceable; drain well. Turn into a heated dish. For the sauce: Blend the sugar, lemon juice and butter in a saucepan over low heat. Pour over the sprouts. Serve hot.

Beets in Sour Cream

Two cups raw beets, grated
Four tablespoons margarine
One-fourth teaspoon sugar
One-fourth teaspoon salt
Three tablespoons lemon juice
Cooking time: Twenty minutes
One-half cup dairy sour cream
Servings: Four

Cook the beets, margarine, sugar, salt and lemon juice in a tightly covered saucepan over very low heat until pierceable, shaking the pan occasionally. Add the sour cream. Serve hot.

French Fried Onions

Four large white onions
One cup milk
Standing time: Thirty minutes
One-half cup flour
Deep fat temperature: 375 degrees
Frying time: Four minutes (about)
One teaspoon salt
Servings: Four

Peel the onions; cut into slices (¼ in. thick). Separate into rings, placing them in a bowl. Pour the milk over them. Let stand. Remove the onions to a paper bag containing the flour. Shake until the rings are well coated. Fry in deep fat

until a golden brown. Drain upon absorbent paper. Keep hot in oven until all are fried. Sprinkle with salt and serve.

Sauteed Summer Squash or Zucchini

Wash and cut (without peeling) the Summer squash or zucchini into slices (¼ in. thick). Dust in seasoned flour. Pan-fry in a small amount of fat in a skillet until brown on all sides, about 10 minutes. Pour into a hot serving dish. Sprinkle with minced parsley or paprika.

Acorn Squash with Applesauce

Wash three acorn squash, dry, cut each crosswise into four slices. Discard seeds. place in a skillet. Add one-third cup water, one bay leaf, and four thin slices of onion; cover. Steam 20 minutes, or until tender. Uncover. Let the water evaporate. Brown the squash quickly on both sides in a little butter or margarine. Season with salt and pepper. Serve a tablespoon of applesauce upon each ring.

Baked Patty Pan Squash

Wash and cut into strips enough patty pan squash to make a full quart (4 cups). Place in a casserole (2 qts.). Mix one teaspoon salt, one-eighth teaspoon

pepper, two cups canned tomatoes and four tablespoons butter or margarine; pour over the squash. Sprinkle one-half cup grated Parmesan cheese over the squash. Cover. Bake in a moderately hot oven (375 degrees) until tender, about forty minutes. Serve immediately.

Baked Butternut Squash

Wash the butternut squash; cut into halves lengthwise. Discard seeds and membrane. Place upon a shallow baking pan. Season. Dot center with butter or margarine. Bake in a moderate oven (350 degrees) until tender, about fifty minutes. Last five minutes of baking put a tablespoon of orange marmalade in the center of each squash. Serve.

Whipped Hubbard or Cocozelle Squash

Wash, peel and cut into pieces (2 in.) enough hubbard or cocozelle squash to make a full quart (4 cups). Cook in a large amount of boiling salted water, covered for 25 minutes. Drain thoroughly. Mash or put through a potato ricer. Mix one teaspoon salt, one-eighth teaspoon pepper and one tablespoon each of butter, brown sugar, evaporated milk and sherry; add. Whip until creamy. Serve immediately.

Caraway Cabbage

One small head cabbage, cut into wedges
Two cups boiling water
One-half teaspoon salt
Cook: Ten minutes, about
Two tablespoons butter or margarine
One-third cup vinegar
One-half teaspoon caraway seeds
One teaspoon sugar or more
One-fourth teaspoon salt
One-eighth teaspoon pepper
Heat: Five minutes
One-half cup dairy sour cream
Servings: Four

Cook the cabbage in the boiling salted water in a covered saucepan until tender. Drain in a colander. Heat the butter, vinegar, caraway seeds, sugar, salt and pepper in the same saucepan until well blended and hot. Stir in the dairy sour cream. Pour over the drained cabbage wedges. Serve at once.

A FAVORITE RECIPE
Hot Slaw

One small head white cabbage, shredded
One cup water
Two teaspoons salt
One-eighth teaspoon pepper
Three tablespoons butter
Cooking time: Ten minutes
One tablespoon flour
Two tablespoons vinegar
Two tablespoons sweet or sour cream
Cooking time Until thickened
Serves: Four

Wash, shred and drain the cabbage. Place in a deep saucepan; add water, salt, pepper and butter. Cook until the cabbage is tender. Sprinkle with flour, mix. Add the vinegar and sour cream. Cook until thick, stirring constantly. Serve hot with pork chops.

MRS. JUNE CONGER
Mt. Crawford, Va.

A FAVORITE RECIPE
King Kohl

Four cups shredded cabbage
One and one-half cups cooked rice
Three tablespoons bacon fat
One-half cup minced onion
One-half cup minced green pepper
Cooking time: Five minutes
One teaspoon salt
One can (No. 2½) tomatoes
Oven temperature: 325 degrees
Baking time: One and one-fourth hours
Servings: Six

In a well greased casserole make layers of the cabbage and rice. Heat the fat in a skillet, cook the onion and green pepper. Spread over the top layer of rice. Season with salt. Pour the tomatoes over the top. Bake in a moderately slow oven. Serve from the casserole.

MRS. DOUGLAS SPINNING, *Bridgeport, Conn.*

Southern Sauced Cabbage

One firm head (1½ lbs.) cabbage
Four cups boiling water
Two teaspoons salt
Cook: Ten to fifteen minutes
One-fourth cup butter or margarine
One-fourth cup mild vinegar
Two tablespoons sugar
One-fourth teaspoon salt
One-eighth teaspoon pepper
Heat: One minute
Two eggs
One cup milk or thin cream
Cook: Six to eight minutes
Serves: Four to six

Wash and trim the cabbage but do not remove all the core. Cut into eight sections or wedges, leaving enough core to hold leaves intact. Place carefully, cut side up, in a wide saucepan; add boiling salted water to depth of two inches. Cover tightly. Cook until tender. While the cabbage cooks, prepare the sauce. Heat the butter, vinegar, sugar and seasoning in the upper half of a double boiler over direct heat one minute, stirring. Take from the heat. Beat the eggs slightly in a bowl; add the milk or cream. Slowly pour in the mixture, stirring; return to the pan, set over simmering water and cook, stirring until thickened. Correct the seasoning. Drain the cabbage well and serve with sauce.

Braised Cabbage and Celery

Two tablespoons butter or margarine
Four cups coarsely sliced cabbage
One cup sliced celery
One-half cup diced green pepper
Two tablespoons boiling water
One-half teaspoon sugar
Three-fourths teaspoon salt
One-eighth teaspoon pepper
Cook: Ten minutes, about
Serves: Four

Melt the butter or margarine in a large heavy skillet. Add the sliced cabbage, celery and green pepper. Pour on the boiling water and sprinkle with the sugar, salt and pepper. Stir to mix well. Cover tightly and cook just until the vegetables are tender. Don't overcook. Serve hot.

Spiced Carrots

Eight or more whole small carrots, scraped
One cup boiling water
One teaspoon salt
One teaspoon sugar
Two whole cloves
One bay leaf
Cook: Fifteen minutes
Two tablespoons butter or margarine
Two tablespoons lemon juice
One tablespoon finely chopped parsley
Serves: Four

Place the carrots in the boiling salted water, to which the sugar, cloves and bay leaf have been added. Cover tightly and cook until tender. Drain. Add the butter and lemon juice and toss lightly. Serve with a sprinkling of the finely chopped parsley.

Marinated Carrots

Eight medium-sized carrots
One-half teaspoon salt
Boiling water
Cook: Ten minutes, about
One-eighth teaspoon black pepper
One-fourth teaspoon oregano, crumbled
One-fourth teaspoon sugar
Two tablespoons olive or salad oil
One tablespoon vinegar
Marinate: Overnight
Serves: Four

Wash and scrape the carrots. Cut into half-inch slices. Place in a saucepan with salt and a half inch of boiling water. Cover and cook until tender. Drain. In a cup stir black pepper, oregano, sugar, olive oil and vinegar together. Pour over cooked carrots and marinate in the refrigerator overnight.

Carrot Celery Pepper Sauté

Two tablespoons salad oil
One cup thinly sliced scraped carrots
One cup thinly sliced celery
One large green pepper, diced
Sauté: Five minutes
Salt
Pepper
One-half teaspoon dill seed
Cook: Five to ten minutes
Serves: Four

Measure the salad oil into a large heavy skillet. Add the thinly sliced scraped carrots, sliced celery and green pepper cut into one inch squares. Stir to coat with oil and sauté five minutes. Sprinkle lightly with salt and pepper, add the dill seed. Cover and continue cooking over low heat for five to ten minutes or until the vegetables are tender.

Sautéed Carrots

Two bunches carrots (10 to 12 medium-sized)
One-fourth cup butter or bacon drippings
Salt and pepper
Simmer: Ten to fifteen minutes
Servings: Six

Wash, scrape and cut the carrots into thin lengthwise slices. Melt the butter or bacon drippings in a large heavy skillet. Add the carrot slices and sprinkle with salt and pepper. Cover lightly and simmer gently until tender. Stir up from the bottom of the pan once during the cooking time. If desired sprinkle with some finely chopped parsley when served.

Pepper Sauced Cauliflower

One medium-sized cauliflower
Boiling salted water
Cook: Ten to fifteen minutes
Three tablespoons wine vinegar
Two tablespoons finely chopped green pepper
Two tablespoons chopped pimiento
One-fourth teaspoon salt
Two tablespoons butter or margarine
Heating time: Five minutes
Serves: Four to six

Wash the cauliflower and separate into flowerets. Cook in the boiling salted water in a saucepan until tender crisp. Drain. In a small saucepan combine the vinegar, green pepper, pimiento, salt and butter and heat until the butter is melted. Serve sauce over the drained cauliflower.

Cauliflower Casserole Superb

One medium-sized cauliflower
Boiling salted water
Cook: Ten minutes, about
Two tablespoons butter or margarine
Two tablespoons flour
One-half teaspoon salt
One-eighth teaspoon pepper
One and one-half cups milk
Cook: Five minutes
Two hard-cooked eggs, chopped
Two tablespoons diced pimiento
One-half cup finely chopped green onions
One tablespoon butter or margarine
One-fourth cup soft bread crumbs
Two tablespoons grated cheese
Oven temperature: 375 degrees
Bake: Thirty minutes
Servings: Four, or more

Wash the cauliflower and separate into flowerets. Cook in boiling salted water until just tender. Remove from heat, drain and place flowerets in a greased casserole (1½ qts.). In a saucepan melt the two tablespoons of butter or margarine. Stir in the flour, salt and pepper and gradually blend in the milk, stirring smooth. Cook, stirring, until sauce is thickened and smooth. Add the chopped hard-cooked eggs, pimiento and chopped green onions (use tops as well). Mix well and pour over the cauliflower in the casserole. Melt the tablespoon of butter or margarine and stir in the soft bread crumbs. Scatter over cauliflower and top off with grated cheese. Bake in a moderately hot oven until nicely browned.

Crisp Crumbed Cauliflower

One medium-sized cauliflower
Boiling salted water
Cook: Twenty minutes, about
Two tablespoons butter or margarine
Two tablespoons flour
One-half teaspoon salt
One-sixteenth teaspoon nutmeg
One cup milk
Two tablespoons butter or margarine
One cup soft bread crumbs
One-half cup grated cheddar cheese
Oven temperature: 500 degrees
Bake: Five to ten minutes
Serves: Four

Wash and separate the cauliflower into flowerets. Cook in a small amount of boiling salted water until tender. Drain. Arrange pieces in a shallow baking dish or pie plate. In a saucepan melt two tablespoons of butter or margarine. Stir in the flour, salt and nutmeg. Gradually blend in the milk, stirring smooth. Cook, stirring constantly, until the sauce thickens. Spoon over the cooked cauliflower. In a saucepan melt the second measure of butter or margarine and stir in the soft bread crumbs. Scatter over the cauliflower. Sprinkle grated cheese over all. Place in the oven just long enough to lightly brown and heat through.

Celery Root

One bunch knob celery (three or four knobs)
Two to three cups boiling water
One teaspoon vinegar
One-half teaspoon salt
Cook: Ten to fifteen minutes
Two tablespoons butter or margarine
One tablespoon finely chopped parsley
Serves: Four

Trim the tops from the knob celery. Scrub the roots with a brush. Peel carefully; cut into small dice or thin slices. Drop the vegetable into a saucepan of boiling water, vinegar and salt. Cover. Bring to a boil, lower heat and cook until tender but not broken. Drain. Stir in the butter or margarine and sprinkle with the chopped parsley. Serve at once. Knob celery also may be mashed and seasoned with butter and a little milk and it may be creamed.

Sautéed Celery

One-fourth cup butter or margarine
Four cups sliced celery
One teaspoon salt
One-eighth teaspoon pepper
Sauté: Fifteen minutes, about
Two tablespoons thinly sliced green onion
Sauté: Five minutes
Two tablespoons butter or margarine
One clove garlic, crushed
Sauté: Five minutes
One-third cup slivered, blanched almonds
Browning time: Five minutes
Two tablespoons dry white wine
Servings: Four or five

In a large heavy skillet melt the fourth cup of butter or margarine. Add the sliced celery and sprinkle with salt and pepper. Cover tightly and cook until celery is almost tender. Add thinly sliced green onion and cook five minutes more. In a small saucepan melt the two tablespoons of butter or margarine. Add crushed garlic and sauté briefly. Add the slivered almonds and cook just until lightly browned. Stir in the dry white wine and spoon over servings of the cooked celery.

Celery au Gratin

Three cups sliced celery
One teaspoon salt
Boiling water
Cook: Twenty minutes, about
One-fourth cup butter or margarine
Three tablespoons flour
Three-fourths teaspoon salt
One-eighth teaspoon pepper
One and one-half cups milk
Cook: Five minutes, about
One cup diced (½ in.) cheddar cheese
One tablespoon butter or margarine
Two tablespoons fine dry bread crumbs
Oven temperature: 350 degrees
Bake: Twenty minutes
Serves: Four to six

Place the sliced celery in a saucepan, sprinkle with salt and cover with boiling water. Cover and cook until tender. Drain. In a saucepan melt the butter or margarine, stir in the flour, salt and pepper and gradually blend in the milk. Cook, stirring constantly until sauce thickens. Remove from heat and add the drained, cooked celery and diced cheddar. Transfer to a shallow baking dish or large pie plate (10 in.). Melt the tablespoon of butter or margarine and stir in the fine dry bread crumbs. Scatter over the celery mixture and bake in a moderate oven until piping hot and lightly browned.

Corn and Pepper Fritters

Two eggs
One-half cup milk
Two cups cooked corn kernels (4 ears)
One tablespoon sugar
One teaspoon salt
One-half cup chopped green pepper
One and one-half cups sifted flour
One and one-half teaspoons baking powder
Two teaspoons oil for frying
Frying time: Five minutes, about
Servings: Six

In a bowl beat the eggs, add the milk, corn, sugar, salt and green pepper. Mix well. Sift together the flour and baking powder and blend into the corn mixture. Beat well. Heat the oil for frying in a large heavy skillet and add the corn mixture by tablespoonfuls. Cook over moderate heat until puffed and browned on both sides. Serve hot. Good with sliced tomatoes or chili sauce.

Crisp Capped Corn

One-fourth cup butter or margarine
One cup packaged seasoned stuffing
Sauté: Until crisp and browned
One can (No. 303) whole kernel corn
Heat: Until piping hot
Finely chopped parsley (optional)
Serves: Four

Melt the butter or margarine in a heavy skillet, add the packaged seasoned stuffing and sauté until crisp and browned. Heat the canned whole kernel corn until piping hot, drain and serve with the crisp crumbs spooned on top and a sprinkling of finely chopped parsley.

Fresh Corn in Cream

Two and one-half cups fresh corn cut from cobs (five or six ears corn)
One-half teaspoon sugar
Three-fourths teaspoon salt
One-sixteenth teaspoon pepper
One-third cup light cream
Cook: Five minutes
Serves: Four or five

Place the cut corn in a saucepan with the sugar, salt and pepper. Pour on the light cream and cover tightly. Place over high heat until steaming starts. Lower heat and cook five minutes over low heat. Serve at once.

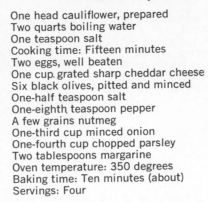

Cauliflower Supreme

One head cauliflower, prepared
Two quarts boiling water
One teaspoon salt
Cooking time: Fifteen minutes
Two eggs, well beaten
One cup grated sharp cheddar cheese
Six black olives, pitted and minced
One-half teaspoon salt
One-eighth teaspoon pepper
A few grains nutmeg
One-third cup minced onion
One-fourth cup chopped parsley
Two tablespoons margarine
Oven temperature: 350 degrees
Baking time: Ten minutes (about)
Servings: Four

Cook the whole cauliflower in boiling salted water in a saucepan until nearly tender. Drain. Set in a shallow baking dish. Pour the combined eggs, cheese, olives, seasonings, onion and parsley over the cauliflower; dot with margarine. Bake in a moderate oven until the sauce is blended with the cauliflower. Place the cauliflower in the center of a hot platter, arranging glazed yams, green beans and grilled tomatoes around it. Serve immediately.

Baked Spinach Ring

Four cups chopped cooked spinach
One-half cup dairy sour cream
One can (10½ oz.) condensed celery soup
One teaspoon onion juice
One teaspoon lemon rind
One teaspoon salt
One-eighth teaspoon nutmeg
Two eggs, well beaten
Oven temperature: 375 degrees
Baking time: Forty-five minutes
Two cups creamed chicken, fish or eggs
Servings: Four, or more

Mix the ingredients in the order given. Pour into a greased ring mold (9 in.). Set the mold in a pan of hot water. Bake in a moderately hot oven until firm. Unmold on a platter. Fill the center with the hot creamed chicken, fish or eggs. Serve with a tossed green salad and wholewheat rolls.

Casserole Nicoise

Six medium-sized potatoes
One teaspoon salt
One-fourth teaspoon pepper
Four tablespoons melted butter or margarine
One can (No. 2½) whole tomatoes
One and one-half cups grated carrots
One and one-half cups chopped green pepper
One-third cup minced onion
One clove garlic, puréed or minced
Three tablespoons minced parsley
One and one-half teaspoons salt
One-fourth teaspoon pepper
One-half teaspoon basil
Four tablespoons olive oil
Oven temperature: 375 degrees
Bake: One and one-half to two hours
Serves: Six, or more

Slice the potatoes paper-thin. Season with salt and pepper. Place in a buttered deep casserole (3 qts.). Pour the melted butter over the potatoes. Combine the tomatoes, carrots, green pepper, onion, garlic, parsley, salt, pepper, basil and olive oil. Spoon over the potatoes. Cover and bake until the potatoes are tender. Uncover last 15 minutes of cooking.

Baked Stuffed Avocados

Two cups diced cooked chicken or turkey
One-fourth cup California sherry
Heat: Until very hot
One and one-half cups sliced celery
One-half cup slivered toasted almonds
One pimiento, chopped
One-half cup real mayonnaise
Two tablespoons lemon juice
One tablespoon grated lemon rind
One teaspoon minced onion
One teaspoon salt
One-fourth teaspoon pepper
Three avocados, peeled, cut lengthwise
Oven temperature: 450 degrees
Baking time: Fifteen minutes (about)
Serves: Six

In a saucepan heat the chicken in the sherry. Add celery, almonds, pimiento and the combined mayonnaise, lemon juice, rind, onion, salt and pepper, blending thoroughly. Fill the avocados. Place in pan, bake in very hot oven until lightly browned. Serve immediately.

A FAVORITE RECIPE

Spinach-Mushrooms Casserole

Two tablespoons butter
One bunch scallions, cut into small pieces
One pound fresh mushrooms, washed, sliced thin
Sautéing time: Twenty minutes, about
Two pounds spinach, washed, chopped, cooked
One teaspoon salt
One-fourth teaspoon pepper

White Sauce

Two tablespoons butter
Two tablespoons flour
One-fourth teaspoon salt
One-eighth teaspoon pepper
One cup milk
Cooking time: Ten minutes
One-half cup buttered bread crumbs
Oven temperature: 350 degrees
Baking time: Twenty minutes
Servings: Six

In a skillet, heat the butter; add scallions and mushrooms; cook, stirring frequently. Cook the spinach in a small amount of boiling salted water; drain thoroughly; chop; season with salt and pepper. In a well buttered casserole, place a layer of the spinach, then a layer of scallions and mushrooms. Repeat the layer. Make a white sauce by blending the butter and flour in the top of a double boiler; add seasonings and milk, cook stirring until thick and smooth. Pour over the spinach mixture. Top with the buttered crumbs. Bake in a moderate oven until the crumbs are lightly browned. Serve from the casserole.

MRS. MARIA SCANDIFFIO, *New York, N.Y.*

Corn Custard

One egg, beaten slightly
One teaspoon salt
One-eighth teaspoon pepper
One-fourth teaspoon paprika
One-fourth teaspoon dry mustard
One tablespoon flour
One tablespoon butter, melted
One cup milk
One can (12 oz.) whole kernel corn
One pimiento, slivered
One-half green pepper, slivered
Oven temperature: 350 degrees
Baking time: Forty minutes
Servings: Four

Combine the ingredients in the order given. Pour into four greased custard cups (8 oz.); set in a pan of hot water. Bake in a moderate oven until nearly firm in the center. Serve hot.

Pineapple Rarebit

One pound cheddar cheese, shredded
One-half teaspoon salt
One-half teaspoon dry mustard
One-sixteenth teaspoon cayenne
One teaspoon paprika
One teaspoon Worcestershire sauce
One-fourth cup warm milk or beer
Cooking time: Five to eight minutes
Six slices canned pineapple
Four slices hot buttered toast
Servings: Four

Cook the cheese and seasonings in the top of the boiler over boiling water, stirring until melting begins. Add the milk or beer, stirring constantly. The serving plates should be very hot. Place a slice of pineapple on a piece of toast on each plate. Pour the rarebit over the pineapple. Garnish with stuffed olives.

Green Beans Amandine

One pound fresh green beans
Boiling salted water
Cook: Twenty minutes, or more
Three tablespoons butter
Three tablespoons slivered blanched
    almonds
Two tablespoons lemon juice
Serves: Four to six

Trim the ends from the beans and cut into short lengths or French. Cook in boiling salted water until just tender. In a small skillet melt the butter, add the slivered almonds and sauté until just browned. Add the lemon juice. Drain the cooked beans and serve with the butter sauce spooned over the top.

Lemon Sauced Green Beans

One package (10 oz.) frozen Frenched
    green beans
Boiling salted water
Cook: Until tender
One package (3 oz.) cream cheese
One egg yolk
One tablespoon lemon juice
Heat: Until blended and smooth
Paprika
Serves: Three or four

Cook the frozen Frenched green beans in boiling salted water according to package directions until tender. In a small saucepan stir softened cream cheese, egg yolk and lemon juice together. Heat until blended and smooth, stirring constantly. Serve over hot, drained cooked beans. Sprinkle a little paprika over sauce.

Schnitzel Beans

Four slices bacon, diced
Fry: Five minutes
One medium-sized onion, sliced
Brown: Five minutes
One package (10 oz.) frozen green beans
One cup canned tomatoes
One teaspoon salt
One-fourth teaspoon pepper
Simmer: Fifteen minutes, or more
Servings: Four

Fry the bacon crisp in a heavy skillet, starting with a cold pan. Add sliced onion and brown lightly. Add the frozen green beans, canned tomatoes broken with a spoon, salt and pepper. Cover tightly and simmer until the beans are tender.

A FAVORITE RECIPE
Green Beans — Tomato Sauce

One-fourth pound salt pork, cut into
    pieces (¼ in.)
One onion, diced
Cooking time: Fifteen minutes, or longer
Two cans (8 oz. each) tomato sauce
Two pounds fresh snap beans, washed,
    broken into pieces (1 in.)
Water to cover
One teaspoon salt
One-fourth teaspoon pepper
One-half teaspoon garlic salt
Cooking time: Twenty minutes
Servings: Eight

In a heavy kettle cook the salt pork and onion, stirring frequently until the pork is brown and the onion well done. Add the tomato sauce, stirring well. Add the beans and enough water to cover the beans. Season with salt, pepper and garlic salt. Bring to a boil; reduce the heat and simmer until the beans are tender. Serve with roast beef or pork.

MRS. SYLVIA TRIPP, *Pawtucket, R.I.*

A FAVORITE RECIPE
Stuffed Green Peppers

Six tablespoons olive oil
One can (10½ oz.) ripe olives, chopped
One can (4 oz.) flat anchovies, chopped
One large or two small tomatoes, peeled,
    chopped
Six slices bread cubed (¼ in.)
Four sprigs parsley
Four large green peppers
Frying time: Until peppers are soft
Servings: Four

Heat two tablespoons of olive oil in a skillet (9 in.). Add the olives, anchovies, tomatoes, cubed bread and parsley. (Add more oil if needed.) Cook, stirring frequently. Cool. Clean the peppers; cut a slice (¼ in.) from the stem end. Remove seeds and membrane. Stuff the pepper with the anchovy mixture. Heat the remaining oil in the skillet; fry the peppers slowly until soft, turning often. Serve hot.

MRS. RITA CARNEVALE, *East Paterson, N.J.*

Quickly Braised Green Peppers

Six medium-sized green peppers
Four tablespoons butter or margarine
Cook: Ten minutes, about
One and one-half teaspoons salt
One-eighth teaspoon pepper
One tablespoon boiling water
Cook: Five minutes
Servings: Five or six

Wash the green peppers, split and remove the seeds and membrane. Cut into half inch strips. In a large heavy skillet heat the butter or margarine. Add the green pepper strips and cook, stirring until they begin to wilt. Add the salt, pepper and boiling water, cover and continue cooking over low heat for about five minutes. Serve at once.

Oven Kasha

One cup roasted buckwheat groats
One egg, beaten
One-half teaspoon salt
One-half teaspoon Ac'cent or Zest
Heating time: Five minutes
One cup boiling water
One tablespoon salad oil
Oven temperature: 350 degrees
Baking time: Twenty minutes
Servings: Four

In a heavy iron skillet combine the groats with the beaten egg, salt and Ac'cent or Zest. Heat briefly, stirring until every grain is separate and dry. Add the boiling water and salad oil. Cover and place in a moderate oven to finish cooking.

Top Stove Kasha

One cup roasted buckwheat groats
Heating time: Five minutes
Two chicken or beef bouillon cubes
Two cups boiling water
One-half teaspoon Ac'cent or Zest
Simmering time: Fifteen minutes
Two tablespoons butter or margarine
Standing time: Five minutes
Servings: Four

In a heavy skillet heat the buckwheat groats briefly, stirring the while. In a bowl dissolve the bouillon cubes in the boiling water and pour into the heated groats. Add the Ac'cent or Zest, cover and simmer over very low heat for fifteen minutes. Stir in the butter or margarine; cover and let stand for five minutes before serving.

Skillet Kasha with Onion

Three tablespoons butter or margarine
One cup chopped onion
Sauté: Five to ten minutes
One egg
One cup buckwheat groats
One and one-half teaspoons salt
Three cups boiling water
Simmer: Fifteen minutes, about
Serves: Four to six

In a large heavy skillet melt the butter or margarine. Add the chopped onion and sauté until golden. In a bowl beat the egg. Stir in the buckwheat groats and salt, mixing well. Add to the sautéed onion with the boiling water, stirring smooth. Cover tightly and simmer until all moisture is absorbed by the groats. Serve at once. If desired the cooked groats may be transferred to a shallow baking dish and lightly browned in the oven before serving.

Baked Limas with Tomato

One pound dry lima beans
Water to cover
Standing time: Overnight
Simmer: One hour, or more
One can (10½ oz.) condensed tomato soup
One-fourth cup salad oil
One cup finely chopped onion
One tablespoon Worcestershire sauce
One-half cup finely chopped celery
One tablespoon salt
One-eighth teaspoon pepper
Oven temperature: 350 degrees
Bake: One hour and fifteen minutes
Servings: Six to eight

Place the dried lima beans in a large bowl, cover with water and let soak overnight. Transfer beans and liquid to a large saucepan and cook gently for about one hour or until beans are tender. Drain the beans reserving one cup of the liquid. In a bowl combine the condensed tomato soup with the one cup of bean liquid, salad oil, chopped onion, Worcestershire sauce, chopped celery, salt and pepper. Add the beans and mix well. Transfer to a casserole or bean pot (2 qts.) and bake in a moderate oven for one hour and fifteen minutes. Good with ham, pork or beef.

Limas and Celery au Gratin

One package frozen lima beans
Two cups sliced celery
Cook: Fifteen to twenty minutes
Four tablespoons butter or margarine
Four tablespoons flour
One teaspoon salt
One-eighth teaspoon pepper
Two and one-half cups milk
One cup grated cheddar cheese
One tablespoon melted butter or margarine
One-half cup soft bread crumbs
Oven temperature: 350 degrees
Bake: Twenty minutes
Servings: Six

Cook the frozen limas and sliced celery in boiling, salted water until tender, fifteen to twenty minutes. Drain well. In a saucepan melt the butter, stir in the flour, salt and pepper; gradually blend in the milk, stirring smooth. Cook, stirring until the sauce thickens. Add the grated cheddar. Place vegetables in a shallow baking dish (1½ qts.), and cover with cheese sauce. Stir the tablespoon of melted butter into the soft bread crumbs and scatter over the sauced vegetables. Bake in a moderate oven until crumbs are lightly browned.

Limas a la Russe

Two cups cooked large dry limas or
Two cans (No. 303) cooked large dry limas
One cup cottage cheese
One cup dairy sour cream
One small onion, chopped
One-eighth teaspoon garlic salt
One teaspoon Worcestershire sauce
One-half teaspoon salt
One teaspoon paprika
One-fourth cup grated cheddar cheese
Oven temperature: 350 degrees
Bake: Forty minutes
Serves: Four to six

Drain the limas well. Combine with the cottage cheese, dairy sour cream, chopped onion, garlic salt, Worcestershire sauce, salt and paprika. Mix thoroughly together and pour into a casserole (2 qts.). Scatter the grated cheddar over the top. Bake in a moderate oven for forty minutes. Serve hot.

Mexican Corn and Limas

Two tablespoons butter or margarine
One small onion, finely chopped
One small green pepper, chopped
Sauté: Five minutes, about
One can (No. 303) whole kernel corn
One can (No. 303) cooked large dry limas
Two chopped canned pimientos
Salt and pepper
Simmer: Ten minutes
Servings: Six

Melt the butter or margarine in a large skillet or saucepan. Add the finely chopped onion and chopped green pepper and sauté five minutes, or until tender. Stir in the drained whole kernel corn, cooked large dry limas and chopped pimientos. Season to taste with salt and pepper. Simmer ten minutes to heat through thoroughly.

Leeks au Gratin

Two bunches leeks (10 to 12)
One teaspoon salt
Boiling water
Cook: Twenty minutes, about
One-fourth cup butter or margarine
One-fourth cup flour
One-half teaspoon salt
One-eighth teaspoon pepper
Two cups milk
Cook: Five minutes, about
One cup grated cheddar cheese
One tablespoon butter or margarine
Two tablespoons fine dry bread crumbs
Oven temperature: 350 degrees
Bake: Twenty minutes
Serves: Four

Trim the roots from the leeks and wash. Cut off all but an inch of green tops and discard. Place trimmed leeks in a skillet. Sprinkle with teaspoon of salt and cover with boiling water. Cover and cook for about 20 minutes or until tender. Drain and arrange in a shallow baking dish or large pie plate (10 in.).

In a saucepan melt the fourth cup of butter or margarine, blend in the flour, salt and pepper. Gradually add the milk, stirring smooth. Cook, stirring constantly until sauce thickens. Add the grated cheddar cheese. Pour over the leeks. Melt the tablespoon of butter or margarine and stir in the fine dry bread crumbs. Scatter over the sauced leeks and bake in a moderate oven until piping hot and lightly browned.

Baked Mushrooms De Luxe

One-third cup butter or margarine
One tablespoon finely chopped parsley
One tablespoon grated onion
One tablespoon prepared mustard
One teaspoon salt
One-eighth teaspoon cayenne pepper
One-eighth teaspoon nutmeg
One and one-half tablespoons flour
One pound mushrooms
One cup heavy cream
Oven temperature: 375 degrees
Bake: Forty-five minutes
Servings: Six

In a bowl cream the butter or margarine until fluffy. Blend in the chopped parsley and onion, mustard, salt, pepper, nutmeg and flour. Wash, dry and trim mushrooms if necessary. Slice. Arrange layers of sliced mushrooms in a casserole (2 qts.) dotting each with the creamed mixture. Pour heavy cream over top and bake in a moderately hot oven for forty-five minutes.

A FAVORITE RECIPE
Mushrooms a la King

Three tablespoons butter, heated
One and one-half cup mushrooms, sliced
Cook: Five minutes
Three tablespoons flour
Two cups milk
Cooking time: Until thickened
Three hard-cooked eggs, chopped
One cup diced cooked celery
One-fourth cup stuffed olives, sliced
One-fourth cup grated American cheese
One tablespoon sherry wine
Cooking time: Until the cheese melts
Servings: Four

Heat the butter in a heavy saucepan. Add the mushrooms, cook, stirring several times. Stir in the flour until well blended. Add the milk slowly, cook until thick. Stir in the eggs, celery, olives, cheese and sherry. Heat thoroughly. Serve on toast or in cups made by cutting bread into four or five-inch slices. Scoop out the centers leaving a bottom and wall ¼-inch deep. Brush with melted butter and toast to a golden brown. Fill with the cooked mushrooms.

MRS. E. C. EISEMAN, *Brooklyn, N.Y.*

A FAVORITE RECIPE
Stuffed Mushrooms

One pound large mushrooms
Three tablespoons olive oil
One small onion, minced
One slice bacon, chopped
Chopped stems from mushrooms
Cooking time: Ten minutes
One-half cup bread crumbs
Two tablespoons grated Parmesan cheese
One tablespoon chopped parsley
One-half teaspoon salt
One-eighth teaspoon pepper
Cooking time: Three minutes
One-half cup plum tomatoes
One egg, beaten lightly
Two tablespoons olive oil
Oven temperature: 350 degrees
Baking time: Thirty minutes, about
Servings: Four

Wash the mushrooms; remove stems, chop fine; set aside. Heat the oil in a skillet; add the onion; bacon and chopped stems of mushrooms. Cook, stirring several times. Stir in the crumbs, cheese, parsley, salt and pepper. Cook. Stir in the tomatoes, mashing them with the egg; cook, stirring until well blended. Fill the mushroom caps with the mixture. Brush each cap with oil. Place on a baking sheet. Bake in a moderate oven. Serve hot.

MRS. F. TANTILLO, *Bronx, N.Y.*

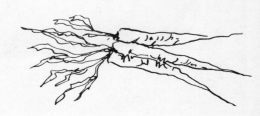

Tomato Falisse

Three large tomatoes
Two hard-cooked eggs, chopped
Six ripe olives, chopped
One tablespoon anchovy paste
Six cold poached eggs
Salad greens
One cup real mayonnaise
One-third cup sour cream
One-half tablespoon horseradish sauce
Serves: Six

Cut the tomatoes into halves crosswise. Scoop out seeds and soft pulp. Invert; drain; chill. Spread in the bottom of each tomato a little of the combined hard-cooked eggs, olives and paste. Place a cold poached egg on top. Serve on salad greens with the combined mayonnaise, sour cream and horseradish sauce.

Corn Custard With Fried Tomatoes

One teaspoon minced onion
Two tablespoons flour
One teaspoon salt
Few grains cayenne
Two cups raw scraped corn
Four eggs, slightly beaten
Two cups milk, scalded
Pimiento strips
Oven temperature: 325 degrees
Baking time: Forty minutes (about)
Two large tomatoes, peeled, halved
One tablespoon flour
One-eighth teaspoon curry powder
One-fourth teaspoon salt
Two tablespoons butter or margarine
Cooking time: Four minutes
Two cups hot, cooked lima beans
Serves: Four

Mix the onion, flour, salt and cayenne with the corn. Add the slightly beaten eggs and scalded milk. Place pimiento strips in the bottom of a greased ring mold (9 in.). With a slotted spoon, arrange corn over the strips. Pour egg mixture over corn. Bake in a moderately slow oven until custard is set. Remove to a rack. Meanwhile, cut the peeled tomatoes in half crosswise. Dust both sides with the combined flour and seasonings. Fry them quickly in the butter over high heat in a skillet for about two minutes on each side. Unmold the custard ring on a platter; fill center with hot lima beans and set fried tomatoes around corn custard. Garnish with crisp bacon strips or curls.

Baked Stuffed Tomatoes

Six ripe tomatoes
Four hard-cooked eggs, chopped
Four scallions or one small sized onion, chopped
Two cans (3¼ ozs. each) Norway sardines
One-half teaspoon dry mustard
Three-fourths teaspoon salt
One-eighth teaspoon pepper
One tablespoon butter, melted
One-half cup soft bread crumbs
Oven temperature: 325 degrees
Baking time: Forty minutes
Servings: Four, or more

Cut off the stem end of each tomato. Scoop out the pulp, leaving a shell. Turn upside down. Dice one-half cup of the pulp; save the remainder for later use in a sauce. Combine the pulp with the eggs, scallions, sardines and seasonings. Fill the tomatoes with the mixture; top with buttered crumbs. Place in a shallow oven-proof dish. Bake in a moderately slow oven until the tomatoes are soft. Remove. Garnish each tomato with a sardine; serve.

A FAVORITE RECIPE
Stuffed Baked Tomatoes

Two tablespoons butter
One medium-sized onion, grated
One tablespoon minced green pepper
Cooking time: Five minutes
Two cups soft bread crumbs
One-half teaspoon salt
One egg, well beaten
One teaspoon minced parsley
Six large tomatoes
Three tablespoons grated sharp cheese
Paprika for garnish
Oven temperature: 350 degrees
Baking time: Twenty minutes, about
Servings: Six

Heat the butter in a skillet, sauté the onion and green pepper until tender. Add the bread crumbs, salt, egg and parsley. Cool. Wash and cut a slice from stem end of tomatoes. Remove pulp leaving ¼ in. rim. (Use the tomato pulp for another dish.) Fill the tomatoes with the cooked mixture. Sprinkle the cheese over the top and garnish with paprika. Place in a well greased shallow pan. Bake in a moderate oven until the cheese is melted and tomatoes are tender. Serve hot.

MRS. PHYLLIS RAFFO, *Union City, N.J.*

Rice with Red Beans

One-fourth cup butter or margarine
One medium-sized onion, chopped
Sautéing time: Five to eight minutes
One and one-third cups quick cooking
   rice (one 5 oz. package)
One teaspoon salt
One-eighth teaspoon pepper
One can (1 lb.) red kidney beans
Tomato juice to make two cups
Cooking time: Three minutes
Standing time: Ten minutes
One-half cup grated cheddar cheese
Servings: Four to six

In a heavy skillet, melt the butter or margarine. Add the chopped onion and sauté until lightly browned. Add the quick cooking rice, salt, pepper and juice from the canned red kidney beans plus tomato juice to yield two cups of liquid. Bring to a boil over high heat, fluffing the rice a few times with a fork. Cover tightly and simmer gently for three minutes. Remove from the heat and let stand for ten minutes. Add the red kidney beans and heat briefly. Serve with the grated cheddar sprinkled over the top.

Squash Crisp

Two packages (12 oz. each) frozen
   cooked squash
Heat: Until defrosted
One tablespoon butter or margarine
Two tablespoons flour
One beaten egg
One tablespoon prepared mustard
One tablespoon brown sugar
One teaspoon salt
One-eighth teaspoon pepper
Two tablespoons butter or margarine
One cup corn flakes
One teaspoon brown sugar
Oven temperature: 350 degrees
Bake: Thirty minutes
Serves: Six

Place the frozen squash in a double boiler and heat over water until defrosted. Stir in the tablespoon of butter or margarine until melted, add the flour, beaten egg, prepared mustard, brown sugar, salt and pepper. Mix thoroughly and transfer to a greased shallow baking dish (8 x 8 x 2 in.) or large pie plate. Melt the two tablespoons of butter or margarine in a saucepan and stir in the corn flakes that have been crushed to half their original volume. Add the brown sugar and mix well. Scatter over the squash mixture and bake in a moderate oven for thirty minutes or until piping hot.

Baked Stuffed Mushrooms

Sixteen large mushrooms
Four tablespoons butter or margarine
Four tablespoons fine bread crumbs
One-fourth cup chopped cooked ham or
   tongue
Two tablespoons minced parsley
Two tablespoons minced onion
Two teaspoons grated Parmesan cheese
One-half teaspoon salt
Few grains cayenne
Cooking time: Ten minutes
One cup white wine or chicken stock
Oven temperature: 400 degrees
Baking time: Twenty minutes
Toast points
Serves: Four, or more

Rinse the mushrooms in cold water, then dry. Remove the stems and chop very fine. In a skillet melt the butter; add the minced stems, bread crumbs, ham, parsley, onion, Parmesan cheese, salt and cayenne. Cook 10 minutes. Blend in one-fourth cup of the wine. Pack the filling into the mushroom caps. Sandwich two filled mushrooms together. Place in a shallow baking dish. Pour the remaining wine around the mushrooms. Bake in a quick oven for 20 minutes. Remove. Place on a platter with toast points. Serve immediately.

Hollandaise á la Blender

Three egg yolks
Two tablespoons lemon juice
One-fourth teaspoon salt
Pinch of cayenne
One-half cup butter
Yield: Three-fourths cup

Place the egg yolks in the blender container with the lemon juice, salt and cayenne. Top with cover and flick switch on and off the high speed to blend. In a saucepan melt the butter until bubbling hot but not brown. Turn the blender on low speed, uncover and add butter gradually in a fine stream. When thoroughly blended together serve with hot cooked vegetables.

Tomato Crunch Casserole

Two large tomatoes
One medium sized onion, thinly sliced
One-fourth pound cheddar cheese, thinly
   sliced
One cup corn flakes
Oven temperature: 350 degrees
Baking time: Thirty minutes
Servings: Four

Slice the tomatoes about one-half inch thick. Arrange half the slices in the bottom of a greased baking dish (1½ qts.). Top with half the onion slices, half the cheese and half the corn flakes. Repeat the four layers. Bake in a moderate oven for thirty minutes.

A FAVORITE RECIPE
Stuffed Onions

Six medium-sized Bermuda onions, peeled
Water to cover
Cooking time: Until almost tender
Three tablespoons chopped onion
    (removed from the centers)
One-half cup chopped, cooked ham
One-fourth cup soft bread crumbs
One-half teaspoon salt
One-eighth teaspoon pepper
One-fourth cup fine dry bread crumbs
One tablespoon, or more, melted butter
One-half cup milk
Oven temperature: 350 degrees
Baking time: Thirty minutes
Servings: Six

Wash, peel and remove a slice (¼ in.) from top of onions. Place in a large saucepan; cover with water; cook until nearly tender. Drain and remove the center from the onions leaving a shell of four rings. For the filling: Combine the chopped onion, ham, soft crumbs and seasonings. Fill the onions with the mixture; cover the top of each onion with the dry crumbs, top with butter. Pour the milk into onions. Place the stuffed onions in a baking dish. Bake in a moderate oven, baking until the onions are tender.

MRS. SALLY FOGLESONG, *Roseville, Ohio*

Creamed Onions

One and one-half pounds small white
    onions, peeled
Two quarts boiling water
Two teaspoons salt
Cook: Twenty minutes, or more
Three tablespoons butter or margarine
Three tablespoons flour
Three-fourths teaspoon salt
One-eighth teaspoon pepper
One and one-half cups milk
Cook: Five to eight minutes
One-fourth teaspoon paprika
Serves: Four to six

Cook the onions in the boiling salted water until tender at the center, drain. In the upper half of a double boiler melt the butter or margarine. Blend in the flour, salt and pepper and gradually add the milk, stirring smooth. Cook over moderate heat, stirring constantly, until the sauce thickens. Add the cooked onions and paprika and place pan over hot water to keep hot.

French Fried Onion Rings

Three or four Spanish type onions peeled,
    thinly sliced
One-half cup milk
One teaspoon salt
One-sixteenth teaspoon pepper
One-half cup flour
Shortening for deep fat frying
Frying temperature: 360-375 degrees
Frying time: One to three minutes
Servings: Six to eight

Separate the onion slices into rings. Dip, a few at a time, into the milk that has been seasoned with salt and pepper; then into the flour. Place rings apart from each other on waxed paper. To fry: Heat shortening in a deep fat fryer or saucepan (2 qts.) to 360-375 degrees. Three inches of fat in the saucepan is sufficient. Fry onion rings a few at a time until a golden brown. Remove from fat and drain on absorbent paper. Transfer to tray in oven (250 degrees) to keep hot while completing the frying.

Crumbed Onions

Two cups (one pound) small white onions
One quart boiling water
One teaspoon salt
Boiling time: Fifteen minutes
Two tablespoons butter or margarine
Three tablespoons stale bread crumbs
Browning time: One to two minutes
One tablespoon minced parsley
Servings: Four

Select small onions of uniform size so they will cook in the same length of time. Peel under water, or pour boiling water over the onions and rinse in cold water before peeling. Cook in the boiling salted water in an open saucepan until tender. Drain in a colander. Place in a heated vegetable dish. Melt the butter or margarine in a small pan over low heat; add the crumbs and brown lightly, stirring the while. Stir in the chopped parsley and scatter over the onions. Serve at once.

Carrots and Peas German Style

Eight medium-sized carrots
One tablespoon butter or margarine
One tablespoon hot water
One-half teaspoon sugar
One-fourth teaspoon salt
Cook: Ten to fifteen minutes
One cup shelled green peas (one-half
    frozen package)
Cook: Five minutes
One tablespoon flour
One-half cup chicken bouillon (made from
    bouillon cube and boiling water)
Cook: Until thickened
Dash of black pepper
One teaspoon chopped parsley
Serves: Four

Wash and scrape the carrots. Cut into julienne strips about two inches long. Place in a shallow saucepan or skillet with the butter, hot water, sugar and salt. Cover tightly and cook ten to fifteen minutes, until carrots are almost tender. Add the shelled fresh or frozen green peas and continue cooking until both vegetables are tender, about five minutes more. Measure the flour into a small saucepan, gradually stir in the chicken bouillon or broth. Cook briefly, stirring constantly, until thickened. Add black pepper and chopped parsley. Spoon over the cooked vegetables when served.

A FAVORITE RECIPE
Peas Creole Style

One can (No. 2) peas
One cup minced celery
One-half, or more, minced green pepper
One-fourth cup minced onion
One teaspoon salt
One-fourth teaspoon pepper
One-sixteenth teaspoon cayenne
Three hard-cooked eggs
One can (10½ oz.) condensed tomato
    soup
One-half cup grated cheese
Oven temperature: 350 degrees
Baking time: One hour
Servings: Four

In a deep heavy saucepan, mix the peas, celery, green pepper and onion. Season with salt, pepper and cayenne. Pour the vegetable mixture alternately with the sliced eggs into a well-greased casserole. Pour the soup over the top. Sprinkle with cheese. Bake in a moderate oven. Serve hot from the casserole.

MRS. W. GOLDBECK, *New York, N.Y.*

A FAVORITE RECIPE
Soufflé of Peas

One can peas (10 oz.)
One-half teaspoon salt
One-eighth teaspoon pepper
Cooking time: Five minutes
Three tablespoons melted butter
Three egg yolks, beaten with
Two cups milk
One-half teaspoon salt
One-sixteenth teaspoon pepper
Three egg whites, beaten stiff
Oven temperature: 350 degrees
Baking time: Twenty minutes
Servings: Four

In a saucepan cook the peas (frozen or canned,) season with salt and pepper. Drain; press through a coarse sieve and add the melted butter. Beat the egg yolks with the milk; mix with the pea mixture. Add salt and pepper to taste. Fold in the stiffly beaten egg whites. Turn into a well-greased baking dish; bake covered for 20 minutes. Uncover and let top brown (optional). Serve hot.

MRS. E. MAZEROLAS, *Kingston, N.Y.*

Savory Peas

Four tablespoons butter or margarine
One cup sliced green onions
Sauté: Five minutes, about
Three pounds fresh peas (3 cups shelled)
One teaspoon sugar
One-half teaspoon powdered savory
One-half teaspoon dried basil
Two tablespoons chopped parsley
One and one-half teaspoons salt
One-fourth teaspoon pepper
Three-fourths cup water
Simmer: Ten to fifteen minutes
Serves: Six

Melt the butter or margarine in a large heavy skillet or saucepan. Add the sliced green onions and sauté until soft. Add the shelled peas, sugar, savory, basil, parsley, salt, pepper and water. Cover and cook over low heat until peas are tender.

Peas and Celery au Gratin

One pound fresh peas
One and one-fourth cups sliced celery
Boiling salted water
Cook: Fifteen minutes, about
Two tablespoons butter or margarine
Two tablespoons flour
One-fourth teaspoon dry mustard
One-fourth teaspoon curry powder
One-half teaspoon salt
One cup milk
Cook: Five minutes, about
One-half cup grated cheddar cheese
One tablespoon butter or margarine
One-half cup soft bread crumbs
Oven temperature: 400 degrees
Bake: Twenty minutes
Serves: Four

Shell the fresh peas and place in a saucepan with the sliced celery and a small amount of salted boiling water. Cook until tender, drain. In a small saucepan melt the two tablespoons of butter or margarine, stir in the flour, dry mustard, curry powder and salt. Gradually blend in the milk. Cook, stirring constantly, until sauce thickens. Add the grated cheese, stir until melted into sauce. Remove from heat and add the cooked peas and celery. Transfer to a shallow baking pan or pie plate. Melt the tablespoon of butter or margarine in a small pan, stir in the soft bread crumbs and scatter over the creamed vegetables. Bake in a quick oven for twenty minutes or until crumbs are nicely browned.

Lyonnaise Potatoes

One and one-half pounds potatoes
Boiling salted water
Cook: Until tender
One-fourth cup butter or margarine
Two-thirds cup finely chopped onion
Sauté: Until golden
Two-thirds teaspoon salt
Freshly ground black pepper
Cook: Five minutes
One-fourth cup finely chopped parsley
Serves: Four

Wash and peel the potatoes, cut in half if large. Cook in boiling salted water to cover until tender. Drain. In the meantime, melt the butter or margarine in a large heavy skillet. Add the chopped onion and sauté until a golden brown. Add the sliced, cooked potatoes. Sprinkle with salt and pepper and cook briefly turning with a broad spatula to coat potatoes with the onion. Sprinkle parsley over the top and serve at once.

A FAVORITE RECIPE
Deviled Potato Cakes

Six medium-sized potatoes, boiled, peeled and shredded
One can (4½ oz.) deviled ham
Three tablespoons finely chopped onion
Two tablespoons flour
One tablespoon prepared mustard
One-half teaspoon salt
One-fourth cup shortening
Frying time: Until a golden brown
One-third cup evaporated milk or light cream
Frying time: Browned on both sides
Serves: Six

Boil, peel and shred the potatoes into a bowl; add the ham, onion, flour, mustard and salt. Toss until well mixed. Form into six cakes. Heat the shortening in a heavy skillet; brown one side of the cakes slowly. Spoon the milk or cream over the cakes; let soak into cakes. Continue to fry until the bottom of cakes are crusty. Turn and cook other side of cakes until crusty. Serve hot.

MRS. SHIRLEY STRIEBER, *Charleston, W. Va.*

Oven Roasted Potatoes

One and one-half pounds small new potatoes
Boiling water
One teaspoon salt
Cook: Ten minutes
One-fourth cup butter or margarine
Salt and freshly ground black pepper
Oven temperature: 375 degrees
Bake: Forty-five to fifty minutes
Serves: Four

Wash and peel the small new potatoes. Place in a saucepan with one inch of boiling water and a teaspoon of salt. Cover and parboil for 10 minutes. Drain. Melt the butter or margarine in a shallow pan or pie tin. Add the potatoes, turning to coat well. Sprinkle with salt and freshly ground black pepper and bake in a moderately hot oven until done. Turn potatoes occasionally to brown all sides.

Scalloped Potatoes

Two tablespoons butter or margarine
Two tablespoons flour
One teaspoon salt
One-eighth teaspoon pepper
Two cups milk
Cook: Ten minutes
Four medium-sized potatoes
One medium-sized onion
Oven temperature: 350 degrees
Bake: One and one-half hours
Serves: Four, or more

In the upper half of a double boiler melt the butter or margarine. Blend in the flour, salt and pepper. Gradually add the milk; place over hot water and cook, stirring constantly until mixture thickens. Cook for 10 minutes. Scrub the potatoes, pare and slice thin. Peel onion and slice thin. Place alternate layers of potatoes,

sauce and onion in a greased casserole (1½ qts.). Bake in a moderate oven for one and one-half hours or until the potatoes are tender.

Browned Rice with Mushrooms

Two tablespoons salad or olive oil
One-fourth pound fresh mushrooms
One-half cup raw rice
Browning time: Five to ten minutes
Four bouillon cubes
Four cups boiling water
One-eighth teaspoon nutmeg
Simmer: Forty minutes
Serves: Four to six

Heat the salad or olive oil in a large heavy skillet. Add the sliced mushrooms and raw rice and cook, stirring constantly, until the rice is golden. Crumble the bouillon cubes in the skillet and add the boiling water and nutmeg. Mix well. Cover tightly and simmer gently until all moisture is absorbed by the rice. Serve with grilled meats or roast.

Splendid Spinach

Two pounds fresh spinach
Cook: Ten minutes, about
One-half cup cream
One-half teaspoon onion salt
One-fourth teaspoon nutmeg
Servings: Six

Pick over the fresh spinach, trimming off roots and thick stems. Discard wilted or old leaves. Place in a large dish pan or sink and fill with warm water. Lift the leaves from the water and repeat until there is no grit or sand settling to the bottom. Place leaves with water that clings to them in a large kettle or saucepan. Cover and place over heat. Cook until leaves wilt down. Chop well and stir in the cream, onion salt and nutmeg. Serve in separate sauce dishes placed beside the dinner plate.

Spinach au Gratin

Two packages (10 oz. each) frozen chopped spinach
Two tablespoons butter or margarine
Two tablespoons flour
One-half teaspoon salt
One cup milk
Three-fourths cup grated cheddar
Four slices bacon, fried crisp
Oven temperature: 350 degrees
Bake: Twenty minutes
Servings: Four to six

Cook the frozen chopped spinach according to package directions; drain. In a saucepan melt the butter or margarine. Stir in the flour and salt and gradually blend in the milk. Cook, stirring, until thickened and smooth. Add the grated cheddar cheese and stir until melted.

Add the drained spinach and transfer to a greased shallow baking pan or pie plate. Crumble the crisp bacon over the top and bake in a moderate oven for twenty minutes.

Soups

Oyster Stew

One bottle (8 oz.) clam juice
One pint oysters with liquid
Two tablespoons Worcestershire sauce
One teaspoon salt or seasoned salt
One-fourth teaspoon pepper
Simmer: Three minutes
Four cups milk
One-half cup heavy or light cream
Heat: To boiling point
Four teaspoons butter or margarine
Paprika
Serves: Four, or more

In a large kettle put the clam juice, oysters, Worcestershire sauce, salt and pepper. Simmer for three minutes. Add milk and cream. Heat to boiling point. Serve in hot bowls. Dot with butter.

Sprinkle paprika on top. Serve immediately.

Montauk Chowder

Two leeks
Two carrots
Four tablespoons butter or margarine
One clove garlic, crushed
Sauté: Five minutes, about
One pound haddock, cod or whiting
One cup water
One bay leaf
One teaspoon salt
One-eighth teaspoon pepper
Simmer: Thirty minutes
Two cups milk
Two tablespoons chopped parsley
Heat: To just below a boil
Serves: Four

Wash, dry and trim the leeks. Scrape the carrots. Slice both thinly. Melt the butter or margarine in a large heavy saucepan. Add the sliced leeks and carrots and the crushed clove of garlic. Sauté until golden. Add the cubed fish (fresh or frozen), water, bay leaf, salt and pepper. Cover and simmer gently for 30 minutes, or until carrots are tender. Most of the water will be absorbed; add more if necessary to prevent sticking. Add milk and parsley and heat carefully until piping hot. Do not permit to boil. Good with buttered pilot crackers.

Oyster Stew Rockefeller

One package frozen spinach
Three cups milk
One slice onion
Cooking time: Twenty minutes
Four tablespoons butter or margarine
Three tablespoons flour
One teaspoon salt
One teaspoon steak sauce
One-half teaspoon celery salt
One-eighth teaspoon white pepper
Few grains nutmeg
Cooking time: Five minutes
One quart oysters
One cup light or heavy cream
Cooking time: Five minutes
Serves: Six, or more

In saucepan cook the spinach, milk and onion for 20 minutes, stir occasionally. Rub through a sieve or press through a ricer. In a large saucepan melt the butter; blend in the flour and seasonings. Stir in the hot pureed spinach mixture cooking until slightly thickened. Add the oysters with their liquor and the cream. Cook until the edge of the oysters curls (about five minutes), stirring occasionally. Serve in hot soup plates.

Bouillabaise American Style

Three pounds fish (sea bass, sole, red
  snapper, haddock)
Three pounds shellfish (lobster, shrimp,
  mussels)·
Two quarts boiling water
One teaspoon salt
Cooking time: Ten minutes
One large onion, chopped
One clove garlic, minced
One-half cup olive oil
Cooking time: Five minutes
One can (No. 2½) whole tomatoes,
  chopped
Six cups fish stock
One tablespoon minced parsley
One tablespoon minced celery
One teaspoon salt
One teaspoon paprika
One-half teaspoon thyme
One-fourth teaspoon sage
One-eighth teaspoon cayenne
Simmering time: Thirty minutes
Serves: Eight, or more

Have the fish filleted at the market
(keep the bones and head for the stock).
Cut the fish in pieces (2 in.). Remove
the shells from the shrimp. Scrub the
mussels in cold water; cut off the beards.
Cook the lobster 10 minutes in boiling
salted water. Remove lobster, break into
serving pieces; crack the shell. In a large
heavy kettle cook the onion and garlic
in the olive oil until straw-colored. Add
the tomatoes, fish stock, parsley, celery
and seasoning. Simmer 20 minutes. Add
the fish and shellfish. Cover and cook
another 10 minutes. Serve in a large
tureen with garlic-buttered croutons.

Chicken Shrimp Gumbo

One broiler chicken (3½ lbs.) quartered
Water to cover
(Sprigs of parsley, onion slice, bay leaf,
  4 peppercorns, celery tops)
Cooking time: One hour
Two pounds raw shrimp
Water to cover
(Sprigs of parsley, onion slice, bay leaf,
  4 peppercorns, celery tops)
Cooking Time: Seven minutes
Standing time: Overnight
Four tablespoons butter or margarine
Two pounds okra or two packages frozen
  okra
One-half cup minced celery
Two cloves garlic, minced
One-half cup minced onion
One-half green pepper, minced
Cooking time: Ten minutes
One tablespoon flour
Heating time: Five minutes
One tablespoon file powder
Four cups cooked rice
Serves: Eight, or more

In a heavy kettle place the chicken,
water to cover and the bouquet garni
(parsley, onion slice, bay leaf, peppercorns and celery tops). Cover; cook until tender. Let cool. Remove skin from
chicken. Cut meat into bitesize pieces;
place in bowl. Strain stock over chicken.
Cool thoroughly. Refrigerate. Cook the
shrimp in a heavy kettle with water to

cover the bouquet garni. Let come to a
boil; cook 7 minutes. Remove shell and
black vein. Place in bowl; strain stock
over shrimp. Cool thoroughly; refrigerate.
The next day in a large skillet melt the
butter; add the okra and cook about 2
minutes; then add celery, garlic, onion,
green pepper; cook 7 minutes. Blend in
the flour. In a large kettle put in the
chicken and stock, shrimp and stock, okra
mixture and file powder. Heat 5 minutes. Pour into a large hot tureen. Ladle
gumbo over cooked rice in soup plates.
Serve immediately.

A FAVORITE RECIPE
Fish Chowder

One pound cod, haddock or whitefish
Water to cover
One teaspoon salt
Cooking time: Five minutes
Two tablespoons butter
Two white onions, chopped
One-half clove garlic, minced
One-fourth cup chopped celery
Two tablespoons minced green pepper
Sauté: Five minutes
Two large potatoes, peeled, diced (¼ in.)
Two teaspoons salt
Two and one-half cups boiling water
Boil: Five minutes
One-fourth teaspoon thyme
One-sixteenth teaspoon sage
One-sixteenth teaspoon cayenne
Simmering time: Fifteen minutes
One and one-half cups tomato juice
Heat: To boiling point
Servings: Four

In a kettle cook the fish in the salted water; drain, reserving the stock. Remove skin and bones from the fish. In a skillet heat the butter, sauté the onions, garlic, celery and green pepper. Sauté five minutes. Add the diced potatoes, salt and boiling water; cook until the potatoes are tender. Add the fish, stock, thyme, sage and cayenne. Simmer. Add the tomato juice. Bring to a boil. Serve in bouillon cups with crisp crackers.

MRS. BURTON DIXON, *Nokesville, Virginia*

A FAVORITE RECIPE
Curried Tuna Chowder

One and one-half cups, peeled, cubed
 (¼ in.) potatoes
Water to cover
Cooking time: Until tender
One cup water
Two cans (10½ oz. each) condensed
 cream of celery soup
One can (8 oz.) peas, with liquid
One can (12 oz.) whole kernel corn
One-fourth cup evaporated milk
One tablespoon minced onion
One-eighth teaspoon pepper
Cooking time: Ten minutes
One and one-half teaspoons curry powder
One can (7 oz.) tuna fish
Cooking time: Until thoroughly heated
Servings: Six

Place the cubed potatoes in a saucepan; cover with water, cook. Drain off the water, measure, adding more water if needed to make one cup. Return the potatoes and water to a kettle (2½ qts.); add the celery soup, peas, corn, milk, onion and pepper; cover. Cook. Mix two tablespoons of the soup with the curry powder, then stir into the soup with the chunk style tuna. Heat thoroughly. Serve in bouillon cups with crackers.

MRS. JOCELYN C. PETERS, *Flushing, N.Y.*

Quick Fish Chowder

One-fourth cup finely chopped salt pork
Fry: Until lightly browned
One-half cup chopped onion
One-half cup chopped green pepper
One cup chopped celery
Sauté: Until tender
One cup clam broth
One cup diced raw potatoes
One pound fish fillets, cubed
One-fourth teaspoon thyme
One teaspoon salt
Dash of cayenne
Cook: Ten to fifteen minutes
Two cups tomato juice
Cook: Five minutes
Servings: Four to six

Place the finely chopped salt pork in a large heavy skillet. Fry until lightly browned. Add the chopped onion, green pepper and celery and sauté until tender. Add the clam broth, diced raw potato and cubed fish fillets. Add the thyme, salt and dash of cayenne. Cover tightly and cook until potatoes and fish are done. Add the tomato juice and heat through thoroughly. Serve at once.

Lobster Chowder

One and one-half cups cubed raw potato
Boiling salted water
Cook: Ten minutes
One package (1½ oz.) onion soup mix
Two cups boiling water
Simmer: Ten minutes
Two tablespoons butter or margarine
Two tablespoons flour
One and one-half cups milk
One-half cup light cream
Cook: Five minutes, about
One-sixteenth teaspoon pepper
One can (5 oz.) lobster
Simmer: Ten minutes
Serves: Four to six

Cook the cubed (1¼ in.), raw potato in boiling, salted water until almost tender; drain. Simmer the onion soup mix in two cups of boiling water for 10 minutes, stirring occasionally. In a large saucepan or skillet melt the butter or margarine, stir in the flour. Gradually stir in the milk and cream. Cook, stirring constantly, until sauce thickens. Season with pepper. Remove cartilage from lobster meat and add with the cooked, drained potato and simmered onion soup mix. Stir together and heat until piping hot. Serve at once. If chowder seems a little thick add additional milk. Good with water biscuits.

Quick Crabmeat Soup

One can (6½ oz.) crabmeat
Three tablespoons lemon juice
One teaspoon Worcestershire sauce
Standing time: Ten minutes
One can (10½ oz.) condensed tomato
 soup
One can (10½ oz.) condensed pea soup
One can light cream
Simmering time: Ten minutes
Servings: Four

In a bowl, flake the crabmeat, removing the cartilage. Add the lemon juice

and Worcestershire sauce and allow to stand for 10 minutes. Add the condensed tomato and pea soup and the light cream or milk. Heat to the boiling point, then simmer briefly. Serve at once.

Cream of Crab Soup

One-fourth cup butter or margarine
One-fourth cup finely chopped onion
Sauteing time: Five minutes or more
One cup boiling water
One bouillon cube
Three tablespoons flour
One teaspoon salt
One-fourth teaspoon celery salt
One-eighth teaspoon pepper
One quart milk
Cook: Ten minutes
Two cans (6 oz. each) crabmeat
Simmer: Ten minutes
Chopped parsley
Servings: Six

In a large saucepan or skillet melt the butter or margarine. Add the finely chopped onion and saute until onion is soft. Pour the boiling water over the bouillon cube and let stand to dissolve. Stir the flour into the sauted onion with the salt, celery salt and pepper. Gradually blend in the milk, stirring constantly. Add the bouillon and cook and stir until the sauce thickens. Add the crabmeat from which the cartilage has been removed. Simmer briefly. Serve in soup plates with a little finely chopped parsley sprinkled on top. Pilot crackers or potato chips are good accompaniments.

Fresh Mushroom and Clam Bisque

Four tablespoons butter or margarine
One-half pound fresh mushrooms, sliced
One-fourth cup finely chopped onion
One-half cup finely chopped celery
Sauté: Five minutes, about
Four tablespoons flour
One teaspoon salt
One-eighth teaspoon pepper
One-eighth teaspoon mace
One teaspoon Worcestershire sauce
Two teaspoons grated lemon rind
Two cups milk
Cook: Ten minutes, or more
One can (7 or 8 ounces) minced clams
Two cups milk
Simmer: Ten minutes
Finely chopped parsley
Serves: Four

In a large heavy skillet melt the butter or margarine. Add the sliced mushrooms, finely chopped onion and celery. Sauté until tender. Stir in the flour, salt, pepper, mace, Worcestershire sauce and grated lemon rind. Gradually blend in two cups of milk, stirring constantly. Cook until mixture thickens, stirring constantly. In a separate saucepan heat the canned minced clams with the other two cups of milk. When heated through, stir into the skillet contents. Blend thoroughly together and serve at once with a sprinkling of finely chopped parsley over each bowlful.

Mushroom and Clam Soup

One-half pound mushrooms, thinly sliced
　or canned
Four tablespoons butter or margarine
Cook: Ten minutes
Three tablespoons flour
Two cups clam juice
Simmer: Ten minutes
One can (7½ oz.) minced clams
One cup light cream or evaporated milk
One-half teaspoon salt
One-fourth teaspoon pepper
One-eighth teaspoon tarragon
Reheat: To the boiling point
One-fourth teaspoon paprika
Serves: Four

Rinse the mushrooms; slice them very thin. In a kettle cook the mushrooms in the butter or margarine over low heat until lightly browned. Blend in the flour. Add the clam juice; add clams; cook, stirring, until slightly thickened. Just before serving, add the light cream, salt, pepper and tarragon; reheat to the boiling point. (Do not boil.) Serve in hot bowls; sprinkle top with paprika.

A FAVORITE RECIPE
Creole Crab Gumbo

Four tablespoons butter
One-half cup sliced onion
Sauté: Ten minutes
Four tablespoons flour
Browning time: Five minutes
One pound crab meat, fresh or canned
　(remove all cartilage)
One pound okra, washed, cut into pieces
　(½ in.)
Five cups canned tomatoes
One cup diced green pepper
Two cloves garlic, crushed
One teaspoon powdered nutmeg
Two teaspoons salt
One-half teaspoon freshly ground black
　pepper
Two cups water
Simmering time: One hour
Servings: Six

In a deep heavy kettle, heat the butter; add onion, cook. Stir in the flour, stirring until browned. Add the crab meat, okra, tomatoes, green pepper, garlic and seasonings. Pour in the water. Bring to a boil; reduce the heat; simmer, covered until serving time.

MRS. MARY LO RE, *Bayonne, N.J.*

Lobster Bisque

One sliced onion
One stalk celery, sliced
One quart milk
Heat: To scalding
Three tablespoons butter or margarine
Three tablespoons flour
One teaspoon salt
One teaspoon paprika
Cooking time: Five to ten minutes
Two cans (6½ oz. each) lobster
　meat, finely chopped
One cup dairy sour cream
Heat: Almost to boiling
Finely cut chives
Serving: Six

Place the sliced onion, celery and milk in a saucepan and heat to scalding. In a skillet or saucepan melt the butter or margarine. Stir in the flour, salt and paprika. Gradually blend in the strained scalded milk and cook while stirring until the soup thickens slightly. Stir in the finely chopped lobster meat and add more salt if needed. Stir in the dairy sour cream and heat almost to boiling. Serve with a sprinkling of finely cut chives spooned on top.

A FAVORITE RECIPE
Chicken-Seafood-Gumbo

One chicken (4 lbs.) disjointed
Five cups water
One clove garlic
One teaspoon salt
Simmer: Two hours
Four slices bacon cut into pieces (1 in.)
Frying time: Until golden brown
One-third cup flour
Cooking time: Until browned
One cup chopped onion
Cooking time: Five minutes
Six cups chicken broth or water
One can (19 oz.) tomatoes
Two teaspoons gumbo file
Simmering time: Thirty minutes
One can (16 oz.) sliced okra
One pint oysters
One can (6 oz.) crab meat (all cartilage
　removed)
One teaspoon salt
One-fourth teaspoon pepper
One-sixteenth teaspoon tabasco sauce
Simmering time: Five minutes
Two cups rice cooked as directed on
　package
Serves: Six

Have chicken prepared. Place in a deep heavy kettle. Add water, garlic and salt. Bring to a boil; reduce heat, simmer until chicken is tender. Remove from pot and discard all heavy skin and bones. Cut into small pieces; set aside. Strain the broth; add enough water to make six cups. In a large kettle fry the bacon until browned. Stir in the flour, brown lightly. Add onion, cook, stirring constantly. Add the broth and water mixture, tomatoes and file. Cover. Simmer: Add the chicken, okra, oysters, crab meat and seasonings. Heat thoroughly and serve with hot rice.

MRS. FLOYD FARISH, *Orrville, Ala.*

Crabmeat Gumbo

Two tablespoons butter
One small onion, chopped
One-fourth cup chopped green pepper
Sauteing time: Five minutes
Two cups water
One-fourth cup raw rice
Cooking time: Fifteen minutes
Three fresh tomatoes, peeled, diced
One can (No. 2) sliced okra
One can (6½ oz.) crabmeat
One-half teaspoon Worcestershire sauce
Simmering time: Twenty minutes
One tablespoon chopped parsley
Yield: Two quarts

In a heavy kettle, melt the butter, add the onion and green pepper and saute until tender. Stir in the water and raw rice and cook. Add the tomatoes, flaked crabmeat, okra and Worcestershire. Cover; simmer. Add parsley and serve hot.

Tomato Bisque with Blue Cheese

Four tablespoons butter or margarine
One-third cup flour
One and one-half teaspoons salt
One-eighth teaspoon pepper
Two cups milk
Cooking time: Five to ten minutes
One can (No. 2½) tomatoes
Three sprigs parsley
One bay leaf
Six whole cloves
One-fourth cup finely chopped onion
Simmering time: Five minutes
One-third cup crumbled blue cheese
Yield: About five cups

In a large heavy skillet melt the butter or margarine. Blend in the flour, salt and pepper. Gradually add the milk, stirring to keep smooth. Cook over moderate heat until the sauce thickens. In a saucepan combine the canned tomatoes, sprigs of parsley, bay leaf, cloves and finely chopped onion and simmer gently for five minutes. Press vegetables through a fine sieve. Add the puree slowly to the cream sauce. Serve at once with a sprinkling of crumbled blue cheese.

Asparagus Roquefort Cheese Soup

Two cans (10½ oz. each) condensed
　cream of asparagus soup
One-fourth cup finely crumbled
　Roquefort cheese
Two soup cans water
Paprika
Heat: To boiling point
Serves: Four

In a saucepan, stir soup, cheese and water until well blended. Heat; stir occasionally. Garnish with paprika.

Tomato Lima Soup

One small onion, sliced thin
Two tablespoons butter or margarine
Sauteing time: Five minutes
Two cups tomato juice
Simmering time: Twenty minutes
Two cups cooked dry limas, pureed
One tablespoon sherry wine
One teaspoon salt
Two cups milk
Heat: To scalding
Yield: Five cups

In a large heavy skillet or kettle, saute the thinly sliced onion in the butter or margarine until transparent. Add the tomato juice and simmer. Add the pureed cooked lima beans, the wine, salt and milk. Heat to scalding and serve at once.

Quick Crab Chowder

One can (10½ oz.) condensed tomato soup
One can (10½ oz.) condensed celery soup
Two bouillon cubes, dissolved in
Five cups boiling water
Heating time: Ten minutes
One cup crab meat
One tablespoon grated onion
One cup light cream
One-half teaspoon salt
One-eighth teaspoon pepper
Heating time: Five minutes
Four teaspoons sherry
Servings: Four, or more

Combine the soups, dissolved bouillon cubes in a large kettle; slowly bring to a boil. Stir in crab meat, onion, cream, salt and pepper; reheat. Serve in hot cups or soup plates, adding a teaspoon of sherry to each. Good with buttered and toasted pilot crackers.

Clam and Corn Chowder

Three tablespoons butter or margarine
One-third cup chopped onion
Sauté: Until golden
Two cups milk
Two cups diced cooked potatoes
One can (1 lb.) whole kernel corn
One teaspoon salt
One-eighth teaspoon pepper
Heat: Thoroughly
One pint clams, chopped
Cook: Five minutes
Servings: Four to six

Melt the butter or margarine in a large heavy skillet. Add the chopped onion and sauté until golden. Stir in the milk, cooked potatoes, whole kernel corn, salt and pepper. Heat thoroughly. Add the chopped clams and liquid and cook only until clams are done, about five minutes. Serve hot with pilot crackers.

Oyster Vegetable Chowder

One pint medium-sized oysters
One-third cup minced salt pork
Two medium-sized onions, sliced
Cooking time: Three minutes
One cup boiling water
One cup diced potatoes
Cooking time: Ten minutes
One cup canned or frozen whole kernel corn
Three cups milk
One teaspoon salt
One-eighth teaspoon pepper
Simmering time: Fifteen minutes
One-eighth teaspoon paprika
Two tablespoons minced parsley
Serves: Six

Drain the oysters, reserving the liquor, and remove any bits of shell. Strain the liquor through a fine sieve; set aside. Brown the salt pork in a large saucepan until crisp. Add onions and cook until straw-colored. Add the water and potatoes. Cover; cook until partially tender. Add corn, milk, oyster liquor, salt and pepper. Cook until the potatoes are tender. Add the oysters; cook over low heat another five minutes. Serve in hot bowls. Garnish with paprika and parsley.

New England Clam Chowder

One-half pound minced salt pork or four
    tablespoons shortening
Cook: Ten minutes
Two medium-sized onions, thinly sliced
Cook: Five minutes
Six medium-sized potatoes, diced
Three cups boiling water
Simmer: Twenty minutes
One quart milk, scalded
Two tablespoons butter or margarine
Two teaspoons salt
One-fourth teaspoon pepper
One quart clams with liquid, coarsely
    chopped or two cans (7½ oz. each)
    minced clams
Simmer: Five minutes
Serves: Twelve

In a kettle cook the fat out of the
minced salt pork. When salt pork is crisp,
remove from pan and reserve. Cook the
onions either in the salt pork fat or
shortening until straw-colored. Add the
potatoes and boiling water. Cover; simmer until the potatoes are tender. Add
the hot milk, butter, salt, pepper, clams
and clam liquor; simmer for about five
minutes or until everything is heated
thoroughly. Serve in a hot tureen.
Sprinkle crisp bits of salt pork on top.

Manhattan Clam Chowder

Two dozen hard-shelled clams, finely cut or
    two cans (7½ oz. each) minced clams
One cup minced salt pork, or six
    tablespoons shortening
Two large onions, chopped
Cook: Eight minutes
Four medium-sized potatoes, diced
Eight cups boiling water
Two cans (No. 2 each) whole tomatoes
Two stalks celery, minced
One green pepper, minced
Two bay leaves
One teaspoon thyme
Two teaspoons salt
One-half teaspoon pepper
Simmer: Twenty minutes
One-half teaspoon caraway seed
Simmer: Five minutes
Serves: Ten, or more

Have the fish man shuck the clams;
reserve the clam liquor. Cut the clams
into fine pieces, or use canned clams. In
a kettle fry out fat from the salt pork.
Remove the browned pieces of salt pork;
reserve. Cook the onion in the fat from
the salt pork or shortening until straw-
colored. Add the potatoes, boiling water,
whole tomatoes, minced celery, green

pepper, bay leaves, thyme, salt and pepper. Cover and simmer over low heat for
thirty minutes. Add the caraway seed,
clams and clam liquor; simmer for another five minutes. Serve in a hot tureen.
Sprinkle top with bits of crisp salt pork.

A FAVORITE RECIPE
Corn Soup

Two cups canned, creamed style corn
One tablespoon grated onion
One cup boiling water
Cooking time: Fifteen minutes
Two tablespoons butter, melted in the
    top of a double boiler
Two tablespoons flour
Three cups milk
One teaspoon salt
One-fourth teaspoon pepper
Cooking time: Ten minutes
Servings: Six

In a saucepan, cook the corn and onion in the boiling water; strain. Set aside. Melt the butter, blend in the flour, add the milk, seasonings and strained broth from the corn and onion. Cook, stirring until smooth and thickened. Serve hot with bread sticks.

MRS. JOHN REED, *Jersey Shore, Pa.*

Corn Chowder

One-half cup chopped salt pork
Browning time: Five minutes
One small onion, thinly sliced
Cook: Two or three minutes
One bay leaf
One-half teaspoon salt
One-fourth teaspoon pepper
One cup raw potatoes, diced
Two cups water
Cook: Ten minutes
Three tablespoons flour
Two cups milk
One can (No. 2) whole kernel corn
Simmer: Ten minutes
Serves: Four, or more

In a large, heavy skillet brown the chopped salt pork thoroughly. Add the sliced onion and cook briefly. Add the bay leaf, salt, pepper, potatoes and water. Cover and cook until the potatoes are tender. In a cup blend the flour with half a cup of the cold milk to make a smooth sauce. Stir into the ingredients in the skillet. Add the remaining milk and corn. Simmer for ten minutes before serving.

A FAVORITE RECIPE
Cheese Corn Chowder

One-fourth cup butter, melted
One-fourth cup chopped onion
Cooking time: Five minutes
One-fourth cup flour
One quart milk
Cooking time: Until thick
Two cans (No. 2) cream style corn
Two cups shredded sharp American
    cheese
One teaspoon salt
One-fourth teaspoon pepper
Cooking time: Until cheese is melted
Servings: Six

In a deep saucepan, melt the butter; add the onion, cook until tender (do not brown). Stir in the flour. Add the milk, cook, stirring until thickened. Add the corn; mix. Stir in the cheese, blending well; cook until the cheese is melted. Add the salt and pepper. Serve in hot bouillon cups with crisp crackers.

MILDRED COULSON, *Bergenfield, N.J.*

Turkey Cheese Chowder

Two tablespoons butter or margarine
One large onion, sliced
One cup sliced celery
Sauté: Ten minutes
Two cups raw potato cubes
One package (10 oz.) frozen lima beans
One cup hot water
Cook: Fifteen minutes
One and one-half cups diced cooked
    turkey*
One can (No. 2½) tomatoes
One can (10½ oz.) condensed cream of
    chicken soup
Two cups grated cheddar cheese
One-fourth teaspoon garlic salt
One-eighth teaspoon pepper
Simmer: Forty-five minutes
Yield: Three and one-half quarts (approx.)

In a large heavy saucepan or kettle (4-5 qts.) melt the butter or margarine. Add the sliced onion and celery and sauté until lightly browned. Add the potato cubes, lima beans and water. Cover and cook until the vegetables are tender. Add the diced cooked turkey, canned tomatoes, condensed cream of chicken soup, cheese, garlic salt and pepper. Cover and simmer gently for forty-five minutes or more. Serve piping hot in soup bowls with toasted rolls.

* No leftover turkey! Then use the canned boned turkey available at supermarket and grocery.

Tomato and Corn Chowder

One can (No. 2) tomatoes
One bay leaf
One-half cup finely chopped celery
One-fourth cup finely chopped green
    pepper
One tablespoon instant minced onion or
    two tablespoons finely chopped fresh
    onion
Boil: Ten minutes
One-fourth cup butter or margarine
One-fourth cup flour
One quart milk
One can (No. 2) cream style corn
Cook: Ten minutes, about
Two teaspoons salt
Simmer: Five to ten minutes
Yield: Two quarts

In a saucepan combine the canned tomatoes, bay leaf, chopped celery, green pepper and onion. Bring to a boil

and boil 10 minutes. In a second pan melt the butter or margarine, blend in the flour; gradually add the milk, stirring constantly. Add the canned cream-style corn and cook, stirring, until the sauce thickens. Add the salt and the tomato mixture and heat until piping hot. Taste; correct seasoning if necessary. Serve with a sprinkling of paprika atop each bowlful.

Fresh Vegetable Chowder

One-half cup diced salt pork
Two slices onion
Browning time: Five minutes
Two cups fresh corn, cut from cob
One cup diced potatoes
One cup chopped celery
One tablespoon minced parsley
Two cups boiling water
Two teaspoons salt
One-eighth teaspoon pepper
One-eighth teaspoon sage
One bay leaf
Simmering time: Twenty minutes
Three tablespoons flour mixed with
One-fourth cup cold milk
Two cups scalded milk
Cooking time: Five minutes
Servings: Four, or more

Brown the salt pork and onion in a heavy kettle, stirring frequently. Add the corn, potatoes, celery, parsley, water and seasoning. Cover; simmer over low heat until the potatoes are tender. Stir in the paste; add the remaining milk. Cool until slightly thickened. Remove the bay leaf. Serve in soup bowls; sprinkle paprika on top.

Tuna Vegetable Soup

One-fourth pound salt pork, minced
Three tablespoons minced onion
One-fourth cup minced celery
Two tablespoons minced green pepper
Cook: Ten minutes
One can (14½ oz.) condensed
    chicken broth
One can (1 lb. 4 oz.) white kidney beans
One can (1 lb.) cream-style corn
Cook: Ten minutes
One can (7 oz.) tuna, drained, flaked
One cup light cream or evaporated milk
One teaspoon salt
One-fourth teaspoon pepper
Reheat: To the boiling point
One tablespoon minced parsley
Serves: Six, or more

In a kettle cook the salt pork until crisp, about 5 minutes. Add the onion, celery and green pepper; cook until the onion is straw-colored. Add the chicken broth, white kidney beans, cream-style corn; cook over low heat about 10 minutes. Just before serving add the flaked tuna, light cream, salt and pepper. Reheat to the boiling point (do not let boil). Serve in hot soup plates. Sprinkle with parsley.

Cream of Carrot Soup

Two tablespoons butter or margarine
Three tablespoons finely chopped onion
Sauté: Five minutes
Three tablespoons flour
Six cups milk
Two cups grated or finely chopped raw
  carrot
One teaspoon salt
One-half teaspoon pepper
Cook: Ten minutes, or more
Serves: Six

In a large heavy skillet melt the butter, add the finely chopped onion and sauté until golden. Stir in the flour. Add the milk gradually, stirring to keep smooth. Add the grated carrot and salt and pepper. Stir the soup and cook, stirring occasionally, until the vegetable is tender. Taste and correct seasoning if necessary. Serve hot.

Cream of Mushroom Soup

One-half pound fresh mushrooms
Two tablespoons butter or margarine
Sauté: Five minutes
Two tablespoons butter or margarine
Two tablespoons flour
One teaspoon salt
One-eighth teaspoon pepper
Three cups milk
One onion, sliced thin
Cook: Ten minutes
One tablespoon lemon juice
Serves: Four

Wash, dry and thinly slice the mushrooms from top to bottom, through cap and stem. In a large heavy skillet heat the butter or margarine, add the sliced mushrooms and sauté until golden. Add the second measure of butter or margarine; when melted stir in the flour, salt and pepper. Gradually add the milk and stir until smooth. Add the sliced onion and cook until thickened. Stir in the lemon juice. Serve piping hot.

Spinach Soup Special

One package (10 oz.) frozen chopped
  spinach
One-third cup condensed beef consomme
Cook: Five to ten minutes
One and one-half teaspoons salt
One-fourth teaspoon pepper
Two cups milk
Heat: Briefly
Four egg yolks
Simmer: Five minutes
Nutmeg
Servings: Four

Cook the frozen chopped spinach in the condensed beef consomme in a saucepan until completely separated and tender. Stir in the milk and beat gently. In a bowl beat the egg yolks well. Stir a little of the spinach mixture into the beaten yolks, return combination to the saucepan and cook over very low heat until heated through. Serve in bowls or cups with a sprinkling of grated nutmeg over top.

Cream of Onion and Cheese Soup

Three tablespoons butter or margarine
Two cups thinly sliced onion
Sauté: Fifteen minutes, or more
Three tablespoons flour
Four cups milk
Cook: Ten minutes
One cup grated cheddar cheese
Simmer: Five minutes
Salt and pepper to taste
Yield: One quart

In a large heavy skillet melt the butter or margarine. Add the thinly sliced onion and sauté over low heat until the onion is soft. Add the flour and blend thoroughly. Gradually add the milk, stirring the while to keep smooth.

Cook, stirring over moderate heat until the soup thickens slightly. Add the grated cheddar cheese and simmer just until the cheese is melted. Check for seasoning needs and use salt and pepper to taste.

Cream of Tomato Soup

Three and one-half cups fresh or canned
  tomatoes (one No. 2½ can)
One-fourth cup chopped onion
Simmer: Twenty minutes
Two tablespoons butter or margarine
Three tablespoons flour
One-half teaspoon sugar
One teaspoon salt
One-eighth teaspoon pepper
Three cups milk
Cook: Ten minutes
Servings: Six

In a saucepan combine the tomatoes with the chopped onion. Simmer together 20 minutes. Rub through a sieve. In the upper half of a double boiler or in a heavy skillet melt the butter or margarine. Blend in the flour, sugar, salt and pepper. Gradually add the milk, stirring to keep smooth. Cook 10 minutes. Add the tomato puree very slowly to the cream sauce, stirring constantly. Heat gently to the boiling point, but do not boil. Serve at once.

Water Cress Soup

Two cups diced raw potato
One-fourth pound fresh water cress (one
  bunch)
Two tablespoons thinly sliced green onion
Two tablespoons chopped parsley
One teaspoon salt
One quart boiling water
Cook: Fifteen minutes
One tablespoon butter
One-half cup heavy cream
Dash of pepper, salt to taste
Heat: Five to ten minutes
Yield: One quart

Place the peeled diced raw potato in a large saucepan with the coarsely chopped washed water cress, sliced green onion, chopped parsley, salt and boiling water. Cook over high heat until the potatoes are tender. Rub through a sieve. Heat the puree with the butter, cream and dash of pepper and salt. Serve hot.

Quick Onion Soup

One-fourth cup shortening
Six medium-sized onions, sliced (four cups)
Browning time: Ten to fifteen minutes
Three bouillon cubes
Four and one-half cups water
One tablespoon Worcestershire sauce
One teaspoon salt
Simmer: Twenty minutes
Melba Toast rounds
Grated Parmesan cheese
Serves: Four

Melt the shortening in a large heavy skillet. Add the sliced onions and cook until lightly browned. Add the bouillon cubes, water, Worcestershire sauce and salt. Cover and simmer gently for twenty minutes. Serve in bowls with floating rounds of Melba toast or sliced French bread and a generous sprinkling of grated Parmesan cheese.

Swiss Onion Soup

Two pounds yellow onions, chopped (4
  cups)
One-half cup butter or margarine
Sauté: Ten minutes, about
One quart milk
Two cups water
Heat: To a boil
Eight ounces Swiss cheese, grated
Six slices stale bread, cubed (½ in.)
Two tablespoons salt
One-half teaspoon paprika
One-fourth teaspoon pepper
Simmer: Twenty minutes
Yield: Three quarts

Peel the onions and chop rather fine. Add to the melted butter or margarine in a large heavy skillet or kettle and sauté until almost soft. Stir in the milk and water. Heat and bring to a boil gradually. Add the grated cheese, cubed stale bread, salt, paprika and pepper. Simmer gently for twenty minutes. Nice served with crusty French bread or rolls and a crisp green salad.

Consomme

One and one-half pounds boiling beef
One veal or beef knuckle bone, cracked
One-half chicken
Few sprigs parsley
Two green onions
Two teaspoons dill seed
Two teaspoons salt
Two quarts water
Two stalks celery, chopped
Two carrots, finely sliced
Simmer: Two and one-half hours
Cool: Thoroughly
Heat: To serve
Serves: Six to eight

Place the boiling beef, knuckle bone and half chicken in a large saucepan or kettle. Add the parsley, onions, dill seed, salt, water, celery and carrots. Cover and simmer gently for two and one-half hours. Remove chicken and use for another meal. Strain the consomme and refrigerate. Lift fat from top of consomme and reheat to serve. Correct seasoning to taste.

Lentil Soup

Two cups dried lentils, washed
Three cups hot water
Soaking time: Three hours
One-fourth pound salt pork, minced
One cup chopped onion
One clove garlic
Cooking time: Five minutes
One cup chopped carrots
One cup chopped potato
One-half cup chopped celery and leaves
Ten cups water
One fresh pork shoulder bone, split
One bay leaf
Two whole cloves
Three peppercorns
One and one-half teaspoons salt
Simmering time: Three hours
Sherry, lemon slices
Servings: Six, or more

Soak the lentils in the water in a bowl. Do not drain. Cook the salt pork, onion and garlic in a kettle until the onion is yellow. Add the remaining ingredients and lentils. Cover and simmer until lentils are soft. Remove the bone. Rub through a sieve; return to kettle. Correct the seasoning and reheat. Ladle into hot soup plates. Add a dash of sherry or serve with a lemon slice. French or pumpernickel bread and salad complete the main course.

Pepper Pot Soup

Two slices bacon, diced
Cook: Five minutes
One medium-sized onion, chopped
One green pepper, chopped
Cook: Five minutes
One-fourth cup beef tea concentrate
Two quarts water
One bay leaf
One teaspoon black pepper
One-half teaspoon salt
One-eighth teaspoon thyme
One-eighth teaspoon cayenne
One-half pound honeycomb tripe, cubed
One cup diced potatoes
Cook: One hour
Three tablespoons butter or margarine
Three tablespoons flour
Cook: Ten minutes
One-half cup light cream
Yield: Two and one-half quarts

In a large heavy kettle, fry the bacon. Add the onion and green pepper and cook for five minutes. Add the beef tea concentrate, the water, seasonings, tripe and potatoes. Cover; cook for one hour. In a small bowl blend the butter with the flour. Dip a cup of the soup from the kettle and gradually add to the blended butter and flour.

Return mixture to the kettle and cook briefly until soup thickens. Add the light cream and serve at once.

Black Bean Soup

One pound dried black beans
Water
Soak: Overnight
Water
Cook: Two hours, or more
Two tablespoons olive oil
One-half cup finely minced cooked ham
Browning time: Five minutes
One clove garlic, crushed
One medium-sized onion, finely chopped
Sauté: Until soft
Two crumbled bay leaves
One-half teaspoon oregano
One-half teaspoon salt
Two bouillon cubes
One cup hot water
Simmer: Fifteen minutes
Servings: Six to eight

Place the dried picked-over black beans in a large kettle, cover with water and let soak overnight. Drain and cover with fresh water. Bring to a boil and cook in plenty of water until beans are very tender. Rub beans through sieve with pan liquid. In a skillet or saucepan heat the olive oil. Add the finely cut ham and brown lightly. Add the garlic and onion and sauté until soft. Add the bean puree, crumbled bay leaves, oregano, salt, bouillon cubes and water. Simmer. Serve with a thin slice of lemon or a dab of whipped or dairy sour cream.

Scotch Broth

One-half cup barley
Three and one-half quarts water
Three and one-half pounds lamb for soup
Three pounds knuckle bone, cracked
Two tablespoons salt
One-half teaspoon pepper
Simmering time: Two hours
Two cups sliced carrots
Three cups sliced celery
One can (No. 2) tomatoes
One-fourth cup coarsely cut parsley
Simmering time: Forty-five minutes
Four tablespoons butter
Four tablespoons flour
Cooking time: Five minutes
Yield: Eight quarts, approx.

In a large kettle, place the barley, water, soup meat and bones, salt and pepper. Cover, simmer for two hours. Remove meat and bones from soup and separate out the meaty portions. Cut, if necessary into uniform size. Return to soup. Add vegetables and simmer until tender. In a small saucepan melt the butter, add the flour and blend well. Stir this mixture into the soup and cook briefly, stirring until well blended. Serve hot.

Old-Fashioned Vegetable Soup

One marrow bone, sawed (one and
    one-half inch pieces)
One knuckle bone, sawed in half
Three pounds beef chuck in one piece
Two carrots, cubed
Two yellow onions, sliced
One large leek, sliced
One large potato, cubed
One parsnip, cubed
One medium-sized yellow onion, sliced
One tablespoon salt
Four peppercorns
Cold water
Simmer: Two and one-quarter hours
Two cups sliced celery
One white turnip, cubed
Simmer: Twenty minutes (about)
One can (No. 2) whole tomatoes
Chopped parsley
Serves: Six

Rinse the marrow bone and knuckle
bone. Put in deep kettle with beef chuck;
add onion, salt and peppercorns. Add
enough water to cover meat. Cover; bring
to a boil; simmer gently until meat is
tender. Remove bones and meat. Place
meat on a platter. Add cubed carrots,
onions, leek, potatoes, parsnips, celery
and turnip. Cover; simmer until vegetables are tender. Add tomatoes; reheat.
Serve in hot soup plates. Garnish with
chopped parsley. Meat may be sliced
and served with horseradish sauce or
made into hash.

Beef Vegetable Soup

One soup bone (1-2 lbs.), cracked
One pound stewing beef (one piece)
Two quarts cold water
One onion, quartered
Three sprigs parsley
Celery tops
One carrot, quartered
One teaspoon salt, or more
Six peppercorns
One bay leaf
Simmering time: Two hours
One cup sliced carrots
One cup sliced celery
One cup quartered potatoes
Simmering time: One hour
One recipe meatballs
Simmering time: Fifteen minutes
One recipe dumplings
Servings: Six

Place the bone, beef and water in a
large kettle; slowly bring to a boil. Skim.
Add the cut vegetables and seasonings;
cover. Simmer gently over low heat.
Skim; remove the vegetables. Add the
sliced vegetables; simmer until the meat
is very tender. Discard the bone. Add
the meatballs; simmer. Cut the beef in
serving pieces. Add the dumplings; reheat. Serve in hot soup plates.

Meat Balls

One-half pound chopped beef chuck
One teaspoon minced onion
One teaspoon minced parsley
One-fourth teaspoon salt
One-eighth teaspoon pepper
Cooking time: Fifteen minutes
Yield: Twelve meat balls

Combine all the ingredients in a bowl.
Shape into balls. Drop into the hot soup;
simmer.

Dumplings

Four tablespoons butter
Six tablespoons milk
One-fourth teaspoon salt
One cup sifted flour
One egg
Cooking time: Ten minutes
Yield: Eighteen

Bring the butter, milk and salt to a
boil in a saucepan. Remove; stir in the
flour all at once until the mixture leaves
the side of the pan. Beat in the egg.
Spoon the mixture into a shallow pan
containing two inches of boiling water.
Simmer until firm. Remove to a plate
with a slotted spoon. Reheat in the hot
soup.

Parmesan Dumplings

One egg
One-half cup grated Parmesan cheese
One teaspoon flour
Cook: Five minutes

Beat the egg in a small bowl and blend in the grated Parmesan cheese and flour. Drop rounded half teaspoonfuls of the mixture into the heated consomme and cook for five minutes. Serve at once.

A FAVORITE RECIPE
Tomato Bouillon Cup

Two cans (10½ oz. each) undiluted beef bouillon
Two and one-half cups canned tomato juice
Two slices lemon
Two whole cloves
One-eighth teaspoon dried basil
One-half teaspoon salt
One-half teaspoon sugar
Cooking time: To the boiling point
Servings: Six

In a heavy saucepan combine the bouillon, tomato juice, lemon slices, cloves and basil. Bring to a boil; reduce the heat; cook for five minutes. Strain, stir in salt and sugar. Serve in bouillon cups with Italian bread sticks.

MRS. MURIEL KISHKILL, *Hillsdale, N.J.*

Potato Soup

Three cups sliced potatoes
One cup sliced onion
One cup diced coarse celery stalks and leaves
Four cups boiling water
Cooking time: Fifteen minutes
One can (14½ oz.) evaporated milk
Two teaspoons salt (about)
Heating time: Five minutes
Two tablespoons butter or margarine
One teaspoon minced parsley
Servings: Four

Measure the sliced vegetables and boiling water into a heavy saucepan; cover. Bring to a boil and cook gently until soft. Mash slightly but do not break up all the potatoes. Add the undiluted evaporated milk and salt to taste. Reheat to the boiling point, stirring. Turn off heat. Stir in the butter or margarine and parsley. Serve in heated soup plates with toasted whole wheat bread.

Potato Soup with Frankfurters

One cup finely chopped onion
Three cups pared, thinly sliced potatoes
Three cups boiling water
Cook: Fifteen minutes, or more
Four chicken bouillon cubes
Three tablespoons butter or margarine
One cup light cream
One cup milk
One teaspoon salt
One-fourth teaspoon pepper
One-half pound frankfurters (four), thinly sliced
Simmer: Fifteen minutes
Yield: Two quarts, about

In a saucepan combine the finely chopped onion, sliced potatoes and boiling water. Cover and cook until potatoes are very tender. Press potatoes and onion with cooking water through a coarse sieve. Return to saucepan and add the bouillon cubes, butter, light cream, milk, salt, pepper and thinly sliced frankfurters. Simmer gently until piping hot but do not boil.

Oxtail Soup

One and one-half pounds oxtail joints
One-fourth cup flour
One teaspoon salt
One-fourth teaspoon pepper
Two tablespoons shortening
Browning time: Ten minutes, about
Two cups water
Three allspice berries
Simmer: Two to three hours
Three carrots, diced
Two stalks celery, diced
One medium-sized onion, sliced
Six cups water
Two tablespoons Worcestershire sauce
Two tablespoons chopped parsley
Simmer: Twenty minutes, or more
Serves: Four

Roll the oxtail pieces in the combined flour, salt and pepper. Heat the shortening in a large heavy skillet or kettle; add the floured oxtail pieces and brown well on all sides. Add the two cups of water and allspice. Cover tightly and simmer for two to three hours or until the meat falls from the bones. Skim off scum and fat. Remove meat from the bones and return to the broth. Add carrots, celery, onion, water, Worcestershire sauce and chopped parsley. Simmer gently until vegetables are tender. Serve hot.

Spicy Vegetable Beef Soup

Four pounds soup beef and bones
Two quarts cold water
Two tablespoons salt
Two tablespoons mixed pickling spice
One medium-sized onion
Simmer: Two hours
Two cups water
One and one-half cups sliced carrots
One and one-half cups sliced celery
One-half cup chopped onion
One can (No. 2½) tomatoes
One can (No. 303) corn
Two cups sliced green beans
One tablespoon salt
Two teaspoons sugar
One-fourth teaspoon pepper
Simmer: Thirty minutes, about
Yield: Approx. four quarts

Place cracked soup bones and meat in a large kettle with two quarts of cold water, two tablespoons of salt, mixed pickling spice tied in cheesecloth and the whole onion. Cover, bring to a boil and simmer for two hours. Remove and discard the spice bag. Cut meat from the bones into cubes and return to the soup with two cups of water, the sliced carrots and celery, chopped onion, tomatoes, corn and green beans. Add salt, sugar and pepper. Cover and simmer gently until vegetables are tender crisp.

Creole Soup

Five tablespoons butter or margarine
One-fourth cup chopped onion
One-fourth cup chopped green pepper
Sautéing time: Five minutes
Six tablespoons flour
Six cups boiling water
Four bouillon cubes
Cooking time: Ten minutes
One can (No. 2½) tomatoes
One cup fine egg noodles
One and one-half teaspoons salt
One-eighth teaspoon pepper
One-eighth teaspoon cayenne pepper
Two tablespoons horseradish
Simmering time: Twenty minutes
Servings: Eight

In a large saucepan or kettle (4 qts.) melt the butter or margarine. Add the chopped onion and green pepper and sauté for five minutes. Stir in the flour and gradually add the boiling water in which the bouillon cubes have been dissolved. Blend smooth and cook, stirring constantly until the sauce thickens slightly. Add the canned tomatoes, noodles, salt, pepper and horseradish and simmer gently for 20 minutes or longer. When the noodles are tender the soup is ready. Serve with hard rolls or French bread and butter.

Italian Vegetable Soup

Two tablespoons butter or margarine
Two tablespoons salad oil
One cup sliced carrots
One cup sliced zucchini
One cup shredded cabbage
One cup chopped celery
Sauté: Fifteen to twenty minutes
Two teaspoons salt
Six beef bouillon cubes
Two quarts water
Simmer: Thirty minutes
One cup chopped tomatoes
One-half cup broken spaghetti
One-half teaspoon thyme
Simmer: Twenty minutes
Grated Parmesan cheese
Servings: Six to eight

In a large heavy skillet or kettle heat the butter and salad oil. Add the prepared carrots, zucchini, cabbage and celery and sauté until vegetables are limp. Add the salt, bouillon cubes and water. Cover and simmer for thirty minutes. Add the tomatoes, spaghetti and thyme and simmer twenty minutes or longer. Serve hot with a sprinkling of grated Parmesan cheese.

Jellied Mushroom Tomato Soup

One-fourth pound chopped mushrooms
(one cup)
Two tablespoons butter or margarine
Sauteing time: Five minutes
One teaspoon finely chopped onion
Cooking time: Three minutes
Two cups tomato juice
Heat: To boiling point
One envelope unflavored gelatin
Chilling time: Two hours
Lemon slices
Servings: Four

In a heavy skillet, saute the mushrooms in the butter. Add the minced onion and cook briefly. In a saucepan, heat the tomato juice to the boiling point, gradually add to the gelatin, stirring to dissolve thoroughly. Add the sauteed mushrooms and chill thoroughly. Break with a fork slightly before serving in cups with lemon slices.

Jellied Sauerkraut Consomme

Two tablespoons unflavored gelatin
Two cans (12 oz. each) sauerkraut juice
One small onion, thinly sliced
One tablespoon chopped parsley
One-half cup diced celery
Simmering time: Ten minutes
Chilling time: Until firm
Dairy sour cream
Chopped olives
Servings: Six, or more

Soften the unflavored gelatin in one cup of the sauerkraut juice. Place the remaining juice in a saucepan with the thinly sliced onion, chopped parsley and celery. Bring to the boiling point, lower the heat and simmer gently for 10 minutes. Strain into a bowl. Add the softened gelatin and stir to dissolve. Pour into a pan (8 x 8 x 2 in.) and chill until firm. Cut into cubes to serve with a dab of dairy sour cream and a sprinkling of chopped olives.

Minted Pea Soup
(Chilled)

Two cups fresh or one package (12 oz.)
frozen peas
Four tablespoons butter or margarine
Two tablespoons finely chopped onion
Sauteing time: Five minutes
Three tablespoons flour
One teaspoon salt
Freshly ground pepper
Three cups milk
Cooking time: Five minutes, about
One-third cup cream (optional)
Chopped fresh mint
Servings: Four

Cook the fresh or frozen peas until tender. Drain and force peas through a sieve into a bowl. In a large saucepan or skillet melt the butter or margarine. Add the finely chopped onion and saute until lightly browned. Stir in the flour, salt and pepper, then gradually blend in the milk, stirring smooth. Cook, stirring constantly, until the sauce thickens. Add

the pea pulp and bring to a boil. Remove from heat and stir in the cream if used. Chill thoroughly. Serve frosty cold with a sprinkling of finely chopped mint over the top.

Frosty Avocado Soup

Four tablespoons butter
Four tablespoons flour
Two teaspoons salt
One-eighth teaspoon pepper
Four cups milk
Cook: Five to ten minutes
Grated rind of one lemon
Two tablespoons lemon juice
One cup sieved ripe avocado
Chill: Thoroughly
Dairy sour cream (optional)
Paprika
Serves: Four, or more

In a saucepan melt the butter. Stir in the flour, salt and pepper and gradually blend in the milk. Cook, stirring constantly until the sauce thickens slightly. Remove from the heat and stir in the grated lemon rind and lemon juice. Add the sieved ripe avocado. Chill thoroughly. Serve in small bowls or cups with a dab of dairy sour cream if desired and a sprinkling of paprika.

Quick Borscht

Two cups diced cooked beets
One teaspoon minced onion
One (10½ oz.) can condensed bouillon
One cup cold water
One-half teaspoon salt
Simmering time: Five minutes
One tablespoon lemon juice
Chilling time: Two hours
Five tablespoons dairy sour cream
One tablespoon minced dill pickle
Servings: Five

In a saucepan, combine the diced cooked beets with the minced onion, condensed bouillon, cold water and salt. Heat to boiling point, reduce the heat and simmer for five minutes. Remove from heat, add lemon juice and chill thoroughly. Serve in cups topped with a tablespoon of dairy sour cream and a sprinkling of minced dill pickle.

Tomato Cucumber Soup

One pound tomatoes, chopped
Three cups water
Cook: Fifteen minutes
One can (8 oz.) tomato sauce
One teaspoon salt
One-fourth teaspoon pepper
One tablespoon sugar
Two teaspoons quick-cooking tapioca
Cook: Ten minutes
Chill: Two hours
One-half cucumber, peeled, seeded,
and sliced
One-half teaspoon basil
One tablespoon parsley
Three-fourths cup dairy sour cream
Serves: Six

In a saucepan, cook the tomatoes and one cup of the water for 15 minutes. Press through a coarse sieve. Add the remaining two cups of water, tomato

sauce, salt, pepper and sugar. Sprinkle in the tapioca, blending well. Cook for 10 minutes; stirring constantly. Chill. Peel cucumbers; remove seeds, slice thin. Add to soup with the basil, parsley and sour cream. Serve warm, or chill until ready to serve.

Cucumber Soup

One-third cup butter
One medium-sized onion, chopped
Four cups thinly sliced peeled cucumber
Sauté: Ten minutes, about
Two tablespoons flour
Two cans (14 oz. each) condensed chicken
broth
One can water
Simmer: Ten to fifteen minutes
One egg yolk
One cup light cream
Simmer: Five minutes
Chopped chives
Yield: Two quarts

In a heavy bottomed large skillet or kettle melt the butter. Add the chopped onion and peeled thinly sliced cucumber. Sauté until golden, not browned. Stir in the flour thoroughly, then the chicken broth and water. Bring to the boiling point, lower the heat and simmer for 10 to 15 minutes or until the cucumber is very tender. Remove from heat and rub through a coarse sieve. Return to heat. In a small bowl beat the egg yolk, add the light cream. Add a cup of the hot soup gradually to the cream mixture stirring to prevent curdling. Return to the rest of the soup, stirring and simmer gently and briefly. Do not allow to boil. Serve in cups or bowls with a sprinkling of chopped chives on top. Excellent when served thoroughly chilled too.

Cucumber Vichyssoise

Three leeks
One large onion, thinly sliced
One-half cup butter or margarine
Cook: Fifteen minutes
Two cucumbers, coarse chopped
One cup water
Cook: Ten minutes
Two potatoes, peeled and sliced
One can (14½ oz.) chicken broth
Four chicken bouillon cubes
Two teaspoons salt
One-fourth teaspoon white pepper
Simmer: Twenty minutes
Chill: Two hours
One cup heavy cream
One-fourth cup chopped chives
Serves: Four, or more

Cut off green part and root ends of leeks; thinly slice white part. In a kettle, saute the leeks and onions in the butter or margarine until straw-colored. Meanwhile, cook the chopped cucumbers in one cup water for 10 minutes. Add the cucumbers and liquid, sliced potatoes, chicken broth and bouillon, salt and pepper to the onion mixture; simmer until the potatoes are tender. Press through a sieve. Chill in refrigerator. When ready to serve add heavy cream; ladle into chilled soup bowls. Garnish top with chives. Serve.

Vichyssoise

Six leeks
One-fourth cup butter or margarine
Cooking time: Five minutes
Two cups thinly sliced potatoes
Four cups chicken stock
One tablespoon salt
Simmering time: Thirty minutes
One cup heavy cream
One-fourth cup chopped chives
Servings: Six

Remove the stem-ends and green tops of the leeks, leaving about two inches above the white portion; slice. Melt the butter in a saucepan; add the leeks and cook until they just begin to turn golden. Add the potatoes, chicken stock and salt; cover; simmer until potatoes are tender. Force the potato mixture through a fine sieve. Stir in the cream. Cool; chill thoroughly. Serve in soup dishes; sprinkle top with chives.

French Onion Soup

Six medium-sized onions
One-fourth cup butter or margarine
Cooking time: Ten minutes
Five bouillon cubes, dissolved in
One quart boiling water
One teaspoon Worcestershire sauce
One-half teaspoon salt
One-half teaspoon paprika
Cooking time: Twenty minutes
Six slices French bread, toasted
One-half cup grated Parmesan cheese
Oven temperature: 400 degrees
Baking time: Ten minutes
Serves: Six

Cook the onions in the butter in a saucepan until straw-colored. Add the dissolved bouillon cubes and seasonings; cover; simmer until the onions are tender. Pour the soup into an earthenware soup dish; place toast on top; sprinkle with cheese. Bake in a quick oven until the cheese melts. Serve.

Gazpacho
(Spanish Cold Soup)

One can (No. 2) tomato juice
Two cups beet juice
One tablespoon white vinegar
One tablespoon sherry
One teaspoon salt
One-eighth teaspoon pepper
Beating time: Three minutes
Chilling time: Three hours
One tomato, diced
One cucumber, diced
One-half cup diced celery
One cup small bread cubes
One tablespoon olive oil
Browning time: Three minutes
One-half cup slivered almonds, toasted
One-half cup crisp, crumbled bacon
One-half cup chopped black olives
Servings: Four, or more

In a bowl mix the tomato and beet juice, vinegar, sherry, salt and pepper. Beat until well blended. Cover and chill in the refrigerator. Dice each vegetable separately; chill. In a saucepan, brown the bread cubes in the olive oil over low heat. Place the toasted cubes, almonds, bacon, olives and chilled vegetables in individual serving dishes on a tray. Serve the chilled vegetable juices in individual soup plates. Each person spoons a portion from each of the small bowls into the soup.

Chicken Salad Bowl

One head Boston lettuce
One head romaine
One small bunch chicory
Two tomatoes, finely sliced
One cup sliced celery
Two cups slivered chicken or turkey
One cup stuffed olives, sliced
One cup slivered, toasted almonds
Two-thirds cup Roquefort cheese, crumbled
Two hard-cooked eggs, chopped with
One pimiento
One cup French dressing
Pimiento, black olives
Serves: Eight

Wash the salad greens; drain and toss dry. Place in plastic bag or foil; store in refrigerator. Prepare tomatoes, celery, chicken, stuffed olives, almonds, Roquefort cheese, eggs and pimiento; chill in separate packets of foil, transparent wrap, or bowls. Chill. When ready to serve, line the bowl with lettuce leaves. Tear the remaining greens and place in chilled salad bowl. Arrange the chilled ingredients over the greens in pinwheel fashion. Garnish with pimiento and black olives. Pour dressing over salad; toss and serve.

Garden Salad Platter

Three cups shelled peas (2 lbs.)
One cup boiling water
One teaspoon salt
One-fourth teaspoon sugar
Simmering time: Ten minutes (about)
Two cucumbers, peeled and sliced
Ten scallions, peeled
Four radishes, thinly sliced
One-half cup seasoned French dressing
Lettuce leaves
Servings: Four

Cook the peas in boiling salted water with the sugar in a tightly covered saucepan. Bring to a boil; then simmer until tender. Remove from the heat; allow to cool in the pan. Drain and chill. Place the chilled cucumbers, scallions and radishes in separate dishes; sprinkle with French dressing. Arrange a bed of lettuce at both ends of a salad platter. Pile the peas on top of the lettuce. Place an overlapping row of cucumber down the center of the platter. Fill the remaining space with scallions and radishes. Serve with oil and vinegar.

Star Salad Bowl

One head crisp lettuce
Eight chicory leaves, broken
One large tomato, cut in sixths
Eight radishes, cut
One-third cup French dressing
Servings: Six

Cut the lettuce into wedges with a sharp knife; arrange in the salad bowl in a star shape design. Tuck the pieces of chicory and tomato between the lettuce wedges. In the center of the star, place radishes which have been sliced almost through. Serve with French dressing.

Zesty Potato Salad

Three-fourths cup sauerkraut juice
Three-fourths cup mayonnaise
Four cups sliced, cooked potatoes
One cup finely grated carrot
One-third cup chopped green pepper
One-third cup finely chopped onion
Chill: Two hours or more
Serves: Six

In a large bowl blend the sauerkraut juice and the mayonnaise. Add the sliced cooked potatoes, grated carrot, chopped green pepper and onion. Mix well and chill before serving.

Cheese Potato Salad

Three cups diced boiled potatoes
Three tablespoons salad oil
One tablespoon vinegar
One and one-half teaspoons salt
One cup thinly sliced celery
One-fourth cup diced green pepper
One-half cup cut ripe olives
One small onion, finely chopped
One-fourth cup mayonnaise
One cup creamed cottage cheese
Chill: Two hours, or more
Servings: Four to six

Place the diced boiled potatoes in a large bowl. In a cup blend together the salad oil, vinegar and salt. Pour over the potatoes, tossing to coat well. Add the sliced celery, diced green pepper and cut olives. In a small bowl combine the onion, mayonnaise and cottage cheese. Add to the potato mixture and toss thoroughly together. Chill well before serving.

Hot Potato Salad (for 12)

Four pounds potatoes, peeled
Boiling salted water to cover
Cook: Twenty-five minutes, about
Twelve slices bacon, diced
One-fourth cup chopped green pepper
One-fourth cup chopped scallions or
  onions
Frying time: Ten minutes
Two tablespoons flour
Two tablespoons sugar
Two teaspoons salt
One and one-half cups water
Cook: Five to ten minutes
Two tablespoons prepared mustard
One-half cup cider vinegar
One-fourth cup salad oil
One-fourth cup dairy sour cream
Servings: Twelve

Cook the peeled potatoes in boiling salted water to cover in a large kettle until tender. In the meantime, in a large heavy skillet partially fry the diced bacon. Add the chopped green pepper and scallions and cook until bacon is crisp and vegetables are tender. Stir in the flour, sugar and salt. Gradually add water and cook, stirring constantly until mixture thickens. Add the prepared mustard, vinegar, salad oil and dairy sour cream. Mix thoroughly together. Slice the hot cooked potatoes in a bowl and sprinkle lightly with salt. Pour hot dressing over potatoes and toss lightly but well. Serve at once.

Standard Potato Salad

Six cups sliced, cooked potatoes
One-fourth cup chopped onion
One-fourth cup finely cut parsley
Three hard-cooked eggs, chopped
Three-fourths cup mayonnaise
One teaspoon prepared mustard
One teaspoon salt
One-fourth teaspoon pepper
Chilling time: Two hours, or more
Servings: Eight

In a large bowl place the sliced cooked potatoes, chopped onion, cut parsley and chopped hard-cooked eggs. In a cup blend the mayonnaise with the prepared mustard, salt and pepper; add to the potatoes. Mix well and chill thoroughly before serving.

Curried Potato Salad

Four cups diced raw potatoes
One teaspoon salt
One teaspoon curry powder
Boiling water to cover
Cook: Ten minutes, about
Two tablespoons lemon juice
Three tablespoons French dressing
One tablespoon grated onion
One and three-fourths teaspoons salt
One-eighth teaspoon pepper
One-eighth teaspoon garlic powder
One-fourth teaspoon curry powder
One and one-half cups diced celery
One-half cup diced green pepper
Two diced hard-cooked eggs
One-fourth cup mayonnaise
Chill: Two hours or more
Crisp lettuce leaves
Paprika or chopped parsley
Servings: Six

Place the peeled, diced (½-inch) potatoes in a saucepan with salt, curry powder and boiling water to cover. Cover and cook until almost tender. Drain. In a bowl combine with the lemon juice, French dressing, grated onion, salt, pepper, garlic and curry powder. Mix slightly and let stand until potatoes are cold. Add the celery, green pepper, eggs and mayonnaise. Mix. Chill thoroughly and serve on crisp lettuce, garnishing each portion with a dash of paprika or finely chopped parsley.

A FAVORITE RECIPE
Dutch Mixed Salad

One cup ripe olives, cut into large pieces
Four slices crisp, fried bacon, diced
One-third cup chopped onion
Frying time: Five minutes
One teaspoon flour
One-fourth teaspoon dry mustard
Two teaspoons salt
One tablespoon brown sugar
One-fourth cup water
Three tablespoons vinegar
Cooking time: To boiling point
Four frankfurters, sliced
Cook: Until heated
Three cups diced, hot boiled potatoes
Three hard-cooked eggs, diced
One cup celery, sliced crosswise, very thin
Serves: Four

In a bowl place the cut olives. Fry the diced bacon until crisp; set aside. Fry the onion in the bacon drippings. Blend in the flour, mustard, salt and brown sugar; stir in the water and vinegar, heat to boiling point; add the sliced frankfurters. Add the diced potatoes to the olives in bowl, add the eggs and celery. Pour the hot dressing and frankfurters over the potatoes and celery. Add the bacon and toss lightly. Serve at once.

ALVENE SAFARIK, *Jackson Heights, N.Y.*

King Crab Stuffed Tomatoes

One pkg. (6 oz.) frozen King crabmeat
  (defrosted)
One and one-half cups diced celery
One-fourth cup chopped ripe olives
One tablespoon finely chopped onion
One-half teaspoon salt
One-half cup mayonnaise
Chill: Thoroughly
Four ripe tomatoes
Crisp lettuce leaves
Two hard-cooked eggs
Potato chips
Serves: Four

In a bowl combine the drained crabmeat with the diced celery, chopped ripe olives, chopped onion, salt and mayonnaise. Toss well to mix and chill thoroughly. At serving time cut the core from the washed, chilled tomatoes and cut each almost through into sixths from top to bottom spreading sections out like the petals of a flower. Place tomatoes on bed of crisp lettuce and fill with chilled crabmeat mixture. Garnish with sliced hard-cooked eggs and potato chips.

A FAVORITE RECIPE
Lobster Stuffed Egg Salad

One pound cooked lobster meat
Two-thirds cup mayonnaise
One tablespoon chili sauce
One teaspoon grated onion
One teaspoon minced green pepper
One teaspoon minced pimiento
One-fourth cup finely chopped nut meats
One and one-half dozen hard-cooked eggs,
  cut into halves lengthwise
One small head crisp lettuce
Mayonnaise
Serves: Eighteen

In a bowl, chop the lobster meat into very small pieces. Add the mayonnaise, chili sauce, onion, green pepper, pimiento and nuts. Stir until the mixture is well blended. Cook, peel, slice lengthwise and remove the hard-cooked yolks from the eggs. Fill each half with the lobster mixture. Break the yolks with a fork; place the stuffed eggs on a platter covered with crisp lettuce. Press the egg yolks through a sieve over the top of stuffed eggs. Place in refrigerator until serving time.

SADIE MC LEAN, *Beverly, Mass.*

A FAVORITE RECIPE
Trio Bean Salad

One cup seashell macaroni cooked as
    directed on package, drained
One-half cup drained cut canned green
    beans
One-half cup drained cut yellow wax beans
One-half cup cooked red kidney beans
    (canned or home-cooked)
One green pepper, cleaned, chopped
One onion, minced
One-half cup celery, chopped
One-half cup real mayonnaise
One-fourth cup wine vinegar
One teaspoon salt
One-half teaspoon pepper
One small green pepper, sliced into strips
    or rings
Servings: Six

Cook the macaroni as directed on package; drain thoroughly. In a bowl mix the
macaroni with the green, wax and kidney
beans, having all well drained. Add the
green pepper, onion and celery. Stir until
well blended. Chill until serving time,
adding the dressing made by blending
the mayonnaise in a bowl with the vinegar, salt and pepper. Fold into the salad
and serve in a glass salad bowl. Garnish
with green pepper.

KAY MESSER, *Danbury, Conn.*

Curried Chicken Salad

Two cups diced cooked chicken
Two hard-cooked eggs, diced
One cup sliced celery
One teaspoon salt
One-half teaspoon curry powder
One tablespoon lemon juice
One-half cup mayonnaise
Chill: Thoroughly
Crisp salad greens
One can (No. 2½) freestone peach halves
One-fourth cup slivered toasted almonds
Serves: Six

In a bowl combine the diced cooked
chicken, eggs, sliced celery, salt, curry
powder, lemon juice and mayonnaise.
Toss lightly to mix well. Chill thoroughly.
At serving time arrange crisp salad greens
on individual plates and place a drained
peach half on each. Fill with the chicken
salad. Garnish with slivered toasted almonds.

Almond Chicken Salad

Three cups cubed, cooked chicken (one
    jar 14 oz. boned)
Two-thirds cup chopped dill pickles
One-third cup blanched, slivered, toasted
    almonds
Two-thirds cup seeded split grapes
One-third cup mayonnaise
One-half teaspoon salt
One and one-half teaspoons cider vinegar
Chill: Thoroughly
Crisp salad greens
Serves: Four

In a bowl combine the cubed, cooked
chicken, chopped dill pickles, toasted
slivered almonds and split seeded grapes.
In a cup stir together the mayonnaise,
salt and vinegar; pour over the chicken
mixture and toss to mix well. Chill. Serve
on crisp salad greens.

Chef's Salad Bowl

Two quarts washed, dried and torn salad
    greens (iceberg and Romaine lettuce)
One-fourth Bermuda onion, thinly sliced
One-fourth green pepper, thinly sliced
Two large ripe tomatoes, cut in slim
    wedges
One-half cucumber, thinly sliced
One carrot, scraped and thinly sliced
Two hard-cooked eggs, sliced
One-half cup julienned cheddar cheese
One-fourth pound julienned boiled ham
Serves: Four, or more

If you wish to toss one large salad
(main course for four, side course for
eight) place the prepared salad greens
in a large bowl and add the thinly sliced
onion, green pepper, tomatoes, cucumber and carrot. (Vegetable peeler will
cut really thin slices of cucumber and
carrot.) Add the sliced hard-cooked eggs,
julienned cheese and ham. Pour on one-
fourth cup or more of salad dressing and
toss thoroughly just before serving.

Note: A self combined salad is enjoyed by many. In that case offer all the
ingredients other than mixed greens in
small bowls on a tray permitting each
diner to combine his own.

A FAVORITE RECIPE
Summer Salad

Three cups diced, cooked chicken
One cup minced celery
One cup orange sections, cut into pieces
    (½ in.)
One can (9 oz.) pineapple tidbits
One-half cup chopped toasted almonds
Two tablespoons salad oil, mixed with
Two tablespoons orange juice
Two tablespoons vinegar
One-half teaspoon salt
One-sixteenth teaspoon marjoram
Standing time: One hour in refrigerator
One-half cup mayonnaise
One head crisp lettuce
Servings: Six

Dice and remove all skin and small
bones from the chicken. In a bowl mix
with the celery, orange, pineapple and
nuts. In a cup mix the salad oil, orange
juice, vinegar, salt and marjoram. Stir
into the chicken mixture. Chill. Drain.
Fold in the mayonnaise. Serve in a salad
bowl, lined with the lettuce.

JENNIS T. OGDEN, *Staten Island, N.Y.*

A FAVORITE RECIPE
Veal Vegetable Salad

Two cups diced (¼ in.) cooked veal
One small onion, minced
One-fourth cup minced celery
One-half cup stuffed olives cut into halves
One teaspoon lemon juice, mixed with
One tablespoon mayonnaise
One head crisp lettuce
Servings: Four

Cook the veal; cut into dice. Place in
a bowl; mix with the onion, celery and
olives. Add the lemon juice to the mayonnaise; fold into the veal mixture. Line a
salad bowl with the lettuce. Turn the
salad into bowl and serve.

MRS. PHILETTA WARD
Methodist Home
Ocean Grove, N.J.

Frankfurter Vegetable Salad

One pkg. (10 oz.) frozen Frenched
    green beans
One pkg. (10 oz.) frozen lima beans
Eight frankfurters
One medium-sized Bermuda onion, thinly
    sliced
Two or three tomatoes, diced
One-half cup French or Italian style
    salad dressing
Chill: Two hours
Crisp lettuce leaves
Servings: Six

Cook the frozen green beans and limas
according to package directions and combine in a large bowl with the thinly
sliced cooked frankfurters, sliced Bermuda onion, diced tomatoes and salad
dressing. Mix well and chill thoroughly
in the refrigerator before serving over
crisp leaves of lettuce.

Pickled Eggs

Six eggs
Simmer: Five minutes
Three-fourths cup canned beet juice
Three-fourths cup vinegar
One-half cup rosé wine
One bay leaf
One-fourth teaspoon ground allspice
Three-fourths teaspoon salt
One-sixteenth teaspoon pepper
One clove garlic (optional)
Chill: Overnight
Yield: Six

Place the eggs in a saucepan and cover
with cold water. Bring slowly to a boil,
reduce heat and simmer for five minutes.
Drain and cover with cold water, crack-
ing each egg shell against the pan. Peel
shells from eggs and place in a screw
top jar.

In a saucepan, combine the beet juice,
vinegar, wine, bay leaf, allspice, salt,
pepper and crushed garlic clove. Heat to
a gentle simmer; do not boil. Pour over
the eggs in the jar. Cool to room temperature and refrigerate overnight before
using.

Serve whole, sliced or quartered
lengthwise with salads or as a garnish on
cold meat plates.

Purple Cabbage Salad

One cup dairy sour cream
One-half cup real mayonnaise
One teaspoon salt
One-fourth teaspoon dry mustard
One tablespoon horseradish sauce
One tablespoon flaked onion
Two teaspoons caraway seed (optional)
One head purple cabbage, finely shredded
Three avocados, peeled and sliced
Four apples, sliced
Serves: Six

In a bowl mix the sour cream, mayonnaise, salt, mustard, horseradish sauce, flaked onion and caraway seed. Let stand for 10 minutes. Pour over crisp purple cabbage, tossing until well mixed. Reserve some of the sliced avocado and apple for garnish. Toss the remaining avocado and apple slices with the purple cabbage. Place green cabbage leaves around rim of platter. Fill with purple cabbage mixture. Garnish with the remaining slices of avocado and apple.

Green Cabbage Salad

One head green cabbage, finely shredded
One cup real mayonnaise
One-half cup French dressing
One teaspoon salt
One package (8 oz.) Switzerland Swiss
  cheese
One package (8 oz.) assorted Italian cold
  cuts
Serves: Six

Carefully remove and wash the outer leaves of cabbage. Use a sharp knife to shred the cabbage. Place leaves and cabbage in a large bowl in refrigerator to crispen. Remove the shredded cabbage; toss with the combined mayonnaise, French dressing and salt, mixing well. Cut the Swiss cheese and cold cuts in squares (1 in.). Add to cabbage; toss together lightly. Place in center of large cold glass platter.

Italian Dressing

Two tablespoons sugar
One and one-half teaspoons salt
One teaspoon mustard
One teaspoon paprika
One teaspoon Worcestershire sauce
One cup catsup
One cup pure vegetable oil
One-half cup wine vinegar
One small onion, minced
One clove garlic, sliced
Let stand: One hour
Yield: Two and one-half cups

Measure ingredients into a jar, cover tightly and shake until well blended. Strain.

California Dressing

Three tablespoons minced anchovies
Three tablespoons minced chives or
  green onion
One tablespoon lemon juice
Three tablespoons tarragon vinegar
One small clove garlic, pureed
One-half cup heavy cream, soured
One cup real mayonnaise
One-third cup minced parsley
One teaspoon salt
One-fourth teaspoon freshly ground
  black pepper
Yield: Two cups

Combine the ingredients. Chill. Shake well before using.

Cheese Salad Dressing

One-fourth cup corn oil
Two tablespoons cider vinegar
One-half teaspoon oregano or thyme
One-fourth teaspoon turmeric
One-fourth teaspoon freshly ground pepper
Four tablespoons crumbled Gorgonzola
  cheese
Serves: Four

In a small bowl blend the oil, vinegar and seasonings. Mix in the crumbled cheese. Serve immediately.

Thousand Island French Dressing

Two tablespoons minced green pepper
Three tablespoons minced pimiento
Two tablespoons capers
Two tablespoons chopped stuffed olives
One teaspoon Worcestershire sauce
One cup French dressing
Yield: One cup

Combine the ingredients. Chill. Shake well before using.

Sour Cream Dressing

One teaspoon salt
One-fourth teaspoon paprika
One-half teaspoon mustard
Few grains cayenne
One tablespoon wine vinegar
One tablespoon lemon juice
One cup dairy sour cream
One tablespoon minced chives
Yield: One cup

Mix the dry ingredients with the wine vinegar and lemon juice. Blend in the sour cream. Chill before using.

Potato Salad

Eight cups cooked new potatoes, diced
Two cups chopped celery
One-third cup chopped onion
Four hard-cooked eggs, chopped
Two packages (1¼ oz. each) Roquefort
    cheese, crumbled
One tablespoon salt
One-half teaspoon pepper
One cup real mayonnaise
Chill: Overnight
Assorted cold cuts
Serves: Eight

In a large bowl, place all the ingredients. Toss gently until well blended. Pack firmly into a bowl. Cover the bowl. Allow to chill overnight. Unmold. Frost entire mold with mayonnaise. Sprinkle chopped parsley over entire mold. Garnish with sieved hard-cooked egg yolks and cucumbers. Arrange cold cuts around salad.

Double Decker Tomato Salad

Two cups chopped, cooked chicken
One cup minced celery
One-fourth cup French dressing
Marinate: Two hours
One cup real mayonnaise
One tablespoon minced parsley
One-half teaspoon onion salt
Few grains cayenne
One pound bacon, fried crisp
One bunch water cress, chopped
Six tomatoes, peeled and chilled
Crisp lettuce
Serves: Six

In a bowl mix the chicken, celery and French dressing. Marinate in refrigerator. Add half the mayonnaise, parsley, salt and cayenne. Reserve. Crumble the bacon; mix with the water cress and remaining mayonnaise. Slice each tomato crosswise into thirds. Sandwich the two bottom slices together with chicken salad and the top layer with the bacon mixture. Repeat procedure for each tomato. Serve on crisp lettuce.

Corned Beef Potato Salad

Three tablespoons vinegar
Three tablespoons salad oil
Five cups hot, cooked cubed potatoes
One can (12 oz.) corned beef
Two cups chopped celery
One-fourth pound Danish blue cheese,
    crumbled
One cup real mayonnaise
One-fourth cup minced onion
One-fourth cup minced parsley
One and one-half teaspoons salt
One tablespoon barbecue mustard
Chill: Two hours
Crisp chicory
Hard-cooked eggs, tomatoes, cucumbers,
    green peppers
Serves: Six

Mixed Salad

Sprinkle the combined vinegar and oil over the hot cubed potatoes. Cool. With a fork break up the corned beef. Add the celery and Danish blue cheese. Add the combined real mayonnaise, onion, parsley, salt and mustard. Mix with the potatoes; chill. Place in a wooden bowl lined with crisp chicory. Garnish with sliced hard-cooked eggs, tomatoes, cucumbers and green pepper. Serve.

Layered Salad

Set aside the broken-up corned beef. Combine the marinated potatoes, celery, Danish blue cheese, mayonnaise, onion, parsley, salt and mustard. Chill. Pack half the potato mixture in a greased loaf pan (8 x 5 x 3 in.); then a layer of corned beef and top with remaining potato mixture; chill. Unmold and garnish.

Tossed Salad

Arrange marinated potatoes, corned beef, celery, Danish blue cheese in separate piles in a chicory lined wooden bowl. Garnish with sliced hard-cooked eggs, tomatoes, cucumbers, green pepper. Combine the real mayonnaise, onion, parsley, salt and mustard. When ready to serve, toss the salad with dressing.

Hot Lettuce Salad

One small head lettuce
Three slices bacon
One tablespoon flour
One teaspoon dry mustard
One teaspoon salt
One teaspoon sugar
Two-thirds cup water
Two tablespoons vinegar
One tablespoon instant minced onion
Serves: Four to six

Wash and dry the lettuce. Break into bite size pieces and place in a large bowl. In a heavy skillet cook the bacon until crisp. Crumble bacon into lettuce. Pour off all but two tablespoons of the drippings in the skillet. Blend flour, dry mustard, salt and sugar into fat in skillet. Gradually blend in the water and vinegar. Add the instant minced onion. Cook, stirring until slightly thickened. Add additional water if necessary. Pour over the lettuce and toss. Serve at once.

Special Green Salad

One small head iceberg lettuce
One small raw leek, sliced
One cup raw chopped spinach
One small clove garlic, crushed (optional)
Two tablespoons olive oil
Two tablespoons vinegar
One-eighth teaspoon dry mustard
One-fourth teaspoon salt
Freshly ground black pepper to taste
Dash paprika
Servings: Four

Wash the lettuce, leek and spinach and dry thoroughly. Tear lettuce into bite-sized pieces and place in salad bowl. Add the thinly sliced raw leek and the chopped raw spinach. In a cup stir together the crushed clove of garlic, olive oil, vinegar, dry mustard, salt and pepper to taste. Just before serving pour over the greens in the salad bowl and toss thoroughly.

Raw Spinach Salad

Two pounds fresh spinach
Two hard-cooked eggs
One-third cup finely chopped celery
One-third cup finely chopped onion
One-half cup finely cubed sharp cheese
One-fourth teaspoon salt
One-fourth teaspoon Tabasco
One teaspoon vinegar
One-third cup mayonnaise
Two tablespoons prepared horseradish
Chill: Well
Crisp leaves of Romaine lettuce
Servings: Six

Trim the roots, coarse stems and bruised leaves from the spinach, using only the fresh inner leaves. Wash well by lifting from several changes of warm water, allowing the sand to fall to the bottom. Dry spinach leaves well and chop fairly fine (you need three cups chopped spinach). Combine chopped spinach with the finely chopped hard-cooked eggs, celery, onion and sharp cheese. Blend the salt, Tabasco and vinegar into the mayonnaise with the prepared horseradish. Fold into the chopped vegetables, mixing well. Chill. Serve on crisp leaves of Romaine lettuce. Good with sliced, boiled or baked ham.

Caesar Salad

One-third cup olive oil
One clove garlic
One and one-half cups bread cubes
Oven temperature: 300 degrees
Bake: Twenty minutes, or more
Three quarts crisp Romaine (torn bite-size)
One-third cup salad oil
Salt
Pepper
One teaspoon Worcestershire sauce
One-third cup grated Parmesan cheese
One egg
One-fourth cup lemon juice
One cup ripe olive pieces
Servings: Four large, eight small

Pour the olive oil into a cup, add the split clove of garlic and let stand for two hours or more if possible. Discard garlic. Scatter the half inch bread cubes on a baking sheet and toast in a slow oven until golden, twenty to thirty minutes. Cool to room temperature and toss with garlic flavored olive oil. Place the washed, dried and chilled greens in a large bowl. Add the plain salad oil, salt and pepper and toss until all pieces are coated with oil. Add Worcestershire sauce, grated Parmesan, raw unbeaten egg, lemon juice, olive pieces and toasted bread cubes. Toss until no trace of egg may be seen. Serve at once.

California Salad

Two cloves garlic, quartered
One-fourth cup olive oil
Standing time: Four hours or overnight
Two cups bread cubes (½ inch)
Oven temperature: 300 degrees
Toast: Fifteen minutes, about
Two quarts salad greens, torn to bite-size
One-third cup crumbled blue cheese
One tablespoon grated Parmesan cheese
One beaten raw egg
Dressing
One-fourth cup salad oil
Three tablespoons lemon juice
Three tablespoons cider vinegar
One teaspoon salt
One-fourth teaspoon ground black pepper
Servings: Four large, eight small

Add quartered cloves of garlic to the fourth cup of olive oil and let stand several hours or overnight. Remove garlic and discard. Scatter the bread cubes over a baking sheet and place in a slow oven until toasted a golden brown. Remove and let cool. Toss bread cubes with the garlic flavored olive oil in a bowl. Wash and trim salad greens (combine Boston and iceberg lettuce with Romaine), dry well and tear into bite-size to loosely fill a four cup measure twice. Chill. At serving time place greens in a large bowl with the toasted bread cubes, crumbled blue cheese, grated Parmesan and beaten egg. Combine the dressing of salad oil, lemon juice, vinegar, salt and pepper in a cup.

Stir to blend well. Add three tablespoons or so to the salad ingredients and toss thoroughly to coat all leaves. Serve at once.

Garden Slaw

One-half cup dairy sour cream
Two tablespoons sugar
Two tablespoons lemon juice
One tablespoon grated onion
One-half teaspoon prepared mustard
Six cups finely sliced cabbage
One cup finely diced celery
One-fourth cup diced green pepper
Salt and pepper to taste
Serves: Six to eight

In a bowl stir together the sour cream, sugar, lemon juice, grated onion and prepared mustard. Chill. Combine the finely sliced cabbage, celery and green pepper. At serving time add dressing to the slaw and toss lightly. Season to taste with salt and pepper.

Crunchy Cauliflower Salad

One small head cauliflower (three cups chopped)
Two tablespoons finely chopped onion
Four radishes, chopped
One tablespoon mayonnaise
One tablespoon lemon juice
One teaspoon prepared horseradish
One-half teaspoon salt
One-eighth teaspoon pepper
Chill: Thoroughly
Crisp lettuce leaves
Finely chopped parsley
Servings: Four to six

Wash the cauliflower and separate into flowerets. Chop the raw vegetable very fine and combine in a bowl with the chopped onion, chopped radishes, mayonnaise, lemon juice, horseradish, salt and pepper. Mix well and chill thoroughly. Serve on lettuce leaves with a sprinkling of finely chopped parsley on top.

Spinach-Bacon Salad

One pound fresh spinach
One-fourth cup finely chopped onion
Salt and pepper
Eight slices bacon, fried crisp
One-fourth cup French dressing, about
Serves: Six, or more

Trim the roots and thick stems from the spinach and discard with any bruised leaves. Drop the crisp leaves into a large dishpan or scoured sink filled with warm water. Move leaves with the hands to permit sand to fall to the bottom. Lift leaves from the water. Repeat two or three times until completely clean. Drain on absorbent towels. Tear into bite size pieces and place in large salad bowl. Add the finely chopped onion, salt, pepper, crumbled crisp bacon and French dressing. Toss until well mixed. Use more French dressing if you wish.

Molded Waldorf Salad

One package apple flavored gelatin
One and one-fourth cups boiling water
One-half cup sherry wine or sauterne
Two tablespoons lemon juice
Chill: Until thickened
One-half cup sliced celery
One-fourth cup chopped walnuts
One red apple, cored, diced
Chill: Until firm
Crisp lettuce leaves
Mayonnaise
Serves: Six

Dissolve the apple flavored gelatin in the boiling water. Add the wine and lemon juice and chill until thickened slightly. Add the sliced celery, chopped nuts and diced red apple with skin left on. Pour into a three cup rinsed mold or six individual molds. Chill until firm. Unmold on crisp lettuce leaves. Serve with mayonnaise.

Roquefort Salad Mold

One envelope unflavored gelatin
One-half cup milk
One and one-half cups milk
Heat: Until dissolved
Two packages (3 oz. each) cream cheese
One-half cup Roquefort cheese (2 oz.)
Chilling time: Until firm
Two large grapefruit
Four oranges
One pint fresh strawberries
Crisp water cress
Servings: Four to six

In a small bowl soften the unflavored gelatin in the half cup of milk. Heat the remaining milk in a saucepan and stir in the softened gelatin. Heat until thoroughly dissolved. In a bowl cream the cheeses thoroughly together and gradually blend in the milk and gelatin mixture. Beat smooth. Pour into a single mold (3 cup) or six individual molds. Chill until firm. Unmold. Surround individual portions of the mold with sections of grapefruit, sections of orange and a mound of sliced fresh strawberries. Garnish with crisp water cress. Pass salad dressing if desired.

A FAVORITE RECIPE
Jellied Chicken Loaf

One chicken (4-5 lbs.) disjointed
Salted water to cover
Cooking time: Two hours, about
Four hard-cooked eggs, shredded
One-half cup minced celery
One-half cup minced sweet pickle
One-half cup cracker meal or bread crumbs
Two tablespoons unflavored gelatin, soaked in
One cup cold water
Two cups hot chicken broth
One teaspoon salt
One-fourth teaspoon pepper
Chill: Four hours
One head crisp lettuce
Two hard-cooked eggs, quartered
Six sprays parsley
Serves: Eight, or more

Place the chicken in a deep kettle; cover with the salted water; bring to a boil, reduce the heat; simmer until the meat falls from the bones. Cool; strain the broth; remove chicken from bones and heavy skin; dice. In bowl mix the chicken with the shredded eggs, celery, pickle and bread crumbs. Soak the gelatin in the cold water; add to the hot chicken broth stirring until dissolved. Add salt and pepper. Pour over the chicken mixture. Pour into a mold (10 in.). Chill until serving time and the loaf is firm. Serve on lettuce leaves, garnished with the hard-cooked eggs and parsley.

ELVA M. STONG SANDERS, *Wichita, Kansas*

A FAVORITE RECIPE
Lime Ham Salad

Four packages (3 oz. each) lime flavored gelatin
Five cups hot water
One cup liquid, drained from sweet pickles
Chilling time: Until it starts to gel
Three-fourths cup chopped, cooked ham
One-half cup thinly sliced sweet pickles
One-fourth cup minced celery
One teaspoon grated onion
One teaspoon celery seed
One-third cup mayonnaise
Chilling time: Until firm
Yield: One mold (2 qt.)
Sliced hard-cooked eggs
Servings: Six, or more

In a bowl, dissolve the lime gelatin in the hot water, stirring well. Cool. Add the pickle liquid, stir. Chill until it starts to gel. Add the ham, sweet pickles, celery, onion, celery seed to one-half the gelatin mixture. Set aside. To the remaining gelatin add the mayonnaise, beating with a rotary beater until fluffy. Turn the mayonnaise mixture into a mold or a tube pan. Top with the ham mixture. Chill until firm. Unmold on a glass plate and garnish with sliced hard-cooked eggs.

MRS. BERTHA SEELY, *Jersey City, N.J.*

A FAVORITE RECIPE
Molded Chicken Mousse

Three envelopes unflavored gelatin
One-half cup cold water
Soaking time: Ten minutes
One can (10½ ozs.) condensed cream of mushroom soup
Two and one-half cups chicken broth
One-fourth teaspoon pepper
Two teaspoons salt
Cooking time: Until boiling point
One cup real mayonnaise
Three cups finely chopped, cooked chicken
One teaspoon Worcestershire sauce
One and one-fourth tablespoons grated onion
Two tablespoons lemon juice
Two tablespoons chopped parsley
One and one-half cups minced celery
One cup heavy cream, whipped
Chilling time: Overnight
One head crisp lettuce
French dressing
Serves: Sixteen

In a cup soak the gelatin in the cold water. In a saucepan combine the mushroom soup, chicken broth, pepper and salt; cook to the boiling point. Add the gelatin, stirring until dissolved; blend in the mayonnaise. Add the chicken, Worcestershire sauce, onion, lemon juice, parsley and celery. Stir until well blended. Fold in the whipped cream. Spoon into one mold (3 qts.) or into three molds (1 qt. each). Rinse the molds in cold water before adding mixture. Serve on crisp lettuce. Serve with French dressing or any other favorite dressing.

MRS. STANLEY HASTE, *East Walpole, Mass.*

A FAVORITE RECIPE
Party Crab Meat Salad

One envelope unflavored gelatin
Two-thirds cup cold water
Three tablespoons lemon juice
One-fourth teaspoon salt
One-sixteenth teaspoon pepper
Three-fourths cup mayonnaise
One hard-cooked egg, chopped
One cup minced celery
One-fourth cup sweet pickle, chopped
One can (7 oz.) crab meat
Chill: Four hours
Yield: Six molds (6 oz. each)

In a cup soften the gelatin in the cold water, dissolving over hot water; cool to lukewarm. Add the lemon juice, salt, pepper and mayonnaise. In a bowl mix the egg, celery, pickle and crab meat (all cartilage removed). Mix with the gelatin and mayonnaise mixture. Turn into six individual molds. Chill until serving time. Serve immediately on crisp lettuce.

MRS. B. A. MC COY, *Elizabeth City, N.C.*

A FAVORITE RECIPE
Jellied Ham Loaf

One tablespoon unflavored gelatin
One-fourth cup cold water
One can (10½ oz.) condensed tomato soup
One cup water
Heating time: To boiling point
One package (3 oz.) softened cream cheese
Cooling time: Until it starts to gel
One-half cup real mayonnaise
Two teaspoons prepared mustard
Two tablespoons lemon juice
Two cups ground cooked ham
Chilling time: Four hours
Six large stuffed olives, sliced
Servings: Six

In a cup soften the gelatin in the cold water. Heat the soup and one cup of water; add the gelatin stirring until dissolved. Add cream cheese, stirring until thoroughly blended. Chill until it starts to gel. Add the mayonnaise, mustard, lemon juice and ground ham; stir until well mixed. Turn into a loaf pan (8 in.), or into a ring mold. Chill until firm; unmold. Serve sliced upon lettuce leaves, garnished with the sliced olives.

MRS. H. B. LITTLEFIELD, *Sante Fe, N. Mex.*

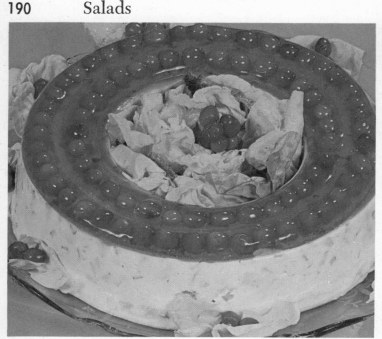

Chicken and Ham Mousse

Two envelopes unflavored gelatin
One-half cup cold water
Two egg yolks, slightly beaten
One-half teaspoon salt
One-half teaspoon dry mustard
One cup chicken stock
One cup milk
Cooking time: Ten minutes (about)
Two cups chopped cooked chicken
One cup chopped cooked ham
Two-thirds cup minced celery
Two teaspoons lemon juice
Chilling time: Thirty minutes (about)
One tablespoon minced parsley
One-fourth cup minced pimiento
One-half cup heavy cream, whipped
Chilling time: Three hours
Servings: Eight, or more

Sprinkle the gelatin over the cold water in cup. Combine the egg yolks and seasonings in the top of a double boiler; add

the stock and milk. Cook over hot water, stirring constantly, until the mixture coats a spoon. Stir in the gelatin. Add the chicken, ham, celery and lemon juice. Chill until it begins to thicken. Fold in the parsley, pimiento and whipped cream. Pour into a ring mold (9 in.). Chill until set. Unmold on a platter; fill the center with salad greens. Garnish with deviled eggs and sliced tomatoes. Serve on chilled salad plates.

Alaska King Crabmeat with Avocado Mousse

Two tablespoons unflavored gelatin
One-half cup cold water
Two cups boiling chicken broth, or
    bouillon
Refrigerate: Until cool
One cup real mayonnaise
Four cups mashed avocado, sieved
One teaspoon salt
Two teaspoons onion juice
One cup heavy cream, whipped stiff
Few drops green coloring
Refrigerate: Overnight
Three packages (6 oz. each) Alaskan King
    Crabmeat, defrosted
One-fourth cup French dressing
Crisp salad greens
Love apples, stuffed olives
Serves: Eight

In a bowl sprinkle the gelatin over the cold water. Let stand; add to boiling chicken broth, stirring until dissolved. Let cool. Stir in the real mayonnaise, sieved avocado, salt and onion juice; beat until smooth. Fold in the whipped cream. If necessary add a few drops of green coloring. Pour into a ring mold (9 in.) rinsed out in cold water. Refrigerate overnight. Defrost the crabmeat; drain and marinate in the French dressing. Unmold salad on a large platter (do not unmold salad until the last minute or it will darken). Fill center with water cress

and love apples. Arrange crabmeat in lettuce cups around salad. Garnish with stuffed olives.

Molded Chicken Salad
Cranberry Topping

Two cups sugar
One cup water
Two cups cranberries
Cook: Ten minutes, about
One envelope unflavored gelatin
One-half cup cold water
Chill: Until somewhat firm

Salad

Two envelopes unflavored gelatin
One-half cup cold water
Two cups boiling chicken broth
Three cups cottage cheese, sieved or
    beaten in blender
One cup dairy sour cream
One cup minced celery
One-third cup minced onion
One-half cup minced green pepper
Four cups chopped cooked chicken
Two teaspoons salt
Few grains cayenne
Chill: Three hours
Crisp lettuce
Serves: Eight

In a saucepan heat the sugar and water stirring until sugar is dissolved. Add the cranberries, cooking until the cranberries begin to burst. Sprinkle the gelatin over the cold water. After 5 minutes stir into cranberry mixture. Pour into a mold (2 qts.). Let stand until it begins to gel. For the salad: Sprinkle the gelatin over the cold water. Stir into the boiling chicken broth until gelatin is dissolved. Add the sieved cottage cheese, dairy sour cream, celery, onion, green pepper, chopped chicken, salt and cayenne. Spoon carefully over the somewhat firm cranberry gelatin. Refrigerate until firm. Unmold. Tuck crisp lettuce in center and around mold.

Tongue and Turkey in Aspic

Two envelopes unflavored gelatin
One-half cup cold water
Two cups condensed canned consomme
One-half teaspoon salt
One-fourth cup vinegar
One beef tongue, cooked according to
  directions on package
Six slices turkey, minced
Chill: Until firm
One cucumber, sliced
One-half cup minced green pepper
One-half cup minced celery
One tablespoon minced scallions
Two tablespoons horseradish sauce
One-fourth teaspoon pepper
One-third cup chopped pimiento
Chill: Two hours
Serves: Four, or more

Sprinkle the gelatin over the cold water in a cup. Heat the consomme to boiling; add salt and vinegar. Add the gelatin, stirring until dissolved. Pour ¼ cup of gelatin mixture in bottom of a loaf pan or mold (6 cup). Chill 5 minutes. Slice the tongue. Alternate six slices of tongue and turkey over the firmed consomme. Pour another fourth cup of gelatin over the tongue and turkey. Arrange cucumber slices around the loaf pan. Chop enough of the tongue to measure one cup. Mix the remaining gelatin mixture with the cup of chopped tongue, green pepper, celery, scallions, horseradish, pepper and pimiento. Spoon over the sliced meat. Refrigerate several hours or overnight. Unmold on lettuce. Garnish as desired. Serve sliced.

Macaroni Egg Salad

One box (8 oz.) macaroni, cooked
Chilling time: Thirty minutes
One cup chopped celery
One-fourth cup chopped green pepper
Eight radishes, sliced
One tablespoon grated onion
One-half cup French dressing
One teaspoon salt
One-sixteenth teaspoon cayenne
Chilling time: Twenty minutes
Six hard-cooked eggs, quartered
Two-thirds cup salad dressing
Servings: Four to six

Drain the macaroni; cool in a dish; separate with a fork; chill. Mix the vegetables, French dressing and seasonings together; chill. Combine the macaroni, vegetables and five of the eggs, moistening with the salad dressing. Arrange upon a chicory-bordered platter. Serve the remaining egg over the salad; garnish with black olives. Serve with cold cuts.

Molded Salmon Salad

One envelope unflavored gelatin
One-half cup cold water
One and one-half cups boiling
  chicken stock
Chilling time: Thirty minutes
Two cups cooked fresh salmon
Two cups cooked peas
Two cups chopped celery
One-third cup French dressing
Three slices cucumber
Three slices radish
Three celery leaves
Chilling time: Three hours, about
Servings: Four to six

Sprinkle the gelatin in the cold water to soften. Add the boiling chicken stock, stirring until dissolved; chill until beginning to gel. Marinate the fish and vegetables separately in the French dressing. Arrange the cucumber, radish and celery leaves in a pattern in the bottom of an oiled pan (10 x 5 x 3 in.), lined with waxed paper. Spoon in one-half cup of gelatin mixture; chill until set. Place the salmon in a layer over the gelatin then add the peas and finely the celery. Pour in the remaining gelatin mixture, chill until firm. Unmold on a tray; garnish with lettuce and tomato. Serve with sour cream and cucumber dressing.

Fruit Salad Supreme

Twelve large cooked prunes
Three ounces cream cheese
Milk
One-sixteenth teaspoon nutmeg
Two grapefruit
Two large oranges
Two large bananas
Green seedless grapes
Two ripe purple plums
Crisp leaves of Romaine
Mayonnaise
Servings: Four

Remove the pits from the cooked prunes. In a small bowl cream the cheese with enough milk to make it light and fluffy, add the nutmeg. Stuff into the prunes. Chill. Peel and section the grapefruit and oranges, removing all membrane. Wash and stem the seedless grapes. Wash, halve and pit the plums, slice. Chill all fruit until serving time. Arrange individual plates attractively, lining each with two or three leaves of Romaine lettuce and arranging alternating sections of grapefruit and orange, a group of stuffed prunes, section of sliced bananas and garnish of sliced plums and seedless grapes. Serve with mayonnaise thinned slightly with fruit juice (orange, pineapple or apricot is good).

A FAVORITE RECIPE
Fruit Salad

One can (No. 2) pineapple chunks
Two small cans Mandarin oranges
One package flaked coconut
One pint sour cream
Marinating time: Three hours
Servings: Four

In a bowl, mix the pineapple chunks, orange slices, coconut and sour cream. Let stand in refrigerator for several hours. Serve on crisp lettuce on individual salad plates.

MRS. IRVING CARTER, *Cos Cob, Conn.*

Holiday Fruit Salad

One cup raw cranberries
Two tablespoons sugar
One red-skinned apple
One grapefruit
One-half cup chopped celery
One small ripe avocado
Crisp lettuce leaves
Mayonnaise, if desired
Servings: Six

Wash and dry the cranberries, cut each in half. Place in a bowl and sprinkle with sugar. Core and dice the unpeeled apple and add with the diced, membrane-free grapefruit, chopped celery and diced avocado. Mix and chill. Serve on crisp lettuce leaves with mayonnaise, if desired.

California Fruit Salad

One and one-half cups red grapes
One large red apple
One can (11 oz.) mandarin orange sections
One-fourth cup chopped or slivered almonds
One-third cup dairy sour cream
One tablespoon honey
One teaspoon lemon juice
One-sixteenth teaspoon salt
Crisp lettuce leaves
Serves: Three or four

Wash and wipe dry the red grapes and apple. Split and seed the grapes. Combine in a bowl with the diced, unpeeled apple, drained canned orange sections and slivered almonds. Chill well. Combine the dairy sour cream, honey, lemon juice and salt and chill. At serving time spoon the combined fruits on crisp leaves of lettuce on individual serving plates and pass the sour cream dressing.

A FAVORITE RECIPE
Stuffed Peach Salad

Eight canned peach halves, drained

Filling

One cup coconut (dry or moist)
One-half cup minced celery
One cup black walnuts or pecans, cut into small pieces
One-half teaspoon salt
Chilling time: Two hours

Topping

One cup heavy cream, whipped
Three tablespoons mayonnaise
Servings: Eight

Remove a small amount of the peach pulp around cavity. Mix in a bowl with the coconut, celery, walnuts and salt. Chill. Arrange the peaches on plates, covered with shredded lettuce; fill with the chilled mixture. Mix the whipped cream and mayonnaise. Garnish each serving with the mixture.

MRS. RUTH H. LLOYD, *White Plains, N.Y.*

Ginger Cream Pear Salad

One pkg. (3 oz.) cream cheese
One tablespoon milk
One-third cup gingersnap crumbs
One can (No. 303) pear halves
Two apples
Crisp lettuce leaves
French dressing
Servings: Six

Blend the softened cream cheese with the milk; form into six small balls. Roll cream cheese balls in the gingersnap crumbs. Chill balls with canned pears and apples. At serving time, arrange crisp lettuce leaves on individual salad plates and place a drained pear half on each. Place several thin slices of cored apple around the pear and top with the gingercheese ball. Serve with French dressing.

Fruit Salad Dressing

One tablespoon sugar
One-fourth teaspoon salt
One and one-half teaspoons lemon juice
One-fourth cup pineapple juice
One-half cup dairy sour cream
Yield: Three-fourths cup

In a bowl stir the sugar and salt together with the lemon juice. Blend in the pineapple juice, then the dairy sour cream, whisking smooth. Chill and serve with fresh or combined fresh and canned fruit salads.

Melon Pear Salad

Two large Bartlett pears
One-half cup orange juice
Three tablespoons lemon juice
One-eighth teaspoon salt
One-eighth teaspoon paprika
One-sixteenth teaspoon nutmeg
One large cantaloupe or medium-sized honeydew melon
Crisp lettuce leaves
One cup stemmed seedless grapes
Two red or purple plums, halved
Servings: Four

Cut the pears into eighths, peel and remove core. Place in a bowl and pour on the orange juice blended with the lemon juice, salt, paprika and nutmeg. Chill. Cut a chilled cantaloupe or honeydew melon in half, remove seeds and fibers. Cut two one-inch circles of melon from each half and peel. Peel and dice the end pieces of melon and add to the pears in juice. At serving time arrange lettuce on serving plates with a ring of melon. Fill center with combined pears and diced melon. Garnish with grapes and plum halves. Sprinkle with remaining fruit juices and serve.

Stuffed Pear Salad

One package (3 oz.) cream cheese
Two tablespoons milk
One teaspoon grated orange rind
One-eighth teaspoon salt
Two-thirds cup fresh dates, pitted and sliced
Eight canned pear halves, chilled
Crisp leaves of Romaine or Boston lettuce
One tablespoon toasted slivered almonds (optional)
Serves: Four, or more

In a small bowl, cream the cheese with a fork, gradually blend in the milk, orange rind and salt. Add the sliced dates. Refrigerate. At serving time spoon the cheese mixture into the centers of the drained pear halves and serve on crisp lettuce leaves. Garnish with the slivered toasted almonds if desired. This makes four main course luncheon or supper salads, eight small side salads.

Stuffed Prune Salad

Two packages (3 oz. each) cream cheese
One-fourth cup orange juice
One-half teaspoon grated orange rind
One-eighth teaspoon salt
Twenty-four large cooked prunes
Four navel oranges, peeled and sectioned
Salad greens
Salad dressing
Serves: Four for luncheon or eight small
    side salads

In a bowl cream the cream cheese until light and fluffy. Gradually blend in the orange juice, stirring smooth. Stir in the grated rind and salt. Remove pits from the large cooked prunes. Fill with the cream cheese mixture; chill in the refrigerator with the sectioned oranges. Just before serving arrange stuffed prunes and orange sections on crisp salad greens.

A FAVORITE RECIPE
Peanut-Prune Salad

Twelve prunes, cooked, pitted, chilled
One-third cup cottage cheese
One teaspoon grated orange rind
Two tablespoons chopped peanuts
Salt to taste
Two tablespoons mayonnaise
One-half head crisp lettuce
Servings: Four

Cook the prunes in enough water to cover. Pit. Chill. In a bowl, combine the cheese, orange rind, peanuts and salt to taste. Add enough mayonnaise to bind the mixture. Stuff the prunes with cheese mixture and place on the crisp lettuce on individual plates.

LOUIS H. KESTENBAUM, *Flushing, L.I., N.Y.*

Pear and Lime Salad Mold

One pkg. (3 oz.) lime flavored gelatin
One and two-thirds cups hot water
One-fourth teaspoon salt
One-fourth cup lemon juice
Two ripe pears
One-fourth cup diced pimiento
One cup finely shredded cabbage
Chill: Until set
Crisp lettuce leaves
Mayonnaise, if desired
Servings: Six

Dissolve the gelatin in the hot water in a bowl. Stir in the salt and lemon juice. Chill until syrupy. When gelatin is thickened, peel, core and dice the pears and add with the diced pimiento and shredded cabbage. Mix well and spoon into individual molds that have been rinsed with cold water. Chill until set. Unmold by dipping the molds to the level of the gelatin in a bowl of hot water. Turn out on crisp lettuce leaves and serve with mayonnaise if desired.

Molded Fruit Salad Chablis

One package (3 oz.) lemon flavored gelatin
One and one-fourth cups boiling water
Three-fourths cup New York state Chablis
Chill: Until syrupy
One cup membrane freed orange segments,
    cut up
One-half cup diced red skinned apple
One-half cup sliced pitted dates
One-fourth cup diced celery
One medium-sized banana, diced
Chill: Until firm
Crisp salad greens
Servings: Six

Place the lemon flavored gelatin in a bowl and add the boiling water. Stir to dissolve. Add the Chablis and chill until syrupy. Stir in the cut up orange segments, diced apples, sliced dates, diced celery and banana; mixing well. Pour into rinsed mold, large single (about five cups) or six individual molds. Chill until firm. Unmold by dipping for a minute or two into a bowl of hot water, up to the level of the contents. Turn out on crisp greens to serve.

A FAVORITE RECIPE
Fruit-Cream Salad

One envelope unflavored gelatin
One-half cup water
Standing time: Five minutes
One cup hot fruit juice, heated to boiling
One-third cup sugar
One-eighth teaspoon salt
One-fourth cup lemon juice
Two small (3 oz. each) packages cream
    cheese (at room temperature)
Chilling time: Until it starts to gel
One cup fruit cocktail, drained
One cup diced canned pineapple, drained
Two oranges, cut into pieces (½ in.)
One cup nuts
Chilling time: Four hours
Serves: Six

Soften the gelatin in the half cup of water. Let stand. Mix into the boiling hot juice, stirring until dissolved. Stir in the sugar, salt and lemon juice. Cream the cheese with a fork; add to the gelatin mixture, stirring until well blended. Chill until it starts to gel. Fold in the fruits and nuts. Pour into six small molds. Chill until serving time. Unmold on glass plates over shredded lettuce.

MRS. KATHRYN M. ELMORE, *Birmingham, Ala.*

Molded Grapefruit Apple Salad

One envelope unflavored gelatin
One-half cup fresh grapefruit juice
Three tablespoons lemon juice
One-fourth cup sugar
One cup hot water
One-sixteenth teaspoon salt
Chill: Until syrupy
One cup fresh grapefruit sections, diced
One-half cup diced red skinned apple
Chill: Until set
Servings: Six small

Sprinkle the unflavored gelatin over the half cup of grapefruit juice in a bowl, let soften. Add the lemon juice, sugar, hot water and salt. Stir to dissolve. Chill until syrupy. Fold in diced grapefruit and apple and chill until set. Use one mold or six small individual ones. Unmold upon crisp lettuce leaves to serve.

A FAVORITE RECIPE
Frozen Pineapple Salad

One cup heavy cream, whipped
One-fourth cup mayonnaise
One teaspoon unflavored gelatin,
    softened in
Three tablespoons syrup from pineapple
One cup crushed pineapple
One-half cup chopped ripe olives
One-half cup minced celery
One-half teaspoon prepared horseradish
One teaspoon salt, or less
Freezing time: Four hours
One head crisp lettuce
Servings: Six

In a bowl, whip the cream; fold in the mayonnaise. Soften the gelatin in the pineapple juice, heated over hot water until dissolved. Cool; fold into the cream mixture. Fold in the crushed pineapple, olives, celery, horseradish and salt to taste. Pour into a refrigerator tray. Set the control to freezing; stir the mixture frequently until frozen. Serve cut into squares on crisp lettuce with a favorite dressing.

MRS. SYLVIA NOVITT, *Wantagh, L.I.*

Apricot Wine Mold

One and one-half tablespoons unflavored
    gelatin
One-fourth cup lemon juice
One can (12 oz.) apricot whole fruit nectar
Heat: To boiling
One-half cup sugar
Three-fourths cup California rosé wine
One can (No. 303) apricot halves
Chill: Until partially set
One large banana, sliced
Chill: Until firm
Serves: Six to eight

Sprinkle the unflavored gelatin over the lemon juice in a cup and let stand to soften. Heat the apricot whole fruit nectar in a saucepan to the boiling point. Dissolve the softened gelatin in the nectar and stir in the sugar. Add the rosé wine. Drain the syrup from the apricot halves and add three-fourths of a cup to the gelatin mixture. Chill until partially set. Cut each apricot half into four pieces and add to the thickened gelatin with the thinly sliced banana. Pour into a six-cup ring or other favorite mold or into individual ones, chill until firm. Serve as dessert or as salad on lettuce leaves with dairy sour cream.

Citrus Salad Hawaiian Style

Three grapefruit, peeled and sectioned
Six oranges, peeled and sectioned
One avocado, peeled and sliced lengthwise
One can (No. 2½) pineapple spears, drained
Three tangerines, peeled and sliced crosswise
One cup dairy cottage cheese
One box kumquats, washed
Servings: Six

On one side of a salad leaf bowl arrange the grapefruit sections, orange sections, and avocado slices. On the other side arrange the pineapple spears and tangerine slices. Fill the smaller section of the leaf dish or a small bowl with cottage cheese and the other section of the leaf dish or bowl with kumquats. To serve: Place a few romaine leaves or salad greens on each salad plate. Then arrange several pieces of each type of fruit, a spoonful of cottage cheese and a couple of kumquats on the romaine leaves. Serve with Fruit French Dressing and mayonnaise.

Fruit French Dressing

One teaspoon paprika
One-half teaspoon salt
One teaspoon sugar
One-half cup salad oil
One-fourth cup orange juice
One tablespoon lime or lemon juice
Yield: Three-fourths cup

Mix the dry ingredients in a bowl; add the oil. Stir until well blended. Add the fruit juices. Beat or shake in a bottle until blended. Pour into a bowl. Garnish with lime or lemon slices. Serve with fruit salad.

Fruit Cottage Cheese Ring

Two envelopes unflavored gelatin
One-half cup cold water
One cup white wine
Four cups creamed cottage cheese, sieved
One cup sour cream
Two tablespoons sugar
One teaspoon salt
Few grains cayenne
Chilling time: Three hours
Four cups cubed fresh fruit
Ten whole strawberries
Six orange slices
Serves: Six, or more

In a cup soften the gelatin in cold water. In a saucepan heat the wine to boiling. Add the gelatin, stirring until dissolved. Stir into the combined cottage cheese, sour cream, sugar, salt and cayenne. Pour into an oiled mold (9 in.). Chill until firm. Unmold on a cold platter. Fill center with fresh fruit. Garnish with calyx leaves, orange slices and strawberries. Serve either as a salad or dessert.

A FAVORITE RECIPE

Mandarin Orange Salad

Two packages orange flavored gelatin
Two cups boiling water
Two cans (6 oz. each) frozen concentrated orange juice
One can (8 oz.) mandarin orange slices
Chilling time: Four hours
One head crisp lettuce
Servings: Six

Empty the orange flavored gelatin into a bowl; add the boiling water, stirring until dissolved. Add the frozen orange juice, stirring until melted. Pour into a mold (10 in.). Add the orange slices. Chill until firm. Serve on crisp lettuce leaves with a favorite dressing.

MRS. ROBERT A. NARDONE, *Bloomfield, N.J.*

A FAVORITE RECIPE

Avocado-Apple Sauce Mold

One package lime flavored gelatin
One package lemon flavored gelatin
Two cups boiling water
Two cups cold water
Chilling time: Until the mixture gels
One can (8 oz.) apple sauce
One ripe avocado, peeled, sliced thin
One cup minced celery
One-half cup chopped walnuts
Chilling time: Four hours
One head crisp lettuce
Berries for garnish
Servings: Six

In a deep bowl, dissolve the lime and lemon gelatin in the boiling water; add the cold water. Chill until the mixture starts to gel, stir and add the apple sauce, avocado, celery and nuts, mixing well. Turn into individual molds and chill until serving time. Unmold on lettuce leaves, garnish with any favorite berry.

MRS. M. W. BUTLER, *New Hyde Pk., L.I., N.Y.*

Molded Fruit Salad

One can (No. 2½) peeled apricots,
    halved and pitted
One-half cup vinegar
Ten whole cloves
Two sticks cinnamon
Simmer: Ten minutes
Three packages lemon flavored gelatin
Chill as directed
One bunch dark grapes, seeded
Two avocados, peeled and sliced
Two bananas, peeled, sliced
Red maraschino cherries, drained and
    halved
Refrigerate: Overnight
Crisp greens
Serves: Eight, or more

Carefully drain apricots, reserving syrup. To the syrup add the vinegar, whole cloves and cinnamon sticks; simmer for 10 minutes. Strain syrup adding enough boiling water to make five cups. Add the lemon flavored gelatin stirring until dissolved. Arrange fruit in bottom of ring mold (9 in.) and a small mold (1 qt.). Pour a portion of gelatin in each. Chill until firm. Repeat procedure until all of the fruit and gelatin mixture is used. Chill until firm. When ready to serve unmold ring on a platter and unmold the smaller one in center of ring. Serve a portion on crisp salad greens with mayonnaise, honey dressing or whipped cream.

Salad in Pineapple Shells

Two ripe pineapples (2 lbs.)
Two cups cooked or canned shrimp, diced
One-half cup chopped celery
One-half cup mayonnaise
Two teaspoons sour or sweet cream
One teaspoon salt
One-fourth teaspoon pepper
One-eighth teaspoon curry powder
Servings: Four

Cut the pineapples into halves lengthwise without removing the leafy tops. Carefully remove the pulp, leaving shells one-half inch thick. Cut the pulp from the core and dice. Place with the shrimp in a bowl. Mix the remaining ingredients and combine with the fruit and shrimp. Heap the pineapple shells with the salad. Place upon salad plates. Garnish with additional mayonnaise, capers and sliced stuffed olives. Serve on plates with potato chips, cheese straws and crisp pickles.

Cheese Fruit Salad

One-half pint cottage cheese
One-half pound Danish blue cheese
One-half cup dairy sour cream
Crisp lettuce
Assorted fruits in season
Serves: Six, or more

Beat the cheeses and cream until well blended. Arrange on bed of crisp lettuce. Arrange fruits around cheese.

Basic French Dressing

One-fourth cup vinegar
Three-fourths cup salad oil
One-fourth teaspoon paprika
One-half teaspoon salt
One teaspoon sugar
Yield: One cup

Combine vinegar, oil, paprika, salt and sugar in a jar with a screw top. Chill thoroughly. Shake well before using.

Roquefort Dressing

One-fourth cup vinegar
Three-fourths cup salad oil
One teaspoon salt
One-fourth teaspoon pepper
One-fourth teaspoon dry mustard
Three tablespoons crumbled Roquefort
  cheese
Yield: One and one-fourth cups

In a small bowl combine the vinegar, salad oil, salt, pepper, dry mustard and crumbled Roquefort cheese. Fork whip until thoroughly blended. Store in a jar that has a tight fitting lid so mixture may be shaken before serving.

Creamy French Dressing

Two cups salad oil
One clove garlic, split
Two teaspoons grated onion
One-half teaspoon powdered dry mustard
One-eighth teaspoon pepper
One teaspoon paprika
One teaspoon salt
One-fourth cup catsup
One tablespoon sugar
Three-fourths cup vinegar
One egg white
Yield: Three cups

In a bowl combine the salad oil, split clove of garlic, grated onion, seasonings and vinegar. Let stand for one hour; remove the garlic and discard. Add the egg white and beat mixture vigorously together with a rotary or electric beater. Transfer to a tightly covered jar and store in the refrigerator.

A FAVORITE RECIPE
Italian French Dressing

One package (3 oz.) Roquefort cheese,
  crumbled
Two tablespoons minced onion
One-fourth cup minced parsley
Four anchovy fillets, cut small
One-half teaspoon coarse black pepper
Three-fourths teaspoon salt
One-sixteenth teaspoon garlic salt
One-fourth cup lemon juice
One teaspoon Worcestershire sauce
One-fourth cup red wine vinegar
One and one-fourth cups salad oil
Yield: Two and one-fourth cups, about

In a jar (with cover) mix the crumbled cheese, onion, parsley and fillet of anchovy. Add the pepper, salt, garlic salt, lemon juice, Worcestershire sauce, vinegar and oil. Shake well before using.

MRS. MILDRED RODEVITZ, *Garfield, N.J.*

Mustard French Dressing

Two teaspoons salt
One teaspoon cracked black pepper
One-fourth teaspoon sugar
One-half teaspoon dry mustard
One teaspoon prepared mustard
One teaspoon lemon juice
Two tablespoons tarragon vinegar
Two tablespoons olive oil
One-half cup vegetable oil
Yield: Three-fourths cup

Measure the salt, pepper, sugar, dry mustard, prepared mustard, lemon juice, vinegar, olive oil and vegetable oil into a screw-top jar. When ready to use shake jar well. Spoon as much as desired of the dressing over mixed salad greens and toss well.

Vinaigrette Salad Dressing

Two teaspoons salt
One-eighth teaspoon pepper
Three-fourths teaspoon dry mustard
One-half teaspoon paprika
Three-fourths teaspoon garlic powder or
  one clove garlic, crushed
One-half cup olive oil
Two tablespoons pickle relish
One tablespoon finely chopped green
  pepper
Three tablespoons vinegar
Two tablespoons lemon juice
Marinate: Two hours
Yield: One cup

Measure all ingredients into a screw-topped jar. Cover and allow to marinate in the refrigerator for two hours or more. Shake well to blend thoroughly before using over mixed greens.

Herbed Dressing

Three tablespoons dried parsley flakes
Two tablespoons dried minced green
  onions
One-fourth teaspoon crumbled dry tarragon
Three tablespoons vinegar
Two tablespoons water
Standing time: Fifteen minutes
One cup mayonnaise
One-half cup dairy sour cream
Two tablespoons anchovy paste
One-half teaspoon salt
Two teaspoons prepared mustard
One-fourth teaspoon ground black pepper
One-eighth teaspoon garlic powder
Chill: Well
Yield: Two cups

Measure the dried parsley flakes; dried minced green onion, and crumbled dry tarragon into a small bowl; add the vinegar and water and let stand for fifteen minutes. In a second bowl combine the mayonnaise, dairy sour cream, anchovy paste, salt, mustard, pepper and garlic powder; mix well. Blend in the herbed vinegar mixture and transfer to a screw top jar. Store in the refrigerator.

Lemon Mayonnaise

One egg
One-fourth cup lemon juice
One teaspoon dry mustard
One teaspoon salt
One tablespoon sugar
One-eighth teaspoon paprika
One pint salad oil
Yield: Two and one-half cups

In a bowl beat together with a rotary or electric beater the egg, lemon juice, dry mustard, salt, sugar and paprika. Continue beating, adding the salad oil very slowly. Beat until the oil is completely incorporated and the dressing is thick. Add it drop by drop for the first half of the oil, then in a very fine stream. Store in a covered jar in the refrigerator.

Cooked Salad Dressing

One egg
One-fourth cup vinegar
Three-fourths cup salad oil
One tablespoon sugar
Two teaspoons dry mustard
One teaspoon salt
One-eighth teaspoon white pepper
One-eighth teaspoon cayenne
Three tablespoons cornstarch
One cup cold water
Cook: Till thick and clear
Yield: Two cups

Break the egg into a medium-sized bowl and beat in the vinegar, salad oil, sugar, dry mustard, salt, pepper and cayenne. Measure the cornstarch into a small saucepan and gradually blend in the cold water. Cook, stirring constantly until the mixture becomes very thick and clear. Beat into the egg and oil mixture until thoroughly blended and smooth.

Green Cream Salad Dressing

One can (2 oz.) flat anchovies, finely
  chopped
Three tablespoons finely chopped green
  onions
Two tablespoons finely chopped parsley
One-fourth teaspoon garlic powder or one
  clove of garlic, crushed
One tablespoon lemon juice
Three tablespoons tarragon or cider
  vinegar
One-fourth teaspoon black pepper
One-half cup dairy sour cream
One cup mayonnaise
Yield: One and one-half cups

Combine the finely chopped anchovies and oil with the finely chopped green onion, parsley, garlic powder, lemon juice, vinegar, pepper, dairy sour cream and mayonnaise. Mix thoroughly together. Use an electric blender if possible. Store in tightly covered jar in the refrigerator to fully develop flavor. Use on mixed green salads.

Blueberry Muffins

One and one-half cups sifted flour
One-half cup sugar
Two teaspoons baking powder
One-half teaspoon salt
One egg
One-half cup milk
One-fourth cup soft shortening
One cup fresh cleaned blueberries, or one can (15 oz.), drained
Oven temperature: 400 degrees
Bake: Twenty minutes
Yield: Twelve

Sift the flour, sugar, baking powder and salt together into a bowl. In a bowl beat the egg and add to the dry ingredients with the milk and soft shortening. Mix together with a pastry blender. Add the blueberries and spoon into well greased muffin pans. Bake in a quick oven until muffins are browned and start to leave the edge of the pans. Turn out on rack and serve warm or thoroughly cooled.

Blueberry Crumb Muffins

Two cups sifted flour
Three teaspoons baking powder
One-half cup sugar
One-half teaspoon salt
One and one-fourth cups washed blueberries
One egg
One-fourth cup salad oil
One cup milk
One-fourth cup butter
One-third cup brown sugar
One-fourth teaspoon cinnamon
One-half cup sifted flour
Oven temperature: 375 degrees
Baking time: Thirty minutes
Yield: Eighteen

Sift together into a bowl the two cups of flour, baking powder, half cup of sugar and salt. Add the blueberries. In a second bowl beat the egg; stir in the salad oil and milk. Add liquid to dry ingredients and stir just until blended. Spoon into greased muffin pans, filling about two-thirds full. In a small saucepan melt the butter. Remove from heat and stir in the brown sugar, cinnamon and half cup of flour. Blend well together; then sprinkle this crumbly mixture over the batter in the muffin pans. Bake in a moderately hot oven for about thirty minutes or until the muffins are nicely browned and away from the edges of the pans. Remove to rack. Serve warm or when completely cooled.

Cranberry Muffins

One cup fresh cranberries
One-half cup sugar
Two cups sifted flour
Three teaspoons baking powder
One-half teaspoon ginger
One-half teaspoon salt
One egg
One cup milk
One-fourth cup salad oil
Oven temperature: 400 degrees
Bake: Twenty-five minutes
Yield: Twelve

Wash and dry the cranberries. Cut each in half with a sharp knife. Mix halved berries with the sugar in a bowl. Sift the flour, baking powder, ginger and salt together over the cranberries. Mix well. In a second bowl beat the egg, add the milk and salad oil. Add to the dry ingredients and mix just enough to moisten all flour. Spoon into greased muffin pans, filling two-thirds full. Bake in a quick oven until nicely browned. Turn out immediately on a rack and serve at once.

Bread

Lemon Muffins

Two cups sifted flour
One-third cup sugar
Three and one-half teaspoons baking powder
One-half teaspoon salt
Two eggs
One cup milk
One-third cup salad oil
One tablespoon grated lemon rind
Oven temperature: 400 degrees
Baking: Twenty minutes
Yield: Twelve

Sift together into a bowl the flour, sugar, baking powder and salt. In a second bowl beat the eggs; add the milk and salad oil. Add the liquid ingredients all at once. Stir together just enough to moisten completely. Spoon into greased muffin pans filling two-thirds full and bake in a quick oven for 20 minutes or until lightly browned and away from the sides of the pans.

Cinnamon Muffins

Two cups sifted flour
One-fourth cup sugar
Four teaspoons baking powder
One-half teaspoon salt
One-half teaspoon cinnamon
One egg
One cup milk
One-fourth cup salad oil
Two tablespoons sugar
One-half teaspoon cinnamon
Oven temperature: 400 degrees
Bake: Twenty minutes
Yield: Twelve

Sift the flour, sugar, baking powder, salt and cinnamon into a bowl. In a second bowl beat the egg, add the milk and salad oil. Pour liquid into dry ingredients and mix just enough to moisten completely. Spoon into greased muffin pans, filling about two-thirds full. Stir remaining sugar and cinnamon together and sprinkle over top. Bake in a quick oven for twenty minutes. Serve while still hot with butter or jam.

Bran Biscuits

Two cups sifted flour
Four teaspoons baking powder
One teaspoon salt
One cup all-bran cereal
Two-thirds cup shortening
Three-fourths cup milk
Oven temperature: 425 degrees
Bake: Ten minutes
Yield: Twelve, or more

Sift flour, baking powder and salt into a mixing bowl. Crush the all-bran cereal into very fine crumbs. Add to the flour. Cut the shortening into the dry ingredients with a pastry blender or two knives until the mixture resembles coarse meal. Add milk and stir only until combined. Turn dough out on floured board and roll out to about half an inch in thickness. Cut with floured biscuit cutter. Bake on ungreased baking sheet in hot oven until lightly browned. Serve at once.

Wheat Germ Surprise Muffins

One and one-half cups sifted flour
One-fourth cup sugar
Three teaspoons baking powder
One teaspoon salt
One-half cup wheat germ
One egg
One cup milk
One-fourth cup salad oil
Peanut butter
Oven temperature: 400 degrees
Bake: Twenty minutes
Yield: Twelve

Sift the flour, sugar, baking powder and salt into a bowl. Stir in the wheat germ. In a small bowl beat the egg, add the milk and salad oil. Pour the liquid into dry ingredients and mix just enough to moisten completely. Place a tablespoon of batter into each greased muffin pan, top with a half teaspoon of peanut butter and a dab of remaining batter. Bake in a quick oven for twenty minutes. Serve while hot. Good with jam.

Baking Powder Biscuits

Two cups sifted flour
Four teaspoons baking powder
One-half teaspoon salt
Four tablespoons shortening
Two-thirds cup milk
Oven temperature: 450 degrees
Baking time: Twelve minutes, about
Yield: Eight to ten

Into a bowl sift together the flour, baking powder and salt. Cut in the shortening using two knives or a pastry blender until the consistency of coarse meal. Add enough milk to give a dough that leaves the sides of the bowl. Turn out upon a floured board; knead gently for a few seconds. Pat or roll out to three-fourths of an inch in thickness. Cut with a floured cutter. Place upon an ungreased baking sheet. Bake in a very hot oven until a delicate brown.

Brioches

One package active dry yeast
One-fourth cup warm, not hot, water
One tablespoon cream
One tablespoon sugar
One-half teaspoon salt
One cup of soft butter
Four eggs
Two and one-half cups sifted all-purpose
    flour
Mixing time: Seven minutes
Chill: Overnight
Rising time: Two hours
Oven temperature: 375 degrees
Baking time: Twenty-five minutes
Yield: Twelve

In a bowl sprinkle the yeast over the warm, not hot, water until softened. Add cream, sugar, salt and butter. Add three eggs and one egg yolk, reserving one egg white. Add the flour. Beat at medium speed of heavy electric beater for about 5 minutes or 7 minutes by hand. Cover. Place in refrigerator overnight. Remove dough from refrigerator. Turn dough out onto a floured board. Cut one-fourth of dough into 12 even-sized pieces. Shape into balls (1 in. diam.). Shape remaining dough into 12 balls. Place larger balls into well-greased floured deep muffin pans (2 in.). Press a deep hole in center of each ball of dough. Place smaller ball in each depression. Brush entire surface with remaining unbeaten egg white. Let rise for 2 hours or until double in bulk. Bake in a moderate oven for 25 minutes. Remove to rack.

Refrigerator Rolls

Two packages active dry yeast
One-half cup warm, not hot, water
One and one-fourth cups scalded milk,
    cooled to lukewarm
One-half cup butter or margarine, melted
Two eggs, slightly beaten
One-half cup sugar
Two teaspoons salt
Five and one-half cups sifted enriched
    flour
Chilling time: Overnight
First rising time: Two hours
Second rising time: One hour
One egg yolk, mixed with
One-fourth cup milk
Poppy, sesame or celery seeds
Oven temperature: 400 degrees
Baking time: Twelve minutes (about)
Yield: Three dozen

In a cup soften the yeast in warm, not hot, water. In a large bowl combine the cooled scalded milk; add the cooled melted butter, eggs, sugar and salt with the yeast. Beat in the flour, a cup at a time. (Dough should be on the soft side.) Knead quickly on a floured board into a smooth dough. Place in a greased bowl; grease the top of the dough. Cover tightly with a bowl cover or waxed paper. Place in the refrigerator. (Dough will actually rise, so punch down and re-cover.) When ready to use within the next few days, continue according to the following directions. Cover with a towel. Set to rise over a pan of warm water in a warm place. Let double in bulk. Shape into rolls. Place on oiled baking sheets or in muffin pans. Brush tops with combined egg yolk and milk. Sprinkle tops with poppy, sesame or celery seeds. Let rise until double in size. Bake in a quick oven until golden. Remove to racks.

Peanut Butter Biscuits

Two cups sifted flour
One teaspoon salt
Two and one-half teaspoons baking powder
Two tablespoons shortening
One-fourth cup peanut butter
Three-fourths cup milk
Oven temperature: 450 degrees
Bake: Ten to twelve minutes
Yield: Twelve

Into a bowl sift together the flour, salt and baking powder. Cut in the shortening and peanut butter, using a pastry blender or two knives. Stir in the milk. Turn dough out on a lightly floured board and knead briefly. Pat or roll dough to the desired thickness and cut into biscuits. Bake on an ungreased baking sheet in a very hot oven until lightly browned.

Cheese Biscuits

Two cups sifted flour
Four teaspoons baking powder
One-half teaspoon salt
Four tablespoons shortening
One-third to one-half cup grated cheddar cheese
Two-thirds cup milk
Oven temperature: 450 degrees
Bake: Twelve minutes, about
Yield: Eight to ten

Into a bowl sift together the flour, baking powder and salt. Cut in the shortening, using two knives or a pastry blender until the consistency of coarse meal. Stir in the grated cheese. Add enough milk to give a dough that leaves the sides of the bowl. Turn out upon a floured board, knead gently for a few seconds. Pat or roll out to three-fourths of an inch in thickness. Cut with a floured cutter. Place upon an ungreased baking sheet. Bake in a very hot oven until nicely browned. Serve hot from the oven.

Raisin Scones

One-half cup raisins
Two cups sifted flour
One-fourth cup sugar
Three teaspoons baking powder
One teaspoon salt
One-third cup shortening
One egg
Milk
Oven temperature: 425 degrees
Bake: Fifteen minutes, about
Yield: Twelve

Cover the raisins with hot water; drain. Sift the flour, sugar, baking powder and salt together into a bowl. Cut in the shortening using a pastry blender or two knives. Add the raisins. Beat the egg slightly in a measuring cup and add milk to make two-thirds cup. Stir into the dry ingredients. Turn dough out on a floured board and divide in two parts. Pat each part into a circle about six inches that is three-fourths of an inch thick. Cut into six wedges. Place on greased baking sheet and brush tops with milk. Bake in hot oven until nicely browned. Serve at once.

Croissants

Two packages active dry yeast
One-half cup lukewarm water
One and one-fourth cups milk, scalded and cooled to lukewarm
One tablespoon sugar
One-half teaspoon salt
Five cups flour (about)
Standing time: Twenty minutes
Three-fourths pound butter, hard
Chilling time: Overnight
Rising time: One and one-half hours
One egg white, unbeaten
Oven temperature: 400-350 degrees
Baking time: Twenty minutes
Yield: Four dozen

In a mixing bowl sprinkle the yeast over the lukewarm water; let stand until dissolved. Add the combined lukewarm scalded milk, sugar and salt. Gradually beat in the flour. On a floured board knead until smooth. Shape into a ball. Cover with a towel. Let rest on board for 20 minutes. Uncover; roll out on a floured board into a rectangle (18x13x⅛ in.). Slice the hard butter into thin pats. Place them over the entire surface of the dough. Roll the buttered dough in jelly roll fashion into a tight roll. Cut the roll in half. Roll out each piece of dough on a floured board into a rectangle (14x10 in.). Fold dough into thirds. Repeat this rolling and folding procedure three more times. Wrap each piece of dough in waxed paper and place in the refrigerator overnight.

Flaky Raspberry Rolls

One cup butter or margarine
Eight ounces cream cheese
One teaspoon salt
Two cups sifted flour
Chill: Until firm
Red raspberry jam (10 oz. jar)
Oven temperature: 425 degrees
Bake: Fifteen minutes, about
Yield: Five dozen

In a bowl cream the butter or margarine with the cream cheese until smooth. Blend in the salt and sifted flour. Mix thoroughly. Chill until firm enough to handle. Roll portions of the dough out on a floured board about one-eighth inch thick. Cut into two and one-half inch squares. Spread each with about a teaspoonful of jam to within one-fourth inch of edge. Roll up tightly and pinch edge to roll or seal. Place on ungreased baking sheet and bake in a hot oven for about fifteen minutes or until nicely browned. Remove to racks to cool thoroughly.

Quick Onion Cheese Rolls
(Beaten Batter)

One and one-fourth cups warm water
One package active dry yeast
Three cups sifted flour
One tablespoon sugar
One teaspoon salt
One-fourth teaspoon celery seed
Two teaspoons instant onion or
Two tablespoons finely chopped fresh onion
Two tablespoons shortening
One egg, beaten
One cup grated cheddar cheese
First rising: One hour, about
Black pitted or stuffed green olives
Second rising: Twenty minutes, about
Oven temperature: 425 degrees
Bake: Fifteen minutes
Yield: Fifteen to eighteen

Measure the warm water into bowl (mixer bowl if electric beater is to be used). Sprinkle on the active dry yeast and let stand to soften. In a second bowl, combine the flour, sugar, salt, celery seed and instant or fresh onion. Cut in the shortening with two knives or a pastry blender. Add the beaten egg to the softened yeast then beat in two-thirds of the flour mixture with grated cheese until smooth. (Beating by hand or electricity takes the place of kneading in this recipe.) Beat in remaining flour until smooth. Scrape the batter down from the sides of the bowl. Cover with a clean cloth, set the bowl in a warm place and allow batter to rise to double its bulk. Beat batter hard and spoon into well greased muffin cups filling just one-half. Press an olive into the center of each. Cover and let rise until batter reaches top of muffin cups. Bake in a hot oven until well-browned. Remove to rack to cool slightly before serving.

Refrigerator Butter Rolls

One package active dry yeast
One fourth cup warm, not hot, water
One-half cup butter
One cup milk
One-half cup sugar
Three eggs, beaten
Four and one-half cups sifted flour
First rising time: One hour, about
Second rising time: One hour, about
Third rising time: One hour
Oven temperature: 375 degrees
Baking time: Twelve minutes
Two tablespoons melted butter
Yield: Thirty-two

In a large bowl, soften the dry yeast in the warm water. In a saucepan, melt the butter in the milk; cool to lukewarm, add to the softened yeast. Add the sugar and beaten eggs; work in the sifted flour. Transfer the mixture to a greased bowl, cover with a cloth and place in a warm spot to allow dough to rise to double in bulk. Punch down; place in refrigerator and allow to rise again. Divide dough into four parts. Roll each piece on a floured board into a circle (9 in.) and

cut into eight wedges. Roll pieces from the wide to the narrow end and place these crescents upon a greased baking sheet to rise again before baking. Bake in a moderately hot oven until browned. Remove from oven, brush with melted butter. (Note: The second rising time may occur in the refrigerator during storage, then the final rising allowed for after forming and previous to the baking.)

Pecan Apple Sauce Rolls

One package active dry yeast
One-fourth cup lukewarm water
One-half cup milk
Three tablespoons shortening
One-fourth cup sugar
One teaspoon salt
One egg
Two and one-half cups sifted flour
First rising time: One hour or more
Two tablespoons butter or margarine
One can (No. 303) apple sauce
Two teaspoons cinnamon
Simmer: Ten minutes
One cup seedless raisins
One teaspoon grated lemon rind
Two tablespoons butter or margarine
Two tablespoons honey
One-fourth cup brown sugar
One cup pecan halves
Second rising time: Thirty minutes, or more
Oven temperature: 375 degrees
Bake: Thirty-five to forty minutes
Yield: Sixteen

Sprinkle the active dry yeast over the lukewarm water in a cup and let stand to soften. Scald the milk in a small saucepan; add the shortening and stir until dissolved. Add sugar and salt. In a large bowl beat the egg. Add the slightly cooled milk mixture gradually. Blend in the softened yeast. Gradually beat in the sifted flour. Turn dough out on a floured board and knead lightly until smooth and satiny.

Shape into a ball and place in a greased bowl, turning over once to grease the top of dough. Cover with a clean cloth and set in a warm spot to rise until double in bulk. Place two tablespoons of butter or margarine in a saucepan with the apple sauce and cinnamon. Simmer gently for ten minutes. Take from heat and add the raisins and grated lemon rind. Set aside to cool. In a small saucepan melt two tablespoons of butter or margarine and stir in the honey and brown sugar. Remove from heat and spread over the bottom of a baking pan (9 x 9 x 2 in.).

Scatter pecans over this. When dough has risen turn out on a floured board and roll out into a rectangle 17 by 9 inches. Spread with apple sauce mixture and roll up from the long side and cut in sixteen slices. Place slices cut side down over pecans in pan. Cover with a cloth and set in a warm spot until rolls rise almost double in height. Bake in a moderately hot oven until well browned, thirty-five minutes or more. Turn out on rack at once.

Pecan Rolls

Two packages active dry yeast
One-half cup lukewarm water
One cup scalded milk
One-third cup shortening
One-half cup sugar
One and one-half teaspoons salt
Five to six cups sifted flour
Two eggs, beaten
Kneading time: Ten minutes
First rising time: One hour
Resting time: Ten minutes
One-half cup butter or margarine, melted
One cup brown sugar
One cup pecan halves
One-fourth cup sugar
Two teaspoons cinnamon
Second rising time: One hour
Oven temperature: 375 degrees
Bake: Thirty minutes
Yield: Eighteen

Sprinkle the dry yeast over the lukewarm water in a small bowl. Pour the scalded milk over the shortening, sugar and salt in a large bowl. Stir to dissolve the sugar and shortening. Stir in two cups of flour and the beaten eggs. Add the softened yeast. Stir in enough additional flour to form a soft dough. Turn out on a floured board and knead until the dough is smooth and satiny. This will take about 10 minutes. Place the rounded dough in a greased bowl, turning over to grease the top surface. Cover and place in a warm spot to rise until double in bulk, about one hour. Punch down; turn out on a floured board, cover and let rest for ten minutes. Combine the melted butter with the brown sugar and spread over the bottoms of two pans (9 x 9 x 2 in.). Sprinkle with pecan halves. Divide the dough in half and roll each piece out into a 12 inch square. Sprinkle with combined sugar and cinnamon and roll up like jelly roll. Slice each roll into nine pieces and place cut side up in the prepared pans. Cover and set to rise in a warm spot until almost double in size. Bake in a moderately hot oven for 25 to 30 minutes. Turn out of pans onto a rack immediately.

Saffron Butter Rolls

Two tablespoons boiling water
One-half teaspoon crumbled saffron shreds
One package active dry yeast
One-fourth cup warm water
One-half cup butter or margarine
One-third cup sugar
One teaspoon salt
One cup milk, scalded
Three and one-half to four cups flour
One egg, beaten
Resting time: Ten minutes
First rising time: Two hours, about
One beaten egg white
Second rising time: One hour, about
Oven temperature: 375 degrees
Bake: Fifteen minutes
Yield: Two dozen

Pour the boiling water over the crumbled saffron in a small bowl or cup and let stand. Sprinkle yeast over the warm water in a cup and let soften. Measure the butter, sugar and salt into a large bowl and pour on the scalded milk, stir until blended. Stir in one cup of flour, then the beaten egg. Add the saffron and liquid and the softened yeast, mix well. Add enough remaining flour to make a soft dough. Turn dough out on a floured board and let rest for ten minutes. Knead until smooth and elastic. Place in a greased bowl, turning dough over once to grease the top. Cover and place in a warm spot until the dough doubles in bulk. Punch down. Knead dough smooth and portion into two dozen rolls, shaping into twists, knots or folds as desired. Place on greased baking sheet and brush with beaten egg white. Cover and let rise until doubled in bulk. Bake in a moderately hot oven for fifteen minutes.

Tea Time Caramel Topped Biscuits

One cup brown sugar
Three tablespoons corn syrup
One tablespoon butter or margarine
Cook: Until sugar melts
Two cups sifted flour
Three teaspoons baking powder
One teaspoon salt
One-third cup shortening
One-half cup raisins
Three-fourths cup milk
Two tablespoons soft butter or margarine
One teaspoon cinnamon
One-fourth cup sugar
Oven temperature: 400 degrees
Baking time: Twenty-five to thirty minutes
Yield: Two and one-half dozen

In a saucepan mix the brown sugar, corn syrup and tablespoon of butter or margarine. Heat gently, stirring the while, until the sugar has melted. Spread over the bottom of a pan (7 x 12 x 2 in.). Sift into a bowl the flour, baking powder and salt. Using a pastry blender or two knives cut in the shortening until the mixture resembles coarse crumbs. Stir in the raisins and milk. Turn dough out on a floured board and knead briefly before dividing in two. Roll each piece into a rectangle (8 x 12 in.). Spread with the butter and sprinkle with the combined cinnamon and sugar. Roll up tightly from long side and cut into half inch slices. Lay side by side on the brown sugar mixture in the pan. Bake in a quick oven for 25 to 30 minutes or until the tops of the biscuits are golden brown. As soon as baked, invert a waxed paper covered rack over the pan of buns and turn out, glaze side up. When cool, cut apart with a sharp knife.

Bagels

One-fourth cup butter or margarine
One and one-half tablespoons sugar
One-half teaspoon salt
One cup scalded milk
Cool: To lukewarm
One package active dry yeast
One egg white, beaten
Three and one-half cups sifted flour
First rising time: Two hours, or more
Second rising time: Thirty minutes
Two quarts water
Cooking time: One-half minute on each side
One egg yolk
One tablespoon water
Oven temperature: 400 degrees
Baking time: Thirty minutes
Yield: Two dozen

Measure the butter or margarine, sugar and salt into a large bowl. Pour the scalded milk into the bowl and stir to melt the butter and dissolve the sugar and salt. When cooled to lukewarm sprinkle on the active dry yeast and let stand to soften. Stir in the beaten egg white and the sifted flour, mix well. Turn dough out on a floured board and knead for about five minutes or until smooth and satiny. Place in a greased bowl, turning dough over once to grease the top. Cover with a cloth and place in a warm spot to rise until doubled in bulk. Divide dough into quarters and each quarter into six pieces. Flour the hands and roll each piece between the palms into a rope about a half inch in diameter and six inches long. Pinch ends together very securely and place rings on a board to rise briefly. Heat water to boiling in a saucepan and reduce heat to just below the boil. Add the rings of dough one at a time. Permit them to cook in the just below boiling water one-half minute on each side. Remove with a slotted cake turner and place on a greased baking sheet. In a cup beat the egg yolk with the tablespoon of water. Brush this over each ring on the baking sheet. Bake in a quick oven for thirty minutes. Remove to racks to cool.

Crusty Rolls

One package active dry yeast
One cup lukewarm, not hot, water
One tablespoon sugar
One teaspoon salt
Two tablespoons melted shortening
Four cups flour, about
Two egg whites, beaten
Kneading time: Five to eight minutes
First rising time: One and one-half hours
Second rising time: Forty-five minutes
Resting time: Ten minutes
Oven temperature: 450 degrees
Baking time: Twenty minutes
Yield: Twelve

Place the lukewarm water in a large bowl, sprinkle the active dry yeast over the top. Let stand until dissolved. Heat the cup of milk in a saucepan to scalding, remove from heat and add the sugar, salt, cinnamon and butter or margarine.

Stir until well blended. Cool to lukewarm and add to the softened yeast. Add the beaten eggs. Add half the sifted flour, beating smooth. Add the raisins or currants and enough flour for a dough thick enough to follow spoon around the bowl. Turn dough out on a floured board and knead until smooth and elastic. Place dough in a greased bowl, turning over once to grease the top surface of the dough. Cover with a cloth and set in a warm place to rise until doubled in bulk. (Note: Bowl may be placed in an unheated oven with a pan of boiling water beneath it. Replace the boiling water as it cools. This creates a warm moist atmosphere that speeds rising time.) When dough has doubled in bulk, punch down. Turn out on floured board and shape into buns, portioning the dough out with a knife and rounding off with the hands. Place in a greased shallow pan or on a baking sheet. Cover with a cloth and let rise until doubled in bulk. When half risen, cut a cross on the top of each with a scissors. Brush the slightly beaten egg white over the top of the buns and bake in a quick oven until browned. Remove to racks. While still warm ice the cross with the combined confectioners' sugar and hot water. Serve warm or cold.

Hot Cross Buns

One-fourth cup lukewarm water
Two packages active dry yeast
One cup milk
Heat: To scald
One-half cup sugar
One and one-half teaspoons salt
One-half teaspoon cinnamon
One-third cup butter or margarine
Two eggs
Five cups sifted flour, about
One-half cup raisins or currants
First rising time: One hour, about
Second rising time: Forty minutes
One egg white, slightly beaten
Oven temperature: 400 degrees
Bake: Fifteen minutes
One cup confectioners' sugar
Two tablespoons hot water
Yield: Two dozen

Soften the yeast in one-fourth cup of water. Place the remaining water in a bowl with the sugar, salt and shortening. Add one cup of flour; beat well. Add softened yeast and beaten egg whites. Mix thoroughly. Add enough flour to make a a soft dough. Knead upon a floured board until smooth and satiny. Shape into a smooth ball and put into a greased bowl. Grease surface of the dough lightly. Cover, and let rise until doubled in bulk. Punch down and let rise again until doubled. Knead down and divide the dough into small portions for rolls. Let rest for ten minutes. Place rolls two inches apart on greased baking sheet. Cover and let rise until doubled. Place a large flat pan filled with water on the bottom of the oven to give crustiness to the rolls. Bake in a very hot oven until well browned.

Apple Kuchen

One box (9 oz.) pastry mix
One-fourth cup cold water (about)
Three apples, peeled and sliced
One cup brown sugar
One teaspoon cinnamon
Two tablespoons margarine
One cup sour cream
Oven temperature: 425 degrees
Baking time: One hour
Servings: Nine

Empty the mix into a bowl; sprinkle the water over it; with a fork stir until blended. Roll out on a floured board into a square (10 in.). Fit into a cake pan (8x8x2 in.). Cover the top with parallel rows of apples, pressing sharp edges into the dough. Sprinkle with the sugar and spice; dot with the margarine. Bake in a hot oven 30 minutes; cover with sour cream and bake until light brown in color. Remove the pan to a rack; cool. Cut into squares.

Blueberry Tea Cake

One and one-fourth cups cool water
One box (14 oz.) muffin mix
One tablespoon lemon juice
One cup frozen blueberries, drained.
One-third cup sugar
One-fourth cup flour
One-eighth teaspoon salt
One-fourth teaspoon cinnamon
Two tablespoons butter
Oven temperature: 375 degrees
Baking time: Forty minutes
Servings: Eight

Add the water to the mix in a bowl; stir only until the mix is moistened. Pat into a greased cake pan (8 in.). Add the lemon juice to the drained berries; sprinkle over the batter. Combine the dry ingredients and butter until crumbly; scatter over the berries. Bake in a moderately hot oven until brown on top and shrunken from the pan. Serve warm.

Tuna Cornmeal Pastries

Two tablespoons shortening
One box (11¾ oz.) corn muffin mix
One-fourth cup cold water (about)
Chilling time: Fifteen minutes
One can (7 oz.) tuna, flaked
One-half cup minced celery
Two tablespoons pickle relish
One-fourth teaspoon tarragon
One-third cup salad dressing
One-half teaspoon salt
Oven temperature: 425 degrees
Baking time: Fifteen minutes
Servings: Four to six

Cut shortening into the mix; sprinkle with the water. Blend with a fork. Chill; then divide into six parts, rolling each into a square (5 in.). Fit into muffin pans. Combine the remaining ingredients; place in the center of the pastries. Fold the opposite edges toward the center. Bake in a hot oven until brown. Serve hot with creamed peas.

Irish Soda Bread

Three cups biscuit mix
One-fourth teaspoon soda
Three-fourths cup cut raisins
One and one-half teaspoons caraway
   seeds
One and one-half cups buttermilk, about
Oven temperature: 375-350 degrees
Baking time: Forty minutes
Yield: One loaf

Blend the mix and soda together in a bowl; raisins and caroway seeds. Stir in enough buttermilk to make a soft dough. Knead one minute on a floured board. Pat into a greased heavy skillet (7 in.); cut a gash on the top with a knife. Bake in a moderately hot oven 10 minutes. Reduce the heat to moderate and bake till the loaf shrinks from the sides of the pan. Cool upon a rack; dust the top with flour. Serve in thin slices with butter.

Raisin Casserole Bread

One-third cup scalded milk
One-third cup orange juice
One-half cup sugar
One and one-half teaspoons salt
One-fourth cup butter or margarine
One tablespoon grated orange rind
Cool: To lukewarm
Two packages active dry yeast
One-half cup warm water (not hot)
One egg, beaten
One cup seedless raisins
Three and one-fourth cups sifted flour
Rising time: Fifty minutes
Oven temperature: 400 degrees
Baking time: Forty-five minutes
Two tablespoons sugar
One-fourth cup honey
One tablespoon butter
Cook: To a boil
One-fourth cup split, toasted almonds
Yield: One loaf

In a bowl, mix the first six ingredients; cool to lukewarm. Sprinkle the yeast over the warm, not hot, water. Add the egg and raisins. Beat in the flour gradually. Beat vigorously for 2 minutes. Let rise in warm place, free from draft until more than double in bulk (looks rough and moist with small bubbles just under the surface). Beat vigorously ½ minute. Turn into greased casserole (1½ qts.). Bake in a quick oven until golden. Remove to rack. Meantime, bring to a boil in a saucepan the sugar, honey and butter. Brush bread while still hot with honey syrup. Sprinkle almonds on top.

Plain Muffins

Two cups sifted flour
Two tablespoons sugar
Three teaspoons baking powder
One-half teaspoon salt
One egg
One cup milk
Four tablespoons butter or margarine, melted
Oven temperature: 400 degrees
Baking time: Twenty-five minutes
Yield: Twelve

In a bowl sift the flour, sugar, baking powder and salt together. Add the combined remaining ingredients stirring only enough to moisten. Spoon into greased muffin pans two-thirds full. Bake in a quick oven until a toothpick inserted in the center comes away clean. Remove to a rack. Serve.

Variations

Peanut Butter Muffins: Blend ¼ cup peanut butter with the milk and combine with other liquid ingredients. Use only 2 tablespoons butter or margarine in place of 4 tablespoons.

Bran Nut Muffins: Use only 1 cup flour and add 1 cup bran, blend into other dry ingredients and ⅓ cup chopped nuts.

Blueberry Poppy Seed Muffins: After the liquid ingredients have been added fold in 1 cup of blueberries and ¼ cup poppy seed.

Spiced Prune Muffins: To dry ingredients, add 1 teaspoon cinnamon and 1 cup chopped cooked prunes.

Upside Down Apricot Muffins: In the bottom of each greased muffin cup put 1 tablespoon butter, 1 teaspoon brown sugar and 1 drained apricot half. Then pour on batter and bake.

A FAVORITE RECIPE
Quick Lemon Rolls

One-third cup sugar
One and one-half teaspoons grated lemon rind
One and one-half teaspoons lemon juice
One and one-half teaspoons melted butter
One dozen ready-to-bake butter dinner rolls
Oven temperature: 400 degrees
Baking time: Fifteen minutes
Servings: Six

In a small bowl combine the sugar, lemon rind and lemon juice. Stir in the melted butter. Spread the mixture over the bottom of a shallow baking pan. Press the top of rolls into the mixture. Bake in a quick oven. Let rolls stand in pan several minutes after taking from oven.

MRS. M. O. ROBINSON, *Dover, Delaware*

Caramel Pecan Muffins

One package active dry yeast
One-half cup warm, not hot, water
One-third cup sugar
One egg
One-half cup butter or shortening, melted
One cup cold water
Five cups sifted flour (about)
First rising time: One hour
Melted butter, brown sugar and pecan meats
Second rising time: One-half hour
Oven temperature: 375 degrees
Bake: Twenty-five minutes
Yield: Three dozen

In a cup sprinkle the yeast over the half cup of warm, not hot, water. In a bowl mix the sugar, egg, butter and cold water. Add the dissolved yeast. Gradually add three cups of sifted flour; beat hard until smooth and elastic. (If heavy electric beater is used, allow to beat 5 minutes until smooth and elastic.) Remove to a floured board. Knead in enough of the remaining flour to make a soft dough. Place in an oiled bowl; brush top of dough with oil. Cover. Place in an oven. Set a pan of boiling water at the side. Reheat the water on top of the stove about every 15 minutes. Let rise until double in bulk. Meanwhile have the muffin pans ready. Fill muffin pans with melted butter not less than ¼-inch deep. Sprinkle one teaspoon brown sugar and pecans over butter. When dough has doubled in bulk, turn out on a floured board. Roll out dough to ¼ inch in thickness. Cut out rounds of dough to fit the muffin pan. Place a round of dough over butter and sugar mixture in muffin pan. Let rise to double in bulk. Bake in a moderately hot oven until a golden brown. Remove. Turn upside-down onto racks immediately.

Butterball Loaves

Two packages active dry yeast
One-third cup warm water
One egg
One-half cup evaporated milk
One-third cup water
Two tablespoons butter, melted
Three cups sifted flour
One-fourth cup sugar
Two teaspoons salt
One-fourth teaspoon mace
First rising time: One hour, about
Three tablespoons butter, melted
Two-thirds cup sugar
One teaspoon cinnamon
One-half cup chopped walnuts
One-half cup raisins
Second rising time: Forty-five minutes
Oven temperature: 325 degrees
Bake: Forty-five minutes
Yield: Two loaves

Sprinkle the active dry yeast over the third cup of warm, not hot water in a small bowl and let stand to soften. In a large mixing bowl beat the egg and blend in the evaporated milk, water and first measure of melted butter. Add the softened yeast. Sift together the flour, sugar, salt and mace and stir into the egg mixture. Mix well. Turn dough out on a floured board and knead briefly until smooth. Place dough in a greased bowl, turning over once to grease the top. Cover with a clean cloth and place in a warm spot to rise. When doubled in bulk punch down and transfer to the board again. With a knife divide the dough into fourths and each piece into 10 small pieces the size of a walnut. Roll these between floured palms into smooth balls.

Dip the balls in the melted butter and then into the mixed sugar and cinnamon and arrange in a layer in two greased loaf pans (5½ x 9½ x 2½ in.). Scatter on the chopped walnuts and raisins and cover with the remaining buttered and sugared balls of dough. Sprinkle any remaining butter or sugar over the top of the loaves and bake in a moderately slow oven for 45 minutes. Remove from oven and turn loaves out on a rack to cool. When cooled wrap in waxed paper or foil to store. This loaf is wonderful hot and may be sliced or broken apart. Wrap in foil and place briefly in the oven to reheat.

Buttermilk Bread

One cup buttermilk
Heat: To scald
One-third cup shortening
Three tablespoons sugar
Two and one-half teaspoons salt
One cup warm water
One package active dry yeast
Three cups sifted flour
One-half teaspoon baking soda
Three cups sifted flour, about
Knead: Until smooth
First rising: Until doubled in bulk
Second rising: Until doubled in bulk
Oven temperature: 400 degrees
Bake: Forty minutes, about
Yield: Two loaves (9 x 5 in.)

Heat the buttermilk in a small saucepan. Add the shortening, stirring to hasten melting. Add the sugar and salt. Measure the warm water into a large bowl. Sprinkle on the active dry yeast and let stand to soften. When milk mixture has cooled to lukewarm stir into the softened yeast. Add the three cups of flour sifted with the baking soda. Add enough additional flour to form a dough that may be turned out on a floured board.

Knead until dough is smooth and elastic. Grease a clean bowl. Place dough in bowl turning over once to grease the top surface. Cover with a clean cloth and place in a warm spot for dough to rise until doubled in bulk, an hour or more. Punch down and shape into loaves on a floured board.

Place in greased loaf pans (9 x 5 x 3 in.) turning dough over to grease the top surface. Cover with cloth and place in a warm spot for dough to rise until center of loaf is slightly higher than edge of pan, about one hour. Bake in a quick oven until loaves are well browned and have a hollow ring when rapped with the knuckles. Turn out on racks to cool thoroughly before slicing. Wrap cooled loaves in waxed paper or foil to store.

Caraway Braid

Two pkgs. active dry yeast
One-fourth cup warm water
Let stand: To soften
Two cups milk
Four teaspoons caraway seed
One teaspoon anise seed
Heat: To boiling
One-fourth cup sugar
One-third cup butter or shortening
One tablespoon salt
Three eggs, beaten
Seven cups sifted flour, or more
Knead: Five minutes, about
First rising time: Two hours, or less
One tablespoon butter, melted
Second rising time: One hour, about
One egg, beaten
Oven temperature: 375 degrees
Bake: Forty minutes
Yield: Two loaves

Sprinkle the active dry yeast over the warm water and let stand to soften. Heat the milk with the caraway and anise seed to the boiling point. Remove from heat and pour into a large bowl. Add the sugar, third cup of butter or shortening and salt. Stir until blended. Beat the eggs in a second bowl and add to milk mixture, When cooled to lukewarm add the softened yeast. Beat in flour two cups at a time, beating until smooth. When dough follows spoon around bowl, turn out on floured board and knead until satiny. Place in a greased bowl, turning over once to grease the top of the dough. Cover with a clean cloth and place in a warm spot until doubled in bulk. Turn dough out on a floured board and divide into two parts. Cut each half in three portions and roll each third into a rope

(14 in.). Make an "x" with two strips on a greased baking sheet, place the third down in the center and braid from center to both ends. Tuck ends under. Brush with melted butter. Cover two braids with piece of waxed paper, then with a clean cloth. Place in warm spot until braids double in bulk. Brush with beaten egg and bake in a moderately hot oven for forty minutes or until well browned. Baked loaf sounds hollow when rapped with knuckles. Remove to rack to cool.

Corn Bread

One cup sifted flour
Three and one-half teaspoons baking powder
One teaspoon salt
Three tablespoons sugar
One cup yellow cornmeal
One egg
One cup milk
One-fourth cup melted shortening, or salad oil
Oven temperature: 400 degrees
Bake: Twenty-five minutes, or more
Yield: Nine squares

Sift together in a bowl the flour, baking powder, salt, sugar and cornmeal. In a second bowl beat the egg; add the milk and the melted shortening or salad oil. Combine the liquid and dry ingredients, mixing just enough to moisten thoroughly. Pour mixture into a greased pan 8 x 8 x 2 in.). Bake in a hot oven until the bread is lightly browned and leaves the edge of the pan. Cut in squares and serve warm.

Garlic Bread

One clove garlic
One-fourth cup soft butter
One loaf French bread
Oven temperature: 400 degress
Heat: Ten minutes

Peel the clove of garlic and crush in a garlic press. Add to the soft butter and let stand an hour to develop full flavor if there is time. Cut one-inch slices of the French bread to within one-half inch of the bottom of the loaf. Spread the butter between the cuts that have been made in the bread. Wrap the loaf in brown paper or in aluminum foil and place in a quick oven until thoroughly heated. Serve at once.

Herbed Batter Bread

One and one-fourth cups warm water
One pkg. active dry yeast
Let stand: Five minutes
Two tablespoons soft shortening
Two teaspoons salt
Two tablespoons sugar
Three cups sifted flour
Beat: Two minutes with mixer
One-half teaspoon nutmeg
One teaspoon poultry seasoning
Two teaspoons caraway seed
First rising time: Thirty minutes, or more
Second rising time: Thirty minutes, or more
Oven temperature: 400 degrees
Bake: Thirty-five minutes
Yield: One loaf

Measure the warm, not hot, water into the mixer bowl. Add the active dry yeast and let stand to dissolve. Add the shortening, salt, sugar and half the flour. Beat with the electric beater at medium speed for two minutes, or use about 300 vigorous strokes by hand. Scrape sides and bottom of bowl frequently. Add remaining flour, nutmeg, poultry seasoning and caraway seed and blend together until smooth with a mixing spoon. Scrape batter down from sides of bowl. Cover with a clean cloth and place in a warm spot until batter doubles in bulk. This will take thirty minutes or more. Stir batter down and transfer to a greased bread pan (9½ x 5 x 2½ in.). Cover and let rise until batter reaches the top of the pan. Bake in a quick oven until well browned. Loaf should sound hollow when tapped with knuckles. Turn loaf out on rack and cool away from draft. (Note: A nice variation of this loaf is made by adding three-fourths of a cup of grated cheddar cheese and eliminating the nutmeg, poultry seasoning and caraway seed.)

Milk Enriched Loaves

One package active dry yeast
One-fourth cup warm water
Two tablespoons butter
Two tablespoons sugar
Two teaspoons salt
One cup boiling water
Three-fourths cup cold water
Five cups sifted flour
One and one-fourth cups non-fat dry milk
First rising time: One hour, about
Second rising time: Thirty minutes, about
Oven temperature: 425 degrees
Baking time: Fifteen to twenty minutes
Yield: Two loaves (8 in.)

Sprinkle the active dry yeast over the fourth cup of warm water in a small bowl or cup. Let stand to soften. Into a large bowl, measure the butter, sugar and salt. Pour on the boiling water and stir until butter is melted. Add the cold water and when contents of the bowl are lukewarm add the softened yeast. Sift together the flour and non-fat dry milk. Add half the dry ingredients to the yeast mixture and beat smooth. Work in the remaining dry ingredients and turn dough out on a floured board to knead until smooth and elastic. Place dough in a greased bowl, turning over once to grease the top of the dough. Cover the bowl and set in a warm spot so the dough can rise to double its bulk. This will take about one hour. Punch dough down and divide into two equal parts. Shape each piece into a round loaf and place in a greased cake pan (8 in.). Cover loaves and place in a warm spot until they have almost doubled in bulk again. Bake in a quick oven for fifteen to twenty minutes or until well browned. Loaf will have a hollow sound when tapped if thoroughly baked. Remove to racks to cool, rubbing a little butter over the top of the loaves if desired.

Oatmeal Bread

One package active dry yeast
One-fourth cup warm water
One cup milk
One cup water
One-fourth cup shortening
One-third cup brown sugar
Two teaspoons salt
Heat: Until blended
One cup rolled oats
Five and one-half cups sifted flour, about
Knead: Five minutes
First rising time: Until double in bulk
Second rising time: Until double in bulk
Oven temperature: 375 degrees
Bake: Forty minutes, about
Yield: Two loaves (9 x 5 in.)

Sprinkle the active dry yeast over the fourth cup of warm water in a cup. Let stand to soften. Measure the milk, water, shortening, sugar and salt into a saucepan. Heat until blended and pour over the rolled oats in a large bowl. Let stand until lukewarm and stir in the softened yeast. Blend in the flour, using enough for a soft dough. Turn dough out on a floured board and knead until smooth and elastic. Shape into a ball and place in a greased bowl, turning dough over once to grease the top. Cover and let stand in a warm spot until dough doubles in bulk. Turn dough onto the floured board and shape into two loaves. Place in greased pans (9 x 5 x 3 in.), cover and let stand in a warm spot until double in bulk. Bake in a moderately hot oven until loaves are nicely browned and sound hollow when rapped with the knuckles. Remove from oven and turn loaves out on rack to cool.

Onion Bread

Four tablespoons dried minced onion
One-fourth cup water
One package active dry yeast
One-fourth cup lukewarm water
Two cups milk
Heat: To scalding
Two tablespoons shortening
Two tablespoons sugar
Two teaspoons salt
Three cups sifted flour
One teaspoon celery salt
One-half teaspoon poultry seasoning
Two to three cups sifted flour
Knead: Ten minutes
First rising time: One and one-half hours
Resting time: Fifteen minutes
Second rising time: One hour, about
Oven temperature: 400 degrees
Bake: Forty minutes
Yield: Two loaves

Measure the dried minced onion into a small bowl, add the fourth cup of water and let stand to soften. In a large bowl sprinkle the active dry yeast over the lukewarm water, let stand until dissolved. Heat the milk to scalding in a saucepan and stir in the shortening, sugar and salt. Cool to lukewarm and stir into the softened yeast. Sift the three cups of flour with the celery salt and poultry seasoning and stir into the yeast mixture,

beating smooth. Add the softened onion and enough additional flour to make a stiff dough.

Turn out on a floured board and knead until dough is smooth and satiny, about 10 minutes. Place dough in a greased bowl, turning over once to grease the top surface. Cover with a clean cloth, wrung out in warm water, and let stand in a warm spot until dough doubles in bulk. Punch down and let dough rest in bowl for fifteen minutes. Turn out on a floured board and form into two loaves. Place in pans (4 x 8 x 2½ in.) and cover with a cloth and let rise in a warm spot until doubled in bulk. Bake in a quick oven until loaf has a hollow sound when rapped with knuckles and is well browned. Turn out on racks to cool. Good served while slightly warm. Also good toasted.

Cornell Bread

Two packages active dry yeast
Three cups warm water
Two tablespoons sugar
Standing time: Five minutes
Six and one-half cups sifted flour
Three tablespoons wheat germ
One-half cup soy flour
Three-fourths cup non-fat dry milk
Four teaspoons salt
Two tablespoons melted shortening
Kneading time: Five minutes
One-half cup flour
First rising time: Thirty-five minutes
Second rising time: Twenty minutes
Resting time: Ten minutes
One-fourth cup melted butter or shortening
Third rising time: Thirty to forty minutes
Oven temperature: 350 degrees
Baking time: Fifty minutes
Yield: Three loaves

In a very large bowl, combine the dry yeast, warm water and sugar. Let stand. Sift together the flour, wheat germ, soy flour and dry milk. Stir half of the dry ingredients into the yeast mixture with the salt. Beat vigorously. Add the rest of the dry ingredients with the two tablespoons of melted shortening. Turn out upon a well floured board using the one-half cup of flour as needed during the kneading. Knead until smooth and elastic. Place in a greased bowl, grease the top of the dough lightly and cover bowl. Let rise in a warm place, 80 to 85 degrees until nearly double in size. Punch dough down, fold over edges and turn upside down in bowl to rise another 20 minutes. Turn dough onto board, divide into three portions. Fold each in to the center to make smooth tight balls. Cover with a cloth and let stand 10 minutes on the board. Shape into three loaves and place in greased bread pans. Brush with melted butter or shortening and let rise until double in size. Bake in a moderate oven. If loaves begin to brown in 15 to 20 minutes, reduce the heat to 325 degrees. When baked, remove the bread to rack to cool. Brush with melted butter if desired.

combined remaining ingredients, mixing only enough to moisten. Pour into a greased loaf pan (9 x 5 x 3 in.). Bake in a moderate oven for one hour. Remove to rack. Cool and slice.

Worcestershire Cheese Bread

Two packages active dry yeast
One-fourth cup warm, not hot, water
One cup milk, scalded and cooled to
    lukewarm
One cup water
Two tablespoons melted butter
Two tablespoons sugar
Three tablespoons Worcestershire sauce
One cup grated Switzerland Swiss cheese
One cup grated Parmesan cheese
Five and one-half to six cups flour (about)
First rising time: Two hours (about)
Second rising time: One hour
Oven temperature: 350 degrees
Bake: Forty to fifty minutes
Yield: Four medium-sized loaves or two
    large loaves

In a bowl sprinkle the yeast over the warm, not hot, water. Scald the milk and cool to lukewarm. Add the water, butter, sugar and Worcestershire sauce. Stir in the dissolved yeast. Mix in the Switzerland Swiss and Parmesan cheese. With a heavy electric beater gradually beat in four cups of the flour until the dough is elastic, or beat in by hand with a wooden spoon. Turn out on a floured board. Knead in the remaining flour until dough is elastic. Place in an oiled bowl and oil the top of the dough. Cover; let rise in a warm place until double in bulk. Punch down. Knead again. Divide dough into four pieces. Shape into loaves. Place in greased and floured bread pans (7½ x 3½ x 2½ in.). Let rise until double in bulk. Bake in a moderate oven until golden, about 40 minutes. Turn out onto racks. The large sized loaves require about 50 minutes to bake.

Cranberry Walnut Bread

Two cups sifted flour
One teaspoon baking soda
One teaspoon salt
Three-fourths cup sugar
One egg, slightly beaten
Two-thirds cup milk
One-fourth cup butter or margarine,
    melted
One cup whole cranberry sauce
One cup chopped walnuts
Oven temperature: 350 degrees
Baking time: One hour (about)
Yield: One loaf

In a large bowl sift the flour, soda, salt and sugar. Add the combined remaining ingredients, mixing only enough to moisten. Pour into a greased loaf pan (9 x 5 x 3 in.). Bake in a moderate oven for one hour. Remove to rack. Cool.

Banana Peanut Bread

Two cups sifted flour
One teaspoon baking powder
One-half teaspoon baking soda
One-half teaspoon salt
One egg, slightly beaten
One cup buttermilk or sour milk
One cup brown sugar
Two tablespoons peanut butter
One cup mashed bananas
One cup chopped peanuts
Oven temperature: 350 degrees
Baking time: One hour
Yield: One loaf

In a large bowl sift the flour, baking powder, soda and salt. Add the combined remaining ingredients, mixing only enough to moisten. Pour into a greased loaf pan (9 x 5 x 3 in.). Bake in a moderate oven for one hour. Remove to rack. Cool.

Avocado Pecan Bread

Two cups sifted flour
One-half teaspoon soda
One-half teaspoon baking powder
One-fourth teaspoon salt
Three-fourths cup sugar
One egg, slightly beaten
One-half cup mashed avocado
One-half cup sour milk or buttermilk
One cup chopped pecans
Oven temperature: 350 degrees
Baking time: One hour
Yield: One loaf

In a large bowl sift the flour, soda, baking powder, salt and sugar. Add the

Irish Soda Bread

Two cups sifted flour
One and one-half teaspoons baking powder
One-fourth teaspoon soda
One-fourth teaspoon salt
One-half cup raisins
One teaspoon caraway seeds
One cup buttermilk (about)
Oven temperature: 375 degrees
Bake: Ten minutes
Oven temperature: 350 degrees
Bake: Forty minutes
Yield: One small round loaf

Sift the flour, baking powder, soda and salt together into a bowl. Stir in the raisins and caraway seeds and enough buttermilk to give a soft dough. Knead lightly on a floured board until stickiness disappears. Form into round flat loaf and place in a greased cake pan (8 in.). Cut an x in the top surface of the loaf with a knife. Bake in a moderately hot oven (375 degrees) for 10 minutes, lower the heat to moderate (350 degrees) and continue baking for 40 minutes. Remove to rack to cool thoroughly before slicing. Serve spread with butter.

Oatmeal Bread

Three cups boiling water
One and one-half cups oatmeal
Three-fourths cup molasses
One tablespoon salt
Six tablespoons butter or shortening
Two packages active dry yeast
One-half cup warm, not hot, water
Seven to eight cups sifted flour
First rising time: Ninety minutes
Second rising time: Thirty minutes
Oven temperature: 425 degrees
Bake: Thirty to forty minutes
Yield: Two loaves

In a large bowl pour the boiling water over the oatmeal. Mix in the molasses, salt and butter. Stir. Let stand until cool. In a cup dissolve the yeast in the warm, not hot, water. Add to the cooled oatmeal mixture. Gradually beat in about five cups of flour. If you have a heavy type electric beater allow dough to beat until smooth and elastic. On a floured board knead in enough of the remaining flour until the dough is smooth and elastic. Shape into a ball. Place in an oiled bowl. Oil the top of the dough. Cover; set in a warm place to double in size. Punch down dough. Divide dough in half. Shape into a ball. Place in two round oiled pans (9 in.). Brush top with oil. Let rise until double in bulk. Bake in a hot oven until done. When tapped it should have a hollow ring. Remove to racks to cool.

Ginger Nut Bread

One cup brown sugar, packed
One egg, well beaten
Two tablespoons melted butter
One-half cup chopped pecans
One-third cup chopped crystallized ginger
Two cups sifted flour
Three-fourths teaspoon soda
One-half teaspoon baking powder
One-fourth teaspoon salt
One cup buttermilk
Oven temperature: 350 degrees
Baking time: Forty-five minutes
Yield: One loaf

In a bowl beat the sugar, egg and butter until smooth and creamy. Add the nuts and ginger to the sifted dry ingredients. Stir the flour mixture alternately with the buttermilk into the egg mixture. Do not beat. Pour into a greased loaf pan (8x5x3 in.). Bake in a moderate oven until a cake tester inserted in the center comes away clean. Remove to a rack. Cool before slicing.

Boston Brown Bread

One cup yellow corn meal
One-half cup quick oats
One-half cup sifted flour
One teaspoon soda
One-half teaspoon salt
Three-fourths cup seedless raisins
One-half cup light molasses
Steam: One and one-half hours, about
Yield: Two loaves

In a bowl stir together the corn meal, quick oats, sifted flour, soda and salt. Mix thoroughly. Measure out one-fourth cup of the dry ingredients and mix with the raisins. Add the molasses and raisins to the bulk of the dry ingredients and blend thoroughly together. Spoon batter into well greased cans filling three-fourths full. No. 303 cans are a good choice, yielding two round loaves four inches long and three inches in diameter. Cover tops of cans with foil, tie on with string. Place in a large kettle on rack with water to one-third the depth of the cans. Cover tightly and steam for one and one-half hours or more after water boils. The firm loaf under the foil may be felt when steaming is completed. Remove from kettle and cool in the cans. Wrap well in foil to store.

Brown Bread with Bran

One cup all-bran cereal
One-half cup seedless raisins
Two tablespoons shortening
One-third cup molasses
Three-fourths cup hot water
One egg
One cup sifted flour
One teaspoon baking soda
One-half teaspoon salt
One-half teaspoon cinnamon
Oven temperature: 350 degrees
Bake: Thirty-five minutes, about
Yield: One loaf (9 x 5 in.)

Measure the all-bran cereal into a bowl and add the raisins, shortening and molasses. Add the hot water and stir until shortening is blended in. Beat in the egg. Sift together the flour, soda, salt and cinnamon. Add to the bran mixture and stir just enough to combine. Transfer to a greased loaf pan (9 x 5 x 2½ in.) or two greased No. 303 cans. Bake in a moderate oven for thirty-five minutes or until the loaves spring back at the touch of a finger and start to leave the sides of the pan.

Chocolate Nut Loaf

Four eggs
One and one-fourth cups sugar
Two and one-half cups sifted flour
Three teaspoons baking powder
One teaspoon salt
Four ounces German sweet chocolate, finely chopped
One and one-half cups pecans, finely chopped (one six-ounce can)
One-half cup milk
Oven temperature: 325 degrees
Bake: One hour, or more
Yield: One loaf (9 x 5 in.)

In a bowl beat the eggs until light. Gradually beat in the sugar. Sift together the flour, baking powder and salt. Dredge the finely chopped sweet chocolate and pecans in the dry ingredients. Beat flour mixture into the egg and sugar combination alternately with the milk. Beat smooth. Pour into a greased loaf pan (9¼ x 5¼ x 2½ in.). Bake in a moderately slow oven for one hour or more until loaf is well browned and starts to leave the sides of the pan. Remove from oven and cool in pan for 10 minutes. Turn out on rack and finish cooling before slicing. Wrap well in aluminum foil or waxed paper to store. Slices well the first day.

Fresh Cranberry Loaf

Juice and grated rind of one orange
Two tablespoons salad oil
Water
One egg, beaten
Two cups sifted flour
One cup sugar
One and one-half teaspoons baking powder
One-half teaspoon soda
One teaspoon salt
One-half cup chopped nuts
Two cups fresh cranberries, halved
Oven temperature: 350 degrees
Baking time: One hour, about
Yield: One loaf

Combine the orange juice and grated rind in a measuring cup. Add the salad oil and enough water to fill the cup to the three-quarter mark. Blend into the beaten egg. Stir together into a bowl the flour, sugar, baking powder, soda and salt. Add the liquid ingredients and stir just enough to dampen completely. Blend in the nuts and the fresh cranberries that have been cut in halves. Transfer the batter to a greased loaf pan (9 x 5 x 2½ in.) and bake in a moderate oven for one hour or until the loaf springs back when touched with a finger. Remove from the oven and from the pan to a rack to cool. Wrap well in waxed paper or foil to store.

Date Nut Bread

One egg
One and one-fourth cups milk
One-fourth cup molasses
One-fourth cup salad oil
Two and one-half cups sifted flour
Three teaspoons baking powder
One teaspoon salt
One-fourth cup sugar
One cup sliced pitted dates
One cup chopped nuts
Two cups corn flakes
Oven temperature: 350 degrees
Bake: One hour
Yield: One loaf (9 x 5 in.)

In a bowl beat the egg, add the milk, molasses and salad oil. Sift the flour, baking powder, salt and sugar together into a large bowl. Add the sliced pitted dates and chopped nuts, stirring to coat with flour. Pour in the egg and milk combination and stir only enough to moisten all flour. Crush the corn flakes to half the volume with the finger tips and stir into the batter. Pour into a greased loaf pan (9 x 5 x 2 in.) and bake in a moderate oven for one hour. Cool in the pan on a rack. Wrap well in waxed paper or foil to store.

Easter Fruit Bread

One-fourth cup lukewarm water
One package active dry yeast
One cup milk, scalded
One-half cup butter
One teaspoon salt
One-half cup sugar
Two eggs, beaten
Five cups sifted flour, or more
Two tablespoons grated lemon rind
One-third cup halved candied cherries
One-third cup chopped citron
One-half cup seedless raisins
Knead: Two minutes
First rising time: One hour
Second rising time: Thirty minutes
One teaspoon sugar
One-fourth teaspoon cinnamon
Oven temperature: 350 degrees
Bake: Forty minutes
Yield: One large ring

Pour the lukewarm water into a large bowl. Sprinkle the active dry yeast over the water and set aside to soften. In a small saucepan scald the milk. Remove from heat, add the butter and stir until dissolved. Stir in the salt and sugar, then the beaten eggs. When lukewarm, add to the softened yeast. Stir in two cups of flour. Add the grated lemon rind, cherries, citron and raisins and enough of the flour to make a soft dough. Turn dough out on a floured board and knead until smooth, elastic and not sticky. Place dough in a greased bowl turning over once to grease the top. Cover with a clean cloth and place in a warm spot to rise. (An unheated oven is a good place with a pan of boiling water beside the bowl to provide the moist, warm atmosphere.)

When the dough has doubled in bulk punch down. Knead briefly and transfer to a buttered tube pan (9 or 10 in.). Permit to rise again in a warm spot. Sprinkle the top with the combined sugar and cinnamon and bake in a moderate oven until well browned on top. Remove to rack to cool thoroughly before slicing.

Marmalade Filled Bran Bread

One cup all bran
Three-fourths cup milk
One cup sifted flour
Two and one-half teaspoons baking powder
One-half teaspoon salt
One-fourth cup sugar
One egg
One-fourth cup salad oil
One-half cup orange marmalade, about
Oven temperature: 400 degrees
Bake: Thirty minutes
Yield: Nine squares

Measure the all bran into a bowl, pour on the milk and let stand until milk is absorbed by bran. Sift the flour, baking powder, salt and sugar together. Beat the eggs and salad oil into the bran mixture, mixing well. Add the dry ingredients, mixing only enough to combine. Spread in a well greased baking pan (9 x 9 x 2 in.). Space nine spoonfuls of orange marmalade over the surface of the batter, pressing in slightly. Bake in a quick oven for thirty minutes. Cut into squares and serve.

Orange Bran Bread

One cup all bran cereal
Three-fourths cup orange juice
One-half cup milk
Two cups sifted flour
One-half cup sugar
Two teaspoons baking powder
One-fourth teaspoon soda
One teaspoon salt
One egg, beaten
One-fourth cup salad oil or melted
    shortening
One tablespoon grated orange rind
Oven temperature: 350 degrees
Bake: One hour
Yield: One loaf (9 x 5 in.)

Measure the all bran cereal into a bowl. Add the orange juice and milk and let stand. Sift the flour, sugar, baking powder, soda and salt into a large bowl. Add the softened bran mixture to the dry ingredients with the beaten egg, salad oil and grated orange rind. Stir only enough to blend and moisten dry ingredients. Transfer mixture to a greased loaf pan (9 x 5 x 3 in.) and bake in a moderate oven for one hour or until lightly browned and leaving the sides of the pan. Cool in the pan for a moister loaf. When cool, wrap well in foil, waxed paper or saran.

Orange Nut Bread

One medium-sized orange
Two tablespoons butter
Three-fourths cup sugar
One egg, beaten
One-half cup hot water
Two cups sifted flour
Two teaspoons baking powder
One-fourth teaspoon salt
One-half teaspoon soda
Two-thirds cup pitted dates, sliced
One-half cup coarsely cut walnuts
Oven temperature: 350 degrees
Bake: Forty minutes or more
Yield: One loaf

Squeeze the orange. Cut the rind in sections and put through the food grinder; set aside with the orange juice. Combine the butter and the sugar in a bowl. Add the beaten egg and the water. Stir in the flour, baking powder, salt and soda that have been sifted together. Add the ground orange, dates and nuts. Transfer to a greased loaf pan (4 x 9 x 3 in.) and bake in a moderate oven until a cake tester inserted in the center of the loaf comes away clean. Remove to a rack to cool. Wrap well to store.

Prune Nut Loaf

Two cups sifted flour
One-half cup sugar
Two and one-half teaspoons baking powder
One-half teaspoon soda
One teaspoon salt
One cup rolled oats
One and one-fourth cups sour milk
Two tablespoons salad oil
One cup diced, drained, cooked prunes
One-half cup chopped walnuts
Oven temperature: 350 degrees
Bake: One hour
Yield: One loaf (9 x 5 in.)

Sift together into a bowl the flour, sugar, baking powder, soda and salt. Add the rolled oats and mix thoroughly. Combine sour milk with the salad oil. Add to the flour mixture with the prunes and walnuts, stirring just enough to moisten the dry ingredients. Batter will not be smooth. Pour into a greased loaf pan (9 x 5 x 3 in.) and bake in a moderate oven until a toothpick inserted in the center comes away clean. Turn out on rack to cool. Wrap well to store.

Peanut Butter Bread

Two cups sifted flour
Two teaspoons baking powder
One-half teaspoon salt
Three-fourths cup sugar
Three-fourths cup peanut butter
One-fourth cup shortening
Two eggs
One cup milk
Oven temperature: 350 degrees
Bake: One hour
Yield: One loaf

Sift the flour, baking powder, salt and sugar together into a bowl. Cut in the peanut butter and shortening with a pastry blender or two knives. In a small bowl, beat the eggs, add the milk. Combine the egg and milk mixture with the dry ingredients, mixing just enough to moisten. Pour into a greased loaf pan (9 x 4 x 3 in.) and bake in a moderate oven until a tester inserted in the center comes away clean. Remove loaf to rack to cool. Wrap well in waxed paper or foil to store.

Raisin Nut Loaf

Three cups sifted flour
Three-fourths cup sugar
Three teaspoons baking powder
One and one-half teaspoons salt
One teaspoon cinnamon
One cup finely chopped walnuts
One cup rinsed and dried raisins
One egg
One and one-fourth cups milk
One tablespoon salad oil or melted
    shortening
Oven temperature: 350 degrees
Bake: One hour, about
Yield: One loaf (9 x 5 in.)

Sift the flour, baking powder, salt and cinnamon into a large bowl. Stir in the finely chopped walnuts and the rinsed and dried raisins. In a second bowl beat the egg and add the milk and salad oil.

Add egg mixture to the dry ingredients and stir just enough to moisten. Transfer to a greased loaf pan (9 x 5 x 3 in.) and bake in a moderate oven for one hour or until the loaf is nicely browned and starts to leave the sides of the pan. Cool in the pan for a moister loaf. When cool, wrap in foil, or waxed paper or saran.

Raisin Tea Bread

One-fourth cup butter
One-fourth cup sugar
Two eggs
Two cups sifted flour
Four and one-half teaspoons baking powder
One-fourth teaspoon soda
One-fourth teaspoon salt
One cup dairy sour cream
One-half cup raisins
One teaspoon caraway seeds (optional)
Oven temperature: 375 degrees
Bake: Ten minutes
Oven temperature: 350 degrees
Bake: Forty to forty-five minutes
Yield: One round loaf (8 in.)

In a bowl cream the butter, blend in the sugar. Beat in the eggs. Sift together the flour, baking powder, soda and salt and add to the creamed mixture alternately with the dairy sour cream. Mix thoroughly. Add the raisins and caraway seeds. Spread in a greased layer cake pan (8 in.) cutting an x in the top surface with a knife. Bake in a moderately hot oven (375 degrees) for 10 minutes. Reduce heat to moderate (350 degrees) and bake for 40 minutes or more, until a cake tester inserted in the center comes away clean. Remove to rack to cool thoroughly before slicing.

Quick Gingerbread

One egg
One-half cup sugar
One-half cup salad oil
One-half cup molasses
Two cups sifted flour
One teaspoon baking powder
One teaspoon salt
One-half teaspoon soda
One and one-half teaspoons ginger
One teaspoon cinnamon
Two-thirds cup boiling water
Oven temperature: 350 degrees
Bake: Forty minutes
Servings: Nine

In a bowl beat the egg, add the sugar, salad oil and molasses; mix thoroughly. Sift together the flour, baking powder, salt, soda, ginger and cinnamon and add to the first mixture alternately with the boiling water. Pour into a greased pan (8 x 8 x 2 in.) and bake in a moderate oven for forty minutes. Serve warm or cold with whipped cream or apple sauce.

corners at the center, pressing firmly. For the filling, combine one cup chopped cooked prunes, one tablespoon each sugar and grated orange rind and one-fourth teaspoon cinnamon. Brush the baked pastries with icing (½ cup confectioners' sugar and one tablespoon hot milk).

French Doughnuts

One package (8½ oz.) prepared cream
　　puff mix
Four tablespoons sugar
One cup boiling water
Four eggs
Shortening or oil
Frying temperature: 385 degrees
Fry: Five minutes
Two cups confectioners' sugar
Two tablespoons water
Yield: Two dozen (about)

Heat bowl by rinsing in hot water and crumble mix into bowl. Blend in sugar. Add all the boiling water at one time; stir with a spoon (not an electric mixer) until well blended. Add one egg at a time beating well after each addition (this is important). Put mixture into pastry bag. Force mixture into rings onto lightly greased aluminum foil squares (3 in.). To fry doughnuts: Turn over the foil squares into the heated oil or shortening releasing the doughnuts (reuse the foil squares). Fry doughnuts on one side until brown, turn and fry until golden on other side. Remove to rack. Repeat procedure. When cool brush the tops of the doughnuts with the combined confectioners' sugar and water. Serve.

Danish Pastry

Two packages active dry yeast
One-fourth cup lukewarm water
One-fourth cup shortening
One-fourth cup sugar
One teaspoon salt
One cup milk, scalded
Two eggs, beaten slightly
Sifted flour (about 4 cups)
First rising time: One hour
One cup sweet butter, mixed with
One-third cup sifted flour
Chilling time: Fifteen minutes
Second rising time: Twenty minutes
Cheese and prune fillings
Third rising time: Thirty minutes
One egg, beaten
Oven temperature: 400 degrees
Baking time: Twenty minutes
Yield: Forty (about)

Sprinkle the yeast over the water in a cup. Place the shortening, sugar, salt and scalded milk in a mixing bowl; cool to lukewarm. Add the yeast and eggs. Gradually add two cups flour; beat well. Then add sufficient flour to make a soft dough. Knead until smooth and elastic. Let rise in a covered bowl until double in bulk. Roll out the dough (¼ in. thick). Spread one-third the chilled butter and flour over the dough. Fold the dough into thirds; pat down and again fold into thirds. Repeat twice, using all the butter and flour. Cover; let rise 20 minutes on board. Roll out half the dough at a time (¼ in. thick); shape and fill. Place on baking sheets; let rise 30 minutes. Brush with egg. Bake in a quick oven to a delicate brown. Remove to racks; cool. Cheese Pastries: Cut the dough into squares (3 in.). Spread a tablespoon cheese filling over each square and fold the corners to the center, pressing them down firmly. For the filling:

Sieve one cup creamed cottage cheese and combine with one egg, beaten, two teaspoons sugar, one tablespoon grated lemon rind and one-eighth teaspoon nutmeg. Prune Pastries: Cut the dough into diamonds (4 in. long). Spread a tablespoon prune filling over the center part of each diamond; overlap the opposite

Baked Doughnuts

One and one-half cups milk,
  scalded and cooled to lukewarm
One-third cup melted butter
One-fourth cup sugar
Two teaspoons salt
Two teaspoons nutmeg
One-half teaspoon cinnamon
Two eggs
Two packages active dry yeast
One-fourth cup warm, not hot, water
Five cups sifted flour
First rising time: One hour
Second rising time: Forty minutes
Oven temperature: 425 degrees
Baking time: Ten minutes (about)
Melted butter
Sugar
Yield: Forty-eight doughnuts

In a saucepan scald the milk and cool to lukewarm. Add the butter, sugar, salt, nutmeg, cinnamon and eggs; mix until blended. In a cup dissolve the yeast in the warm, not hot, water. Blend into the milk mixture. Add the flour gradually. Toss on a floured board and knead until smooth and elastic. If heavy electric beater is used add four cups of flour; beat until smooth and elastic. Knead in the remaining cup of flour into the dough on the board. The dough is a soft mass. Shape into a ball. Place in a greased bowl; grease the top. Cover. Let stand until double in bulk. Roll out half the dough to ½ inch in thickness. Cut with doughnut cutter. Place on a greased cookie sheet one inch apart. Brush with melted butter. Repeat procedure for the remaining dough. Let rise until double in bulk. Bake in a hot oven until golden. Remove to racks. Brush with melted butter; dip in sugar.

Buttermilk Doughnuts

Four egg yolks, beaten
One cup sugar
Two tablespoons butter, melted
Two tablespoons orange rind
Three and one-half cups sifted flour
Two teaspoons baking powder
One teaspoon soda
One-half teaspoon salt
One-fourth teaspoon nutmeg
One-eighth teaspoon cinnamon
Three-fourths cup buttermilk
Chilling time: One hour
Deep fat temperature: 375 degrees
Frying time: Three minutes (about)
Yield: Twenty-four (3 in.)

Beat the egg yolks in a bowl. Blend in the sugar, butter and orange rind. Add the sifted dry ingredients alternately with the buttermilk to make a soft dough as for biscuits. Chill. Roll out the dough (¼ in. thick) upon a floured board. Cut with floured cutter (3 in.). Fry three or four at a time in hot deep fat until brown, turning with a fork. Drain. Place on absorbent paper. Reheat the fat to the proper temperature after each frying operation. Serve plain, sugared or glazed. To sugar: Place the cold doughnuts, a few at a time, in a bag containing a little sugar. Close the bag and shake gently. To glaze: Gradually add one-third cup boiling water to a cup of confectioners' sugar. Mix well. Brush each doughnut with the warm glaze.

Crullers

One egg
One-third cup sugar
Two tablespoons butter, melted
One tablespoon grated lemon rind
One and one-half cups sifted flour
One teaspoon baking powder
One-third cup cream
Chilling time: Thirty minutes
Deep fat temperature: 375 degrees
Frying time: Three minutes (about)
Yield: Eighteen

Beat the egg in a bowl. Blend in the sugar, butter and lemon rind. Add the sifted dry ingredients alternately with the cream. Chill. Roll out (¼ in. thick) upon a floured board. Cut into strips (2 x 4 in.) Twist each one. Fry three or four at a time in hot fat until brown, turning with a fork. Drain. Place on absorbent paper. Reheat the fat to the proper temperature after each frying operation. Serve plain or sugared.

Glazed Quick Apple Bread

One-half cup shortening
One cup sugar
Two eggs
One teaspoon vanilla
Two tablespoons milk
Two cups sifted flour
Two teaspoons baking powder
One-fourth teaspoon salt
One cup finely chopped red skinned apple
One-fourth cup chopped nuts
Oven temperature: 350 degrees
Bake: Fifty to sixty minutes
Cool: Thoroughly
Two tablespoons butter, melted
One-half cup sifted confectioners' sugar
One tablespoon water
Yield: One loaf (9 x 5 in.)

In a bowl cream the shortening, gradually beat in the sugar. Beat in the eggs one at a time. Add the vanilla and milk. Sift together the flour, baking powder and salt and blend into the creamed mixture. Add the chopped apple and nuts. Bake in a greased loaf pan (9 x 5 x 4 in.) in a moderate oven for fifty or sixty minutes, until the loaf leaves the sides of the pan and springs back in the center from the touch of a finger. Let loaf cool in the pan on a rack. When cool, turn out. Combine the melted butter with the sifted confectioners' sugar and tablespoon of water. Beat smooth and pour over loaf, letting it drip down the sides. When glaze has set, wrap loaf to keep fresh.

Butterball Coffee Cake

One package active dry yeast
One-fourth cup warm water
One-third cup shortening
One-third cup sugar
One teaspoon salt
One cup scalded milk
Three and one-half cups sifted flour
Two eggs, beaten
One cup corn meal
Kneading time: Ten minutes
First rising time: One hour, or more
One-half cup butter, melted
One cup sugar
One and one-half teaspoons cinnamon
One cup finely chopped nuts
One-half cup raisins
Second rising time: Forty minutes, about
Oven temperature: 375 degrees
Bake: Forty minutes, about
Yield: One large cake

In a small bowl sprinkle the active dry yeast over the warm water. Let stand to soften. Into a large mixing bowl measure the shortening, sugar and salt. Pour on the scalded milk and stir until shortening is melted. Cool to lukewarm. Stir in one cup of the flour, the beaten eggs and softened yeast. Add the corn meal and enough flour to make a soft dough. Turn out on a floured board and knead until satiny, about ten minutes. Place rounded dough in a greased bowl, turning over once in the bowl to grease the top. Cover and set in a warm spot until dough doubles in bulk, about one hour. Punch down. Pinch off bits of dough and shape into balls the size of walnuts. Dip the balls in the melted butter, then in the mixed sugar and cinnamon and finally in the finely chopped nuts. Arrange layers of the coated balls of dough in a greased tube pan (10 in.) with the raisins scattered between. Cover and let rise until almost doubled in bulk. Bake in a moderately hot oven about forty minutes. Serve hot or cold.

Cinnamon Breakfast Cake

One-third cup shortening
One cup sugar
Two eggs
One and one-fourth cups sifted flour
Two and one-half teaspoons baking powder
One teaspoon cinnamon
One-fourth teaspoon salt
One-half cup milk
Oven temperature: 350 degrees
Baking time: Forty to forty-five minutes
One tablespoon butter or margarine, melted
One tablespoon sugar
One-fourth teaspoon cinnamon
Servings: Nine

In a bowl cream the shortening, gradually blend in the sugar. Beat in the eggs one at a time. Sift together the flour, baking powder, cinnamon and salt. Add to the creamed mixture alternately with the milk. Pour into a greased pan (8 x 8 x 2 in.) and bake in a moderate oven for 40 to 45 minutes or until the cake springs back when touched with a finger. Remove from oven and allow to cool in the pan. Brush the top with the melted butter or margarine and sprinkle with the combined sugar and cinnamon. Serve warm or cooled.

Crown Coffee Cake

One package active dry yeast
One-fourth cup warm water
One third cup shortening
One-third cup sugar
One teaspoon salt
One cup scalded milk
Three and one-half cups sifted flour
Two eggs, beaten
One cup corn meal
Kneading time: Ten minutes
First rising time: One hour
One-half cup butter, melted
One cup sugar
One and one-half teaspoons cinnamon
One cup finely chopped nuts
One-half cup raisins
Second rising time: Forty minutes
Oven temperature: 375 degrees
Baking time: Forty minutes, about
Yield: One large cake

In a small bowl, sprinkle the active dry yeast over the warm water. Let stand to soften. Into a large mixing bowl, measure the shortening, sugar and salt. Pour on the scalded milk and stir until shortening is melted. Cool to lukewarm. Stir in one cup of the flour, the beaten eggs and softened yeast. Add the corn meal and enough flour to make a soft dough. Turn out on a floured board and knead until satiny, about ten minutes. Place rounded dough in a greased bowl, turning over once in the bowl to grease the top. Cover and set in a warm spot until the dough doubles in bulk, about one hour. Punch down. Pinch off bits of dough and shape into balls the size of walnuts. Dip the balls in the melted butter, then in the mixed sugar and cinnamon and finally in the finely chopped nuts. Arrange layers of the coated balls of dough in a greased tube pan (10 in.) with the raisins scattered between. Cover and let rise until almost doubled in bulk. Bake in a moderately hot oven for about forty minutes. Serve hot or cold.

Danish Coffee Cake

One pkg. active dry yeast
One-fourth cup lukewarm water
One and three-fourths cups milk
One cup butter or margarine
Six cups sifted flour
Three tablespoons sugar
One teaspoon salt
One teaspoon ground cardamom
First rising time: Two hours, or more
Kneading time: Three to five minutes
Filling
One-half cup butter or margarine
One-fourth cup sugar
One tablespoon cinnamon
One cup raisins
One-half cup chopped walnuts (optional)
Second rising time: One hour, or more
One egg, beaten
Sugar
One-third cup slivered almonds
Oven temperature: 350 degrees
Bake: Forty-five minutes
Yield: Two coffee cakes

In a large bowl dissolve the yeast in the lukewarm water. In a saucepan scald the milk with the butter or margarine until well blended: cool to lukewarm. Combine with yeast. Add the sugar, salt, ground cardamom and enough of the flour for a stiff dough. Turn out on a floured board and knead until smooth.

Place in a greased bowl, turning over once to grease top of dough. Cover with a clean cloth and place in a warm spot until dough has risen to double in bulk. Turn out on floured board again and knead for several minutes. Divide into two parts and roll each into a long strip about 24 x 6 inches.

Spread with softened butter or margarine and sprinkle with sugar, cinnamon, raisins and chopped nuts. Roll up like jelly roll from long side. Arrange in twists on baking sheets. Allow dough to rise a second time in a warm spot covered with a cloth until almost doubled in size. Brush with beaten egg and sprinkle with sugar and almond slivers. Bake in a moderate oven until a golden brown. Cool slightly on cake racks before cutting.

Prune Filled Coffee Cake

One-fourth cup warm water
One package active dry yeast
One-fourth cup sugar
One-half teaspoon salt
Two and one-fourths cups sifted flour
One-fourth cup shortening
One beaten egg
One-fourth cup scalded milk
First rising time: One and one-half hours, or more
One and one-half cups chopped, stewed prunes
Three tablespoons sugar
Three tablespoons lemon juice
One-half teaspoon grated lemon rind
Second rising time: One hour
Oven temperature: 350 degrees
Baking time: Twenty minutes
One cup sifted confectioners' sugar
One-fourth teaspoon vanilla
One tablespoon milk, or less
Yield: One large flat cake (12 x 15 in.)

Place the warm water in a small bowl or cup, sprinkle on the active dry yeast and allow to soften. Sift together into a bowl the sugar, salt and flour and cut in the fourth cup of shortening using a pastry blender or two knives until the mixture resembles coarse crumbs. In a bowl beat the egg, add the scalded milk then the softened yeast. Stir combination into the dry ingredients and blend thoroughly. Transfer dough to a greased bowl, turning dough over once to grease the top, cover and place in a warm spot to rise until doubled in bulk.

Punch down and divide the dough in half. Roll each piece out to about one-fourth-inch in thickness to cover a greased baking sheet about 12 x 15 inches. In a bowl combine the chopped stewed prunes, sugar, lemon juice and grated lemon rind. Spread over the sheet of dough and top with the second half rolled out equally thin. Cover and let rise in a warm spot to about double in bulk, then bake in a moderate oven until a golden brown. Remove from the oven and cool on the baking sheet. In a bowl blend the confectioners' sugar with the vanilla and enough milk to make a thin icing that may be brushed over the cooled coffee cake. Cut into squares to serve.

Swedish Lattice Coffee Cake

One-half cup butter or margarine
One-half cup chopped almonds or pecans
One-half cup sugar
One-half cup orange marmalade
Cooking time: Five minutes
One package active dry yeast
One-half cup warm milk
Two-thirds cup butter or margarine
One-third cup sugar
Four eggs, beaten
Four cups sifted flour
One teaspoon salt
One-fourth cup flour
Rising time: One hour
Oven temperature: 375 degrees
Baking time: Twenty minutes, about
Yield: Two coffee cakes

In a saucepan, combine the butter, chopped nuts, sugar and orange mar-

malade. Bring to a boil and cook for five minutes. Set aside to cool. In a small bowl, soften the active dry yeast in the warm milk. In a large bowl, cream the butter or margarine with the sugar. Blend in all but two tablespoons of the beaten eggs. Add the sifted flour and salt, mixing well. Spread the batter (reserving about one-fifth) in two greased square pans (9 x 9 x 2 in.). Add the one-fourth cup of flour to the reserved batter. Take small amounts and roll into strips of about one-fourth inch in diameter. Spread the batter in the pans with the cooled marmalade mixture. Arrange strips of dough in lattice pattern over the filling. Brush top with the beaten egg. Cover and let rise in a warm spot until almost doubled in bulk. Bake in a moderately hot oven for twenty minutes or until a golden brown.

Panetone

One and one-half cups seedless raisins
Boiling water
One and one-half cups milk
One-third cup shortening
One-half cup sugar
Two teaspoons salt
One beaten egg
One package active dry yeast
Two cups sifted flour
Standing time: One hour, about
One-half teaspoon nutmeg
One-fourth teaspoon anise seed, chopped or crushed
One-half cup chopped almonds
One-half cup chopped citron
Three cups sifted flour, about
First rising time: One hour, or more
One tablespoon butter, melted
Second rising time: One hour
Oven temperature: 350 degrees
Baking time: Forty-five minutes, about
Yield: One very large or two (10-in.) loaves

Place the raisins in a bowl and cover with boiling water. Let stand. Heat the milk in a saucepan to scalding; pour into a large mixing bowl. Stir in the shortening, sugar and salt. When slightly cooled, add the beaten egg. When lukewarm sprinkle on the active dry yeast and stir to dissolve.

Beat in two cups of sifted flour, beating smooth. Cover and let stand in a warm place until light and bubbly. Beat in the nutmeg, chopped or crushed anise seed, chopped almonds, citron and enough flour for a non-sticky dough. Place in a greased bowl, turning dough over once to grease the top. Cover and let rise in a warm spot until doubled in bulk. Punch down and form into one large or two medium sized round loaves.

Place on greased baking sheet, brush top with melted butter. Cover and let rise in a warm spot until almost doubled in bulk. Bake in a moderate oven for 45 minutes or until well browned and until the loaf gives a hollow ring when tapped with a finger. Remove to rack to cool thoroughly. Best yet if given a day or so (well wrapped) to mellow before cutting to develop full fruit flavor.

Banana Bread

One-third cup shortening
Two-thirds cup sugar
Two eggs
One and three-fourths cups sifted flour
Two teaspoons baking powder
One-fourth teaspoon baking soda
One-half teaspoon salt
One cup mashed ripe banana, two to three
Oven temperature: 350 degrees
Bake: One hour, about
Yield: One loaf

In a bowl cream the shortening, gradually blend in the sugar and the eggs. Beat well. Sift together the flour, baking powder, soda and salt and add alternately to the creamed mixture with the mashed ripe bananas. Pour into a well greased loaf pan (9 x 4 x 3 in.) and bake in a moderate oven until a cake tester inserted in the center comes away clean. Remove to a rack to cool. Wrap in waxed paper or foil to store. Slices best the second day. Wonderful spread or sandwiched with butter or cream cheese.

Banana Walnut Bread

One-fourth cup shortening
Three-fourths cup sugar
Two eggs
One cup mashed ripe banana
Two cups sifted flour
Two teaspoons baking powder
One-half teaspoon salt
One-fourth teaspoon baking soda
One cup chopped walnuts
Oven temperature: 350 degrees
Bake: Fifty to sixty minutes
Yield: One loaf (9 x 5 in.)

In a bowl cream the shortening, gradually beat in the sugar. Beat in the eggs one at a time. Add the mashed banana. Sift the flour, baking powder, salt and baking soda together and add to the first mixture, blending smooth. Add the walnuts. Bake in a greased loaf pan (9 x 5 x 3 in.) in a moderate oven for about one hour. Cool on rack. Wrap well to store.

Wheat Banana Tea Loaf

One-third cup shortening
Three-fourths cup sugar
Two eggs
One and one-half cups sifted flour
Two teaspoons baking powder
One-fourth teaspoon baking soda
Three-fourths teaspoon salt
Three-fourths cup wheat germ
One cup mashed ripe banana
Grated rind of one lemon
Oven temperature: 350 degrees
Bake: One hour
Yield: One loaf (9 x 5)

In a bowl cream the shortening, gradually blend in the sugar. Beat in the eggs until thick and creamy. Sift the flour, baking powder, baking soda and salt together in a bowl. Stir in the wheat germ. Add dry ingredients alternately with the mashed banana to the creamed mixture. Add grated lemon rind. Spoon into greased loaf pan (9 x 5 x 2½ in.), and bake in a moderate oven for one hour. Cool in the pan on a rack. Remove and wrap in waxed paper or foil to store.

Almond Coffee Cake

One package active dry yeast
One-fourth cup warm, not hot, water
One teaspoon salt
One-fourth cup sugar
Six egg yolks
One-half cup milk, scalded and cooled to
    lukewarm
One cup softened butter or margarine
Four cups sifted flour
First rising time: Two hours
Three-fourths cup chopped almonds
One cup currants
One-half cup Sultana raisins
One egg white
Second rising time: Thirty minutes
Oven temperature: 350 degrees
Baking time: Thirty minutes
One cup confectioners' sugar
Two tablespoons hot water
Maraschino cherries
Yield: One large coffee cake

In a cup sprinkle the yeast over the warm, not hot water. In a bowl mix the salt, sugar, egg yolks, milk (scalded and cooled to lukewarm) and butter. Add the yeast. Gradually add only 3 cupfuls of flour, beating vigorously by hand or with heavy type electric beater for 10 minutes. By using the electric beater the dough is smooth and satiny and does not require as much kneading as when the dough is beaten by hand. Remove dough to a board and knead in remaining flour. It is now a soft, pliable, elastic dough. Place in a greased bowl; oil top of dough. Cover. Set in a warm place to rise until double in bulk. Divide dough in half; roll out on a floured board into a rectangle (18x24 in.). Sprinkle half the combined almonds, currants and raisins over the dough. Roll dough lengthwise, jelly roll fashion. Repeat procedure for the remaining dough. Twist the two long rolls on a cookie sheet and form a circle, tucking the ends under. Brush with egg white. Set in a warm place until double in bulk. Bake in a moderate oven for 30 minutes. Remove to a rack. Combine confectioners' sugar and water; spoon over hot coffee cake. Garnish with cherries.

Tube Pan Coffee Cake: After the dough has been rolled jelly roll fashion, brush with melted butter and sprinkle with brown sugar. Cut into slices (½ in.). Place slices cut-side down in a greased tube pan (10 in.). Repeat procedure until all slices are used. Allow to rise in a warm place until double in bulk. Bake in a moderate oven for 30 minutes. Remove to a rack. Sprinkle top with confectioners' sugar.

Spicy Whirligig Loaves

Two packages active dry yeast
One-half cup warm, not hot, water
One-half cup sugar
Two teaspoons salt
Two cups scalded milk, cooled to lukewarm
One-half cup soft butter or shortening
Two eggs, slightly beaten
Seven cups sifted flour (about)
First rising time: One hour (about)
One-fourth cup milk
One-half cup sugar
One tablespoon cinnamon
Two tablespoons sesame seed
Second rising time: Forty-five minutes
    (about)
Oven temperature: 350 degrees
Baking time: Forty-five minutes
Yield: Two loaves

In a bowl dissolve the yeast in warm, not hot, water. Add sugar and salt. Allow the combined milk, butter and eggs to be lukewarm. When cooled, add to yeast mixture. Add enough flour to make a soft ball of dough. Knead on a floured board until smooth and elastic. Place in a greased bowl. Oil top of dough. Cover. Place in oven alongside a saucepan of boiling water. At intervals reheat the water to boiling. When double in bulk divide the dough in half. Knead and roll out each piece of dough into a rectangle (14x9 in.). Brush each surface of dough with milk; spread a fourth of the combined sugar, cinnamon and sesame seed over the dough. Roll as for jelly roll. Place in greased and floured pans (9x5x3 in.). Brush tops of loaves with remaining milk and sprinkle with remaining cinnamon and sesame seed. Let rise until it reaches top of pan. Bake in moderate oven for 45 minutes. Remove from oven to racks. Allow to cool before removing from pans. Slice and serve.

Cakes

Blueberry Orange Shortcake

Three cups sifted flour
Six teaspoons baking powder
One-half teaspoon salt
Four tablespoons sugar
One-half cup butter or margarine
One tablespoon grated orange rind
One-half cup orange juice
Two egg yolks, well beaten
Melted butter
Oven temperature: 450 degrees
Bake: Twelve minutes
Three cups blueberries
One cup heavy cream, whipped
One-fourth cup sugar
Serves: Six, or more

In a bowl sift the flour, baking powder, salt and sugar. Blend in the butter or margarine until the consistency of cornmeal. Add the combined orange rind, juice and egg yolks. Turn out on a floured board; divide dough in half. Pat half the dough into a round cake pan (9 in.). Brush with melted butter. Pat other half of dough on top. Bake in a very hot oven until golden. Remove to rack. Split. Put some blueberries between layers. Whip the cream and sugar together until stiff. Cover top with cream and garnish with the remaining berries.

Fragrant Strawberry Shortcake

One quart strawberries, hulled and washed
One cup sugar, or less
Let stand at room temperature: One hour
Two cups sifted flour
Four teaspoons baking powder
One-half teaspoon salt
One-third cup sugar
One tablespoon grated orange rind
One-fourth teaspoon cinnamon
One-fourth teaspoon nutmeg
One-third cup butter
One egg, well beaten
One-third cup milk (or more)
Melted butter
Oven temperature: 425 degrees
Bake: Twelve minutes
One cup heavy cream, whipped or light cream
Yield: Six servings

Put the hulled and washed berries in a bowl. Reserve a few for garnish. Crush the remaining strawberries slightly; sprinkle the sugar over them and let stand at room temperature one hour before serving time. Sift the flour, baking powder, salt and sugar into a bowl. Add grated orange rind, cinnamon, and nutmeg. Cut the butter into the mixture with a blender until it resembles cornmeal. Add the combined egg and milk. Pat dough into two greased and floured cake pans (8 in.). Brush with melted butter. Bake in a hot oven until golden. Spread strawberries between layers and on top. Serve with whipped or light cream.

Genoise Cake with Peaches

Six eggs
One cup sugar
One-eighth teaspoon salt
One-half teaspoon vanilla
Beating time: Ten minutes
One cup sifted cake flour
One-fourth cup melted butter
Oven temperature: 350 degrees
Baking time: Thirty minutes (about)
Two cups frozen or fresh peach slices
One-fourth cup confectioners' sugar
One cup heavy cream, whipped
Refrigerate: Two hours
One package (10 oz.) frozen raspberries
Serves: Eight, or more

In a bowl beat the eggs until thick and lemon-colored, gradually add the sugar, beating until fluffy (this step is most important). Add the salt and vanilla. Fold in the sifted cake flour. Fold in the butter. Pour into two greased and floured layer cake pans (9 in.). Bake in a moderate oven until a cake tester inserted in the center comes away clean. Immediately remove from pans to cake racks to cool. (If cake is allowed to remain in pans, it will become moist and heavy.) When cold, split the layers with a bread knife. Fill layers with combined peaches and sweetened whipped cream. Remove to cake plate. Slice into wedges. Refrigerate. Serve a spoonful of raspberries over each slice.

Sunshine Cake

One cup sifted flour
One teaspoon baking powder
Six egg yolks
One and one-half cups sugar
One teaspoon almond extract
One-fourth cup boiling water
Six egg whites
One-half teaspoon cream of tartar
One-fourth teaspoon salt
Oven temperature: 350 then 325 degrees
Bake: One hour
Serves: Eight, or more

Sift the flour and baking powder together. In a bowl beat the egg yolks until thick and lemon-colored. Gradually beat in the sugar and the almond extract. Add the boiling water and flour alternately. In a bowl beat the egg whites with the cream of tartar and salt until they form soft peaks. Fold them carefully into the rest of the batter. Pour into an ungreased tube pan (10 in.). Bake 45 minutes in a moderate oven (350 degrees); reduce the heat to moderately slow (325 degrees) and bake until a delicate brown. Remove from oven, invert the pan and let stand for one hour. Loosen the cake around the edges, remove from pan and place on a cake plate. Frost if desired or serve with fruit sauce or whipped cream.

Note: A simple frosting may be made by reserving one of the egg whites called for in the cake recipe and beating it with a half cup of currant or mint jelly, using a rotary or electric beater until light and fluffy. Spread over top and sides of the cake.

Sponge Layers

Five eggs
One cup sugar
Rind of one-half lemon
One teaspoon lemon juice
Rind of one-half orange
One tablespoon orange juice
One-half cup sifted potato flour (potato starch)
Oven temperature: 350 degrees
Bake: Thirty minutes
Yield: Two layers (8 in.)

Using two bowls, separate the yolks from the whites of four eggs. Add the remaining whole egg to the bowl of yolks. Beat the yolks until very thick and continue beating while gradually adding the sugar. Beat until the sugar is thoroughly dissolved (10 to 15 minutes). Add the grated rinds and fruit juices. Add the potato flour a few tablespoons at a time, cutting and folding into the batter until it disappears. Beat the egg whites until they form soft peaks; fold into the cake batter carefully. Pour into two ungreased layer cake pans (8 in.) and bake in a moderate oven for 30 minutes. Remove from oven and invert on a rack for five minutes. Run a spatula around the edge to release and shake the layers out on rack. Put layers to-

gether with fruit and whipped cream. If desired bake in a square pan (9 x 9 x 2 in.) for about 45 minutes.

Chiffon Layer Cake

Two cups sifted flour
One cup sugar
One teaspoon salt
Three teaspoons baking powder
One-third cup salad oil
One-half cup milk
One and one-half teaspoons vanilla
Beat: Till smooth
One-half cup milk
Two egg yolks
Beat: Till smooth
Two egg whites
One-half cup sugar
Oven temperature: 350 degrees
Baking time: Thirty minutes, or more
Yield: Two layers (8 or 9 in.)

Sift together into a bowl the flour, one cup of sugar, salt and baking powder. Add the salad oil, half cup of milk and vanilla. Beat by hand or with electric mixer until smooth, scraping the bowl well. Add the remaining milk and egg yolks and beat smooth again. In a second bowl beat the egg whites with a rotary beater until frothy. Gradually beat in the half cup of sugar until a glossy stiff meringue results. Fold this meringue carefully into the batter. Pour into two greased and floured cake pans (8 or 9 in.) and bake in a moderate oven until cake springs back when touched with a finger. Remove from oven and turn out on racks to cool. Frost and fill as desired.

Orange Layers

Three-fourths cup shortening
One and three-fourths cups sugar
Three eggs
Three cups sifted flour
Four teaspoons baking powder
One-half teaspoon salt
Grated rind of one orange
One-half cup orange juice
One-half cup water
One tablespoon lemon juice
Oven temperature: 350 degrees
Bake: Thirty minutes
Yield: Three layers (8 in.)

In a bowl cream the shortening. Gradually blend in the sugar, beating until light and fluffy. Beat in the eggs one at a time. Sift together the flour, baking powder and salt. Add dry ingredients to the creamed mixture alternately with the combined grated orange rind, orange juice, water and lemon juice. Beat until batter is very smooth. Divide between three well-greased layer cake pans (8 in.) and bake in a moderate oven for thirty minutes or until cake starts to leave sides of pan and springs back when touched with a finger. Remove from oven. Let cool for ten minutes before turning cakes out on racks to finish cooling. We enjoyed this light cake sandwiched with a mixture of orange marma-

lade and chopped walnuts. One cup of each blended together with a tablespoon or two of honey if desired will make sufficient filling for the three-layer cake. Dust top with confectioners' sugar.

Orange Cake

One-half cup butter or margarine
One and one-half cups sugar
Two eggs
Two cups sifted flour
Three teaspoons baking powder
One teaspoon salt
One cup milk
Grated rind of one orange
Oven temperature: 350 degrees
Bake: Forty-five minutes
Yield: One cake (9 x 12 in.)

In a bowl cream the butter or margarine. Beat in the sugar gradually until light and fluffy. Beat in the eggs one at a time. Sift together the flour, baking powder and salt and add to the creamed mixture alternately with the milk. Beat in the grated orange rind. When thoroughly mixed pour into a greased and floured baking pan (9 x 12 x 2 in.) and bake in a moderate oven until cake is nicely browned and springs back at the touch of a finger. The baked cake shrinks away from the sides of the pan slightly. Remove cake from oven and cool thoroughly on rack in pan. Frost is desired.

Chocolate Orange Frosting

One-fourth cup butter or margarine
Two squares (2 ounces) unsweetened chocolate
Heat: Until blended
Three tablespoons orange juice
Two and one-half cups sifted confectioners' sugar
Yield: Frosting for cake (9 x 12 in.)

In a saucepan over low heat melt the butter or margarine and unsweetened chocolate together. Remove from the heat and add the orange juice, mixing well. Gradually beat in the confectioners' sugar, until smooth and creamy and thickened enough to spread over the cake.

Orange Cake Filling

One-third cup sugar
Two tablespoons flour
One-half cup orange juice
One-fourth cup water
Cook: Five minutes, or more
One egg yolk
One or two tablespoons lemon juice
Two tablespoons butter
One teaspoon grated orange rind
Cook: Two minutes
Yield: Three-fourths cup

In a saucepan, combine the sugar and flour, blend in the orange juice and water. Cook over medium heat stirring constantly, until mixture thickens. In a small bowl beat the egg yolk with the lemon juice. Add a small amount of the cooked mixture to the egg. Return the combination to the saucepan with butter and grated orange rind. Cook for two minutes. Cool slightly and spread between cake layers.

Fluffy Butter Layers

One-half cup butter
Two cups sugar
Three cups sifted flour
Four teaspoons baking powder
One and one-half cups milk
One teaspoon vanilla
Five egg whites
Oven temperature: 350 degrees
Bake: Thirty minutes
Yield: Three layers (9 in.)

In a bowl cream the butter until soft. Gradually beat in the sugar until light and fluffy. Sift the flour and baking powder together and add to the creamed mixture alternately with the milk, and vanilla. When beaten smooth, fold in the eggs which have been beaten until they hold soft peaks. Spoon batter into three greased and floured layer cake pans (9 in.). Bake in a moderate oven for thirty minutes or until nicely browned and shrinking away from the sides of the pans. Remove from oven and cool ten minutes in the pans on racks. Turn cakes out on racks and cool thoroughly before frosting.

Coconut Layer Cake

One-half cup butter or margarine
One and one-half cups sugar
Two eggs, beaten
Two and one-fourth cups sifted flour
Three teaspoons, baking powder
One teaspoon salt
One cup milk
One teaspoon vanilla
Oven temperature: 375 degrees
Bake: Twenty-five minutes
Yield: Two layers (9 in.)
Orange Filling
Seven Minute Frosting
Freshly grated or flaked canned coconut
   (1½ cups)

In a bowl cream the butter, gradually add the sugar. Add the beaten eggs, beat well. Sift together the flour, baking powder and salt and add to the creamed mixture alternately with the milk to which the vanilla has been added. Beat the batter until thoroughly blended and pour into two greased and floured or greased and waxed paper-lined cake pans (9 in.). Bake in a moderately hot oven until a toothpick inserted in the center of the cake comes away clean. Remove from the oven, cool briefly in pans then remove to racks to cool. Spread filling between layers and frost with Seven Minute Frosting. Scatter generous amounts of freshly grated or flaked canned coconut over the frosting, pressing it against the sides with the hands.

Butter Layers

One-half cup butter or margarine
One and one-half cups sugar
Two eggs, beaten
Two and one-fourth cups sifted flour
Three teaspoons baking powder
One teaspoon salt
One cup milk
One teaspoon vanilla
Oven temperature: 375 degrees
Bake: Twenty-five minutes
Yield: Two layers (9 in.)

In a bowl cream the butter or margarine well, gradually blend in the sugar, beating until light and fluffy. Beat in the eggs. Sift together the flour, baking powder and salt and add to the creamed mixture alternately with the milk to which the vanilla has been added. Beat the batter until thoroughly blended and pour into two greased and floured or greased and waxed paper lined cake pans (9 in.). Bake in a moderately hot oven until a cake tester inserted in the center comes away clean and the cake starts to leave the sides of the pan. Remove from oven and cool for ten minutes in the pans. Remove to racks to finish cooling before frosting.

Easy Soft Chocolate Frosting

Two packages (6 oz. each) semi-sweet
   chocolate pieces
One cup dairy sour cream
One-fourth teaspoon salt
One-fourth teaspoon cinnamon
One teaspoon instant powdered coffee
Yield: Frosting for two layers (9 in.)

In the upper part of a double boiler over hot water melt the semi-sweet chocolate. Remove from the heat and blend in the dairy sour cream, salt, cinnamon and instant powdered coffee. Beat smooth. Cool, stirring occasionally until frosting is thick enough to hold soft peaks. To hasten this, bowl of frosting may be placed in larger bowl of ice.

Butterscotch Ice Box Cake

One package butterscotch pudding mix
Two cups milk
Two dozen ladyfingers (two three-ounce
   packages)
Chill: Four or more hours
One cup heavy cream, whipped
Serves: Eight to ten

Prepare the packaged butterscotch pudding mix with the milk according to package directions. Arrange half the baker's ladyfingers over the bottom of a shallow baking dish (7 x 12 x 2 in.) over a piece of waxed paper. Pour on the butterscotch pudding and press remaining ladyfingers into the pudding. Chill thoroughly. To serve turn out on a large plate or platter and peel off the waxed paper. Decorate with the whipped cream and cut into squares or slices to serve.

Cinnamon Layers

One-half cup shortening
One and one-fourth cups brown sugar
Two eggs
Two cups sifted flour
One teaspoon soda
One-half teaspoon salt
One tablespoon cinnamon
One cup soured milk
Oven temperature: 375 degrees
Bake: Twenty-five minutes
Yield: Two layers (8 in.)

In a bowl cream the shortening, gradually beat in the brown sugar. Beat in the eggs. Sift together the flour, soda, salt and cinnamon and add to the creamed mixture alternately with the soured milk (fresh milk needs but a teaspoon of lemon juice or vinegar added to curdle it). Beat thoroughly. Pour into two greased layer cake pans (8 in.) and bake in a moderately hot oven for 20 to 25 minutes or until the cake starts to leave the sides of the pan and springs back in the center when touched with a finger. Remove from oven to cool in pans on racks for ten minutes. Turn cakes out on racks to finish cooling. Frost as desired or cut each layer into wedges and top with vanilla ice cream. (The two layers and a quart of ice cream will serve twelve.)

Maple Layer Cake

One-half cup butter or margarine
One-half cup sugar
Two eggs
Two cups sifted flour
Three teaspoons baking powder
One teaspoon salt
One cup maple syrup
One-half cup milk
Oven temperature: 350 degrees
Bake: Thirty minutes
Yield: Two layers (8 or 9 in.)

In a bowl cream the butter or margarine until light, gradually blend in the sugar, beat in the eggs. Sift the flour, baking powder and salt together. Combine the maple syrup and milk. Add the sifted dry ingredients to the egg mixture alternately with the maple syrup and milk. Blend thoroughly together. Pour batter into two well greased and floured layer cake pans (8 or 9 in.). Bake in a moderate oven for thirty minutes or until the cake springs back at the touch of a finger and begins to leave sides of pan. Remove to rack to cool in pans for ten minutes. Turn cakes out on racks to finish cooling. Frost if desired.

Josie's Cheesecake

One and one-half cups rusk crumbs
One-third cup soft butter
One-fourth cup sugar
One can (3½ oz.) flaked coconut
One-half cup finely chopped almonds
Six eggs, separated
One cup sugar
Rind of one lemon
One and one-half pounds cream cheese,
    mashed
Oven temperature: 350 degrees
Baking time: Fifty minutes (about)
Serves: Eight

In a bowl mix the crumbs, butter, sugar, coconut and almonds. Butter heavily the bottom and sides of a spring form pan (9 in.). Line the bottom and sides with the crumb mixture. In a bowl beat the egg yolks until thick and lemon-colored; gradually beat in only one-half cup sugar; add lemon rind. Add the mashed cream cheese, beating until smooth. Beat the egg whites until soft, but not stiff peaks are formed. Gradually add the remaining half cup sugar, beaten until mixture is satiny. Fold into the egg yolk mixture. Pour into the lined crumbed pan. Bake in moderate oven until the mixture is golden and slightly set in center. Remove to rack. Allow to cool in pan; then loosen edges of crust from pan with a spatula. Release spring; remove outer rim. Serve in wedges.

Black Bottom Parfait Cheese Cake

Two cups zwieback crumbs
One-fourth cup sugar
One-half cup melted butter or margarine
Two packages (6 oz. each) chocolate bits
One-half cup strong brewed coffee
Heat: Until melted
Two tablespoons rum
Two envelopes unflavored gelatin
One-half cup cold coffee
Three egg yolks
One cup sugar
One-half cup milk
One-eighth teaspoon salt
Cook: Five minutes
One square (1 oz.) unsweetened chocolate
One pint coffee or vanilla ice cream
One-fourth cup rum
Four cups creamy cottage cheese, sieved
Let stand: Until partially set
Chill: Overnight
Whipped cream, shaved chocolate
Yield: One cake (9 in.)

In a bowl mix the beaten eggs, sugar, salt and corn syrup. On the bottom of the unbaked pastry shell spread the applesauce. Pour the egg mixture over the applesauce. Arrange the nuts on top. Bake in a hot oven for 10 minutes. Reduce the temperature to moderate and continue baking for another 35 minutes. Remove to a rack. Serve plain or with whipped cream.

Cheese Cake

One box (6 oz.) zwiebach, rolled fine
Three tablespoons sugar
Three tablespoons soft butter
Four eggs, separated
One cup sugar
One pound dry cottage cheese, sieved
One-half pint heavy cream
One-fourth cup sifted flour
One-fourth teaspoon salt
One tablespoon grated lemon rind
Three tablespoons lemon juice
One-half teaspoon vanilla
Oven temperature: 275 degrees
Baking time: One and one-half hours, or
    more
Standing time: Five hours
Servings: Eight, or more

Roll the zwiebach into fine crumbs. There will be one and one-half cups crumbs. Combine the crumbs, sugar and butter; reserve one-third cup for the top of the cake. Pat the rest of the crumbs on the bottom and sides of a buttered spring form pan (8 in.) from which the side can be removed. Beat the egg yolks until very thick; gradually beat in one-half cup sugar. Force the cheese twice through a fine sieve; beat in the cream, and add to the egg yolks. Stir in the flour, salt, lemon rind and juice and vanilla. Beat the egg whites until stiff; gradually beat in the rest of the sugar, and fold into the cheese mixture. Pour into the crumb-lined pan. Sprinkle the reserved crumbs over the top. Bake in a very slow oven until set in the center. Turn off the heat. Let the cake remain in the oven until cold, leaving the door ajar. Remove from the oven. The cake will settle slightly. Loosen the cake from the side of the pan and remove side. Do not remove the bottom of the pan. Let stand five hours before cutting. Lift the cake to dessert plate and serve in wedges with hot coffee and cream.

Pineapple Cheese Cake: Scatter one cup thoroughly drained crushed pineapple over the crumbs in the pan before adding the cheese mixture. Bake as for plain cheese cake.

Refrigerator Cheese Cake

One and one-half cups zwieback crumbs
One tablespoon sugar
One teaspoon cinnamon
One-fourth cup melted butter
Two packages unflavored gelatin
One-half cup cold water
Three egg yolks
One teaspoon salt
Three-fourths cup sugar
One-half cup milk
Cook: Three minutes
Two cups creamy cottage cheese, sieved
One-half pound cream cheese
One-fourth cup lemon juice
One tablespoon grated lemon rind
Chill: Until it starts to gel
One cup heavy cream, whipped
One pint strawberries, halved
Serves: Eight, or more

Line sides and bottom of an oiled spring form pan (8 in.) with combined crumbs, sugar, cinnamon and melted butter. In a cup sprinkle the gelatin over the cold water; let stand until softened. In a heavy saucepan mix the egg yolks, salt, sugar and milk. Cook over low heat stirring constantly for three minutes (do not let it boil). Remove; stir in softened gelatin until dissolved. Add the combined cottage cheese, cream cheese, lemon juice and rind. Chill until it starts to thicken. Fold in the whipped cream. Pour half the cheese mixture in the crumb lined pan. Reserve a few halved strawberries for garnish. Place remaining halved strawberries, cut side up, over cheese mixture. Pour remaining mixture on top. Place in refrigerator to set. Garnish with berries; serve.

Schaum Torte

Six egg whites
One-fourth teaspoon salt
One teaspoon baking powder
One cup sugar
One tablespoon vinegar
One cup sugar
Oven temperature: 300 degrees
Baking time: One and one-fourth hours
One-half pint heavy cream, whipped
Fresh or canned fruit
Servings: Twelve, approx.

In a large bowl, beat the egg whites with the salt and baking powder until frothy. Gradually beat in the sugar, adding about a tablespoon at a time and beating in thoroughly after each addition. When one cup of sugar has been well beaten in, add the vinegar. Then continue beating in the second cup of sugar gradually. When meringue is very thick and somewhat dull in appearance, spread over a shallow baking pan (12 x 16 in.) or in two square pans (9 x 9 in.) that have been buttered and dusted with flour. Bake in a slow oven for about one and one-fourth hours or until delicately browned. Remove and cool in the pan on a cake rack. When ready to serve cut into squares, after trimming off the outer edges if necessary. Remove from pan with cake turner. It will seem brittle and cracked. Top with slightly sweetened whipped cream or ice cream and sauce with sliced, slightly sweetened strawberries or other fruit.

Coconut Lemon Torte

One cup finely crushed graham cracker
    crumbs
One-half cup flaked coconut
One-half cup chopped salted cashews or
    walnuts
Four egg whites
One-eighth teaspoon salt
One cup sugar
One teaspoon vanilla
Oven temperature: 325 degrees
Bake: Forty-five minutes
One-half cup heavy cream
One tablespoon sugar
One teaspoon grated lemon rind
One-fourth cup grated coconut
Servings: Nine

In a bowl stir together the crushed graham cracker crumbs, half cup of flaked coconut and chopped nuts. In a second bowl beat the egg whites until foamy, add the salt and gradually beat in the cup of sugar. Beat until meringue holds stiff glossy peaks. Add the vanilla and fold in the graham cracker mixture. Spread in a greased baking pan (9 x 9 x 2 in.) and bake in a moderately slow oven for forty-five minutes or until the top appears dry. Remove from oven and cool torte in pan on rack. Whip the heavy cream with the tablespoon of sugar, add grated lemon rind and coconut. Cut torte into squares with a spoonful of the whipped cream on top.

Zwieback Nut Torte

Three eggs
Three-fourths cup sugar
One cup finely rolled zwieback crumbs
One cup finely chopped walnuts
One teaspoon baking powder
One-fourth teaspoon salt
One-half teaspoon cinnamon
Oven temperature: 325 degrees
Bake: Forty minutes
One-half cup strawberry jam
One-half cup heavy cream, whipped
Serves: Nine

In a bowl beat the eggs until light, beat in the sugar. In a second bowl stir together the zwieback crumbs, walnuts, baking powder, salt and cinnamon. Fold into egg mixture. Transfer to a greased square baking pan (9 x 9 x 2 in.) and bake in a moderately slow oven for 40 minutes. Cool in pan on a rack. To serve spread top with jam and cut in squares. Serve garnished with slightly sweetened whipped cream.

Graham Nut Torte

Three eggs, separated
One cup sugar
One cup fine graham cracker crumbs
Three-fourths cup coarsely chopped nuts
One-fourth teaspoon salt
Oven temperature: 325 degrees
Bake: Forty minutes
Serves: Six, or more

In a large bowl beat the egg whites until they form soft peaks. In a second bowl beat the egg yolks until light, gradually beating in the sugar. Fold yolks into whites with the graham cracker crumbs, chopped nuts and salt. Pour into a well greased and floured cake pan (9 in.) and bake in a moderately slow oven for 40 minutes. Remove from oven and cool cake in pan on a rack. To serve cut in wedges and top with ice cream, whipped cream or a lemon sauce.

Strawberry Torte

One-half cup butter or margarine
One-half cup sugar
Three egg yolks
One teaspoon vanilla
One cup sifted flour
One and one-fourth teaspoons baking
    powder
One-fourth teaspoon salt
One-fourth cup milk
One cup sliced strawberries
Three egg whites
One-half cup sugar
Oven temperature: 350 degrees
Baking time: Thirty-five minutes
One cup heavy cream, whipped
Servings: Ten

In a bowl cream the butter or margarine with the half cup of sugar until light and fluffy. Beat in the egg yolks and vanilla. Sift together the flour, baking powder and salt and add to the creamed mixture alternately with the milk. Spread batter in two greased and waxed paper lined cake pans (8 in.). Arrange sliced strawberries over the batter. In a bowl beat the egg whites until foamy, gradually beat in the remaining sugar until a glossy meringue results. Spread this over the strawberry slices and bake in a moderate oven for 35 minutes. Remove from oven and cool for 10 minutes before loosening the edges and removing to racks to finish cooling. Place layers together so meringue toppings are together and thus form the filling. Frost with the slightly sweetened whipped cream.

Strawberry Banana Angel Torte

One small baker's angel food ring cake
One pint ripe strawberries
One-half cup dairy sour cream
One-fourth cup sugar
One medium-sized banana (three-fourths
    cup sliced)
One cup heavy cream, whipped
Chill: Three hours, about
Serves: 10 or 12

Slice the angel food ring cake into four or five layers. Wash, dry and hull the strawberries. Slice some into a cup and crush to measure one-fourth cup. Slice more to measure one-half cup. Reserve remainder for garnish. Add the dairy sour cream and fourth cup of sugar to the crushed berries, mixing well. Fold this combination with the sliced berries and sliced banana into the whipped cream. Spread about a half cup of the mixture between the layers of angel food cake and over the top. Chill in the refrigerator for several hours. Garnish with cut reserved berries at serving time.

Angel Food Cake

One and one-half cups egg whites (10-12)
One and one-half teaspoons cream of tartar
One-fourth teaspoon salt
One and one-half teaspoons vanilla
One-half teaspoon almond extract
Three-fourths cup sugar
One cup sifted flour
Three-fourths cup sugar
Oven temperature: 350 degrees
Bake: Forty minutes
Serves: Twelve, or more

In a large bowl combine the egg whites with the cream of tartar, salt, vanilla and almond extract. Beat until foamy. Gradually add the first measure of sugar, spoonful by spoonful, beating in thoroughly after each addition until a very stiff meringue results. Beat until the mixture will stand in stiff points. Sift together the flour and the second measure of sugar. Add to the meringue a few tablespoons at a time, folding into the mixture with a half dozen cut and fold strokes of a rubber spatula with each addition. Transfer the batter to an ungreased tube pan (10 in.) and bake in a moderate oven for forty minutes. Remove from oven and invert and let hang with tube of pan resting on a bottle or funnel to cool thoroughly before removing from the pan. When cool, loosen the edges with a spatula and shake the cake from the pan. Serve plain, frosted or with ice cream or sauces as desired.

Coconut Cream Angel Cake

One cup heavy cream
One-fourth cup instant cocoa mix
Pinch of salt
One purchased angel food cake (6 to 8 in.)
One-half cup flaked coconut
Chilling time: One hour
Servings: Eight, or more

In a bowl beat the heavy cream rapidly with the instant cocoa mix and pinch of salt until the cream begins to thicken. Beat more slowly until cream holds its shape. Split the angel food cake into three layers. Fill layers and frost top and sides with the cream mixture, sprinkle with the flaked coconut and chill for one hour before serving.

Blueberry Angel Cake Roll

Three-fourths cup egg whites (5 to 6)
Three-fourths teaspoon cream of tartar
One-eighth teaspoon salt
Three-fourths teaspoon vanilla
One-fourth teaspoon almond flavoring
Six tablespoons sugar
One-half cup sifted cake flour
Six tablespoons sugar
One cup cleaned blueberries
Oven temperature: 350 degrees
Baking time: Fifteen to twenty minutes
Servings: Six, or more

In a bowl beat the egg whites, cream of tartar, salt, vanilla and almond flavoring with a rotary or electric beater until foamy. Gradually add the first measure of sugar spoonful by spoonful, beating thoroughly after each addition until a very stiff meringue results. Beat until the mixture will stand in stiff peaks. Sift together the cake flour and the second measure of sugar. Add to the meringue a few tablespoons at a time, folding into the mixture with a half dozen cut and fold strokes of a rubber spatula with each addition. Add the blueberries. Line a jelly roll pan (10 x 15 x ½ in.) with waxed or oiled brown paper. Pour in the batter, spreading it well into the corners. Bake in a moderate oven until a delicate brown. Remove from oven. Turn out upon a wire rack. Strip off the paper, cool. Spread with lemon filling or softened ice cream and roll up. Slice into serving portions.

Lemon Filling

Three egg yolks
One-half cup sugar
Two tablespoons flour
One-half cup water
Juice and grated rind of one lemon
Cooking time: Ten minutes
Yield: One cup

In the upper half of a double boiler beat the egg yolks. Stir in the sugar, flour and water. Add the lemon juice and grated rind. Cook over hot water, stirring constantly until the mixture thickens. Remove from heat and cool thoroughly. Use as filling for angel roll.

Mocha Filled Sponge Roll

Six eggs
One cup sugar
One-fourth teaspoon salt
One-half teaspoon vanilla
One-half cup sifted flour
Oven temperature: 350 degrees
Bake: Fifteen minutes, about
Confectioners' sugar
One cup heavy cream
One tablespoon cocoa
Two tablespoons sugar
One-half teaspoon instant powdered coffee
Serves: Eight

Separate the whites from the yolks of the eggs, placing whites in a large bowl and yolks in a small bowl. Beat the whites until foamy. Add the sugar gradually, beating well after each addition until a thick glossy meringue is the result. In a small bowl beat the yolks with the salt and vanilla until lemony in color and thick. Fold beaten yolks into the meringue carefully. Fold flour into the batter carefully in four additions. Line a jelly roll pan (10 x 15 x 1 in.) with oiled brown paper. Pour in the batter, spreading well into the corners. Bake in a moderate oven until the cake springs back when touched with a finger and is a golden brown. Remove from oven. Turn cake out upon waxed paper or paper toweling sprinkled with sugar. Tear off the paper on the cake and cut one-half inch of cake from each of the sides. Using paper as a lever roll up the cake. Leave rolled until cooled.

In a bowl beat the heavy cream until almost thick, gradually add the combined cocoa, sugar and instant powdered coffee and beat until stiff. Chill until cake is cooled. To serve, unroll cake and spread with the flavored whipped cream. Roll up, dust with confectioners' sugar and slice into individual portions.

Sweet Chocolate Roll

Seven egg yolks
One-half cup sugar
Seven ounces dark sweet chocolate
Five tablespoons water or brewed coffee
Seven egg whites
One-half cup sugar
Oven temperature: 350 degrees
Bake: Fifteen minutes
Rest: Five minutes
Three tablespoons cocoa
One cup heavy cream
Two tablespoons confectioners' sugar
Two teaspoons vanilla
Servings: Twelve

In a bowl beat the egg yolks with the half cup of sugar until light and fluffy. Place the cut up dark sweet chocolate

in a small saucepan with the water or coffee and heat until blended smooth. Add to the egg yolk mixture. In a bowl beat the egg whites until foamy. Gradually beat in the remaining half cup of sugar until stiff. Fold into the first mixture. Oil a large jelly roll pan (14 x 18 in.), line with waxed paper and oil paper. Spread batter evenly over oiled paper and bake in a moderate oven for fifteen minutes. Turn off oven heat and let cake remain in oven with door open for five minutes. Place pan on rack and cool cake to room temperature under a damp cloth or wrung out paper toweling. Loosen edges of cake and sprinkle with cocoa. Turn cake out on double layer of waxed paper. Peel off paper baked on the cake. Beat the heavy cream with the confectioners' sugar and vanilla until stiff. Spread over the cake. Lift the waxed paper to roll up the cake. Chill if desired.

Snow Cake

Three-fourths cup shortening
One cup sugar
One and one-half teaspoons vanilla
Three cups sifted flour
One and one-half teaspoons salt
Four teaspoons baking powder
One and one-fourth cups milk
Three egg whites
One-fourth teaspoon cream of tartar
One-fourth cup sugar
One cup golden raisins
Oven temperature: 350 degrees
Bake: One hour, about
Yield: One tube cake (8 in.)

In a bowl cream the shortening, gradually blend in the sugar and vanilla. Sift together the flour, salt and baking powder and add to the creamed mixture alternately with the milk. Beat smooth. In a second bowl beat the egg whites with the cream of tartar until foamy, gradually beat in the fourth cup of sugar. Fold stiffly beaten whites into the cake batter with the golden raisins. Transfer to a greased and floured tube pan (8 in.) or two-layer cake pans (9 in.). Bake tube cake in a moderate oven for about one hour or until the cake is nicely browned and leaves the sides of the pan. The layer cakes will take about 30 minutes. Allow cake to cool in pan for about 10 minutes, then remove to racks to cool thoroughly. Tube cake may be frosted or not as you wish; if desired sprinkle cooled cake top with confectioners' sugar.

Blueberry Chiffon Dessert

Twenty-four ladyfingers (3 pkgs)
One-fourth cup cognac or sherry
Two packages unflavored gelatin
One-half cup cold water
Four eggs, separated
One cup sugar
One-half teaspoon salt
One tablespoon grated lemon rind
One-half cup lemon juice
Cook: Five minutes
Chill: Until it starts to jell
Two cups blueberries
One-half cup heavy cream, whipped, or
    dessert topping
Serves: Six, or more

Shape a 14 inch circle of aluminum foil in a pie or spring form pan (10 in.). Arrange ladyfingers on the bottom and sides of foil. Sprinkle the cognac or sherry over the ladyfingers. Set aside. Sprinkle the gelatin over the cold water in a cup. In the top of a double boiler mix the egg yolks, one-half cup of the sugar, salt, lemon rind and juice. Cook over hot water until the mixture is hot, stirring constantly. Add softened gelatin; stir until dissolved. Chill in refrigerator until the mixture is consistency of unbeaten egg whites. Beat the egg whites and remaining sugar until stiff and satiny. Fold the meringue into the gelatin mixture. Reserve a half cup of blueberries for garnish. Fold in remaining berries. Pour mixture over ladyfingers. Chill in refrigerator until firm. When ready to serve, lift the dessert out of the pan. Place on a platter. Gently pull the foil from the sides of the ladyfingers. Cut off excess foil. Garnish with whipped cream and remaining blueberries.

Lemon Strawberry Sherbet Cake

Two eggs
One cup sugar
One tablespoon grated lemon rind
One-half cup light corn syrup
One-fourth cup lemon juice
One and one-half cups milk
Two pints strawberries, washed, sliced
One cup heavy cream, whipped
Freeze: Until mushy
Freezing time: Two hours
Two sponge cake layers
Serves: Twelve

In a bowl beat the eggs and one-half cup of sugar and lemon rind until thick and lemon-colored. Add the combined corn syrup and juice. Add the milk slowly. Pour into refrigerator trays. Freeze until mushy in freezing compartment with the control set at the coldest point. Wash and hull strawberries. Reserve some of the berries for garnish. Crush remaining berries. When lemon mixture is mushy remove to a chilled bowl; beat until smooth. Fold in whipped cream and half the strawberries. Add remaining sugar to berries; let stand. Pour mixture back into trays, freezing until firm. When ready to serve, quickly pack the berry sherbet into a cake pan (8 in.), then place sherbet between lay-

ers of cake. Place on cake plate; garnish with strawberries. Serve immediately cutting cake into wedges and serving with a spoonful of crushed strawberries.

Mincemeat Cake

Two cups prepared mincemeat
Two cups walnuts, chopped
One teaspoon vanilla
One-fourth cup rum or cognac
One tablespoon grated orange rind
One-fourth cup orange juice
One cup buttermilk
One cup real mayonnaise
Three cups sifted all-purpose flour
One and one-half cups sugar
Three-fourths teaspoon soda
One teaspoon salt
Oven temperature: 325 degrees
Baking time: Two hours
Yield: One tube cake (9 in.)

In a bowl mix the mincemeat, walnuts, vanilla, rum or cognac, rind, orange juice, buttermilk and mayonnaise. Sift the flour, sugar, soda and salt into the mixture, blend thoroughly. Pour into a tube pan (9 in.) which has been greased and floured. Bake in a moderate oven for two hours. Remove to rack to cool. Press out frosting into a design with a cooky press. Garnish with candied cherries and angelica.

Frosting

One-fourth cup shortening
One and one-half cups confectioners' sugar
One tablespoon milk

In a bowl beat the shortening, sugar and milk. The frosting should be quite stiff. Put into cooky press. Press out designs on top of cake. Garnish.

Orange Chiffon Cake

Two and one-fourth cups sifted cake flour
One and one-half cups sugar
Three teaspoons baking powder
One teaspoon salt
One-half cup salad oil
Five egg yolks, unbeaten
One cup orange juice
Four tablespoons grated orange rind
One cup egg whites (7 to 8)
One-half teaspoon cream of tartar
Oven temperature: 325-350 degrees
Baking time: Seventy minutes (about)
One-third cup soft shortening
Three cups sifted confectioners' sugar
Yield: One large cake

In a mixing bowl sift the flour, sugar, baking powder and salt. Make a depression in the center of the dry ingredients, filling it with oil, egg yolks, three-fourths cup orange juice and three tablespoons grated rind. Beat until smooth. In a large bowl, whip the egg whites with the cream of tartar until very stiff. Add the egg yolk mixture gradually to the whites, folding carefully. Pour into an ungreased tube pan (10 in.). Bake in a moderately slow oven for 55 minutes; increase the temperature to moderate; bake until the cake springs back when touched lightly with a finger. Remove. Invert upon a cake rack; cool. Loosen side of cake with spatula and place upon a cake plate. To make the frosting: In a bowl blend the shortening and sugar. Stir in the remaining orange juice, beating until smooth. Frost the top and sides of the cake. Garnish with the remaining grated orange rind.

Fresh Coconut Cake

Two-thirds cup butter or margarine
One cup sugar
Four eggs, separated
Two cups sifted cake flour
Three teaspoons baking powder
One-half teaspoon salt
One-half cup coconut milk
One teaspoon vanilla
One-half cup grated coconut
Oven temperature: 375 degrees
Baking time: Twenty-five minutes
Topping
One-half pint heavy cream, whipped
One tablespoon sugar
One-half teaspoon vanilla
One fresh coconut, shredded or grated
Yield: One layer cake

In a bowl cream the butter until fluffy. Add one-half cup sugar, beating until light and fluffy. Add egg yolks, beating vigorously. Add the sifted dry ingredients alternately with the coconut milk. Add vanilla and coconut. Beat the egg whites with the remaining half cup of sugar until meringue-like. Fold into batter. Pour into two greased and floured layer pans (8 in.). Bake in a moderately hot oven until a cake tester inserted into the center comes away clean. Remove to racks. In a bowl beat the cream and sugar until thick. Add vanilla. Spread between layers, top and sides of cake. Sprinkle coconut on top and sides. Serve.

Chocolate Cream Layers

Three squares (one oz. each) unsweetened
   chocolate
One-half cup water
Melting time: Five to eight minutes
One-half cup butter
Two-thirds cup brown sugar
One cup sugar
Three eggs
Two teaspoons vanilla
Two cups sifted flour
One and one-half teaspoons baking powder
One teaspoon soda
One teaspoon salt
One cup dairy sour cream
Oven temperature: 350 degrees
Bake: Forty minutes, about
Yield: Two layers (9 in.)

In a small saucepan heat the baking chocolate and water over low heat until well combined. Remove from heat and allow to cool. In a bowl cream the butter; gradually add the brown and white sugar, beating until light and fluffy. Beat in the eggs one at a time. Add the vanilla. Sift together the flour, baking powder, soda and salt. Stir the dairy sour cream into the chocolate blending well. Add the sifted dry ingredients and the chocolate mixture alternately to the creamed mixture. Beat well together. Divide batter between two greased and floured cake pans (9 in.). Bake in a moderately hot oven until cake springs back in the center when touched with a finger. Remove from oven and let stand ten minutes before removing to cake racks to cool thoroughly. Spread Marshmallow Cream Filling between layers and over top. Chill.

Fudge Layers

One-half cup butter or margarine
One and one-fourth cups sugar
Two egg yolks
Three ounces unsweetened chocolate,
   melted
Two and one-fourth cups sifted flour
Three tablespoons baking powder
One teaspoon salt
One and one-half cups milk
Two teaspoons vanilla
Two egg whites
One-fourth cup sugar
Three-fourths cup finely chopped pecans
Oven temperature: 350 degrees
Bake: Thirty-five minutes
Yield: Two layers (9 in.)

In a bowl cream the butter or margarine. Blend in the one and one-fourth cups of sugar until light and fluffy. Beat in the egg yolks. Add the melted chocolate. Sift together the flour, baking powder and salt and add to the creamed mixture alternately with the combined milk and vanilla. Mix thoroughly. Beat the egg whites in a bowl until foamy, gradually beat in the sugar until a stiff meringue is formed. Fold meringue and finely chopped nuts into the cake batter. Divide between two greased and floured cake pans (9 in.). Bake in a moderate oven until cake tester comes

away clean and cake leaves the edge of pan. Allow cake to cool in pans for ten minutes then remove to racks to finish cooling. Put layers together with slightly sweetened whipped cream or seven-minute frosting.

Seven Minute Frosting

Two egg whites
One and one-half cups sugar
One-eighth teaspoon salt
One-fourth cup water
One tablespoon light corn syrup
One teaspoon vanilla
Cook: Seven minutes, about

In the upper half of a double boiler stir together the unbeaten egg whites, sugar, salt, water, corn syrup and vanilla. Place over boiling water and beat with rotary or an electric beater for seven minutes or until the frosting stands in stiff peaks. Spread between and over cake layers.

Black Eggless Cake

One and two-thirds cups sifted flour
One cup sugar
One-half cup cocoa
One teaspoon soda
One-half teaspoon salt
One-half cup salad oil or melted shortening
One cup sour milk
One and one-half teaspoons vanilla
Oven temperature: 375 degrees
Baking time: Thirty minutes
Servings: Nine

Sift together into a bowl the flour, sugar, cocoa, soda and salt. Beat in the salad oil or melted shortening, the sour milk and vanilla. Beat thoroughly until batter is smooth. Pour into a greased and floured baking pan (9 x 9 x 2 in.) and bake in a moderately hot oven for thirty minutes. Remove from oven and cool in the pan on a rack. Frost or not as desired.

Semi-Sweet Devil's Food Cake

One and one-half cups semi-sweet
   chocolate pieces
One-third cup butter or margarine
One and one-half cups brown sugar
Two eggs
One and one-half teaspoons vanilla
One and three-fourths cups sifted flour
One and one-fourth teaspoons baking soda
One teaspoon salt
One-half cup buttermilk
Three-fourths cup boiling water
Oven temperature: 375 degrees
Bake: Thirty-five minutes, about
Yield: Two layers (8 in.)

Place the semi-sweet chocolate pieces in the upper half of a double boiler and melt over hot water. In a bowl cream the butter, add the sugar gradually. Beat in the eggs one at a time.
Add the vanilla and melted chocolate. Sift the flour, soda and salt together and add to the creamed mixture alternately

with the buttermilk. Mix well. Blend in the boiling water. Pour into two greased and floured layer cake pans and bake in a moderately hot oven for about thirty-five minutes, or until a cake tester inserted in the center comes away clean. Remove to cake rack and cool in pans for ten minutes. Turn out and complete cooling on rack before frosting cake.

Fudge Frosting

Four squares (one ounce each)
   unsweetened chocolate
Three tablespoons butter or margarine
One-eighth teaspoon salt
One teaspoon vanilla
Three cups sifted confectioners' sugar
Four tablespoons milk, or more
Yield: Frosting for two layers

In the upper half of a double boiler over hot water melt the chocolate with butter or margarine. Stir in the salt and vanilla. Remove from heat and blend in the confectioners' sugar and the milk. Beat until smooth and thick. Spread between and over cake layers.

Chocolate Cake

One-half cup vegetable shortening
One and three-fourths cup cake flour
Two teaspoons double-acting baking
   powder
One-fourth teaspoon soda
One teaspoon salt
One and one-half cups sugar
One and one-quarter cups undiluted
   evaporated milk
Beating time: Two minutes
One teaspoon vanilla
Two eggs, unbeaten
Two squares (2 oz.) unsweetened
   chocolate, melted
Beating time: One minute
Oven temperature: 350 degrees
Baking time: Thirty minutes (about)
Servings: Eight, or more

Place the vegetable shortening in a mixing bowl, stirring just to soften. Add the sifted flour, baking powder, soda, salt and sugar with the one cup of evaporated milk. Mix until the flour is dampened. Beat two minutes. Add the remaining milk, vanilla, eggs and melted chocolate. Beat for one minute longer. Pour into two layer pans (9 in.), lined with waxed paper. Bake in a moderate oven until a cake tester inserted in the center comes away clean. Remove to racks. Cool. Remove waxed paper. Put layers together and frost with icing.

Quick Bittersweet Frosting

Three-fourths cup instant cocoa mix
One tablespoon cornstarch
Three-fourths cup warm water
Two and one-third tablespoons butter
Yield: One cup (about)

In a saucepan blend the coca, cornstarch, warm water and butter; cook until slightly thick. Frost cake.

Poppy Seed Cup Cakes

One-half cup butter or margarine
One and one-fourth cups sugar
One teaspoon vanilla
Two cups sifted flour
Two teaspoons baking powder
One-eighth teaspoon salt
One-half cup poppy seed
One cup milk
Four egg whites
One-fourth cup sugar
Oven temperature: 375 degrees
Bake: Twenty minutes
Yield: Two and one-half dozen

In a bowl cream the butter or margarine. Gradually add the sugar. Beat until fluffy. Add the vanilla. Sift together into a bowl the flour, baking powder and salt. Stir in the poppy seed. Add the dry ingredients to the creamed mixture alternately with the milk. In a bowl beat the egg whites until they hold soft peaks; gradually beat in the sugar until a smooth meringue results. Fold this into the cake batter carefully. Spoon into well greased and lightly floured cup cake tins. Bake in a moderately hot oven until the cakes are browned and leave the sides of the pan. Remove pan from oven, let stand for five minutes. Remove cakes from pan to rack to cool. Frost with simple confectioners' frosting. Store in tightly covered tin.

Banana Orange Cup Cakes

Three tablespoons shortening
One-third cup sugar
One egg
One-fourth teaspoon orange extract
Three-fourths cup sifted flour
One-half teaspoon baking soda
One-fourth teaspoon salt
One-third cup mashed ripe banana
Two tablespoons vinegar
Three tablespoons confectioners' sugar
One-half teaspoon grated orange rind
Oven temperature: 375 degrees
Bake: Fifteen minutes or more
Yield: Twelve small cup cakes

In a bowl cream the shortening, gradually blend in the sugar. Beat in the egg and orange extract. Sift together the flour, baking soda and salt. Stir the mashed banana and vinegar together. Add the flour alternately with the banana to the creamed mixture beginning and ending with the flour. Beat until smooth. Stir the confectioners' sugar and grated orange rind together until thoroughly blended. Spoon the cake batter into greased cup cake pans; sprinkle the confectioners' sugar over top. Bake in a moderately hot oven for fifteen minutes or more, until cakes are nicely browned and start to leave the sides of the pans. Remove to rack to cool thoroughly before serving.

Blueberry Cakes

One-third cup shortening
One cup sugar
One and one-third cups sifted flour
One and one-half teaspoons baking powder
One-fourth teaspoon salt
One-half cup milk
One teaspoon vanilla
Three egg whites, stiffly beaten
One cup fresh blueberries
Oven temperature: 375 degrees
Bake: Twenty minutes
Yield: Twelve

In a bowl cream the shortening thoroughly, gradually add the sugar. Sift together the flour, baking powder and salt and add alternately to the creamed mixture with the milk. Add the vanilla. Fold in the stiffly beaten egg whites. Spoon into greased cup cake pans filling about half. Drop a spoonful of blueberries into each pan and top with about a teaspoon of batter. Bake in a moderately hot oven until golden brown. Remove to rack to cool. Dust with powdered sugar. Note: This recipe will make 18 to 24 dainty tea cakes (1½ in.).

Creamy Butter Frosting

One-fourth cup butter
Two cups sifted confectioners' sugar
One teaspoon vanilla
One-sixteenth teaspoon salt
Two tablespoons milk, or more
Yield: Frosting for two to three dozen cup cakes

In a bowl cream the butter until light and fluffy. Gradually blend in the confectioners' sugar with the vanilla, salt and as much milk as necessary for a smooth frosting. Spread in a swirl over the cooled cup cakes.

Gingerbread Men

Two-thirds cup shortening
One-half cup sugar
One egg
Three-fourths cup molasses
Three cups sifted flour
One and one-half teaspoons salt
One teaspoon soda
One-half teaspoon baking powder
Two teaspoons ginger
One teaspoon cinnamon
One-half teaspoon nutmeg
Chill: Two hours, about
Raisins
Oven temperature: 375 degrees
Bake: Ten minutes, about
Yield: Eighteen (3½ x 5 in.)

In a bowl cream the shortening with the sugar. Beat in the egg and molasses. Sift together the flour, salt, soda, baking powder, ginger, cinnamon and nutmeg. Add to the molasses mixture and blend thoroughly together. Chill the dough for easier handling. Turn out half the dough

at a time on a floured board and roll out to one-fourth inch thickness. Cut out the gingerbread men with a floured cutter and transfer to an ungreased baking sheet. Decorate with pieces of raisin and bake in a moderately hot oven for about ten minutes. Remove to racks to cool. Pipe on ornamental frosting for further decorating if desired.

Shiny Topped Brownies

Two squares (ounces) unsweetened chocolate
One-third cup shortening
Heat: Until melted
One cup brown sugar
One teaspoon vanilla
Two tablespoons milk
Two eggs, beaten
Two-thirds cup sifted flour
One-eighth teaspoon soda
One-half teaspoon salt
One teaspoon allspice
One-half cup chopped walnuts
One-fourth cup seedless raisins
Oven temperature: 350 degrees
Baking time: Thirty-five minutes
Yield: One pan (9 in.)

In a double boiler over hot water, melt the unsweetened chocolate with the shortening. Remove from heat and stir in the brown sugar and vanilla, then the milk and the beaten eggs. Sift together the flour, soda, salt and allspice; blend into the chocolate mixture. Add the chopped walnuts and raisins and mix well. Spread in a greased pan (9 x 9 x 2 in.) and bake in a moderate oven until cake springs back at the touch of a finger and leaves the sides of the pan. Cool in the pan. Cut into squares or bars.

Miracle Brownies

Three-fourths cup sifted flour
One cup sugar
One-half cup cocoa
One-half teaspoon baking powder
Three-fourths teaspoon salt
Three-fourths cup shortening
Two eggs
One teaspoon vanilla
One cup nuts, coarsely cut
Oven temperature: 350 degrees
Baking time: Forty minutes
Yield: One pan (9 in.)

Sift together into the mixing bowl the flour, sugar, cocoa, baking powder and salt. Add the shortening, eggs and vanilla and beat until well blended. Add the nuts, reserving two tablespoons. Mix well. Pour into a greased square baking pan (9 x 9 x 2 in.). Sprinkle with reserved nuts and bake in a moderate oven until a cake tester inserted in the center comes away clean. Remove pan to rack to cool. Cut brownies into squares or bars.

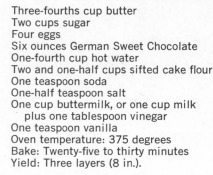

German Sweet Chocolate Cake

Three-fourths cup butter
Two cups sugar
Four eggs
Six ounces German Sweet Chocolate
One-fourth cup hot water
Two and one-half cups sifted cake flour
One teaspoon soda
One-half teaspoon salt
One cup buttermilk, or one cup milk
   plus one tablespoon vinegar
One teaspoon vanilla
Oven temperature: 375 degrees
Bake: Twenty-five to thirty minutes
Yield: Three layers (8 in.).

In a bowl cream the butter until soft. Gradually add the sugar beating until well blended. Add the eggs one at a time beating well after each addition. Melt the chocolate with the hot water over low heat; add. Gradually add the mixed and sifted cake flour, soda and salt alternately with the combined buttermilk and vanilla. Pour into three greased and floured pans (8 in.). Bake in a moderately hot oven until a cake tester inserted in the center comes away clean. Remove from pans onto racks. Spread between and on top with whipped cream frosting. Garnish with chocolate curls.

Note: The cake may be baked in a greased and floured rectangular baking pan (9 x 11 x 2 in.) at 350 degrees for 40 to 50 minutes.

Whipped Cream Frosting

Two cups heavy cream
One-fourth cup sugar
Three tablespoons cocoa
One teaspoon vanilla
Yield: Three cups

In a bowl mix the heavy cream, sugar, cocoa and vanilla. Place in a refrigerator for one hour. Beat until thick. Spread between and on top of cake.

Midnight Cake

One-half cup shortening
One and one-fourth cups sugar
Two eggs, beaten
One-half cup cocoa
One cup hot water
One and one-half cups sifted flour
One teaspoon baking powder
One teaspoon soda
One-half teaspoon salt
One teaspoon vanilla
Oven temperature: 350 degrees
Bake: Fifty-five minutes
Yield: One cake (8 x 8 in.)

In a bowl cream the shortening, gradually add the sugar and cream until fluffy. Blend in the beaten eggs. Place the cocoa in a small bowl, add the hot water gradually, mixing until smooth. Sift together the flour, baking powder, soda and salt. Add the dry ingredients alternately with the cocoa to the creamed mixture. Add vanilla. Pour into a greased and floured square pan (8 x 8 x 2 in.). Bake in a moderate oven until a cake tester inserted in the center comes away clean. Frost or not as preferred.

Rich Chocolate Roll

Four eggs
Three-fourths cup sugar
One package (6 oz.) semi-sweet chocolate
   bits
One square (1oz.) unsweetened chocolate
One-fourth cup cold water
One teaspoon vanilla
One-fourth cup cocoa
Oven temperature: 350 degrees
Baking time: Twenty minutes
One cup heavy cream, whipped
One-fourth cup sugar
Serves: Eight, or more

In a bowl beat the eggs and sugar until thick and lemon-colored (about 10 minutes with electric beater). In a saucepan melt the chocolate bits, unsweetened chocolate and cold water, stirring until smooth. Add vanilla. Blend the chocolate mixture into the egg mixture. Line the bottom of a jelly roll pan (11 x 7 in.) with heavily coated, greased and floured brown paper. Pour the chocolate mixture into pan. Bake in a moderate oven 20 minutes. Remove to rack. Cover top with a cloth which has been wrung out in cold water. Allow to stand 30 minutes. Remove cloth carefully. Loosen cake from sides of pan. Dust the top heavily with cocoa. Place a piece of waxed paper on top. Turn upside down. Carefully remove brown paper. In a bowl beat the cream and sugar until thick. Spread over cake. Roll up like a jelly roll by lifting the waxed paper. Garnish with whipped cream. Slice and serve.

Rich Chocolate Cake

One-half cup butter or margarine
One box (1 lb.) dark brown sugar
Two eggs, unbeaten
Two squares (2 oz.) chocolate, melted
One-half cup buttermilk or sour milk
One teaspoon vanilla
Two and one-half cups sifted cake flour
One-half teaspoon salt
Two teaspoons soda
One cup boiling water
Oven temperature: 375 degrees
Baking time: Twenty-five minutes (about)
Serves: Eight, or more

Work the butter in a bowl until soft. Gradually add the sugar, creaming until light and fluffy. Add the eggs one at a time, beating well after each addition. Stir in the melted chocolate, buttermilk and vanilla. Gradually add the sifted flour and salt. Add the soda to the boiling water. Stir into the batter. Pour the very thin batter into three greased and lightly floured pans (8 in.). Bake in a moderately hot oven until a cake tester inserted in the center comes away clean. Invert upon racks; remove from pans. Cool. Put layers together with frosting.

Seven Minute Coffee Icing

One and one-half cups sugar
Five tablespoons strong brewed coffee
Two teaspoons light corn syrup
Two egg whites, unbeaten
One teaspoon vanilla
Cooking time: Seven minutes
Yield: Icing for three layer cake

Mix the first four ingredients in the top of a double boiler. Cook over boiling water; beat with a rotary beater for seven minutes. Remove from the heat. Add the vanilla. Spread between layers and over side and top of cake.

Devil's Food Cake

Two-thirds cup butter or margarine
One and three-fourths cups sugar
Four eggs
One-half cup cocoa
One-half cup warm water
Two and one-half cups sifted cake flour
One teaspoon soda
One-half teaspoon salt
Three-fourths cup sour milk
One teaspoon vanilla
One package (6 oz.) semi-sweet chocolate bits
Six tablespoons hot coffee
One can (3½ oz.) flaked coconut
Oven temperature: 350 degrees
Bake: Forty-five minutes
Yield: Two layers (8 in. each)

In a bowl cream the butter until soft. Gradually add the sugar beating until light and fluffy. Add the eggs one at a time, beating well after each addition. Add the cocoa to the warm water stirring until smooth. Add to the creamed mixture. Add the sifted flour, soda and salt alternately with the combined sour milk and vanilla. Pour into greased and floured square pans (8 in.). In a saucepan heat chocolate bits, coffee and coconut until bits are melted. Dot top of cake with mixture. Bake in a moderate oven until a cake tester inserted in the center comes away clean. Remove to racks. Frost between layers, top and sides of cake with tinted favorite frosting. Garnish with chocolate curls.

Fruit Cake

One-half pound citron
One-half pound candied lemon peel
One-half pound candied orange peel
One-fourth pound candied pineapple slices
One-fourth pound candied cherries
One-fourth pound dried figs
One pkg. (7½ oz.) chopped dates
　　(one and one-third cups)
Two cups seedless raisins
One cup currants
One cup pecan halves
Four cups sifted flour
Two tablespoons baking powder
One-half teaspoon salt
One cup butter
Two cups sugar
Six eggs
Two teaspoons vanilla
One-half cup orange juice
Oven temperature: 300 degrees
Bake: Two hours
Yield: Six pounds

Cut the citron, lemon and orange peel into thin slices. Cut the pineapple slices into narrow wedges, the cherries in halves. Combine in a very large bowl or deep kettle with the chopped dried figs, chopped dates, raisins, currants and pecan halves. Sift the flour, baking powder and salt together and add to the fruit mixture. Toss thoroughly together with a pair of wooden spoons to mix well. In a bowl cream the butter and gradually beat in the sugar. Add the eggs one at a time, beating in thoroughly. Add the vanilla. Combine creamed mixture with the floured fruit and nuts and the orange juice and mix thoroughly together. Divide the batter between two well-greased loaf pans (9 x 5 x 3 in.) and bake in a slow oven for two hours or until the cake starts to leave the sides of the pan and springs back when touched with a finger. Remove from oven and cool in pans on rack. Turn out and wrap well when cool in waxed paper or foil. If you prefer bake batter in a large tube pan for about three hours. Fruit cakes keep well stored in the refrigerator.

A FAVORITE RECIPE
Fruit Cake

One-half pound butter or shortening,
　　creamed
One-half pound brown sugar
Six eggs, beaten well
Five cups candied fruit peels, cherries,
　　dates, raisins cut into small pieces
Two cups broken nut meats, (walnuts or
　　almonds)
Two tablespoons honey
One-fourth teaspoon cloves
One teaspoon nutmeg
One teaspoon cinnamon
Two and one-half cups flour, sifted with
One-fourth teaspoon baking powder
Grated rind and juice ½ lemon
Grated rind and juice ½ orange
One-half cup rum or brandy
Oven temperature: 275 degrees
Baking time: Two and one-half hours
Yield: One tube cake (12 in.)

Heat the oven. In a large bowl, cream the butter; add sugar and beaten eggs, a little at a time, beating well after each addition. Have the fruits prepared, cutting the cherries into fourths. Stir in the fruits, nuts, honey and spices, blending well. Sift the flour and baking powder, stirring into the mixture. Add the rind and juice of lemon and orange. Stir in the rum. Turn into a well greased tube pan (12 in.). Bake in a slow oven. Cool and wrap in waxed and foil paper. Store in a tight container until needed.

MRS. MIRIAM MAZZANO, *Brooklyn, N.Y.*

Fruit Cake

Two cups butter or margarine
Three cups sugar
Ten eggs (at room temperature)
One tablespoon vanilla
Five and one-half cups sifted flour
Two and one-half teaspoons salt
One teaspoon baking powder
One-half teaspoon soda
Four teaspoons cinnamon
Two teaspoons nutmeg
One teaspoon mace
One teaspoon cloves
One pound citron, finely sliced
One-half pound candied cherries, halved
One-half pound candied pineapple, sliced
One-fourth pound candied lemon peel,
　　finely sliced
One-fourth pound candied orange peel,
　　finely sliced
One pound shelled walnuts or pecans
One pound seedless raisins
One pound currants
One cup thick currant jelly
One-fourth cup brandy or rum (optional)
Oven temperature: 250 degrees
Bake: Three and one-half hours, about
Yield: Ten pounds, approx.

In a bowl cream the butter or margarine until light. Gradually beat in the sugar. Add the eggs, one at a time, beating thoroughly. (Note: eggs cold from the refrigerator can cause a separation of the batter.) Add the vanilla. Sift together the flour, salt, baking powder, soda, cinnamon, nutmeg, mace and cloves. Blend half of the dry ingredients into the creamed mixture, mixing thoroughly. In a large bowl combine the finely sliced citron, cherries, candied pineapple, lemon peel, orange peel, walnuts, raisins and currants. Mix in the currant jelly and brandy or rum, if used. Stir the second half of the dry ingredients into the fruit mixture. Combine the batter with the floured fruit and mix thoroughly, transferring to a larger kettle if necessary or dividing between two large bowls. When thoroughly mixed spoon batter into well-greased and floured loaf pans filling three-fourths and smoothing the top with the back of a spoon. Bake in a very slow oven until cake springs back from the touch of a finger, starts to leave the edge of the pan and is nicely browned on top. Remove from oven and cool in the pans for thirty minutes. Run spatula around edge of cakes, shake loose and turn out

on racks to finish cooling. When thoroughly cooled wrap in waxed paper, foil or saran wrap to store. From this recipe we made two loaves (10 x 4 x 3 in.) and three loaves (7 x 4 x 2½ in.). The batter could be baked in two tube pans (9 in.) for about the same length of time.

Buttermilk Fruit Cake

One orange
One and one-half cups seedless raisins
One cup chopped pecans
One-half cup butter
One cup brown sugar
One egg
Two cups sifted flour
One teaspoon baking soda
One-half teaspoon baking powder
One-half teaspoon salt
One cup buttermilk
One teaspoon vanilla
Oven temperature: 350 degrees
Bake: Fifty to sixty minutes
Yield: One cake (9 x 9 in.)

Cut up the orange, removing seeds. Put all of orange, including peel through a grinder or chop very fine. Combine in a bowl with the raisins and chopped pecans. In a bowl cream the butter, gradually beat in the sugar until light and fluffy. Beat in the egg. Sift together the flour, baking soda, baking powder and salt. Add dry ingredients to the creamed mixture alternately with the buttermilk to which the vanilla has been added. Add the fruit mixture and mix well. Pour into a greased square pan (9 x 9 x 2 in.) and bake in a moderate oven for fifty to sixty minutes. Remove from oven and cool cake in pan on rack. When thoroughly cooled slice and serve or wrap well in foil to store.

Golden Walnut Cake

One-third cup butter or margarine
One cup sugar
Two eggs
Two cups sifted flour
Two teaspoons baking powder
One teaspoon salt
One-third cup orange juice
One-third cup evaporated milk
Grated rind of one orange
One cup chopped walnuts
Oven temperature: 350 degrees
Bake: Fifty minutes, about
Yield: One ring cake (9 in.)

In a bowl cream the butter or margarine. Blend in the sugar. Beat in the eggs. Sift together the flour, baking powder and salt. Add to the creamed mixture alternately with the orange juice and evaporated milk. Beat smooth. Stir in the grated orange rind and chopped walnuts. Pour into a greased and floured tube or ring pan (9 in.). Bake in a moderate oven for 50 minutes or until cake springs back when touched with a finger and starts to leave the sides of the pan. Remove from oven and let cool for 10 minutes in the pan. Turn out on rack to cool completely. Serve plain, top dusted with confectioners' sugar or frosted.

Refrigerator Fruit Cake

Sixteen marshmallows
One-half cup evaporated milk
One-fourth cup orange juice
Four cups graham cracker crumbs (one
    pound)
One teaspoon cinnamon
One and one-half cups diced mixed
    candied fruit
One cup chopped walnuts
One cup seedless raisins, rinsed
Chill: Two days
Yield: Two and one-half pound loaf

Cut the marshmallows into small pieces and place in a bowl. Pour on the evaporated milk and orange juice and let stand. Roll the graham crackers into fine crumbs and combine in a bowl with the cinnamon, diced candied fruit, chopped walnuts and well drained raisins. Add the marshmallow mixture and mix thoroughly together. Line a loaf pan (9 x 4 x 3 in.) with waxed paper and chill for at least two days before cutting.

California Fruit Cake

One cup chopped walnuts
One cup chopped toasted almonds
Three cups seedless raisins
One cup chopped citron
One cup whole candied cherries
One cup cooked, chopped prune pulp
One cup cooked dried apricots, chopped
Two tablespoons grated orange rind
One cup butter or margarine
One and one-half cups brown sugar
Five eggs
Two and one-half cups sifted flour
One teaspoon salt
One teaspoon baking powder
One teaspoon allspice
Two teaspoons cinnamon
Oven temperature: 250 degrees
Baking time: Three to three and one-half
    hours
Yield: Two loaves (9 x 5 x 3 in.)

In a very large bowl combine the chopped walnuts, chopped toasted almonds, seedless raisins, chopped citron, whole candied cherries, chopped prune and apricot pulp and grated orange rind. In a second bowl cream the butter or margarine; gradually blend in the brown sugar and then the eggs, adding one at a time. Sift together the flour, salt, baking powder, allspice and cinnamon. Gradually beat into the creamed mixture. Pour well mixed batter over the fruits and nuts and mix thoroughly. Line two greased loaf pans (9 x 5 x 3 in.) with greased waxed paper. Pour in the cake mixture. Bake in a very slow oven for three hours or more until a cake tester inserted in the cake comes away clean. Remove pans from oven to racks to cool. When thoroughly cooled remove from pans, strip off waxed paper and wrap in aluminum foil to store for ripening in the refrigerator. Moisten from time to time with brandy if you wish.

Cranberry Nut Cake

One-half cup shortening
One cup brown sugar
Two eggs
Two and one-half cups sifted flour
One teaspoon baking soda
One teaspoon baking powder
One teaspoon salt
One-fourth teaspoon nutmeg
One-fourth teaspoon cinnamon
One-half cup milk
One can (one and one-half lbs.) whole
    cranberry sauce
One tablespoon lemon juice
One cup chopped nuts
Oven temperature: 350 degrees
Baking time: One hour, or more
Servings: Twelve

In a bowl cream the shortening, gradually blend in the brown sugar and beat in the eggs. Sift together the flour, soda, baking powder, salt, nutmeg and cinnamon. Add to the creamed mixture alternately with the milk. Beat until smooth. Add the cranberry sauce, lemon juice and chopped nuts and blend thoroughly. Pour into a greased tube pan (10 in.) and bake in a moderate oven for one hour or more until the cake leaves the sides of the pan and springs back at the touch of a finger. Cool for 10 minutes in the pan, then remove to rack to finish cooling. Frost with a simple confectioners' frosting made by stirring two tablespoons or more of lemon juice into one cup of confectioners' sugar. This is enough to frost the top with trickles of frosting running down and decorating the sides.

Brazil Nut Loaf

Three cups shelled Brazil nuts (one pound)
Two packages (6½ oz. each) pitted dates
One cup maraschino cherries, drained
Three-fourths cup sifted flour
Three-fourths cup sugar
One-half teaspoon baking powder
One-half teaspoon salt
Three eggs
One teaspoon vanilla
Oven temperature: 300 degrees
Bake: Two hours, about
Yield: One loaf (9 x 5 in.), or two loaves
    7½ x 3¾ in.)

Combine in a large bowl the shelled Brazil nuts, pitted dates and drained maraschino cherries. Sift together the flour, sugar, baking powder and salt. Add to the fruit and dredge thoroughly. In a second bowl beat the eggs well with the vanilla. Add to the flour and fruit mixture and blend in thoroughly. Spread evenly and well into the corners of a greased and waxed paper lined loaf pan (9 x 5 x 3 in.) or two prepared pans (7½ x 3¾ x 2 in.). Bake in a slow oven for two hours or more, until a cake tester inserted in the loaf comes away clean. Remove from oven and cool thoroughly in pan. When cool, strip off waxed paper and wrap in foil to store. Stores well in refrigerator.

Citron Nut Loaf

Two-thirds cup butter or margarine
One cup sugar
Three eggs
Two cups sifted flour
Two teaspoons baking powder
One-fourth teaspoon salt
One-half cup milk
One teaspoon vanilla
One-third cup finely sliced citron
One cup chopped nuts
Oven temperature: 350 degrees
Bake: One hour, or more
Yield: One loaf (9 x 5 x 2½ in.)

In a bowl cream the butter or margarine, gradually beat in the sugar. Beat in the eggs one at a time. Sift together the flour, baking powder and salt and add to the creamed mixture alternately with the milk. Add the vanilla, citron and chopped nuts and mix thoroughly. Transfer to a greased and lightly floured loaf pan (9 x 5 x 2½ in.). Bake in a moderate oven for one hour or until the loaf is well browned and shrinks slightly away from the edge of the pan. Cool on a rack and wrap well in waxed paper or foil to store. If possible let stand one day to develop full flavor before slicing.

Fruit Nut Specials

One-third cup shortening
One-third cup brown sugar
Three-fourths cup sifted flour
Two teaspoons lemon juice
Oven temperature: 350 degrees
Baking time: Eight minutes
Two eggs
One cup brown sugar
One-half teaspoon vanilla
Two tablespoons flour
One teaspoon baking powder
One-half teaspoon salt
One-half cup shredded coconut
One-half cup chopped walnuts
One-half cup chopped dates
Baking time: Twenty-five minutes
Servings: Nine

In a bowl, cream the shortening and blend in the third cup of brown sugar, then the flour and lemon juice. Mix well. Pack in the bottom of a baking pan (8 x 8 x 2 in.). Bake in a moderate oven for eight minutes. In a bowl, beat the eggs until light and fluffy. Beat in the cup of brown sugar, then the vanilla, flour, baking powder and salt. Mix well. Stir in the coconut, walnuts and dates. Pour over the baked mixture and return to the moderate oven for twenty-five minutes. Cut in squares and serve warm or cold with whipped cream or ice cream if desired.

Dobostorte

Six egg yolks
One-half cup sugar
Six egg whites
One-third cup sugar
One cup sifted cake flour
Oven temperature: 350 degrees
Bake: Fifteen minutes (about)

Chocolate Butter Cream

One package (6 oz.) semi-sweet chocolate
　bits
Three tablespoons brewed coffee
Cook: Three minutes
Four egg yolks
One-half cup sugar
Cook: Five minutes
One cup sweet butter, creamed
One and one-half cups slivered
　almonds, or chopped nuts

Topping

Three-fourths cup sugar, caramelized
One tablespoon butter
Chill: Twelve hours
Serves: Twelve, or more

In a bowl beat the egg yolks until thick and lemon-colored. Gradually add the sugar, beating until thick and fluffy. In another bowl beat the egg whites and one-third cup sugar until stiff and satiny. Fold into the egg yolk mixture. Gradually fold in the flour. Grease and flour the bottoms of cake pans (9 in.). Spread batter as thinly as possible. Bake in a moderate oven for 15 minutes. Remove cake layers onto racks. Repeat procedure until all the cake batter is used (makes 7 or 8 layers). Place layers on paper toweling. Let cool.

In the top of a double boiler melt the chocolate with the coffee over boiling water until the mixture is smooth. Beat the egg yolks until light and lemon-col-

ored. Gradually beat in the sugar until mixture is thick. Quickly stir into the melted chocolate. Cook over hot water until the mixture is thick and smooth. Remove from the heat. Add the creamed butter bit by bit, beating rapidly after each addition. Chill until the cream reaches a spreading consistency, stirring occasionally. Spread the chocolate cream between the layers and sides of the cake. Place nuts on side of cake.

In a heavy pan melt the three-fourths cup sugar with one tablespoon of butter. Stir over medium heat until golden. Remove from heat. With a spatula quickly spread the carmelized sugar over the top. Cut the wedge-shaped markings through the carmelized coating. When cold, place in the refrigerator. Let stand for at least 12 hours before serving. Will stay fresh for a week in the refrigerator. You may also store in freezer for future use.

Walnut Torte

Six eggs, separated
One cup sugar
One teaspoon vanilla extract
Two cups ground walnuts
One tablespoon fine dry bread crumbs
One-half teaspoon salt
One-eighth teaspoon nutmeg
Oven temperature: 350 degrees
Baking time: Fifty minutes
Serves: Eight, or more

In a bowl beat the egg yolks with one-half cup of the sugar until thick and fluffy (about 10 minutes with an electric beater). Fold in the combined vanilla extract, ground walnuts, fine dry bread crumbs, salt and nutmeg. In another bowl beat the egg whites and the remaining half cup of sugar until satiny. Fold the egg yolk mixture into the egg white mixture. Pour into a buttered and crumb lined spring form pan (8 in.). Bake in a moderately slow oven for 50 minutes. Remove to a rack (it will shrink). When cool, remove rim from pan. Cut the torte crosswise into three layers. Fill with vanilla or chocolate butter cream frosting or fill with sweetened whipped heavy cream. Garnish with whole walnuts. Serve in wedges.

Eight Layer Blueberry Torte

Four eggs
One cup sugar
One-half cup water
One teaspoon vanilla
One cup sifted flour
Two teaspoons baking powder
One-eighth teaspoon salt
One box (2 cups) blueberries
Oven temperature: 375 degrees
Baking time: Twelve minutes
One cup heavy cream, whipped
One-fourth cup confectioners' sugar
One tablespoon Grand Marnier (orange
　liqueur)
Refrigerate: Overnight
Serves: Eight

In a bowl beat the eggs until thick and lemon-colored, about 10 minutes. Gradually add the sugar, beating thoroughly after each addition. Add the combined water and vanilla. Add the sifted flour, baking powder and salt. Line eight-inch cake pan with waxed paper. Grease and flour the waxed paper. Spread three-fourths cup of batter into each lined pan; sprinkle one-fourth cup blueberries over the batter in each pan. Bake in a moderately hot oven until edge is slightly brown. Remove to racks. Remove paper immediately. Repeat procedure until all batter is used. There should be eight layers. In a bowl beat the cream and sugar until stiff. Add the Grand Marnier. Spread between layers. Refrigerate. Serve in wedges.

Eight-Layer Torte
(Schicht Torte)

One cup butter or margarine
One cup sugar
Four eggs, separated
Two cups sifted flour
One-half pint dairy sour cream
One cup finely ground almonds
One teaspoon vanilla extract
Marmalade, apricot jam, mint, apple and
　currant jelly
Oven temperature: 350 degrees
Baking time: Twelve minutes (about)
Standing time: Overnight
Two squares (1 oz. each) unsweetened
　chocolate, melted
One tablespoon butter
One-half cup milk
Cooking time: Three minutes
Two cups confectioners' sugar (about)
One-half teaspoon vanilla extract
Refrigerate: Until ready to serve
Yield: One eight-layer torte

In a bowl cream the butter until light and fluffy. Add the sugar gradually, beating until well blended. Beat in the egg yolks. Mix in the flour. Beat the egg whites until stiff but not dry; fold into the mixture. With a spatula spread a thin layer of batter over the bottom of two inverted greased and floured cake pans (9 in.). Bake in moderate oven until edge is a light brown. Remove from cake pan carefully to a rack. Repeat until 8 layers are baked. Spread three tablespoons of jelly over bottom layer. In a bowl combine the sour cream, almonds

and vanilla. Top jellied layer with two tablespoons of the almond mixture. Now, place the next baked layer on top and continue spreading alternate colored jams and almond mixture between layers. Then place a piece of foil over the cake. Let stand overnight with a weight on top (heavy telephone directory). Using a sharp knife trim the edges of the cake. Cut a round small cake (3 in. in diam.) from the center. Remove carefully, insert an inverted glass custard cup in the hole. Place the piece of cake on top of the glass. For the frosting: Put the chocolate, butter and milk in a saucepan. Cook until the chocolate melts. Let stand until lukewarm. Beat in sugar until mixture is thick enough to spread. Add vanilla extract. Frost the entire cake. Garnish with frosted almonds. Refrigerate. Remove to cake platter. Serve in bars (1 in.).

Baba au Rum

One-half cup milk
One envelope active dry yeast
Two egg yolks
One egg
One-third cup sugar
One-fourth cup butter, melted
One teaspoon grated orange rind
Two cups sifted flour
First rising time: Two to three hours
Second rising time: One hour, about
Oven temperature: 350 degrees
Baking time: Thirty-five minutes, about
Cool: Thoroughly
One-third cup sugar
Two-thirds cup orange juice
One teaspoon lemon juice
Simmering time: Fifteen minutes
One-fourth cup rum, or more
Standing time: One hour, or more
Servings: Eight

Scald the milk in a small saucepan, cool to lukewarm. Sprinkle the active dry yeast over the lukewarm milk. In a bowl beat the egg yolks and whole egg well with a rotary beater. Blend in the sugar, melted butter and orange rind. Add the softened yeast and the sifted flour; mix well. Transfer the batter to a clean greased bowl and cover with a clean cloth. Set in a warm spot until the dough has doubled in bulk. This may take several hours. Transfer to a greased mold or tube pan (10 in.) and allow to rise once more. Bake in a moderate oven until well browned. Remove to rack to cool thoroughly. In a saucepan combine the sugar with the orange juice and lemon juice. Bring to a boil, lower heat and simmer gently for 15 minutes. Remove from heat and add rum. Pour over the cooled cake slowly and carefully, permitting the cake to absorb as much as possible. Or, pour the liquid into a shallow pan and set the cake on top, turning on all sides. Serve cake with whipped cream or ice cream, if desired.

Cherry Loaf Cake

Two-thirds cup shortening
One cup sugar
Two eggs
One teaspoon vanilla
One-half teaspoon almond extract
One and three-fourths cup sifted flour
Three-fourths teaspoon baking soda
One teaspoon salt
One-half cup chopped, well-drained
   maraschino cherries
One-fourth cup vinegar
One-third cup milk
Oven temperature: 350 degrees
Bake: Sixty minutes, about
Yield: One loaf (9 in.)

In a bowl cream the shortening, gradually blend in the sugar. Beat in the eggs, vanilla and almond extract. Sift together the flour, baking soda and salt. Add the well-drained and chopped cherries to these dry ingredients and add combination alternately with the vinegar, then with the milk to the cream mixture. Pour the thoroughly mixed batter into a greased and floured loaf pan (9 x 5 in.). Bake in a moderate oven until the cake springs back when pressed with a finger and leaves the sides of the pan. Cool in the pan.

Pear Upside-Down Cake

Two tablespoons butter or margarine
One-half cup brown sugar
Two teaspoons grated lemon rind
Two teaspoons grated orange rind
One-half teaspoon ginger
Two ripe pears
Two cups biscuit mix
One-fourth cup sugar
One egg
Two-thirds cup milk
Oven temperature: 400 degrees
Bake: Twenty-five minutes
Servings: Six to eight

Melt the butter or margarine in the bottom of a square baking pan (9 x 9 x 2 in.), spreading well over the surface. In a small bowl stir together the brown sugar, lemon rind, orange rind and ginger. Sprinkle half the mixture over the butter in the pan, reserve remaining mixture. Peel and core the two pears. In a bowl stir the biscuit mix and fourth cup of sugar together. In a small bowl beat the egg, add the milk. Stir combination into the dry ingredients until smooth. Spoon over the fruit in baking pan. Scatter remaining brown sugar mixture over batter. Bake in a quick oven for twenty five minutes. Turn out on serving plate at once. Cut into squares to serve.

Easy Blueberry Kuchen

One egg
One-half cup sugar
One-half teaspoon vanilla
One-third cup milk
One-fourth cup melted butter or margarine
One and one-half cups sifted flour
Two teaspoons baking powder
One-fourth teaspoon salt
Two cups fresh blueberries
One-half cup confectioners' sugar
Two tablespoons lemon juice
Oven temperature: 350 degrees
Bake: Forty-five minutes
Serves: Nine

In a bowl beat the egg with a rotary beater, beat in the sugar, vanilla, milk and melted butter or margarine. Sift together the flour, baking powder and salt and stir into the egg mixture just enough to blend. Spread in a greased pan (9 x 9 x 2 in.) and scatter the washed berries evenly over the top, pressing gently into the batter. Sprinkle with confectioners' sugar and lemon juice. Bake in a moderate oven until a cake tester, tried at the center comes away clean. Remove from oven; let stand for 10 minutes. Cut into squares and serve from pan with a broad spatula while still warm. Good topped with spoonful of whipped or ice cream.

Lemon Glazed Upside-down Cake

Two tablespoons melted butter
   or margarine
One cup sugar
Three tablespoons cornstarch
One-half teaspoon salt
One cup water
Heat: To boiling
One egg
Grated rind of one lemon
One-fourth cup lemon juice
Heat: To boiling
One-half cup shortening
One cup sugar
Two eggs
Two cups sifted flour
Three teaspoons baking powder
One teaspoon salt
Three-fourths cup milk
One teaspoon vanilla
Oven temperature: 375 degrees
Bake: Thirty-five minutes
Yield: One large cake (9 x 13 in.)

Place the melted butter or margarine in the bottom of a baking pan (9 x 13 x 2 in.) spread evenly. In a saucepan stir together the sugar, cornstarch and salt. Gradually blend in the water. Cook over low heat until mixture boils, stirring constantly. In a small bowl beat the egg, add the grated lemon rind and lemon juice. Add a small amount of the cooked mixture to the egg, return combination to the saucepan. Bring to a boil, stirring smooth. Pour over the butter in the baking pan. Prepare the cake by creaming the shortening in a bowl until fluffy. Beat in the sugar gradually, beat in the eggs one at a time. Sift together the flour, baking powder and salt and add to the creamed mixture alternately with the milk. Mix thoroughly. Add the vanilla. Pour batter over the lemon mixture in the baking pan and bake in a moderately hot oven for thirty-five minutes, or until cake leaves the edge of the pan slightly and springs back at the touch of a finger. Turn out immediately on a rack and serve cut in squares while slightly warm or when cooled to room temperature.

Honey Applesauce Cake

One-half cup shortening
One cup honey
Three cups sifted flour
One and one-half teaspoons soda
One-half teaspoon salt
One teaspoon cinnamon
One teaspoon nutmeg
One-half teaspoon cloves
One and one-half cups thick applesauce
One cup seedless raisins
Oven temperature: 350 degrees
Bake: Forty minutes, about
Yield: One large cake

In a bowl cream the shortening, gradually blend in the honey. Sift together the flour, soda, salt, cinnamon, nutmeg and cloves and add to the creamed mixture alternately with the applesauce. When well mixed add the raisins. Transfer to a greased and floured baking pan (9 x 15 x 2 in.) and bake in a moderate oven for forty minutes or until the cake springs back at the touch of a finger and leaves the edge of the pan. Cool thoroughly in the pan and cut into squares to serve. When cooled the top may be dusted with confectioners' sugar if you wish.

Apple Sauce Nut Cake

One cup shortening
One and one-half cups sugar
One-half cup brown sugar
One egg
Three cups sifted flour
Two teaspoons baking soda
One-half teaspoon salt
One teaspoon cinnamon
One teaspoon nutmeg
One-fourth teaspoon cocoa
Two teaspoons vanilla
Two cups apple sauce
One cup chopped nuts
Oven temperature: 325 degrees
Bake: One hour
Yield: Cake 9 x 13 in.

In a bowl cream the shortening until light, gradually beat in the sugars. Beat in the egg. Sift together the flour, baking soda, salt, cinnamon, nutmeg and cocoa. Stir the vanilla into the apple sauce. Add the sifted dry ingredients and apple sauce alternately to the creamed mixture, mixing thoroughly after each addition. Add the chopped nuts. Pour into a greased and floured rectangular pan (9 x 13 x 2 in.) and bake in a moderately slow oven for one hour or until cake springs back when touched with a finger and has begun to leave the sides of the pan. Cool in pan on a rack. Cut in squares to serve. Good with whipped cream topping or a favorite frosting.

Apple Bran Cake

One-half cup shortening
One cup sugar
One egg
One-half cup all bran cereal
One cup coarsely grated raw apple
One and one-half cups sifted flour
One teaspoon salt
Two teaspoons baking powder
One-fourth teaspoon soda
One-half teaspoon cinnamon
One-half teaspoon cloves
One-half cup cooled, brewed coffee
One teaspoon vanilla
Oven temperature: 375 degrees
Bake: Thirty minutes
One tablespoon butter or margarine
One-third cup fine sugar
One-half teaspoon cinnamon
Bake: Ten minutes
Serves: Eight

In a bowl cream the shortening, blend in the sugar gradually, beat in the egg. Stir in the all bran cereal and grated apple. Sift together the flour, salt, baking powder, soda, cinnamon and cloves. Add to the creamed mixture alternately with the coffee and vanilla. Spread in a greased pan (9 x 9 x 2 in.) and bake in a moderately hot oven for thirty minutes. Blend tablespoon of butter or margarine with the fine sugar and cinnamon and sprinkle over the cake. Continue baking for ten minutes more. Cool in pan. Cut into squares to serve.

Prune Coffee Cake

Fifteen large cooked prunes
Three tablespoons butter or margarine
One tablespoon grated orange rind
One-third cup brown sugar
Two eggs
One-half cup milk
One-third cup salad oil
One teaspoon vanilla
One and one-half cups sifted flour
Three-fourths cup sugar
One and three-fourths teaspoons baking powder
Three-fourths teaspoon salt
Oven temperature: 375 degrees
Bake: Forty-five minutes
Serves: Nine

Cut the prunes in half and remove the pits. Arrange halves cut side up in the bottom of a greased pan (9 x 9 x 2 in.). Melt the butter or margarine in a small saucepan; add the grated orange rind. Spoon evenly over the prunes. Sprinkle evenly with the brown sugar. In a bowl beat the eggs, add the milk, salad oil and vanilla. Sift together the flour, sugar, baking powder and salt. Add to the liquid ingredients and beat until smooth. Pour over the prunes in the baking pan. Bake in a moderately hot oven for 45 minutes. Remove from oven. Let stand on cake rack for about five minutes. Loosen edges and turn out on rack to finish cooling. Dust with confectioners' sugar if desired. Cut in squares to serve.

Dutch Apple Cake

One and one-half cups sifted flour
Three tablespoons sugar
Two teaspoons baking powder
One teaspoon salt
One-third cup shortening
One egg
One-half cup milk
Three medium-sized apples
Three tablespoons sugar
One-half teaspoon cinnamon
Two tablespoons butter or margarine
Oven temperature: 375 degrees
Bake: Forty-five minutes
Two tablespoons corn or maple syrup
Whipped cream (optional)
Serves: Six

Sift the flour, three tablespoons of sugar, baking powder and salt together into a bowl. Cut in the shortening using two knives or a pastry blender until the consistency of coarse meal. Beat the egg in a small bowl, add the milk and stir into the dry ingredients. Mix well and spread in a greased baking pan (8 x 8 x 2 in.). Wash, dry, core and peel the apples. Slice apples and press pieces into the dough in even rows. Stir in the remaining sugar and cinnamon together and sprinkle over the apples. Dot with butter or margarine. Bake in a moderately hot oven until well browned. Sprinkle syrup over top. Serve while still slightly warm with a whipped cream topping if desired.

Nut Crusted Apple Sauce Cake

One-third cup butter or margarine
Two tablespoons sugar
One-half cup chopped walnuts
Two cups sifted flour
One teaspoon baking powder
One teaspoon baking soda
One teaspoon cinnamon
One-half teaspoon salt
One-fourth teaspoon nutmeg
One-fourth teaspoon cloves
One-half cup shortening
One cup sugar
One egg
One cup thick apple sauce
One teaspoon grated lemon rind
Oven temperature: 350 degrees
Bake: Forty-five minutes
Yield: One cake (9 x 9 in.)

Melt the butter or margarine in baking pan (9 x 9 x 2 in.). Sprinkle with two tablespoons sugar and chopped nuts. Sift together the flour, baking powder, soda, cinnamon, salt, nutmeg and cloves. In a bowl cream the shortening and sugar together until light and fluffy. Beat in the egg. Add the sifted dry ingredients alternately with the apple sauce and grated lemon rind. Mix well. Turn batter into baking pan spreading evenly over nuts. Bake in a moderate oven for 55 minutes. Allow to cool in the pan for five minutes before turning out on a rack to cool.

Chocolate Upside-Down Cake

One-third cup butter or margarine
One cup light brown sugar
Pecan halves
One-half cup butter or margarine
One and one-half cups light brown sugar
Three eggs
Three squares (1 oz. each) unsweetened chocolate
One-half cup strong hot black coffee
Two cups sifted cake flour
One teaspoon soda
One teaspoon baking powder
One-half teaspoon salt
One-half cup buttermilk
One teaspoon vanilla
Oven temperature: 350 degrees
Bake: Thirty minutes, or more
Yield: One cake

In the bottom of a heavy skillet (10 in.) melt the butter. Stir in brown sugar (1 cup). Put pecan halves on the bottom. Set aside. In a bowl cream the half cup butter until soft. Gradually add the brown sugar, creaming until light and fluffy. Add the eggs one at a time, beating well after each addition. Melt the chocolate in the hot coffee, stirring until smooth; let cool slightly. Stir into the creamed mixture. Add the mixed and sifted flour, soda, baking powder and salt alternately with the combined buttermilk and vanilla, stirring until smooth. Spoon over the butterscotch mixture in pan. Bake in a moderate oven until a cake tester inserted in the center comes away clean. Remove to rack. Release sides with spatula. Turn upside-down. When cool, serve in wedges.

Lemon Layer Cake

Two-thirds cup butter or margarine
One cup sugar
Three eggs
Two cups sifted cake flour
One teaspoon soda
One-fourth teaspoon salt
One-half cup milk
Three tablespoons lemon juice
One tablespoon grated lemon rind
Oven temperature: 375 degrees
Bake: Twenty-five minutes
Yield: Two layers (8 in.)

In a bowl cream the butter until soft and creamy. Gradually add the sugar, beating until light and fluffy. Add the eggs one at a time, beating well after each addition. Add the mixed and sifted flour, baking powder, soda and salt alternately with the combined milk, lemon juice and rind. Pour into two greased and floured layer pans (8 in.). Bake in a moderately hot oven until a cake tester inserted in the center comes away clean. Remove layers onto racks. Put layers together with Strawberry Seven Minute Frosting.

Apple Butter Squares

One-half cup butter or margarine
One cup sugar
Three eggs
Two and one-half cups sifted flour
One and one-half teaspoons soda
One teaspoon cinnamon
One-half teaspoon cloves
One-half teaspoon nutmeg
One-half teaspoon salt
One cup buttermilk
One cup apple butter
Oven temperature: 350 degrees
Baking time: Fifty minutes (about)
Yield: One square cake (9 in.)

Frosting

One-half stick (2 oz.) cream cheese
One egg white
Three cups confectioners' sugar (about)
One-fourth teaspoon vanilla
Yield: Frosting for one square cake (9 in.)

In a bowl beat the butter until creamy. Add the sugar; beat until fluffy. Add the eggs one at a time beating well after each addition. Add the sifted dry ingredients alternately with the buttermilk. Fold in the apple butter, blending well. Pour into a greased pan (9 in.). Bake in a moderate oven until a cake tester inserted in the center comes away clean. Remove to a rack.

To Frost: In a bowl work the cheese with a fork until soft; add the remaining ingredients. Beat until smooth. Frost the top of the warm cake that has been placed on a cake plate. Use a fork to make the indentations in the frosting. Garnish as desired. Cut into squares.

Upside-Down Gingerbread
Topping

One-fourth cup butter or margarine
One-fourth cup brown sugar
One-fourth cup evaporated milk or heavy
  cream
Four slices canned pineapple, drained
Twelve canned apricot halves, drained
Maraschino cherries, drained

Gingerbread

Two cups sifted flour
One teaspoon soda
One-fourth teaspoon salt
One and one-half teaspoons ginger
One teaspoon cinnamon
One-fourth teaspoon nutmeg
One-half cup brown sugar, packed
Two eggs, slightly beaten
One-half cup molasses
One cup buttermilk or sour milk
One-half cup butter or margarine, melted
Oven temperature: 350 degrees
Bake: Fifty minutes
Serves: Nine

For the topping: Melt the butter in the bottom of a square pan (9 in.). Blend in the brown sugar and milk. Arrange the pineapple slices, apricot halves and cherries in the bottom of pan. In a bowl sift the dry ingredients; mix in the combined eggs, molasses, buttermilk and butter. Pour over the arranged fruit. Bake in a moderate oven for 50 minutes. Turn upside-down on rack. Serve slightly warm in squares.

Pineapple Upside Down Cake

Three tablespoons margarine
One cup coconut
One-half cup light brown sugar
One-third cup heavy cream
One-fourth teaspoon ginger
One can (No. 2) pineapple spears, drained
Nine maraschino cherries
Ten blanched, peeled almonds
Three eggs, well beaten
One and one-half cups sugar
Three-fourths cup milk
One and one-half tablespoons butter
One and one-half cups sifted flour
One and one-half teaspoons baking powder
One teaspoon salt
Oven temperature: 350 degrees
Baking time: Thirty minutes (about)
Servings: Eight

Melt the margarine in the bottom of a skillet (9 in.). Sprinkle the coconut around the edge of the pan forming a circle. In the center of the pan pour the combined brown sugar, cream and ginger. Arrange the pineapple spears, cherries and almonds in a pattern over the mixture. Set aside. Beat the eggs until thick and lemon-colored. Gradually beat in the sugar. Heat the milk and butter to boiling. Add the sifted dry ingredients alternately with the hot milk mixture. Pour over the prepared mixture in the skillet. Bake in a moderate oven until a cake tester inserted in the center comes away clean. Remove to a rack; let stand three minutes. Loosen edge of cake with a spatula; turn upside-down on serving plate. Serve in wedges.

A FAVORITE RECIPE
Lemon Date Squares

One-half cup butter or margarine
One-fourth cup confectioners' sugar
One cup sifted flour
One teaspoon grated lemon rind
Oven temperature: 350 degrees
Baking time: Twenty minutes
Two eggs, beaten until foamy
One cup sugar
Two tablespoons flour
One-half teaspoon baking powder
One-half teaspoon salt
One cup shredded coconut
One-half cup pitted dates
One tablespoon lemon juice
Oven temperature: 350 degrees
Baking time: Twenty-five minutes
Yield: One cake (8 x 8 x 2 in.)

In a bowl, cream the butter and sugar until light and fluffy. Blend in the flour and lemon rind. Pat into the bottom of a well greased square pan (8 x 8 x 2 in.). Bake in a moderate oven. Remove from the oven. Have the topping ready. Beat the eggs in a bowl; add the sugar, flour, sifted with the baking powder and salt, coconut, dates and lemon juice. Blend thoroughly. Spoon the mixture over the pastry baked crust. Bake until the top is firm and brown. Cool on a wire cake rack. Cut into squares. Store in tight container until needed.

MRS. MARY PIDRO, *Utica, N.Y.*

Strawberry Shortcake

One quart strawberries
One-third cup sugar, or more
Standing time: Fifteen minutes
Two cups sifted flour
Three teaspoons baking powder
One teaspoon salt
Two tablespoons sugar
One-third cup shortening
Two-thirds cup milk
One tablespoon melted butter
Oven temperature: 425 degrees
Baking time: Twelve minutes
One-half pint heavy cream, or more
Sugar
Servings: Eight, or more

Wash, drain and hull the strawberries. Save a few for garnish; slice majority into a bowl. Sweeten to taste and let stand while preparing the biscuits. Sift together into a bowl the flour, baking powder, salt and sugar. Cut in the shortening using two knives or a pastry blender until the mixture resembles coarse crumbs. Stir in the milk. Turn dough out on a floured board and pat or roll out to between one-fourth and one-half inch in thickness. Cuts out biscuits and place on baking sheet. Brush half the biscuits with the melted butter and top with another to make the double individual shortcakes. Bake in a hot oven for about twelve minutes or until delicately browned. Remove from oven. While still slightly warm split and put together with the sweetened strawberries and slightly sweetened heavy cream.

Lady Fingers

Three egg whites
One-third cup fine granulated sugar
Three egg yolks
One-fourth teaspoon vanilla
Three tablespoons hot water
One-half cup sifted flour
One teaspoon baking powder
One-fourth teaspoon salt
Confectioners' sugar
Oven temperature: 350 degrees
Bake: Ten minutes, about
Yield: Two dozen, or more

In a bowl beat the egg whites until foamy. Gradually beat in the fine granulated sugar until a satiny meringue is formed. Beat the egg yolks in a bowl until thick and lemon colored. Fold carefully into the meringue with the vanilla and hot water. Sift the flour, baking powder and salt together and fold into the egg mixture in two or three parts. Spoon onto brown paper on a baking sheet or press mixture through a moistened pastry bag forming fingers about four by one inch. Sprinkle confectioners' sugar over top. Bake in a moderate oven for ten minutes or until delicately browned. Remove from oven and let stand for about one minute. Remove from paper with a spatula and let cool on a rack. Put together in pairs with slightly beaten egg white or jam.

Special Cheese Cake

One pound cream cheese
One pound creamed cottage cheese
One and one-half cups sugar
Four eggs, beaten light
Two tablespoons lemon juice
One teaspoon vanilla
Three tablespoons flour
Three tablespoons cornstarch
One-fourth pound butter, melted
One pint dairy sour cream
Oven temperature: 325 degrees
Bake: One hour, or more
Rest in oven: Two hours
Chill: Thoroughly
Servings: Twelve, or more

Cream the cream cheese in a bowl until light and fluffy. Rub the creamed cottage cheese through a fine sieve into a bowl. Add to the fluffy cream cheese. Beat in the sugar gradually. Add the beaten eggs, lemon juice and vanilla. In a cup stir the flour and cornstarch together. Gradually beat into the cheese mixture. Add the melted butter and finally the dairy sour cream. Mix well. Pour into a greased spring form pan (9 in.) and bake in a moderately slow oven until set in the center. Turn off the oven, leaving cake in for two hours more. Remove from oven and let come to room temperature; chill thoroughly in the refrigerator before removing the spring form sides of the pan and serving.

Jamaica Spice Cake

One cup butter or margarine
One cup sugar
Three egg yolks
One-half cup molasses
One-half teaspoon soda
One tablespoon water
Two cups sifted flour
One-half teaspoon cinnamon
One-half teaspoon ginger
One-half teaspoon allspice
One-third cup Jamaica rum
Three egg whites
Oven temperature: 350 degrees
Bake: Fifty minutes, about
One-fourth cup confectioners' sugar
Yield: One cake (9 x 9 in.)

In a bowl cream the butter or margarine thoroughly. Gradually blend in the sugar. Beat in the egg yolks, then the molasses. Dissolve the soda in the water and add. Sift together the flour, cinnamon, ginger and allspice and add alternately with the rum to the creamed mixture. Beat the egg whites until they hold soft peaks and fold into the batter carefully. Pour into a greased pan (9 x 9 x 2 in.) and bake in a moderate oven for about fifty minutes or until the cake starts to leave the sides of the pan and springs back in the center when touched with a finger. Remove to rack to cool. Stir the confectioners' sugar through a sieve over the top of the cake. Cut into slices or squares to serve.

Spiced Cream Cake

One-half cup butter
Two cups brown sugar
Three egg yolks
Two cups sifted flour
One teaspoon baking soda
One-fourth teaspoon salt
Two teaspoons cinnamon
One-half teaspoon allspice
One-half teaspoon nutmeg
One-fourth teaspoon cloves
One cup dairy sour cream
Three egg whites
Oven temperature: 350 degrees
Baking time: Thirty minutes
Yield: Two layers (8 in.)

In a bowl cream the butter; gradually add the brown sugar, beating until light and fluffy. Beat in the egg yolks one at a time. Sift together the flour, soda, salt, cinnamon, allspice, nutmeg and cloves and add to the creamed mixture alternately with the dairy sour cream, beating well. In a bowl beat the egg whites until they hold soft peaks; fold into the batter carefully. Divide batter between two greased and floured cake pans (8 in.) and bake in a moderate oven until the cake springs back in the center when touched with a finger. Remove from oven and let stand for ten minutes before removing to cake racks to cool thoroughly before frosting as desired.

Spiced Marble Cake

One cup shortening
One and one-half cups sugar
Three eggs
Two teaspoons vanilla
Two and one-half cups sifted flour
Two teaspoons baking powder
One and one-half teaspoons salt
Three-fourths cup milk
One tablespoon cocoa
Three-fourths teaspoon cinnamon
One-fourth teaspoon allspice
One-fourth teaspoon nutmeg
One-eighth teaspoon cloves
Oven temperature: 375 degrees
Bake: Forty-five minutes, or more
Serves: Twelve

In a bowl cream the shortening until fluffy. Gradually beat in the sugar, then the eggs one at a time. Add the vanilla. Sift together the flour, baking powder and salt. Add dry ingredients to the creamed mixture alternately with the milk. Mix well. Place one-third of the batter in a smaller bowl and stir in the cocoa, cinnamon, allspice, nutmeg and cloves. Spoon both mixtures alternately by tablespoon into the greased and floured tube pan (9 in.). Run a spatula through batter several times to marble. Bake in a moderately hot oven until a cake tester inserted in the cake comes away clean or when the cake springs back when touched with a finger. Remove to rack to cool. When cool, dust with confectioners' sugar or frost as desired. Bake in two eight-inch layer cake pans if preferred for about thirty minutes.

Raspberry Cream Tart

One and one-half cups sifted flour
One-fourth cup sugar
One-half teaspoon baking powder
One-half teaspoon salt
One-half teaspoon cinnamon
One-half cup brown sugar
One-half cup butter or margarine
One egg
One-third cup finely ground or chopped almonds
Cream Filling
Raspberry Sauce
Flour
Oven temperature: 375 degrees
Baking time: Thirty or thirty-five minutes
Servings: Eight, or more

Sift together into a bowl the flour, sugar, baking powder, salt and cinnamon. Using a pastry blender or two knives, cut in the brown sugar and butter until the mixture resembles coarse meal. Add the egg and ground or finely chopped almonds and blend thoroughly. Set aside and chill one-third to one-half cup of the mixture. Press the rest of the dough into the bottom and part way up the sides of a pie plate (10 in.). Fill with the Cream Filling and carefully spread Raspberry Sauce over the top. Roll out the chilled dough using flour as necessary to a thickness of one-eighth inch. Cut into one-fourth inch strips with a knife or pastry wheel and arrange a lattice top. Lay a long continuous strip around the outer edge sealing the lattice as it comes in contact with the side crust. Press edge with finger-tips to seal and make a shallow tart. Do not build up edge around rim. Bake in a moderately hot oven for 30 to 35 minutes. When nicely browned remove to rack to cool. Let chill thoroughly before serving.

Cream Filling

One and one-half cups milk
One egg
One-third cup sugar
One-fourth cup sifted flour
One-fourth teaspoon salt
Cooking time: Ten minutes, or more
One teaspoon vanilla

Scald the milk in the upper half of a double boiler. In a bowl beat the egg well, gradually beat in the sugar until thick and lemony. Blend in the flour and salt. Gradually add the scalded milk, then return the combination to the double boiler. Place over boiling water and cook, stirring constantly until thick. Cover and continue cooking for five minutes, stirring occasionally. Add vanilla and cool slightly.

Raspberry Sauce

One package (10 oz.) frozen raspberries, thawed
Two tablespoons sugar
Two tablespoons cornstarch
One tablespoon lemon juice
Cooking time: Five minutes, or more

In the upper half of a double boiler beat the egg yolks until light. Beat in the sugar and lemon juice. Add the butter and cook over hot water until blended, stirring constantly. Continue cooking, stirring occasionally until sauce thickens. It will thicken considerably more on cooling. Serve in tart shells, as a cake filling or as a spread for biscuits.

Little Hats
(Hammentaschen)

One pound prunes
Water to cover
Simmer: Twenty minutes
Two tablespoons sugar
Juice and grated rind of one lemon
One-half cup finely chopped nuts
One-half cup butter or margarine
One-fourth cup sugar
One egg
Two and one-half cups sifted flour
Three teaspoons baking powder
One-half teaspoon salt
Oven temperature: 375 degrees
Bake: Ten to twelve minutes
Yield: Twenty-four

Place the prunes in a saucepan, cover with water and simmer until tender, about 20 minutes. Drain, cool and pit. Chop coarsely and blend in a bowl with the sugar, lemon juice and rind and chopped nuts. In a mixing bowl cream the butter or margarine and blend in the sugar. Beat in the egg. Sift together the flour, baking powder and salt and blend into the creamed mixture. Turn dough out on a floured board and roll out to thickness of one-fourth inch. Cut with three or three and one-half inch cutter. Lay circles of dough on a baking sheet. Spoon some of the fruit filling on each circle and fold up three sides to form the little three-cornered hat shape. Bake in a moderately hot oven 10 to 12 minutes. Remove to racks to cool. Store in a tightly covered container.

Mandarin Orange Cream Puffs

One-half package cream puff mix
One package vanilla pudding mix
One and one-half cups milk
Chill
One-half cup heavy cream, whipped
Two cans (11 oz. each) mandarin orange slices, chilled
Serves: Eight

Prepare one-half package (one stick) of cream puff mix according to directions, shaping into eight puffs. Prepare the vanilla pudding mix using one and one-half cups of milk and cook until thickened. Remove from heat and chill to room temperature. Fold in the whipped cream and chill thoroughly. At serving time cut the top from the puffs, spoon in the filling and orange slices. Replace tops and serve at once.

Pies and Pastries

Banbury Tarts

One cup seedless raisins, chopped
One cup sugar
Three tablespoons fine cracker crumbs
Two egg yolks
One tablespoon soft butter
Two tablespoons lemon juice
One tablespoon grated lemon rind
One package prepared pie pastry (2 cups)
Oven temperature: 450 degrees
Bake: Twelve minutes
Yield: Eighteen

In a bowl mix the raisins, sugar crumbs, yolks, soft butter, lemon juice and rind. Roll out pastry into a square 24 x 24". Cut into squares (4 in.). Spread filling over half of each square. Moisten edges. Fold into triangles. Press edges together with fork tines. Prick tops. Place on cooky sheet. Bake in a very hot oven until golden. Remove to racks.

Butterscotch Pecan Tarts

Two-thirds cup sugar
One-third cup butter or margarine
One-fourth cup hot water
One-third cup sugar
One-half teaspoon salt
Two tablespoons flour
One tablespoon cornstarch
One cup hot water
Cooking time: Four to five minutes
Two egg yolks, beaten
One cup pecan halves
Cooking time: Two or three minutes
Eight baked two and one-half inch tart shells
Servings: Eight

In a small heavy skillet place the two thirds cup of sugar. Stir over heat until melted, then stir in the butter or margarine and the fourth cup of hot water. In saucepan blend the third cup of sugar with the salt, flour and cornstarch. Stir in the cup of hot water. Cook over low heat, stirring constantly, until the mixture thickens and comes to a boil. Stir in the caramel mixture. Add a little of the combination to the beaten egg yolks, return to the saucepan with the pecans. Cook, stirring constantly, over low heat for two to three minutes, until the mixture comes to the boiling point. Remove from heat and cool before spooning into the baked and cooled tart shells. Note: Graham cracker crust may be packed into eight fluted paper cups and bake in muffin pans if desired. For this blend together one-fourth cup soft butter, one-fourth cup sugar and one and one-half cups graham cracker crumbs. Bake for eight minutes in a moderate hot oven (375 degrees).

Chess Tarts

Three egg yolks
One egg white
One cup sugar
Two tablespoons flour
One-half cup melted butter or margarine
Five tablespoons milk
One-half teaspoon vanilla
One package pastry mix for tart shells
Twelve unbaked tart shells (3½ in.)
Oven temperature: 375 degrees
Baking time: Thirty-five minutes (about)
Two egg whites
One-fourth cup sugar
Oven temperature: 325 degrees
Yield: Twelve tarts

Beat the egg yolks and white until thick. Gradually add the combined sugar and flour. Stir in the butter, milk and vanilla. Fill each tart shell two-thirds full. Bake in a moderately hot oven until the pastry is done and the filing light brown. Take from the oven. The filling will settle slightly. Beat the egg whites until stiff; gradually adding the sugar; beating until glossy. Pile over the filling. Brown lightly in a moderately slow oven.

Glazed Fruit Tarts

One-third cup sugar
Three tablespoons flour
One-eighth teaspoon salt
Two cups milk, scalded
Cooking time: Fifteen minutes in a
    double boiler
Two egg yolks, beaten slightly
Cooking time: Three minutes
One-fourth teaspoon almond extract
Twelve baked tart shells (3 in.)
Four whole peeled apricots, stoned
Two cups halved seeded green grapes
Two cups fresh blueberries
Eight slices banana (1 in. thick)
Two cups strawberries, halved
One-half cup apple or currant jelly, melted
Servings: Twelve

Mix the sugar, flour and salt in a double boiler; gradually stir in the hot milk. Cook, stirring, until thickened. Pour half the mixture over the beaten egg yolks in a bowl. Return to the boiler; stir until thick. Cool; add the extract. Fill the tart shells. In the center of four tarts place an apricot and edge with grapes. Fill four tarts with blueberries and decorate with banana. Cover the tops of the remaining four tarts with strawberries. To glaze, spoon the melted jelly over the fruit and berries.

Puff Pastry

One cup sifted flour
One-fourth teaspoon salt
One-third cup ice water
Ten tablespoons butter (1¼ sticks)
Turn: Five times (rolling and folding dough)
Refrigerate: Twenty minutes
Oven temperature: 450 degrees
Yield: Ten horns, eight napoleons, twelve
    butterflies, eight pastry shells

In a bowl mix the flour and salt. Add the ice water. Form into a ball of dough, handling as little as possible. Place on bread board. Meanwhile cut butter lengthwise into fourths. (When cut, butter should hold its shape but not be soft enough to melt. Dough and butter must be at about same temperature, otherwise butter will break through the dough.) On a floured board roll dough into rectangle (10 x 6 in.). Place cut butter on half the dough; fold over dough; seal edges securely. You must be careful to see that the butter does not break through the dough, especially during the first time the dough is rolled out into a rectangle (18 x 8 in.). Roll and fold into thirds (this is called a turn); mark the turn with spatula or thumb print; wrap in

foil or transparent paper; refrigerate for 20 minutes. Repeat procedure four more times. Then make puff specialties.

To Make Pastry Shells

Roll out puff pastry into a rectangle (18 x 10 in.). Cut out rounds with a cutter (4 in.). Remove centers from ⅔ of rounds to make rims. Set aside. Place plain rounds on cooky sheet, moisten edges with cold water; put on half of the rims, moisten again and place remaining rims on top; press edges slightly. Chill 15 minutes. Bake shells in very hot oven for 12 minutes; reduce heat to moderate and continue to bake for 25 minutes longer. Remove. Makes eight.

Lay centers and trimmings carefully on top of each other; refrigerate to use for other pastries.

To Make Horns

Roll out puff pastry into rectangle (18 x 10 in.). Cut into strips (¼ in.). Shape heavy foil into cones. Wrap two strips of pastry around each foil cone. Brush with unbeaten egg white and sprinkle with sugar. Place on cooky sheet. Chill 15 minutes. Bake in a very hot oven until golden brown (about 12 minutes). Re-

move to racks to cool. Remove foil cones. Fill with sweetened whipped cream. Yield: Ten horns (about).

To Make Napoleons

Divide the dough into thirds. On floured cooky sheets roll out each piece of dough (9 x 7 in.). Prick entire surface of dough. Chill 15 minutes. Bake in a very hot oven for 12 minutes. Remove to racks to cool. Spread cream filling between layers; top with thin confectioners' icing. Trim edges with a sharp knife. Cut into rectangles. Yield: Eight.

To Make Butterflies

Roll out puff pastry into a rectangle (18 x 10 in.). Brush surface of dough with confectioners' sugar. Fold each 10 inch side of dough to center; fold again to center making four folds in all. With a sharp knife cut into strips (½ in.). Dip cut side of each strip of folded dough into unbeaten egg white, then into sugar. Place sugared side up on cooky sheet. Chill 15 minutes. Bake in a very hot oven for 8 minutes; turn and bake another 4 minutes on other side. Remove to rack to cool. Yield: Eighteen (about).

Pineapple Cheese Pie

One package (8 oz.) cream cheese
One-half cup sugar
One-half teaspoon salt
Two beaten eggs
One-half cup milk
One-half teaspoon vanilla
One cup pineapple preserves (one 12 oz. jar)
One unbaked pastry shell (9 in.)
One-fourth cup chopped pecans
Oven temperature: 400 then 325 degrees
Bake: One hour
Serves: Six to eight

In a bowl cream the cheese until light and fluffy. Beat in the sugar and salt. Gradually blend in the beaten eggs, milk and vanilla. Spread the pineapple preserves over the bottom of an unbaked pastry shell (9 in.) and top with the cream cheese mixture. Scatter the finely chopped pecans over all and bake in a quick oven for 10 minutes to set the crust. Reduce the heat to moderately slow and continue baking for 50 minutes. Remove from oven and allow to cool, then chill thoroughly before serving.

Nut Topped Sour Cream Pie

Two eggs
One cup sugar
One teaspoon flour
One-fourth teaspoon salt
One-fourth teaspoon cinnamon
One cup dairy sour cream
One unbaked pie shell (9 in.)
One-half cup finely chopped walnuts or pecans
Oven temperature: 425-350 degrees
Baking time: Forty-five to fifty-five minutes
Servings: Six

In a bowl beat the eggs, gradually beat in the sugar. Add the flour, salt, cinnamon and dairy sour cream. Mix well. Pour into an unbaked pastry shell (9 in.). Scatter the finely chopped nuts over the top. Bake in a hot oven (425 degrees) for 10 minutes to set the pastry, reduce the heat to moderate (350 degrees) and continue baking until the center of the filling is set, about 35 to 45 minutes. Cool before serving.

Chess Pie

One cup sifted flour
One-half teaspoon salt
One-third cup shortening
Two or three tablespoons ice water
One-half cup butter or margarine
One and one-half cups sugar
Three eggs
One teaspoon vanilla
Oven temperature: 375 degrees
Bake: Forty minutes
Servings: Six

Sift the cup of flour and half teaspoon of salt into a bowl. Cut in half the shortening until as fine as cornmeal, cut in remaining shortening until the size of small peas. Stir in enough ice water to bind crumbs together. Turn out on floured board and roll out pastry to fit a pie plate (9 in.) Trim and flute the edge. In a saucepan melt the butter or margarine. Stir in the sugar. In a bowl beat the eggs until foamy, add the vanilla and gradually beat in the butter and sugar combination. Pour into the pastry lined pie plate and bake in a moderately hot oven for forty minutes or until nicely browned. Chill thoroughly before serving.

Buttermilk Pie

One cup sifted flour
One-half teaspoon salt
One-third cup shortening
Two or three tablespoons ice water
Three egg yolks
One-fourth cup butter or margarine, melted
Two cups buttermilk
One cup sugar
Three tablespoons flour
One-half teaspoon salt
Three egg whites
Oven temperature: 375 degrees
Bake: Forty-five minutes
Servings: Six

Sift the cup of flour and half teaspoon of salt into a bowl. Cut in half the shortening until as fine as cornmeal, cut in remaining shortening until the size of small peas. Stir in enough ice water to bind the crumbs together. Turn out on floured board and roll out pastry to fit a pie plate (10 in.). Trim and flute the edge. In a bowl beat the egg yolks, blend in the slightly cooled melted butter or margarine. Stir in the buttermilk. Sift the sugar, flour and salt together and blend into the egg and milk mixture. Beat the egg whites until stiff but not dry and fold into the first mixture. Pour into the pastry lined pie plate and bake in a moderately hot oven until set in the center and well browned. Chill thoroughly before serving.

Shoo Fly Pie

One cup sifted flour
One-half teaspoon flour
One-third cup shortening
Two to three tablespoons ice water
One and one-half cups sifted flour
One-half cup sugar
One-fourth cup shortening or butter
One-half teaspoon soda
One tablespoon boiling water
One-half cup molasses
One-half cup boiling water
Oven temperature: 425 then 350 degrees
Bake: Forty minutes
Servings: Six

Sift the cup of flour with the salt into a bowl. Cut in half the one-third cup measure of shortening using a pastry blender or two knives until mixture is consistency of coarse meal. Cut in second half until size of small peas. Stir in enough of the ice water with a fork to bind crumbs together. Transfer to a floured board and roll out crust to fit a pie plate (9 in.). Trim and flute the edge. Sift the remaining flour and sugar into a small bowl. Use pastry blender or two knives to cut in the fourth cup of shortening or butter until the consistency of fine crumbs. Measure the soda into another bowl. Add the tablespoon of boiling water and stir to dissolve. Add the molasses and beat until a golden color. Blend in the half cup of boiling water. Pour molasses mixture into the unbaked pie shell; scatter the crumbs over the top. Bake in a hot oven (425 degrees) for ten minutes to set the crust, reduce the heat to moderate (350 degrees) and continue baking for thirty minutes more. Remove from oven to rack to cool before serving.

Toasted Almond Chiffon Pie

One-half cup blanched almonds
Oven temperature: 350 degrees
Toast: Ten minutes, about
One tablespoon unflavored gelatin
One-fourth cup milk
Three egg yolks
One-fourth cup sugar
One cup evaporated milk
One-fourth teaspoon nutmeg
Cook: Five to eight minutes
Two teaspoons vanilla
Three egg whites
One-eighth teaspoon salt
One-fourth cup sugar
One baked pie shell (9 in.)
Chill: One hour, or more
Serves: Six

Place blanched almonds on a shallow tray in a moderate oven for about ten minutes to toast a light brown. Remove, cool, and chop fairly fine or grind in an electric blender. Sprinkle the unflavored gelatin over the fourth cup of milk in a cup. Allow to stand to soften the gelatin. In a saucepan beat the egg yolks with the fourth cup of sugar, evaporated milk and nutmeg. Place over direct heat and cook, stirring constantly, until the mixture thickens. Remove from heat and add the softened gelatin, stirring until dissolved. Add the vanilla. Chill until the mixture is considerably thicker. In a bowl, beat the egg whites with the salt until foamy, add the sugar gradually, beating until the meringue is glossy and stiff. Fold meringue into the chilled mixture. Add about three fourths of the ground or finely chopped toasted almonds. Pile mixture into the baked pie shell. Sprinkle with remaining almonds. Chill thoroughly before serving.

Cherry Chiffon Pie

Twenty graham crackers, crushed
One-fourth cup soft butter or margarine
One-fourth cup sugar
Oven temperature: 350 degrees
Baking time: Ten minutes
One envelope unflavored gelatin
One-fourth cup cold water
One can (No. 2) sour pie cherries
One-half cup sugar
One-eighth teaspoon salt
Heat: To boiling point
One tablespoon lemon juice
Chill: Until syrupy
One-half cup heavy cream, whipped
Chilling time: Two hours
Servings: Six

In a bowl combine the crushed graham crackers with the soft butter and sugar. Blend with the fingers if you wish. Pack the mixture into the bottom and against the sides of a pie plate (9 in.) and bake in a moderate oven until lightly browned. Remove and permit to cool. Soften the unflavored gelatin in the water. In a saucepan heat the sour cherries and juice with the sugar and salt to the boiling point. Add the softened gelatin and lemon juice and stir to dissolve. Chill until syrupy, then fold in the whipped cream. Pour into the prepared pie shell. Chill until the filling is set.

Black Bottom Pie

One cup sifted all-purpose flour
One-half teaspoon salt
One-third cup shortening
Three or four tablespoons ice water
Oven temperature: 425 degrees
Bake: Ten to fifteen minutes
Three-fourths cup sugar
One-fourth cup flour
Four egg yolks
Three cups milk
Cook: Ten to fifteen minutes
One tablespoon unflavored gelatin
One-fourth cup cold water
One and one-half ounces unsweetened chocolate
One teaspoon vanilla
Four egg whites
One-fourth cup sugar
Two teaspoons rum extract
Chill: Until thickened
Chill: Five hours
One-half cup heavy cream, whipped
One-half ounce unsweetened chocolate
Serves: Six or eight

Sift the cup of flour and salt into a bowl. Cut in half the shortening until as fine as corn meal. Cut in second half of the shortening until the size of small peas. Add enough water to bind the crumbs together into a ball that follows the fork around the bowl. Turn out on floured board and roll out. Fit pastry into a pie plate (9 in.), trim and flute the edge. Prick all over with the tines of a fork. Bake in a very hot oven until nicely browned. Remove from oven and let cool. Prepare the filling by combining the three-fourths cup of sugar and fourth cup of flour in a saucepan. Add the beaten egg yolks and the milk. Cook,

stirring constantly, until the mixture thickens. Sprinkle the unflavored gelatin over the fourth cup of cold water and let stand to soften. Add to the cooked mixture stirring until dissolved. Divide the mixture in half. Stir the ounce and a half of unsweetened chocolate and the vanilla into one part, stirring until chocolate is melted. In a bowl beat the egg whites until foamy, gradually beat in the fourth cup of sugar until they hold stiff peaks. Add the rum extract. Fold into second part of cooked mixture. Pour the slightly cooled chocolate mixture into the pie shell. Let the rum flavored mixture chill and thicken slightly and mound over the chocolate filling. Chill pie for five hours. To serve garnish with the whipped cream and grated half ounce of unsweetened chocolate.

Orange Chiffon Pie

Two envelopes unflavored gelatin
One-half cup cold water
Three egg yolks
One-fourth cup sugar
One-half teaspoon salt
One-fourth cup orange juice
Cook: Ten minutes, about
Chill: Until syrupy
Three egg whites
Six tablespoons sugar
One tablespoon lemon juice
One cup finely diced orange pulp
One baked pie shell (9 in.)
Chill: Until set
Servings: Six

Sprinkle the unflavored gelatin over the cold water in a cup. Let stand to soften. In the upper half of a double boiler beat the egg yolks with the fourth cup of sugar, salt and orange juice. Place over hot water and cook, stirring constantly, until mixture thickens. Remove from heat, add the softened gelatin and stir until dissolved. Chill until mixture is syrupy. Beat the egg whites until foamy, gradually beat in the sugar until a stiff and glossy meringue is formed. Fold meringue, lemon juice and diced orange pulp (membrane removed) into the gelatin mixture carefully. Pile into the baked pie shell. Chill until set before serving.

Strawberry Chiffon Pie

One package strawberry-flavored gelatin
One cup hot water
One pint fresh ripe strawberries
One tablespoon sugar
Chill: Until syrupy
Two egg whites
One-eighth teaspoon cream of tartar
Three tablespoons sugar
One-half teaspoon vanilla
One baked pastry shell (9 in.)
Chill: Until firm
Whipped cream (optional)
Servings: Six

Dissolve the strawberry gelatin in one cup of hot water in a bowl. Wash, dry, hull and slice the strawberries into a bowl. Add the tablespoon of sugar and let stand to draw the juices. When the

gelatin is at room temperature add the strawberries and chill until syrupy. In a bowl beat the egg whites with the cream of tartar until foamy. Gradually beat in the sugar and vanilla until a stiff meringue is formed. Fold into the thickened gelatin and pour into the baked pastry shell (or crumb crust). Chill until firm. Serve with whipped cream if desired.

Coco-Mint Chiffon Pie

One pie shell (9 in.)
One tablespoon unflavored gelatin
One-fourth cup cold water
One-half cup sugar
Four tablespoons cocoa
One-eighth teaspoon salt
One and three-fourths cups milk
Cook: Five minutes
Two egg yolks, beaten
Cook: Until slightly thickened
One-fourth teaspoon mint flavoring
Chill: Until thick
Two egg whites
One tablespoon sugar
Chill: Until set
Serves: Six

Prepare a baked pastry shell or crumb crust in a nine inch pie plate. Sprinkle the unflavored gelatin over a fourth cup of cold water and let stand to soften. In the upper half of a double boiler stir the sugar, cocoa and salt together. Gradually blend in the milk, stirring smooth. Cook for five minutes or until well blended. Add a little to the beaten egg yolks and return combination to the pan. Cook until slightly thickened. Add the mint flavoring and softened gelatin, stirring until dissolved. Chill until thick. Beat the egg whites until foamy, add the tablespoon of sugar and beat until they hold stiff peaks. Fold into the thickened gelatin mixture carefully. Transfer to pie shell and chill until set. Serve with a garnish of whipped cream if desired.

Lime Chiffon Pie

One envelope unflavored gelatin
One-fourth cup cold water
Three egg yolks
Three-fourths cup sugar
One-half cup lime juice
Cook: Ten minutes
Six drops green food coloring
Three egg whites
One-fourth teaspoon salt
Baked pie shell (9 in.)
Chill: Two hours, about
Serves: Six

Sprinkle the gelatin over the cold water in a cup. In the upper half of a double boiler, beat the egg yolks slightly, add half the sugar and the lime juice. Cook over boiling water, stirring constantly until thickened slightly. Remove from the heat, add the softened gelatin and stir until dissolved. Add the green food coloring. When cool, fold in the meringue made by beating the egg whites in a bowl with the salt until foamy and gradually beating in the remaining sugar until stiff. Pile mixture into the baked pie shell and place in the refrigerator to chill thoroughly before serving.

Fluffy Lemon Pie

Four eggs, separated
One cup sugar
One-half cup lemon juice
Cooking time: Fifteen minutes
One tablespoon grated lemon rind
One-eighth teaspoon cream of tartar
One baked pastry shell (9 in.)
Oven temperature: 350 degrees
Baking time: Fifteen minutes
Refrigerate: Overnight
One-half cup heavy cream, whipped
Serves: Eight

In the top of a double boiler beat the egg yolks and ½ cup sugar until thick and lemon-colored. Add the lemon juice. Cook over hot water until slightly thick; add rind. Set aside to cool. Beat the egg whites, with the cream of tartar, until soft peaks are formed. Gradually beat in the remaining sugar until satiny. Fold into the egg yolk mixture. Pour into the baked pie shell. Bake in a moderate oven until delicately browned. Remove to rack. When cold, place in refrigerator overnight; spread whipped cream on top and cut into wedges.

Fluffy Lime Pie

Four egg yolks
One-fourth cup lime juice
Three tablespoons cold water
One-half sugar
Cook: Until thickened
Few drops green food coloring
Four egg whites
One-eighth teaspoon salt
One-half cup sugar
One baked pastry shell (9 in.)
Oven temperature: 300 degrees
Bake: Twenty minutes, about
Chill: Thoroughly
Servings: Six

In a saucepan beat the egg yolks until thick and light. Stir in the lime juice, cold water and sugar. Cook over low heat, stirring constantly, until thickened. Remove from heat and add a few drops of food coloring, about six. In a bowl beat the egg whites until frothy with the salt. Gradually beat in the remaining sugar until a stiff, glossy meringue is formed. Fold half the meringue into the lime mixture and pour into a cooled pastry shell. Spoon balance of meringue around the edge of the pie like a wreath. Bake in a slow oven for twenty minutes or until lightly browned. Chill thoroughly before serving.

Ambrosia Pie

One-third cup sugar
One-half cup flour
One-fourth teaspoon salt
Three cups milk
One cup flaked coconut
Cooking time: Fifteen minutes
Two egg yolks, slightly beaten
Cooking time: Two minutes
Two teaspoons grated orange rind
One tablespoon butter
One baked pastry shell (9 in.)
Two egg whites, unbeaten
One-half cup sugar
One-eighth teaspoon salt
Three tablespoons water
Beating time: Three minutes
One-half teaspoon vanilla
One-half cup flaked coconut
Serves: Eight

In the top of a double boiler mix sugar, flour and salt, gradually add the milk, stirring until smooth. Add one cup of coconut. Cook over rapidly boiling water, stirring constantly until thickened. Mix a small amount with the egg yolks, return to double boiler; cook 2 minutes longer. Remove; add grated rind and butter. When cool, pour into a pastry shell. With a rotary beater, beat the egg whites, sugar and salt until thoroughly mixed. Place over rapidly boiling water one minute. Remove from heat and continue beating for 2 minutes. Add vanilla. Pile lightly on filling. Garnish with coconut, orange slices and grapes. Serve in wedges immediately.

Lemon Meringue Pie

One and one-fourth cups sugar
One-half cup flour
One and three-fourths cup water
Cooking time: Ten minutes in a double
    boiler
Three eggs, separated
Cooking time: Two minutes
One and one-half tablespoons butter
One-fourth cup lemon juice
Two tablespoons grated lemon rind
One baked pie shell (9 in.)
Six tablespoons sugar
Oven temperature: 325 degrees
Baking time: Twenty minutes
Servings: Six

Sift the sugar, flour and salt into the top of a double boiler. Add the water, stirring until smooth. Cook over direct heat, stirring constantly until beginning to thicken. Set over boiling water; cook until very thick, stirring often. Gradually add the hot mixture to the beaten egg yolks. Return to the boiler; cook, stirring until the mixture coats a spoon. Add the butter, lemon juice and rind. Cool. Beat the egg whites until stiff; gradually add the sugar, beating until glossy. Pour the filling into the baked pie shell. Pile meringue over the filling. Brown lightly in a moderately slow oven. Remove to a rack. Allow to stand for two hours before cutting.

Vanilla Wafer Pie Crust

One and one-third cups vanilla wafer
    crumbs
One-fourth cup butter, melted
Chill: Thirty minutes, or more
Yield: One pie shell (9 in.)

Mix the finely rolled vanilla wafer crumbs with the melted butter and pack evenly into the bottom and sides of a pie plate (9 in.) with the back of a spoon. Chill in the refrigerator at least thirty minutes before filling.

Baked Alaska Pie

Two tablespoons soft butter
One box (4 oz.) shredded coconut
Oven temperature: 350 degrees
Baking time: Ten minutes (about)
Three egg whites
One-eighth teaspoon salt
Three tablespoons sugar
One cup chopped candied cherries
One pint strawberry ice cream, frozen
    hard
Oven temperature: 450 degrees
Baking time: Five minutes
Servings: Six

Spread the butter evenly on the bottom and sides of a glass pie plate (8 in.). Sprinkle in the coconut, pressing it into

the butter. Cover with two thicknesses of heavy brown paper. Bake in a moderate oven until golden. Cool 20 minutes on a rack. For the meringue: Beat the egg whites and salt until foamy; gradually add the sugar, beating until stiff. Set aside. Arrange the cherries in the coconut pie shell; over them place the ice cream. Quickly spread the entire pie with the meringue. Bake in a very hot oven until lightly brown. Cut and serve at once.

Cranberry Meringue Pie

Two tablespoons cornstarch
One-eighth teaspoon salt
One can (1 lb.) whole cranberry sauce
Cook: Ten minutes, or more
One tablespoon butter or margarine
One-half teaspoon vanilla
One baked pastry shell (8 in.)
Two egg whites
Four tablespoons sugar
Oven temperature: 325 degrees
Bake: Twenty-five minutes
Servings: Five or six

In a saucepan stir together cornstarch and salt, gradually blend in the canned whole cranberry sauce, stirring smooth. Bring slowly to a boil and cook, stirring constantly, until thickened. Remove from heat, add the butter or margarine and the vanilla and cool. Transfer the cooked filling to the baked pastry shell. In a bowl beat the egg whites until foamy. Gradually beat in the sugar until a stiff glossy meringue is formed. Heap this over the pie filling, taking care to fuse it to the pastry all around the edge. Bake in a moderately slow oven until nicely browned. Remove from the oven and cool away from draft.

Orange Meringue Pie

Three-fourths cup sugar
Six tablespoons cornstarch
One-half teaspoon salt
Two cups milk
Cook: About ten minutes
Three beaten egg yolks
Cook: Two minutes
Two tablespoons butter
Grated rind one orange
One-third cup orange juice
Cool: Thoroughly
One baked pastry shell (9 in.)
Three egg whites
One-eighth teaspoon salt
Two teaspoons lemon juice
Six tablespoons sugar
Oven temperature: 325 degrees
Bake: Twenty minutes, about
Serves: Six

In the upper half of a double boiler, stir together the three-fourths cup of sugar, cornstarch and half teaspoon of salt. Gradually blend in the milk. Place over boiling water and cook, stirring constantly until mixture is thick. Cover and cook for two minutes more. Remove from heat. In a bowl, beat the egg yolks. Gradually, add the cooked mixture to the yolks, beating smooth. Return combination to the pan and continue cooking, stirring for two minutes more. Add the butter, orange rind and orange juice. Cool. Spoon into the baked pastry shell. In a bowl, beat the egg whites until foamy with the salt. Add the lemon juice. Gradually beat in the sugar until a stiff, glossy meringue is formed. Pile meringue over the filling in the pie, taking care to fuse it to the pastry shell around the edge.

Pineapple Meringue Pie

Three-fourths cup sugar
Four tablespoons cornstarch
One-half teaspoon salt
One can (No. 2) unsweetened pineapple
    juice
Three beaten egg yolks
Cook: Until thickened
One tablespoon butter
Cool: Thoroughly
One baked pastry shell (9 in.)
Three egg whites
One-eighth teaspoon salt
Six tablespoons sugar
Oven temperature: 325 degrees
Bake: Twenty minutes, about

In a saucepan, stir together the sugar, cornstarch, and salt. Gradually blend in the unsweetened pineapple juice, stirring smooth. Add the beaten egg yolks and place over low heat stirring until thickened. Remove from heat, add butter and let cool to room temperature. Spoon into baked pastry shell. In a bowl, beat the egg whites until foamy, add the salt and gradually beat in the sugar until the meringue is stiff and satiny. Spoon over the filling, taking care to fuse it to the pastry all around the edge. Bake in a moderately slow oven until a golden brown. Remove to rack to cool.

Rich Mocha Angel Pie

Three egg whites
One-fourth teaspoon cream of tartar
Three-fourths cup sugar
Oven temperature: 275 degrees
Bake: One hour or more
Two packages (6 oz. each)
    semi-sweet chocolate pieces
One tablespoon instant coffee
One-fourth cup boiling water
One cup heavy cream
One teaspoon vanilla
Chill: Until set
Servings: Ten to twelve

In a bowl beat the egg whites with the cream of tartar until frothy. Gradually beat in the sugar until a glossy smooth meringue is formed. Spread half of the meringue over the bottom and halfway up the sides of a well-buttered pie plate (9 in.). Drop mounds of remaining meringue along the rim of the plate. If desired pipe this on using a pastry bag. Bake in a very slow oven until the meringue is crisp and lightly browned. Remove from oven and cool thoroughly but slowly before filling. Prepare the filling by melting the chocolate pieces in the upper half of a double boiler. Dissolve the instant coffee in the boiling water and blend into the melted chocolate. Cool mixture slightly. In a bowl beat the cream until stiff. Add the vanilla and chocolate mixture. Pour into the cooled meringue shell. Chill until set. Note: Meringue pies are usually easier to cut and serve in the kitchen as you must carefully loosen the shell from the plate.

Strawberry Cream Pie

One pint strawberries
One tablespoon sugar
Cream Filling:
Two-thirds cup sugar
One-third cup flour
One-fourth teaspoon salt
Two cups milk
Cooking time: Ten minutes
Two eggs, beaten
Cooking time: Two minutes
Chilling time: Forty minutes
One teaspoon vanilla
One baked pie shell (9 in.)
One-half cup heavy cream, whipped
Servings: Eight

Wash, hull and slice the strawberries into a bowl. Add the tablespoon of sugar and let stand. To make the cream filling combine in the upper half of a double boiler the sugar, flour and salt. Gradually stir in the milk. Cook over hot water, stirring constantly, until the mixture thickens. Cover and continue cooking, without stirring for ten minutes. Add a small amount of the mixture to the beaten eggs, then return combination to the pan. Cook for two minutes more. Chill thoroughly; add vanilla. Pour filling into baked pie shell, spread sliced berries over filling and top with slightly sweetened whipped cream. Chill and serve.

Easy Strawberry Pie

One-fourth cup butter or margarine
Two tablespoons sugar
Four cups corn flakes, crushed
Chilling time: One hour, about
One quart strawberries
One-fourth cup sugar
One-half pint heavy cream
Servings: Eight, or more

In a bowl cream the butter or margarine, blend in the sugar. Work in the very finely crushed corn flakes using a spoon or pastry blender. Pack into a pie plate (9 in.) and chill thoroughly in the refrigerator. Wash, drain and hull the strawberries. Save a dozen for garnish, slice the majority into a bowl. Sweeten to taste. When ready to serve fill the chilled crust with the drained sweetened sliced berries. Top with the whipped and slightly sweetened heavy cream; garnish with reserved whole berries. Serve at once.

Honey Prune Pie

One unbaked pastry shell (9 in.)
Two eggs
One-half cup dairy sour cream
One-fourth teaspoon salt
Two-thirds cup honey
Two tablespoons lemon juice
Two cups cooked prunes
Oven temperature: 450 degrees
Bake: Ten minutes
Oven temperature: 375 degrees
Bake: Thirty minutes
Servings: Six

Prepare pastry to line a nine-inch pie plate. Flute edge. In a bowl beat the eggs, beat in the dairy sour cream. Add the honey, salt and lemon juice. Remove pits from the cooked prunes leaving fruit in large pieces. Add to the egg mixture. Pour into the pastry shell and bake in a very hot over for ten minutes to set the crust. Reduce temperature to moderately hot and continue baking for thirty minutes. Remove from oven and cool to room temperature. Chill, before serving. May be topped off with spoonfuls of dairy sour cream if you wish.

Maple Walnut Chiffon Pie

Twenty graham crackers
One-fourth cup sugar
One-fourth cup butter or margarine, melted
Oven temperature: 375 degrees
Baking time: Eight minutes
One envelope unflavored gelatin
One-fourth cup water
One and one-half cups milk
One-fourth teaspoon salt
One-fourth cup sugar
Three egg yolks
Cooking time: Ten minutes, about
Chilling time: Until syrupy
Three egg whites
One-fourth cup sugar
One-third cup maple syrup
One-half cup finely chopped walnuts
Chilling time: Several hours
Servings: Eight or more

Crush the graham crackers to very fine crumbs on a board with rolling pin. Combine in a bowl with the one-fourth cup of sugar and the melted butter or margarine. Pack into the bottom and sides of a pie plate (10 in.) using a nine-inch pie plate as a firmer. Bake in a moderately hot oven for eight minutes; set aside to cool. Soften the unflavored gelatin in the water. In the upper half of a double boiler scald the milk with the salt and one-fourth cup of sugar. Beat the egg yolks in a small bowl. Add a little of the scalded milk to the egg yolks, stirring with a spoon. Return to the remaining milk in the pan. Cook, stirring constantly, over hot water until the custard thickens. Add softened gelatin and stir until dissolved. Cool until the mixture is syrupy. Beat the egg whites until foamy. Add the remaining one-fourth cup of sugar gradually, beating well after each addition. Fold into the syrupy custard mixture with the maple syrup and chopped nuts, reserving two tabelspoons of the nuts. Pile into the baked crumb shell and scatter reserved chopped nuts over the top. Chill several hours before serving. Should you have more filling than the shell will hold, spoon into custard cups or dessert dishes.

Raisin Pear Pie

Two cups sifted flour
One teaspoon salt
Two-thirds cup shortening
Four to six tablespoons cold water
Two cups seedless raisins
One can (No. 2) pears
One cup water
One-half cup pear syrup
Two tablespoons orange juice
Two tablespoons lemon juice
Boil: Five minutes
One cup sugar
One-fourth cup cornstarch
One-half teaspoon salt
One tablespoon butter
Oven temperature: 375 degrees
Bake: Thirty minutes
Serves: Six or more

Sift the flour and teaspoon of salt into a bowl. Cut in half the shortening with a pastry blender or two knives until the mixture resembles coarse meal. Cut in second half of shortening until the size of small peas. Gradually stir in the cold water, using enough to hold dough together. Dough will follow fork around the bowl in a ball. Turn out on floured board and roll out half to line pie plate (9 in.).
Roll out second half of dough for top crust. Cover raisins with hot water and drain. Drain syrup from the pears, dice fruit. In a saucepan combine the water, half cup of pear syrup, orange and lemon juice. Bring to a boil. Add the raisins and boil for five minutes. In a small bowl stir the sugar, cornstarch and salt together. Add to the raisin mixture and cook, stirring until thick and clear. Add the diced pears and butter. Cool slightly and pour into the pastry lined pie plate. Affix the top crust, trim and flute. Cut vents for the escape of steam. Bake in a moderately hot oven for thirty minutes or until nicely browned. Remove from oven and serve slightly warm.

Apple Raisin Pie

Three-fourths cup sugar
Four tablespoons cornstarch
One-eighth teaspoon salt
One cup apple juice
Two cups sliced, peeled apples
One-half cup raisins
One-inch piece cinnamon stick
Cook: Five minutes
Two tablespoons lemon juice
Cool: Fifteen minutes
One baked pie shell (9 in.)
Whipped cream (optional)
Serves: Six

In a saucepan, combine the sugar with the cornstarch and salt. Gradually blend in the apple juice. Add the sliced apples, raisins and cinnamon stick. Cook over low heat, stirring constantly until the mixture thickens. Remove the cinnamon stick and add the lemon juice. Cool briefly before pouring into a baked pastry shell. Serve with sweetened whipped cream if desired.

Molasses Rum Pie

Two tablespoons sugar
One envelope unflavored gelatin
One-eighth teaspoon salt
Three egg yolks
One cup milk
One-third cup molasses
Cook: Ten minutes, about
One and one-half teaspoons rum flavoring
  or
One tablespoon rum
Chill: Until thicker
Three egg whites
One-third cup sugar
One cup heavy cream
One baked pastry shell (9 in.)
Chill: Until set
Servings: Six, or more

In the upper half of a double boiler stir the two tablespoons of sugar with the unflavored gelatin and salt. Beat in the egg yolks, blend in the milk and molasses. Place over boiling water and cook, stirring constantly until mixture is slightly thickened. Remove from the heat and add the rum flavoring or rum. Chill until slightly thicker. In a bowl beat the egg whites until foamy, gradually beat in remaining sugar. Fold into the chilled custard with the whipped cream. Pour into baked pastry shell and chill until set.

Peach Crumb Pie

One cup sifted all purpose flour
One-half teaspoon salt
One teaspoon sugar
One-third cup shortening
Two to three tablespoons ice water
Four cups sliced fresh peaches (six large)
One-fourth cup sugar
Two tablespoons lemon juice
One-half cup brown sugar
Three-fourths cup flour
One-third cup butter or margarine
Oven temperature: 425 then 350 degrees
Baking time: Forty minutes, about
Servings: Six

Sift together into a bowl the flour, salt and sugar. Cut in half the shortening with a pastry blender or two knives until the mixture resembles coarse meal. Cut the remaining shortening in until it is the size of small peas. Gradually add the ice water; stir with a fork until the dough follows around the sides of the bowl. Turn dough out on a floured board and roll out to fit a nine inch pie plate. Trim and flute. In a large bowl, mix the sliced peaches with the fourth cup of sugar and the lemon juice. Place in the prepared pie shell. In a bowl combine the brown sugar and three-fourths cup of flour. Cut in the butter or margarine using a pastry blender or two knives. Scatter this crumbly mixture over the fruit in the pie shell. Bake in a hot oven (425 degrees) for ten minutes to set the pastry, reduce the heat to moderate (350 degrees) and continue baking until the peaches are tender. Remove and cool thoroughly before serving.

the ice cream cut into pieces, stirring until melted. Chill in the refrigerator until slightly thickened, but not set. Turn into the cooled almond pie crust. Chill until set. When ready to serve, garnish with whipped cream and nuts.

Nesselrode Pie

One envelope unflavored gelatin
One-fourth cup cold water
Two cups light cream, scalded in
    double boiler
Two eggs, separated
Cooking time: Three minutes
One tablespoon rum
Chilling time: One hour
One-fourth cup sugar
One-fourth cup Nesselrode sauce, mixed
    glazed fruit
One cup macaroon crumbs
One baked pie shell (9 in.)
Chilling time: Three hours, or more
One-half cup heavy cream, whipped
Servings: Six to eight

Sprinkle the gelatin over the cold water in a cup. Add the hot cream; stir until dissolved. Beat the egg yolks slightly; gradually stir in the hot cream mixture. Return to the double boiler; stir until creamy. Cool; add the rum. Chill until slightly thickened. Beat the egg whites until stiff, gradually add the sugar. Fold the meringue, Nesselrode sauce and crumbs into the gelatin mixture. Pour into the pie shell. Chill. When ready to serve, spread cream on top and garnish with unsweetened chocolate shavings or curls.

Butterscotch Parfait Pie

One and one-half cups blanched almonds,
    finely chopped
One egg white
Four tablespoons sugar
Oven temperature: 375 degrees
Baking time: Twelve minutes (about)
Six tablespoons butter
One cup dark brown sugar, packed
One and one-fourth cups water
One egg yolk
One envelope unflavored gelatin
One-fourth cup cold water
One pint vanilla or coffee ice cream
First chilling time: Twenty-five minutes
    (about)
Second chilling time: Twenty-five minutes
One-half cup heavy cream, whipped
Slivered toasted almonds
Serves: Six

Chop the blanched almonds very fine (do not put through a food grinder). In a bowl beat the egg white until stiff; gradually add the sugar. Fold in the almonds. Press the mixture into an oiled pie pan (9 in.), pressing firmly over the bottom and sides. Bake in a moderately hot oven until lightly browned. Remove to a rack; cool. For the filling: In a saucepan melt the butter. Add the sugar and water; heat to boiling. Combine a little of the mixture with the egg yolk and then stir into the mixture in the saucepan. In a cup soften the gelatin in the cold water. Stir into the brown sugar mixture until the gelatin is dissolved. Add

Sweet Sour Rhubarb Pie

Two eggs, separated
One-third cup flour
One pint strawberries, stemmed and
    washed
One teaspoon grated lemon rind
One-eighth teaspoon salt
Two pounds rhubarb, washed
One unbaked pie shell (9 in.)
Oven temperature: 425-350 degrees
Baking time: One hour
Cooling time: Two hours
One and one-half cups sugar
One-eighth teaspoon cream of tartar
Five tablespoons water
Cooking time: Seven minutes (about)
One-eighth teaspoon almond extract
Servings: Six, or more

With a fork mix the egg yolks and flour. Add and crush half of the strawberries. Blend in the lemon rind and salt. Cut the rhubarb into pieces (1 in. long). Place the combined mixture and rhubarb in the pie shell. Bake in a hot oven 15 minutes; reduce to moderate. Continue baking until the rhubarb is tender. Remove to a rack. Cool. Stir the remaining egg whites, sugar, cream of tartar and water in the top of a double boiler until well blended. Place over hot water. Beat with a rotary beater until the icing will hold its shape. Add the almond extract. Spread over the cold pie. Garnish with the remaining strawberries. Cut into wedges; serve.

Deep-Dish Peach Pie

One recipe pastry (2 cups), or one
    package pastry mix
Two tablespoons lemon juice
Six cups sliced fresh peaches
One cup sugar
Three tablespoons flour
One-half teaspoon cinnamon
One-eighth teaspoon ginger
One-eighth teaspoon nutmeg
Two tablespoons butter or margarine
Oven temperature: 425 degrees
Bake: Forty-five minutes
Serves: Six

Roll out three-fourths of the pastry. Line a deep casserole (1½ qts.) with pastry. Sprinkle the lemon juice over the peaches. Mix together the sugar, flour, cinnamon, ginger and nutmeg; mix lightly into the peaches. Spoon the peach mixture into the casserole. Dot with butter. Cover with remaining pastry which has been rolled out. Slit top crust or insert the china bird into crust (keeps juices in pie). Bake in a hot oven until brown on top. Remove to rack. Serve slightly warm with cream.

A FAVORITE RECIPE
Apricot and Banana Pie

Pastry for two crust pie
Two large cans (10 oz. each) apricots, halved, drained
Two or three ripe bananas, sliced (¼ in.)
Juice (¼ cup) from apricots
Juice ½ lemon
One-half teaspoon cinnamon and nutmeg, mixed
Two tablespoons butter
Oven temperature: 400 degrees
Baking time: Forty to fifty minutes
Servings: Six

Line a pie plate (9 in.) with pie pastry. Arrange the apricots over the pastry; cover with the sliced bananas. Sprinkle with the apricot and lemon juice. Sprinkle with cinnamon and nutmeg. Add the top crust, seal the edges. Dot with butter. Bake in a quick oven until a golden brown. Serve cold.

MRS. E. W. SMITH, *Saint James, L.I., N.Y.*

Pie Crust

Two cups sifted flour
One teaspoon salt
Two-thirds cup shortening
Six tablespoons cold water, about
Yield: Pastry for two crust pie

Sift the flour with the salt into a bowl. Add the shortening and cut into the flour with a pastry blender or two knives until the mixture resembles coarsely ground meal. Take a table fork and stir in the cold water, tablespoon by tablespoon until the mixture holds together and follows the fork around the bowl in a ball. Place dough on a floured board and cut in half. Roll each piece out with a floured rolling pin, turning between rolling to maintain the circular form needed for a pie plate. When rolled slightly larger than the pie plate fold pastry over in half and once more into quarters. Lift into pie plate and unfold. Fit loosely into the plate, trimming the crust with a half-inch extension beyond the rim. Fill with fruit sugared and spiced to taste and dot with bits of butter. Roll out remaining dough in same way and lay over the fruit. Trim top crust and tuck under the lower one. Flute all around the edge pressing with the thumbs and forefingers of both hands. If you prefer you may press the edges together with the tines of a fork against the rim. Cut two or three slits in top to permit escape of steam. Bake in a hot oven at 425 degrees for 10 minutes to set the crust; reduce the heat to 375 degrees and continue baking until fruit is tender and crust nicely browned.

If pie shells are wanted fit the dough into two (9 in.) pie plates and flute the edge. Prick pastry all over with a fork to prevent shrinkage during baking.

If possible chill the unbaked shells thoroughly before placing in a hot oven (425 degrees) to bake about 15 minutes or until lightly browned. Remove from oven and cool on rack before filling.

Double Crust Lemon Pie

Pastry for two crust pie
Three-fourths cup sugar
One-third cup cornstarch
One-fourth teaspoon salt
Three eggs
Two tablespoons melted butter or margarine
One can (6 oz.) frozen concentrate for lemonade
One and one-half cups water
Oven temperature: 425 then 350 degrees
Bake: Ten minutes, then fifty minutes
Yield: One pie (10 in.)

Line a pie plate with pastry, roll out the top crust. In a small bowl combine the sugar with the cornstarch and salt. In a large bowl beat the eggs. Gradually add the sugar and cornstarch to the beaten eggs, beating thoroughly after each addition. Add the melted butter and the thawed lemonade concentrate. Stir in the water. Pour into the pastry lined pie plate and top with the pricked pastry. Bake in a hot oven for ten minutes, reduce the temperature to moderate and continue baking for 50 minutes more. Remove pie to rack to cool thoroughly before serving.

Cherry Pie

Two cups sifted flour
One teaspoon salt
Two-thirds cup shortening
One-fourth cup water
Two cans (No. 303) water pack sour red cherries
One-half cup cherry juice
Three tablespoons quick-cooking granular tapioca
Two-thirds cup sugar, or more
One-half teaspoon salt
One-fourth teaspoon almond extract
One teaspoon lemon juice
Two tablespoons butter
Oven temperature: 425 degrees
Bake: Thirty-five minutes
Serves: Six

Sift together into a bowl the flour and salt. Cut in the shortening using a pastry blender or two knives until the mixture resembles coarse meal. Stir in the water with a fork, pressing together to form a ball of dough. Divide into two parts and roll each out into a circle on a floured board. Line a pie plate (9 in.) with one piece. In a bowl mix the drained sour red canned cherries with the cherry juice, tapioca, sugar to taste, salt, almond extract and lemon juice. Mix well and transfer to pastry lined pie plate. Dot with bits of butter. Affix the top crust; trim and flute the edge. Cut vents in top crust for escape of steam. Bake in a hot oven until nicely browned.

Apricot Cream Pie

Pastry for one crust pie
One can (No. 2½) apricots
One egg
One-fourth cup sugar
Three tablespoons flour
One-fourth teaspoon salt
One-half cup dairy sour cream
One-half cup honey
Oven temperature: 425 degrees
Bake: Ten minutes
Oven temperature: 350 degrees
Bake: Thirty minutes
Yield: One pie (9 in.)

Roll out pastry and fit into a pie plate (9 in.), flute the edge. Drain the canned apricots, remove pits and cut into cubes. Arranging in bottom of pastry shell. In a bowl beat the egg. Beat in the sugar, flour and salt. Stir in the dairy sour cream and honey. Pour over the fruit. Bake in a hot oven (425 degrees) and continue baking 30 minutes or until pie is set in center. Remove from oven and cool on rack to room temperature. Chill thoroughly before serving.

Spiced Raisin Pie

One tablespoon cornstarch
Five tablespoons sugar
One-half teaspoon salt
One-half teaspoon cinnamon
One-eighth teaspoon cloves
Two cups raisins, rinsed
One tablespoon lemon juice
One teaspoon grated lemon rind
One tablespoon butter
One and one-half cups water
Cooking time: Five minutes
One recipe pastry
Oven temperature: 425 degrees F.
Baking time: Twenty-five minutes
Servings: Six

Mix the ingredients in a saucepan in the order given. Cook until slightly thickened, stirring. Pour into a pastry-lined pie pan (8 in.). Cover with the top crust; slash in several places. Press edges together. Bake in a hot oven until brown. Remove to a rack. Cool before cutting. Serve with slices of Edam cheese.

Pineapple Pie

One-half cup sugar
Two tablespoons cornstarch
One-fourth teaspoon salt
One can (No. 2) crushed pineapple and juice
One tablespoon lemon juice
One teaspoon grated lemon rind
Pastry for two crust pie
Oven temperature: 425 degrees
Bake: Twenty to thirty minutes
Serves: Four to six

In a saucepan stir together the sugar, cornstarch and salt. Blend in the pineapple, lemon juice and grated lemon rind. Cook, stirring constantly, until mixture clears and thickens. Roll half of the pastry out to fit a pie plate (8 in.). Trim and flute the edge. Pour cooked filling into the shell. Cut strips of dough and arrange over top in lattice fashion. Crimp to edge. Bake in hot oven for 20 to 30 minutes or until pastry is nicely browned.

A FAVORITE RECIPE
Country Prune Pie

Two and one-half cups cooked prunes, pitted
One-half cup chopped blanched almonds
Three-fourths cup packed brown sugar
One-fourth teaspoon salt
One-half teaspoon cinnamon
One cup dairy sour cream
One-third cup liquid from cooked prunes
One egg, beaten light
One pie shell (9 in.) baked
Oven temperature: 450 degrees
Baking time: Thirty minutes
Servings: Six

Cut the cooked prunes into small pieces (¼ in.). In a bowl, combine the prunes, almonds, sugar, salt and cinnamon. Stir in the cream, prune juice and beaten egg. Bake the pie shell, but do not brown. Pour the mixture into the baked pie shell. Bake in a hot oven for 30 minutes. Cool and serve.

MISS C. CURRY, *Bronx, N.Y.*

Pear Pie

Pastry for a double crust
Five or six Anjou or Bosc pears
One cup sugar
One teaspoon grated orange rind
One and one-half tablespoons quick-cooking tapioca
One-fourth cup orange juice
One-half teaspoon nutmeg
Two tablespoons butter
Oven temperature: 425 degrees
Baking time: Forty minutes
Yield: One pie (9 in.)

Line a pie plate (9 in.) with pastry. Roll out top crust. Pare, core and slice the Anjou or Bosc pears into a large bowl. Add the sugar, grated orange rind, tapioca, orange juice and nutmeg and mix well. Transfer to pastry lined pie plate and dot with butter. Affix top crust, seal and flute edge. Bake in a hot oven for forty minutes or until crust is delicately browned and pears are tender. Permit to cool for at least an hour before serving.

Fresh Peach Pie

Pastry for two crust pie
Four cups thinly sliced peeled fresh peaches
Three-fourths cup sugar
Three tablespoons quick-cooking tapioca
One-fourth teaspoon salt
Two tablespoons butter or margarine
Oven temperature: 425 degrees
Bake: Thirty-five to forty minutes
Serves: Six

Roll half pastry out into a circle to fit a pie plate (9 in.). In a bowl combine the thinly sliced peeled fresh peaches with the sugar, tapioca and salt, mixing well. Transfer to the pastry lined pie plate and dot with butter or margarine. Roll out remaining pastry for top crust, cutting vents for escape of steam, trimming and fluting edge. Bake in a hot oven for thirty-five to forty minutes or until crust is nicely browned. Remove to rack to cool to room temperature before serving. Good topped off with vanilla ice cream.

Short Peach Pie

One cup sifted flour
One-half teaspoon salt
One-half teaspoon baking powder
One-third cup shortening
One egg
One teaspoon lemon juice
One can (No. 2½) peach halves, drained
Two tablespoons sugar
One tablespoon flour
Three-fourths teaspoon cinnamon
Two tablespoons butter or margarine
Oven temperature: 400 degrees
Bake: Thirty minutes
Servings: Six

Sift the flour, salt and baking powder together into a bowl. Cut in the shortening with a pastry blender or two knives until mixture resembles coarse meal. Stir in the unbeaten egg and lemon juice. Turn dough out on a floured board and roll out into a circle to fit a pie plate (9 in.). Fit into the pie plate, trimming and fluting the edge. The fluted edge may be pressed down toward the bottom crust with this pie as it is relatively shallow. Cut the drained peach halves into four pieces and arrange over the bottom crust. In a bowl stir the sugar, flour and cinnamon together. Cut in the butter until crumbly and sprinkle over the fruit. Bake in a quick oven until pastry is browned. Serve warm or chilled.

Rhubarb Cream Pie

Pastry for two crust pie
One cup sugar
Two tablespoons flour
One-eighth teaspoon salt
Two eggs, beaten
Three cups rhubarb, cut in ½ inch pieces
Oven temperature: 425 then 325 degrees
Bake: Forty minutes
Yield: One pie (9 in.)

Line a pie plate (9 in.) with pastry. In a bowl combine the sugar, flour and salt. Add the beaten eggs and rhubarb. Pour into the pastry lined pie plate and cover with top crust or lattice arrangement of pastry strips. Slit the solid crust to allow steam to escape. Bake in 425 degree oven for 10 minutes, reduce the heat to 325 degrees and bake for 30 minutes more. Remove from oven to rack to cool before serving.

Pecan Pie

One-fourth cup butter or margarine
One cup sugar
One-half cup corn syrup
Three eggs, well beaten
One-fourth teaspoon salt
One teaspoon vanilla
One cup chopped pecans
One unbaked pastry shell (9 in.)
Oven temperature: 400 then 350 degrees
Bake: Forty minutes, about
Serves: Six

In a saucepan melt the butter or margarine. Remove from the heat and blend in the sugar and corn syrup. Add the well beaten eggs, salt, vanilla and chopped pecans. Pour into the unbaked pastry shell and bake in a quick oven for 10 minutes to set the crust. Reduce the heat to moderate and continue baking for 30 minutes more. Remove from oven and allow to cool thoroughly before serving.

Raisin Cranberry Pie

One and one-half cups seedless raisins
Two cups fresh cranberries
One and one-half cups water
Three tablespoons cornstarch
One and one-fourth cups sugar
One-half teaspoon salt
Cook: Five to ten minutes
One-fourth teaspoon almond extract
One tablespoon butter or margarine
Pastry for two-crust pie
Oven temperature: 425 degrees
Bake: Thirty minutes, about
Serves: Six or more

Rinse the raisins and cranberries and place in a saucepan with the water. Stir the cornstarch into the sugar with the salt. Blend into the fruit mixture. Heat to boiling point and cook, stirring constantly for three or four minutes or until thickened and smooth. Remove from heat and stir in the almond extract and butter. Let cool slightly before pouring into a pastry lined pie plate (9 in.). Affix top crust and bake in a hot oven until crust is crisp and nicely browned.

Pretzel Crumb Crust

One and one-half cups pretzel crumbs
One-fourth cup sugar
One-fourth cup softened butter or margarine
Two tablespoons water
Oven temperature: 400 degrees
Baking time: Ten minutes
Yield: One pie shell (9 in.)

Crumble pretzels into fairly fine crumbs with a rolling pin. In a bowl blend the crumbs with the sugar and with the softened butter or margarine, using a pastry blender or your fingers as you prefer. Stir in the water; mix thoroughly. Press firmly against the bottom and sides of a pie plate (9 in.). Bake in a quick oven for 10 minutes. Remove and cool crust before filling.

ening in coarse particles the size of navy beans. Sprinkle the water, a tablespoon at a time, over the mixture. Work lightly and quickly with a fork until the dough forms a mass that leaves the bowl clean. Turn out on a piece of waxed paper; with the hands shape into a ball. Roll two-thirds of the dough out of a floured board into a circle (11 in.). Fit loosely in a pie plate (9 in.); fill as desired. Roll out the remaining dough for the top crust.

Lemon Apple Pie

One recipe pastry (2 cups)
Four cups apples, peeled and cored
One cup sugar
Two tablespoons flour
One-eighth teaspoon nutmeg
One-eighth teaspoon salt
Grated rind and juice of a lemon
Oven temperature: 400 degrees
Baking time: Fifty minutes (about)
Serves: Six, or more

Roll out two-thirds of pastry on a floured board to fit a pie pan (9 in.). Put apples through coarsest blade of food grinder, mixing the juice and apples together or chop the apples fine with a knife. Mix with the combined remaining ingredients. Pour into pie shell. Arrange slit top crust on apple mixture; sealing edges of pastry. Bake in a quick oven until brown on top. Remove to a rack. Serve with a wedge of cheese.

Apple Pie

Spice or plain pastry dough for two crust pie
Six or seven cups sliced apples (about 2-2½ lbs.)
One cup sugar
Four teaspoons flour
One-half teaspoon cinnamon
One-fourth teaspoon nutmeg
One tablespoon lemon juice
One teaspoon grated lemon rind
Three tablespoons butter or margarine
Oven temperature: 450-350 degrees
Baking time: One hour
Servings: Six

Line a pie plate (9 in.) with pastry. Roll out dough for upper crust; set aside. Half-fill the pie shell with sliced apples placed close together. Mix the sugar, flour, spices, lemon juice and rind. Sprinkle half the sugar mixture over the apples. Dot with half the butter or margarine. Add enough apples to fill the pastry liberally. Sprinkle with the remaining sugar mixture; dot with the rest of the butter. Cover with the top crust. Slash in several places to allow the steam to escape. Bake in a very hot oven 10 minutes; reduce the heat to moderate. Bake until the apples are tender and the crust is brown. Remove to a rack. Serve warm or cold.

Pastry

Two cups sifted all-purpose flour
Three-fourths teaspoon salt
Two-thirds cup shortening
Seven tablespoons ice water (about)
Yield: Two crusts (9 in.)

Sift the flour and salt into a bowl. Cut in half the shortening with a pastry blender or two knives to the consistency of cornmeal. Cut in the remaining short-

Mock Apple Pie

Two cups sugar
Two cups apple juice, water or cider
Two teaspoons cream of tartar
Cooking time: Fifteen minutes
One tablespoon grated lemon rind
Two tablespoons lemon juice
Four tablespoons butter or margarine
One teaspoon cinnamon
One-sixteenth teaspoon salt
One recipe pastry (2 cups)
Forty saltine crackers, broken coarsely
Oven temperature: 425 degrees
Baking time: Twenty-five minutes
Serves: Six, or more

In a saucepan cook the sugar, juice and cream of tartar for 15 minutes. Remove; add rind and lemon juice, butter, cinnamon and salt. Line a pie pan (9 in.) with pastry. Break the saltines into coarse pieces, filling the pastry-lined pie pan. Pour the hot sugar mixture over the crackers. Cover with pastry; seal edges. Cut a few gashes on top to allow steam to escape. Bake in a hot oven until golden on top. Remove to rack: Serve.

Crumb Topped Apple Mince Pie

One and one-half cups prepared mince-
    meat
One unbaked pie shell (9 in.)
One-third cup flour
One-half cup brown sugar
Three tablespoons butter or margarine
Three medium-sized green apples
Oven temperature: 400 degrees
Bake: Thirty to thirty-five minutes
Serves: Six

Spread the prepared mincemeat over the bottom of the unbaked pie shell. In a bowl stir together the flour and brown sugar. Cut in the butter or margarine until the mixture is crumblike in texture. Peel and core the apples; slice. Arrange apple slices over the mincemeat. Sprinkle crumbs over all. Bake in a quick oven for thirty to thirty-five minutes until apples are tender and crumbs lightly browned. Good served while slightly warm.

Apple Pecan Pie

Three eggs, slightly beaten
One-half cup brown or white sugar
One-fourth teaspoon salt
One cup light corn syrup
One unbaked pastry shell (9 in.), chilled
One cup fresh or canned applesauce
Two cups pecan halves
Oven temperature: 425-350 degrees
Baking time: Forty-five minutes
One-half cup heavy cream, whipped
Serves: Eight

In a bowl mix the beaten eggs, sugar, salt and corn syrup. On the bottom of the unbaked pastry shell spread the applesauce. Pour the egg mixture over the applesauce. Arrange the nuts on top. Bake in a hot oven for 10 minutes. Reduce the temperature to moderate and continue baking for another 35 minutes. Remove to a rack. Serve plain or with whipped cream.

Danish Pastries

One-fourth cup sugar
One-fourth cup butter
One teaspoon salt
One cup milk, scalded
Two packages active dry yeast
One-third cup warm water
One egg, beaten
One-fourth teaspoon vanilla
One teaspoon grated lemon rind
Three and one-half cups sifted flour
First rising time: One and one-half
     hours, about
Three-fourths cup butter
Second rising time: Twenty minutes
One cup chopped walnuts
One cup sugar
Two teaspoons cinnamon
Third rising time: Thirty minutes
Oven temperature: 375 degrees
Bake: Fifteen to twenty minutes
Yield: Three to five dozen

Measure the fourth cup each of sugar and butter into a bowl and add the salt and scalded milk, stirring to completely blend. Sprinkle the yeast over the warm, not hot, water in a cup and let stand to dissolve. Add the beaten egg, vanilla and grated lemon rind to the milk mixture and when it is lukewarm stir in the dissolved yeast. Beat in one and one-half cups of sifted flour. Blend in the remaining flour gradually to make a moderately stiff dough. Turn out on a floured board and knead lightly until smooth and elastic. Place in a greased bowl, turning dough over once to grease the top. Cover with a cloth and place in a warm spot to rise. When dough has doubled in bulk roll out on floured board to one-fourth inch in thickness. Dot center third of the dough with half the butter cut in small pieces.

Fold one end of dough over to cover the butter. Dot this with remaining butter, folding over last third to cover this layer. Press edges together firmly. Turn the dough one-fourth way around on the board and roll out to one-fourth inch in thickness. Fold each end to center; fold to make four layers. Turn one-fourth way around. Roll out again and fold three times. Cover with a cloth and let rise for twenty minutes. Combine the finely chopped walnuts, sugar and cinnamon.

To form the pastries roll dough out to one-fourth inch in thickness and cut as desired. Two or four inch squares of the dough may be cut from each corner almost to the center and have each alternating point pressed firmly to the center. Roll carefully in the sugar and nut mixture to coat.

Place on a piece of brown paper cut to fit a baking sheet. Let rise for thirty minutes before baking in a moderately hot oven for fifteen to twenty minutes. Remove to racks to cool. Vary the shaping of the pastries to suit your taste making coils or figure eights or twists from strips of the dough.

Baked Peach Dumplings with Sauce

Two cups sifted flour
Four teaspoons baking powder
One-half teaspoon salt
One-fourth cup shortening
Two tablespoons butter
Two-thirds cup milk (about)
One-half cup sugar, mixed with
One-eighth teaspoon nutmeg
Eight whole peaches, peeled
One-half cup water
Oven temperature: 450 degrees
Baking time: 20 minutes (about)
Serves: Eight

In a bowl, sift the flour, baking powder and salt. Blend in the shortening and butter to the consistency of corn meal. Add enough milk to make a stiff dough. On a floured board, roll out (⅛ in. thick) into a rectangle. Cut into strips with a pastry wheel. Sprinkle the sugar and nutmeg over fresh whole peeled peaches in a bowl; let stand a few minutes. Place three pastry strips around each peach, tucking the ends under the peach. Place in a buttered baking dish. Pour one-half cup water in the bottom. Bake in a hot oven until peaches are tender. Remove and serve immediately with raspberry sauce.

RASPBERRY SAUCE

One box frozen raspberries, defrosted
One tablespoon lemon juice
One tablespoon cornstarch, mixed with
One cup cold water
Cooking time: Five minutes
Yield: Two cups (about)

To make the sauce: Combine all ingredients in a saucepan; cook until thickened. Serve with peach dumplings.

Peach and Raspberry Dumplings

Two cups sifted flour
One-half teaspoon salt
Four teaspoons baking powder
One tablespoon sugar
One-half cup shortening
Three-fourths cup milk, about
Two tablespoons sugar
One-fourth teaspoon nutmeg
One-fourth teaspoon grated lemon rind
One can (No. 2½) peach halves, drained
Five tablespoons raspberry jam
Oven temperature: 400 degrees
Bake: Twenty-five to thirty minutes
Yield: Five

Sift together into a bowl the flour, salt, baking powder and tablespoon of sugar. Cut in the shortening until the mixture resembles coarse meal. Stir in enough of the milk with a fork to form a stiff dough. Transfer to a floured board and roll out into a rectangle (12 x 18 inches). Cut into five six inch squares. In a cup stir together the sugar, nutmeg and grated lemon rind. Place a drained peach half on each square of dough. Sprinkle with some of the sugar mixture. Place a tablespoonful of raspberry jam in each peach hollow, top with another peach half, sprinkle with remaining sugar mixture.

Crimp edges of the dough together around the fruit and place on a baking sheet. Bake in a quick oven until nicely browned. Remove and serve cooled to room temperature or while still warm with milk or cream poured over top.

Peach Cobbler

Three pounds ripe peaches
One cup sugar
One-fourth teaspoon salt
Two tablespoons butter or margarine
One and one-half cups sifted flour
Three-fourths teaspoon salt
Three teaspoons baking powder
One tablespoon sugar
One-third cup shortening
One egg
One-half cup milk
Oven temperature: 425 degrees
Bake: Forty minutes
Serves: Eight

Peel and slice the ripe peaches into a bowl. Add the sugar and fourth teaspoon of salt and mix well. Transfer to a baking pan (9 x 13 x 2 in.). Dot fruit with the butter or margarine. Sift together into a bowl the flour, salt, baking powder and tablespoon of sugar. Cut in the shortening using two knives or a pastry blender. In a small bowl beat the egg; add the milk. Add combination to the dry ingredients and stir together. Drop mixture by tablespoonfuls over the fruit and bake in a hot oven for thirty minutes or until browned. Cover with a piece of foil and bake ten minutes more. Serve while still warm with cream if desired.

Raisin Applesauce Cobbler

Four cups applesauce
One cup seedless raisins, rinsed
One-fourth to one-half cup sugar
One-fourth teaspoon allspice
One-eighth teaspoon salt
Oven temperature: 350 degrees
Bake: ten minutes
One-fourth cup shortening
One-half cup sugar
One egg, beaten
One-half teaspoon vanilla
One-half cup milk
One and one-fourth cups sifted
     all-purpose flour
Two teaspoons baking powder
One-half teaspoon salt
Bake: Forty minutes
Serves: Six, or more

Combine the applesauce, drained raisins, sugar, allspice and salt in a bowl. Pour into a greased baking dish (12 x 8 x 2 in.). Place in a moderate oven while preparing the batter. Cream the shortening and remaining sugar together in a mixing bowl. Stir in the beaten egg, vanilla and milk. Add the sifted dry ingredients and stir just enough to blend. Remove the baking dish from the oven and place the batter over the hot applesauce and raisins. Return to the oven and bake until the crust is done thoroughly and browned on top. Serve hot or cold, plain or with cream.

Apple Cranberry Crisp Pie

One can (1 lb. 4 oz.) sliced apples
One cup canned whole cranberry sauce
One-half cup brown sugar
One tablespoon flour
One-half teaspoon nutmeg
One-half teaspoon cinnamon
One unbaked pastry shell (9 in.)
One-half cup brown sugar
Three-fourths cup flour
One-fourth teaspoon salt
One-fourth cup butter or margarine
Oven temperature: 400 degrees
Bake: Thirty-five minutes
Servings: Six

In a bowl combine the canned sliced apples, cranberry sauce, half cup of brown sugar, tablespoon of flour, nutmeg and cinnamon. Mix well. Pour into the unbaked pastry shell. In a bowl, stir together the second measure of brown sugar, flour and salt. Cut in the butter or margarine with a pastry blender or two knives until crumbly. Scatter over the fruit mixture in the pie shell. Bake in a quick oven for thirty-five minutes. Good served while slightly warm with a spoonful of vanilla ice cream.

French Apple Cream Pie

One cup brown sugar
Three tablespoons flour
Three-fourths teaspoon cinnamon
One-half teaspoon salt
One unbaked pastry shell (9 in.)
Five large apples
One cup heavy cream
Oven temperature: 425 degrees
Baking time: 40 minutes (about)
Serves: Six

In a bowl mix the sugar, flour, cinnamon and salt. Sprinkle half the mixture on the bottom of an unbaked pastry shell. Arrange the pared, cored and sliced apples over the dry mixture. Sprinkle the remaining mixture over the apples. Pour one-half cup of cream over the top. Bake in a hot oven until the apples are tender. Remove to rack to cool. Whip the remaining cream; spoon over the pie; serve.

Sour Cream Apple Pie

Two-thirds cup brown sugar
One-fourth teaspoon cinnamon
One-eighth teaspoon nutmeg
One-fourth teaspoon salt
Two tablespoons cornstarch
Four cups pared and sliced tart apples
One unbaked pastry shell (9 in.)
One cup dairy sour cream
One-fourth cup butter
Three tablespoons sugar
Three tablespoons brown sugar
One-half teaspoon cinnamon
One-half cup flour
Oven temperature: 400 degrees
Bake: Thirty-five minutes
Yield: One pie (9 in.)

In a bowl, stir together the brown sugar, cinnamon, nutmeg, salt and cornstarch. Mix well. Alternate layers of the sliced tart apples and the sugar spice mix in the unbaked pastry shell. Cover with the dairy sour cream. In a saucepan, melt the butter or margarine. Stir in the sugar, cinnamon and flour and mix well. Sprinkle over the sour cream. Bake in a quick oven until apples are tender.

Crunchy Topped Apple Pie

Five apples, peeled and sliced
   (Six cups sliced apples)
One-half cup brown sugar
One-fourth teaspoon cinnamon
Two tablespoons lemon juice
One unbaked pastry pie shell (9 in.)
One-half cup flour
One-third cup brown sugar
One-eighth teaspoon nutmeg
One-fourth cup butter or margarine
One-half cup slightly crushed corn flakes
Oven temperature: 425 then 350 degrees
Baking time: Forty minutes, about
Servings: Six

In a bowl combine the peeled, thinly sliced apples with the brown sugar, cinnamon and lemon juice. Transfer to the unbaked pastry pie shell. In a bowl mix the flour, brown sugar and nutmeg. Cut in the butter or margarine using a pastry blender or two knives. Stir in the slightly crushed corn flakes. Scatter over the top of the sliced apples in the pie shell and bake in a hot oven (425 degrees) for 10 minutes. Reduce heat to moderate (350 degrees) and continue baking until apples are tender.

Three-Inch Apple Pies

One cup canned apple sauce
One-third cup flaked coconut
One-fourth cup seedless raisins
One-third cup sugar
Two tablespoons lemon juice
One teaspoon grated lemon rind
Two cups sifted all purpose flour
One teaspoon salt
Two-thirds cup shortening
Six tablespoons cold water, about
Oven temperature: 400 degrees
Bake: Twenty minutes
Yield: Two dozen

In a bowl stir together the apple sauce, flaked coconut, raisins, sugar, lemon juice and grated rind. Set aside. In a bowl combine the flour with the salt. Cut in half the shortening with two knives or a pastry blender until it has the consistency of coarse meal. Cut in second half until the size of small peas. Gradually stir in the water until the dough holds together and follows the fork around the bowl. Turn dough out on a floured board, half at a time and roll out to one-eighth inch in thickness. Cut circles of pastry with three-inch cutter and spoon a rounded teaspoonful

of the apple sauce mixture on each. Top each with second circle of dough and press together all around the edge with the tines of a fork. Place on a baking sheet and bake in a quick oven for 20 minutes or until pastry starts to brown. Remove to racks to cool.

German Apple Pie

Four medium-sized pie apples
One unbaked pie shell (9 in.)
One teaspoon cinnamon
One-half cup sugar, or more
Two eggs
One-half cup heavy cream
One tablespoon butter
Oven temperature: 375 degrees
Baking time: One hour
Servings: Six

Pare, core and slice the apples into thin pieces. Arrange in an orderly fashion (overlapping) in the bottom of an unbaked pie shell (9 in.). Sprinkle with the cinnamon and the sugar, varying the latter depending upon the tartness of the apples. In a bowl, beat the eggs, stir in the heavy cream. Pour carefully over the fruit, spreading evenly over all. Dot the top with small bits of butter. Bake in a moderately hot oven for about one hour or until apples are tender and top well browned. Remove to rack and serve while still slightly warm or thoroughly chilled.

Upside-Down Apple Pie

Two tablespoons butter
Two-thirds cup dark brown sugar
One-half cup pecan halves
Pastry for two crust pie
Six cups peeled, sliced apples
Four tablespoons lemon juice
One-third cup dark brown sugar
One-half teaspoon cinnamon
One tablespoon flour
One-half teaspoon nutmeg
One-fourth teaspoon salt
Oven temperature: 450 then 350 degrees
Bake: Forty to forty-five minutes
Servings: Six, or more

Spread the soft butter over the bottom and sides of a pie plate (9 in.). Sprinkle the brown sugar in an even layer over the butter. Arrange pecan halves in a pattern on top and press into the brown sugar. Cover this with a layer of pastry and proceed to make the apple pie. In a bowl combine the sliced apples with lemon juice. In a bowl mix the one-third cup of brown sugar with the flour, cinnamon, nutmeg and salt. Stir mixture into the apples, mix well. Place apples in pastry-lined pie plate; top with second layer of pastry. Trim and flute crust as usual. Prick crust with fork in several places to permit steam to escape. Bake in a 450-degree oven for ten minutes to set the crust, then reduce heat to 350 degrees and continue baking until the apples are tender. Remove from oven and invert upon a serving dish.

Cherry Strudel

One and one-half cups sifted flour
One-fourth teaspoon salt
One tablespoon salad oil
One egg, beaten with
One-third cup warm water
Kneading time: Fifteen minutes
Standing time: Thirty minutes
One can (No. 2) sour pitted cherries, drained
One-half cup sugar
One-half cup flour
One teaspoon almond extract
One-fourth cup butter or margarine, melted
One-half cup fine bread crumbs
One-half cup chopped pecans
One-half cup brown sugar
Oven temperature: 400 degrees
Baking time: Thirty minutes
Serves: Eight

Make a dough of the first five ingredients. Turn the dough out on a floured board. Knead with both hands until the dough comes away clean, elastic and silky to touch. Then throw or beat dough against the board until it blisters (about 100 times with great force). Cover with a warm bowl; keep in a warm place for 30 minutes.

Prepare the filling: In a bowl combine the drained cherries with the sugar, flour and almond extract. Cover the table with a small white cloth; flour the cloth slightly. Place the dough on the cloth. Pull out and stretch the dough very gently to the thickness of tissue paper, working around the dough and pulling easily from underneath. Stretch the dough a little larger than a two-foot square. Allow to dry slightly and then spread with some of the melted butter. With a scissors trim off the thick edges of the dough.

Sprinkle the bread crumbs, nuts and brown sugar over the dough. Spoon the

cherry mixture along one end of the dough. Let the dough roll by lifting the cloth high with both hands. Roll onto a greased baking sheet. Twist roll to form a crescent. Brush with melted butter. Bake in a quick oven until brown and crisp. Remove to a rack. Spread top again with melted butter and dust with confectioners' sugar. Serve warm or cold.

Apple Strudel filling: Four cups thinly sliced apples mixed with one cup sugar, one-half cup raisins, one-half cup chopped walnuts, one tablespoon grated lemon rind and one teaspoon cinnamon. Spread the paper-thin dough with melted butter or margarine and one-half cup fine bread crumbs. Then proceed as directed in the above Cherry Strudel Recipe.

Apple Dumplings with Ginger Crust

Three cups sifted flour
One-fourth cup non-fat dry milk (optional)
One-half teaspoon salt
One teaspoon ginger
One teaspoon cinnamon
One teaspoon cloves
One-fourth teaspoon nutmeg
One cup shortening
Ten tablespoons ice water (about)
Four large apples, peeled and cored
One-half cup sugar
One teaspoon cinnamon
Two tablespoons butter or margarine

Syrup Mixture

One cup sugar
Two cups water
Three tablespoons butter or margarine
Boil: Three minutes
Oven temperature: 425 degrees
Bake: Forty minutes (about)
Serves: Four

In a bowl sift the flour, non-fat dry milk, salt and spices. With a blender cut

in one-half cup of the shortening to the consistency of cornmeal. The other half cup of shortening is cut into the mixture in coarse pieces. With a fork work in the ice water a tablespoon at a time. Shape into a ball. Divide into four pieces. Roll out each piece of pastry into a square (9 in.). Place apple on each square of pastry. Fill cavity with sugar and cinnamon mixture. Dot with butter. Bring opposite points of pastry up over the apple. Overlap; moisten and seal. Place in a shallow baking dish. Boil sugar, water and butter. Pour mixture in bottom of dish. Bake in a hot oven until crust is crisp and brown. Serve with any of the following sauces.

Lemon Sauce

Mix one tablespoon cornstarch, one-half cup sugar and one-fourth teaspoon salt. Stir in one cup cold water; cook over low heat until clear. Beat in one tablespoon finely grated lemon rind, three tablespoons lemon juice and two tablespoons butter. Serve hot. Yield: One cup.

Fluffy Sauce

Beat two egg yolks and one cup confectioners' sugar until fluffy. Beat in three tablespoons cognac or Spanish sherry. Fold in one-half cup heavy cream that has been whipped. Yield: One cup.

Raisin Orange Sauce

In a heavy saucepan mix two beaten egg yolks, one-fourth cup sugar, one tablespoon grated orange rind, one-half cup orange juice and 2 tablespoons rum. Cook over low heat until mixture coats a spoon, stirring constantly. Add one-half cup raisins. Cool slightly in pan of cold water. Fold in two stiffly beaten egg whites. Serve. Yield: One cup.

Apricot Cobbler

Two cups sifted flour
Three teaspoons baking powder
One-half teaspoon salt
Four tablespoons butter or shortening
Three-fourths cup milk (about)
Two cans (No. 2½ each) whole apricots,
    peeled, pitted; well-drained
Four tablespoons brown sugar
One-fourth teaspoon ginger
Four tablespoons cognac
Two tablespoons butter or margarine
Oven temperature: 425 degrees
Baking time: Thirty minutes (about)
One cup heavy cream, whipped, or dairy
    sour cream
Serves: Six

In a bowl sift the flour, baking powder and salt. With a blender or two knives cut in the butter until the mixture is the consistency of cornmeal. Stir in the milk gradually to make a smooth dough. Turn out on a floured board. Roll out two-thirds of the dough into a rectangle (10 x 8 in.). Fit into a shallow baking dish (8 x 6 in.); crimping the edge of the dough. Arrange the apricots in the dish. Spread the combined brown sugar, ginger and cognac over apricots. Dot with butter. Roll out remaining dough (7 x 5 in.). Slit the dough; lay on top of apricots. Bake in a hot oven until brown on top. Remove to rack. Cut into squares and serve hot with whipped or dairy sour cream.

Cranberry Apple Cobbler

Two cups fresh cranberries
Five medium-sized tart apples
One and one-fourth cups sugar
One-half teaspoon salt
Two and one-half tablespoons quick-
    cooking tapioca
One teaspoon vanilla
Two tablespoons butter or margarine
One cup sifted flour
One-half teaspoon salt
One-third cup shortening
Three tablespoons cold water, about
Oven temperature: 425 degrees
Bake: Fifteen minutes
Oven temperature: 350 degrees
Bake: Thirty minutes
Serves: Six, or more

In a bowl combine the washed and drained cranberries, the peeled and sliced apples, sugar, salt, tapioca and vanilla. Mix well together and transfer to a baking pan (10 x 6 x 2 in.). Dot with butter or margarine. Prepare a pastry topping by sifting the flour and salt together into a bowl. Cut in half the shortening until as fine as cornmeal, cut in second half until size of small peas. Add enough cold water to bind dough together so it follows a fork around the bowl. Roll dough out on a floured board into a rectangle that will cover the friut in the baking pan. Cut vents for escape of steam and crimp dough to the edge of the pan. Bake in a hot oven for fifteen minutes to set the dough. Reduce heat to moderate and continue baking until crust is brown and apples tender. Serve warm or cold.

Citrus Cobbler

Two large grapefruit
Four medium-sized oranges
One cup sugar
One-eighth teaspoon salt
Two tablespoons butter
Two cups sifted flour
One-half teaspoon salt
Four teaspoons baking powder
One tablespoon sugar
One-third cup shortening
One egg
One cup milk
Oven temperature: 425 degrees
Baking time: Thirty minutes
Servings: Nine

Peel and section the grapefruit and oranges, taking care to remove as much of the membrane as possible. Mix in a bowl with the sugar and salt. Transfer to a greased baking dish (7½ x 12 x 2 in.) and top with bits of butter. Sift into a bowl the flour, salt, baking powder and sugar. Using a pastry blender or two knives cut the shortening into the dry ingredients until the mixture resembles corn meal. In a small bowl beat the egg; add the milk. Stir into the dry mixture. Spoon over the fruit in the baking dish. Bake in a hot oven for 30 minutes or until a golden brown. Serve warm in dessert dishes with a whipped cream topping if you wish.

A FAVORITE RECIPE
Peach Lexington

Two cups flour, sifted with
One-fourth teaspoon baking powder
Two tablespoons sugar
One-half cup butter or margarine
Twelve peach halves (canned) drained
One cup sugar
One tablespoon cinnamon, or less,
Oven temperature: 400 degrees
Baking time: Fifteen minutes
One cup heavy cream, beaten with
Two egg yolks, beaten until frothy
Baking time: Thirty minutes
Servings: Six

Sift the flour, baking powder and sugar into a bowl. Add the butter, cutting into the flour until mealy. Press an even layer of the mixture into the bottom and sides of a layer cake pan (9 in.). Place 12 peach halves, drained over the mixture, cut side up, in pan. Sprinkle the sugar and cinnamon over peaches. Place in a hot oven and bake for 15 minutes. Remove from the oven and pour the cream mixed with the egg yolks over the peaches. Return to oven and continue baking. Serve warm or cold.

MRS. G. B. DWYER, *Hartford, Conn.*

Coffee Meringue Tarts

One cup sifted flour
One-half teaspoon salt
One-third cup shortening
Three tablespoons cold water, or less
Oven temperature: 425 degrees
Bake: Ten to fifteen minutes
Two-thirds cup sugar
Five tablespoons cornstarch
One-half teaspoon salt
One cup milk
One and one-half cups strong brewed
 coffee
Cook: Ten minutes, about
Two egg yolks
Cook: Two minutes
Two egg whites
One-eighth teaspoon salt
Four tablespoons sugar
Oven temperature: 325 degrees
Bake: Twenty minutes, about
Yield: Six tarts

Sift the flour into a bowl with the half teaspoon of salt. Cut in half the shortening until mixture resembles coarse meal. Cut in second half of shortening until size of small peas. Stir in the cold water with a fork using just enough to hold dough together. It will follow fork around the bowl. Turn out on a floured board and divide into six parts. Roll each out into a circle about five inches across. Fit into tart of muffin pans, pressing against the sides and crimping the edge. Prick all over with a fork and bake in a hot oven until crisp and lightly browned. Remove from oven and cool. Prepare the filling by stirring the sugar, cornstarch and salt together in the upper half of a double boiler. Gradually blend in the milk, stirring smooth, then the strong coffee. Cook over hot water, stirring constantly, until thickened. Beat the egg yolks in a bowl, stir in a little of the cooked mixture and return combination to the saucepan. Cook, stirring, for two minutes. Remove from heat and cool to room temperature before spooning into the baked tart shells. Prepare the meringue by beating the egg whites in a bowl with the salt until foamy, gradually beat in the sugar until thick and glossy. Spoon over the filled tarts taking care to seal with the pastry all around the edge. Bake in a moderately slow oven until a golden brown. Cool at room temperature. Chill further in the refrigerator if desired before serving.

Coconut Rum Tarts

Pastry for two crust pie
Three eggs
One-fourth cup rum
One-half cup brown sugar
One-eighth teaspoon nutmeg
One-eighth teaspoon cinnamon
One cup flaked coconut
Oven temperature: 375 degrees
Bake: Twenty minutes
Yield: Twelve, or more

Prepare the pastry for two crust pie and roll out. Cut circles of dough that measure four inches across. Cut double thickness of aluminum foil the same measure and place a circle of dough on each. Fold up the foil on four sides and pinch corners of dough together with foil to form a shallow square tart. Place these on a baking sheet. In a bowl beat the eggs well and stir in the rum, brown sugar, nutmeg and cinnamon, mixing well. Add the flaked coconut and spoon into the tart shells, filling about two thirds. Bake in a moderately hot oven for 20 minutes or until lightly browned. Remove from oven, peeling off the foil and permit to cool on a rack. If desired serve with a topping of rum flavored whipped cream and toasted coconut.

Lemon Fruit Tarts

One cup sifted flour
One-half teaspoon salt
One-third cup shortening
Two or three tablespoons ice cold water
Chill: Thoroughly
Oven temperature: 450 degrees
Bake: Ten to twelve minutes
One-fourth cup sugar
One tablespoon cornstarch
One-eighth teaspoon salt
One can (1 lb.) fruit cocktail
Cook: Five minutes, about
One egg yolk
Cook: Two to three minutes
One tablespoon lemon juice
One-fourth teaspoon grated lemon rind
Three maraschino cherries
Chill: Thoroughly
Yield: Six

Sift flour and salt into a bowl. Cut in half the shortening until the mixture resembles coarse meal. Cut in second half of shortening until the size of small peas. Stir in just enough water to hold dough together. It will follow the fork around the bowl. Turn out on a floured board and roll out quite thin. Cut pastry into circles and fit into six tart shells or muffin pans. Crimp the edge and prick all over with the tines of a fork. Chill thoroughly and bake in a very hot oven for 10 minutes or more until lightly browned. Remove from oven and allow to cool to room temperature. Prepare the filling by stirring sugar, cornstarch and salt together in a saucepan. Drain the syrup from the canned fruit cocktail and stir one-half cup into the saucepan. Set fruit aside for later use. Cook the sugar and syrup mixture, stirring constantly over low heat, until clear and thickened. Beat the egg yolk in a small dish with a fork; stir into the cooked mixture and continue cooking, stirring constantly, for two or three minutes. Remove from heat and add the lemon juice and grated lemon rind. Add the well drained fruit. Mix well and spoon into the baked tart shells. Garnish top of each with a maraschino cherry half and chill completely before serving.

Rhubarb Tart with Hard Sauce

Pastry for two crust pie
Four cups one-inch cuts fresh rhubarb
 (2 lbs.)
One-half cup sugar, or more
Oven temperature: 425 degrees
Bake: Forty minutes
One-half cup butter
Two-thirds cup brown sugar
Two teaspoons lemon juice
Servings: Six

Line a pie plate (9 in.) with pastry. Fill with cut rhubarb. Sprinkle with the half cup of sugar, using somewhat more if desired. Cut pastry into strips and arrange a lattice top. Bake in a hot oven until lightly browned. Remove from oven and serve at once. To make the sauce cream the butter in a bowl and gradually beat in the brown sugar. Stir in the lemon juice and serve spoonfuls atop each portion of the hot pie.

Banana Cream Tarts

Pastry for two crust pie (your own or
 package mix)
Chill: Thoroughly
Oven temperature: 425 degrees
Bake: Fifteen minutes, about
One-half cup sugar
One-fourth cup cornstarch
One-fourth teaspoon salt
Two cups milk
Cook: Fifteen minutes, about
Three egg yolks
Cook: One minute
One tablespoon butter or margarine
One-half teaspoon vanilla
One-half pint heavy cream
One teaspoon sugar, or more
Three medium-sized ripe bananas
Yield: Eight

Prepare the pastry and roll out. Fit into or over tart shells (3 inch). Prick all over with a fork and chill thoroughly. Bake in a hot oven until lightly browned. Cool on a rack. Make the filling by combining the sugar, cornstarch and salt in the upper half of a double boiler. Gradually stir in the milk. Place over boiling water and cook, stirring constantly, until thickened and smooth. Continue cooking, stirring, for 10 minutes.

In a bowl beat the egg yolks. Spoon in a little of the cooked mixture at a time, blending in until about half has been added. Return combination to a double boiler and cook and stir for one minute. Remove from heat and stir in the butter and vanilla. Cover and cool filling thoroughly. Whip cream and sweeten slightly; refrigerate. Just before serving spoon a little of the filling into each tart shell. Arrange a layer of banana slices and top with additional filling. Spoon slightly sweetened whipped cream over filling. Chill until ready to serve. Garnish with additional banana slices when served as banana will darken when exposed to air.

Fruit Melange

One can (No. 2) grapefruit sections
Two bananas
Two red apples
Three peaches
One cup blueberries
Sugar (one to two tablespoons if necessary)
Servings: Eight

Place the grapefruit sections in a two-quart bowl. Stir in the sliced bananas, diced apples, sliced peaches and blueberries. Mix well to coat with grapefruit juice. Taste to see if it is necessary to add sugar. Chill thoroughly before serving. Garnish each portion, if desired, with a few mint leaves or a small ball of sherbet. Note: Red or green grapes, plums or other berries as well as fresh or canned pineapple and melon balls are excellent additions.

Poached Pears

Six Anjou or Bosc pears
Juice of one lime
One and one-half cups sugar
Three cups water
One-sixteenth teaspoon salt
Simmering time: Twenty minutes, about
One cup Emperor grapes, halved and seeded
Chill: Thoroughly
Servings: Twelve

Wash pears and cut in half lengthwise, cutting through the stems and leaving them attached to the fruit. Remove the cores in each half, using a measuring teaspoon as a scoop. Brush the cut surface of the fruit with lime juice and salt to the boiling point. Add the pears. Cover and simmer until the fruit is tender. Transfer to a large serving bowl, add the seeded grape halves and chill thoroughly in the refrigerator. Delicious served with a small scoop of lemon sherbet atop each pear half.

Peaches Supreme

One-fourth cup brown sugar
One-half cup corn syrup
One-third cup sherry wine
Two tablespoons butter or margarine
Simmer: Five minutes
Six fully ripened peaches
Standing time: Ten minutes
Whipped or dairy sour cream
Serves: Six

In a saucepan combine the brown sugar, corn syrup, sherry wine and butter or margarine. Bring to a boil, lower heat and simmer for five minutes. Add the peeled ripe peach halves and let stand in the hot sauce until serving time. Garnish peaches in sauce with a dab of whipped or dairy sour cream.

Creme Supreme

One cup dairy sour cream
Three tablespoons brown sugar
One pound grapes, split and seeded
Chill: Thoroughly
Servings: Six

In a small bowl combine the dairy sour cream with the brown sugar, blending smooth. Add remaining sour cream. Wash, split and seed the grapes. Place about a third cup of split grapes in each of six serving dishes. Spoon the cream over the fruit and chill thoroughly before serving.

Pears Poached in Orange Juice

Six large Anjou or Bosc pears
One and one-half cups sugar
One-half cup water
One-half cup orange juice
Two tablespoons lemon juice
Boil: Three minutes
Simmer: Twenty minutes, about
Chill: Thoroughly
Whipped cream
Finely shaved unsweetened chocolate
Serves: Twelve

Wash pears and cut in half lengthwise. Remove cores in each half using a measuring teaspoon as a scoop. Peel. In a large skillet or saucepan combine the sugar, water, orange and lemon juice. Bring to a boil and boil for three minutes. Add the prepared pear halves, turning over once in the syrup to coat. Cover and simmer gently for about twenty minutes or until fruit is tender. Cool thoroughly in the syrup. Serve pear halves in the syrup with a dab of whipped cream and garnish of finely shaved unsweetened chocolate.

Poached Pears with Grapes

Six large Anjou or Bosc pears
Juice of one lime
One and one-half cups sugar
Three cups water
One-sixteenth teaspoon salt
Boil: Three minutes
Simmer: Twenty minutes, about
One cup Emperor grapes, halved and seeded
Chill: Thoroughly
Serves: Twelve

Wash pears and cut in half lengthwise, cutting through the stems and leaving them attached. Remove the cores in each half, using a measuring teaspoon as a scoop. Brush the cut surface of the fruit with lime juice to prevent discoloration. In a large saucepan or skillet combine the sugar, water, remaining lime juice and salt and bring to the boiling point. Add the pears. Cover and simmer until the fruit is tender. Transfer to a large serving bowl, add the seeded grape halves and chill thoroughly in the refrigerator. Delicious served with a small scoop of lemon sherbet atop each pear half.

Baked Pears with Lemon Sauce

Six ripe Anjou pears
One-fourth cup sugar
One-fourth cup water
Oven temperature: 375 degrees
Bake: Forty-five minutes

Lemon Sauce

One-half cup sugar
Two tablespoons cornstarch
One-eighth teaspoon cinnamon
One cup boiling water
Boiling time: One minute
One tablespoon butter
One-fourth cup lemon juice
One teaspoon grated lemon rind
One egg
Cooking time: One minute
Yield: One and one-half cups sauce

Wash and core the pears, place in a baking dish. In a small saucepan, heat the sugar with the water until dissolved. Pour this syrup over the pears and bake in a moderately hot oven until fruit is tender. Make the sauce by combining the sugar, cornstarch and cinnamon in a saucepan. Add the boiling water and heat until the boiling point is regained. Cook for one minute. Stir in the butter, lemon juice and rind. In a small bowl, beat the egg. Add the sauce gradually to the beaten egg, stirring constantly. Return the mixture to the saucepan and cook for one minute. Remove from heat and chill. Serve with baked pears.

Minted Poached Apples

One and one-fourth cups sugar
Two cups water
Heat: To boiling point
Two teaspoons peppermint flavoring
Three or four drops red food coloring
Six large cooking apples
Cook: Ten minutes, about
Three-fourths cup seedless raisins
Simmer: Five minutes
Chill: Thoroughly
Six ounces cream cheese
One-half cup chopped nuts
Serves: Six

In a large shallow skillet or saucepan heat the sugar and water to the boiling point. Stir in the peppermint and food coloring. Core and peel the apples. Add to the syrup in the pan and cook slowly until tender, spooning the syrup over the fruit most of the cooking time, turning fruit over once. Remove apples to a plate and chill. Chill syrup separately. Place the raisins in a small saucepan, cover with water and bring to a boil. Simmer five minutes and drain. At serving time blend some of the syrup into the cream cheese in a bowl to make it light and fluffy. Add the raisins and chopped nuts. Fill apple centers with the cream cheese mixture and serve with some of the syrup spooned over top.

Chocolate Meringue Cake

One-half cup butter or margarine
Three-fourths cup sugar
Four eggs, separated
Four squares (1 oz. each) unsweetened
   chocolate, melted
One teaspoon vanilla
One-half cup sifted cake flour
One-fourth teaspoon salt
One-half teaspoon soda
One-fourth cup hot water
One-fourth cup sugar
One package (6 oz.) chocolate bits
Oven temperature: 350 degrees
Baking time: Thirty-five minutes
One-fourth cup confectioners' sugar
One cup heavy cream, whipped
Serves: Eight, or more

In a bowl cream the butter and first
measure of sugar (¾ cup) until fluffy and
creamy. Beat in the egg yolks. Add the
melted chocolate and vanilla. Mix in the
sifted dry ingredients. Stir in the hot
water. Pour into two greased and floured
layer cake pans, (8 in.). Beat the egg
whites and the remaining one-fourth cup

sugar until satiny. Sprinkle the chocolate
bits over the batter in each pan; spread
the meringue over the top. Bake in a
moderate oven for 35 minutes. Remove
from oven and cool for 10 minutes before
loosening the edges and removing to racks
to finish cooling. Place layers together so
meringue toppings are together and thus
form the filling. Frost with the slightly
sweetened whipped cream.

Banana Meringue Cake

Six egg whites
One-eighth teaspoon salt
One-fourth teaspoon cream of tartar
One and one-half cups sugar
One teaspoon vanilla
Oven temperature: 250 degrees F.
Baking time: Thirty minutes (about)
One cup heavy cream, whipped
One-half cup sugar
One cup blueberries or other berries
One cup sliced bananas
Servings: Eight, or more

In a large bowl beat the egg whites
with the salt until stiff but not dry. Beat
in the cream of tartar; gradually beat in
the sugar, one tablespoon at a time. Add
the vanilla. Trace two circles (8 in.) on
two baking sheets, lined with waxed
paper. Cover the circles with meringue.
Bake in a slow oven until the edges are
very light brown. With a spatula remove
the circles of meringue carefully and
quickly from the waxed paper. Cool on
racks. Put the meringue layers together
with the combined cream, remaining
sugar, berries and fruit. Set upon serving
plate. Garnish the top with cream, blueberries and bananas.

Meringue Lemon Dessert

Six egg whites
Two cups sugar
Two teaspoons vanilla
Two cups vanilla wafer-crumbs
Two cups chopped pecans
Oven temperature: 350 degrees
Bake: Thirty minutes

Lemon Filling

Six egg yolks
Six tablespoons sugar
Six tablespoons lemon juice
Pinch of salt
Cook: Five minutes
Whipped cream and strawberries
Serves: Eight

In a bowl beat the egg whites until
foamy. Gradually add the sugar beating
well after each addition. Beat until thick
and satiny. Add the vanilla. Fold in the
crumbs and pecans. Spoon mixture into
two pie plates (9 in.) lined with oiled
foil, to form a shell. Bake in a moderate
oven for 30 minutes. Remove to racks.
For the filling: Beat the yolks, sugar,
lemon juice and salt until thick. Cook
over hot water until thick and smooth.
Cool. Spread filling in each pie shell. Fill
with strawberries and whipped cream
between layers and on top. Serve in
wedges.

Pink Meringues

Two egg whites
One-eighth teaspoon salt
One-half teaspoon vanilla
Four tablespoons currant jelly
Oven temperature: 325 degrees
Bake: Twenty minutes

In a bowl beat the egg whites until
they hold soft peaks. Add the salt and
vanilla and gradually add the currant
jelly beating until stiff. (Add a drop or
two of red food coloring to intensify pink-
ness, if you wish.) Drop meringue by
spoonfuls on a half inch of boiling water
in a baking pan. Bake in a moderately
slow oven for twenty minutes. Lift from
water to a plate with a slotted spoon or
turner and allow to cool slowly and thoroughly to room temperature. Chill in the
refrigerator. Serve on top of chilled custard.

Meringue Delight

Six egg whites
One-sixteenth teaspoon salt
One-fourth teaspoon cream of tartar
One and one-fourth cups superfine
    granulated sugar
One-eighth teaspoon almond extract
Oven temperature: 250 degrees
Baking time: One hour, or longer
One quart ice cream, or one cup heavy
    cream, whipped
One cup sweetened sliced strawberries
Servings: Eight, or more

In a large bowl, beat the egg whites
and salt until foamy. Add the cream of
tartar and beat until stiff, but not dry.
Beat in the sugar, a tablespoon at a time.
Add the extract. It should be satiny in
appearance and stiff. Spoon the meringue
into a pastry bag. Cut a piece of brown
paper to fit a cooky sheet; oil the paper.
Force the meringue through the bag onto
the sheet, making individual nest-like
shells (4 in. in diameter). Bake in a very
slow oven one hour or until crisp. Remove. Cool. Fill with ice cream or
whipped cream. Garnish with strawberries. Serve immediately.

Note: Make the meringue shells on
cool, dry days only.

Gingercake Peach Meringue

One-fourth cup butter or margarine
One-half cup sugar
Three egg yolks
One and one-half cups sifted all-purpose
    flour
One-half teaspoon soda
One-fourth teaspoon salt
One teaspoon ginger
One teaspoon cinnamon
One-third cup molasses
One-half cup buttermilk
Oven temperature: 350-325 degrees
Baking time: Thirty minutes
Three egg whites
One-eighth teaspoon cream of tartar
One-half cup sugar
Two cans (No. 2) halved cling peaches,
    well drained
One-half cup heavy cream, whipped
Serves: Six. or more

In a bowl cream the butter and sugar
until fluffy. Add the egg yolks, beating
thoroughly. Add the mixed and sifted
flour, soda, salt, ginger and cinnamon
alternately with the combined molasses
and buttermilk, beating until smooth.
Pour into a greased and floured layer
pan (9 in.). Bake in a moderate oven
350 degrees until a cake tester inserted
in the center comes away clean. Remove
to rack. Beat the egg whites and cream
of tartar until stiff but not dry. Gradually
beat in the sugar until meringue is satiny.
Spoon meringue into waxed paper lined
layer pan (9 in.), shaping it into a ring.
Bake in a moderately slow oven 325 degrees until golden. Remove to rack. Place
layer on a serving plate, arranging well-
drained peaches on top. Crown with
meringue. Fill center with whipped
cream and peaches. Serve immediately.

Baked Alaska Brownie

One pan (8 in.) baked brownies
One pint coffee, or vanilla ice cream
    cut into sixths
Five egg whites
One-eighth teaspoon cream of tartar
Two-thirds cup sugar
Oven temperature: 500 degrees
Baking time: Two minutes (about)
Few drops of red coloring
One can (3½ ozs.) flaked coconut
Serves: Six

Cut the brownies into six oblong pieces.
Space them 3 inches apart on a cookie
sheet. In the center of each brownie,
spoon a sixth of a pint of hard ice cream.
Beat the egg whites with cream of tartar
until stiff, but not dry; gradually add
sugar beating until satiny in appearance.
Cover the ice cream with a thick layer
of meringue. Bake in a very hot oven
until brown. Meanwhile, in a bowl rub the
red food coloring into the flaked coconut.
Then top each Alaskan brownie with the
pink flaked coconut. Serve immediately.

Baked Apples

Eight baking apples
One-half cup brown or white sugar
One-half teaspoon cinnamon
One cup hot water
One-fourth cup light corn syrup
Oven temperature: 400 degrees
Bake: Forty-five minutes
Serves: Eight

Wash the apples, wipe dry, remove stems, core. Cut away one inch of the peel around the top of each apple. Place fruit close together in a baking dish a little deeper than the height of the apples. Fill the centers with the combined sugar and cinnamon. Mix the water and corn syrup; pour half of this in the bottom of the dish, reserving the rest to baste the fruit. Bake in a quick oven until apples are tender. Baste with the syrup mixture from time to time. If a browned top is desired, sprinkle the apples lightly with sugar and place under broiler just until the sugar melts. Remove. Serve hot or cold with milk or cream.

A FAVORITE RECIPE
Prune Stuffed Baked Apples

Six cooked pitted prunes
Three tablespoons peanut butter
Six cooking apples
Twenty-four whole cloves
One-half cup brown sugar
Three tablespoons butter
One cup water
Oven temperature: 375 degrees
Baking time: Fifty minutes, about
One cup cream
Servings: Six

Cut the prunes into small pieces. Mix the prunes and peanut butter in a bowl. Wash and remove cores from the apples; fill the cavities with the prune and peanut mixture. Place the apples in a baking pan; stick four cloves into each apple. Sprinkle the brown sugar over apples and dot the centers with butter. Pour the water into the pan. Bake in a moderately hot oven until the apples are tender. Serve warm with cream.

MRS. JESS KEMPER, *Stendal, Ind.*

Baked Apple Slices with Apricot

Six cups peeled and sliced cooking apples
One-half cup water
Oven temperature: 375 degrees
Bake: Thirty minutes
Two tablespoons butter or margarine
Two teaspoons vanilla
One-eighth teaspoon salt
One-fourth cup apricot jam
Chill: Thoroughly
Serves: Six, or more

Wash, peel, core and slice the cooking apples to measure six cups. Place in a casserole (1½ qts.) with the water and cover tightly. Bake in a moderately hot oven for thirty minutes or until fruit is tender. Remove from oven and stir in the butter or margarine, vanilla, salt and apricot jam until well blended. Chill thoroughly before serving.

A FAVORITE RECIPE
Rum Sauce Superb

Two eggs, beaten until thick
One cup confectioners' sugar
One cup heavy cream, whipped
Four tablespoons rum
Chilling time: Two hours
Yield: One and one-half cups

In a bowl beat the eggs until thick and lemon-colored. Gradually add the sugar, beating constantly. In a separate bowl whip the cream until stiff; add the rum. Combine the cream mixture with the egg and sugar. Blend thoroughly. Chill until serving time. Serve over baked apples, rice or fruit puddings.

MRS. ANDREW BEHARI, *Danbury, Conn.*

A FAVORITE RECIPE
Orange Baked Apples

Six large apples
One-half cup sugar
One-sixteenth teaspon salt
One-half teaspoon cinnamon
One tablespoon melted butter
Two tablespoons chopped nuts
One cup orange juice
Grated rind one orange
Oven temperature: 375 degrees
Bake: Forty-five minutes
Serves: Six

Wash and core the apples, taking care not to puncture through blossom end. Pare around the center of each apple. In a bowl combine the sugar, salt, cinnamon, butter and nuts. Fill the center of apples with the mixture. Combine the orange juice and rind; pour over the apples, after placing in a shallow pan. Bake in a quick oven, basting frequently with pan liquid.

MISS KATHRYN BEUCHAT, *La Valle, Wisconsin*

Skillet Baked Apples

Four Rome beauty apples
Four tablespoons sugar
One-half teaspoon cinnamon
Four tablespoons water
Simmer: Fifteen to twenty minutes
Cream (optional)
Servings: Four

Wash and core the apples. Place in a heavy skillet or saucepan. In a cup mix the sugar and cinnamon and spoon into each of the apple centers. Add four tablespoons of water to the pan, cover tightly and cook over gentle heat until the apples are tender. The time will vary somewhat depending on the size, type and maturity of the apples used. Remove fruit from the pan spooning pan syrup over the top of each. Serve hot or cold with cream or milk.

Fresh Fruit Compote

One cup sugar
Three cups water
Boil: Five minutes
Grated rind of one lemon
Juice of one lemon
One large grapefruit
Three large oranges
Three cups slivered fresh pineapple
One cup split and seeded grapes
Chill: Thoroughly
One cup hulled strawberries, split
Two large bananas, sliced
Servings: Twelve, about

Measure the sugar and water into a saucepan. Bring to a boil and boil, stirring occasionally, for five minutes. Remove from heat and add the grated lemon rind and juice. Cool. Peel the grapefruit and oranges with a very sharp knife, cutting away skin and membrane at same time. Then cut toward the center of the fruit along the separating membrane to release each segment. If these are too large, cut in two. Place in a large bowl. Add the slivered fresh ripe pineapple and split seeded grapes. Pour one cup of the prepared thin syrup over the fruit and chill thoroughly in the refrigerator. An hour or so before serving add the hulled and halved strawberries and the bananas (running tines of fork down side before cutting into half inch slices). Serve fruit very cold with a crisp rich cookie or two.

Cranberry, Orange and Pear Compote

Three cups fresh cranberries
Two cups orange sections
Three cups sliced peeled pears
One cup sugar
One-fourth cup water
Oven temperature: 350 degrees
Baking time: One hour
Chill: Thoroughly
Servings: Eight

Wash and pick over the fresh cranberries. Layer in a large casserole (3 qts.) with the membrane-free orange sections and pear slices, repeating each fruit twice. In a saucepan combine the sugar and water and bring to a boil to dissolve the sugar thoroughly. Pour over the fruit in the casserole, cover and bake in a moderate oven until the fruit is tender. Chill thoroughly before serving.

Spanish Cream with Strawberries

One envelope unflavored gelatin
One-half cup cold milk
One and one-half cups hot milk
One-eighth teaspoon salt
Two egg yolks, beaten
Cook: Ten minutes, about
One teaspoon vanilla
Three tablespoons sugar
Chill: Until syrupy
Two egg whites
One tablespoon sugar
Chill: Two hours, about
One quart fresh ripe strawberries
Sugar
Servings: Eight

Sprinkle the unflavored gelatin over the cold milk in the upper half of a double boiler. Stir in the hot milk and salt. Place over hot water and stir until softened gelatin is thoroughly dissolved. Pour slowly into beaten egg yolks, stirring constantly. Return to top of double boiler and cook over hot water until the mixture coats a metal spoon. Remove from heat. Add vanilla and three tablespoons of sugar. Stir to dissolve completely. Chill until syrupy. In a bowl beat the egg whites with the tablespoon of sugar until they hold soft peaks. Fold into the thickened custard mixture. Pour into a four cup mold or eight individual molds. Chill until firm. Wash, dry and hull the strawberries. Slice into a bowl and sweeten to taste. Chill. Serve as sauce with the unmolded Spanish Cream.

Coconut Bavarian Cream

Two tablespoons cold water
One tablespoon unflavored gelatin
Four egg yolks
One-half cup sugar
One-eighth teaspoon salt
One cup scalded milk
Cook: Five to eight minutes
One teaspoon vanilla
Cool: Until thickened
One cup flaked coconut (one can 3½ oz.)
One cup heavy cream, whipped
Chill: Until set
Two cups melon balls or fruit sauce
Mint sprigs
Serves: Eight

Measure the cold water into a cup. Sprinkle on the unflavored gelatin and let stand to soften. Beat the egg yolks in the upper half of a double boiler. Beat in the sugar and salt, gradually blend in the scalded milk. Place over boiling water and cook, stirring constantly, until custard coats spoon. Remove from heat and add the softened gelatin, stirring until dissolved. Add the vanilla. Chill in the refrigerator until thickened, then fold in the flaked coconut and whipped heavy cream. Pour into a rinsed mold (5 cup) or individual molds and chill until set. Unmold to serve with tiny melon balls or a fruit sauce.

Kentucky Cream

One-half cup sugar
One envelope unflavored gelatin
Three egg yolks
One-fourth cup milk
One-half cup bourbon whisky
Cook: Five to eight minutes
Three egg whites
One-fourth cup sugar
One cup heavy cream, whipped
Chill: Until set
Fresh strawberries
Servings: Eight

In the upper half of a double boiler stir the half cup of sugar into the unflavored gelatin. Beat in the egg yolks. Blend in the milk. Add the bourbon whisky very slowly, stirring smooth. Place over gently simmering water and cook, stirring constantly, until the mixture thickens slightly and coats a metal spoon. Remove from heat and pour into a bowl to speed cooling. Beat the egg whites in a bowl until foamy, gradually beat in the fourth cup of sugar until stiff. Carefully fold room temperature custard into the stiff whites. Fold in the whipped cream and transfer to a rinsed mold (five cups) or individual molds. Chill until set. Turn out on serving platter or individual dessert plates and garnish with whole strawberries. If you prefer spoon into custard cups or parfait glasses and serve without unmolding.

Raspberry Bavarian Cream

One package (10 oz.) frozen raspberries, thawed
One envelope unflavored gelatin
One-fourth cup sugar
One-fourth teaspoon salt
One-fourth cup water
One cup milk
Cook: Ten minutes, about
Two egg yolks
Cook: Two or three minutes
Chill: Until syrupy
One cup heavy cream, whipped
One teaspoon vanilla
Two egg whites
One-fourth cup sugar
Chill: Until set
Serves: Six

Place the frozen raspberries in a bowl to thaw. In the upper half of a double boiler stir together the unflavored gelatin, fourth cup of sugar and salt. Blend in the water and milk. Place over boiling water and cook, stirring constantly until the mixture coats a metal spoon. In a bowl beat the egg yolks. Gradually blend some of the cooked mixture into the beaten yolks, stirring constantly. Return combination to the pan and cook, stirring constantly for two to three minutes. Remove from heat and transfer to a large bowl. Chill until syrupy. Fold in the beaten cream and vanilla. In a bowl beat the egg whites until foamy, gradually beat in the fourth cup of sugar until a glossy meringue is formed. Fold into the cream and custard with the thawed berries and syrup. Pour into a rinsed mold

(5 cup) and chill until firm. Unmold on platter to serve with garnish of additional berries and whipped cream if desired.

Grape Bavarian Cream

One tablespoon unflavored gelatin
One-fourth cup cold water
Three-fourths cup boiling water
One-half cup sugar
One can (6 oz.) frozen grape juice concentrate
Two tablespoons orange juice
One tablespoon lemon juice
Chill: Until thick and syrupy
One-third cup heavy cream, whipped
Chill: One and one-half hours
Serves: Six

Sprinkle gelatin over cold water in a bowl to soften. Add boiling water and sugar and stir until dissolved. Stir in fruit juices. Chill until thick and syrupy. Beat with rotary beater. Fold in whipped cream. Pour into custard cups or individual molds. Chill until set.

Pineapple Sponge

One envelope unflavored gelatin
One-fourth cup cold water
One cup pineapple juice
One tablespoon lemon juice
One-fourth teaspoon salt
One and one-half teaspoons vanilla
Chill: Until syrupy
One-half cup crushed pineapple
Two egg whites
Three tablespoons sugar
Chill: Until set
Servings: Eight

Sprinkle the unflavored gelatin over the fourth cup of cold water in a cup. Let stand to soften. Heat the pineapple juice to the boiling point, stir in the softened gelatin, lemon juice, salt and vanilla. Chill in the refrigerator until syrupy. Beat gelatin until fluffy. In a bowl beat the egg whites until foamy, gradually beat in the sugar until meringue holds soft peaks. Fold meringue into the beaten gelatin with the crushed pineapple. Rinse a one quart mold with cold water. Pour gelatin mixture into mold and chill until set. Turn out on a serving plate, releasing the edges with the finger first and applying a hot towel to the outside of the mold if necessary. Garnish with pieces of pineapple and maraschino cherries if desired.

Molded Blueberry Pineapple Cheese Cake

*One can (1 lb. 4½ oz.) pineapple spears, drained
Two envelopes unflavored gelatin
One-half cup cold water
Two egg yolks
One-half cup sugar
One teaspoon salt
One cup milk
Cook: Five minutes
Two cups creamy cottage cheese (sieved)
Three tablespoons lemon juice
One tablespoon grated lemon rind
One teaspoon vanilla
One cup heavy cream, whipped
Two egg whites, beaten stiff
Two cups blueberries
One-fourth cup gingersnap crumbs
One tablespoon melted butter
Chill: Four hours
Serves: Eight

Split the pineapple spears in half lengthwise. Place eight of them in a mold. Mince the remaining spears. In a bowl sprinkle the gelatin over the cold water. In the top of a double boiler blend the egg yolks, sugar, salt and milk. Cook over hot water for five minutes. Add the softened gelatin, stirring until dissolved. Sieve the cottage cheese, add the lemon juice, rind and vanilla. Stir into the gelatin mixture. Fold in whipped cream and beaten egg whites. Reserve a cup of blueberries for garnish. Add the other cup of blueberries and minced pineapple. Carefully spoon the mixture into the mold. Cover with combined gingersnap crumbs and butter. Chill; until set. Garnish. Unmold on a cold plate; serve in wedges.

* Note: Use only canned pineapple — will not jell with fresh pineapple.

A FAVORITE RECIPE
Molded Fruit Salad

One package lemon flavored gelatin
One cup boiling water
One package (8 oz.) cream cheese (room temperature)
One can (7 oz.) crushed pineapple
One teaspoon sugar
One teaspoon vanilla
Three drops food coloring
One-half cup chopped pecans
One cup lemon flavored soda
Chilling time: Four hours
Servings: Six

In a bowl dissolve the gelatin in the boiling water, stirring until cooled. Add the cream cheese, mashing and stirring until well blended. Add the pineapple, sugar, vanilla, food coloring and pecans. Blend well while adding the soda. Turn into a mold; chill; stirring several times until molded.

MRS. H. H. MILLER, *Beaver, W. Va.*

Strawberry Coeur A La Creme

One pound creamy cottage cheese
One pound cream cheese
One tablespoon confectioners' sugar
Two cups heavy cream
Few grains salt
Chilling time: Overnight
One quart strawberries, washed and hulled
One cup sugar
Standing time: Three hours
Serves: Eight, or more

Force the cheeses through sieve into bowl. Add sugar and heavy cream. Beat until smooth. Add the salt. Line a heart shaped wicker basket with a dampened piece of cheesecloth. Fill the basket with the mixture. Place the basket on a plate. Place in the refrigerator overnight, allowing it to drain. Reserve 12 berries for garnish. Wash and hull remaining berries. Cut them in half; place in a bowl. Pour the sugar over the berries; allow to stand. Chill. When ready to serve the dessert, unmold the heart upon a platter, removing the cheesecloth. Garnish with the whole berries. Slice cheese heart; serve with sugared, chilled berries.

Coffee Bavarian

One envelope unflavored gelatin
One-fourth cup cold water
Two tablespoons instant coffee
One cup boiling water
Two eggs, separated
Two-thirds cup brown sugar
One-half teaspoon salt
Cooking time: Five minutes
Chilling time: Until beginning to set
One cup heavy cream, whipped
Two tablespoons rum
Chilling time: Three hours
Serves: Six

In a cup soften the gelatin in the cold water. Dissolve the coffee in the boiling water. Add the gelatin; stir until dissolved. In a bowl beat the egg yolks, sugar and salt; gradually stir in the coffee mixture. Cook and stir over hot, not boiling water until slightly thickened. Chill. When mixture begins to set, fold in the stiffly beaten egg whites. Fold in the whipped cream. Add the rum. Pour into a mold (1 qt.). Chill until firm. Unmold; garnish with whipped cream.

A FAVORITE RECIPE
Bridge Dessert

One cup strained cranberry sauce, crushed
Eight marshmallows, cut into fourths
(or 32 miniature marshmallows)
One teaspoon grated lemon rind
Sixteen blanched almonds, chopped
One-half cup sieved banana pulp
One-half cup heavy cream, whipped
Chilling time: Two hours
Serves: Six

In a bowl crush the cranberry sauce with a fork; add the marshmallows, lemon rind, almonds and banana pulp. Mix thoroughly. Fold in the whipped cream. Chill until serving time.

MISS LORETTA SMITH, *Montour Falls, N.Y.*

White Velvet Cream

One envelope unflavored gelatin
Three-fourths cup sugar
Two cups heavy cream
Let stand: Five minutes
Heat: Until gelatin dissolves
One tablespoon vanilla
Two cups sour cream
Refrigerate: Two hours
Three pints strawberries
One-half cup sugar
Four tablespoons Kirsch or cognac
Serves: Eight, or more

In a saucepan mix the gelatin and sugar. Stir in the heavy cream. Let stand for 5 minutes. Place saucepan over low heat; heat and stir until the gelatin is dissolved. Remove; cool to lukewarm. Add vanilla and sour cream blending until smooth. Pour into a mold (1½ qts.). Refrigerate until set. Meanwhile wash, hull and slice the strawberries, preserving a few whole ones for garnish. Sprinkle the sugar and Kirsch over the strawberries.

Unmold; garnish. Serve with the sweetened strawberries or serve with chocolate sauce. Serve immediately.

Rum Mold

One envelope unflavored gelatin
One-half cup milk
Four egg yolks
One-half cup sugar
One cup scalded milk
Cook: Five to ten minutes
Two or three tablespoons rum
Cool: Until syrupy
One cup heavy cream, whipped
Chill: Two hours or more
Shaved bitter chocolate or Raspberry
    Sauce
Servings: Twelve

Sprinkle the unflavored gelatin over the half cup of milk in a small bowl. In the upper half of a double boiler beat the egg yolks until lemon colored. Stir in the sugar. Add the scalded milk gradually, stirring the while. Place over boiling water and cook, stirring constantly, until the mixture is smooth and thickened. Remove from heat and add the softened gelatin stirring to dissolve. Cool slightly. Add the rum gradually, stirring while adding. Let cool in the refrigerator, stirring occasionally to keep smooth. When custard begins to get syrupy, fold in the whipped cream. Pour mixture into a rinsed mold (four cups) and chill until firm. Unmold on a platter and serve with a generous dusting of shaved bitter chocolate or the following Raspberry Sauce. Mold for individual servings if preferred.

Raspberry Sauce

One tablespoon cornstarch
One tablespoon cold water
One-half cup currant jelly
Cooking time: Five minutes
One package (10 oz.) frozen raspberries
Yield: One and one-half cups

In a small saucepan blend the cornstarch with the cold water. Stir smooth and blend in the currant jelly. Place over moderate heat and cook stirring constantly, until jelly melts and sauce thickens slightly. Remove from heat and add the berries. Chill before using.

Coconut Honey Custard Molds

One envelope unflavored gelatin
One-fourth cup sugar
One-fourth teaspoon salt
Three egg yolks
Two cups milk
Cook: Ten minutes, about
One teaspoon vanilla
One-half teaspoon almond extract
Chill: Until firm
Honey
Flaked coconut
Servings: Four

In the upper half of a double boiler, stir together the unflavored gelatin, sugar and salt. In a bowl, beat the egg yolks and blend in the milk. Stir into the sugar mixture. Cook over hot water, stir-ring constantly, until the custard coats the spoon. Remove from heat and allow to cool. Add vanilla and almond extract and pour into custard cups or molds. Chill until firm. Unmold on dessert plates, spoon a little honey on top of each and sprinkle with flaked coconut.

Eggnog Mold

One envelope unflavored gelatin
One-half cup milk or water
Four egg yolks
One-half cup sugar
One cup scalded milk
Cooking time: Five to ten minutes
Three tablespoons fruit-flavored brandy
Cooling time: Until syrupy
One cup heavy cream, whipped
Chilling time: Two hours, or more
Shaved bitter chocolate
Servings: Eight

Sprinkle the unflavored gelatin over the half cup of milk or water in a small bowl. In the upper half of a double boiler beat the egg yolks until lemon colored. Stir in the sugar. Add the scalded milk gradually, stirring the while. Place over boiling water and cook, stirring constantly, until the mixture is smooth and thickened. Remove from heat and add the softened gelatin stirring to dissolve. Cool slightly. Add the brandy gradually to the cooled custard, stirring while adding. Let cool in the refrigerator, stirring occasionally to keep smooth. When custard begins to get syrupy, fold in the whipped cream. Pour mixture into a rinsed mold (four cup) and chill until firm. Unmold on a platter and decorate with shaved bitter chocolate. Note: Individual molds may be made with eight rinsed custard cups.

A FAVORITE RECIPE
Molded Plum Pudding

One package lemon flavored gelatin,
    dissolved in
Two cups hot water
Three cups grapenuts cereal
Three-fourths cup seedless raisins
Three-fourths cup chopped walnuts
Three-fourths cup chopped prunes
One-fourth cup chopped citron
One-half teaspoon cinnamon
One-fourth teaspoon cloves
One-half teaspoon salt
Chilling: Overnight
Serves: Six

In a bowl dissolve the lemon gelatin in the hot water; stir constantly. While the mixture is still hot, add the grapenuts, raisins, walnuts, prunes, citron and seasonings. Turn into a mold rinsed with cold water. Let chill overnight. Unmold on a platter. Serve with whipped cream or a favorite sauce.

MRS. S. OLSEN, *Long Island Beach, L.I., N.Y.*

Party Fruit Mold

One package lime flavored gelatin
One cup hot water
One-half cup cold water
Chill: Until firm
One cup pineapple juice
One-fourth cup sugar
Heat: To dissolve sugar
One package lemon flavored gelatin
One-half cup cold water
Chill: Until syrupy
One cup finely rolled graham cracker
    crumbs
One-fourth cup butter, melted
One cup diced canned pears, drained
One cup diced canned peaches, drained
One cup pineapple tidbits, drained
Two cups heavy cream, whipped
Chill: Eight hours, or more
Serves: Twelve, or more

Dissolve the lime gelatin in a bowl with the hot water. Add the half cup of cold water and pour into a cake pan (8 x 8 x 2 in.). Chill until firm. In a small saucepan heat the pineapple juice with the fourth cup of sugar until dissolved. Remove from heat and stir in the lemon gelatin and finally the half cup of cold water. Chill until syrupy. Mix the graham cracker crumbs with the melted butter and pack into the bottom of a spring form pan (9 in.). Prepare the canned fruits. Cut the lime gelatin into half-inch cubes, using a sharp knife dipped frequently into hot water. Run knife around edge of pan. Remove by running spatula under gelatin.

Fold the whipped cream into the thickened lemon gelatin carefully. Add the fruits and the diced lime gelatin and pour into the spring form pan. Chill for eight hours or more before serving. Run a knife around the edge of the pan before removing sides. Serve from the base of the spring form pan set upon a large platter. Decorate with peach slices and other fruits if desired.

Rhubarb Cream

One package frozen rhubarb (one pound)
One and one-third cups canned crushed
    pineapple
One-eighth teaspoon salt
One-third cup sugar
Simmering time: Twenty minutes
One can (13 oz.) evaporated milk, chilled
One-eighth teaspoon mace
Chill: Three hours
Servings: Eight, or more

In a saucepan combine the frozen rhubarb, crushed pineapple, salt and sugar. Bring to a boil on top of the stove, then simmer gently until rhubarb is soft. Remove from heat, allow to cool. Pour the thoroughly chilled evaporated milk into a large bowl and beat with a rotary or electric beater until very stiff. Fold the fruit mixture and mace into the whipped milk and pour into refrigerator trays. Place in coldest part of refrigerator to chill thoroughly.

Pineapple Custard

One-half cup sugar
One and one-half tablespoons cornstarch
One-fourth teaspoon salt
One cup pineapple juice
Cook: Twenty minutes
Four eggs
Cook: Five minutes
One cup crushed pineapple, drained
Two teaspoons lemon juice
One and one-half teaspoons vanilla
One cup heavy cream
Chill: Thoroughly
Servings: Six to eight

In the upper half of a double boiler stir together the sugar, cornstarch and salt. Gradually blend in the pineapple juice. Place over hot water and cook, stirring constantly, until slightly thickened. In a bowl beat the eggs. Add the cooked mixture gradually to the beaten eggs then return combination to the pan. Place over hot water and cook about five minutes more until thickened. Remove from heat and add the crushed drained pineapple, lemon juice and vanilla. In a bowl beat the cream until stiff. Fold into the custard mixture. Spoon into custard cups or small individual dessert dishes. Chill thoroughly before serving.

Baked Custard

Two cups milk
One-fourth cup sugar
One-fourth teaspoon salt
Scald: Two to three minutes
Three eggs
One and one-half teaspoons vanilla
Nutmeg
Oven temperature: 300 degrees
Bake: Fifty minutes
Serves: Five

In a saucepan heat the milk, sugar and salt to scalding. In a bowl beat the eggs, add the vanilla and gradually stir in the scalded milk. Pour mixture through a strainer into five individual custard cups or one large baking dish. Sprinkle nutmeg over the top. Place in a baking pan and pour hot water around the cups to the depth of one inch. Bake in a slow oven until custard is set. Remove from water bath and cool.

Peach Creme Brulee

Three-fourths cup evaporated milk
Three-fourths cup water
Two eggs
One-fourth cup granulated sugar
One tablespoon cornstarch
One-fourth teaspoon salt
Cook: Until thickened
One-half teaspoon vanilla
One can (No. 2½) sliced peaches
Brown sugar
Broiler temperature: 500 degrees
Broil: Three to five minutes
Chill: Thoroughly
Servings: Six

In the upper half of a double boiler heat the evaporated milk with the water. Beat the eggs in a bowl. Stir the sugar, cornstarch and salt together and beat into the eggs. Stir eggs into the hot milk and place over boiling water. Cook and stir until thickened. Remove from heat, stir in the vanilla and cool to room temperature. Drain the peach slices well and arrange in a shallow heat proof dish or pie plate. Spoon cooled custard over fruit and cover completely about one-fourth inch with brown sugar. Place about six inches from broiler heat and broil until sugar melts and bubbles. Remove from broiler and chill thoroughly.

Chocolate Custard Pudding

Three tablespoons butter or margarine
Three-fourths cup sugar
One-fourth cup sifted flour
One-fourth cup cocoa
One-half teaspoon salt
Three egg yolks
One and one-fourth cups milk
One teaspoon vanilla
Three egg whites
Oven temperature: 350 degrees
Bake: Thirty-five minutes
Serves: Six

In a bowl cream the butter or margarine and blend in the sugar, flour, cocoa and salt. Add the beaten egg yolks, milk and vanilla. In a bowl beat the egg whites until stiff but not dry, fold into the first mixture carefully. Pour into a greased baking dish (1½ qts.) or square pan (8 x 8 x 2 in.) or individual custard cups. Place dish, pan or custard cups in a large pan in an inch of hot water. Bake in a moderate oven until set on top. Time will be slightly less for custard cups. Serve warm or cold. A light sponge layer will cover the chocolate sauce.

Lemon Custard Pudding

Three tablespoons butter or margarine
One cup sugar
One-third cup sifted flour
One-half teaspoon salt
Three egg yolks
One cup milk
One-fourth cup lemon juice
One-fourth teaspoon grated lemon rind
Three egg whites
Oven temperature: 350 degrees
Bake: Thirty-five minutes
Serves: Six

In a bowl cream the butter or margarine and blend in the sugar, flour and salt. Add the beaten egg yolks and milk. Gradually add the lemon juice and grated rind, stirring the while. In a bowl beat the egg whites until stiff but not dry; fold into the creamed mixture carefully. Pour into a greased baking dish (1½ qts.) or square pan (8 x 8 x 2 in.) or individual greased custard cups. Place dish or pan or custard cups in a large pan in an inch of hot water. Bake in a moderate oven until lightly browned on top. Time will be slightly less for custard cups. Serve warm or cold. A light sponge layer will cover the lemon sauce.

Sherry Custard Trifle

Four egg yolks
One-half cup sugar
Cook: Until thickened
One-half cup medium sherry
One-half cup lemon juice
Chill: Thoroughly
Four egg whites
One-half cup heavy cream
One package (3 oz.) lady fingers
Six large canned peach halves
Nutmeg
Chill: Thoroughly
Servings: Six

Beat the egg yolks in the upper half of a double boiler until thick and lemon colored. Gradually beat in the sugar. Place over hot water and cook, stirring, until thickened. Remove from heat and slowly stir in the sherry and lemon juice. Pour into a bowl and chill thoroughly. Beat the egg whites in a bowl until they hold soft peaks; fold in stiffly beaten heavy cream. Fold custard into the cream and egg white mixture. Split the lady fingers and arrange in individual dessert dishes. Place a peach half in each. Spoon custard mixture over fruit and sprinkle with nutmeg. Chill thoroughly before serving.

A FAVORITE RECIPE
Fruit Pudding

One cup flour
One cup sugar
One-half teaspoon salt
One egg, well beaten
One cup fruit cocktail with juice
One-half cup brown sugar
One-half cup chopped walnuts
Oven temperature: 325 degrees
Baking time: One hour
One cup heavy cream, whipped
Serves: Six

Sift the flour, sugar and salt together three times. Add the beaten egg and fruit cocktail, mixing well. Pour into a well buttered loaf pan (8 in.). Cover with the brown sugar, mixed with the walnuts. Bake in a moderately slow oven. Serve warm, garnished with whipped cream.

MRS. CHARLOTTE MILLER, *West Rutland, Vt.*

The Sunday News
Velvet Souffle

Two envelopes unflavored gelatin
One-half cup cold water
Six eggs, separated
Three-fourths cup sugar
Four cups milk
One-eighth teaspoon salt
Cook: Ten minutes
One-fourth cup cognac or sherry
Chill: Until beginning to set
One cup heavy cream
One-fourth cup confectioners' sugar
Chill: Until firm
Jelly and whipped cream
Serves: Six, or more

In a bowl sprinkle the gelatin over the cold water. In the top of a double boiler mix the egg yolks, one-fourth cup of sugar, milk and salt. Cook over hot water, stirring occasionally for 10 minutes. Add the softened gelatin, stirring until dissolved. Remove; cool. Beat the egg whites with the remaining measure of sugar (½ cup) until meringue-like. Fold into the cool egg yolk mixture. Add the cognac. Chill until the mixture is the consistency of unbeaten egg white. Beat the heavy cream and confectioners' sugar until stiff. Fold into the jellied mixture. Make a collar with waxed paper and tie it tightly around the top of souffle dish. Pour in mixture so the jellied mixture is about one inch above the rim of the dish. Set in refrigerator. Chill until firm. Remove the waxed paper. Serve plain or garnish with jellied diamonds and whipped cream.

A FAVORITE RECIPE
Charlotte Russe

Twelve ladyfingers, split into halves
Two envelopes unflavored gelatin
Two-thirds cup sugar
One-fourth teaspoon salt
Three cups milk
Cooking time: Until gelatin and sugar are dissolved
One-fourth cup brandy, or one teaspoon vanilla
Chilling time: Until mixture starts to set
Two cups heavy cream, whipped
Serves: Six

Butter a spring-form pan (8 in.). Cut ¼ inch from end of the split ladyfingers. Arrange the ladyfingers around the sides of pan. In a saucepan mix the gelatin, sugar and salt. Stir in the milk. Place over a low flame, stirring constantly until the gelatin and sugar are dissolved. Remove from the heat. Stir in the brandy or vanilla. Chill until the mixture starts to mold. Fold in the whipped cream. Turn into the spring form pan; chill until firm. Garnish with whipped cream and maraschino cherries.

MISS THELMA RICHARDS, Louisville, Ky.

Macaroon Chocolate Souffle

One package (4 oz.) macaroons
Three tablespoons butter
Three tablespoons flour
One cup milk
Two squares (1 oz. each) unsweetened chocolate
One-fourth cup sugar
One-fourth teaspoon salt
One teaspoon vanilla
Cooking time: Ten minutes
Four egg yolks, slightly beaten
Four egg whites, beaten stiff
One-fourth cup sugar
Oven temperature: 400-375 degrees
Baking time: Thirty-five minutes
One-half cup heavy cream, whipped
One can (8 oz.) chocolate syrup
Serves: Six

Butter souffle dishes (2 cups); sprinkle sides and bottom with sugar. Place a layer of macaroons on the bottom of the dish. Set aside. In a heavy saucepan melt the butter. Blend in the flour; gradually add the milk; stirring constantly. Add chocolate stirring until melted. Add sugar, salt and vanilla. Cook until thickened and smooth. Add the egg yolks, one at a time, beating well after each addition. Beat the egg whites and remaining measure of sugar until stiff. Fold into chocolate mixture. Pour into souffle dishes. Set dishes in a pan of hot water. Bake in a quick oven 15 minutes; reduce the oven to moderately hot and bake for 20 minutes longer. Serve immediately with whipped cream and chocolate syrup.

Strawberry Blintzes
Pancakes

One cup sifted flour
One tablespoon sugar
Few grains salt
Two eggs, plus two egg yolks, beaten
One and three-fourths cups milk
Two tablespoons melted butter or
   margarine
Standing time: Two hours
Bake: Until browned on one side only

Filling

Two 8 oz. cartons cottage cheese
One tablespoon sugar
One-half cup sour cream
One-eighth teaspoon cinnamon
Eight whole strawberries
One tablespoon cognac
One cup strawberries, or raspberries, halved
Four tablespoons butter or margarine
Cook: Ten minutes
Serves: Six

Sift the flour, sugar and salt into a bowl. Add eggs and half the measure of milk. Beat until smooth. Add remaining milk and butter, beating until smooth. Let stand. Brush a small hot skillet (7 in.) with melted butter. Pour a generous tablespoon of batter into pan, tipping to coat bottom of pan. Cook until slightly browned on one side. Flip over onto paper toweling. Keep baking until all the batter is used. For the filling: Mix the cottage cheese, sugar, two tablespoons of the sour cream and cinnamon. Reserve 8 strawberries. Pour cognac over halved strawberries. Put a tablespoon of filling in center of each browned side of pancake. Roll it up and fold in ends. Brown in hot butter, turning to cook on both sides. Serve with remaining sour cream and garnish with the reserved strawberries.

Crepe Suzettes
Orange Butter

One-half pound butter or margarine
One tablespoon grated orange rind
One tablespoon grated lemon rind
One-fourth cup orange juice
Standing time: Three hours

Thin Pancakes

One cup sifted flour
Two tablespoons sugar
One-half teaspoon salt
One and one-fourth cups milk
Three eggs
Butter for frying

Liqueur Sauce

Five tablespoons Grand Marnier
Five tablespoons Benedictine
Five tablespoons cognac
Serves: Four, or more

In a bowl cream the butter or margarine until soft and fluffy. Add grated rinds and juice. Let stand three hours to develop flavor.

In a bowl mix and sift flour, sugar and salt. Gradually beat in the combined

milk and eggs, stirring until smooth. Each time a pancake is baked grease the bottom of a small skillet (5 in.) with butter, using a paper napkin. Pour three tablespoons at a time into pan tilting the pan on all sides so batter spreads out to the edge of the pan. The pancake browns very quickly. Turn pancake with spatula and brown other side. Remove to paper towel. Repeat procedure until all the pancake batter is used. Makes about 14 pancakes.

In a frying pan or electric skillet melt two tablespoons of orange butter over an alcohol burner or low heat. Place six pancakes in orange butter. With a spoon and fork toss and turn them around until thoroughly heated. Add two tablespoons each Grand Marnier, Benedictine and cognac. Ignite. Fold pancakes in half and then fold again; place on hot platter. Repeat procedure for the remaining pancakes. Serve three pancakes per person.

Floating Island with Fruit

Three egg whites
One-eighth teaspoon salt
Six tablespoons sugar
Two and one-half cups milk
Poach: Ten minutes
One-fourth cup sugar
Two teaspoons cornstarch
One-fourth teaspoon salt
Cook: Ten minutes, about
Three egg yolks
Cook: Five minutes, about
One-half teaspoon vanilla
One-fourth teaspoon almond extract
Pinch of nutmeg
Chill: Thoroughly
Sliced fresh bananas, pears or plums
   slightly sweetened
Servings: Six

In a bowl beat the egg whites with the salt until foamy, gradually beat in the sugar until they hold a peak. Pour the milk into a large skillet and heat to simmering. Drop spoonfuls of meringue into the hot milk and poach with gentle heat without covering for ten minutes. Remove meringues with slotted spoon to drain off liquid and place on platter or tray. Cool to room temperature then refrigerate until serving time. Strain the milk in skillet and add to it if necessary to measure two cups. In the upper half of a double boiler stir the fourth cup of sugar, cornstarch and salt together. Gradually blend in the milk. Place over hot water and cook, stirring constantly, until slightly thickened.

Chocolate Pot de Creme

One-fourth pound sweetened chocolate
One tablespoon sugar
One-eighth teaspoon salt
Heat: Until melted
One cup heavy cream
Three egg yolks
Cook: Five minutes
Chill: Thoroughly
Servings: Six (three ounce)

In the upper half of a double boiler place the sweetened chocolate broken into small chunks, the sugar and salt. Place over hot water and cook until all is melted and smooth. Blend in the heavy cream, stirring smooth. In a bowl beat the egg yolks until light. Add the chocolate mixture slowly and carefully to the beaten egg yolks. Return combination to the pan, place over hot water and cook, stirring for five minutes. Pour into six small pot de creme containers or the three ounce souffle bakers or custard cups. Chill thoroughly before serving. Note: If you prefer bake the combined chocolate and egg yolk mixture in small custard cups surrounded by hot water in a slow oven (300 degrees) for twenty minutes. Chill before serving.

Rich Chocolate Pudding

Six ounces semi-sweet chocolate
One-half cup butter
Four egg yolks
One ond one-half teaspoons vanilla
Four egg whites
One-fourth cup sugar
Chill: Thoroughly
One cup heavy cream, whipped
Servings: Six to eight

Melt the semi-sweet chocolate in the upper half of a double boiler over hot water. Remove from the heat and gradually beat in small pieces of the butter, beating and stirring well after each addition. Beat in the egg yolks, one at a time. Add the vanilla. In a bowl beat the egg whites until foamy, gradually beat in the sugar. Beat until stiff. Fold the chocolate mixture into the egg whites carefully. Chill in the refrigerator. To serve layer alternate spoonfuls of the chocolate with the whipped cream in small parfait glasses.

Steamed Chocolate Pudding

One-fourth cup butter or shortening
Two-thirds cup sugar
One egg
Two squares (two ounces) unsweetened
   chocolate, melted
One teaspoon vanilla
One and one-half cups sifted flour
Three teaspoons baking powder
Three-fourths teaspoon salt
Three-fourths cup milk
Three-fourths cup chopped walnuts
Steaming time: One hour and a half
Servings: Six, or more

In a bowl cream the butter or shortening, gradually blend in the sugar. Beat in the egg. Add the melted chocolate and vanilla and stir smooth. Sift together the flour, baking powder and salt and add to the first mixture alternately with the milk. Blend smooth and stir in the chopped walnuts. Transfer to a greased pudding mold (1½ qts.) or bowl. Cover tightly and place in large pan on rack. Pour on boiling water to the depth of half the mold or bowl. Cover pan and steam pudding for two hours or until it seems light and leaves the sides of the mold slightly. Turn out on a serving platter and serve at once with soft vanilla ice cream or the following sauce.

Foamy Vanilla Sauce

One egg
One tablespoon water
One-half cup sugar
One-fourth teaspoon salt
Cook: Three minutes
One teaspoon vanilla
Yield: One cup, about

In a small saucepan beat the egg with the water. Stir in the sugar and salt. Cook over direct heat, stirring constantly, until slightly thickened. Remove from heat and stir in vanilla. Beat until foamy and serve immediately over pudding.

Chocolate Mint Creme

Three ounces unsweetened chocolate
Heat: To melt
One cup sugar
Three cups milk
Four egg yolks
One-fourth teaspoon salt
Cook: Thirty to forty minutes
One teaspoon peppermint extract
Chill: Thoroughly
Serves: Six

Melt the unsweetened chocolate in the upper half of a double boiler over hot water. Stir in the sugar and gradually blend in the milk. Remove from heat. In a bowl beat the egg yolks; stir in the milk mixture and salt and return to double boiler. Cover and cook over simmering water until the mixture is medium thick, stirring occasionally. It will take from 30 to 40 minutes. Add peppermint and pour into custard cups. Chill. Serve with cream if desired.

A FAVORITE RECIPE
Chocolate Dessert

One-half pound sweet chocolate, cut
   into pieces
Four tablespoons water
Two tablespoons confectioners' sugar
One-sixteenth teaspoon salt
Cooking time: In a double boiler until
   the chocolate melts
Four egg yolks
Cooling time: One hour
One teaspoon vanilla
Four egg whites, beaten stiff
Chilling time: Three hours
One-half cup heavy cream, whipped
Servings: Four

In the top of a double boiler mix the chocolate, water, sugar and salt. Cook until the chocolate is melted, stirring frequently. Add the egg yolks, one at a time, beating with the chocolate after each addition. Cool. Beat the egg whites until very stiff. Add the vanilla to chocolate and fold in the beaten egg whites. Turn into individual serving dishes. Chill. Serve garnished with whipped cream.

MRS. MARY NOLTE, *Jersey City, N.J.*

Soft Custard

Four eggs
One-fourth cup sugar
One-eighth teaspoon salt
Two cups milk
Cook: Ten minutes, or more
One teaspoon vanilla
Serves: Four, or more

In the upper half of a double boiler beat the eggs, stir in the sugar and salt. Add the milk and place over hot, not boiling water and cook until the mixture thickens, stirring constantly. When cooked, the mixture will coat a metal spoon. Remove from the heat, add vanilla and cool. Pour into a cold bowl or individual serving dishes; chill.

Lemon Vanilla Bombe

Two egg yolks
One-fourth cup sugar
One-fourth cup lemon juice
One-eighth teaspoon salt
Cook: Five to ten minutes
Chill: Thoroughly
Two-thirds cup heavy cream, whipped
One quart vanilla ice cream
Freeze: Firm
Serves: Six to eight

In the upper half of a double boiler beat the egg yolks. Beat in the sugar, lemon juice and salt. Place over hot water and cook, stirring constantly until thickened. Remove from the heat and chill thoroughly. Fold into the whipped heavy cream carefully. Pack the slightly softened vanilla ice cream against the bottom and sides of a five or six cup pudding or melon mold. Pour cream mixture into the center. Cover with lid or with a piece of aluminum foil and freeze in the freezer until firm. Unmold by inverting over serving plate and pressing a cloth wrung out in hot water against the mold.

Vanilla Ice Cream Special

One-half cup sugar
One tablespoon cornstarch
One and one-half cups milk
Cook: Until thickened, then ten minutes more
Two egg yolks, beaten
Cook: Five minutes
Two teaspoons vanilla
Two egg whites
Pinch of salt
First freezing time: Until firm
One cup heavy cream, whipped
Second freezing time: Until firm
Serves: Six

In the upper half of a double boiler combine the sugar and cornstarch. Gradually stir in the milk. Place over boiling water and cook until mixture thickens, stirring constantly. Cover, continue cooking, stirring occasionally, for ten minutes. Add a small amount of the cooked mixture to the beaten egg yolks. Return combination to the pan. Cook over hot, but not boiling water for five minutes. Remove from heat, add vanilla and cool. In a bowl beat the egg whites with salt until they form soft peaks. Fold into the chilled cooked mixture. Pour into refrigerator tray and freeze firm. Remove to a bowl and beat smooth with a wooden spoon. Fold in the whipped cream and return to the refrigerator tray to freeze until firm.

Fudge Sauce

Two squares (2 oz.) unsweetened chocolate
Two tablespoons butter or margarine
One-half cup corn syrup
One cup sugar
Two-thirds cup water
One-eighth teaspoon salt
Boil: Five minutes
Yield: One and one-half cups

In a small saucepan melt the unsweetened chocolate with the butter or margarine over low heat, stirring constantly. Blend in the corn syrup and sugar, water and salt. Heat to the boiling point and cook, stirring constantly for five minutes. Add the vanilla and use hot or cold.

Mocha Almond Ice Cream

One envelope unflavored gelatin
One-fourth cup water
One cup strong coffee
One square unsweetened chocolate
Heat: To melt chocolate
Three-fourths cup brown sugar
One-fourth teaspoon salt
One teaspoon vanilla
One can (14½ oz.) evaporated milk
One and one-half cups heavy cream
Freeze: Until set
Three-fourths cup slivered toasted almonds
Freeze: Firm
Serves: Eight, or more

Sprinkle the unflavored gelatin over the fourth cup of water and let stand to soften. In a small saucepan heat the coffee with the unsweetened chocolate until thoroughly blended. Add the softened gelatin and stir to dissolve. Remove from heat and add brown sugar and salt, stirring until dissolved. Cool to room temperature and add the vanilla, evaporated milk and heavy cream. Pour into a deep refrigerator tray and freeze to a mush. Transfer to a bowl and beat smooth with a wooden spoon. Add the slivered toasted almonds and return to the freezing section to freeze firm.

Butter Rum Sauce

One cup sugar
One-half cup water
Boiling time: Five minutes
Four tablespoons butter
One teaspoon grated orange rind
Two tablespoons orange juice
One-fourth cup rum
Heating time: Two minutes
Yield: One cup

In a small saucepan boil the sugar and water together for five minutes. Stir in the butter, orange rind, juice and rum.

Cherry Sauce

Three-fourths cup sugar
One and one-half tablespoons cornstarch
One can (No. 2) tart red cherries
Cook: Five to ten minutes
One tablespoon lemon juice
Yield: Two cups sauce

In a small saucepan stir the sugar and cornstarch together. Drain the juice from the canned cherries and add one cup to the sugar mixture gradually, stirring smooth. Cook, stirring, until the sauce thickens and is clear. Remove from heat and add the cherries and lemon juice. Chill thoroughly before serving.

Fruit Sauce

Three-fourths cup orange juice
One-fourth cup lemon juice
One-half cup canned pineapple juice
One cup sugar
Simmer: Twenty minutes
One-fourth cup sauterne
Two teaspoons light corn syrup
Simmer: Ten minutes
Cool: Slightly
One cup washed, hulled and sliced strawberries
One cup well drained canned pineapple (crushed or tidbit cut)
One large banana, thinly sliced
Yield: Three cups, approx.

In a saucepan combine the orange, lemon and pineapple juice with the sugar. Stir over moderate heat until sugar is melted. Simmer gently for 20 minutes. Add the sauterne and corn syrup and continue to simmer for 10 minutes more. Cool slightly and add the sliced strawberries, drained pineapple and sliced bananas. Chill thoroughly before serving over ice cream filled cream puffs.

Lemon Cream Filled Meringues

Three egg whites
One-fourth teaspoon cream of tartar
One-fourth teaspoon salt
Three-fourths cup sugar
Oven temperature: 250 degrees
Bake: One hour
Three egg yolks
One-fourth cup sugar
One-fourth cup lemon juice
Cook: Five to ten minutes
Chill: Thoroughly
Two-thirds cup heavy cream
Chill: Overnight
Serves: Six, or more

In a bowl beat the egg whites until foamy. Add the cream of tartar and salt. Add the sugar gradually and beat until very stiff and glossy. Cover a baking sheet with aluminum foil and form the individual meringues from the mixture with a spoon, shaping up the sides and scooping out the centers to create a hollow. You can make six large meringues or up to twelve smaller ones. Bake for one hour in a very slow oven. They do not need to brown. Remove from oven and cool on the foil on a rack. When cooled peel off the foil. Prepare the filling by beating the egg yolks in the upper half of a double boiler. Beat in the sugar, then the lemon juice. Place over hot water and cook, stirring constantly until thickened.

Remove from heat and chill thoroughly. Beat the heavy cream until stiff and fold into the chilled lemon mixture. Spoon into the hollows of the cooled meringues and chill thoroughly, preferably overnight. Serve plain or with the colorful cherry sauce.

Layered Jellied Fruit Cocktail

Two packages strawberry flavored gelatin
Two packages lemon flavored gelatin
Two packages lime flavored gelatin
Chill: Until it begins to gel
One can (No. 2½) fruit cocktail, drained
Flaked coconut and Jordan almonds for
    garnish
One-half pint heavy cream
One-fourth cup sugar
Serves: Eight, or more

Prepare the strawberry, lemon and lime flavored gelatins according to directions on the package using ½ cup less liquid. Chill until each one begins to jell (the consistency of unbeaten egg white). Add a third of the fruit cocktail to each. Line three cake pans (8 in.) with aluminum foil. Oil the foil on bottom and sides. Fill each layer with different flavored gelatins. Chill until firm. When firm, lift out the foil; loosen edges. Place the strawberry flavored gelatin on bottom, then lemon flavored gelatin and top with the lime flavored gelatin. Set in refrigerator. When ready to serve, garnish with flaked coconut and colored Jordan almonds. Beat the heavy cream and sugar together until stiff. Cut the layered gelatin into wedges; serve with sweetened whipped cream.

Chocolate Pudding Mint Parfait

One package prepared chocolate pudding
    mix
One package prepared vanilla pudding mix
Few drops mint flavoring
Few drops green coloring
Chill: Until ready to serve
Serves: Eight

Prepare both pudding mixes according to directions on package using ½ cup less liquid in each case. To the vanilla pudding add a few drops of mint flavoring and green coloring. Allow the pudding to cool. Spoon layers of each kind of pudding in parfait glasses. Garnish with whipped cream and green cherries.

Vanilla Pudding Strawberry Parfait

One package prepared vanilla pudding
    mix
One package strawberry flavored gelatin
One cup strawberries
Chill: Until it begins to gel
One-half cup flaked coconut
Chill: Until ready to serve
Serves: Eight

Prepare the pudding mix according to the directions on the package. Cool. Prepare the strawberry gelatin according to directions on package using ½ cup less liquid. Chill. Wash and hull the berries. Reserve eight berries. Slice remaining berries. When the strawberry gelatin starts to gel (the consistency of unbeaten egg whites) add the sliced strawberries; spoon the cold vanilla pudding in bottom of each parfait glass. Then arrange a layer of strawberry gelatin over the pudding; then another layer of pudding mix. Sprinkle coconut on top. Garnish with whole berries.

Fruit Chiffon Tarts

One package prepared pastry mix
One package prepared lemon chiffon mix
Fruit (strawberries, grapes, apricots)
One-half cup apricot jam, or currant jelly
Serves: Seven

Prepare the packaged pastry mix according to directions on package for tart shells. Prepare the lemon chiffon mix according to directions on package. When tart shells are cold, fill each with lemon chiffon mix; top with strawberries, grapes, with apricots. Heat the jam or jelly; brush over fruit to glaze.

Floating Island

Three cups milk, scalded
Six eggs, separated
Three-fourths cup sugar
Cook: Two minutes
Chill: Until serving time
One cup heavy or light cream, scalded
One-half cup sugar
One teaspoon vanilla
Cook: Until mixture coats a metal spoon
    (about 10 minutes)
Chill: Three hours
One can (11 oz.) Mandarin oranges
Serves: Six

In a heavy skillet (9 in.) heat the milk until bubbles appear around the edge. Beat the egg whites until soft and fluffy. Add the three-fourths cup sugar gradually, beating until satiny. Drop rounded spoonfuls of meringue on the hot, not boiling, milk using very low heat. Cook about two minutes for meringues. Remove carefully to a towel to drain. When cool, chill on a plate. Strain milk into top of a double boiler; add scalded heavy cream. Beat vigorously the combined egg yolks and sugar into the mixture. Cook until the mixture coats a metal spoon. To stop the cooking, pour into another dish. Cool. Add vanilla. Chill until serving time. Serve custard in a wide shallow glass bowl. Top with meringue. Garnish with Mandarin oranges and mint.

Praline Ice Cream

One and three-fourths cups light cream
One package (4 oz.) vanilla frozen
    dessert mix
Freezing time: Thirty minutes, or more
Beating time: Three minutes (about)
One cup praline candy pieces (½ in.)
Freezing time: Two hours, or more
Servings: Four

Set the cold control of the automatic refrigerator at freezing temperature. Pour the light cream into a mixing bowl. Add the frozen dessert mix; beat with a rotary beater until smooth. Pour into a shallow tray. Place in the freezing compartment and freeze until solid one inch or more from the sides of the tray. Put the mixture into a medium-sized bowl (1½ qts.). Mash thoroughly. Beat with a rotary beater until the volume is about doubled. Fold in the pieces of praline candy. Return to the tray and freeze until firm.

To vary this ice cream, fold in one-third cup crushed peppermint stick candy, one-half cup peanut brittle or one-fourth cup finely cut candied ginger in place of the praline candy.

A FAVORITE RECIPE
Biscuit Tortoni

Three egg yolks, slightly beaten
One-third cup confectioners' sugar
Two cups milk, heated to scalding
Cooking time: Until it starts to thicken
    in the top of a double boiler
One teaspoon almond extract
Chilling time: One hour
One egg white, beaten stiff with
One-eighth teaspoon salt
One pint heavy cream, beaten with
One-third cup confectioners' sugar
One-half cup finely chopped almonds
Freezing time: Four hours
Yield: Twenty-four cups (2 in.)

In a bowl, beat the egg yolks slightly; add the sugar, stirring until dissolved. Heat the milk slowly until scalding. Pour over the egg mixture in the bowl. Return to the top of double boiler; cook stirring constantly until the mixture begins to thicken. Strain. Cool to room temperature. Add the extract, mix. Chill thoroughly. Beat the egg white and salt in a bowl until the egg holds its shape. Beat the cream with the sugar until thick. Combine with the egg white. Add the cooked egg mixture, blending well. Pour into the cups. Sprinkle the top with the almonds. Set the refrigerator control to freezing. Freeze until serving time. Store the other two egg whites in refrigerator for future use.

MRS. JAMES MARCHETTI, *Brooklyn, N.Y.*

Orange Ice Cream

One envelope unflavored gelatin
One-half cup water
One-half cup evaporated milk
One can (6 oz.) concentrated orange juice
Two-thirds cup sugar
One-eighth teaspoon salt
Freezing time: Thirty minutes
One cup heavy cream, whipped
Freezing time: Three to four hours
Servings: Six, or more

Soften the gelatin in one-fourth cup water. Scald the remaining water and milk; add to the gelatin mixture, stirring until the gelatin is dissolved. Blend in the juice, sugar and salt. Pour into the freezing trays of the automatic refrigerator, setting the cold control at freezing temperature. Freeze rapidly until thickened. Turn the mixture into a chilled bowl; beat with a heavy rotary beater until fluffy. Fold in the whipped cream. Return to the trays and freeze until firm.

Cranberry Sherbet

One pound (four cups) cranberries
Two and three-fourths cups boiling water
Cook: Five to ten minutes
One tablespoon unflavored gelatin
One-fourth cup cold water
Two cups sugar
One-third cup lemon juice
Freeze until firm
Yield: One quart

Cook the cranberries in the boiling water until all have popped. Rub through a sieve or food mill into a large bowl. Add the gelatin that has been softened in the cold water, then the sugar. Stir to dissolve thoroughly. Add the lemon juice. Pour into refrigerator trays and freeze until firm. Serve with chicken or turkey or as a dessert.

Melon Sherbet

One-half cup sugar
One and one-half cups water
Boil: Five minutes
Three cups ripe melon pulp and juice
One-third cup lemon juice
Freeze: Until solid
Freeze: Firm
Servings: Six or eight

Combine the sugar and water in a saucepan, bring to a boil, boil five minutes. Cool to room temperature. Chop the meat of a ripe melon (cantaloupe, honeydew, cranshaw) very fine, measure with juice. (Ideally put the melon meat in an electric blender and reduce to a pulp electrically.) Combine melon pulp with the cooled syrup and lemon juice. Pour into a deep freezer tray and freeze solid. Remove, cut into cubes and transfer to a bowl. Beat smooth with a wooden spoon. Return to tray and freeze until firm.

Sherry Lemon Dessert

One envelope unflavored gelatin
One-fourth cup cold water
Three egg yolks
One-half cup sugar
One-half teaspoon salt
One-half teaspoon grated lemon rind
One-fourth cup lemon juice
One-half cup cream or medium sherry
Cook: Five to ten minutes
One cup marshmallow fluff
Chill: Until almost set
Three egg whites
One-fourth cup sugar
One-fourth cup chopped walnuts
Chill: Until firm
Servings: Eight

Sprinkle the unflavored gelatin over the cold water in a cup, let stand to soften. In the upper half of a double boiler beat the egg yolks, stir in the half cup of sugar, salt, grated lemon rind, lemon juice and sherry. Place over hot water and cook, stirring constantly until thickened. Remove from heat and stir in the softened gelatin until blended; add the marshmallow fluff. Chill in the refrigerator until almost set. In a bowl beat the egg whites until foamy, gradually

beat in the fourth cup of sugar until stiff. Fold into the thickened gelatin mixture and spoon into individual sherbet glasses. Sprinkle a few chopped nuts over each serving and refrigerate until set.

Cherries Jubilee

One can (No. 2½) Bing cherries and syrup
One-fourth cup cognac
Heating time: Five minutes, about
One-fourth cup cognac
One tablespoon cognac
One quart vanilla ice cream
Servings: Eight

In a saucepan heat the Bing cherries and syrup. Add one-fourth cup of cognac. Pour the sauce into a shallow heat proof serving bowl and carefully pour second measure of cognac over the top. Ignite the tablespoon of cognac by holding a match under the spoon. Use the flaming cognac to ignite that on the top of the cherry sauce. Spoon flaming sauce over individual portions of vanilla ice cream.

A FAVORITE RECIPE
Frozen Peach Custard

Two cups milk
Four egg yolks, beaten light with
Four tablespoons brown sugar
One-fourth teaspoon salt
Cooking time: Fifteen minutes in a double boiler
Two cups ripe peaches, mashed, fresh or canned
One cup sugar
One-half teaspoon almond extract
Two cups heavy cream, whipped
Freezing time: Four hours
Servings: Eight

In the top of a double boiler, scald the milk. Beat the eggs in a bowl, add the brown sugar and salt, beat. Pour the hot milk over the egg, beating constantly. Strain into the double boiler, cook, stirring frequently until as thick as custard. Cool. Crush the peaches thoroughly in a bowl with the sugar. Press through a coarse sieve. Add the almond extract. Combine the custard and peach mixture, folding in the whipped cream. Turn into a tray and set the refrigerator control to freeze. Serve sliced on glass plates.

MRS. CARL HAUSER, *East Islip, L.I., N.Y.*

Creme de Menthe Pear Sundaes

One can (No. 2½) pear halves
One-third cup sugar
One and one-half tablespoons cornstarch
One cup pear syrup
Cook: Five minutes, about
One tablespoon butter
One-fourth cup creme de menthe liqueur
Chill: Thoroughly
One pint vanilla ice cream
One pint chocolate ice cream
Serves: Eight

Drain the syrup from the canned pear halves and set aside. Refrigerate the

fruit until serving time. In a saucepan stir together the sugar and cornstarch. Gradually blend in one cup of the pear syrup. Cook, stirring constantly until the sauce thickens and is clear. Remove from the heat and stir in the butter and creme de menthe. Chill thoroughly. At serving time place a pear half in each individual serving dish. Fill with several small scoops of vanilla and chocolate ice cream and spoon on the creme de menthe sauce. Serve at once.

Broadway Bombe

One quart coffee ice cream
One pint chocolate ice cream
Freeze: Firm
One-half cup heavy cream
One-fourth teaspoon vanilla
One-eighth teaspoon salt
Two tablespoons sugar
Two tablespoons cocoa
Chill: Thirty minutes
Serves: Six to eight

Pack the slightly softened coffee ice cream against the bottom and sides of a five or six cup pudding mold. Spoon chocolate ice cream into the center. Cover with lid or with a piece of aluminum foil and freeze in freezer until firm. Measure the heavy cream into a bowl and add the vanilla, salt, sugar and cocoa. Let chill for thirty minutes before beating with rotary beater until stiff enough to hold its shape. Refrigerate until serving time. Unmold ice cream by inverting over serving plate and pressing a cloth wrung out in hot water against the mold. Garnish with the chocolate whipped cream.

Toasted Snow Balls

One and one-half cups flaked coconut
Oven temperature: 400 degrees
Bake: Eight to ten minutes
One quart coffee ice cream
Serves: Six

Scatter the flaked coconut over a baking sheet and toast a golden brown in a quick oven, checking occasionally to prevent scorching. Remove from oven and cool. At serving time roll balls of coffee ice cream in the toasted coconut and serve with Mocha Sauce.

Mocha Sauce

One-half cup sugar
One tablespoon cocoa
One tablespoon cornstarch
One-eighth teaspoon salt
One cup brewed coffee
Boil: Three minutes
Two tablespoons butter
Yield: One cup

In a small saucepan stir together the sugar, cocoa, cornstarch and salt. Blend in the coffee. Bring to a boil; boil, stirring constantly for three minutes. Remove from the heat and add butter. Serve warm or cold over the Toasted Snow Balls.

Bread and Jam Pudding

Four or five slices white bread
Soft butter
One-fourth cup jam or less (apricot, raspberry, grape)
Two eggs
Three tablespoons sugar
One-sixteenth teaspoon salt
Two cups milk
Oven temperature: 375 degrees
Baking time: Twenty minutes
One-fourth cup flaked coconut
Baking time: Twenty minutes
Servings: Six

Trim the crusts from the bread and spread each slice with the softened butter and some of the jam or preserves. Cut each slice in two and fit into a baking dish (1 qt.) lining the bottom and sides. Place a second trimmed and spread slice over that in the bottom. In a bowl beat the eggs. Stir in the sugar and salt. Scald the milk in a saucepan and add gradually to the egg and sugar mixture, stirring constantly while adding. Pour over the bread in the baking dish. Place dish in a pan of hot water and bake in a moderately hot oven for 20 minutes. Sprinkle the top of the pudding with the flaked coconut and continue baking for 20 minutes more. Remove from the oven when coconut is lightly browned and custard is set. Cool, then chill thoroughly in the refrigerator before serving.

Lemon Rice Pudding

Two cups cooked rice
One tablespoon grated lemon rind
One cup water
One-fourth cup lemon juice
One-half cup sugar
One-half teaspoon salt
Cook: Twenty minutes, or more
Two eggs
Cook: Five minutes
Chill: One hour, about
One cup heavy cream
One-half teaspoon vanilla
One-fourth teaspoon almond flavoring
Chill: Thoroughly
Serves: Six, or more

In the upper half of a double boiler combine the cooked rice, grated lemon rind, water, lemon juice, sugar and salt. Cover. Place over boiling water and cook until most of the liquid is absorbed. In a bowl beat the eggs. Add a small amount of the cooked mixture to the eggs, return the combination to the saucepan. Cook for five minutes or until thickened, stirring the while. Remove from heat and chill thoroughly before folding in the whipped cream flavored with vanilla and almond flavoring. Spoon into dessert dishes and chill before serving. Garnish with a maraschino cherry or nutmeat.

Cranberry Orange Tapioca

Two cups fresh cranberries
One cup water
Cook: Eight to ten minutes
Three tablespoons quick-cooking tapioca
Three-fourths cup sugar
One cup boiling water
Cook: Three to five minutes
One-half cup diced orange
One teaspoon vanilla
Chill: Thoroughly
Serves: Six

Wash and pick over the cranberries. Place in a saucepan with the cup of water and cook until all the skins burst, about eight to ten minutes. In a second saucepan stir the quick-cooking tapioca and sugar together. Add the boiling water and cook over medium heat, stirring constantly for about three to five minutes or until transparent. Cool slightly. Stir into the cranberries with the diced orange and vanilla. Chill thoroughly before spooning into dessert dishes.

Walnut Tapioca

Three cups milk
Heat: To scalding
Three tablespoons quick-cooking tapioca
One-half teaspoon salt
Cook: Twelve minutes
Three egg yolks
One-fourth cup sugar
Cook: Three to five minutes
One teaspoon vanilla
Cool: Thoroughly
Three egg whites
One-fourth cup sugar
One-half cup chopped walnuts
Whipped cream (optional)
Serves: Six

In the upper half of a double boiler, heat the milk to scalding. Add the quick-cooking tapioca and salt and cook over hot water for twelve minutes, stirring constantly. In a bowl beat the egg yolks slightly with the one-fourth cup of sugar. Gradually add the hot tapioca to the egg yolks, stirring constantly, return combination to double boiler and cook until mixture thickens. Cool slightly and add vanilla. Chill thoroughly. Just before serving beat the egg whites until foamy, gradually beat in the remaining one-fourth cup of sugar until a satiny meringue is formed. Fold into the chilled tapioca with the chopped walnuts. Spoon into serving dishes and garnish with whipped cream if desired.

Chocolate Bread Pudding

Two cups milk
Two tablespoons butter
One-half cup sugar
Scalding time: Three to five minutes
Two eggs beaten
Two cups bread cubes (½ in.)
One-fourth teaspoon salt
Two squares unsweetened chocolate, melted
Oven temperature: 350 degrees
Bake: Forty minutes
Serves: Four, or more

In a saucepan combine the milk, butter and sugar. Heat to scalding, melting the butter and sugar. Remove from the heat. In a bowl, beat the eggs. Add a small amount of the milk to the eggs then return to the saucepan. Add the bread cubes, salt and melted chocolate. Pour into a greased baking dish (1½ qts.). Place dish in a large pan that contains an inch of hot water. Bake in a moderate oven until set in center. Serve warm or cooled with thin or whipped cream.

Lemon Coconut Crunch Bread Pudding

One pkg. (4 oz.) lemon pie filling
Two and one-half cups water
One-third cup sugar
Two beaten egg yolks
Cook: Five minutes, about
Two cups soft bread cubes (½ in.)
One-third cup brown sugar
One-third cup flaked coconut
One-fourth cup butter or margarine, melted
Oven temperature: 350 degrees
Bake: Twenty-five minutes
Serves: Six

Prepare the lemon pie filling with the water, sugar and egg yolks according to the directions on the package. Pour cooked pudding into a shallow baking dish (8 x 8 x 2 in.). In a bowl combine the soft bread cubes, brown sugar, flaked coconut and melted butter. Toss thoroughly to mix well. Scatter over the pudding in the baking dish and bake in a moderate oven until nicely browned on top. Serve at room temperature or thoroughly chilled.

A FAVORITE RECIPE
Matzo Apple Pudding

One-half cup unsalted, crushed matzo square
One-fourth cup hot water
Two eggs, beaten light
One-eighth teaspoon salt
Four teaspoons light brown sugar
Three apples, peeled, cored, chopped
One-fourth cup seeded raisins
One cup milk
One teaspoon vanilla
One tablespoon sugar, mixed with
One teaspoon cinnamon
Six pats (1 in.) butter
Six whole, candied cherries
Oven temperature: 350 degrees
Baking time: One hour
Servings: Six

Roll the matzo on a bread board; place in a bowl; add the water. Stir until matzo is soft. Add the eggs, salt, sugar, apple and raisins. Fold lightly until well blended. Add the milk and vanilla. Turn into a well greased pan (8 x 8 in.); sprinkle the sugar and cinnamon over the top. Dot with the pats of butter; top with the whole cherries. Bake in a moderate oven until lightly browned. Serve warm or cold.

MRS. FAY BAGDON, *Bronx, N.Y.*

Peach Coupe

Six ripe peaches, peeled
Boiling water
Boil: One minute
One bottle Bordeaux sauternes wine
Chill: Two hours
Serves: Six

Put peaches into a saucepan of boiling water. Let boil one minute. Drain. Put peaches into ice water. Peel the peaches. With a toothpick punch holes in the peaches. Place in a dish, cover with sauternes. Place a piece of transparent Saran over peaches so as to prevent discoloring. Chill. Serve in chilled glasses with sauternes wine. Garnish with triangular-shaped wafers.

Fresh Fruit with Strawberry Ice

Sprinkle one cup sugar over one quart of strawberries or raspberries. Let stand two hours; rub through a sieve. Add one tablespoon of lemon juice. Freeze mixture. Arrange an assortment of sweetened chilled fresh fruit in a sherbet glass. Place a scoop of strawberry or raspberry ice on top.

Melon Supreme

Scoop out melon balls from four wedges of honey dew melon, leaving the holes intact. Fill the holes with an assortment of melon balls (watermelon, cantaloupe, honey dew) soaked in white wine. Chill. Serve with a wedge of lime or lemon.

Strawberries Romanoff

Pour one-half cup cognac or kirsch over four cups strawberries; chill one hour. Beat one-half pint ice cream to semi-soft stage; fold in one-half cup heavy cream which has been beaten until stiff. Add berries. Serve at once in sherbet glasses.

Ambrosia Medley

Six medium-sized oranges, sectioned
Two grapefruit, sectioned
One cup freshly grated or shredded coconut
Nine maraschino cherries, drained
Serves: Six

In a bowl arrange the orange and grapefruit sections. Place the coconut in the center and garnish with cherries. Chill.

Poached Fruit Medley

Four peaches
Four green gage plums
Eight apricots
Three pears, split and cored
Four blue plums
One small pineapple, cut into spears
Four cups water
Two cups sugar
Cooking time: Three minutes
Simmering time: Three to six minutes
One tablespoon lemon juice
Cooking time: Three minutes
Serves: Six, or more

Dip the peaches in boiling water, remove the skins; split in half; stone. Wash and prick with a fork the green plums, apricots and blue plums. Cut the pineapple into spears. In a heavy large skillet boil the water and one cup of sugar until the sugar is dissolved. Put in all the fruit except the blue plums into the boiling syrup. After about three minutes of cooking over low heat, carefully remove the green plums and apricots to a bowl. Continue cooking the peaches, pears, and pineapple spears about three minutes longer or until tender. Remove; place in the bowl with the apricots. Add the blue plums; cook about two minutes. Remove to a separate small bowl for they discolor the other fruit. Add the remaining sugar and lemon juice to the syrup; cook until the sugar is dissolved. Cover the fruit in the bowls with the syrup. Let cool. When cold, serve in glass dessert dishes.

*Note. If some of the fresh fruit is not available use canned fruit.

A FAVORITE RECIPE
Fruit Cocktail Dessert

One cup sugar
One cup flour
One teaspoon baking soda
One-half teaspoon salt
One egg, beaten light
One can (1 lb. 1 oz.) fruit cocktail

Topping

One cup sifted brown sugar
One cup ground nuts
Oven temperature: 300 degrees
Baking time: One hour
One cup, or more, heavy cream, whipped
Servings: Six

In a bowl, mix the sugar, flour, soda and salt. Stir in the beaten egg. Add the fruit cocktail (2 cups); mix thoroughly. Turn into a well greased baking pan (7 x 13 or 8 x 13 in.). Sprinkle the top with the brown sugar. Spread the nuts over all. Bake in a slow oven for one hour. Serve on glass plates topped with the whipped cream.

MARIE MURPHY, *New York City, N.Y.*

Chilled Melon Compote

One watermelon
Two cups honey dew melon balls
Two cups cantaloupe balls
Two cups white wine
Chilling time: Sixty minutes
One bunch green grapes, seeded
One bunch red grapes, seeded
One bunch mint
Eight red cherries with stems
Servings: Eight, or more

Cut the watermelon in half lengthwise with a large sharp knife. Make balls of the pink watermelon, using a French ball cutter, or a standard measuring tablespoon. Place in a shallow bowl with the honeydew and cantaloupe balls. Pour the white wine over them. Chill, turning them occasionally. Then hollow out one-half of the melon, making a shell. Fill the shell with chilled assorted melon balls and seeded grapes. Garnish with mint and cherries.

Pear Pineapple Crisp

Four cups peeled, sliced pears
One can (8 oz.) crushed pineapple
One tablespoon lemon juice
One teaspoon grated lemon rind
One cup sugar
Three-fourths cup flour
One teaspoon cinnamon
One-third cup butter or margarine
Oven temperature: 375 degrees
Baking time: Thirty minutes
Servings: Six

In a bowl, mix the sliced pears with the pineapple, lemon juice and rind. Sift together into a bowl the sugar, flour and cinnamon. Using a pastry blender or two knives cut the butter or margarine into the flour mixture until the consistency resembles coarse meal. Place half the fruit in the bottom of a greased baking pan (8 x 8 x 2 in.) sprinkle with half the crumbly mixture. Repeat. Bake in a moderately hot oven until brown on top. Serve warm with milk or cream if desired.

A FAVORITE RECIPE
Blueberry Dessert

Sixteen graham crackers, crushed fine
One-fourth cup melted butter
One-half cup powdered sugar
One package (8 oz.) cream cheese (room temperature)
Two eggs, beaten light
One-half cup white sugar
Oven temperature: 350 degrees
Baking time: Twenty minutes
One can blueberry pie mix
One teaspoon lemon juice
Chilling time: Eight hours
One cup heavy cream, whipped
One-half teaspoon vanilla
One teaspoon sugar
Serve: Six, or more

Roll the crackers until rather fine. In a bowl mix with the melted butter and powdered sugar. Pat the mixture into a pan (9 x 13 in.); sides and bottom covered. In a bowl mix the cream cheese with the beaten eggs and sugar, beating until smooth. Spread over the graham cracker crust in pan. Bake in a moderate oven. Cool thoroughly. Mix the blueberry mix and lemon juice, spread over the top and chill. When ready to serve spread on the whipped cream beaten with the vanilla and teaspoon of sugar.

BETTY TOYCEN, *Swan Lake, Montana*

Blueberry Betty

One and one-half cups corn flakes
One teaspoon cinnamon
One-fourth cup sugar
Two tablespoons melted butter
Two cups blueberries (fresh or canned)
One tablespoon lemon juice
Oven temperature: 350 degrees
Bake: Twenty minutes
Cream
Servings: Six

In a bowl combine the corn flakes, cinnamon, sugar, and melted butter. Sprinkle the blueberries with lemon juice. Place half the blueberries in the bottom of a baking dish, cover with half the corn flakes. Repeat. Bake in a moderate oven for twenty minutes. Serve warm with cream.

Brown Betty

Two tablespoons butter or margarine
One cup soft bread crumbs
Heating time: Five minutes
Three cups thinly sliced peeled apples
One-third to one-half cup sugar
One-eighth teaspoon salt
One-eighth teaspoon cinnamon
One-half cup water, about
One tablespoon butter
Oven temperature: 350 degrees
Baking time: Thirty minutes, or until brown
Servings: Four

Melt the butter or margarine in a skillet. Add the soft bread crumbs and crisp slightly. Sprinkle one-third in the bottom of a casserole (1 qt.). Add half the sliced apples, sprinkle with half the mixed sugar, salt and spice. Repeat layers and finish off with remaining crumbs. Pour on the water and dot with butter. Cover and bake in a moderate oven until the apples are soft. Uncover and bake until the crumbs on top have browned. Serve hot or while still warm with milk or cream as preferred.

A FAVORITE RECIPE
Pineapple-Cherry Squares

One and one-half cups fine vanilla wafer crumbs
One can (1½ cups) flaked or shredded coconut
One-half cup butter or margarine
One and one-half cups sifted confectioners' sugar
Two eggs
One cup heavy cream, whipped
One cup maraschino cherries, well drained
One cup (9 oz.) crushed pineapple, drained
One cup broken walnut meats
Chilling time: Four hours or longer
Servings: Eight

Roll the wafers between waxed paper until fine. Place half the crumbs in the bottom of a pan (9 x 9 in.); sprinkle one-half of the coconut over the crumbs. Cream the butter in a bowl, adding the sugar gradually, creaming until light. Add the eggs, one at a time, beating well after each addition. Spread the mixture over the coconut. Whip the cream in a deep bowl; add the cherries, drained pineapple and nuts, folding until well blended. Spread over the top, sprinkling with the remaining coconut and crumbs. Chill in refrigerator until serving time.

MRS. DOROTHY BERGER, *Bronx, N.Y.*

A FAVORITE RECIPE
Strawberry Loaf

One large loaf unsliced white bread cut lengthwise into three slices
One quart fresh ripe strawberries
One-third cup sugar
Simmering time: Ten minutes
Six tablespoons soft butter
Foil to wrap bread
Chill: Overnight
One-half pint heavy cream, whipped
One tablespoon sugar
Servings: Six

With a sharp knife cut the crust from the loaf of bread. Slice lengthwise. Wash the berries, place in a saucepan with the sugar. Cook slowly, crushing gently. Butter the bottom slice of bread; top with half the warm berries. Butter the middle slice, set over berries. Place top slice over berries. Press together lightly. Wrap in foil or plastic wrap. Chill. Just before serving whip the cream. Spread over the top and sides of loaf. Garnish with whole berries. Slice crosswise and serve.

MRS. G. G. CRABTREE, *Lansing, Mich.*

A FAVORITE RECIPE
Cherry-Peach Dessert

Two cups peeled sliced peaches
One cup fine graham cracker crumbs
One cup light brown sugar
One teaspoon cinnamon
One-half teaspoon nutmeg
One can (1 lb. 4 oz.) sour cherries, drained
Two tablespoons butter
Juice drained from cherries (heated)
Oven temperature: 350 degrees
Baking time: Thirty minutes
Servings: Eight

In a well buttered baking dish (8 x 8 x 2 in.) place a layer of the peaches; sprinkle with the crumbs mixed with the sugar and spice; add a layer of the cherries and a layer of crumbs. Continue the layers until all ingredients are used; top with crumbs, dot with butter. Pour the hot juice over the top. Bake in a moderate oven. Serve with hard or lemon sauce.

MRS. CHRISTINE MALAST, *Brooklyn, N.Y.*

Creamy Rice Pudding

One-half cup rice
One quart milk
One-half cup sugar
One-half teaspoon salt
Oven temperature: 300 degrees
Bake: One hour
One-half cup seedless raisins
Bake: One and one-half hours
Serves: Six

Mix the rice, milk, sugar and salt in a greased baking dish (2 qts.). Bake in a slow oven, stirring every 15 minutes. After the first hour of baking add the raisins and bake until creamy without stirring. Serve warm or cold with milk or cream poured over top. If desired sprinkle with one-eighth teaspoon of nutmeg after adding the raisins.

A FAVORITE RECIPE
Lamb Chops Indian Style

Two tablespoons cooking oil, heated
Four large shoulder lamb chops
Seasonings to taste
Browning time: Fifteen minutes
One-fourth cup water
Simmering time: Forty minutes
One tablespoon curry powder
One can (10½ oz.) cream style corn
Simmering time: Fifteen minutes
Servings: Four

In a heavy skillet, heat the oil. Season the chops; brown on each side; reduce the heat; add the water. Cover, cook until almost tender. Mix the curry with the corn. Remove water from skillet and corn; simmer until the chops are tender. Serve with mashed potatoes and a green salad.

MRS. MATTHEW GREEN, *Brooklyn, N.Y.*

Chili Con Carne

One-fourth pound kidney fat, diced
One and one-half pounds chopped beef chuck
One cup water
Cooking time: Thirty minutes
Two small onions, chopped fine
Two cloves garlic, minced
Four tablespoons chili powder
One can (No. 2) tomatoes
Simmering time: One hour
One tablespoon paprika
Three-fourths tablespoon salt
One-sixteenth teaspoon cayenne
Servings: Four, or more

In a large heavy skillet cook the kidney fat until melted. Add the meat and water; cook uncovered over low heat for 30 minutes. Stir in the onion, garlic, chili powder and tomatoes. Simmer for 60 minutes. Blend in the paprika, salt and cayenne. Serve with kidney beans, enchiladas, or tamales.

Shrimps in Green Sauce

One-third cup wine vinegar
Two-thirds cup olive oil
One clove garlic, cut and crushed
One-fourth cup finely minced parsley
One small onion, cut and crushed
One teaspoon anchovy paste
One-fourth teaspoon salt
One-fourth teaspoon pepper
Chilling time: Overnight
Two cups small cooked shrimp, chilled
Servings: Six

Mix all the ingredients in a jar except the shrimps. Shake well. Chill. Pour the sauce into small glass dishes; set each on a plate. Arrange the shrimps around the sauce. Serve.

Chicken Pilaf

One frying chicken, cut up (2½ to 3 lbs.)
One-half cup butter or margarine
One-half cup chopped onion
Sauté: Until browned
One green pepper, chopped
One tablespoon turmeric
One teaspoon ginger
One teaspoon cinnamon
One teaspoon salt
One-fourth teaspoon pepper
One-eighth teaspoon crushed hot peppers
One can (No. 2½) tomato puree
Cook: One hour
Two cups cooked rice
Oven temperature: 375 degrees
Bake: Twenty minutes
Serves: Four

Rinse and dry the pieces of chicken. Melt the butter or margarine in a large heavy skillet. Add the chicken and chopped onion and cook until chicken is browned. Add the chopped green pepper, turmeric, ginger, cinnamon, salt, pepper, crushed hot peppers and tomato puree. Stir to blend, cover and simmer gently until the chicken is very tender. Cook regular or quick cooking rice. When chicken is tender remove to a plate. Stir cooked rice into the sauce and transfer to a shallow casserole. Lay chicken over the rice and bake in a moderately hot oven until piping hot and well browned. Serve with the uncooked chutney.

Food from Other Lands

Canadian Chutney

Two pounds, seeded raisins, cut coarsely
One pound dried figs, shredded
Two pounds apples, diced
Three tablespoons minced garlic
Two pounds brown sugar
Four tablespoons salt
Two tablespoons ginger
One teaspoon cayenne pepper
One quart cider vinegar
Cooking time: One and one-half hours
Yield: Five pints, about

In a large kettle combine the prepared raisins, figs, apples and garlic. Add the sugar, salt, ginger, cayenne pepper and vinegar. Bring to a boil, stirring, boil slowly until the chutney begins to thicken. Reduce the heat, simmer to the consistency of jam, stirring often. Seal in hot sterilized jars as for canned fruit.

A FAVORITE RECIPE
Bombay Salad

One cup shredded coconut
Two cups diced cooked chicken
One-half cup cooked rice
One-half cup India relish
One-fourth cup mayonnaise
One tablespoon light cream
One head crisp lettuce
One small can pimiento, cut into strips
Serves: Six

In a bowl combine the coconut, chicken, rice and relish, tossing until well blended. Mix the mayonnaise and cream together and add to salad, tossing again. Line a salad bowl with the lettuce; turn salad into bowl; garnish with pimiento.

ELIZABETH HOWSER, *Colorado Springs, Colo.*

Lamb with Spiced Rice

One cup rice
One-fourth cup butter or margarine
One and one-half pounds boneless lamb
Two onions, thinly sliced
Browning time: Ten minutes, about
One pint yogurt or sour milk
One clove garlic, crushed
One-half teaspoon coriander
One teaspoon ground ginger
One-eighth teaspoon pepper
One clove garlic
Two cardamon seeds
One and one-half teaspoons salt
One-half teaspoon saffron
One tablespoon boiling water
Cook: Ten minutes
One and one-half cups boiling water
Simmer: Forty-five minutes, about
Serves: Six

Place the rice in a bowl, cover with cold water and let stand for 15 minutes, drain well. Melt the butter or margarine in a large heavy skillet. Cut the boneless lamb into one inch cubes and add to the melted butter with the thinly sliced onion. Sauté until brown on all sides. Add the yogurt, garlic, coriander, ginger, pepper, clove, cardamon seeds, salt, rice and saffron dissolved in the tablespoon of boiling water. Stir well together to mix. Cover tightly and cook over medium heat for 10 minutes. Reduce heat to low for 10 minutes. Add the hot water and simmer for 45 minutes, or until rice and lamb are very tender.

Chow Mein

Six tablespoons salad, peanut or olive oil
One-half cup minced onion or scallion
One cup chopped celery or green pepper
Cooking time: Five minutes
Two cups bean sprouts (drained) or
    chopped water chestnuts
One-half cup broth or water
One can (10½ oz.) condensed cream of
    chicken, mushroom or celery soup
One can sliced mushrooms, pimiento or
    slivered toasted almonds
One-fourth teaspoon salt or Ac'cent
Cook: Fifteen minutes
One teaspoon cornstarch or potato starch,
    mixed with
Two tablespoons water, bouillon or stock
Cooking time: Five minutes
Two cups canned flaked crabmeat,
    chicken, turkey, tuna, lobster or shrimp
Heat: To the boiling point
Two cups hot crisp noodles or potato chips
Serves: Four, or more

In a heavy skillet heat the oil; cook the onion and celery until the onion is straw-colored. Add the bean sprouts, broth, soup, mushrooms and salt. Cook until celery is tender. Stir in the combined cornstarch and water; cook until slightly thickened. Remove cartilage from crabmeat; flake (saving a few pieces for garnish). Gently add the crabmeat; heat to the boiling point. Over hot crisp noodles serve crabmeat mixture. Garnish with crabmeat and green pepper rings.

Seafood Casserole

Four tablespoons butter
One-half cup sherry wine
One cup cooked or canned lobster meat
One cup cooked shrimp
One cup cooked crabmeat
Heat: Fifteen minutes
Two tablespoons flour
One and one-half cups light cream
Two egg yolks
One-half teaspoon salt
One-fourth teaspoon white pepper
Cook: Until thickened
One pound cooked snow peas or
    Italian beans

Topping

Four tablespoons butter or margarine
One-half teaspoon paprika
One-half cup seasoned bread crumbs
One tablespoon grated Parmesan cheese
One-fourth cup sherry wine
Two tablespoons crushed potato chips
Oven temperature: 325 degrees
Bake: Twenty minutes, or more
Serves: Six

In the top of a double boiler, put the butter, sherry, lobster, shrimp and crabmeat. Place over simmering water for 15 minutes. Stir in the combined flour, light cream, egg yolks, salt, white pepper; cook until slightly thickened, stirring occasionally. Remove. Put the seafood mixture and snow peas into a casserole. For the topping: Combine the melted butter, paprika, seasoned bread crumbs, Parmesan cheese and sherry wine. Add the potato chips. Sprinkle mixture around edge of casserole. Bake in a moderately slow oven until hot. Serve with rice.

Shrimp Sukiyaki

Two tablespoons fat
Two pounds cooked shrimp, deveined
One-half cup hot meat or chicken stock
One tablespoon soy sauce
One tablespoon sugar
Heating time: Five minutes
Six scallions, thinly sliced lengthwise
One leek, thinly sliced lengthwise
Six stalks celery, thinly sliced
One cup washed spinach leaves
One cup thinly sliced mushrooms
One cup thinly sliced bamboo shoots
Cooking time: Five minutes
Serves: Six, or more

Rub the fat on the inside surface of an electric skillet. Set the control at medium heat. Add the shrimp, stock, soy sauce and sugar, heat until the shrimp is hot. Add the remaining prepared ingredients. Cook five minutes at medium heat stirring occasionally. Serve with cooked rice and green tea.

Chinese Egg Roll Pancakes

Six eggs, beaten
One cup water
Two cups sifted flour
Two teaspoons salt
Two tablespoons fat
Cooking time: One minute
Yield: Twenty small pancakes
Serves: Eight

Beat the egg and water in a bowl; sift in the flour and salt; beat smooth with a rotary beater. Grease a small skillet (7 in.) lightly; heat over a moderate flame. Pour in enough batter to cover the bottom of the skillet with a thin layer. Cook on one side only until the pancake will hold together. Remove to a flat surface to cool. Repeat until all the batter is cooked. Fill.

Chinese Egg Roll Filling

One-half cup salad oil
One-half pound pork, shredded or ground fine
Cook: Three minutes (about)
One-half pound bean sprouts, canned or fresh
One-fourth cup bamboo shoots, shredded
Saute: Two minutes
One tablespoon sherry
One-fourth pound raw shelled shrimp, minced
Four dried Chinese mushrooms, soaked in water, shredded
Two tablespoons "Oyster Sauce"
One teaspoon sesame oil
One teaspoon salt
One tablespoon cornstarch, mixed with Three tablespoons cold water
Cook: five minutes
One-half teaspoon Ac'cent
Two large scallions, split, chopped (1 in. pieces)
Yield: Filling for twenty pancakes

Paste for Sealing

One tablespoon flour or cornstarch
Two tablespoons cold water
One package egg roll skins or pancakes
Oil for frying
Frying temperature: 375 degrees
Frying time: Five minutes
Yield: Twenty rolls

Heat the oil in a pan. Add shredded pork. Cook over a high flame until pork is pale in color. Remove meat, leaving two tablespoons of oil in the pan. Add the bean sprouts and bamboo shoots; saute two minutes. Add sherry, shrimp, mushrooms and pork, stirring thoroughly. Add oyster sauce, sesame oil and salt. Cook until shrimp turns pink. Stir in the cornstarch paste. Cook until it thickens. Add Ac'cent. Spread out on platter to cool. When cool, add the scallions. In making rolls, put one tablespoon of fill-ing on one sheet of egg roll skin or pancake, in the center. Moisten edge of dough with paste. Fold one corner of dough over filling. Fold over two corners envelope fashion; roll up. Repeat procedure for remaining skin or pancakes. Fry in hot deep oil until golden. Serve with a mustard sauce. They may be reheated in the oven.

Note: For those interested in buying Egg Roll Skins readymade, they may be purchased in some Chinese Specialty shops.

Chinese Egg Roll

Pancake batter:
One cup sifted flour
One-half teaspoon salt
Two eggs, well beaten
One cup water
One-fourth cup salad oil (about)
Frying time: Three to four minutes
Yield: Eight, or more

In a bowl, combine the flour and salt. Combine the beaten eggs with the water; blend into the flour, beating until smooth. Heat a skillet (8 in.), grease lightly with oil. Cover the bottom of the skillet with a very thin layer of batter, tipping the pan to spread batter as thin as possible. Fry until lightly brown on one side only. Remove from pan and put aside to cool. Grease skillet before frying each pancake. Reserve two tablespoons of batter for sealing the rolls later.

Filling

Three tablespoons shredded carrots
Three tablespoons finely diced celery
One-fourth cup boiling water
Simmering time: Four minutes
One tablespoon finely sliced green onions or scallions
One-half cup finely chopped cooked meat (chicken, ham or beef)
One-half cup finely diced cooked shrimp
One-half teaspoon salt
One-fourth teaspoon pepper
One tablespoon salad oil
One teaspoon sugar
Chilling time: Two hours
Fat for frying
Frying temperature: 370 degrees
Frying time: Three minutes, or more
Yield: Eight to ten rolls
Four tablespoons dry mustard
Three tablespoons water
Servings: Four

In a small saucepan, combine the shredded carrots and diced celery with the boiling water. Cook briefly; drain. Add sliced onion, meat, shrimp, salt, pepper, tablespoon of salad oil and sugar. Mix well. Place one tablespoon of this filling in the middle of each pancake on the browned side. Roll the pancakes, folding in the ends while rolling. Seal with remaining batter. Chill in the refrigerator thoroughly. Heat fat in a medium-sized saucepan to the depth of two inches to 370 degrees. Insert a toothpick in each chilled egg roll to keep it tightly wrapped. Slip rolls one at a time into the hot fat and cook rapidly, turning once to brown evenly. Remove to absorbent paper to drain. Serve with a mustard sauce made by combining the dry mustard with the water and beating until smooth.

Chinese Vegetable Soup with Pork

One-half pound lean pork
One cup water
Simmer: Ten minutes
One-half pound mushrooms
One and one-half cups fresh spinach, torn into small pieces
One carrot, scraped and slivered
Three tablespoons canned bamboo shoot cubes
Two teaspoons soy sauce
One teaspoon ginger
Two cans (10½ oz. each) condensed bouillion
Simmer: Ten to fifteen minutes
Serves: Four, or more

Cut the lean pork into julienne strips about two by one-half by one-half inches. Place in a saucepan with the cup of water and simmer for ten minutes. Add the trimmed and sliced mushrooms, washed and torn spinach, carrot strips cut like the pork, cubed bamboo shoots, soy sauce, ginger and bouillon. Simmer gently until carrots are just tender.

A FAVORITE RECIPE
Chinese Roast Pork

Two pounds pork chops or pork cutlets (¼ in. thick)

Sauce

Four tablespoons sugar
Four tablespoons honey
Four tablespoons soy sauce
One teaspoon salt
Oven temperature: 325 degrees
Baking time: Forty-five minutes
Servings: Four

Place the chops in a roasting pan. For the sauce: Mix the sugar, honey, soy sauce and salt in a small bowl. Pour over the chops. Bake in a moderately slow oven, baste frequently with the pan sauce. Serve hot with rice and stewed tomatoes.

MRS. FRED SCHWARTZ, *Lee, Mass.*

Chinese Fried Rice

Two tablespoons salad oil
One-fourth cup finely chopped onion
Four cups cooked rice
One-half cup finely chopped cooked ham
Two tablespoons soy sauce
Cook: Ten minutes
One beaten egg
Cook: One or two minutes
Chopped parsley (optional)
Servings: Six or more

In a large skillet combine the salad oil, finely chopped onion, cooked rice, chopped ham and soy sauce. Cook slowly, stirring frequently for 10 minutes or until well heated through. Add the beaten egg and cook one or two minutes longer, stirring the while. Serve at once sprinkled with finely chopped parsley if desired.

Chinese Pork with Mushrooms

One pound lean pork
Three tablespoons butter
Sauté: Ten minutes, about
One small onion, finely chopped
One and one-half cups thinly sliced celery
One-half pound fresh mushrooms, sliced
One teaspoon salt
One-eighth teaspoon pepper
One-eighth teaspoon ginger
One-eighth teaspoon nutmeg
One-fourth cup sherry
Simmer: Twenty minutes or less
Hot cooked rice
Serves: Four

Cut the lean pork into thin slices, then into finger sized strips. Heat the butter in a large heavy skillet, add the pork and sauté for ten minutes, or until pork is slightly browned. Add the finely chopped onion, thinly sliced celery and mushrooms. Sprinkle with salt, pepper, ginger, nutmeg and sherry. Cover tightly and simmer gently until celery is tender crisp, stirring occasionally. Add more sherry or water if dry. Serve over hot cooked rice.

A FAVORITE RECIPE
Pork Chow Mein

Four medium-sized onions, sliced into eighths
One bunch celery, cut into one inch lengths
Sauté: Fifteen minutes
One-half pound fresh mushrooms, sliced thin
Sauté: Five minutes
One pound fresh pork, diced (¼ in.)
Cooking time: Ten minutes
Three tablespoons soy sauce
One can bean sprouts with liquid
Cooking time: To boiling point
Two tablespoons molasses
Two tablespoons cornstarch mixed with
Three tablespoons water
Cooking time: To the boiling point
Three cups cooked rice
One-fourth pound salt pork, rendered in a Dutch oven
Servings: Six

In a deep heavy skillet render the salt pork. Remove the salt pork; sauté the onions and celery in the hot fat; add the mushrooms, sauté. Brown the pork in the fat in a separate skillet, stir several times until browned on all sides. Add the soy sauce. Turn the mixture into skillet with the onion mixture. Add the bean sprouts with the liquid. When the mixture boils, add the molasses, stirring until well blended. Mix the cornstarch and water, stir into the mixture, stirring until smooth and thickened. Serve hot over hot rice or with Chinese noodles.

SHARON CHESTNUT, *Dumont, N.J.*

A FAVORITE RECIPE
Shrimp Chinese

One cup minced boiled shrimp
One-third cup finely minced boiled ham
One tablespoon minced scallions
    (optional)
One-fourth teaspoon salt
One-sixteenth teaspoon pepper
Whites of two eggs, beaten stiff
Ten slices bread, crust removed, cut
    into wedges
Oil for cooking, heated
Frying time: Until browned on both sides
Servings: Eight, or more

In a bowl, mix the shrimp, ham and scallions. Season with salt and pepper and fold in the beaten egg whites. Spread on the bread wedges. Cook in the hot oil over a medium flame until lightly browned on both sides. Drain on absorbent paper. Serve hot. This may be prepared hours ahead of serving time, just reheat in oven.

MRS. DOUGLAS C. SHAFFER, *New York, N.Y.*

Chinese Chicken

One frying chicken (2½-3 lbs.) cut up
Two tablespoons cornstarch
One-half teaspoon ginger
One-fourth teaspoon powdered garlic
One teaspoon sugar
One-half teaspoon salt
Two tablespoons butter or margarine
Browning time: Five to ten minutes
Three tablespoons soy sauce
One-half cup apple juice
One-half cup water
Simmering time: Twenty minutes, about
One can (4 oz.) diced bamboo shoots,
    drained
Heating time: Ten minutes, about
Hot cooked rice
Servings: Four

Rinse off and dry thoroughly the chicken pieces. Stir together the cornstarch, ginger, powdered garlic, sugar and salt. Dust chicken pieces with cornstarch mixture, reserving any excess. In a large heavy skillet heat the butter or margarine, add the seasoned chicken and brown quickly on all sides. Stir together the soy sauce, apple juice and water and pour over the chicken. Cover and simmer gently until chicken is tender, about twenty minutes. Add the drained canned diced bamboo shoots. Stir in a little of the pan liquid into the reserved cornstarch mixture. Stir into the liquid in the skillet. Cook briefly, stirring smooth. Serve chicken and sauce over fluffy hot rice.

Chicken Chow Mein

Three tablespoons butter
One-fourth cup chopped onion
One cup sliced celery
One medium-sized green pepper, sliced
One-half cup mushrooms, sliced
Sautéing time: Five minutes
One and one-half cups shredded, cooked
    chicken
One and one-half cups chicken broth
Two teaspoons soy sauce
One teaspoon salt
Simmering time: Fifteen minutes
One and one-half tablespoons cornstarch
Three tablespoons water
Cooking time: Three to five minutes
One can (4 oz.) fried Chinese noodles,
    heated
Servings: Four

Melt the butter in a heavy skillet with onion, celery, green pepper and mushrooms; sauté. Add chicken, broth, soy sauce and salt; simmer. Mix cornstarch with water and add to the cooked mixture. Cook until slightly thickened and clear. Serve hot over heated chow mein noodles.

A FAVORITE RECIPE
Chinese Vegetable Casserole

One medium-sized eggplant (2 lbs.)
    peeled, cut into chunks (1 in.)
One small can (10 oz.) water chestnuts,
    drained
One green pepper cut, cleaned, cut into
    strips
One large tomato, peeled, cut into pieces
One medium-sized onion, peeled and
    quartered
One-fourth pound small mushrooms,
    washed (do not cut)
Oven temperature: 300 degrees
Baking time: Forty minutes (until tender)
Three-fourths cup hot white sauce,
    seasoned
One-half teaspoon soy sauce (optional)
Baking time: Ten minutes
Servings: Four

In a casserole (10 in.) place the prepared eggplant, water chestnuts, green pepper, tomato, onion and mushrooms. Cover tightly. Bake in a slow oven until the vegetables are nearly soft. Make a white sauce; pour over the vegetables, return to oven; bake 10 minutes longer. If desired canned cream of mushroom soup may be used, diluting the soup with milk; add the soy sauce, mix. Serve hot from the casserole.

FRED H. MC DONALD, *New York, N.Y.*

Eggs Foo Young

One cup diced cooked turkey
One-half cup finely diced celery
One-third cup finely diced green pepper
Two medium-sized mushrooms, chopped
One-fourth cup peeled and diced water
    chestnuts
One-fourth cup coarsely cut bamboo
    shoots (optional)
Six eggs
One teaspoon salt
One-eighth teaspoon pepper
Oil or fat for frying
Cooking time: Five minutes, about
Servings: Four to six

In a bowl, combine the diced, cooked turkey with the cut celery, green pepper, mushrooms, water chestnuts and bamboo shoots if used. In a large bowl, beat the eggs well, add the salt and pepper and the mixed vegetables and turkey. Heat a little oil or fat in a large skillet and spoon in the egg mixture, cooking six medium-sized omelets (approximately six inch) separately, turning once to brown on the second side. Serve with soy sauce.

Chicken Cantonese

One frying chicken (2½-3 lbs.), cut up
Paprika
Salt and pepper
Flour
One-third cup salad oil
Frying time: Fifteen minutes, about
One-half teaspoon salt
One-fourth teaspoon cloves
One-fourth teaspoon nutmeg
One-fourth cup pineapple juice
One-fourth cup orange juice
Simmering time: Twenty-five minutes
One-fourth cup flour
One-half cup water
One cup pineapple juice
One cup orange juice
Cooking time: Five minutes, about
Two-thirds cup pineapple chunks
One-third cup slivered almonds
Cooking time: Ten minutes
Servings: Four

Rinse and dry thoroughly the pieces of chicken. Lay on a board or platter and sprinkle generously with paprika, salt, pepper and flour on both sides. Heat the salad oil in a large heavy skillet, add the seasoned chicken pieces and brown well on both sides. In a small bowl stir together the half teaspoon of salt, cloves and nutmeg. Blend in the fourth cup each of pineaple and orange juice and pour over the browned chicken in the skillet. Cover and simmer over low heat for twenty-five minutes or until chicken is tender. Measure the flour into a saucepan. Gradually blend in the water, taking care to beat out any lumps. Stir in the remaining pineapple and orange juice and cook over moderate heat, stirring constantly until thickened. Add the pineapple chunks and slivered almonds and pour over the chicken that has simmered tender. Cook over low heat without a cover for ten minutes more before serving. Cook with fluffy rice.

Chinese Pork with Broccoli

One-half pound lean pork, thinly sliced
One tablespoon salad oil
Browning time: Three minutes
One-half teaspoon salt
One-half teaspoon Ac'cent
Three-fourths cup chicken broth
One small onion, sliced
Simmering time: Ten minutes
One-half cup chopped celery
Two cups cut broccoli (1 in. pieces)
Cooking time: Five minutes
Two teaspoons cornstarch, mixed with
Two tablespoons cold water
One-half teaspoon soy sauce
Cooking time: Three minutes
Servings: Four

The pork must be cut into paper-thin strips. Brown in the oil in a skillet over high heat. Add the seasonings, broth and onion. Cover; then cook gently until the onions are soft. Add the celery and broccoli; cover. Cook until the broccoli is tender yet crisp. Blend in the cornstarch paste and soy sauce; stir until slightly thickened. Serve with a bowl of rice.

Shrimp Tempura with Sauce

Sixteen large shrimp
One cup sifted flour
One egg, slightly beaten
Two-thirds cup water (about)
Deep fat temperature: 365 degrees
Frying time: Six minutes (about)
One-fourth cup soy sauce
One-fourth cup water
One teaspoon sugar
One-fourth teaspoon salt
One teaspoon white wine or sherry
One eighth teaspoon minced ginger root
  or grated horseradish
One teaspoon Ac'cent
Servings: Four

Wash and drain the shrimp. Remove the shell, leaving the tail and last segment of shell intact. Split down the back; remove the vein. Set aside. In a bowl combine the flour, egg and water to make a medium batter. Dip in the shrimp, four at a time, holding each by the tail. Fry each batch in the hot deep fat until brown on both sides. Drain on absorbent paper. To make the sauce: Bring the remaining ingredients to a boil in a saucepan. Serve with shrimp.

Lobster Cantonese Style

Two small live lobsters
Three quarts water
Cooking time: Three minutes
Four tablespoons oil
One clove garlic, minced
One-half pound ground pork
Browning time: Five minutes
One tablespoon soy sauce
One teaspoon sugar
One teaspoon Ac'cent
One-fourth teaspoon pepper
One cup hot chicken broth
Cooking time: Ten minutes
One tablespoon cornstarch, mixed with
One-half cup cold water
Cooking time: Three minutes
One egg, slightly beaten
Four scallions, chopped
Standing time: Two minutes
Servings: Four

Drop the lobsters in the boiling water, cook; drain. Remove the vein and sack behind the head. Cut into edible portions. Crack the claws. Set aside. Brown the garlic and pork in the oil in a large skillet. Add the soy sauce, seasonings, broth and lobster. Cover; cook slowly until the lobster turns a deep red. Stir in the cornstarch paste; cook, stirring, until thickened. Turn off the heat. Pour the beaten egg over the lobster; stir. Add the scallions. Cover; let stand. Serve with rice.

Lamb Curry

Two pounds cubed shoulder lamb
Browning time: Ten minutes
Two tablespoons butter
One cup chopped onion
One clove garlic, crushed
Cooking time: Five minutes
One teaspoon curry powder, or more
Two teaspoons salt
One-sixteenth teaspoon thyme
Two bay leaves
Four cups hot stock
Two tablespoons tomato puree
Simmering time: One and one-half hours
One green apple, peeled and chopped
Cooking time: Five minutes
One-half cup light cream
Servings: Four, or more

Trim excess fat from the lamb. Brown the meat on all sides in a heavy saucepan; remove meat. Add butter, cook onions and garlic until soft. Add the lamb, seasonings, stock and tomato puree. Cover; cook gently until the meat is tender. Remove the meat to a hot serving dish. To the sauce in the pan, add the apple; cook until soft. Stir in the cream; reheat. Pour over the meat; serve with fluffy rice and an assortment of four or more condiments, such as chutney, chopped peanuts, sieved hard-cooked egg, shredded or chipped coconut, minced parsley, candied ginger, preserved kumquats, watermelon pickle.

Shrimp Curry

Six tablespoons butter or margarine
Three-fourths cup diced onion
Two cups minced apple
One-half cup minced celery
Cook: Ten minutes
One tablespoon flour
One tablespoon curry powder
One teaspoon salt
Two cups chicken broth or bouillon
Cook: Ten minutes
One tablespoon minced chutney
Two pounds cooked shrimp
Fluffy rice
Parsley, peanuts, raisins, hard-cooked
    eggs, flaked coconut, chutney
Serves: Four

In a heavy skillet heat the butter, add the onion, apple and celery. Cook until the apple is soft, stirring constantly. Blend the flour, curry and salt into the chicken broth; stir until smooth. Add to the apple mixture; cook until slightly thickened. Add the chutney and shrimp; reheat until hot and bubbly. Serve on a nest of fluffy rice with chopped parsley; peanuts, raisins, hard-cooked eggs, flaked coconut and chutney.

NOTE: To cook shrimp. In a kettle heat to boiling enough water to cover the shrimp. Add sprigs of parsley, slice of onion, five peppercorns, half a sliced lemon and one teaspoon salt. Add shrimp; bring to a boil. Turn down heat to simmer and cook six minutes. Shell and devein.

A FAVORITE RECIPE
Lasagne

One-half pound lasagne
Three cups boiling water
Two tablespoons salt
Cooking time: Until tender
One pound pot cheese
One small mozzarella cheese, sliced thin
One can (8 oz.) tomato sauce

Meat Balls

One pound chopped meat (¼ pound pork
  and ¾ pound beef)
One clove garlic, minced
One teaspoon salt
One-fourth teaspoon pepper
Two tablespoons water
Two eggs
Olive oil for frying, heated
Frying time: Until browned
Oven temperature: 300 degrees
Baking time: Thirty minutes
Servings: Four

In a large kettle, cook the lasagne in the boiling salted water until tender. Drain thoroughly. Alternate layers of the lasagne, pot cheese, mozzarella cheese, tomato sauce and meat balls in a large square oven dish. For the meat balls: Mix the meat, garlic, salt and pepper. Add the water and eggs, mix well and form into small balls. Heat the olive oil in a skillet, fry the balls until browned. Place over the lasagne and bake in a very slow oven. Serve from oven dish.

MRS. JANE AGUSTA, *New York, N.Y.*

A FAVORITE RECIPE
Neopolitan Fish

One pound fillet of sole, cut into pieces
  (2 inch)
One dozen large shrimp, cleaned, split
  part way down
One-half dozen clams, quartered
One-half pound scallops, sliced (½ in.)
One tablespoon minced parsley

Sauce

One-half cup olive oil, heated
One clove garlic, mashed
Browning time: Three minutes
One can (No. 2) plum tomatoes, mashed
One-half teaspoon salt
One-fourth teaspoon oregano
Simmering time: Ten minutes
Oven temperature: 400 degrees
Baking time: Twenty minutes
One and one-half cups cooked rice
Servings: Four

In a large flat baking dish, place the sole. Spread the shrimp, clams and scallops over the top; sprinkle with parsley. For the sauce: Heat the oil in a skillet; add the garlic, mash to a pulp; brown. Add the tomatoes, salt and oregano; bring to a boil, reduce the heat, simmer, stirring frequently. Pour the sauce over the fish, covering each piece. Bake in a quick oven until fish is flaky. Serve hot over cooked rice or spaghetti.

MRS. D'EUSTACHIO, *New Hyde Pk., L.I.,N.Y.*

A FAVORITE RECIPE
Italian Rice Pie

Two cups cooked rice
Five eggs, beaten light
One cup Parmesan cheese, grated
One pound hot Italian sausage, fried
  until browned
One whole Mozzarella cheese (8 oz.) cut
  into chunks (¼ in.)
One teaspoon salt
One-fourth teaspoon pepper
Oven temperature: 350 degrees
Bake: Forty minutes
Yield: One pie (9 in.)
Serves: Six

Place the rice in a bowl; add the beaten eggs and grated cheese. In a skillet, cook the sausage until well done. Cut the sausage into ¾-inch pieces. Add with the cut mozzarella cheese, salt and pepper to the rice, mixing well. Turn into a well buttered pie plate (9 in.); bake in a moderate oven until lightly browned. Serve hot.

MRS. ADELINE TULLIO, *Bronx, N.Y.*

Italian Style Pizza

One-half cup milk, scalded and cooled to
  lukewarm
One tablespoon oil
One teaspoon sugar
One teaspoon salt
One package active dry yeast
One-fourth cup lukewarm water
One and three-fourths cups sifted flour
Rising time: Fifty minutes
One cup canned tomatoes, drained
Two tablespoons grated Parmesan cheese
One tablespoon olive oil
One-half teaspoon oregano
Few grains cayenne pepper
One-half pound mozzarella cheese
One teaspoon minced parsley
Oven temperature: 400 degrees
Baking time: Twenty minutes, about
Servings: Six or more

In a bowl combine the milk, oil, sugar and salt; cool to lukewarm. Sprinkle the yeast over the lukewarm water in a cup; let stand five minutes. Add to the mixture in a bowl. Beat in the flour to make a dough that can be handled. Knead upon a floured board five minutes or until smooth and elastic. Shape into a ball; place in a greased bowl. Grease the top of the dough. Cover and let rise in a warm place until the dough doubles in size. Divide the dough in half. Roll each piece into a circle (8 in.) on a floured board and place in an oiled pan (8 in.). Stretch to fit. Spread half the drained tomatoes, Parmesan cheese, olive oil, oregano and cayenne pepper over each piece of dough, leaving one-half inch of the uncovered dough around the edge. Arrange thinly sliced mozzarella cheese on top. Sprinkle with parsley. Bake in a quick oven until bubbly and brown. Cut in wedges and serve at once.

A FAVORITE RECIPE
Potato Croquettes Italian

Four potatoes, peeled, diced, cooked,
  mashed with
Two eggs, well beaten
One-half teaspoon salt
One-eighth teaspoon pepper
One-half cup bread crumbs
One clove garlic, minced, or less
One teaspoon minced parsley
One tablespoon grated Parmesan cheese
Three slices salami, minced
Oil for frying, heated
Frying time: Until golden brown
Serves: Four

Wash, peel and cook the potatoes. In a bowl mash and add the egg, salt, pepper, bread crumbs, garlic, parsley and cheese; beat until well blended. Fold in the minced salami. Roll in hands to desired shape. Heat the oil; brown the croquettes on all sides. Serve hot.

MRS. JOHN C. PONTICELLO, *Roselle, N.J.*

Caffe Tortoni

One cup heavy cream
One-half cup confectioners' sugar
One teaspoon instant espresso coffee
Two tablespoons rum
One egg white
Two tablespoons finely chopped almonds,
  toasted
Chill: Until firm
Servings: Six

In a bowl whip the cream and sugar until stiff. Dissolve the instant espresso coffee in the rum and add to the cream. In a bowl beat the egg white until it holds soft peaks. Fold into cream mixture. Spoon into six paper cups (4 oz.). Scatter the toasted almonds over top and chill in the freezing unit of the refrigerator until firm.

A FAVORITE RECIPE
Italian Rice Cake

One-half cup rice, cooked as directed on
  package; drain
Eight eggs, beaten light
Two pounds ricotta
Two cups sugar
Grated rind one orange
Grated rind one lemon
Juice one-half lemon
One-fourth teaspoon cinnamon
One teaspoon vanilla
One pie crust (10 or 12 in.)
Oven temperature: 350 degrees
Baking time: One hour
Serves: Eight

Cook the rice as directed; drain and cool. Beat the eggs in a bowl until light and fluffy. In a bowl mix the rice, eggs, ricotta, sugar, orange and lemon rind, lemon juice and cinnamon; add vanilla. Make a favorite pie crust, or use the prepared mix. Line the pie plate. Fill with the rice mixture. Bake until firm in a moderate oven. Cool; serve.

MISS JOAN PETRUZZELLI, *Fort Lee, N.J.*

Stuffed Cabbage Mexicana

One large head cabbage
Boiling salted water
Cook: Ten minutes, about
One pound sausage meat
One-half pound ground beef
One-half cup rolled oats
One can (6 oz.) tomato sauce
One teaspoon salt
One-eighth teaspoon pepper
Two tablespoons shortening or oil
One large onion, finely chopped
One green pepper, finely chopped
Sauté: Five to ten minutes
One cup hot water
One teaspoon chili powder
Simmer: One and one-fourth hours
Servings: Six

Remove 12 leaves from a large head of cabbage and add to the boiling salted water in a large kettle or saucepan. Cook until pliable and almost translucent. Drain. In a bowl mix the sausage meat, ground beef, raw oats, tomato sauce, salt and pepper well together. Spoon the meat mixture on each cabbage leaf at the stem end. Fold over once, turn in the sides of the leaf and roll up snugly. If necessary use wooden picks to hold together. In a large heavy skillet heat the shortening or oil. Add the chopped onion and the green pepper and sauté until tender. Add the water, chili powder and cabbage rolls. Cover and simmer gently for one and one-fourth hours. Serve piping hot with creamy mashed potatoes and green beans.

Spanish Lamb

Four slices bacon, diced
Fry until crisp
One-fourth cup flour
One teaspoon salt
Four shoulder lamb chops (one inch thick)
One cup chopped onion
Browning time: Ten minutes, about
Four small scraped carrots
One can (No. 303) tomatoes
One and one-half cup diced celery
One-half teaspoon poultry seasoning
One tablespoon vinegar
Simmer: One hour
One-half cup water
Cook: Five minutes
Servings: Four

In a large heavy skillet cook the diced bacon until crisp. Push to one side of pan. Combine the flour and salt and dredge chops in the combination; reserve remaining flour. Brown the chops and onions in the bacon fat. Add the carrots, tomatoes, celery, poultry seasoning and vinegar. Cover tightly and cook slowly for about one hour or until lamb and carrots are tender. Remove chops and carrots to serving platter. Combine water and remaining seasoned flour to form a paste. Add to the sauce in the skillet and cook, stirring until thickened. Serve hot gravy with the chops and carrots.

Chicken with Rice
(Arroz con Pollo)

One (3 pound) frying chicken, cut up
One-half cup salad oil
Browning time: Ten to fifteen minutes
One cup finely chopped onion
One-half cup chopped green pepper
One clove garlic, crushed
Browning time: Five to ten minutes
One can (No. 2½) tomatoes
One-fourth cup tomato paste
Two bay leaves
Two teaspoons salt
Simmer: Forty minutes
One cup raw rice
One teaspoon vinegar
One-half cup sliced mushrooms
Cook: Fifteen minutes
One package (10 oz.) frozen peas
Cook: Ten minutes
Serves: Six

Rinse and dry the pieces of cut-up chicken, removing the wing tips if preferred. Heat the salad oil in a large, heavy skillet, add the chicken and brown quickly on all sides. Remove chicken to a platter and add the chopped onion, green pepper and crushed garlic to the skillet. Brown lightly. Add the canned tomatoes, breaking up with a fork, tomato paste, bay leaves and salt. Stir to blend. Lay browned chicken pieces on top, cover and simmer gently for 40 minutes. Stir in the rice, vinegar and sliced mushrooms; cover and simmer 15 minutes. Add the frozen peas, cover and cook until rice and peas are tender. Serve at once, spooning rice and vegetable mixture on individual plates and topping with pieces of chicken.

A FAVORITE RECIPE
Chili Con Carne

Two tablespoons olive oil, heated
One clove garlic, minced
One large onion, minced
One green pepper, cleaned, chopped
Cooking time: Five minutes
Two pounds ground chuck beef
Cooking time: Ten minutes
Two cans (8 oz. each) tomato sauce
Two cans (No. 303 each) red kidney beans
One-eighth teaspoon allspice
One-half teaspoon basil leaves
One-fourth teaspoon chili powder
Simmering time: One and one-half hours
Servings: Eight

In a large deep skillet or a Dutch oven, heat the olive oil. Add the garlic, onion and green pepper; cook. Add the ground meat, cook, stirring frequently. Stir in the tomato sauce, kidney beans, allspice, basil and chili powder. Simmer, stirring frequently. Serve with crisp rolls.

MRS. GERALDINE KARAHALIAS, *Reading, Pa.*

A FAVORITE RECIPE
Stuffed Potatoes Puerto Rican

One tablespoon oil or margarine
One onion, minced
One-half green pepper, minced
Two cloves garlic, minced
Sauté: Five minutes
One-fourth teaspoon black pepper
One-half teaspoon oregano
One teaspoon salt
One ounce seedless raisins
Six to eight stuffed olives, chopped
One pound chopped meat
Cooking time: Ten minutes
Three potatoes, peeled, cooked, mashed
Three eggs
One teaspoon salt
One-half cup flour
Fat for deep frying (2 lbs. about) heated
Frying time: To a golden brown
Servings: Six

Heat the oil in a skillet, add the onion, green pepper and garlic. Sauté, stirring several times. Add pepper, oregano, salt, raisins, chopped olives and ground meat. Mix well, breaking the meat with a fork, cook. Cool. Cook and mash the potatoes. Add the eggs and salt, mix thoroughly. Take two tablespoons of the mashed potatoes into hands, make a hollow in the center, add one tablespoon of the meat mixture. Form into a ball, roll in flour. Continue with the mashed potatoes and meat until all the mixture is used. Fry in deep fat, heated to 350 degrees. Drain on absorbent paper.

MRS. AMELIA TORO, *Philadelphia, Pa.*

A FAVORITE RECIPE
Mexican Cookies

One cup vegetable shortening
One and one-half cups sugar
One egg, beaten light
Grated rind, one orange
Four cups sifted flour
One teaspoon salt
One teaspoon cinnamon
One teaspoon powdered cloves
One-half cup ground pecans
Juice one orange
Oven temperature: 400 degrees
Baking time: Eight to ten minutes
Yield: Ten dozen (1½ in.) cookies

In a deep bowl cream the shortening; add the sugar, beating until light and fluffy; add the egg and finely grated orange rind. Beat. Sift the flour, salt, cinnamon and cloves. Add with the pecans to the creamed mixture, alternately with enough orange juice to moisten the ingredients. Mix well. Roll out very thin on a floured board. Cut into fancy shapes with a floured cooky cutter. Bake in a quick oven for 8 minutes.

MRS. DOLORES MC CONNELL, *Roslyn, N.Y.*

Minestrone

One cup dried pea beans
Four cups cold water
Soaking time: Overnight
One-fourth pound salt pork, diced
One-half cup chopped onion
One clove garlic, minced
Cooking time: Five minutes
Simmer: One hour
Three quarts beef stock with soup meat
Two cups chopped cabbage
One cup julienne carrots
One cup diced celery
One package (10 oz.) frozen lima beans
One cup elbow macaroni
One-half cup raw rice
One-fourth cup minced parsley
One tablespoon salt
One-half teaspoon pepper
One-half teaspoon oregano
Cooking time: Thirty minutes
One can (1 lb.) kidney beans
Parmesan cheese
Serves: Eight, or more

In a bowl soak the pea beans in cold water. In a saucepan fry the salt pork until crisp. Remove salt pork; reserve. Cook the onion and garlic in the fat until the onion is straw-colored; add the pea beans. Cover; simmer until tender. In a large kettle combine the beef stock, soup meat, pea bean mixture, cabbage, carrots, celery, lima beans, macaroni, rice, parsley, salt, pepper and oregano. Cook for 30 minutes. Add kidney beans, heat to boiling. Pour into a tureen. Sprinkle with crisp salt pork. Serve with Parmesan cheese.

Beef Stock

Three to four pounds soup bones, cracked
One pound soup meat
Three quarts cold water
Four sprigs parsley
One large onion, quartered
Three stalks celery and leaves
One carrot, halved, lengthwise
One tablespoon salt
Six peppercorns
Simmering time: Four hours
Yield: Three quarts stock

In a large kettle place all the ingredients. Bring to a boil, lower the heat. Cover; simmer gently for 4 hours. Remove from heat; strain into a large bowl. Discard the bones and peppercorns. Rub the vegetables through a sieve; add to stock. Uncover; let soup cool. When cold place in refrigerator. Remove fat from top. Reheat and serve.

Antipasto

A highly flavored assortment of foods, arranged on a platter, consisting of: Black olives wrapped in anchovy fillets, green olives, Prosciutto, salami, Mortadella, pickled mushrooms, artichoke hearts, pimiento, capers and shrimp. To be served with wine vinegar and olive oil, bread or bread sticks and wine.

Spaghetti with Sausage Sauce

One package (1 lb.) quick-cooking
  sausage links
Cooking time: Five minutes
Two tablespoons minced green pepper
Two tablespoons minced onion
One clove garlic, crushed
Cooking time: Three minutes
One can (2 lbs. 3 oz.) Italian plum
  tomatoes
One can (7 oz.) tomato paste
One cup California red wine or water
One-half teaspoon basil
One-half teaspoon salt
One-eighth teaspoon pepper
One bay leaf
One teaspoon steak sauce
Two teaspoons sugar
Few drops angostura bitters
Simmering time: Two hours
One package (8 oz.) spaghetti
Parmesan cheese
Serves: Four

Cook sausage in a heavy skillet until
brown. Remove sausage; slice; reserve.
Add the green pepper, onion and garlic
in the skillet; cook until the onions are
straw-colored. Add the tomatoes, paste,
wine, basil, salt, pepper, bay leaf, steak
sauce, sugar and bitters. Let simmer uncovered over low heat until mixture is
thick. Stir occasionally to prevent sticking. Add sausages which have been
sliced. Reheat until very hot. Cook spaghetti as directed on package; rinse,
drain; arrange on hot platter. Pour sauce
in center of dish. Remove bay leaf. Garnish with chopped parsley. Serve with
Parmesan cheese.

Italian-Style Garlic Bread

Heat one-half cup of olive oil with one
clove crushed garlic in a saucepan. Then
brush the oil over Italian bread (cut
lengthwise). Sprinkle chopped parsley,
grated Parmesan cheese over oil. Replace
the top, wrap in foil. Heat in a hot oven
(5 minutes). Remove; slice and serve.

Manicotti

One can (No. 3) Italian plum tomatoes,
  sieved
One can (6 oz.) tomato paste
One can (6 oz.) water
One-half teaspoon salt
One-eighth teaspoon pepper
One-half teaspoon oregano
One-half teaspoon sugar
Simmer: One hour, about
One and one-fourth pounds ricotta
One-half pound mozzarella, cut in small
  cubes
Two eggs
One-half cup grated Parmesan cheese
One tablespoon chopped parsley or parsley
  flakes
One-half teaspoon salt
One-eighth teaspoon pepper
One-half teaspoon nutmeg
Six quarts boiling water, salted
One package (8 oz.) manicotti
Boiling time: Four minutes
Oven temperature: 350 degrees
Bake: Twenty minutes
Parmesan cheese, grated
Serves: Six, or more

In a saucepan simmer the sieved tomatoes, paste, water, salt, pepper, oregano and sugar for one hour. In a bowl,
blend until smooth the ricotta, mozzarella, eggs, Parmesan cheese, parsley,
salt, pepper and nutmeg. Bring the salted
water to a rolling boil in a large kettle;
add manicotti, four at a time, and boil
4 minutes (do not overcook). Lift very
carefully from the boiling water with a
slotted spoon, saving the water for remaining manicotti to be cooked. Fill the
parboiled manicotti immediately with
the cheese filling mixture, using a teaspoon. Repeat procedure until all manicotti has been cooked and filled. Cover
the bottom of a baking dish (15 x 9 x
2 in.) with tomato sauce; arrange stuffed
manicotti side by side in a single layer in
the baking dish. Cover with sauce and
bake in a moderate oven for 30 minutes.
Sprinkle with grated cheese and serve
piping hot with a helping of additional
sauce, if desired.

A FAVORITE RECIPE
Armenian Vegetable Stew

Two pounds lean lamb shoulder, cut into
    pieces (one inch)
Three tablespoons butter
Browning time: Twenty minutes
One eggplant (1½ lbs.) peeled, cut into
    one inch pieces
One-half cup green beans, cut (1 in.)
One-half cup sliced carrots
One-half cup green pepper, cut into one
    inch pieces
One-half cup zucchini peeled, cut into
    one inch pieces
One-half cup washed small whole okra
Two medium-sized onions, sliced
Two fresh tomatoes, peeled, sliced
One or more teaspoons salt
One-fourth teaspoon garlic salt
One-half can (4 oz.) tomato sauce
Oven temperature: 350 degrees
Baking time: Two hours
Servings: Six

Wipe the lamb with a damp cloth.
Heat the butter in a Dutch oven. Brown
the meat, turning frequently. Add the
prepared vegetables, seasonings and tomato sauce. Mix well. Cover tightly. Bake
in a moderate oven. Serve with hot biscuits.

MRS. P. SARKISIAN, *Hasbrouck Heights, N.J.*

Pilaf

One-fourth cup butter or margarine
One medium-sized onion, chopped
Sautéing time: Five to eight minutes
One cup of raw rice
Browning time: Five minutes, about
One can (10 oz.) consomme
One-half cup warm water
One-eighth teaspoon pepper
Heat: To boiling
Oven temperature: 300 degrees
Baking time: Thirty to forty minutes
Servings: Four to Six

In a heavy skillet, melt the butter or
margarine. Add the chopped onion and
sauté until lightly browned. Add the rice
and brown slightly. Pour in the consomme, warm water and pepper and
heat to boiling. Pour into a casserole (1½
qts.), cover and bake in a slow oven
until all the liquid is absorbed by the
rice. Good with chicken or lamb.

Green Beans Mediterranean

One cup boiling water
One bouillon cube
One-half teaspoon salt
One-eighth teaspoon pepper
Two tablespoons olive oil
Two tablespoons catsup
One package (10 oz.) frozen green beans
Simmering time: Fifteen minutes, or more
Servings: Four

Bring water, bouillon cube, salt, pepper, olive oil and catsup to a boil in a
heavy saucepan. Add the beans; mix well.
Cover tightly and cook gently until the
beans are tender.

Greek Spice Cookies

One cup butter
Two cups confectioners' sugar
One egg yolk
Two cups sifted flour
One teaspoon cinnamon
One teaspoon cloves
One-eighth teaspoon salt
Two cups ground almonds
Angelica (optional)
Oven temperature: 350 degrees
Baking time: Fifteen minutes
Yield: Thirty-six

In a bowl, cream the butter. Gradually beat in the confectioners' sugar
then the egg yolk. Sift together the flour,
cinnamon, cloves and salt and blend into
the creamed mixture. Add the nuts. Mix
well. Shape into small balls with the
hands dusted with confectioners' sugar.
Place on greased baking sheets three
inches apart. Place a piece of angelica in
the center of each cooky. Bake in a moderate oven until a golden brown. Remove
to racks to cool. Store in a tightly covered tin.

A FAVORITE RECIPE
Greek Meat Rolls

One pound lean lamb, ground
One-half cup soft bread crumbs
One-half cup dry white wine
Two cloves garlic, minced
One-half teaspoon salt
One-fourth teaspoon pepper
One-half teaspoon caraway seed
Olive oil or butter for frying
Frying time: Until lightly browned on
    all sides
One can (8 oz.) tomato sauce
One-half teaspoon sugar
One-half cup water
Simmering time: Ten minutes, about
Servings: Four

In a bowl, mix the ground lamb, bread
crumbs, wine and garlic. Add salt, pepper and caraway seed. Form into six rolls
(5 in. x 1 in.). Heat the oil or fat in a
heavy skillet, brown rolls on all sides.
Add the tomato sauce, sugar and water.
Heat slowly to boiling point. Simmer.
Serve with rice or mashed potatoes.

MRS. MARY DOUMAS, *Bayside, N.Y.*

Syrian Lamb Stew

Two tablespoons olive or salad oil
Three pounds lamb shoulder, cubed
    (1½ in.)
Browning time: Five minutes, about
Four large onions, sliced
One tablespoon salt
One-fourth teaspoon pepper
One tablespoon paprika
Two cups water
Simmer: One and one-half hours
Two cans (8 oz. each) tomato sauce
One green pepper, diced
One-half pound mushrooms, sliced
One pound green beans or
Two pkgs. (10 oz. each) frozen green beans
Cook: Twenty minutes, or more
Two cups rice, cooked
Serves: Eight

Heat the olive or salad oil in a large
heavy skillet or Dutch oven. Add the
lamb and brown quickly on all sides.
Add the sliced onions, salt, pepper, paprika and water. Cover and bring to a
boil. Lower the heat and simmer gently
until lamb is tender, about an hour and
a half. Add the canned tomato sauce,
diced green pepper, sliced mushrooms
and Frenched green beans (if frozen are
used thaw first and add for the final ten
minutes). Cook until vegetables are tender and serve spooned over the hot fluffy
rice.

A FAVORITE RECIPE
Syrian Style Eggplant

One eggplant (3 lbs.), unpeeled sliced
    (½ in. thick)
One teaspoon salt
Standing time: One-half hour
Three tablespoons oil, heated
Browning time: Five minutes
One green pepper, cleaned, sliced
Two onions, sliced thin
Six trimmed shoulder lamb chops
Two tomatoes, peeled, sliced
One-half cup boiling water
One teaspoon salt
One-fourth teaspoon pepper
One-half cup buttered bread crumbs
Oven temperature: 350 degrees
Baking time: One hour, about
Serves: Four

Slice the eggplant; sprinkle with salt;
let stand. Rinse, dry. In a skillet brown
the eggplant in the oil on each side. In
a casserole (2 qts.), make layers of the
eggplant, green pepper and onions. Arrange the lamb chops over the top, place
the sliced tomatoes on the chops. Pour
the water over all. Season with salt and
pepper. Sprinkle the bread crumbs over
the top. Bake in a moderate oven. Serve
hot from the casserole with baked potatoes and crisp rolls.

MRS. R. K. TELAGE, *New London, Conn.*

A FAVORITE RECIPE
Spareribs Caribbean

Three pounds lean spareribs
Oven temperature: 350 degrees
Bake: One and one-fourth hours
One-half cup minced yellow onion
One teaspoon salt
One-fourth teaspoon pepper
One-fourth cup diced green pepper
Two cans (8 oz. each) tomato sauce
One tablespoon Worcestershire sauce
One-third cup cider vinegar
One can (No. 2) pineapple tidbits with
    syrup
One-fourth cup brown sugar
One-fourth teaspoon dry mustard
Marinating time: One hour
Bake: Fifty minutes, about
Serves: Four

Place the ribs in a shallow roasting pan. Bake for 1¼ hours. Drain off excess fat. Cut every third rib half-way through. Pour the prepared sauce over the ribs. For the sauce: In a saucepan combine the onion, salt, pepper, green pepper, tomato and Worcestershire sauce, vinegar, pineapple tidbits with syrup, sugar and mustard. Let marinate. Return to oven and bake for 40 minutes, or more, basting frequently with the sauce. Serve hot.

MRS. L. MC DOUGALL, *Cardiff By the Sea, Calif.*

Jamaican Chicken

Four pound fricassee chicken or two
   broiler-fryers (2 pounds each)
One and one-half teaspoons salt
Three cups water
Simmer: Forty to sixty minutes
Two tablespoons butter or margarine
One-half cup sliced green olives
One-half cup diced green pepper
One-fourth cup finely chopped onion
One clove garlic, crushed
Sauté: Five to ten minutes
One-half teaspoon salt
One-fourth teaspoon pepper
One tablespoon vinegar
Two and one-half tablespoons cornstarch
Two cups chicken broth
Cook: Until thickened
Oven temperature: 350 degrees
Bake: Thirty minutes
Servings: Six

Cut the chicken into serving pieces and place in a large saucepan with the teaspoon and a half of salt and the water. Cover and simmer gently until chicken is tender, 40 to 60 minutes. In a large heavy skillet melt the butter or margarine, add the olives, green pepper, onion and garlic and sauté until soft. Stir in the half teaspoon of salt, pepper and vinegar. Measure cornstarch into a bowl and gradually stir in the two cups of broth drained from the chicken. Add to the contents of the skillet. Cook, stirring constantly, until sauce thickens slightly. Place chicken pieces in a single layer in a large shallow pan. Pour sauce over top and bake in a moderate oven for 30 minutes. Serve piping hot.

Saffroned Beef and Beans

One cup dry navy beans
Water
One teaspoon salt
Simmering time: Three hours
Two tablespoons salad oil
One pound cubed beef for stew
Browning time: Ten minutes, about
Two ripe tomatoes, quartered
One medium-sized onion, thinly sliced
One teaspoon salt
One-eighth teaspoon pepper
One-fourth teaspoon crumbled saffron
One teaspoon brown sugar
One cup dry white wine
Simmering time: One and one-half hours,
   about
One can (No. 2) whole kernel corn and
   liquid
One-half large green pepper, thinly sliced
Cooking time: Fifteen minutes
Servings: Four

Place the dry navy beans in a saucepan, cover with water, cover and cook slowly until tender, adding more water as needed. It will take about three hours. Add the teaspoon of salt during the last hour. In a large heavy skillet heat the salad oil, add the cubed stewing beef and brown quickly on all sides. Add the quartered ripe tomatoes, thinly sliced onion, salt, pepper, saffron, brown sugar and dry white wine. Cover and simmer gently until the meat is tender. When the beans are well cooked add to the skillet after draining off any excess water. Add the canned corn, thinly sliced green pepper and continue cooking until pepper is tender.

Hawaiian Chicken

One frying chicken, cut in serving pieces
One-third cup flour
One teaspoon salt
One-eighth teaspoon pepper
One teaspoon paprika
One-fourth cup salad oil
Frying time: Twenty minutes, about
One-eighth teaspoon nutmeg
One-eighth teaspoon cloves
One-half cup orange juice
One-half cup canned unsweetened
   pineapple juice
One-fourth cup unsweetened grapefruit
   juice
Cook: Two minutes
One-fourth cup sauterne
Salt and pepper to taste
One large orange
One-half cup pineapple chunks
Two tablespoons blanched almonds,
   shredded and toasted
Oven temperature: 350 degrees
Bake: One hour
Serves: Four

For this casserole dish use only the meaty pieces of the chicken. Use the breast pieces boned and cut in half, second joints and drumsticks (8 pieces). Rinse with cold water, wipe dry. In a bowl mix the flour, salt, pepper and paprika. Set two tablespoons of seasoned flour aside. Dust pieces of chicken evenly with what remains in bowl. Heat salad oil in a large heavy skillet, add the coated chicken and fry quickly until a golden brown on all sides. Place browned chicken in a casserole with a tight fitting cover. Stir the reserved seasoned flour into the fat remaining in the skillet. Blend in the nutmeg and cloves. Gradually add the fruit juices, stirring until smooth. Cook, stirring constantly until thickened. Add the sauterne, salt and pepper to taste, peeled and sectioned orange, pineapple chunks and toasted almonds. Pour over the chicken in the casserole. Cover and bake in a moderate oven until very tender.

A FAVORITE RECIPE
Ham Hawaiian

Two tablespoons butter
Two and one-half cups slivered, uncooked
   ham
One-half cup chopped green pepper
Cooking time: Until slightly browned
Three-fourths cup pineapple juice
Three-fourths cup water
Three tablespoons vinegar
Two tablespoons brown sugar
Two tablespoons cornstarch
One-half teaspoon dry mustard
One-sixteenth teaspoon pepper
Cooking time: Until thickened
One and one-half cups pineapple chunks
One and one-third cups hot water
One-half teaspoon salt
One-sixteenth teaspoon pepper
Two teaspoons chopped scallions
One and one-third cups quick-cooking
   rice
Standing time: Until rice is soft
Serves: Four

In a heavy skillet melt the butter; sauté the ham and green pepper until lightly browned, stirring frequently. In a bowl combine the pineapple juice, water, vinegar, sugar and cornstarch. Add the mustard, salt and pepper, mixing thoroughly. Cook, stirring until thick. Add the pineapple chunks, (drained). Pour over the mixture. In a saucepan combine the hot water, salt, pepper, scallions and the quick-cooking rice. Pour into the center of the ham and sauce mixture; cover and bring to a boil. Cover and stand until the rice is fluffy. Serve with hot rolls.

MRS. GEORGE F. HALL, *Asheville, N.C.*

A FAVORITE RECIPE
Polynesian Steak

One pound or more, tender steak cut into
   chunks (2 x 2 in.)

Sauce

One cup water
Two large onions, sliced thin
Two tablespons soy sauce
Two tablespoons honey or syrup
Two tablespoons cooking sherry or
   sauterne
Two cloves garlic, minced
One-half teaspoon salt
Marinating time: Three hours or longer
Broiling oven temperature: 375 degrees
Servings: Two

Have the steak cut in the market. In a bowl, mix the water, onions, soy sauce, honey, wine and seasonings. Pour into a metal or heavy oven baking dish (1 or 2 in. deep). Add the meat to mixture, turning each piece until coated with the sauce. Let stand, turning several times. Broil in the sauce, turning the meat until all sides are browned. Serve with hot rice.

CAROLE LEVY, *Bayside, L.I.*

Lasagna
Meat Balls

One and one-half cups chopped beef
One-half cup pork, chopped
Three eggs, slightly beaten
One clove garlic, crushed
Two tablespoons minced parsley
One-half teaspoon oregano
Two tablespoons Parmesan cheese
Three tablespoons olive oil
Browning time: Five minutes

Sauce

One can (17 oz.) Italian tomatoes
Two cans (8 oz. each) tomato sauce
One can (7 oz.) tomato paste
One teaspoon basil
One teaspoon oregano
One teaspoon salt
One-fourth teaspoon pepper
One bay leaf
Simmering time: Two hours
One package (1 lb.) ribbed lasagna, cooked
One pound ricotta cheese
One-half pound mozzarella cheese, sliced
Six Italian cooked sausages, sliced
One-fourth cup grated Parmesan cheese
Oven temperature: 350 degrees
Baking time: Forty-five minutes
Serves: Eight

In a bowl combine the first seven ingredients. Shape into very small balls (½ in.). Heat the oil in a large heavy skillet; brown the meat balls on all sides (about five minutes). Add the Italian tomatoes, tomato sauce and paste, herbs and seasonings to the meat balls. Cover; simmer over low heat two hours, stirring occasionally. Follow directions on the package for cooking the lasagna. Pour one cup of the tomato sauce in which the meat balls were cooked into a shallow buttered baking dish (11 x 9 x 2 in.). Over it arrange a layer of lasagna, one layer of meat balls; spread with ricotta cheese and sauce. Cover with lasagna. Spread a little tomato sauce over the lasagna; top with sliced mozzarella. Cover with lasagna, sauce and sliced sausages. Repeat the layers until all the ingredients have been used, finishing with tomato sauce and sprinkle the top with grated Parmesan cheese. Bake in a moderate oven until brown on top.

A FAVORITE RECIPE
Italian Bean Salad

One can (1 lb.) red kidney beans
One can (1 lb.) white kidney beans
One large green pepper, cleaned, minced
One large red onion, minced
Two medium-sized tomatoes, peeled, diced
One tablespoon capers
One cup Italian dressing
Chilling time: Twelve hours
Servings: Six

In a large bowl mix the prepared vegetables and capers. Pour the salad dressing (your favorite) over the vegetables. Toss until the vegetables are well coated with the dressing. This salad is better prepared the day before serving.

MISS DORIS R. BRINKDOPKE, *New York, N.Y.*

Scaloppine Marsala

One and one-half pounds veal, sliced thin
One-half cup grated Parmesan cheese
One-fourth cup butter or margarine
Cooking time: Fifteen minutes
One cup thinly sliced mushrooms
Two tablespoons butter
One-half teaspoon salt
Few grains cayenne
Cooking time: Five minutes
One chicken bouillon cube
One-half cup Marsala or sherry wine
Cooking time: One minute
Serves: Six

Have the butcher pound the veal very thin. Dip the veal on both sides in the cheese. In a heavy skillet melt the butter. Over low heat cook the meat slowly on both sides. In another skillet cook the mushrooms in the butter; add salt and cayenne. Arrange the veal on a hot platter overlapping the slices. Crush the bouillon cube with the back of a spoon in the skillet; mix in the wine. Stir and cook for one minute over high heat. Pour the sauce over the veal; garnish with mushrooms. Serve at once.

Pizza

One cup milk, scalded and cooled to
    lukewarm
Two tablespoons oil
Two teaspoons sugar
Two teaspoons salt
One package active dry yeast
One-fourth cup warm, not hot, water
Three and one-half cups sifted enriched
    flour (about)
Rising time: One hour
One package (6 oz.) mozzarella cheese,
    sliced
One can (6½ oz.) spaghetti sauce
One fourth teaspoon oregano
Twelve stuffed olives, sliced
Eight cooked mushrooms, sliced
One can (3¾ oz.) Norwegian sardines,
    drained
Two cans (2 oz. each) Norway rolled
    anchovies
Oven temperature: 400 degrees
Baking time: Fifteen minutes
Parmesan cheese, grated
Yield: Two pizzas

In a bowl combine the milk, oil, sugar
and salt; cool to lukewarm. Sprinkle the
yeast over the warm, not hot, water in
a cup; let stand five minutes. Add to the
mixture in the bowl. Beat in the flour to
make a dough that can be handled.
Knead upon a floured board until smooth
and elastic. Shape into a ball; place in a
greased bowl. Grease the top of the
dough. Cover; let rise in a draft-free
warm place until double in size. Divide
the dough in half. On a lightly floured
board roll out each half into a circle (12
in.). Place in two round pans (12 in.);
stretch to fit the pans. Place the sliced
mozzarella cheese over the dough saving
eight pieces for the top. Spread half the
combined spaghetti sauce and oregano
over dough, leaving one-half inch of the
dough uncovered around the edge. In
separate sections arrange over the sauce,
slices of olives, mushrooms, Norway sardines and anchovies. Top with the remaining mozzarella cheese. Bake in a
quick oven until bubbly and brown.
Serve right from the oven. Cut into
wedges and sprinkle with grated Parmesan cheese.

Shrimp Fra Diavolo

One-third cup olive oil
One medium-sized onion, finely minced
Two cloves garlic, finely minced
Cook: Four minutes
One can (2 lb. 3 oz.) Italian-style tomatoes
Two tablespoons chopped parsley
One and one-half teaspoons salt
Few grains cayenne
One teaspoon oregano
One teaspoon basil
Simmer: Thirty minutes
Two pounds fresh shrimp
One-fourth cup olive oil
Cook: Six minutes (about)
One package (1 lb.) cooked fusilli
    (fancy spaghetti)
Serves: Six

Heat the olive oil in a heavy saucepan.
Add the onion and garlic; cook until the
onion is straw-colored. Add the Italian-

style tomatoes, parsley, salt, cayenne,
oregano and basil; simmer gently over
low heat for thirty minutes, stirring occasionally. Peel the shrimp leaving the shell
piece on the tail and the first segment
next to the tail. Devein the shrimp. In a
skillet heat the one-fourth cup of olive
oil. Put in shrimp. Cook over low heat for

three minutes or until the shrimp turn
pink; turn and cook on the other side.
Add to the tomato sauce, saving a few
shrimp for garnish. Follow the directions
for cooking the fusilli on the package.
Place fusilli in center of dish with the
shrimp sauce around the edge of the
dish. Garnish with remaining shrimp.

Barbecued Spareribs

Two-thirds cup chopped onion
One clove garlic, crushed
One cup chopped green pepper
One-half cup finely chopped celery
One cup tomato juice
One cup water
One cup red wine vinegar
One-half cup catsup
One-fourth cup butter or margarine
One teaspoon salt
One-fourth cup Worcestershire sauce
Simmer: Twenty minutes
Four pounds spareribs
Grill: Forty to sixty minutes
Serves: Six

In a saucepan combine the chopped onion, garlic, green pepper, celery, tomato juice, water, wine vinegar, catsup, butter, salt and Worcestershire sauce. Simmer over low heat for 20 minutes. Cut the spareribs into serving sized pieces, trimming off excess fat. Place ribs on grill over coals that have been permitted to develop about 40 minutes. Baste ribs with the barbecue sauce, turning and basting frequently so the ribs cook slowly and thoroughly.

Coconut Curry Sauce

One fresh coconut, grated or two cans
   (3½ oz. each) flaked coconut
One quart milk, scalded
Standing time: One hour
Two tablespoons butter
One-half cup finely chopped onion
One clove garlic, pureed
One teaspoon minced fresh ginger root
Cook: Three minutes
One-fourth cup flour
One tablespoon curry powder
One teaspoon brown sugar
Cook: Ten minutes
Yield: Four cups

Grate the coconut meat; add scalded milk. Let stand. In a heavy skillet melt the butter; add onion, garlic and ginger root; cook until straw-colored. Blend the flour, curry powder and sugar then add to onion and garlic mixture. Pour coconut mixture through a cheesecloth. Squeeze dry. Gradually stir in the liquid. Cook until it thickens. Serve over chicken laulau.

Chicken Laulau

Four chicken fryers (2 lbs. each)
   quartered
Three tablespoons flour
One teaspoon ginger
Six tablespoons butter or margarine
Browning time: Twenty minutes
Ti leaves, foil squares or corn husks
Four packages (10 oz. each) frozen
   spinach, defrosted
Four medium-sized onions, minced
Six teaspoons soy sauce
Salt and pepper
Oven temperature: 400 degrees
Steaming time: One and one-fourth
   hours
Serves: Twelve, or more

Dredge each piece of chicken in the blended flour and ginger. In a heavy skillet melt the butter; brown the chicken. In the center of ti leaves or a square of heavy aluminum foil (10 in.) place a fourth of a package of defrosted spinach, one tablespoon onion; top with a piece of chicken. Sprinkle each with soy sauce; season with salt and pepper. Bind leaves and tie in a packet or bring up all four corners of foil together; twist tightly. Repeat procedure. Place all packets on oven rack in a quick oven. Let steam 75 minutes. Place on hot platter. Serve with coconut curry sauce.

A FAVORITE RECIPE
Sukiyaki

Three tablespoons salad oil
Three medium-sized onions, sliced thin
Sautéing time: Five minutes
Three-fourths pound round steak, sliced
   cross grain, thin as possible
Browning time: Ten minutes
One-half pound fresh mushrooms, sliced
   through caps
One-half pound fresh spinach, chopped
   coarsely
Six stalks celery, cut into lengths (1 inch)
One bunch green onions, cut into pieces
   (2 inch)
One can (8 oz.) bamboo shoots, cut
One-fourth cup soy sauce, blended with
One-half cup beef consomme
Two tablespoons sugar
Cooking time: Fifteen minutes or until
   vegetables are tender
Servings: Six

In a heavy deep skillet, sauté the onions in the oil. Add the prepared steak, browning well on both sides. Add the cut vegetables in separate layers across the skillet. Blend the soy sauce with the consomme and sugar; pour over the mixture in skillet. Cook uncovered until the vegetables are tender, stirring gently several times. Serve on hot plates from the skillet with rice.

MRS. JOSEPH M. CARLE, *Kingston, N.Y.*

Fried Rice and Shrimp

One-half cup minced scallions or onion
One-fourth cup minced green pepper
Four tablespoons salad oil
Cook: Three minutes
Two pounds cooked shrimp, cut into
   pieces (reserve a few whole ones for
   garnish)
Four cups cold cooked rice
One can (4 oz.) sliced mushrooms, drained
Four tablespoons soy sauce
Cook: Ten minutes
Two eggs, beaten
Cook: One, or two minutes
Shredded fried egg pancakes
Servings: Ten, or more

In a large heavy skillet cook the scallions and green pepper in the oil for three minutes. Reserve a few shrimp for garnish. Add the combined shrimp, rice, drained mushrooms and soy sauce. Cook slowly, stirring frequently for 10 minutes or until heated through. Add the eggs; cook one or two minutes longer, stirring constantly. Place in a hot dish. Garnish with hot shrimp and shredded egg pancakes.

A FAVORITE RECIPE
Beef-Mushrooms-Chinese

Three tablespoons shortening, heated
One clove garlic, minced
Sautéing time: Three minutes
One and one-half pounds steak, cut into
   pieces (⅛ x 4 in.)
Three tablespoons diced onion
Simmering time: Fifteen minutes
One and one-half cups beef broth (or
   bouillon)
One-half pound fresh mushrooms, washed,
   sliced thin
Cooking time: Ten minutes
Five tablespoons cornstarch, mixed with
One tablespoon soy sauce
One-fourth cup water
Cooking time: Until as thick as desired
One cup rice, cooked as directed on
   package
Serves: Four

In a deep heavy skillet, heat the shortening; sauté the garlic until light brown. Remove the garlic. Add the steak and onion; cooking over a slow fire until lightly browned, tossing frequently with a fork while cooking. Add the broth and mushrooms. Cover the skillet, tightly; simmer. In a cup mix the cornstarch with the soy sauce and water; add to the ingredients in the skillet, stirring until well blended. Cook. Serve on hot fluffy rice.

MRS. TOM W. RUGH, *Lakeside, Oregon*

Chinese Almond Cookies

Four cups sifted flour
One and one-fourths cups sugar
Two teaspoons salt
One-half teaspoon baking powder
One and one-half cups lard
One beaten egg
Two tablespoons water
Sesame seeds
Whole blanched almonds
Oven temperature: 325 degrees
Baking time: Twenty minutes
Yield: Six dozen, approx.

Sift together into a bowl the flour, sugar, salt and baking powder. Cut in the lard using two knives or a pastry blender until the mixture resembles corn meal. Stir in the beaten egg and water. Mix well. Form dough into small balls using a rounded teaspoonful for each. Dip part of each ball into the sesame seeds and place on a ungreased baking sheet. Flatten slightly with the bottom of a glass. Press an almond into the center of each. Bake in a moderately slow oven for about 20 minutes or until lightly browned on edges. Remove to racks to cool.

Holiday Fare

High Temperature Foil-Roasted Turkey

Sprinkle the inside cavity of a turkey with salt; rub the outside skin with unsalted butter or shortening. Tie the legs to the tail with a soft cord. Neatly fold back the neck skin and skewer under the bird. Tuck the wing tip under the wing. Wrap the turkey in heavy aluminum foil. Place the turkey in a shallow pan. Cook the turkey in a very hot oven according to the chart given below. 20 minutes before the end of the cooking period, open the foil and allow turkey to brown.

Time Table For Cooking Foil-Wrapped Turkey

Turkey Weight (without stuffing)	Oven Temperature
8 to 10	450 degrees
10 to 12	450 degrees
14 to 16	450 degrees
18 to 20	450 degrees
22 to 24	450 degrees

Cooking Time (minutes per lb.)	Total Cooking Time (hours)
16 to 15	2¼ to 2½
14 to 13	2¾ to 3
13 to 12	3 to 3¼
10 to 9	3¼ to 3½
9 to 8	3¼ to 3¾

Readying the Bird

For the person who has roasted two or three, the turkey poses no problem, it is strictly a matter of preparing it properly and letting the oven do the work. To the novice, however, it may seem a frightening undertaking.

Take heart first timer, the bird responds well to the application of some of the simplest techniques.

In the first place you'll want to select a bird of appropriate size. With an aversion to the cold sliced meat (one we do not share at all) you will be well advised to keep the size of the bird small. If the cold buffet with a contribution from the holiday bird is in the plan you may want the large economy size. In any event allow at least one pound of turkey as purchased per person.

You can choose from fresh or frozen birds but remember to allow time to defrost the latter. With a large (15 to 20 pound) frozen turkey it will take more than a full day for defrosting.

Check the bird over for pin feathers; there are always a few. Let cold water run through the bird and dry well. Put the giblets in a saucepan, cover with water, add salt, celery and peppercorns and let simmer until tender. These are splendid finely chopped and added to the gravy made just before serving time.

Sprinkle the cavities in the bird with salt and stuff loosely to allow for expansion during the roasting. A tightly packed bird will often split before it is thoroughly cooked.

Sew the opening closed or use several small skewers, threading them together with clean white string. Wooden picks may be substituted for the skewers if bird is small.

Tuck the wing tips under the body and tie the legs to the tail piece. Thus trussed, the bird is compact and ready for oven roasting.

Rub the bird all over with butter, bacon grease or shortening and place on a rack in a shallow roasting pan. Spoon drippings over the bird from time to time during the roasting.

We recommend the moderately slow oven, set at 325 degrees. Usually an eight pound bird will take three hours at this setting, a twelve pounder — four hours and a fifteen pound turkey, five hours. You'll know it is thoroughly cooked (and poultry is not at its best unless it is) when the drumstick can be moved up and down easily, and when the meat on the thickest part of the leg is very soft when you press it with your fingers protected with several thicknesses of paper toweling.

You'll want to allow the bird a twenty minute "rest period" upon leaving the oven. It will carve better with it. This is a fine opportunity to make the gravy.

Bring your prize to the table on a hot platter with all cords and skewers removed for the convenience of the carver. With a truly sharp knife the serving can be a most pleasant ritual.

Gravy Making

You really complete the picture of the browned bird of Thanksgiving when you offer it with savory bread stuffing and flavorsome gravy. Giblets may be added to the gravy if you wish.

We're inclined to feel that the simplest stuffing is the best, especially when so many other specialties crowd the table for attention. Well seasoned bread crumbs held together with a liberal measure of butter and roasted to a fare-thee-well within the holiday turkey is our choice. The recipe has stood the test of innumerable Thanksgivings.

Gravy making is not nearly the problem you might think when you have a good collection of nicely browned pan drippings. Several hours of oven roasting usually guarantees these.

When the roasted bird has been transferred to a platter pour all the drippings in the roasting pan into a bowl. Place the pan on a top burner and measure a tablespoon of drippings and tablespoon of flour into it for each cup of gravy wanted. Blend these together and gradually stir in a cup of milk for each cup of gravy aimed at. Cook until thickened and smooth, seasoning to taste with salt and pepper. The browned bits in the pan will dissolve and color the gravy. Add cooked, finely chopped giblets and heat well before serving.

Giblet Gravy

Turkey giblets (liver, gizzard and heart) and neck
Eight cups water
One onion, halved
Three celery tops
One teaspoon salt
Simmer: Two hours
One-fourth cup drippings
One-third cup flour
Brown: Two minutes
Two and one-half cups stock, or water
One teaspoon salt
One-fourth teaspoon pepper
Cook: Five minutes
Yield: Three cups (about)

In a saucepan over low heat simmer the giblets and neck in water with the onion, celery tops and salt for 2 hours or until tender; remove the liver after 20 minutes. Cool. Remove the meat from the neck; chop. Cut the giblets into small pieces. Place meat in a refrigerator jar; strain liquid over it. Cover; reserve until ready to make the gravy. Remove all except one-fourth cup drippings from the roasting pan. Stir the flour into the drippings and scrape sides of pan, stirring until slightly brown. Remove from heat. Add stock from giblets or water and seasonings. Return to heat; cook until thickened. Add giblets; reheat. Pour into gravy boat.

Cornbread Dressing

One cup crumbled cornbread
Five cups crumbled day-old bread
One and one-half teaspoon salt
One-fourth teaspoon pepper
One tablespoon poultry seasoning
One-half cup chopped celery
One-half cup minced onion
One-half cup butter or fat
Cooking time: Three to five minutes
One egg, slightly beaten
Three-fourths cup stock or water
One-half cup chopped pecans
Yield: Seven cups (about)

Combine the breads and seasonings in a large bowl. Cook the celery and onion gently in the butter or fat; mix in with the breads. Add the egg, stock or water, and nuts. Pack lightly into a turkey (8 lbs.). Sew or skewer the edges.

A Thanksgiving Buffet

A Thanksgiving Setting

Thanksgiving Pies

A FAVORITE RECIPE
Spiced Cranberry Relish

Four cups ripe cranberries, washed,
    stems removed
One winesap apple, cored
One can (8½ oz.) pineapple, drained
One teaspoon rum, or rum flavoring
One-half teaspoon cinnamon
One-fourth teaspoon ground ginger
One-fourth teaspoon ground cloves
One cup sugar
Standing time: Overnight, or longer
Yield: Six cups

Prepare the cranberries and apple. Run through the food grinder. In a bowl, mix with the pineapple, rum, spices and sugar. Blend thoroughly. Turn into a glass serving dish; cover. Chill until serving time.

ELIZABETH REHM, *Jamaica, N.Y.*

A FAVORITE RECIPE
Yam Puffs

Two cups hot mashed yams
Three tablespoons butter or margarine
One-fourth teaspoon salt
One-eighth teaspoon pepper
Six canned pineapple chunks
Two-thirds cup crushed corn flakes
Oven temperature: 350 degrees
Bake: Twenty minutes
Serves: Six

In a bowl mash the yams with the butter and seasonings. Form into balls, pressing the yams around the pineapple chunks. Roll in the crushed corn flakes. Place on a well greased baking sheet. Bake until a golden brown. Serve at once.

MRS. B. F. NORTON, *Belpre, Ohio*

Sweet Potato Marshmallow Scallop

Six medium-sized sweet potatoes
Boiling water
One and one-half teaspoons salt
Cook: Twenty minutes, or until tender
Two tablespoons butter
One-third cup milk
One cup crushed pineapple and juice
One-fourth cup chopped nuts
Twelve marshmallows
Oven temperature: 350 degrees
Bake: Twenty minutes
Serves: Six

Scrub the sweet potatoes; do not peel. Place in a saucepan with the boiling water to cover and salt. Cover, cook until tender. Drain. Peel. Mash thoroughly or press through a potato ricer into a bowl. Add the butter, milk, crushed pineapple and juice and chopped nuts. Transfer to a greased casserole (2 qts.) and top with the marshmallows. Bake in a moderate oven until the marshmallows are lightly browned and slightly melted. Serve at once from the casserole.

Spice Pastry

Two cups sifted all-purpose flour
Three-fourths teaspoon salt
One-eighth teaspoon cinnamon
One-fourth teaspoon nutmeg
Two-thirds cup shortening
Five to seven tablespoons ice water
Yield: Two crusts (9 in.)

Sift the flour, salt and spices into a bowl. Cut half the shortening into the dry ingredients with a pastry blender or two knives to the consistency of cornmeal. Cut in the remaining shortening until the coarse particles are the size of navy beans. Sprinkle the water, a tablespoon at a time, over the mixture. Work lightly and quickly with a fork until the dough forms a mass that leaves the bowl clean. With the hands shape into a ball. Roll half of the dough out on a floured board into a circle (11 in.). Fit loosely in a pie plate (9 in.). Repeat with remaining dough for second pie shell or upper crust.

Mince Pie

Pastry dough for two crust pie
One jar (1 lb. 2 oz.) mincemeat
One cup thinly sliced apples
One-fourth cup brown sugar
Two tablespoons sherry or lemon juice
Oven temperature: 425 degrees
Baking time: Thirty-five minutes
Servings: Six

Line a pie plate (9 in.) with pastry. Roll out dough for upper crust. Using a ruler, mark and cut even strips of pastry for lattice top. In a bowl mix the mincemeat, apples, sugar and sherry or lemon juice. Pour into pastry-lined pie plate. Arrange lattice strips on top. Bake in a hot oven until the crust is brown. Remove to a rack. Serve hot or cold.

Pumpkin Pie

Spice or plain pastry dough for one crust
    pie
One and one-half cups cooked or canned
    pumpkin
Three-fourths cup sugar
One-half teaspoon salt
One teaspoon cinnamon
One teaspoon ginger
One-fourth teaspoon nutmeg
One-fourth teaspoon cloves
Three eggs, lightly beaten
Three-fourths cup evaporated milk
One cup milk
Oven temperature: 450-350 degrees
Baking time: One hour
Servings: Six

Line a pie plate (9 in.) with pastry. Chill. Combine the pumpkin, sugar, salt and spices. Add the combined eggs and milk. Pour into the unbaked pie shell. Bake in a very hot oven 10 minutes; reduce the temperature to a moderate oven. Bake until knife inserted in the center comes away clean. Serve slightly warm or cold with or without spiced whipped cream.

Apple Pie

Pastry for two crusts
Six or seven cups sliced apples (about
    2-2½ lbs.)
Two-thirds cup sugar
Four teaspoons flour
One-eighth teaspoon salt
One-eighth teaspoon cinnamon
One-eighth teaspoon nutmeg
Three tablespoons butter
Oven temperature: 450-350 degrees
Bake: One hour
Serves: Six

Line a pie plate (9 in.) with pastry. Half fill with sliced apples placed close together. Mix the sugar, flour, salt and spices; sprinkle half over the apples. Dot with half the butter. Add enough apples to fill the pastry liberally, having the center higher than the sides. Sprinkle with the remaining sugar mixture; dot with the rest of the butter. Cover with the top crust; tuck the bottom crust over the top crust; flute the edge of the pastry. Slash in several places to allow the steam to escape. Bake in a very hot oven 10 minutes; reduce the heat to moderate. Bake until the apples are tender and the pastry is brown. Remove to a rack; serve warm or cold. Serve with a piece of sharp cheddar cheese.

Mincemeat-Pumpkin Pie

One recipe pastry (2 cups), or one
    package pastry mix
Chill: One hour
One jar (1 lb. 12 oz.) prepared mincemeat
One cup canned pumpkin
One-half cup sugar
One-fourth teaspoon salt
Three-fourths teaspoon cinnamon
Three-fourths teaspoon ginger
One-eighth teaspoon nutmeg
One-eighth teaspoon cloves
Two eggs, slightly beaten
One-half cup evaporated milk or
    heavy cream
Three-fourths cup milk
Oven temperature: 450-350 degrees
Baking time: One hour
Edam cheese, whipped cream
Servings: Six, or more

Line a pie plate (9 in.) with pastry. Make a divider out of heavy cardboard or corrugated paper (8x10x3 in.). Cover with foil. Securely set the divider across the center of the pastry. Roll out the remaining pastry; cut into strips (5x¼ in.). Roll into rosettes. Place the rosettes around dampened edge of pie crust. Secure with toothpicks. Chill. Combine the pumpkin, sugar, salt and spices. Add the combined eggs and milk. Fill one side with the mincemeat, the other side with the pumpkin mixture. Bake in a very hot oven 10 minutes; reduce the temperature to a moderate oven and bake for another 50 minutes. Remove to a rack. Cool. Remove toothpicks. Arrange Edam cheese slices on the mincemeat half and whipped cream on the pumpkin. Serve in wedges.

Light Eggnog

Six eggs, beaten well
Three-fourths cup sugar
One cup brandy or sherry
Two cups milk
Two cups heavy cream
One-eighth teaspoon nutmeg
Servings: Twenty-five

Beat the eggs until they are as thick as mayonnaise. Gradually beat in the sugar. Add the brandy or sherry slowly. Then stir in the milk and half the cream. Whip the remaining cream until stiff and fold into the eggnog mixture. Pour into a punch bowl; sprinkle lightly with nutmeg. Serve in small punch cups.

Bottled eggnog is offered by some milk companies during the holidays. To this add a little brandy, sherry or rum and fold in some whipped cream.

Mulled Wine Punch

Two cups sugar
One cup water
Two sticks cinnamon
Two dozen whole cloves
Boil: Five minutes
Eight cups hot fruit juices (lemon, orange, pineapple, apple juice)
Two bottles Bordeaux red wine
Heat: To boiling point (do not boil)
Few drops red food coloring
Lady apples, studded with cloves, and lemon slices
Yield: Four quarts

In a saucepan cook the sugar, water, cinnamon and whole cloves for 5 minutes. Strain the syrup. Add two quarts of blended hot fruit juices. Heat, but do not boil the red wine. Combine the fruit and wine mixture in a punch bowl. Add a few drops of red food coloring if needed. Garnish with Lady apples and lemon slices. Serve hot.

Braided Christmas Bread

One cup milk, scalded and cooled
One-half cup shortening, melted
Three-fourths cup sugar
One-half teaspoon salt
Two packages active dry yeast
One-fourth cup lukewarm water
Two eggs, beaten
Five and one-half cups sifted flour
One-fourth cup chopped citron
One-fourth cup currants or raisins
One-fourth cup chopped almonds
First rising time: One hour (about)
One egg yolk, slightly beaten
One tablespoon water
One-fourth cup blanched almonds
Oven temperature: 375 degrees
Baking time: Forty-five minutes
Yield: One braided bread

In a large bowl combine the milk, shortening, sugar and salt. Sprinkle the yeast over the lukewarm water in a cup; let stand five minutes. Combine the two mixtures in the bowl. Beat in the eggs and three cups of flour until smooth. Stir in the citron, currants and almonds. Add enough of the remaining flour to make a dough that can be handled. Knead on a floured board until smooth and elastic. Shape into a ball; grease the top lightly. Place in a greased bowl; cover. Let rise in draft-free, warm place until double in size. Punch down. Divide the dough in half. Divide one-half into three equal pieces. Roll each piece into three strips (18 in. long). Place strips on greased baking sheet; braid. Grease top lightly. Divide two-thirds of remaining dough into three equal parts. Form into a second braid. Place on top of first braid; grease lightly. Form the remaining dough into a third braid; place on top of second braid and grease lightly. It is necessary to use toothpicks to hold braid in place. Let rise until double in bulk. Brush top with the combined egg yolk and water. Decorate with almonds. Bake in a moderately hot oven until golden. Remove to a rack. If desired, ice and garnish with cherries.

Kugelhopf

One package active dry yeast
One-fourth cup lukewarm water
Three-fourths cup milk, scalded and cooled to lukewarm
Seven cups sifted flour (about)
Rising time: One and one-half hours
One cup seedless raisins, washed
One-half cup dried currants, washed
One tablespoon cognac
Three-fourths cup sugar
One cup soft butter
Six eggs
One-half teaspoon salt
One tablespoon grated lemon rind
One-half cup chopped blanched almonds
Three tablespoons confectioners' sugar
Three tablespoons powdered cinnamon
Second rising time: Two hours
Oven temperature: 350 degrees
Baking time: Fifty to sixty minutes
Serves: Eight, or more

In a cup sprinkle the yeast over the lukewarm water. Scald and cool the milk to lukewarm. Beat in one cup of flour. Cover the bowl with a towel. Let rise in a draft-free, warm place until spongy. In a bowl soak the raisins and currants in the cognac. Cream the sugar and butter in a large bowl until light and fluffy. Beat in the eggs, one at a time, beating well after each addition. Add the yeast sponge, remaining flour and salt; mix until smooth. Add the lemon rind, and raisin mixture. On a floured board knead until smooth and elastic. Shape half the dough into one piece, making a hole in the center. Place in a greased tube pan (8 or 9 in.). Sprinkle with the almonds. Shape remaining dough just like first piece, making a hole in the center and place on top of dough in pan. Sprinkle with combined confectioners' sugar and cinnamon. Let rise until double in bulk. Bake in a moderate oven for fifty min-

utes. Remove to a rack. Decorate with simple confectioners' icing, candied cherries and angelica.

NOTE: During the rising period, a constant moist temperature (80-82 degrees) is required. To maintain this, place the bowl of dough, and later the pans of dough, in a cold oven alongside a kettle of boiling water and close oven door. The water is heated to boiling every half hour.

Holiday Pound Cake

Two cups butter (one pound)
Two cups sugar
Two teaspoons vanilla
Eight to ten eggs (two cups)
Four cups sifted flour
One and one-half teaspoons salt
One-half pound shelled walnut meats
Eight ounces glazed cherries
One and one-half cups currants
Oven temperature: 325 degrees
Bake: Two hours, or less
Yield: One large cake (10 in.) or two or more smaller loaves

Have the butter and eggs at room temperature before starting to make cake. Cream the butter in a bowl very thoroughly. Gradually blend in the sugar, beating well. Add the vanilla. In a second bowl beat the eggs until light and fluffy, add to the butter and sugar mixture alternately with the flour and salt that have been sifted together. Beat smooth after each addition. Beat until the batter has a satiny smoothness in appearance. In a bowl mix the slightly broken walnut meats, the whole glazed cherries and the currants thoroughly together. Grease and flour a 10-inch tube pan or several loaf pans. Sandwich three layers of batter with two layers of the fruit in the prepared pans, filling about three fourths. Bake in a moderately slow oven for two hours for the large single cake, about an hour and a half for the loaves (9 x 5 x 3 in.) and an hour and a quarter for loaves (7½ x 3¾ x 2 in.). Bake until the cake springs back when touched with a finger, and is nicely browned on top. Let cool in the pan for 10 minutes, then remove to rack to cool thoroughly. Wrap in foil or waxed paper to store. Large cake will cut as many as 40 slices.

Party Punch

One package (12 oz.) frozen strawberries
Two teaspoons grated lime rind
Two tablespoons lime juice
Simmer: Ten minutes
One bottle each New York state sparkling burgundy, champagne and sauterne
Block of ice
Serves: Twenty-five

Combine strawberries, grated lime rind and lime juice in a saucepan. Simmer 10 minutes. Cool. Pour fruit mixture over ice in punch bowl. Add wines just before serving. Garnish with lime slices.

Light Eggnog

Mulled Wine Punch

Braided Christmas Bread

Kugelhopf

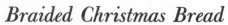

Italian Easter Ring

Two packages active dry yeast
One-fourth cup warm, not hot, water
One cup scalded milk, cooled to lukewarm
One-half cup soft butter
One-half cup sugar
Three-fourths teaspoon salt
Four egg yolks, slightly beaten
Two tablespoons slivered citron
One tablespoon slivered orange peel
One-half cup Sultana raisins
Four cups sifted flour (about)
First rising time: Two hours
Eight hard-cooked eggs, colored
Second rising time: One hour
Oven temperature: 350 degrees
Baking time: Thirty-five minutes
One cup confectioners' sugar
One tablespoon milk
Yield: Two rings

In a bowl soften the yeast in the warm, not hot, water. Scald the milk and cool to lukewarm; combine with the butter, sugar, egg yolks, citron, orange peel and raisins. Beat in one cup flour. Add the softened yeast. Beat in the remaining flour. Toss on a floured board, knead until smooth and elastic. Shape into a ball. Place in an oiled bowl; brush top of dough with oil. Cover. Let rise in a warm place until double in bulk. Take two-thirds of the dough and divide into four pieces. Shape each piece into a long roll (18 x 1 in.). Twist two of the rolls to form a circle or nest. Place on a greased baking pan. Place colored eggs in the dough. Repeat procedure. Shape the remaining dough into six thin long rolls. Place three rolls over the eggs in a criss-cross fashion. Repeat procedure. Brush top of dough with oil or melted butter. Cover. Let rise until double in bulk. Bake in a moderate oven until golden. Remove to racks. While warm, brush top with combined confectioners' sugar and hot milk.

Easter Dinner
Apricot Glazed Ham

One ready-to-eat ham (10-12 lbs.)
Oven temperature: 325 degrees
Heating time: One hour
One cup apricot puree
One-half cup brown sugar
One-fourth teaspoon dry mustard
One-fourth cup lemon juice
Glazing time: One-half hour
Servings: Twenty, or more

Place the ham upon a rack in a shallow pan; bake in a moderately slow oven until heated through. Take from the oven. Pour off the drippings. Score the ham diagonally in a diamond pattern, using a sharp knife. Mix the apricot puree and the remaining ingredients; spread over the ham. Return to the oven and bake until glazed, basting twice with the apricot mixture. Transfer to a platter; garnish with cress nests filled with aspic colored eggs.

Sugar Topped Coffee Cake
Topping

One-half cup brown sugar
One teaspoon cinnamon
One-half cup chopped nuts

Cake

One-half cup butter or margarine
One cup sugar
Two eggs
Two cups sifted flour
One teaspoon soda
One teaspoon baking powder
One-fourth teaspoon salt
One cup dairy sour cream
One teaspoon vanilla
Oven temperature: 350 degrees
Bake: Thirty minutes (about)
Yield: Sixteen squares

Mix the ingredients for the topping. Set aside. In a bowl cream the butter, gradually add the sugar, beating until light and fluffy. Add the eggs, one at a time, beating well after each addition. Add the sifted flour, baking soda, baking powder and salt alternately with the combined sour cream and vanilla. Pour into a greased and floured square pan (9 in.). Sprinkle topping over the cake. Bake in a moderate oven until a cake tester inserted in the center comes away clean. Remove to rack. Cut into squares. Serve.

Macaroons

One pound almond paste
Three-fourths cup egg whites (5 to 6)
One and one-half cups confectioners' sugar (½ lb.)
One cup granulated sugar (½ lb.)
Oven temperature: 325 degrees
Bake: Twenty minutes (about)
Yield: Sixty (2 in.)

Put the almond paste and a third of the egg whites into a bowl. Beat until smooth. Add the confectioners' and granulated sugars alternately with the remaining egg whites. Beat until thick and smooth. The consistency should be stiff and hold its shape, but not runny. With a spatula drop level tablespoonfuls of dough (2 in. apart) onto a brown paper lined cookie sheet. To flatten dough: Dip the bottom of a glass in water then press down lightly on each cookie. Bake in a moderately slow oven until the edges are a delicate brown. When cool, dampen back of paper and remove the macaroons. Store in a tightly covered container. Baked macaroons put into plastic bags keep in perfect condition in a deep freezer.

Aspic Colored Eggs

For six eggs, prepare one package of lemon-flavored gelatin. Divide and tint in delicate Spring colors. Carefully pierce both ends of an egg with a skewer, making one hole larger than the other. Blow out the yolk and white into a bowl; use for baking. Repeat with the other eggs. Cover the small end of each egg with melted paraffin. Make a funnel of waxed paper; insert in the larger hole and fill the shell with tinted gelatin. Set the filled eggs in the carton and chill until firm. At serving time remove the shell and use the aspic as a garnish.

Sunshine Coconut Cake

One cup sifted cake flour
One teaspoon baking powder
Six egg yolks, beaten
One and one-half cups sugar
One-half teaspoon vanilla extract
One-half teaspoon almond extract
One-fourth cup boiling water
Six egg whites
One-half teaspoon cream of tartar
One-fourth teaspoon salt
Oven temperature: 350-325 degrees
Baking time: One hour
Mint Jelly Frosting
One cup coconut, toasted
Servings: Twelve

Sift the flour and baking powder together three times; set aside. Beat the egg yolks until thick and lemon-colored; gradually beat in the sugar; add the extracts. Fold in the boiling water and flour mixture alternately. Beat the egg whites, cream of tartar and salt together until stiff and shiny, but not dry. Carefully fold this into the egg yolk mixture.

Pour into an ungreased tube pan (9 in.). Bake 45 minutes in a moderate oven; reduce the heat to moderately slow; bake until delicate brown on top. Invert the pan; let stand one hour; loosen the cake from the pan; remove to a plate. Spread with mint jelly frosting; sprinkle with toasted coconut.

Mint Jelly Frosting

One-half cup mint jelly
One egg white
Yield: Frosting for a tube cake

Mash the jelly in a bowl; add the egg white. Set the bowl in a pan containing two inches of hot water. Beat with a rotary beater until the frosting is light and fluffy. Spread over the top and sides of the cold cake.

Kulich

One package active dry yeast
One-fourth cup warm, not hot, water
One cup scalded milk, cooled to lukewarm
Two-thirds cup sugar
One-half teaspoon salt
Three egg yolks
Three-fourths cup soft butter or margarine
Four cups sifted flour (about)
One-half cup raisins
Three-fourths cup candied fruit (citron, orange peel, cherries)
One-fourth cup toasted almonds, chopped
Two tablespoons cognac
First rising time: One and one-half hours
Second rising time: Two hours
Oven temperature: 350 degrees
Baking time: Thirty to thirty-five minutes (about)
Yield: One large and two small coffee cakes

Soften the yeast in the warm, not hot, water. In a large bowl mix the scalded, cooled milk, sugar, salt, egg yolks and soft butter. Beat in half the flour. Add the raisins, citron, orange peel, cherries, almonds, cognac and yeast. Beat in remaining flour. Turn out on a floured board; knead until dough is smooth and elastic. Place in an oiled bowl, lightly oil top of dough. Cover, let rise until double in bulk. Shape two-thirds of the dough into a ball. Place into a greased and floured shortening can (3 lb. size). The can should be half-filled. Divide remaining dough into two balls. Place each ball into a greased and floured can (No. 2 in size). Let rise until dough reaches the top of the can. Bake in a moderate oven until brown. Remove from can to rack. If desired, frost top of bread with confectioners' sugar mixed with a little warm milk and allow to dribble down the sides.

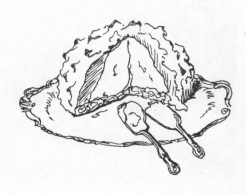

Roasted Stuffed Broilers

Three whole roaster broilers, drawn
Four tablespoons butter or margarine
One-third cup chopped onion
One-fourth pound chopped boiled ham
Cooking time: Five minutes
Three cups cooked Frenched green beans
One-half teaspoon salt
One-fourth teaspoon dry mustard
One-sixteenth teaspoon pepper
Oven temperature: 325 degrees
Roasting time: Two hours
Serves: Six

Remove the pin feathers, singe and wash quickly. Dry inside and out. In the butter in a saucepan cook the onions and ham until the onions are straw-colored. Add the cooked beans and seasonings. Stuff the broilers three-fourths full with the mixture. Skewer and truss. Place and wrap each broiler, breast side up, in aluminum foil. Place the broilers in a shallow roasting pan. Bake in a moderately slow oven for one and one-half hours. Remove the foil and finish roasting in the oven until a golden brown. Serve on a hot platter.

Easter Menu

Assorted Raw Appetizers
Chilled Tomato Cocktail
Roast Leg of Lamb
Pineapple Mint Sauce
Asparagus Amandine
Roast New Potatoes
Hot Rolls
Spring Salad
Strawberry Chiffon Tarts
Coffee

Roast Leg of Lamb

One leg lamb (6 to 7 lbs.)
One clove garlic slivered
Two teaspoons salt
One-fourth teaspoon pepper
Oven temperature: 325 degrees
Roasting time: Three hours (about)
Servings: Ten, or more

Ask the butcher to prepare the leg of lamb French style. Trim excess fat. Wipe the leg with a damp cloth. Do not remove the skin. Wrap foil around the exposed bone to prevent charring. Insert slivers of garlic into the meat. Sprinkle with salt and pepper. Place upon a rack, skinside down, in an open roasting pan. Roast in a moderately slow oven until medium or well done, allowing 30 to 35 minutes to the pound. Place on a hot platter; garnish with mushrooms and mint. Remove the foil; adjust the frill.

Roast New Potatoes

Three pounds new potatoes, peeled
Six tablespoons fat, melted
Oven temperature: 325 degrees
Baking time: One hour
One teaspoon salt
One-eighth teaspoon pepper
Servings: Eight, or more

Place the potatoes in a baking dish (2 qt.). Pour the fat over the potatoes. Cover tightly. Bake 30 minutes in a moderately slow oven; uncover and bake until pierceable. Sprinkle with salt and pepper; turn several times. Return to the oven; let remain 10 minutes. Serve immediately in a hot vegetable dish.

Pineapple Mint Sauce

Eight slices pineapple, slivered
Six tablespoons sweet relish
One tablespoon sugar (about)
One-half cup minced mint leaves
Standing time: One hour
Yield: Two cups

Combine all the ingredients in a pint jar; cover. Let stand until the mint has penetrated the sauce.

Asparagus Amandine

One bunch (3 lbs.) asparagus
Two cups boiling water
One teaspoon salt
Cooking time: Fifteen minutes
One-half cup almonds, slivered
Four tablespoons butter
Heating time: One minute
Servings: Eight

Wash and snap the tough ends from the asparagus stalks. Tie the stalks into four bunches with a soft cord. Stand them upright in a tall saucepan (2 qts.) containing the boiling salted water. Cover; cook until the stalks are tender. Drain. Arrange upon a heated dish; remove the cord. Saute the almonds in the butter in a small pan over low heat. Pour over the asparagus. Serve.

Strawberry Tarts

Two cups flour
One teaspoon salt
Two thirds cup shortening
Six tablespoons ice water, about
Oven temperature: 425 degrees
Bake: Ten to fifteen minutes
Four cups washed hulled strawberries
One-half cup water
Cook: Three to five minutes
One and one-third cups strawberry juice
One cup sugar
One-fourth teaspoon salt
Three tablespoons cornstarch
Cook: Five to eight minutes
Chill: Thoroughly
One cup heavy cream, whipped
Eight perfect strawberries (optional)
Servings: Eight

Sift the flour and salt into a bowl. Cut in half the shortening until as fine as cornmeal, cut in second half until the size of small peas. Stir in enough ice water to bind crumbly mixture together. Turn out on floured board and cut in eight portions. Roll each out to cover a tart shell (3½ in.). Trim and press firmly against shell. Prick all over with a fork.

Chill thoroughly if possible and bake in a hot oven for fifteen minutes or until nicely browned. Remove from oven and cool on rack. In a saucepan mash two cups of strawberries with a potato masher. Add the half cup of water and place over heat. Bring to a boil and simmer for three to five minutes. Remove from heat and strain. Measure the strawberry juice (adding water if necessary). In a saucepan stir together the sugar, salt, and cornstarch. Gradually blend in the strawberry juice, stirring smooth. Place over moderate heat and cook, stirring constantly until thickened and clear. Remove from heat and cool to room temperature.

Place whole strawberries (halved or quartered if large) in the baked tart shells, spoon the cooked strawberry sauce over the fruit and chill thoroughly. At serving time garnish with slightly sweetened whipped cream and a perfect whole strawberry.

Rabbit Baked in Sour Cream

One frozen frying rabbit (approx. 2½ lbs.)
Two teaspoons Ac'cent or Zest
Standing time: Fifteen minutes
One-fourth cup butter or margarine
Browning time: Fifteen minutes, about
One small onion, finely chopped
Sautéing time: Five minutes
Three tablespoons flour
One cup water
One cup dairy sour cream
One teaspoon paprika
Salt and pepper to taste
Cooking time: Ten minutes
Oven temperature: 350 degrees
Baking time: One hour, or more
Two tablespoons chopped parsley
Servings: Four

Defrost the frozen rabbit, rinse off and wipe dry. Sprinkle generously with the Ac'cent or Zest and let stand for 15 minutes. Melt the butter or margarine in a large heavy skillet, add the pieces of rabbit and brown carefully on all sides. Remove meat from pan to casserole. Add the onion to the drippings and sauté for about five minutes. Add the flour. Gradually blend in the water, stirring to keep smooth. Add the dairy sour cream, paprika and salt and pepper to taste. Cook, stirring constantly until the gravy thickens. Pour over the meat in the casserole. Cover and bake in a moderate oven for one hour or more. Serve baked rabbit with the sour cream gravy and a sprinkling of finely chopped parsley.

Roasted Stuffed Broilers

Roast Leg of Lamb

*Traditional
Passover
Tables*

Cranberry Stuffing for Capon

One cup chopped onion
One cup diced celery
One-fourth cup chicken fat
Cook: Five minutes
Three cups matzoth farfel
One-half cup condensed clear chicken
    soup, heated
One-half teaspoon sage
One teaspoon salt
One egg, slightly beaten
One can (1 lb.) Passover cranberry jelly
One capon (8 lbs.)
Oven temperature: 325 degrees
Roast: Three hours, or longer
Serves: Eight

In a skillet saute the onion and celery in the chicken fat until lightly browned. Add farfel and the hot chicken soup, sage, salt and egg, blending thoroughly. With a fork break up the cranberry jelly; add the farfel mixture. Stuff the capon, skewer and truss. Place on a rack in a shallow roasting pan. Bake in a moderately slow oven until a fork is easily inserted in the thickest part of the thigh joint and no red color in juice is evident. Remove to hot platter. Serve.

Golden Sponge Cake

One package Passover prepared sponge
    cake mix
Six eggs, separated
One-fourth cup cold water
One cup finely grated carrots
One-half cup chopped walnuts
Oven temperature: According to package
    directions
Bake: One hour and ten minutes

Frosting

One egg white
One-half cup canned Passover cranberry
    jelly
Five strawberries, halved
Serves: Eight

Combine the prepared sponge cake mix, egg yolks and water according to directions on the package. Fold in the finely grated carrots and walnuts. Fold in the stiffly beaten egg whites. Bake and cool according to directions on the package. To frost: In a bowl beat the egg white and cranberry jelly for 10 minutes or until thick. Spread on top of cooled cake; garnish with halved strawberries.

Matzo Balls in Chicken Soup

Two eggs, beaten
One tablespoon chicken fat, melted
One-half cup matzo meal
One-half teaspoon salt
One-sixteenth teaspoon pepper
Chilling time: One hour
Four cups boiling chicken broth
Cooking time: Fifteen minutes
Servings: Four to six

In a bowl beat the eggs until light; add the fat, meal, salt and pepper, stirring until blended. Chill. Form into balls (1½ in.). Cook in boiling soup till the balls come to the surface. Serve immediately; garnsh with parsley.

Gefillte Fish

Three-fourths pound carp
Three-fourths pound whitefish
Three-fourths pound yellow pike
Two teaspoons salt
Standing time: Two hours
Two medium-sized onions
Two medium-sized carrots
One-fourth cup matzo meal
One egg, beaten
One-third cup water
One-eighth teaspoon pepper
Three cups boiling water
One bouquet: One slice onion, carrot
    parsley sprig
Cooking time: One and one-half hours
Servings: Four to six

Scale, remove the bone and keep the skin intact. Wash and sprinkle half the salt over the fish; let stand. Put the fish and vegetables through the food chopper. Add the meal, egg, water, pepper and remaining salt. Form into patties; wrap with the skin. Add the bones to the boiling water; lay the patties on top. Cover; cook slowly until firm. Remove; serve hot or cold. Garnish with cooked carrots and parsley.

Seder Menu

CONCORD GRAPE WINE

GEFILTE FISH WITH
    BEET HORSERADISH

CLEAR CHICKEN SOUP WITH
    MATZOTH BALLS

ROAST CAPON WITH
    CRANBERRY STUFFING

PARSLEY POTATOES

ASPARAGUS GOLDENROD

KOSHER PICKLES

MATZOTH

GOLDEN SPONGE TORTE

TEA OR BLACK COFFEE

Matza Meal Pie Crust

One-fourth cup vegetable fat
Two tablespoons sugar
One-fourth teaspoon salt
One cup matza meal
Two tablespoons water (about)

Cream fat; add sugar and salt and mix well. Gradually work in the matza meal. Add water, drop by drop, sufficient only to hold mixture together. Press into a 9 or 10-inch pie plate, shaping well into the bottom and sides. Bake in a moderate oven (350 degrees) for about 10 minutes, or until lightly browned. Fill shell as desired.

Passover Lemon Meringue Pie

Four eggs, separated
One cup sugar
One tablespoon potato starch
Dash of salt
Two tablespoons water
Two teaspoons grated lemon rind
Six tablespoons lemon juice
One baked matza pie shell (9 in.)

Mix the slightly beaten egg yolks with one-half cup of the sugar, the potato starch, salt, water, lemon rind and lemon juice. Cook over boiling water, stirring constantly, until the mixture is thick and smooth. Then remove from heat. Prepare a meringue by beating the egg whites with the remaining one-half cup of sugar. Beat the sugar in gradually, beat well after each addition. Fold about one-half of this meringue into the yolk mixture and turn into the baked matza pie shell. Cover with remaining meringue, piling it on lightly, but covering all the edges. Bake in a slow oven (325 degrees) for about 15 minutes—until delicately brown. If preferred, all of the meringue can be folded into the yolk mixture, and baked as above.

Passover Stuffing

Three cups matza farfel (bit pieces)
    or four matzoth broken into bits
Three-fourths cup cold water
One medium-sized onion, diced
Three tablespoons poultry fat (or
    vegetable fat)
Two eggs, slightly beaten
One teaspoon salt
One-fourth teaspoon pepper
One-fourth teaspoon ginger
One-fourth cup celery, diced
Two tablespoons minced parsley

Moisten the farfel with cold water. Brown onion in the fat in a very large frying pan. Press water from the farfel, gently; do not mash. Add to the onions; add remaining ingredients and mix lightly. Stuff, with a light touch, into poultry or meats.

Ginger Ice Cream Cake

One-fourth cup shortening
One tablespoon sugar
One egg
One and one-fourth cups sifted flour
One-half teaspoon soda
One-fourth teaspoon salt
One-half teaspoon ginger
One-half teaspoon cinnamon
One-half cup dark molasses
One-half cup boiling water
One-third cup flaked coconut or more
Oven temperature: 325 degrees
Bake: Thirty minutes
One pint vanilla ice cream
Servings: Six to eight

In a bowl cream the shortening with the sugar. Beat in the egg. Sift together the flour, soda, salt, ginger and cinnamon. Add to the creamed mixture alternately with the molasses and boiling water combined. Beat well. Pour batter into a greased and floured pie plate (9 in.). Scatter the flaked coconut over top. Bake in a moderately slow oven for 30 minutes. Allow cake to cool partially in pie plate then turn out on cake rack to finish cooling. To serve: Split cake and fill with slightly softened ice cream. Serve at once or wrap and keep in freezer until serving time.

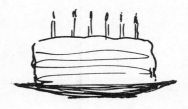

Flower Cake

Two-thirds cup butter or margarine
One cup sugar
Three eggs, unbeaten
Two cups sifted cake flour
Three teaspoons baking powder
One-half teaspoon salt
One-half cup milk
One teaspoon vanilla extract
Oven temperature: 375 degrees
Baking time: Twenty-five minutes (about)
Coconut Filling
Royal Icing
Twelve varicolored mints
Twelve varicolored almonds
Servings: Twelve, or more

To the creamed butter or margarine in a bowl gradually add the sugar, beating until fluffy. Beat in the eggs, one at a time. Add the sifted dry ingredients alternately with the combined milk and vanilla. Pour into two greased layer pans (8 in.), lined with waxed paper. Bake in a moderately hot oven until a cake tester comes away dry. Invert upon racks; remove the pans and paper. Cool. Put the layers together with coconut filling. Place on a cake plate. Ice. Place a circle of yellow paper (8 in.) on top of the cake. Lay a doily (9 in.) over the paper and on it arrange the decorated mints, almonds and leaves. To serve: Remove the doily with the candies. Slice the cake and serve a candy with each portion.

Coconut Filling

Two tablespoons sugar
Three tablespoons flour
One cup evaporated milk, scalded
Cooking time: Five minutes
Two tablespoons margarine
Two egg yolks, beaten
Cooking time: Two minutes
One-half cup shredded coconut
One teaspoon rum
Yield: One and one-half cups

Mix the sugar and flour together in a double boiler; blend in the milk. Cook, stirring until thickened. Add the margarine. Stir into the egg yolks. Return to the boiler; cook until thick. Cool. Add the coconut and rum. Spread between layers of cake.

Royal Icing

Three egg whites, unbeaten
Three cups confectioners' sugar
One and one-half teaspoons lemon juice
One-half teaspoon almond extract
One and one-half tablespoons glycerine
Yield: Two cups, or more

Beat the egg whites and one-third cup sugar in a large bowl until smooth. Gradually beat in the remaining sugar. Add the other ingredients, beating until the icing holds its shape. Cover the bowl with a damp cloth to keep the icing moist while decorating the cake. Tint half the icing green; spread thinly on top and sides of the cake. Divide and tint the remaining icing pink, lavender and yellow, and use in a cake decorator set to make flowers on top of the mints, leaves on waxed paper and buds on the almonds. Set the almonds upright to let the icing harden.

Vanilla Ice Cream

Two cups milk, scalded
One cup sugar
Two teaspoons flour
One-eighth teaspoon salt
Cooking time: Ten minutes in a
  double boiler
Two egg yolks, beaten slightly
Cooking time: Two to three minutes
Two teaspoons unflavored gelatin
Two tablespoons cold water
Chilling time: Thirty minutes
Two teaspoons vanilla
Two cups heavy cream, whipped
Freezing time: Two to four hours
Servings: Twelve

Stir the hot milk into the mixed sugar, flour and salt in the top of a double boiler. Cook and stir. Briskly stir into beaten egg yolks. Return to boiler; cook until slightly thickened. Remove from hot water. Sprinkle gelatin over cold water; let stand a few minutes. Stir into hot mixture until dissolved. Chill. Add vanilla,

fold in whipped cream. Pour into refrigerator trays. Place in freezing unit with control set at lowest point. Freeze until firm. Serve plain or with sauce.

Circus Wagons

Pre-packaged ice cream is cut into blocks for the wagons, one package making 4 wagons. For the wheels, attach gum drop discs to the wagon with toothpicks. Use gum drop sticks for the wires and gum drop slices for the top of the cage. A piece of licorice candy whip makes the wagon tongue. Set immediately on colored plates and serve.

Coconut Angel Squares

One and one-eighth cups sifted cake flour
One and one-half cups sifted sugar
Ten egg whites
One-fourth teaspoon salt
One and one-fourth teaspoons cream
  of tartar
One teaspoon vanilla extract
One-fourth teaspoon almond extract
Oven temperature: 375 degrees
Baking Time: Thirty-five minutes
Servings: Eighteen squares

Mix the sifted flour and one-half cup of the sugar; sift together four times. Beat egg whites and salt until foamy. Sprinkle in the cream of tartar; continue beating until the egg whites form soft peaks. Fold in the remaining sugar in four installments. Add the extracts. Gradually fold in the flour mixture. Turn into an ungreased pan (13x9x2 in.). Bake in a moderately hot oven until light brown on top. Cool on a rack; remove from the pan. Cut into 18 squares; frost with a seven-minute icing; generously cover with coconut. Decorate the top with a candle, a wee toy, a pennant with the child's name, or a tiny American flag.

White Birthday Cake

One cup butter or margarine
Two cups sugar
Three and one-half cups sifted cake flour
Two teaspoons baking powder
One-fourth teaspoon salt
One cup milk
One-half teaspoon almond extract
Six egg whites
Oven temperature: 375 degrees
Baking time: Thirty-five minutes (about)
Serves: Ten, or more

In a large bowl, work the butter until soft. Gradually add the sugar; cream until fluffy. Add the mixed and sifted flour, baking powder and salt alternately with the combined milk and extract. Beat the egg whites stiff but not dry (soft peaks); fold into the mixture. Pour into two greased and floured cake pans (9 in.). Bake in a moderately hot oven until a cake tester inserted in the center comes away clean. Remove from the pans onto racks. Fill the center with a cream fruit filling and frost with a boiled icing. Decorate as desired.

Shamrock Cake

One cup butter or margarine
Two cups sugar
Three cups sifted cake flour
Three teaspoons baking powder
One-half teaspoon salt
One cup milk
One-half teaspoon almond extract
Six egg whites
Oven temperature: 375 degrees
Bake: Thirty-five minutes (about)
Serves: Eight, or more

In a bowl cream the butter until light and fluffy. Gradually add one and one-half cups sugar. Add the sifted dry ingredients alternately with the combined milk and almond extract, stirring until smooth. Beat the egg whites and remaining half cup of sugar until stiff. Fold into mixture. Pour into two greased and floured cake pans (9 in.). Bake in a moderately hot oven until a cake tester inserted in center comes away clean. Turn out onto a rack. Spread cream filling between cake layers. Frost with Royal Icing.

Cream Filling

In a heavy saucepan mix until well-blended two-thirds cup sugar, two tablespoons flour, one cup milk and three egg yolks. Add two tablespoons butter. Cook over low heat until thick, stirring constantly. Add one teaspoon vanilla. Spread between layers of cake.

Royal Icing

One cup sugar
One tablespoon light corn syrup
One-third cup water
Boil: To 242 degrees
Two egg whites

Shamrock

Two tablespoons soft butter
One cup confectioners' sugar
One tablespoon hot milk
Few drops green coloring
Yield: Enough icing for top and sides of
    layer cake (9 in.)

In a saucepan stir the sugar, water and light corn syrup together. Bring to a boil. Boil without stirring until syrup reaches 242 degrees, or a little syrup dropped from tip of spoon forms a fine thread (about 6 in. long). Start beating egg whites into soft peaks when syrup reaches 230 degrees. Add syrup in a thin stream, in beaten egg whites beating constantly. Do not scrape bottom or sides of pan or icing will become sugary. Continue beating until icing is of spreading consistency. Spread on top and sides of cake. Draw and cut out a large paper shamrock. Place on cake; trace around it. Beat the butter, sugar and milk until smooth. Tint green. Spread over marked area for the shamrock. Place on cake dish. Place small ribbon bows around base of cake.

Baked Alaska Firecracker

One packaged sponge or pound cake
Four egg whites
One-eighth teaspoon salt
Three-fourths cup sugar
Two pints strawberry ice cream, frozen firm
Oven temperature: 500 degrees
Bake: Three to five minutes
A piece of heavy cord
Blueberry sauce
Serves: Six, or more

Have the cake cut so it fits an area 12" x 16". Keep in saran wrap. When ready to prepare dessert, place the unwrapped cake to the proper dimensions on a cooky sheet. In a bowl beat the egg whites and salt until foamy. Sprinkle in sugar a tablespoon at a time, beating constantly until satiny. Preheat oven. Place the rounds of firmly frozen ice cream, lengthwise, in the center of the cake. Cover the ice cream with a thick coating of meringue. Bake in a very hot oven until golden. Remove to a platter. Put in the fuse. If desired, garnish with frosted leftover cake pieces. Immediately serve in slices with Blueberry Sauce.

Blueberry Sauce

In a saucepan cook a package of frozen blueberries or one and one-half cups fresh blueberries with three-fourths cup sugar and a dash of nutmeg for five minutes. Serve hot or cold.

Wedding Cake

One pound Sultana raisins
One pound seedless raisins
One and one-half pounds currants
One-third cup orange juice
One-third cup apple juice
One-fourth cup lemon juice
One-half pound candied orange peel
One-half pound candied lemon peel
One-half pound candied pineapple
One pound citron
One-half pound chopped walnuts
Three cups sifted flour
One teaspoon salt
Two teaspoons cinnamon
One and one-half teaspoons nutmeg
Three-fourths teaspoon allspice
One and one-half cups butter or margarine
One and one-half cups sugar
Nine eggs
Oven temperature: 250 degrees
Bake: Two to three hours
Yield: Three layers (9 in. 6 in. 3 in.)

Put the raisins and currants in a large bowl or pan; pour the orange, apple and lemon juice over them. Slice the candied orange and lemon peels, pineapple and citron very thin; add to raisin mixture. Add the nuts; mix thoroughly. Sift flour, salt, cinnamon, nutmeg and allspice over the fruit mixture; mix thoroughly. In a bowl work the butter until soft and creamy. Gradually add the sugar beating until light and fluffy. Add the eggs, one at a time, beating well after each addition. Blend in remaining measure of dry ingredients. Add to the fruit and mix thoroughly. Pack into three heavily greased and floured round deep cake pans (9, 6 and 3 inches). Bake in a slow oven. After two hours take out the smaller cakes; remove to a rack. After three hours remove the large cake to a rack. Frost with ornamental icing.

Ice Cream Heart Cake

Two and one-fourth cups sifted cake flour
One and one-half cups sugar
Three teaspoons baking powder
One teaspoon salt
One-half cup vegetable oil
Five egg yolks
One-fourth cup cherry liquid
One-half cup milk
One-fourth teaspoon almond extract
One cup egg whites (7 or 8 whites)
One-half teaspoon cream of tartar
Eight maraschino cherries, chopped fine
Oven temperature: 350 degrees
Bake: Thirty minutes
Two pints ice cream
Two cups heavy cream
Two tablespoons confectioners' sugar
Cherries or cinnamon drops
Yield: One three-layer cake

Sift the dry ingredients into a bowl. Make a well in the center; add oil, yolks, cherry liquid, milk and almond extract. Beat until smooth. Beat egg whites and cream of tartar until very stiff. Gradually fold into first mixture until well blended. Pour into three greased and floured heart-shaped cake pans (8 in.). Bake in a moderate oven until a cake tester inserted in center comes away clean. Remove to cake racks. Cool. When cold, layer with ice cream. Place in a freezer. Place a weight on top. Beat the heavy cream with the confectioners' sugar until stiff. Remove cake and quickly frost. Place in freezer immediately. Decorate as desired.

Log Nut Roll

Six egg yolks
Three-fourths cup sugar
One and one-half cups finely chopped nuts
Two teaspoons vanilla
One teaspoon baking powder
Six egg whites
Oven temperature: 350 degrees
Bake: Fifteen to twenty minutes
One cup heavy cream, whipped
One tablespoon confectioners' sugar
Serves: Eight

In a bowl beat the egg yolks and one-half cup sugar until thick and lemon-colored. Fold in the finely chopped nuts, vanilla and baking powder. Beat the egg whites and the remaining fourth cup of sugar until stiff, but not dry. Fold into the mixture. Pour the mixture into a pan (10x15x½ in.) lined with oiled brown paper. Bake in a moderate oven for 15 minutes. Turn out on a paper, sprinkled with confectioners' sugar. Remove paper. Roll as for jelly roll. When cold, unroll. Beat the cream and sugar together until thick. Spread over roll. Re-roll. Cover with a frosting to simulate a log.

Frosting

One-half cup soft butter
One egg yolk
Two tablespoons cocoa
Two and one-half cups confectioners' sugar
Brewed coffee
Melted unsweetened chocolate (¼ oz.)
Yield: One cup frosting

In a bowl beat the butter, egg yolk, cocoa and confectioners' sugar. Add enough coffee for a spreading consistency. Frost the nut roll with mixture so it looks like a log. With a toothpick work in melted chocolate.

Velvet Cream Cheese Cherry Pie

One envelope unflavored gelatin
One-fourth cup cold water
One cup heavy cream
Heat: Until hot, not boiling
One-half cup sugar
One-half teaspoon salt
One-half pound cream cheese
One cup dairy sour cream
One-fourth teaspoon almond extract
Chill: One hour
One baked pastry shell (9 in.)
Two jars (8 oz. each) maraschino cherries
Serves: Six

In a cup sprinkle the gelatin over the cold water. Heat the heavy cream until hot, not boiling. Remove from heat. Stir in gelatin, stirring until dissolved. Add sugar and salt. In a bowl beat the cream cheese and sour cream until smooth. Stir into the gelatin mixture. Add extract. Place in refrigerator and allow to chill. When cold, pour into baked pastry shell. Garnish top with cherries. Place in refrigerator. Serve in wedges.

A FAVORITE RECIPE
Cherry Bars

One-half cup butter
One-fourth cup brown sugar
One cup flour, sifted with
One-half teaspoon salt
One-half teaspoon baking powder
Oven temperature: 350 degrees
Baking time: Ten minutes
One package (6 oz.) candied cherries, cut into thirds
Two egg whites, beaten stiff
One-half teaspoon cream of tartar
One-fourth teaspoon baking powder
One cup light brown sugar
Oven temperature: 350 degrees
Baking time: Until lightly browned
Yield: One pan (8 x 8 in.) cut into bars

In a bowl cream the butter and sugar. Add the sifted flour, salt and baking powder. Pat into a well greased pan (8 x 8 in.). Bake in a moderate oven for 10 minutes; remove from oven. Place the cherries on top of the baked mixture. Beat the egg whites, with cream of tartar and the baking powder. Gradually beat in brown sugar. Spread over the cherries. Bake until browned in a moderate oven. Cut into bars. Cool. Store in a tight container.

MRS. G. A. GOGO, *Montreal, P.Q., Canada*

Cherry Cream Pie

One package vanilla pudding mix
Two cups milk
Baked pie shell (9 in.)
One-half cup halved, pitted bing cherries
Three and one-half tablespoons cherry flavored gelatin
One-half cup boiling water
One-half cup cold water
Chill: Until syrupy
Chill: Until firm
Whipped cream (optional)
Serves: Six

Prepare the packaged vanilla pudding with the milk according to directions on the package. Chill slightly, covered with a piece of waxed paper to prevent the formation of a skin on top. Pour into a baked pie shell (9 in.). Arrange halved, pitted bing cherries on top. In a bowl, dissolve the cherry flavored gelatin in the boiling water, add the cold water and chill until syrupy. Spoon thickened gelatin over the cooled vanilla filling in the pie. Chill pie thoroughly before serving. Whipped cream may be piled around the edge of the pie at serving time, if desired.

Cherry Turnovers

One can (No. 2) sour red pitted cherries
One and one-half tablespoons cornstarch
One-fourth cup sugar
One-fourth teaspoon salt
One-eighth teaspoon nutmeg
One-third cup cherry juice
One teaspoon grated lemon rind
One teaspoon lemon juice
Cooking time: Five minutes, about
Two tablespoons margarine or butter
Two cups sifted flour
One-half teaspoon salt
Two-thirds cup margarine or butter
One-third cup ice water
Oven temperature: 425 degrees
Baking time: Twenty minutes, about
Yield: Eight

Drain the liquid from the canned cherries into a bowl. In a saucepan stir together the cornstarch, sugar, salt and nutmeg. Blend in one-third cup of the cherry juice, lemon rind and lemon juice. Cook over moderate heat, stirring constantly, until thick and clear. Remove from heat and stir in the two tablespoons of margarine or butter. Add the drained cherries and set aside. Sift together into a bowl the flour and salt. Cut in the two-thirds cup of margarine or butter, using two knives or a pastry blender until mixture resembles coarse crumbs. Stir in the ice water. Divide the dough into two balls. Roll each ball out on a floured board to about 12 by 12 inches. Cut into four six-inch squares. Roll out the other half of the dough the same way. Spoon the cherry mixture onto each piece of dough, folding pastry over to make triangle. Crimp edges together; cut slit in top for escape of steam. Place on baking sheet and bake in a hot oven for twenty minutes or until lightly browned. Remove to racks to cool.

Classified Index

Appetizers

Beverages

Nog

Coffee

Hot Chocolate, Cocoa

Punch

Tea

Wine

Bread

Biscuits

Bread

Coffee Cake

Doughnuts

Muffins

Rolls

Cheese

Cookies and Candy

Candy

Cookies

Desserts

Cream

Crepe Suzettes

Custard

Fruit

Eggs and Breakfast Dishes

Fish and Shellfish

Veal Roulees, 95
Veal Sauté over Rice, 96
Veal Scallops with Cream, 104
Veal Stew, 98
Veal Stew, Parsley Dumplings, 98

Pie and Pastry

Cheese Pie

Pineapple Cheese Pie, 240

Chiffon Pie

Cherry Chiffon Pie, 241
Coco-Mint Chiffon Pie, 241
Lime Chiffon Pie, 241
Maple Walnut Chiffon Pie, 245
Orange Chiffon Pie, 241
Strawberry Chiffon Pie, 241
Toasted Almond Chiffon Pie, 240

Cobbler

Apricot Cobbler, 255
Citrus Cobbler, 255
Cranberry Apple Cobbler, 255
Peach Cobbler, 252
Raisin Applesauce Cobbler, 252

Cream Pie

Apricot Cream Pie, 248
Black Bottom Pie, 241
Buttermilk Pie, 240
Butterscotch Parfait Pie, 246
Fluffy Lemon Pie, 242
French Apple Cream Pie, 253
Molasses Rum Pie, 245
Nesselrode Pie, 246
Nut Topped Sour Cream Pie, 240
Rhubarb Cream Pie, 249
Sour Cream Apple Pie, 253
Strawberry Cream Pie, 244

Dumplings

Apple Dumplings, Ginger Crust, 254
Baked Peach Dumplings with Sauce, 252
Peach and Raspberry Dumplings, 252

Fruit Pie

Apple Cranberry Crisp Pie, 253
Apple Pie, 250
Apple Raisin Pie, 245
Apricot and Banana Pie, 248
Cherry Pie, 248
Country Prune Pie, 249
Crumb Topped Apple Mince Pie, 251
Crunchy Topped Apple Pie, 253
Deep-Dish Peach Pie, 247
Double Crust Lemon Pie, 248
Easy Strawberry Pie, 244
Fresh Peach Pie, 249
German Apple Pie, 253
Honey Prune Pie, 244
Lemon Apple Pie, 250
Mock Apple Pie, 251
Peach Crumb Pie, 245
Peach Lexington, 255
Pear Pie, 249
Pineapple Pie, 248
Raisin Cranberry Pie, 249
Raisin Pear Pie, 245

Short Peach Pie, 249
Spiced Raisin Pie, 248
Sweet Sour Rhubarb Pie, 247
Upside-Down Apple Pie, 253

Meringue Pie

Baked Alaska Pie, 243
Cranberry Meringue Pie, 244
Fluffy Lime Pie, 242
Lemon Meringue Pie, 243
Orange Meringue Pie, 244
Pineapple Meringue Pie, 244
Rich Mocha Angel Pie, 244

Pastry

Cherry Strudel, 254
Danish Pastries, 252
Mandarin Orange Cream Puffs, 237
Pastry, 250
Puff Pastry, 239
To Make Butterflies, 239
To Make Horns, 239
To Make Napoleons, 239
To Make Pastry Shells, 239

Pie Crust

Pie Crust, 248
Pretzel Crumb Crust, 249
Vanilla Wafer Pie Crust, 243

Sauce

Fluffy Sauce, 254
Lemon Sauce, 254
Raisin Orange Sauce, 254
Raspberry Sauce, 237

Specialty Pie

Ambrosia Pie, 242
Chess Pie, 240
Pecan Pie, 249
Shoo Fly Pie, 240

Tarts

Banana Cream Tarts, 256
Banbury Tarts, 237
Butterscotch Pecan Tarts, 237
Chess Tarts, 238
Coconut Rum Tarts, 256
Coffee Meringue Tarts, 256
Glazed Fruit Tarts, 238
Lemon Cheese, 237
Lemon Fruit Tarts, 256
Little Hats (Hammentaschen), 237
Raspberry Cream Tarts, 237
Rhubarb Tart, Hard Sauce, 256
Three-Inch Appie Pies, 253

Poultry

Chicken

Baked Chicken Americana, 125
Baked Chicken and Corn Casserole, 125
Baked Chicken and Mushrooms, 121
Baked Chicken Salad, 125
Baked Chicken with Rosemary, 125
Browned Fricassee of Chicken, 129
Branswick Stew, 124
Cashew Chicken, 120
Chicken à la King, 127
Chicken and Veal, Duchess Potatoes, 124

Chicken Cacciatore, 129
Chicken Dinner, 118
Chicken Fricassee, 126
Chicken in Red Wine, 122
Chicken in Wine Sauté, 128
Chicken Kiev, 122
Chicken Loaf, 129
Chicken Marengo, 129
Chicken Mousse, 128
Chicken Noodle Supreme, 129
Chicken Paprika, 126
Chicken Parisian, Asparagus, 121
Chicken, Sherry, 121
Chicken Specialty, 124
Chicken Supreme, 126
Chicken Tetrazzini, 129
Chicken Venetian, 120
Chicken with Lemon and Rosemary, 128
Chicken with Tarragon, 125
Chiffon Chicken Pie, 127
Crown of Chicken, Rice Mold, 119
Deviled Chicken, 123
Floating Chicken, 128
Glazed Roast Chicken, 124
Honey Wine Broiled Chicken, 121
Individual Chicken Roasts, 120
Lemon Broiled Chicken, 128
Mushroom Olive Stuffed Chicken, 121
Noodle Fruit Stuffed Roast Chicken, 120
Orange-Dipped Chicken, 128
Oven Fried Spiced Chicken, 125
Paprika Chicken, 125
Peasant Style Chicken, 120
Pot Roasted Chickens, 120
Roasted Capon, 119
Spiced Chicken, 128
Sweet and Pungent Chicken, 122
Western Chicken Pie, 124

Duck

Baked Oranges, 134
Barbecued Duckling, 133
Best Roast Duckling, 130
Duckling in Wine, 133
Duckling, Purple Plum Sauce, 134
Ducklings, Green Grapes, 130
Flared Duckling, 133
Oven Barbecued Duckling, 130
Roast Duck, 133
Sweet and Sour Duckling, 133

Rock Cornish Hen

Rock Cornish Hen, Olive Wine Sauce, 131

Stuffing, Dressing

Fruit Dressing, 124
Poultry Stuffing, 121

Turkey

Oven-Fried Turkey, Giblet Gravy, 131
Spicy Sauced Turkey Curry, 132
Turkey Casserole, 133
Turkey Divan, 132
Turkey Hash with Cream, 132
Turkey Macaroni Skillet Meal, 132
Turkey Patties, 132
Turkey Supreme, 132
Turkey Tetrazzini, 132
Turkey Turnovers, 132

Vegetables

French Boule de Neige
(Snow Ball)

Six eggs, separated
One cup sugar
One cup sifted cake flour
One-eighth teaspoon salt
One tablespoon grated lemon rind
One teaspoon lemon juice
One teaspoon vanilla
Oven temperature: 350 degrees
Bake: Fifty minutes (about)

Filling

Two tablespoons kirsch or cognac
One jar (8 oz.) minced, glazed fruit
Let stand: Fifteen minutes
Four tablespoons butter or margarine
Six tablespoons flour
One-fourth cup sugar
Two cups milk
Two egg yolks
Cook: Ten minutes
One pint heavy cream
One-third cup sugar
Crystalized violets
Serves: Eight, or more

In a bowl beat the egg yolks until thick and lemon-colored. Gradually beat in a half cup of the sugar. Beat the egg whites with the remaining half cup sugar, until stiff. Fold the egg white mixture into the egg yolks. Fold in the mixed and sifted flour, salt, grated lemon rind, juice and vanilla. Pour into two bowls (1½ qts. each) lightly greased and floured. Bake in a moderate oven until golden. Turn upside down on rack. When cool loosen edges with spatula; remove from dish. Use shears to hollow out center of each cake. Leave a shell one inch thick. Fill with creamy glazed fruit mixture.

To make filling: in a bowl pour the kirsch over the glazed fruit. In a heavy saucepan melt the butter; blend in the flour and the sugar. Gradually stir in the milk, cooking until smooth and thick. Add some of mixture to the egg yolks, stirring briskly. Blend into the creamed mixture. When cool, add the glazed fruits. Fill shells of cake with filling. Place one cake over the other to form a sphere. Beat the cream and sugar until thick. Rosette the entire surface of cake with the whipped cream. Arrange candied violets on cake. Chill until ready to serve. Cut into wedges.

Creamed Turkey and Ham
Casserole

One-half cup butter or margarine
One-half cup flour
One teaspoon salt
One-fourth teaspoon pepper
Two cups milk
Two cups turkey broth
Cook: Ten minutes
Four cups cooked, cubed turkey
Two cups boiled ham, cut julienne style
Cook: Five minutes
Four tablespoons butter or margarine
One-half pound medium-sized mushrooms, quartered
Cook: Ten minutes
Serves: Eight

In a large heavy saucepan melt the butter. Blend in the flour, salt and pepper until smooth. Gradually stir in the milk and broth, stirring constantly until mixture is smooth and thickened. Add the turkey and ham; reheat. In a heavy pan melt the butter, add the quartered mushrooms; cook until tender. Place the creamed mixture in a chafing dish. Arrange the mushrooms around the edge of the dish. Garnish as desired. Serve hot.